EMPLOYMENT DISCRIMINATION LAW

Problems, Cases, and Critical Perspectives

EMPLOYMENT DISCRIMINATION LAW oclc record

Problems, Cases, and Critical Perspectives

Janis L. McDonald, Associate Professor of Law
Syracuse University College of Law

Frank S. Ravitch, Professor of Law
Michigan State University College of Law

Pamela Sumners, Esquire
Chicago, Illinois

Pearson
Prentice Hall
Legal Series

PEARSON
Prentice
Hall

Upper Saddle River, New Jersey 07458

Library of Congress Cataloging-in-Publication Data

McDonald, Janis (Janis L.)
    Employment discrimination law : problems, cases, and critical perspectives/Janis
McDonald, Frank S. Ravitch, Pamela Sumners.—1st ed.
      p. cm.
    ISBN 0–13–974866–0
  1. Discrimination in employment—Law and legislation—United States—Cases. I. Ravitch,
Frank S., 1966- II. Sumners, Pamela. III. Title.
KF3464.A7M33 2006
344.7301'133—dc22

                                                            2004026584

Director of Production and Manufacturing: Bruce Johnson
Senior Acquisitions Editor: Gary Bauer
Editorial Assistant: Jacqueline Knapke
Editorial Assistant: Cyrenne Bolt de Freitas
Senior Marketing Manager: Leigh Ann Sims
Managing Editor—Production: Mary Carnis
Manufacturing Buyer: Ilene Sanford
Production Liaison: Denise Brown
Production Editor: Judy Ludowitz/Carlisle Publishers Services
Composition: Carlisle Communications, Ltd.
Senior Design Coordinator/Cover Design: Christopher Weigand
Cover Printer: Coral Graphics
Printer/Binder: Hamilton Printing

The information provided in this text is not intended as legal advice for specific situations, but is meant solely for educational and informational purposes. Readers should retain and seek the advice of their own legal counsel in handling specific legal matters.

Pearson Prentice Hall™ is a trademark of Pearson Education, Inc.
Pearson® is a registered trademark of Pearson plc
Prentice Hall® is a registered trademark of Pearson Education, Inc.

Pearson Education LTD.   Pearson Education Australia PTY, Limited
Pearson Education Singapore, Pte. Ltd.   Pearson Education North Asia Ltd.
Pearson Education Canada, Ltd.   Pearson Educacíon de Mexico, S.A. de C.V.
Pearson Education—Japan   Pearson Education Malaysia, Pte. Ltd

10 9 8 7 6 5 4 3 2 1
ISBN 0-13-974866-0

To Ryan Rafael, my wonderful college bound son, and to Kokkie Buur, who continues to help professional women keep their mental health and sanity as we shatter glass ceilings.

Janis McDonald

To Jamie, my wife, and my daughters, Elysha and Ariana.

Frank Ravitch

To Georgia Catherine Sumners, my beautiful baby daughter.

Pamela Sumners

Pearson Legal Series

Pearson Legal Series provides paralegal/legal studies students and educators with the publishing industry's finest content and best service. We offer an extensive selection of products for over 70 titles and we continue to grow with more new titles each year. We also provide:

- online resources for instructors and students
- state-specific materials
- custom publishing options from Pearson Custom Publishing group

To locate your local Pearson Prentice Hall representative, visit www.prenhall.com

To view Pearson Legal Series titles and to discover a wide array of resources for both instructors and students, please visit our website at:

www.prenhall.com/legal studies

Pearson
Prentice Hall
Legal Series

Contents

CD Contents

PART TWO   Additional Materials on Procedure and Exhaustion of Administrative Remedies

Problem 62

    G. What about the charge-filing deadlines for federal employees?

    H. What about aggregating the number of employees at two different worksites?

    I. What about a successor corporation's liability for Title VII claims?

Problem 63

    J. Does the pendency of an EEOC charge toll the statute of limitations for non-Title VII causes of action?

Problem 64

    K. What if the right to sue is issued by the EEOC before it has had the charge for 180 days or before conciliation has occurred?

    L. Can someone who knows of or has observed discrimination, but who has not personally experienced it, file an EEOC charge?

    M. Can EEOC make a charge of discrimination public?

    N. How does EEOC's conciliation process work?

    O. Can individuals be sued under Title VII for monetary damages or recover under other federal statutes based on the exact same events that gave rise to the Title VII claim?

    P. What about Title VII liability with independent contractors?

    Q. Is a temporary-placement agency an employer for Title VII purposes?

    R Are there limits on the amount of damages that can be imposed for Title VII violations?

    S. Can a plaintiff use the experiences of other employees, or what she learned from them, as a basis for imposing liability in her Title VII suit?

PART THREE   Additional Materials Related to Public Employees and Discrimination

Problem 65

Problem 66

I. Private Race Discrimination in the Formation or Fulfillment of Contractual Relationships and a Brief Overview of 42 United States Code Section 1985(3)

    A. 42 U.S.C. § 1981 Requirements

      Fadeyi v. Planned Parenthood Ass'n of Lubbock, Inc., 160 F.3d 1048 (5th Cir. 1998)

      Raggs v. Mississippi Power & Light Co., 278 F.3d 463 (5th Cir. 2002)

      Sledge v. Goodyear Dunlop, 275 F.3d 1014 (11th Cir. 2001)

Problem 67

    B. A Note on Section 1985: Conspiracy to Interfere with Civil Rights

Preface

Employment discrimination law is a dynamic and ever-changing field. The impact of these changes is a matter of both intense scholarly and practical interest. Society generally, and businesses specifically, may be greatly affected by developments in the law of employment discrimination. These effects are occasionally predicted, or even intended, but are at times unforseen and far-reaching.

This book presents, from a legal perspective, law affecting much of employee/manager relations. A clear understanding of the rights of all persons in an organizational hierarchy is fundamental to the sound management of any company's most valued asset, its people. Students at all levels of study will benefit from a consideration of the legal structures that help to shape those relationships.

Employment discrimination laws affect everything from how employers conduct business and how they respond to employees who perceive themselves as victims of discrimination to how employees exercise their rights inside and outside the workplace. Issues such as disparate treatment, or intentional discrimination, in decisions to hire, promote, or terminate employees; workplace harassment; disability discrimination; affirmative action; and religious accommodation in the workplace need to be understood by those entering the work force as well as by those who will represent the employer, the employee, or other persons involved in a conflict. A practical and theoretical understanding of these complex issues will provide the necessary flexibility with which to more effectively face the future decisions required in an ever-changing work force. Lawyers, employees, businesspeople, social scientists, union management and union representatives, and policy makers alike need to be equipped to address the significant and often difficult issues that arise from the myriad of federal and state statutes, constitutional concepts, and common law doctrines relevant to discrimination in the workplace.

This book is written to provide students with a framework for a practical and foundational understanding of employment discrimination law. It is structured around issues of current significance rather than more outdated, and now rarely used, legal claims. The book does, however, cover the earlier important concepts as well. Instead of devoting hundreds of pages to the development of issues in their original form, the book examines the modern treatment or rejection of the particular approach.

For example, the Supreme Court, during the 1970s, interpreted the main employment discrimination law, Title VII of the Civil Rights Act of 1964, to

For example, the Supreme Court, during the 1970s, interpreted the main employment discrimination law, Title VII of the Civil Rights Act of 1964, to include claims of discrimination even where there was no intent to discriminate on the part of the employer. The Court recognized that neutral employment policies had a damaging impact on groups of minority employees, creating discrimination of a different type. The claim was heavily used for a period of time and has been the subject of intense criticism and modification ever since. The chapter on disparate impact introduces the student to the concept and the history of its use, but we devote more time to the modern context within which disparate impact analysis operates in discrimination law. These ideas are conceptually quite important, and the critiques by scholars of the current difficulties and possibilities of this doctrine are explored as a way to further the discussion.

The book devotes considerable attention to the case law that developed and now refines current issues such as hostile work environment and disparate treatment. We focus appropriate attention on the issues that are likely to matter to students who will practice law or deal with these issues as employers or employees in the twenty-first century. The incorporation of excerpts from scholars of law and economics, law and race, law and feminism, and law and society, among others, enables students to explore the impact of antidiscrimination laws on the real world and to question whether such laws have changed the social biases and bigotry that gave rise to them. Throughout, we have been careful to give useful hypotheticals that will enable students to analyze and apply what they learn from the cases and materials in each section. Each of the main chapters begins with hypotheticals to give the students working problems that will help them assimilate the difficult case material that follows. These hypotheticals are often based on real cases. We have generally used hypotheticals rather than note questions (which are common in casebooks) to further explore the material in the book. Notes are utilized at times, however, especially in connection with narrower issues that do not command as much attention in the main text.

We wrote this book because we felt it important to have a text available that focuses appropriate attention on the future, rather than simply updating an organizational structure that reflects the law 20 years ago. We did, however, contextualize these issues within the historical development of antidiscrimination law. Thus, it is our hope that this book will provide a practical, analytical, and theoretical understanding of this fascinating and dynamic area of law.

As co-authors, we bring a unique mix of legal experience and scholarship to the task of preparing this book. We are scholars and litigators who have committed our professional lives to issues that relate directly to employment discrimination law. It is our hope that both students and teachers will find this to be an exciting and thought-provoking aid to the study of this important subject.

Janis L. McDonald
Frank S. Ravitch
Pamela Sumners

Jan/2005

Acknowledgments

Janis L. McDonald: My son, Ryan Rafael, is always the inspiration for my work. I continue to grow and learn from him. I would also like to thank my secretary, Marie Zurowel, my research assistants at the Syracuse University College of Law, Tracy Sanders, Class of 2002, Yukiko Sakamoto, Class of 2003, and Chanel Hudson, Class of 2005 for their assistance on this project. A special thanks to Susannah Furnish for her assistance in proofreading the entire book. I am grateful to Syracuse University College of Law, particularly Dean Hannah Arterian, for the support I received during the development of this project.

I know I speak on behalf of my co-authors in thanking all of the scholars and the publishers who gave permission to reprint segments of their published work: Gary Blasi, Paul Brest, Kingsley R. Browne, Devon Carbado, Erwin Chemerinsky, Margaret M. Chon, Kimberle Williams Crenshaw, the late Jerome McCristal Culp, Jr., John J. Donohue III, Maxine Eichner, Richard Epstein, Lucinda M. Finley, Barbara Flagg, Lani Guinier, Mitu Gulati, Elizabeth M. Iglesias, Charles R. Lawrence III, Orly Lobel, Deborah C. Malamud, Richard Posner, Laura L. Rovner, Mary Ellen Turpel, Susan Sturm, Francisco Valdes, and Frank H. Wu. I believe each of them shares our hope that this generation of students will benefit from a wide range of views about the challenges of discrimination in the workplace.

Frank S. Ravitch: There are many people I would like to thank. My wife, Jamie, has been supportive and understanding throughout the writing of this book. She has provided excellent comments and has been an inspiration and source of strength for everything I have written. My daughters, Elysha and Ariana, have also been a source of pride and joy; their smiles always make a long day brighter. My parents, Arline and Carl Ravitch, have been supportive and are a source of constant support and inspiration. They are the best parents any child could ever hope to have. My mother- and father-in-law (yes, some people actually love their in-laws), Barbara and Gerry Grosslicht, provide constant support. My sisters, Elizabeth and Sharon, and their families, my grandmother-in-law, Hilda Sorhagen and my Uncle Gary and Aunt Mindy and Aunt Jackie and Uncle Ken are always curious and supportive of my endeavors.

I am also grateful to many colleagues who have been helpful in this process, either by getting me interested in this area of law or by providing support and inspiration while I was writing this book. These include Lucinda Finley, Charles Abernathy, Gary Gildin, Daniel Hall, Douglas Huron (who was my professor for this course—and an excellent one at that), Brian Kalt, Charles Ten

Brink and Dean Terence Blackburn, who has fostered an environment at Michigan State that has been immensely supportive of my writing. Special thanks go to Jacklyn Beard, my secretary, who worked tirelessly to reformat parts of this manuscript. Special thanks also go to Sarah Belzer and Amy Benedict for their able and immensely useful research assistance.

Special thanks to the reviewers of this text: C. Suzanne Bailey of Western Illinois University, IL; Eli C. Bortman of Babson College, MA; Deborah A. Howard of University of Evansville, IN; Reginald Oh of Appalachian School of Law, VA; Robert Diotalevi of Florida Gulf Coast University, FL; Kent Kauffman of Ivy Tech State College, IN; Taylor L. Morton.

Note on Editing

We want to make this book as accessible as possible to a wide variety of readers. Case books are generally intended for law students only, but we have made an attempt to edit these cases to make them more readily understandable by students of employment law in many disciplines. Employment discrimination is an issue of importance in our society, and the more the law is understood, the better we can address problems presented. We have edited and rearranged the cases in this book so that **"The Employment Problem"** is presented at the beginning of each case, using the facts that the court thought were relevant to tell the story of the employee's experience with the employer. Sometimes judges bury the facts in their opinion, and we think it helps to place the story of the people involved in the case up front so that we can all focus on the problems faced in the employment context before we address the way the law treated the problem.

We have also rearranged each case to present what each court did in the process of trying to get to a final answer in the case. We present the decision of the trial court first. Every case that is brought before the courts has to start in a trial court after "exhausting administrative remedies." The federal court system, where these cases are usually litigated, consists of the U.S. district court (the trial court), an appellate court in the trial court's circuit (the U.S. court of appeals for the trial court's circuit) and the U.S. Supreme Court, which will hear a case if the Court decides there is an important reason for considering it. Our editing of the cases rearranges the material in the opinion of the court to reflect, first **"The Employment Problem,"** the **"Decision of the Trial Court,"** second, **"The Decision of the U.S. Court of Appeals;"** and, if it went that far, **"The Decision and Rationale of the U.S. Supreme Court."** We have also added a section in most cases entitled **"The Legal Issue,"** which contains the court's language that most closely identifies the legal issue. The language under each section is the language of the final appellate court, depending on how far the case was appealed, unless the language is in brackets, which indicates language added by us as editors.

During a law student's first year in law school, there is much attention devoted to the craft of finding out these categories by carefully reading the cases to understand these distinctions; however, even when studying a more advanced topic such as employment discrimination law, law students as well as students of other disciplines can benefit from the presentation of the material in an ordered way. This is not meant to be a casebook devoted to learning how to read a legal opinion; it is meant to help students understand the way the courts have interpreted the federal laws that deal with employment discrimination and the societal problems that may or may not have been addressed by these efforts.

We have tried to avoid overediting the cases contained in this book, but virtually every case in the book has been edited, some to a significant degree. Some will feel that there are cases that are too long, and some might feel that there are cases that should have included additional material. We have included material we think is important for the task at hand. We have tried to note where text has been cut in cases by inserting an ellipsis— . . . —We have deleted parallel citations within cases without so denoting. The above-referenced notations are for the benefit of readers who wish to consult the full case to review the material that was edited.

Moreover, the articles presented throughout this book have been edited, and some of them significantly so. These articles were all reprinted with permission of the law reviews and/or the authors, but the authors and the law reviews are not responsible for any of the editing and thus have no responsibility for editing errors. Additionally, the full articles are heavily footnoted and contain more information and attributions to other sources than the edited version in this book. Thus, if you are especially interested in a particular article, we encourage you to read the full article (citations are provided for all articles).

Additional materials are available on the CD. A complete Contents for the CD material is available on pp. xvi–xxii. The materials, in Part One, include the relevant federal statutes prohibiting discrimination in employment. In Part Two we have included a detailed description of the Equal Employment Opportunity Commission procedures required to exhaust administrative remedies prior to commencing a lawsuit in federal court. Legal issues raised about these procedures are included. These materials are helpful to the practitioner as well as the student of the subject. In Part Three we have provided information specifically related to government employment.

EMPLOYMENT DISCRIMINATION LAW

Problems, Cases, and Critical Perspectives

ONE

Solving the Problem
The Meaning of Discrimination

chapter

1

The Goals of Antidiscrimination Laws

A. The History of Title VII of the Civil Rights Act of 1964

The history of civil rights movements in the United States provides a foundation for the study of laws prohibiting discrimination in employment. The most familiar of these movements is the struggle by African Americans to claim social, political, civil, and human rights. Almost every library today owns a copy of the much-acclaimed documentary production of the video series by Blackside, Inc./PBS, EYES ON THE PRIZE, AMERICA'S CIVIL RIGHTS YEARS 1954 TO 1965. It is recommended that any serious student of employment discrimination issues view this series of interviews and documentary videos of the period. Other videos exist documenting the civil rights movements and the experiences of Asian Americans, Latina/os, women, and those with disabilities. (See, for example, Christine Choy and Renee Tajima, WHO KILLED VINCENT CHIN?, Elizabeth Martinez, 500 YEARS OF CHICANO HISTORY, Emiko Omori, RABBIT IN THE MOON (a new documentary on the internment of Americans of Japanese descent in World War II and WHEN BILLY BROKE HIS HEAD, AND OTHER TALES OF WONDER, a documentary about disabilities).

Entire courses and a tremendous wealth of literature exist that cover the historical, cultural, political, economic, religious, philosophical, and ethnocentric perspectives on this period and the similar struggles of other minority groups in the United States. There is a wealth of material about the struggles by Asian Americans, Latino/a Americans, women, homosexuals, and persons with disabilities, among others, to claim the rights guaranteed to them by the U.S. Constitution and federal, state, and local laws.

The emphasis during the civil rights movement led by Dr. Martin Luther King, Jr. was not initially on employment discrimination but on more immediate concerns of safety, desegregation in all aspects of American life, and education. The protests and the economic boycotts of busses and stores that enforced segregation began with other issues and then moved to worker strikes like the one in Memphis, Tennessee, and the assassination of Dr. King in 1968.

Despite some failed attempts at legislative reform, discrimination in the early 1940s was widespread in transportation, housing, public accommodations, and the armed services. In 1948, President Harry S. Truman issued a presidential executive order to desegregate the armed forces. Congress passed the Civil Rights Acts of 1957 and 1960 with a focus on preventing the denial of voting rights and discrimination on the basis of race. The U.S. Civil Rights Commission was established and created a gradual expectation that the federal government might become more involved in the protection of civil rights. In 1962, President John F. Kennedy issued a presidential executive order prohibiting discrimination in some forms of housing. President Kennedy also began work on a new, comprehensive civil rights bill. He sent a message on civil rights to Congress along with a proposed bill, (H. R. Doc. No. 124, 88th Cong., 1st Sess.), which was introduced in the House of Representatives as H.R. 7152 and in the Senate as S. 1731. Substantial hearings were held by the House Judiciary Committee, and a subcommittee recommended further action. In October of 1963, the full Judiciary Committee considered the matter, but it was not until January of 1964, almost two months after President Kennedy's death, that the House began to consider and debate the bill as amended in committee. Although he had voted against the Civil Rights Acts of 1957 and 1960, President Lyndon B. Johnson became a key leader in the passage of the Civil Rights Act of 1964. The Act was passed on July 2, 1964 and provided for full voting rights, full access to public accommodations, desegregation of public facilities, desegregation of public education, nondiscrimination in federally assisted programs, nondiscrimination in employment, the establishment of the Equal Employment Opportunity Commission (EEOC), and future authorization of the existing Civil Rights Commission. These agencies were charged with the implementation of Title VII. Full information on the legislative history of the Civil Rights Act of 1964 may be obtained at the website *www.thomas.gov* and in the Equal Employment Opportunity Commission document *Legislative History of Titles VII and IX of the Civil Rights Act of 1964* (1968) or Charles Whalen and Barbara Whalen, THE LONGEST DEBATE: A LEGISLATIVE HISTORY OF THE 1964 CIVIL RIGHTS ACT (1985).

Title VII of the Civil Rights Act of 1964, which is devoted to employment discrimination, prohibits discrimination on the basis of race, color, sex, religion, and national origin. One of the concerns noted in the hearings on this section of the bill was the disparity between nonwhites, who were unemployed at a rate of 11.4 percent, and whites, who had an unemployment rate of 4.9 percent, based on Department of Labor statistics. Salary discrepancies were also noted between nonwhites and whites as well as between men and women. The final reports on the bill contained very little information about the specific purposes of Title VII because it was a combination of efforts by several committees and political compromise in a very contested battle.

Congress continued to consider amendments to Title VII and new legislation that related to employment discrimination for additional unlawful reasons. The Equal Employment Opportunity Act of 1972 added federal, state, and local government employees to the scope of coverage of Title VII and gave the Equal Employment Opportunity Commission more powers to enforce its provisions. The Pregnancy Discrimination Act of 1978, which became law as an amendment to Title VII, was a reaction to an unpopular U.S. Supreme Court decision that determined pregnancy discrimination was not covered by Title VII.

Implementation of Title VII

After Title VII became law, cases began to surface in the federal courts. A person who claims that he or she has been discriminated against on the basis of race, color, sex, religion, or national origin must first file a charge with the Equal Employment Opportunity Commission, which gives the Commission an opportunity to notify the employer, investigate the charge, and either attempt to settle the case or make a finding that there is cause to believe discrimination did or did not occur. The EEOC did not have power to fix the problem if the parties did not agree; only the courts could do that. The employee had to wait for a fixed amount of time before a lawsuit could be filed in the U.S. district court, a federal court located in the vicinity of the employee's place of employment. Attorneys for the employers began to file motions in court to get the claims dismissed, and the courts had to interpret the meaning of Title VII. This was not an easy job because the language of the law was vague. The courts had to determine what certain language meant and how a case of employment discrimination based on Title VII could be proved.

Title VII did provide that the EEOC, as part of its responsibilities, could develop procedures to implement the intent of the law. The EEOC could not create new law, but could develop ways to make sure that Title VII's demands were met. Eventually the EEOC drafted regulations that helped to detail the procedures required by the words of Title VII. Those regulations can be found in the Code of Federal Regulations, along with the regulations of all other government agencies.

The courts were left with the responsibility of interpreting this new federal law. Each time a new case came before the courts, issues were raised by the case that required the court to announce the meaning of certain language of Title VII as applied to that controversy. The earliest cases did not distinguish between the ways of proving Title VII cases with nearly the precision or formulas that the U.S. Supreme Court eventually developed. Much of the time, the cases concerned blatant forms of discrimination that could be dealt with in a straightforward fashion. Gradually, as those employers who intended to discriminate became more sophisticated about the way the laws were going to be interpreted, they learned not to provide "evidence" of their intent to discriminate.

B. Critical Perspectives on the Goals of Antidiscrimination Laws

The problem of discrimination continues to be a major source of conflict in today's society. Vehement disagreement exists about the goals of established and proposed antidiscrimination laws and about the nature of the problem of discrimination itself. No one perspective on the problem existed among the legislators who enacted the civil rights laws of the 1960s and 1970s. The language of these laws is vague and open to broad or narrow interpretation, and it is often left to judges to interpret the meaning of the language.

Before studying the language of the antidiscrimination laws or the interpretations of the courts, it is useful to understand the different foundational assumptions that influence perspectives on the meaning of discrimination. Equality, for example, is a very attractive term and may well be adopted as a goal of antidiscrimination laws. But what does equality mean? What are the consequences if one thinks equality means treating all races as if they are exactly the same but another interprets equality to demand taking account of those differences? What are the consequences of adopting any one definition of equality for purposes of implementing the antidiscrimination laws?

This chapter provides an introduction to a number of different critical perspectives that are important to understand in studying employment discrimination law and policy. These articles are examples of feminist theory, law and economics theory, critical race theory, and liberal theory and the way those theories intersect to provide insight on and a critique of employment discrimination laws. Within each theory, there exists a broad range of opinion. There are, however, generalizations that can be made about some of the positions taken by adherents of one theory or the other. For example, liberal theory, as presented by Professor Paul Brest, seems to endorse the antidiscrimination principle and the idea of a colorblind approach to equality. The colorblind approach is often criticized by race scholars such as the late Professor Jerome McCristal Culp, Jr., who was a strong advocate of taking race into account in order to address the very realities faced by minorities in society and in the workplace today. An edited version of his critique is presented in this chapter.

Feminists analyzed the sameness/difference difficulties raised by interpretations of equality and take different positions on what to do about the problem. Professor Lucinda Finley focused on this problem in the context of pregnancy discrimination early in the debate. What does equality mean when we face the real physical difference that pregnancy means for women as opposed to men? Are differences in the workplace to be defined only when they mirror men's experiences? How should employers account for these potential differences between men and women in order to ensure equal opportunity and equal treatment? How relevant should it be that only some women become pregnant? Another approach examines the problems of equality in the workplace and in society from a very different perspective. Professor Maxine Eichner, for example, describes different approaches of Catharine Mackinnon and Drucilla Cornell on the problem of dominance and power in institutional structures that produce discrimination.

Antidiscrimination laws began to be critiqued by law and economics theorists in the 1980s. Some scholars, including Richard Epstein and Edwin Chemerinsky, disagreed about whether the market would and should be allowed to deal on its own with problems related to employment discrimination. Interference by federal or state government in the way markets handle the problems of the workplace would only exacerbate the results.

Critical race feminist scholars began to identify the problems caused by the total failure of Title VII to deal with the overlap between race or national origin and gender. Black women, including Professor Kimberlé Crenshaw, led in identifying the way the law ignored their experiences, forcing them to choose between their identities based on race or gender. In recent years, critical white scholars, including Professor Barbara Flagg, have begun to examine the layers of assumptions and privilege that have prevented white people from understanding their relative positions of power in the structure and interpretation of employment discrimination laws.

The scholarship offers an overwhelming array of insightful and dynamically diverse perspectives on the meaning of discrimination in our society.

Each of these topics is a useful tool when learning to appreciate the foundational questions that must be answered as the legal system exerts a profound influence on the workplace. It is recommended that the reader return to these articles and think about the ways the perspectives may affect the resolution of the problems identified throughout this book.

1. The Antidiscrimination Principle and the Meaning of Colorblind Equality

Paul Brest, *Foreword: In Defense of the Antidiscrimination Principle,* 90 Harv. L. Rev. 1 (1976)

(This is an edited version of the article and footnotes are deleted.)

By the "antidiscrimination principle" I mean the general principle disfavoring classifications and other decisions and practices that depend on the race (or ethnic origin) of the parties affected. . . . The heart of the antidiscrimination principle is its prohibitions of race-dependent decisions that disadvantage the members of minority groups. . . .

My "defense" of the antidiscrimination principle is that it prevents and rectifies racial injustices without subordinating other important values. At the risk of stating the obvious, the antidiscrimination principle is not the only principle of justice that should guide policymaking. For example, I believe that governments should assure that people are not denied fundamental needs because of their poverty and, more generally, should promote greater equalization in the distribution of wealth among individuals. To adopt the antidiscrimination principle as the exclusive principle of racial justice surely does not preclude adopting these or other principles concerned with economic justice.

Throughout this essay I use the word "race" as a shorthand for race and ethnic origin. However, the antidiscrimination principle can be and has been extended to encompass a variety of other traits, including alienage, illegitimacy, and sex. By limiting my concern to race-dependent decisions I do not imply that the antidiscrimination principle should not be so extended; but the inquiries necessary to evaluate such extensions lie beyond the scope of this essay.

1. The Antidiscrimination Principle

The antidiscrimination principle rests on fundamental moral values that are widely shared in our society. Although the text and legislative history of laws that incorporate this principle can inform our understanding of it, the principle itself is at least as likely to inform our interpretations of the laws. . . .

Stated most simply, the antidiscrimination principle disfavors race-dependent decisions and conduct—at least when they selectively disadvantage the members of a minority group. By race-dependent, I mean deci-

sions and conduct (hereafter, simply decisions) that would have been different but for the race of those benefited or disadvantaged by them. Race-dependent decisions may take several forms, including overt racial classifications on the face of statutes and covert decisions by officials.

A. Rationales for the Antidiscrimination Principle

The antidiscrimination principle guards against certain defects in the process by which race-dependent decisions are made and also against certain harmful results of race-dependent decisions. Restricting the principle to a unitary purpose vitiates its moral force and requires the use of sophisticated reasoning to explain applications that seem self-evident.

1. *Defects of Process.* The antidiscrimination principle is designed to prevent both irrational and unfair infliction of injury. . . . The unequal treatment could be justified only if one group were in fact more worthy than the other. This justification failing, such treatment violates the cardinal rule of fairness—the Golden Rule.

2. *Harmful Results.* A second and independent rationale for the antidiscrimination principle is the prevention of the harms which may result from race-dependent decisions. Often, the most obvious harm is the denial of the opportunity to secure a desired benefit—a job, a night's lodging at a motel, a vote. But this does not completely describe the consequences of race-dependent decisionmaking. Decisions based on assumptions of intrinsic worth and selective indifference inflict psychological injury by stigmatizing their victims as inferior. Moreover, because acts of discrimination tend to occur in pervasive patterns, their victims suffer especially frustrating, cumulative, and debilitating injuries.

. . . I have argued that the prevention of stigmatic and cumulative harms, as well as concerns for process, support the antidiscrimination principle. Individuals may, however, be stigmatized by non-race-dependent practices that appear to be discriminatory and may also suffer cumulative disabilities from various non-race-dependent practices. Whereas the process rationales for the antidiscrimination principle apply only to race-dependent decisions, the result-oriented rationales seem to disfavor all practices that produce these harms and thus to support a doctrine broader than the antidiscrimination principle. . . .

. . . I believe that an individual's moral claim to compensation loses force as the nature, extent, and consequences of the wrongs inflicted become harder to identify and as the wrongs recede into the past. Not only does the image blur as the focus shifts from a specific claim based on an identifiable act to encompass amorphous wrongs, but new kinds of claims enter the field of vision. For racial discrimination is hardly the only injury that our society has inflicted on its members. The minority's claim to compensation for past discrimination must now share the field with the claims of all persons whose present position is the result of economic exploitation and other social injustices.

Indeed, as claims to compensation based on the past injustices of human institutions become attenuated, they begin to compete with claims based on the vagaries of fate, and thus become indistinguishable from demands for greater distributive justice among all individuals. If we are to compensate people for the adverse effects of their environments, there is no reason to distinguish among the causes of the environments. One major function of compensation is to remedy the upset or outrage occasioned by the wrongdoer's frustration of the victim's justified expectations—to remedy the loss of the an-

ticipated enjoyment of benefits possessed or reasonably expected. But a person cannot, in this sense, "expect" to be brought up from the start in an environment different from the one in which he or she was in fact raised.

The poor, nonpreferred white and the black beneficiary of a preferential program are like two children raised as brothers in an impoverished household. It is later discovered that one or the other is probably the heir to a small fortune, which is given to the one with the more likely claim, the other taking nothing. All parties concerned would regard the occurrence as a windfall, and certainly not based on desert. So, too, is a preference premised on a greater probability that the minority's situation is the result of past injury. . . .

Certainly, the paradigm model of compensatory justice is not concerned with issues of equity between the victim of a wrong and others who are similarly situated for different reasons; but only with equity between the wrongdoer and the victim, whose claim has priority over most other beneficial uses of the wrongdoer's resources. But the thrust of the preceding discussion is that a general preferential treatment or reparations program moves well beyond this paradigm to a point where the distinction between compensatory and distributive justice becomes untenable. . . .

Question

1. Does this idea of equality work the same for everyone? Why? Why not? What are the strengths of the antidiscrimination principle? What are its weaknesses?

2. The Critique of the Colorblind Principle of Equality

Jerome McCristal Culp, Jr., *Colorblind Remedies and the Intersectionality of Oppression: Policy Arguments Masquerading as Moral Claims*, 69 N.Y.U. L. Rev. 162 (1994)

(This is an edited version of the article and footnotes are deleted.)

One of the myths we tell children and law students is that the law is or can be colorblind. This myth posits colorblindness, or inattention to race, as a moral requirement of all "right" thinking people and all good law. The truth, however, is that racial justice and colorblindness are not the same thing. Race-neutral policies are only as good or bad as the results they produce. No one thinks that economic efficiency or the labor theory of value are moral requirements independent of their impact on the components of justice. In like manner, to assume that ignoring race in making social policy will bring about justice or achieve morality is legal fantasy.

There are several reasons that Americans nonetheless have come to mythologize colorblindness as racial justice. First, many people believe that participants in

the Civil Rights Movement sacrificed their blood, sweat, and tears for a colorblind world. This view of the Civil Rights Movement is best captured by Martin Luther King, Jr.'s famous exhortation that people ought "not to be judged by the color of their skin but by the content of their character." If colorblindness was good enough for Martin Luther King, many argue, then it ought to be good enough for a society that still aspires to the movement's goals of equality and fair treatment.

A second reason people see colorblindness as a moral requirement is that it is easy: the colorblind principle permits judges to decide difficult issues without discussing the kind of moral system to which we aspire. In a colorblind world of mythic justice, will black people be assimilated or remain distinct? Will racial distinctions be seen as interesting flavoring in the melting pot or as important components of an individual's personality? How are race and culture connected? Rather than providing answers to these important questions, colorblindness permits us to avoid any discussion of the morality or justice of assimilation, nationalism, or cultural difference. Instead, its proponents simply assert that justice and morality are vested within colorblindness.

A final and related reason for the persistence of the colorblind myth is that Americans simply do not have a concept of justice that can take account of racial difference. Colorblindness, therefore, is thought to embody racial justice fully. Black leaders are in part to blame for this state of affairs. In fashioning policy prescriptions to end racial oppression, many civil rights leaders criticized the policy of racial separation for limiting the economic, legal, and social opportunities of blacks. Some people have used that criticism to bolster a claim that attention to color is always and everywhere evil, and that colorblindness is always and everywhere a moral good.

These justifications for colorblindness are all overly simplistic. Dismantling Jim Crow does not require an acceptance of colorblindness. As our history shows, colorblindness has often not been a defense against the oppressive effects of racism. Martin Luther King, Jr., worked for civil rights for almost fifteen years. Much of his work required black people to become more, rather than less, race-conscious in their thinking in order to achieve change, and much of his program included race-conscious responses to the existing evil of racism. Still, people have created a mythic Martin Luther King, Jr., and associated him with a fictional notion of colorblindness. In a similar fashion, the Supreme Court has adopted colorblindness as a legal watchword, even as it systematically limits the access of blacks to jobs and jury duty, and permits racially disparate and onerous police interrogation and investigation of black Americans.

Myths are often created to fill a necessary psychological space. Colorblindness has been created to help us get over the difficulty of race in a society where race is particularly powerful. In our post-civil rights legal world, race is like the nakedness in the fairy tale of the emperor's new clothes—something only the bold or the unsophisticated are willing to acknowledge. The "grownups" tell us that we are clothed with a nonracial reality; indeed, we are told by many that we too could see that "race doesn't matter" if only we were appropriately committed to individual achievement and liberal justice. Many individuals argue that if we simply were to extend principles of colorblindness to all aspects of our private lives, the issue of race would go away as an important legal and social phenomenon. Some would extend this principal to a whole array of concerns, from gender to appearance. However, this effort to make the world colorblind (or blind to any

number of issues) has to confront the fact that, in general, we refuse to limit private actions that produce consequences in both the private and public sphere. Proponents of colorblindness call for restrictions on the legal use of race in public policy, even though they know that private actors will continue to use race for negative purposes. In short, race-neutral principles cannot prevent covert, oppressive uses of race.

This essay argues that the colorblind principle is not a moral requirement, but rather a policy argument resting on several invalid assumptions. In particular, I want to advance the seditious idea that we will not change the racial present until we adopt an effective program of race-conscious policies, for only race-conscious policies can alter the racial status quo in this country. I contend that the argument for colorblindness ultimately argues in favor of a racialized status quo that leaves black people and other racial minorities in an unequal position. By the phrase "racial status quo," I mean the economic reality that African Americans are twice as likely to be unemployed and are more likely to be fired than are white Americans. They are also less likely to be employed in positions that provide status or higher income. Despite the many antidiscrimination laws passed since 1964, black Americans still earn substantially less income than whites. Indeed, even in pure market transactions where the race of the purchaser would not seem to matter—such as the purchase of an automobile—there is significant evidence that it does: black purchasers are treated very differently than are white purchasers by sales staff.

A Brief History of the Colorblind Principle

. . . The genuine moral goal associated with race is to end race-based oppression. Colorblindness may sometimes accomplish this moral goal, but it is not the goal itself. Therefore, the colorblind principle in modern constitutional discourse must be seen as a policy argument and not a moral precept.

It is easy to see that the colorblind ideal is not sufficient to protect us from the moral dilemmas if one examines early efforts of our citizens to be colorblind. The white men who adopted the Constitution refused to put the words "race," "color," or "slavery" anywhere in its text. The Constitution was thus formally "neutral" towards race, slavery, and color. This conscious decision to be colorblind, of course, did not prevent the creators of the American constitutional order from accepting the pernicious American form of slavery. The Constitution was, in modern constitutional parlance, facially neutral while protecting subjugation by private parties and even governmental entities.

Moreover, the Constitution is colorblind in a particular inapt and improper way. Although the text's silence on race might allow the superficial appearance of racial "equality," in fact the colorblindness serves to enforce the racial present. By denying the law the power to take account of and, therefore, to rectify the status quo, colorblind morality sustains a racially subordinate present for African Americans.

When courts and commentators argue for colorblindness, they implicitly are making both a public policy claim and a moral statement. The policy assertion is that colorblindness will achieve social goals effectively, and the moral claim is that the society so produced will be an objectively good one. If we understand, however, that the public policy claim ultimately reinforces the status quo of a society that is racially oppressive, then it is clear that the moral claim actually defends the white supremacy reflected in existing social arrangements. In such a "race-neutral" world, subordination of black people becomes the natural state unchangeable by public policy or other efforts by governmental agents. . . .

. . . In thinking and talking about how to deal with race, courts and commentators often confuse the notion of colorblindness—the removal of race from the legal and governmental discourse—with the antidiscrimination principle—the elimination of deprivations based on race. The antidiscrimination principle can be read in a colorblind way; i.e., we could have written Title VII to require, for example, that people be hired on production and merit-based grounds. The statute would not mention race, but would implicitly eliminate racial choices in an employer's "meritorious" and "production-based" decision. However, Congress did not adopt this approach in passing the Fourteenth Amendment and Title VII of the 1964 Civil Rights Act. Instead, the Reconstruction amendments and the Civil Rights Acts of the modern era mandated the elimination of social and economic race privilege.

This aspect of the antidiscrimination principle is explicitly color conscious. Thus, race is a salient issue for courts when deciding whether the thirteenth or fourteenth amendments apply in constitutional interpretation. The antidiscrimination principle aims to change the present by enforcing different norms on some decisionmakers. However, the antidiscrimination principle cannot fulfill this aim when it is colorblind, precisely because it cannot then acknowledge the racial present. Although a colorblind antidiscrimination principle would perhaps prevent an increase in racial subordination, it cannot hope to change the status quo. The antidiscrimination principle therefore loses its power to effect real societal change when it becomes colorblind.

The question many of you must be asking is: do we know how to use race consciousness to eliminate the status quo? The answer is that it depends on the circumstances. The appropriate race-conscious policy will depend on how deeply entrenched racial subordination is in a particular context. The intersection of race and other issues of oppression, like gender and class, also means that fashioning an appropriate race-conscious policy is more complicated than some have assumed; it requires ultimately that policymakers and judges apply practical policy, instead of simple bright-line rules, to eliminate the consequences of racial subordination.

Traditionally, courts and commentators have assumed that colorblind policies are superior because they are effective policies which will lead to morally just results. . . .

I should end by pointing out that not all race-conscious policies need to occur through government action. When blacks create communities of influence to alter the existing structure of life, those communities are engaging in a form of race-conscious policymaking. The eradication of the racial present ultimately requires a careful balancing of sophisticated programs that rely neither on the formalism of colorblindness nor on the naive notion that the status quo is easily remediable. . . .

3. White Assumptions

Relative power is also at the center of the growing scholarship on critical white legal studies. There have been numerous critiques of the failure of members of the white race to look inward to discover previously unacknowledged privileges and bias. Many critical race scholars have pointed out that those who are white aren't even aware of the privileges that are built into their lives on a daily basis. Because these privileges remain unacknowledged, many whites cannot accept or understand why they should be the ones to suffer in competition with blacks as a result of affirmative action efforts, which they view as giving blacks undeserved advantages.

The efforts to develop critical white scholarship began with minority critical race scholars. Very few white scholars joined their ranks until Professor Barbara Flagg and others began exploring the problem of their own privilege.

Barbara Flagg, 'Was Blind, But Now I See': White Race Consciousness and the Requirement
of Discriminatory Intent, 91 Michigan Law Review 953 (1993)

(This is an edited version of the article and footnotes are deleted.)

. . . White people externalize race. For most whites, most of the time, to think or speak about race is to think or speak about people of color, or perhaps, at times, to reflect on oneself (or other whites) in relation to people of color. But we tend not to think of ourselves or our racial cohort as racially distinctive. Whites' "consciousness" of whiteness is predominantly unconsciousness of whiteness. We perceive and interact with other whites as individuals who have no significant racial characteristics. In the same vein, the white person is unlikely to see or describe himself in racial terms, perhaps in part because his white peers do not regard him as racially distinctive. Whiteness is a transparent quality when whites interact with whites in the absence of people of color. Whiteness attains opacity, becomes apparent to the white mind, only in relation to, and contrast with, the "color" of nonwhites. . . .

I do not mean to claim that white people are oblivious to the race of other whites. Race is undeniably a powerful determinant of social status and so is always noticed, in a way that eye color, for example, may not be. However, whites' social dominance allows us to relegate our own racial specificity to the realm of the subconscious. Whiteness is the racial norm. In this culture, the black person, not the white, is the one who is different. The black, not the white, is racially distinctive. Once an individual is identified as white, his distinctively racial characteristics need no longer be conceptualized in racial terms; he becomes effectively raceless in the eyes of other whites. Whiteness is always a salient personal characteristic, but once identified, it fades almost instantaneously from white consciousness into transparency.

The best "evidence" for the pervasiveness of the transparency phenomenon will be the white reader's own experience: critically assessing our habitual ways of thinking about ourselves and about other white people should bring transparency into full view. The questions that follow may provide some direction for the readers' reflections.

In what situations do you describe yourself as white? Would you be likely to include white on a list of three adjectives that describe you? Do you think about your race as a factor in the way other whites treat you? For example, think about the last time some white clerk or salesperson treated you deferentially, or the last time the first taxi to come along stopped for you. Did you think, "That wouldn't have happened if I weren't white"? Are you conscious of yourself as white when you find yourself in a room occupied only by white people? What if there are people of color present? What if the room is mostly nonwhite?

Do you attribute your successes or failures in life to your whiteness? Do you reflect on the ways your educational and occupational opportunities have been enhanced by your whiteness? What about the life courses of others? In your experience, at the time of Justice Souter's nomination, how much attention did his race receive in conversations among whites about his abilities and prospects for confirmation? Did you or your white acquaintances speculate on the ways his whiteness might have contributed to his success, how his race may have affected his character and personality, or how his whiteness might pre-dispose him to a racially skewed perspective on legal issues?

. . . Do you try to understand the ways your shared whiteness affects the interactions between yourself and your white partner, friends, and acquaintances? For example, perhaps you have become aware of the absence of people of color on some occasion. Did you move beyond that moment of recognition to consider how the group's uniform whiteness affected its interactions, agenda, process, or decisions? Do you inquire about the ways white persons you know have dealt with the fact, and privilege, of their whiteness?

. . . White people can do better than to continue to impose our beliefs, values, norms, and expectations on black people under the rubric of race neutrality. Recognizing transparency for the defining characteristic of whiteness that it is ought to impel us to a radical skepticism concerning the possibility of race-neutral decision-making. Operating from the presumption that racially neutral criteria of decision are in reality race-specific can prompt whites committed to the realization of racial justice to search for and adopt more racially inclusive ways of doing business. In this way, the skeptical stance can be instrumental in the development of a positive white racial identity, one that comprehends whiteness not as the (unspoken) racial norm, but as just one racial identity among many. . . .

Questions

1. What are the differences between discrimination against Caucasians and that against various minority racial groups? The answer to this question shapes many legal interpretations of Title VII, reverse discrimination, affirmative action, and the recognition of the injury of discrimination. The U.S. Supreme Court has interpreted the protection accorded to victims of discrimination on the basis of race to members of all races, including Caucasians, in both Title VII cases and claims arising under the

equal protection clause of the Fourteenth Amendment to the U.S. Constitution. *McDonald v. Santa Fe Trail Transp. Co,* 424 U.S. 952 (1976).

2. What are the underlying assumptions that you think are inherent in the idea of equality? What role, if any, should the ideas of white privilege play in the identification of those underlying assumptions? How could the law begin to address these assumptions in a fair and equitable manner?

3. Do you identify with Barbara Flagg's questions? What privileges do you have compared to other races? What about your privileges with respect to people whose sexual orientations are different from yours? Do you have privileges with respect to your physical strengths and weaknesses? Which of Professor Flagg's questions upset you the most? Which of these privileges affect the way the law interprets the existence of discrimination or the need for affirmative action?

4. The Sameness/Difference Dilemma in Developing the Ideal of Equality

Feminist critical legal theory offered a different perspective on the legal idea of equality and the goals of antidiscrimination laws. In addition to forcing an examination of the way the law recognized a dichotomy between the public and private spheres of society, feminist critical legal scholars focused on equality doctrine and brought into question the requirements that opened fields of opportunity to women who could show their similarities to men and the male standard. Lucinda Finley, currently a professor of law at the University of Buffalo School of Law, made an early contribution to the sameness/difference debate about equality for women. She suggests that equal treatment does not necessarily mean substantive equality for women if all it means is that they are equal when they are the same as men. Her article, which is excerpted here, describes the debate and recognizes the ways in which it influenced the plight of pregnant women in the workplace under the law. The sameness/difference dilemma discussed in this and other scholarly articles continues to be an unresolved issue and affects the way the courts interpret Title VII. Think about why this is an important perspective for understanding the goals of discrimination laws.

Lucinda M. Finley, *Transcending Equality Theory: A Way Out of the Maternity and the Workplace Debate,*
86 Colum. L. Rev. 1118 (1986)

(This is an edited version of the article and footnotes are deleted.)

The Equal Treatment/Special Treatment Debate and a Critique of Equality Analysis

The ideal of equality—that similarly situated individuals should be treated alike—is basic to our political and legal system. By appealing to equality and the doctrine of antidiscrimination, women have been able to make great strides toward the goal of improving their social status and power. Equality theory has been particularly useful for gaining access to traditionally male prerogatives within the public sphere. It works well and should continue to be the guide when the goal is assimilation of women into male institutions. Assimilation, however, too often means the creation of "a world in which persons of both genders are encouraged to act as men currently do and in which current 'female behavior' will gradually

wither away." This conception of the ideal world that underlies equality jurisprudence is precisely why it is limited and problematic in the pregnancy context, and in other gender contexts where women have qualities or perspectives that can enhance the male sphere and should not be dispensed with. Pregnancy is essential to the human race, and it is an area in which women cannot and should not act like men. It is "female behavior" that is not going to gradually wither away. Where gender distinctions arise from biological facts, or where they have culturally existed, women are not similarly situated to men. Existing institutional structures therefore have distinct implications for women and men. Given this reality, equality doctrine is not going to advance women very far. The doctrine inherently assumes that the goal is assimilation to an existing standard without questioning the desirability of that standard, and thus it limits the debate to what policies will best achieve the assimilation.

The Special Treatment/Equal Treatment Debate Summarized

The special treatment/equal treatment debate reflects the limiting focus of equality analysis. Each side agrees that women should have the right not to be penalized as workers for being childbearers and for having principal childrearing responsibility. The split comes over how to realize that right and about what constitutes a penalty: is it not being treated as men are, or is it not being treated as a woman? The answer, however, is that it can be both, depending on the situation, and what one considers male-like or "equal" treatment, and on what form the female-like or "special" treatment will take.

Essentially, the debate is between two strands of traditional liberal equality theory—formal versus substantive equality, or equal opportunity versus equal outcomes. By formal equality I mean the doctrinal model that would treat likes alike. The rule requires us first to identify relevant similarities and then to treat two similar individuals the same. By substantive equality I mean the doctrinal model which acknowledges that parceling out goods such as workplace benefits according to egalitarian distributive principles may not result in people's positions actually coming out equal in the end. To make the competition equal, people may need varying underlying substantive entitlements. Individual needs and positions may have to be taken into account in any particular situation in order to achieve equality of outcome.

In many respects, each side of the debate accepts the notion that the public world of the workplace and the private world of the home are separate spheres. They both see the problem as the relegation of women to the private sphere through barriers erected in the public sphere. The goal, then, is to make women more equal in the workplace sphere. Both agree that one way to achieve this goal is to support legislative initiatives to make parenting leaves available to men and women.

. . . There is an insoluble quality to this debate, reminiscent of many means-ends disputes. The conundrum in which feminists have found themselves is attributable to the limitations and flaws inherent in the doctrinal tradition that we have been given for attempting to "solve" pressing social problems that emerge out of the fact that we are not a perfectly homogeneous society of similarly situated equals. Both sides of the debate appeal to aspects of the doctrinal framework of equality analysis, yet that very framework provides no objectively principled, apolitical basis for making a general choice between the sometimes competing visions of equality of opportunity and equality of outcome.

The Special Treatment/Equal Treatment Debate as a Device for Critiquing Equality Analysis

The limitations of equality analysis as a transformative device for challenging the economic and social subordination of women and attendant limitations on male roles stem from its inability to come to terms in any acceptable, unproblematic manner with the reality of human variety. We are all different, and distinctions of gender are one type of difference that is unlikely ever to disappear. . . .

The ideal of homogeneous assimilation has been a motivating force behind our legal system's definition of equality as the similar treatment of those who are similar. The search for categories of similarity means that there must be a standard against which similarities are to be measured, and the choice of the standard will determine the nature of the outcome of the comparison. But there is something inherent in the concept of a standard for assessment that views the standard as the norm, and everything that is dissimilar from the standard as the deviate "other." "Different" and "other" consequently have pejorative connotations in our tradition of equality jurisprudence.

The idea that to be "different" is undesirable leads to the "difference dilemma." Our tradition of equality has too often meant prejudice toward those whom the dominant group has labelled as different. Thus, to be considered different can mean being stigmatized or penalized. "Difference" is stigmatizing because the assimilationist ideal underlying our society's conception of equality presumes sameness. Thus, the recognition of difference threatens our conception of equality, and the proclamation or identification of difference can serve as a justification for existing inequities. On the other hand, to hide the fact of difference from the prevailing norm means being treated according to a "faulty neutrality," or a standard that, because it was not created with the difference in mind, advances the dominant group to the detriment of those who are not, in fact, like it.

The special treatment/equal treatment debate reflects each side of the difference dilemma. The equal treatment position, by emphasizing sameness, is designed to avoid further instances of discrimination in the male dominated and defined workplace because of ways in which women are different from men. The special treatment position recognizes the disadvantage of this emphasis on sameness, which is to recreate and entrench instances of discrimination that occur because the standards of the workplace have not been determined according to the needs and perspectives of women. To be treated as if you were the same as a norm from which you actually differ in significant ways is just as discriminatory as being penalized directly for your difference.

The very idea of a norm implies that whatever is considered "normal" can take on a quality of objective reality, so that it is no longer possible to see that the standard of measurement reflects simply one group of qualities out of the infinite variety of human experience. The qualities chosen as the standard for measurement for legal equality analysis have been determined by those who have had the power to define or to imprint their view of what is real, important, and normal, on others. . . .

There is yet a deeper level, however, that has been obscured by equality analysis. The context in which gender hierarchy problems arise includes the need to question why we value some kinds of human activity as "work" and not others of equal societal value, and why some kinds of "work" are considered appropriate for one sex rather than the other. It is also necessary to question why we view those who are engaged in the remunerative kinds of work as abstract individuals with little responsibility to each other and with totally separate lives "outside" work. A central aspect of the problem that eludes equality analysis is the maintenance of separate spheres of work and home, and the devaluation of the home sphere and values associated with it in the work world. Consequently, the values of interdependence, care, and responsibility that are characteristic of the home sphere are absent from the public sphere of the workplace and the legal system.

Suggestions for Transcending Equality Analysis

. . . [T]he current conception of the ideal articulated by the equality doctrine has taken on a meaning that keeps referring us to a male norm. The word has come to equate difference with stigma, and to exalt similarity as the ideal. In the process, the idea of "equality" overlooks the socially constructed nature of difference. The inherited language of equality does not easily convey the meanings of those who urge a broader definition of "equality." The language seduces us into the circularity of the special treatment/equal treatment debate. Thus, we need to acknowledge that the borrowed language is no longer well suited to expressing many of the problems women must address, now that women have advanced in ever increasing numbers into previously male domains and privileges. Once our society's conceptions of sameness and difference, male and female, have undergone some change, it may be profitable to start talking about "equality" again. . . .

How to Think About Differences

The point of thinking about differences in a legal system that accepts human variety should be to try to avoid the dilemma of people being stigmatized or penalized by, or burdened in their access to, the domain of the "not dif-

ferent" by the fact of their difference. Gender differences should not burden women in the work world and keep men trapped in a world that denies to them the values of the home world.

Present equality analysis asks which differences count and which do not; or, what are the relevant similarities and differences? This approach diverts attention from the need to ask how acknowledged differences should count and how the law should respond to the variety of differences between people. What do we make of the differences between men and women, using both, rather than just men, as a reference point? To start thinking about what the significance of a perceived difference should be, we have to question the valuation assigned to a particular difference. To do this we have to remain sensitive to the fact that the attribution of difference is one of perspective, and that the attribution is constructed out of a relationship between the "normal" and the "different," a relationship affected by the power to label.

These questions about differences represent a significant change in emphasis from the question posed by equality analysis. They move us away from an orientation toward sameness and an acceptance of the premises underlying the labels "same" and "different," to one focused on thinking about the norms or prevailing values embraced by the attribution of difference.

Thinking about the meaning of the attribution of difference means that we must constantly subject to critical scrutiny the idea of a normal standard of measurement, defined by those with the power to define. We must scrutinize structures such as job requirements and expectations, and assumptions about human capabilities, to see to what extent they are determined not by the real needs of the job or of society, but by the idea of a norm that does not actually reflect job functions or the composition of society or the workforce. For example, the prevailing norm that a worker is an able-bodied person who should rarely get sick and who has someone else who can devote full time to taking care of children, food, laundry, repairs, errands, and family illnesses, describes very few men today and even fewer women. Once the false nature of the norm around which workplaces are structured is realized, the answer to the question of "how should an employer or the law respond to the differences between men and women" starts to change. It becomes less significant that women are "not men." It can be understood that, in relationship to each other, there may be more commonalities than supposed, and that a policy adopted to respond to the needs of women can be inclusive of, and benefit men too. It also might make apparent the need to start changing the values and structures of the workplace to incorporate some of the values of the world traditionally associated with women. . . .

In order to appreciate better the relational nature of differences, legal decisionmakers will have to be encouraged to make a conscious effort to listen to and to appreciate the perspective of those they have labeled different. In antidiscrimination law the perspectives of the victims of discrimination have too often been ignored; the voices of women, in particular, have too often been unheard by our legal system. Because of this lack of attention to the perspectives of the "different," the concrete way in which various attributions of difference have harmed those so labeled has often been overlooked in judicial opinions. While it is certainly problematic for those in power, who are used to thinking of themselves as part of the norm, to put themselves within the perspective of someone they have been taught to view as different, simply being asked to make the effort to think in those terms can broaden one's horizons and enrich one's own perspective. Being conscious of the fact that attributions of difference are largely a matter of power and one's perspective can make us less certain that the "other" is really so different. It can help break through the barriers of distrust and misunderstanding that reinforce the idea of difference as something undesirable and deserving of penalty. This will probably require new terminology, since current preconceptions are firmly embedded in the word "different." If we start talking about varieties and nuances rather than differences, it may be easier to see the necessity and desirability of many human distinctions. It will also become less important to rank qualities or people, such as putting the feminine into a less valued home sphere, and the masculine into a more valued public sphere. It will also make us less comfortable with accepting generalizations about each gender. . . .

The trap that equality analysis has become for women in the seemingly unique context of pregnancy highlights the need for a new conception for evaluating gender issues. Any approach, to be adequate, must not mask, as equality analysis does, the deeper underlying aspects of the value choices and the vision of society at stake in debates over gender roles. We need a legal framework that offers a richer conception of human needs than the theory of human nature that undergirds equality analysis. Such a framework must perceive not only our essential interconnectedness, but must start from the premise that work and family are the two most important defining aspects of the lives of men and women. Consequently, the idea that these two aspects of human existence occupy separate spheres must be replaced with legal policies and a framework for evaluating them that appreciates that public and private are a continuum, with each defining and affecting the other. If we supplement our existing conception of rights with a concept of responsibility to others arising out of our interconnectedness, we can begin to move toward workplace policies that make it possible for both women and men to combine their work lives with involvement in the family. Maternity leave laws should be understood as examples of such policies, because rather than being "special treatment" for women, they redound to the benefit of men and children, as well.

5. Post Modern Theory: The "Dominance" and "Discourse" Attacks on Basic Assumptions of Power

One important critique of the unstated goals of antidiscrimination laws, and of equality law in particular, has focused on the power imbalance that shapes the structure of society and the relationships between men and women and between powerful majority groups and relatively less powerful minority groups in today's society. Professor Eichner discusses the approach introduced by Catharine MacKinnon has been a leader in the legal discourse on power, dominance, and the relationships between men and women in society at large, and on the problem of sexual harassment in the workplace, in particular.

Maxine Eichner, *on Postmodern Feminist Legal Theory*, 36 Harvard Civil Rights-Civil Liberties Law Review 1 (2001)

(This is an edited version of the article and footnotes are deleted.)

. . . Prior to the rise of poststructuralist accounts of power, the prevailing model of power in feminist theory was what I call the "dominance" model. This model was developed in the 1970s and 1980s, largely in the work of radical feminists. The dominance model was developed in response to the mainstream conception of power that existed in both political theory and popular thought during that time, which conceived of power as something that people or groups possess and can wield consciously for their own ends against others. As Max Weber describes this view, "we understand by 'power' the chance of a man or a number of men to realize their own will in a social action even against the resistance of others who are participating in the action." Dominance in this model is sustained from above, as the less powerful are forced to comply with the edicts of those in power. Power's effects, however, extend only to external obedience: it does not affect an individual's interior wants and desires. Power in this way was seen as repressive, acting through prohibitions on what the individual may do and how she may act, while individuals were seen as having an autonomous, internal existence that precedes and remains aloof from power.

While liberal feminists generally accepted the mainstream model at the inception of second wave feminism in the 1960s and 1970s, radical feminists subsequently rejected it. The dominance conception they developed, which received its most theoretically sophisticated legal treatment in the work of Catharine MacKinnon in the 1980s, adopted the mainstream model's view that power is something possessed by some and wielded against others. It further stratified the lines of power, however. Under this model, men hold power and intentionally wield it against powerless women: "[M]en oppress women to the extent that they can because it is in their interest and to their advantage to do so."[28]

Male power, according to the dominance view, is univocal and completely totalizing, creating the world, including women, in its image. In contrast to the mainstream model, the dominance model jettisons the humanist notion that the powerless have selves that precede and exist apart from power. Instead, the dominance model conceives of women, their wants and needs, as completely constructed by patriarchal power. According to MacKinnon, "In feminist terms, the fact that male power has power means that the interest of male sexuality constructs what sexuality as such means, including the standard way it is allowed to be felt and expressed and experienced, in a way that determines women's biographies, including sexual ones."[30] Women's differences from men, in this reading, are the result of male power: women are different from men because men desire them to be different and subordinate them to produce this effect.

The dominance model made considerable gains for feminist theory by responding to the serious deficiencies in the mainstream view of power. The mainstream view, in holding that power operated externally on individuals, failed to link power with women's characteristics, aims, and desires, all of which it saw as preceding power. It therefore allowed opponents of feminism to argue that women's differences from men demonstrated that women either were "naturally" the weaker sex (an argument also phrased in terms of how women's delightfully feminine nature led them to gravitate to certain roles), or that women themselves were responsible for the choices that left them in second-class positions in society. The dominance model of power put forth by radical feminists effectively countered these arguments. Under it, the suffering of women could no longer be ascribed to women's nature or women's choices. In Susan Bordo's words, "the insistence that women are the done to, not the doers, here; that men and their desires bear the responsibility; and that female obedience to the dictates of [women's stereotypical roles] is better conceptualized as bondage than choice— was a crucial historical moment" for feminism.[33] At the same time, this position allowed feminists to deal with ways in which women were different from men without giving up the fight for equality. In doing so, the dominance model opened up a complete range of issues for the feminist agenda—sexuality, abortion, domestic violence—that liberal feminism could not consider because it had largely emphasized women's similarities to men.

Despite these virtues, however, it has become increasingly clear that the dominance model of power is inadequate to address the complexity of the situation of men and women in contemporary Western society. Since the late 1980s, a number of critics, including many postmodern feminist legal theorists, have spelled out the problems with this model. They point out, first, that MacKinnon's oppressor/oppressed view of power fails to take into account differences among women. In MacKinnon's theory, all women are oppressed, and oppressed in the same way, without regard to differences in age, ethnicity, religion, geography, and a host of other factors. Yet, as a number of feminist theorists argue, gender is only one of a number of axes of power that exist in our society. Accordingly, different women are differentially situated with respect to power: while white women may experience oppression on account of their sex, they also share privilege on account of their race.[36] As Drucilla Cornell points out, the meaning of gender is "always modified."

---

[28] Catharine MacKinnon, TOWARD A FEMINIST THEORY OF THE STATE (1989) at 260 n. 65. Additionally, MacKinnon writes, "It is not only that men treat women badly, although often they do, but that it is their choice whether or not to do so." Id. at 94.
[30] Id. at 129.

[33] Susan Bordo, Unbearable Weight: Feminism, Western culture, and the body 22–23 (1993).
[36] Drucilla Cornell, Beyond Accommodation: Ethical Feminism, Deconstruction, and the law (1991) at 130.

Further, the dominance model totalizes the grasp of patriarchy and misses the myriad ways in which women, in actual fact, diverge from dominant images of the feminine. One consequence of MacKinnon's monolithic view of power is that she cannot explain the emergence of a feminist viewpoint. In Drucilla Cornell's words, "[i]f women as a gender are defined as victims, as fuckees, as voiceless, and if, as MacKinnon argues, the feminist 'point of view' is an impossibility within our system of male dominance, then it would be impossible to provide the condition for repair." Women, in other words, if they are truly the passive victims MacKinnon theorizes, could never become feminists capable of resisting male dictates. Further, even when women do conform to these images, for example in their role as children's caretakers, MacKinnon's theory cannot recognize the value of these activities.

The dominance model also overstates men's power, even while it ignores women's. Her account ignores the way in which men are themselves constructed within the system of gender hierarchy rather than its conscious creators for their own interests. In Steven Winter's words, "it should follow from [MacKinnon's] analysis that men, too, are subjected to the regulation and control of this system of gender relations (although, obviously, in very different ways). MacKinnon, however, balks at this conclusion. Thus, for example, she gives short shrift to 'the phenomena of "compulsive masculinity."'"

Finally, the dominance account of power fails to recognize the multiplicity of meanings in current gender practices. For example, there is no single, acceptable notion of how women in our society should behave, but rather there are a welter of different, sometimes contradictory notions that emerge from a multitude of sites. While many of these are disempowering, certainly some are empowering. . . . The dominance model, with its black-and-white conception of power, is not up to this task.

Poststructuralist Models of Power

In place of the dominance view of power, postmodern legal theorists, most notably Drucilla Cornell and Steven Winter, seek to substitute a version of power premised on the poststructuralist notion of discourse. Broadly speaking, this notion of discourse links power to shared patterns of language and thought that, by constructing the way in which subjects see the world, construct social reality. Specific poststructualist accounts of how discourse operates to perpetuate inequalities of power differ widely, however. In drawing on widely disparate strands of poststructuralism, Drucilla Cornell and Steven Winter produce very different accounts of power and power's relation to gender hierarchy. . . .

Drucilla Cornell's discourse theory has the virtue of recognizing that women are more complex than either the dominant images of women in contemporary society or the dominance view of power allows. Her discursive account of the formation of gender hierarchy is also promising in its recognition that the meanings of gender and sex are contestable and open to reinterpretation. Yet despite these qualities, Cornell's version of discourse theory is ultimately of limited use to feminist legal theory. . . .

In reading gender hierarchy as either remetaphorizable or subvertible at will, both Cornell and Winter fail to realize crucial gains that discursive theories of power offer feminism. By focusing on the way in which power is manifested in social relations rather than held by some and not by others, such theories of power provide a better description of contemporary power. At the same time, in focusing on the links among power, identity, desire, and resistance, discourse theories provide feminist legal theory with the opportunity to construct a more useful account of power by recognizing the implications of power for the possibilities of resistance. To take advantage of the gains from discursive theories of power, such an account would recognize that women often internalize what Foucault would call "the gaze"—that is, they impose their own discipline, such that their senses of self are structured by normalizing forces in society. In this way, they adapt their preferences to conform with the status quo and the limited opportunities it provides. Further, this account would recognize the ways in which women's actions and choices may be more or less constrained depending on the range of discourses and identities available to them. Finally, it would recognize the extent to which, through discourse circulating among a multitude of sites and subcultures, dominant gender images are already continually being contested in women's lived reality.

A few feminist theorists, though not specifically identifying themselves as postmodernists, have begun the necessary reconstruction of feminist theory to take into account the complex ways in which identity, agency, and choice are related to power. In a recent article, Kathryn Abrams embarks on the difficult project of theorizing agency in the context of power inequalities. She directs her article against liberal conceptions of autonomy and, in the process, sets out a theory of socially inscribed agency. Along similar lines, several theorists have called attention to the ways in which resistance can be limited by social factors but still exist in circumscribed form. These theorists argue that women's resistance has often been overlooked because theorists have failed to recognize the options for resistance that women have available to them in particular circumstances, or have defined resistance too narrowly. For example, Martha Mahoney demonstrates that women's experience of battering is far more complex than is conveyed by the legal system's presentation of such women as passive victims. These women, even if they do not immediately end the battering relationship, may still resist the batterer in a number of ways that protect themselves and their children, both physically and psychologically, in the short and long term.

Conceived in this manner, discourse theories of power can provide direction for a postmodern feminist legal agenda. Such a discourse theory would demonstrate that because power is inherently unstable and scattered through multiple processes and locations, and because dominant meanings are never completely monolithic, subjects can sometimes both gain access to and internalize divergent interpretations on which resistance to dominant norms can be grounded. Resistance can therefore be fostered in particular situations. The function of feminist legal theory, then, is not simply to assert that women can transcend expected gender roles, but to locate the social, political, and legal conditions that will foster women's ability to subvert traditional gender identities. This formulation of a postmodern feminist legal agenda would therefore require explicit focus on strategies that would call attention to subversive gender discourse in actual women's lives and strengthen women's ability to resist dominant discourses. . . .

Questions

1. What does the dominance theory suggest about today's workplace? What does the "discourse" theory suggest? How would either of these theories deal with the problem of single mothers who are fired because they come in late when their children are sick or because they can't travel out of town for business meetings on a regular basis?
2. What are the effects of this kind of a theory, if incorporated in law, for employers? Are there any ways in which this could have positive effects for employers and the economy? What are the negative aspects of this theory from an employer perspective?
3. How does Professor Finley approach the problem of the marketplace? What do you think are the major differences, if any, between Professors Finley, MacKinnon, and Cornell in their approaches to the problems women face in the workplace?

6. The Marketplace as a Regulator of Discrimination in Employment

Law and Economics has become a pervasive force in legal theory. It has not played as significant a role in the formation of current employment discrimination laws, but it has been used by a variety of scholars to analyze such laws. Law and Economics analysis of employment discrimination laws has been heavily focused on efficiency and the market but not in a monolithic way. Various scholars have approached these issues from a number of perspectives, with some analyses assigning more or less importance to economic efficiency, externalities, and the operation of the market. We can provide only a brief glimpse of this material, but it is significant to note that many voices in the Law and Economics area would disagree with some or all of the material that follows.

This section will focus on a debate between two prominent scholars: Professor Richard Epstein and Professor Erwin Chemerinsky. The material raise the following questions: Can the marketplace regulate employment discrimination? Even if it can't do so without the help of government regulation—i.e., employment discrimination laws—are there trade-offs that must occur as we add more groups to the list of protected classes? Do similar trade-offs occur if we shift our views of the goals of employment discrimination law, and can the market account for these trade-offs? Finally, even if we accept that employment discrimination laws have benefits for those protected under them, are there costs to those protected, and how might we balance the economics and social benefits vis-à-vis the costs? As you read the material, think about these questions and whether economics provides an answer and, if so, whether that answer is adequate. How do you think these Law and Economics scholars would view each other's approaches?

Richard A. Epstein & Erwin Chemerinsky, *Should Title VII of the Civil Rights Act of 1964 Be Repealed?*,
2 S. Cal. Interdisc. L.J. 349 (1993)

(This is an edited version of the article and footnotes are deleted.)

Professor Richard Epstein's 1992 book, *Forbidden Grounds: The Case Against Employment Discrimination Laws*, boldly challenges the existing social consensus in favor of laws against employment discrimination. On November 19, 1992, the University of Southern California chapter of the Federalist Society sponsored a debate on Professor Epstein's proposal to repeal all employment discrimination laws. . . . [The debate was between Professor Epstein and Professor Erwin Chemerinsky.]

Professor Epstein: Employment Discrimination Laws Should Be Repealed

In this brief talk, I want to outline some of the reasons why I think that the present body of antidiscrimination laws should be repealed insofar as it applies to private employers who operate in competitive markets. The simplest way to justify that position is to give a comparison between the operation of the antidiscrimination laws and the usual tort prohibitions against the use of force. In my view the differences in the operation of these two types of laws largely explain why the antidiscrimination laws should be repealed. The fact that there is a strong social consensus in favor of the civil rights acts, and the antidiscrimination principle they are said to embody, offers, if anything, an additional reason for their repeal, and none for their continued enforcement.

In making this general claim I want to stress again that the focus here is on private employment. I am not concerned with voting rights or with any other subject, such as aid to educational institutions that are covered by the Civil Rights Acts themselves. In many cases the analysis that I have given will carry over, but in other cases it may not. It is best therefore to focus on one area, and leave all else aside.

Returning then to our basic inquiry, I should state at the outset that my basic political orientation is libertarian, but that as a limited-state libertarian, I do not believe that there should be no government at all. I do not believe that we could endure a state of affairs in which all individuals have no legal rights and no legal duties. I do not believe in a legal regime of anarchy, without any regime of government. But I do think that the central legal prohibition on certain individual conduct does derive directly from the Hobbesian concern with the use of force and, I will add, fraud, in a state of nature.

Given this orientation, the central question is a comparison in the positions of two kinds of victims, those of force and those of discrimination in employment markets. The dissimilarities will dominate. In order to see why, ask first why it is that we all fear the use of force. I think that the explanation is not difficult or complicated: some people could kill us. So now the question is, what steps do we have to take in order to control these people. One approach is to adopt a market orientation and to say that we should all enter private contracts to secure our self-protection. But immediately the question is, with whom should the contract be made? In a world in which you are looking at force as the major source of horror, the people you are concerned with are not your friends, but generally speaking, your enemies. So the first person with whom you must contract has to be the person who is most intent on doing you harm. You would have to find some mix of bribes and threats that would lead him to renounce the use of force against you, and to keep his promise. Only then could you start to breathe easily.

But not for long, for there are lots of people out there who could do you ill, so that even if you enter into a contract with one or another of them, there will remain others who are every bit as hostile to you, and with the same designs on your person and property. So what now? It turns out that you need a second arrangement, and then a third, and then a fourth. In a world in which, I am sorry to say, there is a great deal of bigotry and a great deal of intolerance, and impatience and stupidity, you will not be able to make, let alone enforce, enough contracts with enough persons to keep all these potential enemies at bay. There is in effect a huge set of transactional barriers that block the voluntary creation of a complicated network of contracts whereby everyone agrees to a mutual renunciation of force. So owing to these barriers, we have come to recognize the need for the state, and the coercive transactions it uses to insure peace. The state imposes taxes (hence the reason for calling me a limited-government libertarian) on us all for the benefit of the common good, which in this particular case is to create a monopoly of force that prohibits the private aggression by one individual against another. It is perhaps somewhat paradoxical that a strong libertarian like myself who generally thinks that state intervention is a "bad" must nonetheless concede that it is possible to identify some circumstances in which the collective use of force is a manifest good. The failure of coordination by private agreement is what drives us to a social contract.

The difficulties here are very pronounced, for even if voluntary agreements could be reached to satisfy ninety-nine percent of the population, the reluctance of the other one percent to go along could undo all or much of the gains from the agreements otherwise reached. Owing to these instabilities, a strong social consensus does not create a viable equilibrium. The misbehavior of a single individual can undo the precarious social peace which commands wide social support. It is truly a case where all must be bound in order for any to be protected.

Now when we switch to the antidiscrimination laws in employment we face a very different social phenomenon. In order to see what it is, it is important to recall what the basic structure of the Civil Rights Acts provides. It does not deal with the punishment of individuals who act out of bad motives; there are indeed many situations (especially those involving the use of force) where the presence of a bad motive can make an illegal action worse. . . .

So now it is important to keep the Civil Rights Acts in perspective. They are not concerned with cases of aggravated assault for racial motives or something of that sort. Instead as the statute itself recognizes, we are dealing with cases where someone "fails to or refuses to" deal with another person because of—and you may now fill in the blanks—race, creed, religion, age, handicap, intelligence, or indeed anything that you want. The precise content of the particular prohibition has relatively little to do with the basic structure of the law.

What basic structure? The key feature concerns the kinds of searches and the kinds of conduct open to individuals to improve their positions. Recall—and it is critical to the argument—that we are in a world in which all persons have secured a liberty of the person by a prohibition against the use of force. What is the analogous danger that we face from private discrimination?

Initially, note that in this situation, you are looking at a world of hundreds, and thousands, and millions of people, some of whom hate you quite as much as they did in an unregulated state of nature. The question still remains, what can they do with their hatred? By definition they can at most refuse to do business with you. The change in the nature of the legal rules changes the nature of the contracts that you must seek in order to better yourself. In effect what you must now do is to search the other side of the market to try to find those individuals whose inclinations are most favorable to your welfare. You can spurn all of those whose inclinations are hostile to your own welfare. In this setting the relevant imagery is very different from that involved when the use of force is allowed. If you can find a tiny segment of the population which will do business with you on favorable terms, then the fact that many others refuse to deal with you will not result generally in any systematic diminution of your wealth. Now you need not enter into a mass of contracts to keep the enemy at bay, but only one, or a few contracts, to sell your labor to some willing employer.

So how should we expect the world to play out even if there is some conscious discrimination so that whites

(for example) prefer to do business with whites? In order to see what is going on here, it is critical to return to a central distinction introduced by Gary Becker in his early analysis of discrimination: one possible outcome of discrimination is a wage differential, and the other is a separation of blacks and whites (to take a simple example) into different firms. His argument was that even if you could show that many employers wished to discriminate against some portion of the population, so long as there is free entry into the market (that is many parties looking for contracts) the wages between the two groups will in equilibrium be the same, adjusting for productivity variables, even though you might find some level of market separation between blacks and whites. In a competitive situation, his position was that you could find market separation, but not wage differentiation.

Now, with some trepidation, I would like to suggest that what Becker said is wrong on one point. He said that in a world of pure competition, you would expect all forms of discrimination to cease, because the firms that engage in discrimination in competitive markets would find themselves at a systematic disadvantage relative to their rivals. He is clearly correct that competition will have an enormous effect on the way in which the market operates, so much so that I am in favor of some antidiscrimination or nondiscrimination provision to the extent that there is monopoly or restricted entry that allows one firm, or union, to have some control over price or contract terms. The point is that once the monopolist is a sole person with whom you can deal, various forms of discrimination do become possible, and these lead to inferior allocative outcomes to situations in which competitive forces are allowed to work.

But does it follow that in a competitive world we would expect to see a color-blind or race-blind equilibrium, of the sort that was generally thought desirable in the social discussion around the time that Congress enacted the 1964 Civil Rights Act. It is of course difficult to predict in the abstract the precise form that the market behavior and discrimination will take. Indeed most of the standard models on the subject tried to identify various imperfections that could explain the persistence of discrimination: all employers were white males with preferences for their own kind; or that all customers had preferences for white over black, or male over female, or some other assumptions that were every bit as austere and improbable.

It turns out that these depictions of the market are, however, wholly inconsistent with any assumption of free entry into the marketplace. If anyone can become an employer, then we should expect to find lots of persons becoming employers whose preferences run very much at cross-currents with the simple, uniform descriptions of the market, and each of these employers will seek out some niche where he or she can enjoy some temporary advantage relative to some equally determined rivals. . . .

But it is said that there are preferences and preferences; that the arguments for diversity are vastly stronger than the arguments in favor of old-fashioned bigotry. One could point to the stain of history and the need for some rectification. And I must say that in general I have sympathy with this position, although I am ever more distressed by the intolerant way in which the case is often made. But by the same token even if the arguments for diversity carry some weight, it is important to recognize their intrinsic limitations: while these arguments may justify the race-conscious practices of the firms that choose to accept their moral force, they do not justify the coercion of others who do not share this view of history. One can make the argument from history on the retail basis and respond to it at that level. There is no reason to make a strong point of view, no matter how sound, official state policy.

The simple point of my argument is that if a large portion of the population thinks that some form of race preference is an appropriate response to past discrimination, then even if one repealed the antidiscrimination laws tomorrow, you would expect to see many more firms engage in these desired forms of discrimination than in the opposite forms. The moral case does not disappear with the statute. But since the forms of discrimination are not wholly voluntary (with no stick in the side of those who disagree with the official policy), then we are freed as a nation of the incredible government colossus that today imposes a huge tax on us all. Likewise, we will be freed of the enormous political risk that the civil rights statutes that were originally defended as a "mild and moderate" intervention in the market will create massive intrusions with respect to testing, pensions, promotions, and every other aspect of the employment relationship.

These remarks are not idle comments. If you start to look at these civil rights statutes and ask yourself to consider the drain that they clearly create, it is necessary to identify some offsetting social improvement that they can deliver. And on this critical point the evidence in favor of the statute is very, very weak. There were some gains attributable to the passage of the civil rights statutes in the years before 1975. I think that it is fair to say that virtually all of those gains had to do with the dismantling of the apparatus of segregation as it existed in the old South, and with the change in union practices throughout the country. But by the same token, if you look at the post-1975 period, there are two critical findings that are in close correlation with each other. There is both a relative stability in black/white wage differentials, and a decline in the overall level of wage growth. The reason why these two phenomena go together is that competitive markets do a far better job in sorting people by tastes, abilities, and preferences than any system of heavy-handed government planning.

The bottom line should be clear. On issue after issue, it is clear that governments cannot move with assurance and wisdom in response to changes in external market and technology forces. We know from the socialist failures of Eastern Europe and the old Soviet Union that centralized planning cannot work. Those arguments carry over to a T with respect to the antidiscrimination laws as they apply to the employment relationship. For that reason—and perhaps for that reason only—I think that these statutes should be forthwith repealed. All of us, regardless of race, regardless of color, would be far better off under a color-blind state that enforces a regime that prohibits the private use of force and fraud, and gives legal protection to voluntary contractual relations in competitive markets.

Professor Chemerinsky: Society Needs Employment Discrimination Laws. . .

Professor Epstein is the foremost libertarian scholar among law professors today. But any idea taken to an extreme gives absurd results. What Professor Epstein is arguing for today is the repeal of all employment discrimination laws. He is arguing that employers should be free to discriminate, in any way they want, based on race, gender, religion, sexual orientation, disability, or age. He does this by focusing on abstractions—freedom of contract, the market in theory—but he ignores the social realities. I would argue that it is imperative that society have laws that prohibit employment discrimination. What I want to do is go step-by-step through the justifications for social prohibition of employment discrimination.

The first step of the analysis is that without legal regulation, significant employment discrimination would exist in the American market system. Racism, sexism, anti-Semitism, and homophobia are realities in this society. They've long manifested themselves in employment discrimination. Professor Epstein argues that the market system left to its own devices will eliminate most of that employment discrimination. I think he is clearly wrong.

Let me point to five flaws in his analysis with regard to the market system. First, history proves him wrong. We long had an unregulated market system. Civil rights laws did not exist until 1964, and employment discrimination was pervasive on all of these grounds. The statistics and real world examples both confirm this. Sandra Day O'Connor graduated high in her class from the Stanford Law School in the early 1950s. No law firm would hire her except as a legal secretary. Where was the market system to provide her a job?

Or consider another example, concerning a mutual friend that Professor Epstein and I share, who is now a chaired professor at Yale Law School. He is about ten years older than I am. He said that when he graduated from Yale Law School near the top of his class, virtually no law firm would offer him a job because he was Jewish. Where was the market system when he needed work? The simple reality is, as history shows us, employment discrimination is pervasive in a free market system.

A second flaw in Professor Epstein's market analysis is that prejudice distorts employers' evaluation of employees. The reality is that because of prejudice, employers discount the skills and talents of minorities. Because of prejudice, employers discount the skills and talents of women, or Jews, or gays and lesbians. And as a result, when prejudice is pervasive throughout society, the market system repeatedly undervalues contributions of these individuals and, as a result, these people never get hired as they should.

Third, Professor Epstein fails to account for customer preferences, and more importantly, perceived customer preferences. A law firm believes that its clients don't want to deal with Jewish lawyers. An employer believes that its customers don't want to deal with those with disabilities. And as a result, throughout the market, you see individuals who are minorities or disabled or Jewish simply not getting hired.

Fourth, Professor Epstein assumes that the market system, through competition, will create enough slots for these individuals. Professor Epstein says the Korean community will create jobs for Koreans; the black community will create jobs for blacks. But why believe that enough jobs will be created within these communities, especially given pervasive discrimination by the white community against these groups.

For all of these reasons I would say Professor Epstein's market theory is wrong. But I add a fifth reason. Professor Epstein fails to account for the fact that at times employers would rather discriminate even if it's costly. Think of a simple example: sexual harassment. Some studies show that over half of all women in the workplace have been harassed. Why do employers do this knowing that they might lose valuable female employees who might quit as a result? The reason is that their short-term perceived benefits are greater than their long-term costs. Perhaps they believe that the workers in the market are sufficiently fungible. Regardless, they believe that the short-term gains are worth the cost to them, and, thus, they go ahead and discriminate. The market system produces discrimination.

As I read Professor Epstein's long book, I was convinced that a key thing he fails to take into account is the pervasiveness of discrimination in the market economy. . . . My second step in the analysis is that laws should prohibit employment discrimination. I reason in two substeps here: Substep A is that employment discrimination

is terribly harmful. I believe the single most outrageous part of this book is that it does not take into account the terrible social harms of employment discrimination.

Professor Epstein refers to employment discrimination as a "preference" or in his words, "a taste of employers." For him, there's no difference between a company choosing white wallpaper as opposed to black wallpaper, and their choosing white employees over black ones. For him there's no difference between picking furniture as opposed to picking employees. And that's wrong. Employment discrimination imposes enormous costs on society. I think of three.

First, think of the cost to workers who are treated unfairly by being discriminated against on account of their race, or their gender, or their religion. Fairness should be one of our concerns in society. An individual who loses income on account of discrimination is being treated unfairly. Think of the loss of human potential in that person. A person is not able to pursue his or her calling and find fulfillment because of discrimination. Think of the enormous dignity harm to that person who can't get a job or can't get a promotion because of discrimination. Nowhere does Professor Epstein speak of that.

Think of a second harm, the harm to society's value of equality. We as a society should be deeply committed to equality. We should adhere to the principle that likes should be treated alike. Any compromise of that is unacceptable. This is something that has acceptance from all parts of the political spectrum. . . .

And third, there's enormous economic cost to society from discrimination. When we think of the cost in terms of the potential unfulfilled, we will never be able to measure what people could have contributed but didn't. We will never be able to measure the people who didn't look for a job because they know of discrimination. But we know that it is enormous. Society loses terribly when there's discrimination. For all of these reasons, discrimination must be regarded as an unacceptable evil.

Substep B of this argument is that freedom of contract should be interfered with to eliminate employment discrimination. Professor Epstein begins by saying that the main normative premise for society should be freedom of contract. But I believe where he goes wrong is that he tremendously overweighs the importance of freedom of contract and he underweighs the harms of discrimination.

At the very least with regard to freedom of contract, I disagree with his premise that it can only be interfered with to stop force or coercion. I certainly agree law is necessary and government is necessary to stop force and coercion. That's not the only time we need laws. The law should prohibit contracts for slavery even if slavery doesn't involve force or coercion. We should and do interfere with freedom of contract to protect the public safety and health. For example, you can't go to the gas station across the street to buy gasoline that has lead any longer. That interferes with freedom of contract, but the public health and the environment demand it. There are numerous instances where we interfere with freedom of contract for the public good. And one of these instances must be prohibiting employment discrimination.

Furthermore, Professor Epstein's argument with regard to freedom of contract only focuses on freedom of contract of employers. He ignores the freedom of contract of employees who are discriminated against. Imagine Sandra Day O'Connor graduating from law school in the early 1950s. What freedom of contract did she have in the market to get hired?

Professor Epstein assumes that the only thing that can interfere with freedom of contract is government laws. Discrimination, even the market system itself, can interfere with freedom of contract. We would expand the protection of freedom of contract for businesses at the expense of decreasing freedom of contract for individuals. But even if that were not true, I believe the evils of employment discrimination justify limiting freedom of contract. The principle of equality is simply more important in this society than the principle of freedom of contract.

The third step in my argument is that employment discrimination laws are successful in outlawing employment discrimination. At the beginning of Professor Epstein's book, he presents the argument that he advanced today: there's no evidence that employment discrimination laws succeed. And then later in his book he proves that employment discrimination laws succeed and he argues they work too well.

He says, for example, that employers are often forced to stop discriminating even when there's no proof of discrimination. He says, for example, with regard to age discrimination, that over twenty percent of the university budgets might have to go to pay the costs of the Age Discrimination in Employment Act. In other words, statistically, employment discrimination laws work. Moreover, he ignores an enormous body of evidence that shows that employment discrimination laws have been successful.

Professor Blumrosen, for example, looks at the success of employment discrimination laws in advancing minorities within professions. He says that within the minority community, millions of dollars of income have been transferred because of employment discrimination laws. He shows, with regard to almost every professional category, the number of minority employees went up as a result of employment discrimination laws. It is always hard to deal with this statistically because it is always very difficult to measure what doesn't exist, or what the world would be like without those laws. So think of examples.

Look at the airline industry. As a result of the laws prohibiting employment discrimination, airlines are now required to hire male flight attendants. If you fly in airplanes you'll see the employment discrimination laws work there. It used to be that the airlines said that flight attendants had to retire and leave the service when they got married. No longer can airlines discriminate in this way. It used to be that airlines had sex-based weight requirements imposed only on women flight attendants. That requirement no longer exists. It used to be that a flight attendant had to leave as soon as she knew she was pregnant. That requirement no longer exists. I could generalize from this industry to almost any industry at which the bottom line point is: employment discrimination laws are successful regarding hiring blacks, women, Jews and those who have been traditionally discriminated against.

My fourth and final major point is that even if employment discrimination laws are unsuccessful, their repeal would be a social disaster. Think of the message that would be conveyed if we repealed all employment discrimination laws. It would be the government implicitly saying racism, sexism, and homophobia are acceptable in this society. It would be giving license to the expression of that. We live in a society already terribly divided over basic characteristics like race and religion. I can't imagine any government action that would more tear at the social fabric and divide a society than repealing them. Even if the employment discrimination laws are nothing but a symbol, their symbol is one society must continue to have.

History shows that the vilest of ideas can be justified with the noblest of rhetoric. Today Professor Epstein comes before you with abstractions. He wants to talk about the market as an abstraction. He wants to talk about freedom of contract as an abstraction. I think you have to look at the reality of American society and what the legacy of discrimination is. We have to say loudly and always that employment discrimination is unacceptable and the laws must prohibit it.

Professor Epstein's Rebuttal

. . . It is not as though the positions I defend have widespread support in either the Republican or Democratic party. What I find so enormously ironic is the effort to place the failures of modern race relations at my doorstep when nothing I believe represents current policy and Professor Chemerinsky's beliefs are dominant on all key issues. There may be explanations for the current racial tensions, but to attribute them to the market is odd when there is no market operating here at all—which might explain why the situation has become so bad.

Professor Chemerinsky also misstated my position as to the current state of affairs. The sentence he quoted referred to overt and institutional discrimination, and noted that it all was in favor of members of protected classes, such as women and minorities. I did not say that there was no individual discrimination, which is how Professor Chemerinsky interpreted my remarks. I think that my original statement is true. I have not been in any firm or institution that has any formal white male preference. I do not know of any such business; neither does anyone else.

Next Professor Chemerinsky chides me for my devotion to moral abstractions and offers his own: namely, that discrimination on the basis of irrelevant characteristics is impermissible and unacceptable. But he is strangely silent on whether he favors affirmative action programs. And we don't know whether he thinks that diversity is a justification for race- and sex-conscious decisions. I suspect that he supports affirmative action and diversity. I do not know how he squares these beliefs with a thoroughgoing defense of the antidiscrimination principle. Yet somehow in his denunciation of my position, these issues all fade to the background, and we once again see the 1964 vision of a color-blind society emerge. I thought that I had made it clear that one of the advantages of getting rid of the antidiscrimination laws in private competitive markets was that it allowed well-intentioned people who favored these programs to adopt them if they so chose.

Now we still must ask what would happen if these statutes were repealed. We are told that there will be a great symbolic failure. I think that the exact opposite is more likely to occur. If we could explain why we want to repeal the statutes, we might enjoy a symbolic success. . . . If I were facing someone as hostile as Professor Chemerinsky. . . . I would stress that these are not color-blind or sex-blind laws. These are laws that say essentially that we do not believe that blacks and women can make it on their own. These are laws that say that explicit legal protection is necessary for their economic success, when in fact it is a barrier to them. These are laws that say that no employer can do a decent thing unless hit over the head by the threat of legal suit. I think that these laws are an insult, or at least an injustice, to every woman, every black, every Hispanic, who has been able to advance by hard work and honest effort.

Professor Chemerinsky stresses that in the past there were all sorts of barriers, many of them informal, to blacks and women who wanted to advance. But before one endorses the political remedy, it must be recognized that in 1951 no one could have passed any antidiscrimination statute: the votes were not there. But today there is a political majority in favor of the statutes, so why think that they are needed when there are huge numbers of employers who actively recruit on a race- and sex-conscious basis?

Professor Chemerinsky also insists that there have been great successes under the civil rights laws. But he does not know the difference between a change and a success. It may well be that we have turned the hiring practices of the airline industry inside and out. But when reliable polling data suggested that ninety-seven percent of your customers—men, women, and children—in 1968 prefer female stewardesses, then why condemn the firms

for responding to these preferences? What else are they supposed to respond to? Are we supposed to tell people when they are anxious or under stress that we are less concerned with their emotions and feelings and more concerned about our abstract ideals? Or should we try to help them? And if it turns out that these preferences do change—and I suspect that they would have changed—there is nothing that forces the airlines to keep their former policies, and many of them will change voluntarily.

Professor Chemerinsky also refers to the age discrimination laws. I can assure each student here that he or she will face enormous barriers to entry into labor markets because of these statutes. I and others have worked for hours at the University of Chicago to formulate plans that will limit their harmful effects so that we can find ways to hire young people without having to pay senior faculty full salaries, full pensions, and social security long after they have passed their most productive periods. Why their wages should shoot up while everyone else suffers a decline is simply beyond me. The age discrimination statutes are bad for you and bad for society at large. They will create major dislocations in future years, and you will bear the brunt of it.

Professor Chemerinsky's Rebuttal

Professor Epstein just shifted positions enormously. He began by telling you that all employment discrimination laws should be repealed. In his rebuttal he shifts away from that and instead wants to argue that particular aspects of the law are undesirable because affirmative action programs have a great cost. We are not arguing about whether particular provisions are good or bad. They can be changed. But what we are arguing about today is whether all employment discrimination laws be repealed and on this he clearly loses the debate.

I advance these four points. First, that without legal regulation, substantial discrimination would exist in the American market system. I pointed to five flaws in Professor Epstein's reasoning; he responded to none of them. Instead he says two things: first, he says we have had racial tensions since 1964 even though we've got the laws, so obviously the laws have failed.

We have racism in this society, we have sexism in this society, and as a result we do have racial and sexual tensions in this society. That doesn't prove that the employment discrimination laws fail. In fact, it's the very existence of racism and sexism that necessitates the laws prohibiting discrimination. And I believe the tensions would be far greater if we didn't have the laws, and infinitely greater if the laws are repealed.

Second, he talks about affirmative action and diversity. That's just not what this debate is about. I'd be glad to invite Professor Epstein back to debate affirmative action with him. But that's not what we are talking about here. We are not saying whether or not there should be preferences given to minorities or women in hiring. We are talking about whether or not employers should be prohibited from discriminating on the basis of race, gender, and religion. And on that ground, Professor Epstein does not deny that the market will inevitably leave discrimination.

With regard to the last quote from his book that I read, where he said there is no institutional discrimination except against white males, he said that he was speaking of institutional discrimination. And that's my point: that he fails to recognize that institutions—employers—will discriminate and do discriminate. The discrimination will increase tremendously if there aren't laws prohibiting employment discrimination. Even if no business has an announced "white-male preference," countless businesses do discriminate against women and racial minorities.

My second major point was that laws should prohibit employment discrimination. I tell you in subpoint A that employment discrimination is a terrible harm. It's harmful to the individual who is discriminated against, it offends society's notion of equality and is enormously costly to society.

I tell you in subpoint B that we should interfere with freedom of contract so as to stop employment discrimination. As I point out, he only wants to protect employers' freedom of contract. He ignores the rights of employees to have freedom of contract. And every time an employer discriminates, the freedom of the employee is compromised. Moreover, even if it means we are interfering with freedom of contract, it's worth doing that in order to stop discrimination in this society.

In my third major point I tell you that the laws that prohibit employment discrimination are successful. There are studies, there are statistics that prove this. In fact, I suggest that Professor Epstein's own book proves this. I say for example that the age discrimination act must be successful if there is an imposed twenty percent cost on the university budgets.

His response is to tell you that that is a terribly burdensome cost that will hurt all of you. Well notice there are two points here: First, he proves therefore that the law is working in eliminating discrimination. It has to

have worked to impose harms on others in order to impose a cost. The second question: Is it desirable to have that? And that really goes to whether or not the law is too strict. Maybe we should relax the terms of the law. Maybe we should have other ways of dealing with that. But the fact that age discrimination laws impose those costs refutes his claim that there is no effect.

I give you the example of the airlines. I said look at all of the ways with regard to the airlines that the airlines have obviously changed. He says, well, that assumes it's good. And this is my view: I use the airlines as an example to show that the laws prohibiting discrimination work. Once we see that they work we now can talk normatively about whether that's desirable.

He says, "What about customers? What if ninety-eight percent of customers only want female flight attendants." I do not believe we should give in to preferences that are discriminatory. I believe that those preferences deserve much less weight in our society than we should give to the right of people to not be discriminated against. I believe that customer preferences should not be a justification for employment discrimination, but our commitment to equality deserves far more weight.

Fourth and finally, I tell you that even if everything else is wrong, the repeal of employment discrimination laws would be a social disaster. That would transmit a symbolic message that racism, sexism and anti-Semitism are acceptable. Frankly, I found Professor Epstein's book outrageous because I think it fails to account for how evil racism, sexism, and anti-Semitism are in this society, and how essential it is that the government now and always be against them. Employment discrimination laws must remain on the books. I think Professor Epstein is simply wrong in urging their repeal.

Questions

1. What are the major points of disagreement between Professors Epstein and Chemerinsky? Which argument do you find more persuasive?
2. Is it possible to fashion employment laws that take into account the concerns identified by all of the excerpts presented in this chapter? How would this be accomplished?

7. The Intersection of Race, Color, Sex, Age, Religion, and/or National Origin Claims

Title VII of the Civil Rights Act of 1964 prohibits discrimination on the basis of either race, color, sex, religion, or national origin. But what of the individual who is claiming that the discrimination is based on a combination of several of these categories of discrimination that are incapable of separation? For example, what if a Latina claims discrimination based on her gender and her Bolivian ancestry? Interpretation of Title VII law required that separate claims be made for the discrimination based on national origin and the discrimination based on gender. Some of these claims were defeated in court because the employer was able to discredit the evidence of gender discrimination by raising the national origin discrimination evidence as providing conflicting reasons for the action. In the national origin claim, the employer could legitimately show that even the employee was confused about the real reasons for the action. No specific provisions were crafted to take care of the reality that some employees are members of several different categories of protection and that the separate treatment of these claims worked to obscure the real reasons for the discrimination.

Critical race feminist scholars began to draw attention to this failure in Title VII law. Kimberle Williams Crenshaw has been at the center of the debate about race, feminism, intersectionality, and equality for over 20 years. Her articles are considered to be foundational pieces for critical race and critical race feminist scholarship, which critique conservative, liberal, and critical legal theory about antidiscrimination discourse. Professor Crenshaw highlights the critical importance of intersectionality of multiple identities in her analysis of civil rights and employment discrimination laws. Consider the difficulties in dealing with a claim of discrimination that may include a combination of age, race, and gender or a combination of national origin, color, race, and gender. How should Title VII resolve these claims?

Kimberlé Williams Crenshaw, *Demarginalizing the Intersection of Race and Sex: A Black Feminist Critique of Antidiscrimination Doctrine, Feminist Theory and Antiracist Politics*, 1989 U. Chi. Legal F. 139.

(This is an edited version of the article and footnotes are deleted)

One of the very few Black women's studies books is entitled, *All the Women Are White; All the Blacks Are Men, But Some of Us Are Brave.* I have chosen this title as a point of departure in my efforts to develop a Black feminist criticism because it sets forth a problematic consequence of the tendency to treat race and gender as mutually exclusive categories of experience and analysis. In this talk, I want to examine how this tendency is perpetuated by a single-axis framework that is dominant in antidiscrimination law and that is also reflected in feminist theory and antiracist politics.

I will center Black women in this analysis in order to contrast the multidimensionality of Black women's experience with the single-axis analysis that distorts these experiences. Not only will this juxtaposition reveal how Black women are theoretically erased, it will also illustrate how this framework imports its own theoretical limitations that undermine efforts to broaden feminist and antiracist analyses. With Black women as the starting point, it becomes more apparent how dominant conceptions of discrimination condition us to think about subordination as disadvantage occurring along a single categorical axis. I want to suggest further that this single-axis framework erases Black women in the conceptualization, identification, and remediation of race and sex discrimination by limiting inquiry to the experiences of

otherwise-privileged members of the group. In other words, in race discrimination cases, discrimination tends to be viewed in terms of sex- or class-privileged Blacks; in sex discrimination cases, the focus is on race- and class-privileged women.

This focus on the most privileged group members marginalizes those who are multiply-burdened and obscures claims that cannot be understood as resulting from discrete sources of discrimination. I suggest further that this focus on otherwise-privileged group members creates a distorted analysis of racism and sexism, because the operative conceptions of race and sex become grounded in experiences that actually represent only a subset of a much more complex phenomenon. . . .

Unable to grasp the importance of Black women's intersectional experiences, not only courts, but feminist and civil rights thinkers as well have treated Black women in ways that deny both the unique compoundedness of their situation and the centrality of their experiences to the larger classes of women and Blacks. Black women are regarded either as too much like women or Blacks and the compounded nature of their experience is absorbed into the collective experiences of either group or as too different, in which case Black women's blackness or femaleness sometimes has placed their needs and perspectives at the margin of the feminist and Black liberationist agendas.

While it could be argued that this failure represents an absence of political will to include Black women, I believe that it reflects an uncritical and disturbing acceptance of dominant ways of thinking about discrimination. Consider first the definition of discrimination that seems to be operative in antidiscrimination law: Discrimination which is wrongful proceeds from the identification of a specific class or category; either a discriminator intentionally identifies this category, or a process is adopted which somehow disadvantages all members of this category. According to the dominant view, a discriminator treats all people within a race or sex category similarly. Any significant experiential or statistical variation within this group suggests either that the group is not being discriminated against or that conflicting interests exist which defeat any attempts to bring a common claim. Consequently, one generally cannot combine these categories. Race and sex, moreover, become significant only when they operate to explicitly *disadvantage* the victims; because the *privileging* of whiteness or maleness is implicit, it is generally not perceived at all.

Underlying this conception of discrimination is a view that the wrong which antidiscrimination law addresses is the use of race or gender factors to interfere with decisions that would otherwise be fair or neutral. This process-based definition is not grounded in a bottom-up commitment to improve the substantive conditions for those who are victimized by the interplay of numerous factors. Instead, the dominant message of antidiscrimination law is that it will regulate only the limited extent to which race or sex interferes with the process of determining outcomes. This narrow objective is facilitated by the top-down strategy of using a singular "but for" analysis to ascertain the effects of race or sex. Because the scope of antidiscrimination law is so limited, sex and race discrimination have come to be defined in terms of the experiences of those who are privileged *but for* their racial or sexual characteristics. Put differently, the paradigm of sex discrimination tends to be based on the experiences of white women; the model of race discrimination tends to be based on the experiences of the most privileged Blacks. Notions of what constitutes race and sex discrimination are, as a result, narrowly tailored to embrace only a small set of circumstances, none of which include discrimination against Black women.

Questions

1. What is intersectionality as identified by Professor Crenshaw? How do you think antidiscrimination laws could approach problems of discrimination encountered by, e.g., older black women?

2. What does Professor Crenshaw mean when she writes that one of the problems is that, but for race or sex discrimination, the decision is assumed to be fair or neutral? Do you agree?

3. Do you think that these authors accurately describe the problem of discrimination in employment today? Which author best reflects your understanding of the problems? Why? What role do you think the law should play in the area of employment relations? Explain your answer.

chapter 2

The U.S. Supreme Court Interpretation of Title VII and the Stages of Proof of a Disparate Treatment Claim

---

Problem 1

Ella Jones, a young, African American female employee, was fired from her job as a financial analyst in a private corporation. Her boss came into her office one day and told her that she was being terminated. He asked her to gather her things and leave by the end of the day. After the initial shock, Ella started clearing her desk and other files that contained her personal papers. She went to the copier to copy her health benefits plan. While she was standing by the machine, she noticed several papers turned face down on the counter beside the machine. She turned them over and discovered a memo written by her boss. As she read the memo, she was stunned to see that it included derogatory terms about women of her race and revealed an intent to get rid of all "nigras" in the workplace. She made a copy and quickly placed it in her file of personal papers.

Problem 2

When Ella applied for her next job, she didn't have much luck. Although she didn't know it, the hiring manager had narrowed the applicants down to Ella and a white male applicant. The manager, an elderly white male, met extensively with both candidates and decided that their qualifications and their experience were identical, but somehow he felt more comfortable with the white male candidate. As he explained to his boss, "I decided on the guy because I felt like he and I had more in common. I just felt more comfortable with him, I don't know why." He told Ella that he had hired someone with far superior qualifications.

A. Title VII Prohibitions Against Discrimination

The law passed by Congress did not apply to all employers. Many small business owners feared that if the law applied to their businesses, they would be subjected to the high costs of litigation, which could wipe out their businesses even if they were successful in defending against charges of discrimination. The small business lobby became very active in bringing their fears to the attention of members of Congress. When the final language was adopted, the law specifically limited the reach of Title VII to employers with more than 20 employees. Employment agencies and unions were also required to apply this nondiscrimination law. The definition section, Section 701, includes definitions of "employer" and "employee" as well as other important definitions that should not be ignored. For example, when Congress amended Title VII in 1978, Section 701(k) was added to make clear that "sex discrimination" included discrimination on the basis of pregnancy. The definitional section does not, however, include a definition of "discrimination."

Section 703 (42 U.S.C. § 2000e–2) is the statute's key statement of the prohibition against discrimination. Section 703(a) provides as follows:

It shall be an unlawful employment practice for an employer—

1. to fail or refuse to hire or to discharge any individual, or otherwise to discriminate against any individual with respect to his compensation, terms, conditions, or privileges of employment, because of such individual's race, color, religion, sex, or national origin; or
2. to limit, segregate, or classify his employees or applicants for employment in any way which would deprive or tend to deprive any individual of employment opportunities or otherwise adversely affect his status as an employee, because of such individual's race, color, religion, sex, or national origin.

The remainder of Section 703 includes exceptions to the main prohibition of Title VII, including exemptions for Native American tribes as employers, exemptions for religious institutions as employers, and exemptions for certain national security interests. It also includes provisions that deal with particular problems that are raised in the employment context: for example, how to treat seniority systems that give preferential treatment to employees based on the length of time they have worked for the employer. There are many different problems addressed in Section 703, but this chapter and Chapter 3 will address the problems that arise regarding the meaning of discrimination itself.

B. The Requirement of Intent to Discriminate

Nothing in the language of Title VII of the Civil Rights Act of 1964 defines discrimination, because the members of Congress who enacted this major piece of legislation could not agree on its meaning. The specific language of the law does not explain how the litigants should go about proving a claim pursuant to the statute. The textual language also is not clear about the precise problems that the statute is attempting to address. Should, for example, the law cover both of the hypothetical situations described above? There were many questions after the enactment of this legislation that had to be interpreted by the courts in the face of specific challenges to the implementation of Title VII. The first major Supreme Court case to address these problems has become a major landmark in the interpretation of Title VII law and is still relied on by the courts.

1. The Employee's "Prima Facie" Hurdle in Establishing a Plausible Claim

---

MCDONNELL DOUGLAS CORP.
v.
GREEN
411 U.S. 792 (1973)

Justice POWELL delivered the opinion of the Court.

[The Employment Problem]

[Mr. Green, an African American from St. Louis, Missouri, worked as a mechanic and laboratory technician for McDonnell Douglas Corporation, an aerospace and aircraft manufacturer, from 1956 until 1964. He was laid off from work when the employer decided to reduce its work force. Mr. Green was a long-time activist in the civil rights movement and participated in protests against McDonnell Douglas Corporation, claiming that the general hiring practices and his own discharge were racially motivated. In particular, he participated in a Congress on Racial Equality demonstration during which they stalled their cars on the main roads to the McDonnell Douglas plant to block access to the plant.

McDonnell Douglas eventually decided it could afford to rehire old employees and hire new ones at this plant. They advertised for qualified mechanics, and Mr. Green applied to be rehired. He was turned down. The employer claimed that he was not hired because he had participated in an illegal protest.]

[The Legal Issue]

[Mr. Green decided to file a legal claim of discrimination. He alleged that he had been discriminated against on the basis of his race in violation of Title VII. The law required that he first make a timely filing of a claim of discrimination with the Equal Employment Opportunity Commission (EEOC). Title VII requires that every claim be made within a specified period of time to the proper government agency (the EEOC) so that the administrative agency could investigate the complaint and attempt to settle the dispute quickly. Since the EEOC failed to resolve the case to Mr. Green's satisfaction, he took advantage of his right to file a lawsuit in federal court, charging a violation of Sections 703(a)(1) and 704(a) of Title VII of the Civil Rights Act of 1964.

The U.S. district court had to consider the relatively new questions that centered on defining the purposes of Title VII and describing how a discrimination case could be proven. Title VII was a new law, and eventually it fell to the U.S. Supreme Court to determine what it meant in Mr. Green's situation. According to the Supreme Court: The case before us raises significant questions as to the proper order and nature of proof in actions under Title VII. . . . The critical issue before us concerns the order and allocation of proof in a private, non-class action challenging employment discrimination. . . .]

[The Decision and Rationale of the U.S. Supreme Court]

[Section 703(a)(1) of the Civil Rights Act of 1964 states that it is "an unlawful employment practice for an employer—(1) to fail or refuse to hire or to discharge any individual, or otherwise to discriminate against any individual with respect to his compensation, terms, conditions, or privileges of employment, because of such individual's race, color, religion, sex, or national origin. . . ."]

. . . The language of Title VII makes plain the purpose of Congress to assure equality of employment opportunities and to eliminate those discriminatory practices and devices, which have fostered racially stratified job environments to the disadvantage of minority citizens. . . . [As the Court noted in *Griggs v. Duke Power Co.*, 401 U.S. 424, 429 (1971):]

Congress did not intend by Title VII, however, to guarantee a job to every person regardless of qualifications. In short, the Act does not command that any person be hired simply because he was formerly the subject of discrimination, or because he is a member of a minority group. Discriminatory preference for any group, minority or majority, is precisely and only what Congress has proscribed. What is required by Congress is the removal of artificial, arbitrary, and unnecessary barriers to employment when the barriers operate invidiously to discriminate on the basis of racial or other impermissible classification. . . .

There are societal as well as personal interests on both sides of this equation. The broad, overriding interest, shared by employer, employee, and consumer, is efficient and trustworthy workmanship assured through fair and racially neutral employment and personnel decisions. In the implementation of such decisions, it is abundantly clear that Title VII tolerates no racial discrimination, subtle or otherwise.

In this case [Mr. Green] charges that he was denied employment "because of his involvement in civil rights activities" and "because of his race and color." . . . [The employer] denied discrimination of any kind, asserting that its failure to re-employ [Mr. Green] was based upon and justified by his participation in the unlawful conduct against it. . . .

The complainant in a Title VII trial must carry the initial burden under the statute of establishing a *prima facie* case of racial discrimination. This may be done by showing (i) that he belongs to a racial minority; (ii) that he applied and was qualified for a job for which the employer was seeking applicants; (iii) that, despite his qualifications, he was rejected; and (iv) that, after his rejection, the position remained open and the employer continued to seek applicants from persons of complainant's qualifications. . . . In the instant case, we agree with the Court of Appeals that [Mr. Green] proved a prima facie case. . . . [The Employer] sought mechanics, [Mr. Green's] trade, and continued to do so after [his] rejection. [The Employer], moreover, does not dispute [Mr. Green's] qualifications . . . and acknowledges that his past work performance in [Employer's] employ was "satisfactory.". . .

The burden then must shift to the employer to articulate some legitimate, nondiscriminatory reason for the employee's rejection. We need not attempt in the instant case to detail every matter, which fairly could be recognized as a reasonable basis for a refusal to hire. Here [the Employer] has assigned [Mr. Green's] participation in unlawful conduct against it as the cause for his rejection. We think that this suffices to discharge [the Employer's] burden of proof at this stage and to meet [Mr. Green's] prima facie case of discrimination. . . .

[The Employer's] reason for rejection thus suffices to meet the prima facie case, but the inquiry must not end here. While Title VII does not, without more, compel rehiring of [Mr. Green], neither does it permit [the Employer] to use [Mr. Green's] conduct as a pretext for the sort of discrimination prohibited by § 703(a)(1). On remand, [Mr. Green] must, as the Court of Appeals recognized, be afforded a fair opportunity to show that [the Employer's] stated reason for [Mr. Green's] rejection was in fact pretext. Especially relevant to such a showing would be evidence that white employees involved in acts against [the Employer] of comparable seriousness to the 'stall-in' were nevertheless retained or rehired. [The Employer] may justifiably refuse to rehire one who was engaged in unlawful, disruptive acts against it, but only if this criterion is applied alike to members of all races.

Other evidence that may be relevant to any showing of pretext includes facts as to [the Employer's] treatment of [Mr. Green] during his prior term of employment; [the Employer's] reaction, if any, to [Mr. Green's] legitimate civil rights activities; and [the Employer's] general policy and practice with respect to minority employment. . . . On the latter point, statistics as to [the Employer's] employment policy and practice may be helpful to a determination of whether [the Employer's] refusal to rehire [Mr. Green] in this case conformed to a general pattern of discrimination against blacks. . . . In short, on the retrial [Mr. Green] must be given a full and fair opportunity to demonstrate by competent evidence that the presumptively valid reasons for his rejection were in fact a cover-up for a racially discriminatory decision. . . .

In sum, [Mr. Green] should have been allowed to pursue his claim under § 703(a)(1). If the evidence on retrial is substantially in accord with that before us in this case, we think that [Mr. Green] carried his burden of establishing a prima facie case of racial discrimination and that [the Employer] successfully rebutted that case. But this does not end the matter. On retrial, [Mr. Green] must be afforded the opportunity to demonstrate that [the Employer's] assigned reason for refusing to re-employ was a pretext or discriminatory in its application. If the District Judge so finds, he must order a prompt and appropriate remedy. In the absence of such a finding, [the Employer's] refusal to rehire must stand.

[At the new trial in U.S. District Court in Missouri, the judge ruled that the evidence showed that the reason Mr. Green was not rehired centered on his unlawful protest activities and not because of his race or lawful civil rights activities. A judgment was entered for McDonnell Douglas Corporation.]

Developing the Law

Gradually the courts began to identify the specific requirements of a *disparate treatment* claim of discrimination. Employees could prevail with direct evidence of discrimination or with indirect, or "circumstantial," evidence of intentional discrimination. The "easiest" form of discrimination was the type of discrimination often proved by the use of evidence referred to as "smoking gun" evidence—that is, the kind of unquestionable proof that the accused employer really did intend to discriminate. One might find a written statement by the employer to that effect or a witness who overheard these statements by the employer. Openly discriminatory acts were so pervasive within the society at the time of the passage of the Civil Rights Act of 1964 that many early cases addressed problems of proof in these terms. Others were the type discussed in Chapter 3, where the discrimination was inferred from exclusionary practices or customs that had the direct result of keeping minorities out of the workplace.

Employees who lacked "smoking gun" evidence had a more difficult claim to prove. While the courts began to recognize that employers who discriminate would not voluntarily provide such evidence of their intent to discriminate, the idea of the need to prove intent remained at the center of judicial inquiry. The disparate treatment claim of discrimination became a search for alternative ways to prove that, more likely than not, the employer was motivated by an intent to discriminate based on the employee's membership in the protected class.

As the Supreme Court analyzed the problems that reached the Court, the opinions began to set out a path for a litigant to follow in trying to establish a claim based on circumstantial evidence. Circumstantial evidence is evidence that, when considered all together, tends to support the conclusion that intentional discrimination did exist. In these cases, the employee had different ways of showing that discrimination operated in the employment decision.

Given the way in which lawsuits are presented, the amount of evidence an employee must demonstrate to withstand challenges by the employer varies at different stages of the litigation. The cases in this chapter interpreted Title VII to require the employee to overcome various hurdles in order for the litigation to go forward. *McDonnell Douglas Corp. v. Green* was the landmark case, the one that is still relied on as a foundation for employment discrimination law, that identified the employee's initial responsibility of proof in cases where there is no direct proof of intentional discrimination.

Questions

1. Reconsider the problems presented at the beginning of this chapter. How do you feel about the quality of proof available in each of these problems? Do you feel more comfortable finding discrimination in one or both

examples? Why? If you feel that these two situations are dramatically different in the nature of the proof of discrimination available, do you feel that both are still cases of discrimination? Why? Since the employer just wants to feel "comfortable" with his choice in Problem 2, why should this be a concern? What difficulty, if any, do you have in placing this in the category of intentional discrimination? How do you feel about omitting it from the category of intentional discrimination?

2. How do you analyze the second problem according to the *McDonnell Douglas* case? What kind of steps (standard) does *McDonnell Douglas* set out for showing a prima facie case? What are the facts of that case that help to show each step? Who has the burden at each of these steps? What is the description of the burden? If you are going to determine what is going on in employment discrimination cases, it will be critical that you understand the answers to these questions. What difficulties will you encounter, and how should they be addressed? Is there enough evidence to survive the screening test of the prima facie case? Does the employer have enough evidence to meet its burden of showing a legitimate reson for not hiring Ella? What can the employee do to respond to the employer's reason for not hiring her?

Discussion Notes

1. The evidence obtained by Ella in Problem 1 is a rare, if ugly, find. Most employers who felt this way wouldn't commit their sentiments to writing. Such a document, written by someone in authority who actually fired the employee, is solid proof of an intent to discriminate that violates Title VII. It is also rare to find an employer who publishes a policy that specifically states a plan to hire only Caucasians or only Hispanic Americans or only African Americans. If that occurred, then it would be proof of intentional discrimination unless the employer could assert a bona fide occupational qualification for that requirement, as discussed in Chapter 8. The disparate impact cases discussed in Chapter 8 are also inappropriate for this kind of analysis. Later, other "mixed motive" cases will be considered. In those cases, proof exists of direct discrimination and proof exists of a legitimate reason for the adverse employment action.

2. Pay attention to how the Court sets out the requirements of a prima facie case. The prima facie requirements are a set of facts and inferences that alert the Court that the employer may have discriminated. The inquiry, of course, does not end there but will require the employer to provide information about its reasons for taking the adverse action against the employee. This will resurface in all cases where the proof of intent to discriminate depends on less than "direct" evidence of discriminatory intent. Notice that the Court recognized in *McDonnell Douglas* that it is not easy to get into the mind of the employer to determine whether he or she has an "intent to discriminate." Inferences may be deduced from evidence that is presented to meet many kinds of legal requirements in both civil and criminal law. It is not uncommon to meet the requirements of a case by proof of circumstantial evidence—that is, proof that creates inferences from which a jury could decide that it is more likely than not,

when considering all the bits and pieces of evidence presented, that the unlawful discrimination did occur. Be alert to (a) what the Court says might happen if the employer fails to offer any explanation and (b) what the plaintiff must do if the employer does present a reason for its actions.

2. The Employer's Burden to Articulate a Legitimate, Nondiscriminatory Reason for Its Adverse Action Against the Employee

Problem 3

Andre Smith, a 25-year-old African American male, has worked for the XYZ Law Firm for the last four years. He has been the only African American paralegal staff member for that entire time. All of the other paralegals are Caucasian. His job description included filing documents in court, assisting with case investigations, and doing document control of cases for attorneys in the firm. His direct supervisor has been Alexa Arden, a Caucasian female, who is a senior associate attorney in the firm. For the last four years, Andre has received exemplary performance review assessments by Alexa. All of these reports were oral and not in written form. He has received two small merit raises in addition to the general cost-of-living increases received by everyone else. In May of this year, Alexa retired, and John Adams, a Caucasian male, became Andre's supervisor. John is a 49-year-old white male. From the beginning of their relationship, John has criticized Andre. After two weeks of supervising Andre, John warned him that he would not last in his job unless he improved his performance, but he never told Andre what he was doing wrong or what he needed to do in the future. None of the other paralegals received criticisms for their work even though Andre knew they were doing the same kind of work. In July, Andre was terminated by John. No further explanation was given.

Problem 4

Kathleen Cifra was the only female industrial hygienist at GE Corporation's three plants in Syracuse, New York. As such, she was responsible for monitoring the health and safety of over 7,000 employees. From 1984 until the summer of 1990, she received two promotions and had excellent performance evaluations. In the summer of 1990, her department was reorganized, and she reported to a new boss. Everyone agreed that he was sharp with many employees but that he singled out Kathleen as a target. He told her early in the fall that she was a problem and that she wasn't doing her job properly. Kathleen responded with professional, written responses to each critique, demonstrating

(continued)

(continued)

the unfairness of his critique. She claimed that no action was taken by GE to remedy the situation. She was placed on a performance improvement plan, and the supervisor set many goals for her to reach during the 60-day "probation." Everyone agreed that Kathleen met those goals, but the supervisor began to find other things that she should have done. Several male employees received criticisms, and one was placed on a performance improvement plan. He never met the goals of that plan to the satisfaction of the same supervisor, yet Kathleen was terminated and this male employee was not terminated.

According to the *McDonnell Douglas* test, Andre and Kathleen must first introduce enough in the record to show a prima facie case. The prima facie case is a screening mechanism to weed out claims that do not even assert basic facts that the law has recognized as "discrimination" under Title VII. If Andre and Kathleen survive that screening test, the employer must "articulate a legitimate nondiscriminatory reason for its actions" against the employee, as identified in *Texas Department of Community Affairs v. Burdine*, the case discussed below.

Questions surfaced immediately after lower federal courts began applying the *McDonnell Douglas* formula. Employees argued that the employer should have to prove that its reason for taking the adverse employment action involved was a legitimate, nondiscriminatory reason. Employers argued that they had no such burden, since it was the plaintiff's responsibility in a civil lawsuit to persuade the judge or jury that it was more likely than not that discrimination had occurred. Employers also argued that they should prevail at the summary judgment stage—that is, without the necessity of a trial—once they articulated a legitimate, nondiscriminatory reason for their action. Focus on the way that the Court in the *Burdine* case describes (a) the employer's burden once the employee has established a prima facie case and (b) the employee's responsibility once the employer has given a reason for its actions. Keep Andre's and Kathleen's problems in mind as you read this case.

TEXAS DEPARTMENT OF COMMUNITY AFFAIRS
v.
BURDINE
450 U.S. 248 (1981)

Justice POWELL delivered the opinion of the Court.

[The Employment Problem]

[Ms. Burdine wanted to be promoted to a supervisor's position when it became vacant. She had several years' experience in employment training at her job with the Texas Department of Community Affairs, a public agency that provided training and employment opportunities in the public sector for unskilled workers. Although she had received previous promotions, she was denied the promotion to Project Director, and the position remained open for six months. At this point, the agency hired a male as Project Director and fired Ms. Burdine and two other employees—but retained one other male, who was the only other professional in that division. Although Ms. Burdine was soon rehired and assigned to another division in the agency and kept her salary and responsibilities at the same level as she would have received as Project Director, she felt that she had been discriminated against as a woman. The employer disagreed. Ms. Burdine made the necessary claim of discrimination with the EEOC, the administrative agency charged with investigating claims before the courts are able to consider them. She then filed her case in a U.S. district court, asserting a violation of Section 703(a)(1) of the Civil Rights Act of 1964 on the basis of sex discrimination. The employer denied her claim.]

[The Legal Issue]

The narrow question presented is whether, after the employee has proved a prima facie case of discriminatory treatment, the burden shifts to the employer to persuade the court by a preponderance of the evidence that legitimate, nondiscriminatory reasons for the challenged employment action existed.

[The Decision and Rationale of the U.S. Supreme Court]

The burden of establishing a prima facie case of disparate treatment is not onerous. The plaintiff/ [employee] must prove by a preponderance of the evidence that she applied for an available position for which she was qualified but was rejected under circumstances which give rise to an inference of unlawful discrimination. The prima facie case serves an important function in the litigation: it eliminates the most common nondiscriminatory reasons for the plaintiff's rejection. See *Teamsters v. United States*, 431 U.S. 324, 358, and n.44 (1977). As the Court explained in *Furnco Construction Corp. v. Waters*, 438 U.S. 567, 577 (1978), the prima facie case "raises an inference of discrimination only because we presume these acts, if otherwise unexplained, are more likely than not based on the consideration of impermissible factors." Establishment of the prima facie case in effect creates a presumption that the employer unlawfully discriminated against the employee. If the trier of fact believes the plaintiff's evidence, and if the employer is silent in the face of the presumption, the court must enter judgment for the plaintiff because no issue of fact remains in the case.[7]

The burden that shifts to the defendant/ [employer], therefore, is to rebut the presumption of discrimination by producing evidence that the plaintiff was rejected, or someone else was preferred, for a legitimate, nondiscriminatory reason. The defendant need not persuade the court that it was actually motivated by the proffered reasons. It is sufficient if the [employer's] evidence raises a genuine issue of fact as to whether it discriminated against the [employee].[8] To accomplish this, the [employer] must clearly set forth, through the introduction of admissible evidence, the reasons for the [employee's] rejection.[9] The explanation provided must be legally sufficient to justify a judgment for the [employer]. If the [employer] carries this burden of production, the presumption raised by the prima facie case is rebutted[10] and the factual inquiry proceeds to a new level of specificity. Placing this burden of production on the defendant/[employer] thus serves simultaneously to meet the employee's prima facie case by presenting a legitimate reason for the action and to

[7] The phrase "prima facie case" not only may denote the establishment of a legally mandatory, rebuttable presumption, but also may be used by courts to describe the plaintiff's burden of producing enough evidence to permit the trier of fact to infer the fact at issue. . . . *McDonnell Douglas* should have made it apparent that in the Title VII context we use "prima facie case" in the former sense.

[8] This evidentiary relationship between the presumption created by a prima facie case and the consequential burden of production placed on the defendant is a traditional feature of the common law. . . . Usually, assessing the burden of production helps the judge determine whether the litigants have created an issue of fact to be decided by the jury. In a Title VII case, the allocation of the burdens and the creation of a presumption by the establishment of a prima facie case is intended progressively to sharpen the inquiry into the elusive factual question of intentional discrimination.

[9] An articulation not admitted into evidence will not suffice. Thus, the defendant cannot meet its burden merely through an answer to the complaint or by argument of counsel.

[10] In saying that the presumption drops from the case, we do not imply that the trier of fact no longer may consider evidence previously introduced by the plaintiff to establish a prima facie case. A satisfactory explanation by the defendant destroys the legally mandatory inference of discrimination arising from the plaintiff's initial evidence. Nonetheless, this evidence and inferences properly drawn therefrom may be considered by the trier of fact on the issue of whether the defendant's explanation is pretextual. Indeed, there may be some cases where the plaintiff's initial evidence, combined with effective cross-examination of the defendant, will suffice to discredit the defendant's explanation.

frame the factual issue with sufficient clarity so that the plaintiff/[employee] will have a full and fair opportunity to demonstrate pretext. The sufficiency of the [employer's] evidence should be evaluated by the extent to which it fulfills these functions.

The [employee] retains the burden of persuasion. She now must have the opportunity to demonstrate that the proffered reason was not the true reason for the employment decision. This burden now merges with the ultimate burden of persuading the court that she has been the victim of intentional discrimination. She may succeed in this either directly by persuading the court that a discriminatory reason more likely motivated the employer or indirectly by showing that the employer's proffered explanation is unworthy of credence. See *McDonnell Douglas*, 411 U.S., at 804–805. . . .

The Court of Appeals has misconstrued the nature of the burden that *McDonnell Douglas* and its progeny place on the defendant. See Part II, *supra*. We stated in *Sweeney* that "the employer's burden is satisfied if he simply 'explains what he has done' or 'produc[es] evidence of legitimate nondiscriminatory reasons.'" 439 U.S. at 25, n.2., quoting *id.*, at 28, 29 (Stevens, J. dissenting). It is plain that the Court of Appeals required much more: it placed on the defendant the burden of persuading the court that it had convincing, objective reasons for preferring the chosen applicant above the plaintiff. . . .

. . . We have stated consistently that the employee's prima facie case of discrimination will be rebutted if the employer articulates lawful reasons for the action; that is, to satisfy this intermediate burden, the employer need only produce admissible evidence which would allow the trier of fact rationally to conclude that the employment decision had not been motivated by discriminatory animus. The Court of Appeals would require the defendant to introduce evidence which, in the absence of any evidence of pretext, would *persuade* the trier of fact that the employment action was lawful. This exceeds what properly can be demanded to satisfy a burden of production. . . .

. . . Title VII prohibits all discrimination in employment based upon race, sex, and national origin. "The broad, overriding interest, shared by employer, employee, and consumer, is efficient and trustworthy workmanship assured through fair and . . . neutral employment and personnel decisions." *McDonnell Douglas, supra*, at 801. Title VII, however, does not demand that an employer give preferential treatment to minorities or women. 42 U.S.C. § 2000e-2j. See *Steelworkers v. Weber*, 443 U.S. 193, 205–206 (1979). The statute was not intended to "diminish traditional management prerogatives." *Id.* at 207. It does not require the employer to restructure his employment practices to maximize the number of minorities and women hired. *Furnco Construction Corp. v. Waters*, 438 U.S. 567, 577–578 (1978).

The views of the Court of Appeals can be read, we think, as requiring the employer to hire the minority or female applicant whenever that person's objective qualifications were equal to those of a white male applicant. But Title VII does not obligate an employer to accord this preference. Rather, the employer has discretion to choose among equally qualified candidates, provided the decision is not based upon unlawful criteria. The fact that a court may think that the employer misjudged the qualifications of the applicants does not in itself expose him to Title VII liability, although this may be probative of whether the employer's reasons are pretexts for discrimination. *Loeb v. Textron, Inc., supra*, at 1012, n.6; see *Lieberman v. Gant*, 630 F.2d 60, 65 (CA2 1980).

Questions

1. What does Andre have to show to make a prima facie case of intentional discrimination under *McDonnell Douglas* and *Burdine*?
2. Does the employer have an obligation to give an explanation for the termination? When does this arise? What happens if the employer refuses to provide any explanation?
3. What burden does the employee have if the employer does give an explanation for the firing?
4. How should Kathleen's attorney evaluate her situation in light of the proof of a circumstantial case of sex discrimination that follows the *McDonnell Douglas/Burdine* formula?
5. Assume a woman was hired to replace Kathleen. Does this mean that the fourth prong of the prima facie case cannot be demonstrated? What else might you use to establish the fourth prong of the prima facie case in order to survive a summary judgment challenge? What form would that take?
6. What happens if the trier of fact becomes convinced of the falsity of the reasons articulated by the employer for terminating

Kathleen? Could the plaintiff claim that she is entitled to summary judgment because (a) the defendant has not come forward with legitimate reasons for the employer's actions? Or (b) the plaintiff has successfully demonstrated pretext, and thus the court is compelled to enter a judgment for the plaintiff as a matter of law? Or (c) the trier of fact may find that the plaintiff has met her ultimate burden of persuasion of intentional discrimination by a combination of the facts that supported the prima facie case, the proof of the lie, and any inferences that the trier of fact makes about those facts? What are the differences among these three options? The following two cases, *St. Mary's Honor Center v. Hicks* and *Reeves v. Sanderson Plumbing Products, Inc.*, address these issues.

Discussion Notes

1. The employer is permitted to submit a motion to the trial court asking the court to dismiss the case if the employee has failed to meet the burden established under *McDonnell Douglas*. Summary judgment motions are the most frequent vehicle for dismissing employment discrimination claims prior to trial. If the plaintiff/employee succeeds in defeating this motion, the burden shifts to the defendant/employer to state some nondiscriminatory reason for its adverse employment action against the employee.

2. Notice that the standard is flexible depending on whether we are talking about discrimination claims in hiring, firing, promotion, or other kinds of adverse action by the employer. The prima facie requirements of a failure to promote claim, for example, have been modified as follows: (a) the employee is a member of the protected class, (b) the employee is qualified for the promotion (that is, she meets the stated promotion criteria), (c) the employee actually applies for the promotion and is denied the promotion, and (d) an inference of discrimination exists. Modifications have also been used where the employee's benefits or working conditions were changed, where the employee quit because of the discrimination, and where the employee claims that disciplinary action was taken against him for discriminatory

reasons. See, e.g., *Goldmeier v. Allstate Ins. Co.*, 337 F.3d 629 (6th Cir. 2003); *Cooley v. Daimler-Chrysler Corp.*, 281 F. Supp. 2d 979 (E.D. Mo. 2003). The Supreme Court in *McDonnell Douglas* stressed that its standard would have to be flexible, given the variety of ways that adverse employment actions take place.

3. Summary judgment orders dismissing employees' cases before trial are entered frequently. The court may determine that the employee has not introduced reasons to believe the employer has given a false excuse or "pretext" for its action. The court may find that the employee has not offered sufficient evidence of any type to create an important factual dispute that could lead a reasonable jury to believe that intentional discrimination occurred. As a result of these determinations, many federal district courts frequently grant an employer's motion for summary judgment, which effectively terminates the claim of discrimination.

4. The standards for determining whether you have enough to show a prima facie case of discrimination are different at the summary judgment stage and at/after a trial of the facts: When a defendant moves for summary judgment claiming that plaintiff has not met the prima facie requirements, how is this evaluated by the court? What is different about the evaluation that takes place when the defendant asks the judge to set aside a jury verdict for the plaintiff or asks an appellate court to reverse the lower court's judgment for plaintiff? An understanding of the various procedural stages of litigation and the standards that will be applied is vital to the practicing attorney, particularly in the field of employment discrimination litigation. The way the standards for summary judgment and judgment notwithstanding the verdict are articulated by the court will usually be a pretty good predictor of the end result. As cases developed, some issues appeared to be procedural in nature and concerned the level of proof needed at various stages of the litigation. But the resolution of these problems also had an impact on the substantive interpretation of the nature of discrimination prohibited under Title VII.

3. The Employee's Requirement to Demonstrate Pretext, Lies, or Other Proof

Problem 5

Raphael Quincy is a male American citizen who was born in the Dominican Republic. He has been a software engineer with Micropile Industries for the last 10 years. During that time, he has received seven promotions and substantial raises. His performance evaluations have always been excellent. Last year, however, his supervisor was replaced, and he began work under the supervision of Alderson Anderson III, a Caucasian male American citizen. Alderson did not seem to like Raphael from the start. Three months after Alderson began to supervise Raphael, Alderson notified Raphael that he would be laid off because of hard economic times in the industry. Raphael did not think this was the real reason he was being laid off, and he filed suit in federal district court after properly filing a charge with the EEOC.

The *Burdine* case identified the nature of the burden on the employer and the effect on the employee's case when the employer meets its burden of giving a reason for its actions. In the usual case, the employer has little difficulty meeting the minimal burden in coming up with a reason for its actions. In Raphael's situation, the employer will easily raise the hard economic times as the basis for the action against Raphael. The responsibility is then shifted back to the employee, who may be able to show that the employer's reason for its actions is not the real reason. This has often been referred to as the "pretext" stage of analysis. Pretext evidence focuses on the validity of the employer's proffered reasons for its adverse action against the employee.

The courts have struggled with issues related to the validity of the employer's reason for the adverse employment action at the crux of any lawsuit, and two major problems needed to be addressed. The first category of issues focused on the validity of the reason offered by the employer. In Raphael's situation, for example, who had the duty to show that the reason given by the employer was not believable, and how could that be done? The second category of issues focused on the need for the employee to prove intentional discrimination as the final burden of persuasion at trial. That is, in Raphael's situation, for example, even if Raphael could prove that the employer's reason for laying him off was not the real reason, was that enough to prove discrimination in violation of Title VII, or did Raphael have to go further to show intentional discrimination? The problem of the employee's overall burden of proving that it was more likely than not that discrimination existed became confused with the issue of pretext.

The preoccupation with the pretext stage of employment litigation masked the real concern: What overall burden of persuasion did the plaintiff need to meet in order to prove her case? The Supreme Court addressed these issues in 1993 in *St. Mary's Honor Center v. Hicks* and in 2000 in *Reeves v. Sanderson Plumbing Products*.

ST. MARY'S HONOR CENTER
v.
HICKS
509 U.S. 502 (1993)

SCALIA, J., delivered the opinion of the Court.

[The Employment Problem]

[Melvin Hicks, an African American-male, was a correctional officer at St. Mary's Honor Center (St. Mary's), a halfway house operated by the Missouri Department of Corrections and Human Resources (MDCHR). Mr. Hicks received a promotion to shift commander, one of six supervisory positions, in February 1980. Mr. John Powell became his supervisor in 1983, and Mr. Steve Long became Mr. Powell's supervisor. Soon thereafter, Mr. Hicks began to be subjected to disciplinary actions by his supervisor. He was suspended for violations of institutional rules by his subordinates, and he received a letter of reprimand for failure to conduct an adequate investigation of a brawl between inmates on his shift. He was later demoted to correctional officer for failing to ensure his subordinates entered their use of a St. Mary's vehicle into the official log book. He was finally discharged for allegedly threatening Mr. Powell during a heated exchange.]

[The Decision of the Trial Court and the U.S. Court of Appeals for the Eighth Circuit]

[Mr. Hicks filed a lawsuit in federal district court after proper exhaustion of administrative remedies with the EEOC. He lost his case in the district court but had that decision reversed by the U.S. Court of Appeals for the Fifth Circuit.

Both the district court judge and the court of appeals determined that the reasons given by the employer were not the real reasons for the demotion in rank and eventual discharge, because Mr. Hicks was the only supervisor disciplined for violations committed by his subordinates; similar and more serious violations were committed by co-workers and were either disregarded or treated more leniently, and the final confrontation was provoked by Mr. Powell. The district court held, however, that the employee had failed to prove that his *race* was the determining factor in the adverse decisions by the employer. The court of appeals disagreed, finding that "[o]nce [the employee] proved all of the [employer's] proffered reasons for the adverse employment actions to be pretextual, [the employee] was entitled to judgment as a

matter of law." 970 F. 2d, at 492. The court of appeals argued that "[b]ecause all of [the employer's] proffered reasons were discredited, [the employer was] in a position of having offered no legitimate reason for [its] actions. In other words, [the defendant was] in no better position than if [it] had remained silent, offering no rebuttal to an established inference that [it] had unlawfully discriminated against [the employee] on the basis of his race." *Ibid.*]

[The Legal Issue]

Did the court of appeals err in holding that rejection of the employer's reasons for terminating the employee compelled judgment for that employee? The Supreme Court considered whether this holding erroneously shifted the burden of proof to the employer when the employee "at all times bears the ultimate burden of persuasion."

[The Decision and Rationale of the U.S. Supreme Court]

. . . By producing evidence (whether ultimately persuasive or not) of nondiscriminatory reasons, [the employers] sustained their burden of production, and thus placed themselves in a "better position than if they had remained silent."

In the nature of things, the determination that a defendant has met its burden of production (and has thus rebutted any legal presumption of intentional discrimination) can involve no credibility assessment. For the burden-of-production determination necessarily *precedes* the credibility-assessment stage. . . .

If, on the other hand, the defendant has succeeded in carrying its burden of production, the *McDonnell Douglas* framework—with its presumptions and burdens—is no longer relevant. To resurrect it later, after the trier of fact has determined that what was "produced" to meet the burden of production is not credible, flies in the face of our holding in *Burdine* that to rebut the presumption "[t]he defendant need not persuade the court that it was actually motivated by the proffered reasons." 450 U.S., at 254. The presumption, having fulfilled its role of forcing the defendant to come forward with some response, simply drops out of the picture. *Id.,* at 255. The defendant's "production" (whatever its persuasive effect) having been made, the trier of fact proceeds to decide the ultimate question: whether plaintiff has proven "that the defendant intentionally discriminated against [him]" because of his race, *id.* at 253. The factfinder's disbelief of the reasons put forward by the defendant (particularly if disbelief is accompanied by a suspicion of mendacity) may, together with the elements of the prima facie case, suffice to show intentional discrimination. Thus, rejection of the defendant's proffered reasons will *permit* the trier of fact to infer the ultimate fact of intentional discrimination,[4] and the Court of Appeals was correct when it noted that, upon such rejection, "[n]o additional proof of discrimination is *required*," 970 F.2d, 493 (emphasis added). But the Court of Appeals' holding that rejection of the defendant's proffered reasons *compels* judgment for the plaintiff disregards the fundamental principle of Rule 301 that a presumption does not shift the burden of proof, and ignores our repeated admonition that the Title VII plaintiff at all times bears the "ultimate burden of persuasion. . . ."

We have no authority to impose liability upon an employer for alleged discriminatory employment practices unless an appropriate factfinder determines, according to proper procedures, *that the employer has unlawfully discriminated.* We may, according to traditional practice, establish certain modes and orders of proof, including an initial rebuttable presumption of the sort we described earlier in this opinion, which we believe *McDonnell Douglas* represents. But nothing in law would permit us to substitute for the required finding that the employer's action was the product of unlawful discrimination, the much different (and much lesser) finding that the employer's explanation of its action was not believable. . . .

In sum, our interpretation of *Burdine* creates difficulty with one sentence; the dissent's interpretation causes many portions of the opinion to be incomprehensible or deceptive. But whatever doubt *Burdine*

might have created was eliminated by *Aikens.* There we said, in language that cannot reasonably be mistaken, that "the ultimate question [is] discrimination *vel non.* 460 U.S., at 714. Once the defendant "responds to the plaintiff's proof by offering evidence of the reason for the plaintiff's rejection, the factfinder must decide" *not* (as the dissent would have it) whether that evidence is credible, but "whether the rejection was discriminatory within the meaning of Title VII." *Id.,* at 714–715. At that stage, we said, "[t]he District Court was. . . in a position to decide the ultimate factual issue in the case," which is "whether the defendant intentionally discriminated against the plaintiff." *Id.,* at 715. The *McDonnell Douglas* methodology was "'never intended to be rigid, mechanized, or ritualistic.'" 460 U.S., at 715 (quoting *Furnco Construction Corp. v. Waters,* 438 U.S. 567, 577). Rather, once the defendant has responded to the plaintiff's prima facie case, "[t]he district court has before it all the evidence it needs to decide" *not* (as the dissent would have it) whether defendant's response is credible, but "whether the defendant intentionally discriminated against the plaintiff. . . . "

Justice SOUTER, with whom Justice WHITE, Justice BLACKMUN, and Justice STEVENS join, dissenting.

Twenty years ago, in *McDonnell Douglas Corp. v. Green,* 411 U.S. 792 (1973), this Court unanimously prescribed a "sensible, orderly way to evaluate the evidence" in a Title VII disparate-treatment case, giving both the plaintiff and the defendant fair opportunities to litigate "in light of common experience as it bears on the critical question of discrimination." *Furnco Constr. Corp. v. Waters,* 438 U.S. 567, 577 (1978). We have repeatedly reaffirmed and refined the *McDonnell Douglas* framework, most notably in *Texas Dept. of Community Affairs v. Burdine,* 450 U.S. 248 (1981), another unanimous opinion. . . . But today, after two decades of stable law in this Court and only relatively recent disruption in some Circuits . . . the Court abandons this practical framework together with its central purpose, which is "to sharpen the inquiry into the elusive factual question of intentional discrimination," *Burdine, supra,* at 255, n.8. Ignoring language to the contrary in both *McDonnell Douglas* and *Burdine,* the Court holds that, once a Title VII plaintiff succeeds in showing at trial that the defendant has come forward with pretextual reasons for its actions in response to a prima facie showing of discrimination, the factfinder still may proceed to roam the record, searching for

---

[4] Contrary to the dissent's confusion-producing analysis . . . there is nothing whatever inconsistent between this statement and our later statements that (1) the plaintiff must show "*both* that the real reason was false, *and* that discrimination was the real reason," *infra,* at 2754, and (2) "it is not enough . . . to *dis*believe the employer," *infra,* at 2754. Even though (as we say here) rejection of the defendant's proffered reasons is enough at law to *sustain* a finding of discrimination, *there must be a finding of discrimination.*

some nondiscriminatory explanation that the defendant has not raised and that the plaintiff has had no fair opportunity to disprove. Because the majority departs from settled precedent in substituting a scheme of proof for disparate treatment actions that promises to be unfair and unworkable, I respectfully dissent. . . .

At the outset, under the *McDonnell Douglas* framework, a plaintiff alleging disparate treatment in the workplace in violation of Title VII must provide the basis for an inference of discrimination. In this case, as all agree, Melvin Hicks met this initial burden by proving by a preponderance of the evidence that he was black and therefore a member of a protected class; he was qualified to be a shift commander; he was demoted and then terminated; and his position remained available and was later filled by a qualified applicant.[1] Hicks thus proved what we have called a "prima facie case" of discrimination, and it is important to note that in this context a prima facie case is indeed a proven case. Although, in other contexts, a prima facie case only requires production of enough evidence to raise an issue for the trier of fact, here it means that the plaintiff has actually established the elements of the prima facie case to the satisfaction of the factfinder by a preponderance of the evidence. See *Burdine*, 450 U.S., at 253, 254, n.7. By doing so, Hicks "eliminat[ed] the most common nondiscriminatory reasons" for demotion and firing: that he was unqualified for the position or that the position was no longer available. *Id.*, at 254; Under *McDonnell Douglas* and *Burdine*, however, proof of a prima facie case not only raises an inference of discrimination; in the absence of further evidence, it also creates a mandatory presumption in favor of the plaintiff.

As we made clear in *Burdine*, "[I]f the employer is silent in the face of the presumption, the court must enter judgment for the plaintiff." *Id.*, at 254. Thus, if the employer remains silent because it acted for a reason it is too embarrassed to reveal, or for a reason it fails to discover, the plaintiff is entitled to judgment under *Burdine*.

Obviously, it would be unfair to bar an employer from coming forward at this stage with a nondis-criminatory explanation for its actions, since the lack of an open position and the plaintiff's lack of qualifications do not exhaust the set of nondiscriminatory reasons that might explain an adverse personnel decision. If the trier of fact could not consider other explanations, employers' autonomy would be curtailed far beyond what is needed to rectify the discrimination identified by Congress. Cf. *Furnco, supra,* at 577–578 (Title VII "does not impose a duty to adopt a hiring procedure that maximizes hiring of minority employees"). On the other hand, it would be equally unfair and utterly impractical to saddle the victims of discrimination with the burden of either producing direct evidence of discriminatory intent or eliminating the entire universe of possible nondiscriminatory reasons for a personnel decision. The Court in *McDonnell Douglas* reconciled these competing interests in a very sensible way by requiring the employer to "articulate," through the introduction of admissible evidence, one or more "legitimate, nondiscriminatory reason[s]" for its actions. 411 U.S., at 802. . . . Proof of a prima facie case thus serves as a catalyst obligating the employer to step forward with an explanation for its actions. St. Mary's, in this case, used this opportunity to provide two reasons for its treatment of Hicks: the severity and accumulation of rule infractions he had allegedly committed. 970 F.2d, at 491.

The Court emphasizes that the employer's obligation at this stage is only a burden of production, and that, if the employer meets the burden, the presumption entitling the plaintiff to judgment "drops from the case," *id.*, at 255, n.10. This much is certainly true . . . but the obligation also serves an important function neglected by the majority, in requiring the employer "to frame the factual issue with sufficient clarity so that the plaintiff will have a full and fair opportunity to demonstrate pretext." 450 U.S., at 255–256. The employer, in other words, has a "burden of production" that gives it the right to choose the scope of the factual issues to be resolved by the factfinder. But investing the employer with this choice has no point unless the scope it chooses binds the employer as well as the plaintiff. Nor does it make sense to tell the employer, as this Court has done, that its explanation of legitimate reasons "must be clear and reasonably specific," if the factfinder can rely on a reason not clearly articulated, or on one not articulated at all, to rule in favor of the employer. . . . " *Id.*, at 258; see *id.*, at 255, n.9 ("An articulation not admitted into evidence will not suffice").

Once the employer chooses the battleground in this manner, "the factual inquiry proceeds to a new

---

[1] The majority, following the courts below, mentions that Hicks's position was filled by a white male. . . . This Court has not directly addressed the question whether the personal characteristics of someone chosen to replace a Title VII plaintiff are material, and that issue is not before us today. . . .

level of specificity." *Id.,* at 255. During this final, more specific enquiry, the employer has no burden to prove that its proffered reasons are true; rather, the plaintiff must prove by a preponderance of the evidence that the proffered reasons are pretextual. *Id.,* at 256. *McDonnell Douglas* makes it clear that if the plaintiff fails to show "pretext," the challenged employment action "must stand." 411 U.S., at 807. If, on the other hand, the plaintiff carries his burden of showing "pretext," the court "must order a prompt and appropriate remedy."[5] *Ibid.* Or, as we said in *Burdine*: "[The plaintiff] now must have the opportunity to demonstrate that the proffered reason was not the true reason for the employment decision. This burden now merges with the ultimate burden of persuading the court that [the plaintiff] has been the victim of intentional discrimination. . . . " 450 U.S., at 256. *Burdine* drives home the point that the case has proceeded to "a new level of specificity" by explaining that the plaintiff can meet his burden of persuasion in either of two ways: "either directly by persuading the court that a discriminatory reason more likely motivated the employer or indirectly by showing that the employer's proffered explanation is unworthy of credence." *Ibid.* . . . That the plaintiff can succeed simply by showing that "the employer's proffered explanation is unworthy of credence" indicates that the case has been narrowed to the question whether the employer's proffered reasons are pretextual. . . . Thus, because Hicks carried his burden of persuasion by showing that St. Mary's proffered reasons were "unworthy of credence," the Court of Appeals properly concluded that he was entitled to judgment. . . . 970 F.2d, at 492.

[5] The Court makes a halfhearted attempt to rewrite these passages from *McDonnell Douglas*, arguing that "pretext for discrimination" should appear where "pretext" actually does. . . . [W]hen the *McDonnell Douglas* Court's focus shifts from what the employer may not do to what the plaintiff must show, the Court states that the plaintiff must "be afforded a fair opportunity to show [that the employer's] stated reason for [the plaintiff's] rejection was in fact pretext," plain and simple. . . . To the extent choosing between "pretext" and "pretext for discrimination" is important, the *McDonnell Douglas* Court's diction appears to be consistent, not sloppy. *Burdine*, of course, nails down the point that the plaintiff satisfies his burden simply by proving that the employer's explanation does not deserve credence. . . .

Questions

1. In Problem 4, does Kathleen have to show something more than that the employer's reasons are false? What more does she have to show?
2. The *Hicks* majority mentioned that the "prima facie presumption disappeared" once the employer met its burden of producing evidence of reasons for taking the adverse action against the employee. What happens to the evidence that supported the prima facie case? In Kathleen's case, what if the fourth prong of the prima facie case had been evidence to support an inference that similarly situated men were not treated the same way that she was treated? Once the prima facie presumption disappears, what happens to that evidence? Could it be used to support a finding that intentional discrimination was more likely than not the reason for the employer's action? Do you think the courts are bound to consider this evidence? How responsible did an employer have to be to give the "true" reason for its actions and what consequences should apply when it was not the true reason?
3. As Justice Souter, writing in dissent, pointed out, there is conflicting language in this opinion, and he warned that the Court's opinion foreshadowed even further confusion. Justice Souter proved to be correct; confusion reigned. The opinions of the appellate courts in the various federal circuits went in opposite directions on how to interpret the nature of the plaintiff's burden after *St. Mary's Honor Center.* Those supporting the "pretext plus" requirement used language in the opinion to support their findings, while those who rejected the "pretext plus" requirement cited different language from *St. Mary's Honor Center* that supported other ways of meeting the plaintiff's final burden of persuasion. As you re-read the edited version of the Court's opinion in *St. Mary's Honor Center* and Justice Souter's dissenting opinion, be on the lookout for the language that supports both views.
4. How would you analyze Raphael's situation in Problem 5?

4. When Can Pretext Evidence Be Enough?

> ## Problem 6
>
> Margo Maynard has worked for the Dew Chemical Company for the last 20 years. She is a 55-year-old chemist who has excelled in the production of numerous lucrative products for the company. Recently she has had a number of offers from competitor companies, yet she has remained loyal to Dew. Michael Dawson, Ms. Maynard's supervisor, has been jealous of Margo's success over the years, and he wants to get rid of her. He doesn't believe that women belong in the ranks of star performers at Dew, and he thinks he should be receiving the credit for her past work. The management at Dew has asked him to suggest a new budget for his department in order to cut costs. Michael decides to get rid of Margo by including her in a reduction in force or RIF of expensive employees. Margo thinks that there are other employees, however, who fall in the same category of performance and salary who are not subjected to the RIF. She has not been able to produce evidence of similarly situated employees being treated differently. She has found a witness who will testify that Michael was jealous of Margo and that is why he wanted to get rid of her.
>
> Margo is in a difficult position because she can prove that Michael was motivated by a reason other than the one produced as the "legitimate, nondiscriminatory reason for the adverse employment action," but can she meet her ultimate burden of proving that Title VII was violated? Although the information provided by the witness may be enough to create an inference of discrimination for purposes of getting past the prima facie requirements and showing that the employer's reason is false, is it enough to prove discrimination on the basis of her sex?

The opinion by the Supreme Court in *Reeves v. Sanderson Plumbing Products, Inc.,* in July 2000, returned to the requirements of the *McDonnell Douglas* model to consider the role of evidence presented at both the prima facie stage and the plaintiff's final burden stage. Facts, the Court reminds us, don't disappear once the prima facie case presumption of discrimination is rebutted by the employer's articulation of a legitimate, nondiscriminatory reason. The facts presented to support the prima facie case remain evidence that can be considered to support the plaintiff's final burden of persuading the factfinder that it is more likely than not that discrimination occurred. The Court also addressed the controversy in the lower courts of appeal about the so-called pretext-plus requirement seemingly supported by *St. Mary's Honor Center v. Hicks*. Some circuits had required proof beyond the falsity of the employer's reason, stating that there must be additional proof of an intent to discriminate.

The Supreme Court in *Reeves* recognized that the employee might meet his ultimate burden of persuasion in some discrimination cases with evidence that was presented to support the prima facie case and evidence that the employer's reason for its actions was false, without the requirement of further evidence of an intent to discriminate.

Notice how the Court is careful not to reject its earlier opinion in *Hicks*. In *Hicks*, the employee was arguing that he was entitled to summary judgment as a matter of law because he had shown that the employer's reason was false, and in *Reeves*, the employer was asking that a jury verdict be overturned because the employee demonstrated only that the reason asserted by the employer was false and did not show additional evidence of an intent to discriminate. What difference should this make to the outcome in these cases? Doesn't *Reeves* say that its ruling applies to summary judgments also?

REEVES
v.
SANDERSON PLUMBING PRODUCTS, INC.
530 U.S. 133 (2000)

O'CONNOR, J., delivered the opinion for a unanimous Court. GINSBURG, J. filed a concurring opinion.

[The Employment Problem]

[Roger Reeves was a 57-year-old male who worked 40 years for Sanderson Plumbing Products, Inc. He worked as a supervisor in the "Hinge Room," where he supervised the "regular line" manufacturing toilet seats and covers. One of his responsibilities included recording and reviewing the attendance and hours of those who worked under his supervision. When management became aware that "production was down" because employees were coming in late or were absent, an audit revealed numerous timekeeping errors and misrepresentations on the part of Reeves, his supervisor, and a co-supervisor. Reeves and his supervisor were terminated. Reeves filed a lawsuit in federal district court, contending that he had been fired because of his age in violation of the Age Discrimination in Employment Act of 1967 (ADEA), 29 U.S.C. 621 et seq. The employer claimed that he was terminated for failing to maintain accurate attendance records, while Reeves attempted to demonstrate that the employer's reason for this action was a pretext for age discrimination.]

[The Legal Issue]

This case concerns the kind and amount of evidence necessary to sustain a jury's verdict that an employer unlawfully discriminated on the basis of age. Specifically, we must resolve whether a defendant is entitled to judgment as a matter of law when the plaintiff's case consists exclusively of a prima facie case of discrimination and sufficient evidence for the trier of fact to disbelieve the defendant's legitimate, nondiscriminatory explanation for its action. We must also decide whether the employer was entitled to judgment as a matter of law under the particular circumstances presented here. . . .

[The Decision of the Trial Court and the U.S. Court of Appeals for the Fifth Circuit]

. . . The [trial] court instructed the jury that "[i]f the plaintiff fails to prove age was a determinative or motivating factor in the decision to terminate him, then your verdict shall be for the defendant." . . . So charged, the jury returned a verdict in favor of [the Employee], awarding him $35,000 in compensatory damages, and found that [the Employer's] age discrimination had been "willful[l]." 197 F.3d, at 691. The District Court accordingly entered judgment for petitioner in the amount of $70,000, which included $35,000 in liquidated damages based on the jury's finding of willfulness *Ibid*. [The employer] then renewed its motion for judgment as a matter of law and alternatively moved for a new trial, while [the employee] moved for front pay. . . . The District Court denied [the employer's] motions and granted [the employee's], awarding him $28,490.80 in front pay for two years' lost income. . . .

The Court of Appeals for the Fifth Circuit reversed, holding that [the employee] had not introduced sufficient evidence to sustain the jury's finding of unlawful discrimination. 197 F.3d at 694. After noting [the employer's] proffered justification for [the employee's] discharge, the court acknowledged that [the employer] "very well may" have offered sufficient evidence for "a reasonable jury [to] have found that [the employer's] explanation for its employment decision was pretextual." *Id.*, at 693. The court explained, however, that this was "not dispositive" of the ultimate issue—namely, "whether Reeves presented sufficient evidence that his age motivated [the employer's] employment decision." *Ibid.* Addressing this question, the court weighed [the employee's] additional evidence of discrimination against other circumstances surrounding his discharge. See, *id.*, at 693–694. Specifically, the court noted that Chesnut's age-based comments "were not made in the direct context of Reeves's termination"; there was no allegation that the two other individuals who had recommended that petitioner be fired (Jester and Whitaker) were motivated by age; two of the decisionmakers involved in [the employee's] discharge (Jester and Sanderson) were over the age of 50; all three of the Hinge Room supervisors were accused of inaccurate recordkeeping; and several of [the employer's] management positions were filled by persons over age 50 when [the employee] was fired. *Ibid.* On this basis, the court concluded that [the employee] had not introduced sufficient evidence for a rational jury to conclude that he had been discharged because of his age. *Id.*, at 694.

[The Decision and Rationale of the U.S. Supreme Court]

We granted *certiorari* to resolve a conflict among the Courts of Appeals as to whether a plaintiff's prima facie case of discrimination (as defined in *McDonnell Douglas Corp. v. Green*, 411 U.S. 792, 802 (1973)), combined with sufficient evidence for a reasonable factfinder to reject the employer's nondiscriminatory explanation for its decision, is adequate to sustain a finding of liability for intentional discrimination. Compare *Kline v. TVA*, 128 F.3d 337 (CA6 1997) (prima facie case combined with sufficient evidence to disbelieve employer's explanation always creates jury issue of whether employer intentionally discriminated) [similar cites from the 11th, 3d, 8th, 7th, and 9th Circuits omitted] with *Aka v. Washington Hospital Center*, 156 F.3d 1284 (CADC 1998) (en banc) (plaintiff's discrediting of employer's explanation is entitled to considerable weight, such that plaintiff should not be routinely required to submit evidence over and above proof of pretext), and with *Fisher v. Vassar College*, 114 F.3d 1332 (CA2 1997) (en banc) (plaintiff must intro-

duce sufficient evidence for jury to find both that employer's reason was false and that real reason was discrimination), cert. denied, 522 U.S. 1075 (1998) [similar cites from the 5th, 4th, and 1st Circuits omitted].

Under the ADEA, it is "unlawful for an employer . . . to fail or refuse to hire or to discharge any individual or otherwise discriminate against any individual with respect to his compensation, terms, conditions, or privileges of employment, because of such individual's age." 29 U.S.C. §623(a)(1). When a plaintiff alleges disparate treatment, "liability depends on whether the protected trait (under the ADEA, age) actually motivated the employer's decision." *Hazen Paper Co. v. Biggins*, 507 U.S. 604, 610 (1993). That is, the plaintiff's age must have "actually played a role in [the employer's decisionmaking] process and had a determinative influence on the outcome." *Ibid.* Recognizing that "the question facing triers of fact in discrimination cases is both sensitive and difficult," and that "[t]here will seldom be 'eyewitness' testimony as to the employer's mental processes," *U.S. Postal Service Bd. of Governors v. Aikens*, 460 U.S. 711, 716 (1983), the Courts of Appeals, including the Fifth Circuit in this case, have employed some variant of the framework articulated in *McDonnell Douglas* to analyze ADEA claims that are based principally on circumstantial evidence. . . . This Court has not squarely addressed whether the *McDonnell Douglas* framework, developed to assess claims brought under §703(a)(1) of Title VII of the Civil Rights Act of 1964 . . . also applies to ADEA actions. Because the parties do not dispute the issue, we shall assume, *arguendo*, that the *McDonnell Douglas* framework is fully applicable here. Cf. *O'Connor v. Consolidated Coin Caterers Corp.*, 517 U.S. 308, 311 (1996).

McDonnell Douglas and subsequent decisions have "established an allocation of the burden of production and an order for the presentation of proof in . . . discriminatory treatment cases." *St. Mary's Honor Center v. Hicks*, 509 U.S. 502, 506 (1993). First, the plaintiff must establish a prima facie case of discrimination. *Ibid.*; *Texas Dept. of Community Affairs v. Burdine*, 450 U.S. 248, 252–253 (1981). It is undisputed that [the employee] satisfied this burden here: (i) at the time he was fired, he was a member of the class protected by the ADEA ("individuals who are at least 40 years of age," 29 U.S.C. §631 (a)), (ii) he was otherwise qualified for the position of Hinge Room supervisor, (iii) he was discharged by [the employer], and (iv) [the employer] successively hired three persons in their 30s to fill [the employee's] position. The burden therefore shifted to [the employer] to "produc[e] evidence that the plaintiff was rejected, or someone else was preferred, for a legitimate, nondis-criminatory reason." *Burdine, supra*, at 254. This burden is one of production, not persuasion; it "can involve no credibility assessment." *St. Mary's Honor Center, supra*, at 509. [The Employer] met this burden by offering admissible evidence sufficient for the trier of fact to conclude that [the employee] was fired because of his failure to maintain accurate attendance records. See 197 F.3d, at 692. Accordingly, "the *McDonnell Douglas* framework—with its presumptions and burdens"—disappeared, *St. Mary's Honor Center, supra*, at 510 and the sole remaining issue was "discrimination *vel non*," *Aikens, supra*, at 714.

Although intermediate evidentiary burdens shift back and forth under this framework, "[t]he ultimate burden of persuading the trier of fact that the defendant intentionally discriminated against the plaintiff remains at all times with the plaintiff." *Burdine*, 450 U.S., at 253. And in attempting to satisfy this burden, the plaintiff—once the employer produces sufficient evidence to support a nondiscriminatory explanation for its decision—must be afforded the "opportunity to prove by a preponderance of the evidence that the legitimate reasons offered by the defendant were not its true reasons, but were a pretext for discrimination." *Ibid.*; see also *St. Mary's Honor Center, supra*, at 507–508. That is, the plaintiff may attempt to establish that he was the victim of intentional discrimination "by showing that the employer's proffered explanation is unworthy of credence." *Burdine, supra*, at 256. Moreover, although the presumption of discrimination "drops out of the picture" once the defendant meets its burden of production, *St. Mary's Honor Center, supra*, at 511, the trier of fact may still consider the evidence establishing the plaintiff's prima facie case "and inference properly drawn therefrom . . . on the issue of whether the defendant's explanation is pretextual," *Burdine, supra*, at 255, n.10.

In this case, the evidence supporting [The Employer's] explanation for petitioner's discharge consisted primarily of testimony by Chesnut and Sanderson and documentation of [The employee's] alleged "shoddy record keeping." 197 F.3d, at 692. Chesnut testified that a 1993 audit of Hinge Room operations revealed "a very lax assembly line" where employees were not adhering to general work rules. . . . As a result of that audit, [the employee] was placed on 90 days' probation for unsatisfactory performance. 197 F.3d, at 690. In 1995, Chesnut ordered another investigation of the Hinge Room, which, according to his testimony, revealed that [the employee] was not correctly recording the absences and hours of employees. . . . [The

Employer] introduced summaries of that investigation documenting several attendance violations by 12 employees under [the employee's] supervision, and noting that each should have been disciplined in some manner. . . . Chesnut testified that this failure to discipline absent and late employees is "extremely important when you are dealing with a union" because uneven enforcement across departments would keep the company "in grievance and arbitration cases, which are costly, all the time." . . . He and Sanderson also stated that [the employee's] errors, by failing to adjust for hours not worked, cost the company overpaid wages. . . . Sanderson testified that she accepted the recommendation to discharge [the employee] because he had "intentionally falsif[ied] company pay records . . . ".

[The Employee], however, made a substantial showing that [the Employer's] explanation was false. First, [the employee] offered evidence that he had properly maintained the attendance records. Most of the timekeeping errors cited by [the Employer] involved employees who were not marked late but who were recorded as having arrived at the plant at 7 a.m. for the 7 a.m. shift. . . . [The Employer] contended that employees arriving at 7 a.m. could not have been at their workstations by 7 a.m., and therefore must have been late. . . . But both [the employee] and Oswalt testified that the company's automated timeclock often failed to scan employees' timecards, so that the timesheets would not record any time of arrival. . . . On these occasions, [the Employee] and Oswalt would visually check the workstations and record whether the employees were present at the start of the shift. . . . They stated that if an employee arrived promptly but the timesheet contained no time of arrival, they would reconcile the two by marking "7 a.m." as the employee's arrival time, even if the employee actually arrived at the plant earlier. *Ibid.* On cross-examination, Chesnut acknowledged that the timeclock sometimes malfunctioned, and that if "people were there at their work station[s]" at the start of the shift, the supervisor would write in seven o'clock. . . ." [The Employee] also testified that when employees arrived before or stayed after their shifts, he would assign them additional work so that they would not be overpaid. See 197 F.3d, at 693.

[The Employee] similarly cast doubt on whether he was responsible for any failure to discipline late and absent employees. [The Employee] testified that his job only included reviewing the daily and weekly attendance reports, and that the disciplinary writeups were based on the monthly reports, which were reviewed by Caldwell. . . . Sanderson admitted that

Caldwell, and not [the Employee], was responsible for citing employees for violations of the company's attendance policy. . . . Further, Chesnut conceded that there had never been a union grievance or employee complaint arising from [the Employee's] recordkeeping, and that the company had never calculated the amount of overpayments allegedly attributable to [the Employee's] errors. . . . [The Employee] also testified that, on the day he was fired, Chesnut said that his discharge was due to his failure to report as absent one employee, Gina Mae Coley, on two days in September 1995. But [the Employee] explained that he had spent those days in the hospital, and that Caldwell was therefore responsible for any overpayment of Coley. Finally, [the Employee] stated that on previous occasions that employees were paid for hours they had not worked, the company had simply adjusted those employees' next paychecks to correct the errors. . . .

Based on this evidence, the Court of Appeals concluded that [the Employee] "very well may be correct" that "a reasonable jury could have found that [respondent's] explanation for its employment decision was pretextual." 197 F.3d, at 693. Nonetheless, the court held that this showing, standing alone, was insufficient to sustain the jury's finding of liability. "We must, as an essential final step, determine whether Reeves presented sufficient evidence that his age motivated [respondent's] employment decision." *Ibid.* And in making this determination, the Court of Appeals ignored the evidence supporting petitioner's prima facie case and challenging respondent's explanation for its decision. . . . The court confined its review of evidence favoring [the Employee] to that evidence showing that Chesnut had directed derogatory, age-based comments at [the Employee], and that Chesnut had singled out [the Employee] for harsher treatment than younger employees. See *ibid.* It is therefore apparent that the court believed that only this additional evidence of discrimination was relevant to whether the jury's verdict should stand. That is, the Court of Appeals proceeded from the assumption that a prima facie case of discrimination, combined with sufficient evidence for the trier of fact to disbelieve the defendant's legitimate, nondiscriminatory reason for its decision, is insufficient as a matter of law to sustain a jury's finding of intentional discrimination.

In so reasoning, the Court of Appeals misconceived the evidentiary burden borne by plaintiffs who attempted to prove intentional discrimination through indirect evidence. This much is evident from our decision in *St. Mary's Honor Center.* There we held that the factfinder's rejection of the employer's legiti-

mate, nondiscriminatory reason for its action does not *compel* judgment for the plaintiff. 509 U.S., at 511. The ultimate question is whether the employer intentionally discriminated, and proof that "the employer's proffered reason is unpersuasive, or even obviously contrived, does not necessarily establish that the plaintiff's proffered reason . . . is correct." *Id.,* at 524. In other words, "[i]t is not enough . . . to *disbelieve* the employer; the factfinder must *believe* the plaintiff's explanation of intentional discrimination." *Id.,* at 519 [emphasis added by the Court].

In reaching this conclusion, however, we reasoned that it is *permissible* for the trier of fact to infer the ultimate fact of discrimination from the falsity of the employer's explanation. Specifically, we stated:

> The factfinder's disbelief of the reasons put forward by the defendant (particularly if disbelief is accompanied by a suspicion of mendacity) may, together with the elements of the prima facie case, suffice to show intentional discrimination. Thus rejection of the defendant's proffered reasons will *permit* the trier of fact to infer the ultimate fact of intentional discrimination. *Id.,* at 511.

Proof that the defendant's explanation is unworthy of credence is simply one form of circumstantial evidence that is probative of intentional discrimination, and it may be quite persuasive. *See id.,* at 517. ("[P]roving the employer's reason false becomes part of (and often considerably assists) the greater enterprise of proving that the real reason was intentional discrimination"). In appropriate circumstances, the trier of fact can reasonably infer from the falsity of the explanation that the employer is dissembling to cover up a discriminatory purpose. . . . Moreover, once the employer's justification has been eliminated, discrimination may well be the most likely alternative explanation, especially since the employer is in the best position to put forth the actual reason for its decision. Cf. *Furnco Constr. Corp. v. Waters,* 438 U.S. 567, 577 (1978). ("[W]hen all legitimate reasons for rejecting an applicant have been eliminated as possible reasons for the employer's actions, it is more likely than not the employer, who we generally assume acts with *some* reason, based his decision on an impermissible consideration"). Thus, a plaintiff's prima facie case, combined with sufficient evidence to find that the employer's asserted justification is false, may permit the trier of fact to conclude that the employer unlawfully discriminated.

This is not to say that such a showing by the plaintiff will *always* be adequate to sustain a jury's finding of liability. Certainly there will be instances where, although the plaintiff has established a prima facie case and set forth sufficient evidence to reject the defendant's explanation, no rational factfinder could conclude that the action was discriminatory. For instance, an employer would be entitled to judgment as a matter of law if the record conclusively revealed some other, nondiscriminatory reason for the employer's decision, or if the plaintiff created only a weak issue of fact as to whether the employer's reason was untrue and there was abundant and uncontroverted independent evidence that no discrimination had occurred. See *Aka v. Washington Hosp. Ctr.*, 156 F.3d, at 1291–1292; see also *Fisher v. Vassar College*, 114 F.3d, at 1338 ("[I]f the circumstances show that the defendant gave the false explanation to conceal something other than discrimination, the inference of discrimination will be weak or nonexistent"). To hold otherwise would be effectively to insulate an entire category of employment discrimination cases from review under Rule 50, and we have reiterated that trial courts should not "treat discrimination differently from other ultimate questions of fact." *St. Mary's Honor Center, supra,* at 524 (quoting *Aikens*, 460 U.S., at 716).

Whether judgment as a matter of law is appropriate in any particular case will depend on a number of factors. Those include the strength of the plaintiff's prima facie case, the probative value of the proof that the employer's explanation is false, and any other evidence considered on a motion for judgment as a matter of law. See infra, at 2110–2111. For purposes of this case, we need not—and could not—resolve all of the circumstances in which such factors would entitle an employer to judgment as a matter of law. It suffices to say that, because a prima facie case and sufficient evidence that supports the employer's case and that properly may be to reject the employer's explanation may permit a finding of liability, the Court of Appeals erred in proceeding from the premise that a plaintiff must always introduce additional, independent evidence of discrimination.

[The discussion in Part III of the standard for overturning a jury verdict for insufficiency of the evidence, which the Court also applied to summary judgment motions, is omitted here.]

Justice GINSBURG, concurring. . . .

. . . I write separately to note that it may be incumbent on the Court, in an appropriate case, to define more precisely the circumstances in which plaintiffs will be required to submit evidence beyond these two categories in order to survive a motion for judgment as a matter of law. I anticipate that such circumstances will be uncommon. As the Court notes, it is a principle of evidence law that the jury is entitled to treat a party's dishonesty about a material fact as evidence of culpability. *Ante,* at 2108. Under this commonsense principle, evidence suggesting that a defendant accused of illegal discrimination has chosen to give a false explanation for its actions gives rise to a rational inference that the defendant could be masking its actual, illegal motivation. Whether the defendant was in fact motivated by discrimination is of course for the finder of fact to decide; that is the lesson of *St. Mary's Honor Center v. Hicks*, 509 U.S. 502 (1993). But the inference remains—unless it is conclusively demonstrated, by evidence the district court is required to credit on a motion for judgment as a matter of law . . . , that discrimination could not have been the defendant's true motivation. If such conclusive demonstrations are (as I suspect) atypical, it follows that the ultimate question of liability ordinarily should not be taken from the jury once the plaintiff has introduced the two categories of evidence described above. Because the Court's opinion leaves room for such further elaboration in an appropriate case, I join it in full.

Questions

1. What should happen in Margo's hypothetical situation? Does she have enough to survive the initial requirement of a prima facie case? What about pretext? What is her ultimate burden and what does she have to support it?
2. Notice that a trial occurred in *Reeves.* Unlike many cases that are reviewed because a lower court has granted a summary judgment motion against the employee, the jury decided that discrimination had occurred here, and the judge made a determination of damages. The court of appeals and the Supreme Court had to review whether there were correct jury instructions on the law and enough evidence to support that verdict. Should there be a difference in the way the Court reviewed this case because there was a jury decision?
3. How do you synthesize the treatment of the problem in *Hicks* with this more recent Supreme Court decision? Are they compatible? What happens to the "pretext plus" requirement used by some courts prior to *Reeves*?

Discussion Notes

1. *Reeves* is a case about age discrimination. Age is not a protected class under Title VII. The Age Discrimination in Employment Act became law

in 1967 after the passage of Title VII. The courts interpreting this Act have borrowed heavily from cases interpreting Title VII. The law interpreting age discrimination has also developed its own set of unique requirements based on the specific language of that statute. Congress decided that the Age Discrimination in Employment Act protected employees over the age of 40 and not those younger than that age.

2. As employment discrimination law has evolved in recent years, many scholars view age discrimination cases as the "trend setters" in the law—that is, the interpretations developed by the courts in age discrimination cases are now borrowed and applied to other kinds of discrimination cases under Title VII. The unanimous decision, with one concurring opinion, by the Supreme Court in *Reeves*, is an example. The Court specifically notes the assumption that their analysis in this age discrimination case can be applied to cases decided under Title VII. They also note the assumption but do not specifically hold that the *McDonnell Douglas* formula applies to Age Discrimination in Employment Act cases.

3. In 2002, the U.S. Supreme Court decided that state employees could not sue their state employers under the Age Discrimination in Employment Act of 1967, 29 U.S.C. § 629 et seq., because of the problem of the Eleventh Amendment, which states that "the judicial power of the United States shall not be construed to extend to any suit in law or equity, commenced or prosecuted against one of the United States by Citizens of another State, or by Citizens or Subjects of any Foreign State." Under Article 1 of the Constitution, which describes Congress's powers, Congress cannot waive a state's immunity in its own courts. *Alden v. Maine*, 527 U.S. 706 (1999). State immunity may be waived when Congress has made its intent explicit and based its action on a specific congressional power (e.g., Section 5 of the Fourteenth Amendment), and such a waiver must be limited to the promulgation of the purposes of the specific amendment implicated. *Kimel v. Florida Bd. of Regents*, 520 U. S. 62 (2000). In *Kimel*, the Supreme Court ruled that the 1974 amendments to the Age Discrimination in Employment Act that applied the ADEA to states could not be justified under this test. *Id.* A similar ruling was applied to the Americans with Disabilities Act of 1990 (ADA) when the Court ruled that a state cannot be sued for damages under the ADA. *Board of Trustees of the University of Alabama v. Garrett*, 531 U.S. 356 (2001).

---

5. Proof of Direct Evidence of Discrimination and a Legitimate, Nondiscriminatory Reason for the Adverse Action: The "Mixed Motives" Claims

Problem 7

Alicia Kaiser sued her former employer, Egyptian Palace, Inc., a casino located in Reno, Nevada. Alicia worked in the warehouse for the casino as the only woman forklift driver. She claimed both gender and race discrimination against her employer for the treatment she endured at work and for the final termination. Her work was evaluated as "excellent" prior to the incidents involved in this case. Her supervisor had written on her most recent evaluation, "We knew that when she was out there the work would get done." Even so, she started experiencing problems with management and her co-workers. A series of events, which included informal comments, refusals to give her privileges received by male employees,

(continued)

and a suspension all finally led to termination. Alicia offered evidence showing that when she was reprimanded for being late, male employees were not reprimanded for the same behavior. She claimed she was subjected to comments about her that reflected racial and gender stereotypes. She was berated for actions, while her male co-workers did not receive the same kind of derision for the same activity. When she was accosted by a co-worker, she was fired, and the co-worker was suspended.

At trial, the Egyptian Palace owners claimed that she was terminated because of her disciplinary history and her altercation with the co-worker. Alicia did not suggest that she was a model employee but asserted that her sex was at least a motivating factor in her treatment and final termination.

Sometimes employers have a legitimate reason for taking the adverse employment action against an employee, but they also act based on discriminatory reasons. The U.S. Supreme Court addressed this problem in the *Price Waterhouse v. Hopkins* case and set forth guidelines for determining whether and how the employee could prevail in these situations. When the employer had a discriminatory reason for its action, Title VII is violated, but when the employer also had a legitimate reason for taking the action against the employee, the employee should not, according to the Court, receive a "windfall" when the action would have taken place anyway.

The Court implied that a different procedure would have to be followed in "mixed motives" cases than the one followed in a *McDonnell Douglas* case. If the employee could establish by direct evidence that the employer based his decision, in part, on a discriminatory reason, the employee would prevail unless the employer could show that the employment action would have been taken even if no discriminatory reason had been involved in the decision. According to the Supreme Court in *Price Waterhouse*, the employee would lose if the employer met this burden.

This raised questions and concerns about the continuing vitality of the *McDonnell Douglas* formula for proving discrimination. Was this an offshoot of *McDonnell Douglas* or a move toward the eventual dismantling of the traditional method of considering proof of intentional discrimination? The Court suggested a procedure for deciding whether this was a mixed motives or a circumstantial *McDonnell Douglas* case. Unfortunately, the Court didn't elaborate on the distinction and has left the lower courts guessing about the process. In the Civil Rights Act of 1991, Congress changed the outcome of a finding of discrimination in a mixed motives case by allowing for liability when the illegitimate discriminatory factor was a part of the decision but limiting the kinds of damages a plaintiff could receive if the employer showed that it would have fired or failed to promote the plaintiff even if the illegitimate factor had not been present.

Employers became concerned about the additional burden imposed on them when the plaintiff was able to convince the judge that there was direct evidence of discrimination at play in the decision not to promote and claimed that it inappropriately shifted the burdens in the case away from the plaintiff and onto the employer in a deviation from traditional burdens of proof. Employers were now required to assert an affirmative defense and prove that they would have taken the employment action contested even if there had been no illegitmate motive present. If they met that burden, no violation of Title VII occurred. Employees argued that an employer should not be able to escape responsibility for its illegitimate motive just because it could meet the new affirmative defense of showing that it would have taken the same action even if no illegal motive had been present.

PRICE WATERHOUSE
v.
HOPKINS
490 U.S. 228 (1989)

BRENNAN, J., announced the judgment of the Court. . . .

[The Employment Problem]

Ann Hopkins was a senior manager in an office of Price Waterhouse when she was proposed for partnership in 1982. She was neither offered nor denied admission to the partnership; instead, her candidacy was held for reconsideration the following year. . . . Ann Hopkins had worked at Price Waterhouse's Office of Government Services in Washington, D.C., for five years when the partners in that office proposed her as a candidate for partnership. Of the 662 partners at the firm at that time, 7 were women. Of the 88 persons proposed for partnership that year, only 1—Hopkins—was a woman. Forty-seven of these candidates were admitted to the partnership, 21 were rejected, and 20—including Hopkins—were "held" for reconsideration for the following year. . . . Before the time for reconsideration came, two of the partners in Hopkins' office withdrew their support for her, and the office informed her that she would not be reconsidered for partnership. Hopkins then resigned. . . . She sued Price Waterhouse under Title VII of the Civil Rights Act of 1964 charging that the firm had discriminated against her on the basis of sex in its decisions regarding partnership.

[The Legal Issues]

[The Supreme Court] granted certiorari to resolve a conflict among the Courts of Appeals concerning the respective burdens of proof of a defendant and plaintiff in a suit under Title VII when it has been shown that an employment decision resulted from a mixture of legitimate and illegitimate motives. . . . [The Court was faced with the difficulty of a "mixed motives" case: Is there a violation of Title VII where there is a legitimate and an illegitimate basis for the decision not to promote and both reasons played a role in the decision? The Court also indirectly addressed the problem of gender stereotyping as a violation of Title VII.]

[The Decision of the Trial Court and the U.S. Court of Appeals for the District of Columbia Circuit]

Judge Gesell in the Federal District Court for the District of Columbia ruled in her favor on the question of liability, and the Court of Appeals for the District of Columbia Circuit affirmed. [The district court recognized that illegal sex stereotyping violated Title VII, but there were other, legitimate reasons for the decision not to promote at that time.

[The Decision and Rationale of the U.S. Supreme Court]

[*The Illegitimate Reason*: Ann Hopkins was an outstanding performer. The Court analyzed her performance by looking at the statements of the jointly prepared report supporting her candidacy. The partners in her office] showcased her successful two-year effort to secure a $25 million contract with the Department of State, labeling it "an outstanding performance" and one that Hopkins carried out "virtually at the partner level. . . ." Despite Price Waterhouse's attempt at trial to minimize her contribution to this project, Judge Gesell specifically found that Hopkins had "played a key role in Price Waterhouse's successful effort to win a multi-million dollar contract with the Department of State." 618F. Supp., at 1112. Indeed, he went on, "[n]one of the other partnership candidates at Price Waterhouse that year had a comparable record in terms of successfully securing major contracts for the partnership." *Ibid.*

The partners in Hopkins' office praised her character as well as her accomplishments, describing her in their joint statement as "an outstanding professional" who had a "deft touch," a "strong character, independence and integrity. . . ." Clients appear to have agreed with these assessments. At trial, one official from the State Department described her as "extremely competent, intelligent," "strong and forthright, very productive, energetic and creative." Tr. 150. Another high-ranking official praised Hopkins' decisiveness, broadmindedness, and "intellectual clarity"; she was, in his words, "a stimulating conversationalist." *Id.*, at 156–157. Evaluations such as these led Judge Gesell to conclude that Hopkins "had no difficulty dealing with clients and her clients appear to have been very pleased with her work" and that she "was generally viewed as a highly competent project leader who worked long hours, pushed vigorously to meet deadlines and demanded much from the multidisciplinary staffs with which she worked." 618 F. Supp., at 1112–1113. . . .

[*Sex Role Stereotyping*:] There were clear signs, though, that some of the partners reacted negatively to Hopkins' personality because she was a woman. . . . One partner described her as "macho"; another suggested that she "overcompensated for being a woman"; a third advised her to take "a course at charm school". Several partners criticized her use of profanity; in response, one partner suggested that those partners objected to her swearing only "because it's a lady using foul language." Tr. 321. Another supporter explained that Hopkins "ha[d] matured from a tough-talking somewhat masculine hard-nosed mgr to an authoritative, formidable, but much more appealing lady ptr candidate. . . ." But it was the man who, as Judge Gesell found, bore responsibility for explaining to Hopkins the reasons for the Policy Board's decision to place her candidacy on hold who delivered the *coup de grace*: in order to improve her chances for partnership, Thomas Beyer advised, Hopkins should "walk more femininely, wear make-up, have her hair styled, and wear jewelry." 618 F. Supp., at 1117.

Dr. Susan Fiske, a social psychologist and Associate Professor of Psychology at Carnegie-Mellon University, testified at trial that the partnership selection process at Price Waterhouse was likely influenced by sex stereotyping. Her testimony focused not only on the overtly sex-based comments of partners but also on gender-neutral remarks, made by partners who knew Hopkins only slightly, that were intensely critical of her. One partner, for example, baldly stated that Hopkins was "universally disliked" by staff . . . and another described her as "consistently annoying and irritating" . . . ; yet these were people who had had very little contact with Hopkins. According to Fiske, Hopkins' uniqueness (as the only woman in the pool of candidates) and the subjectivity of the evaluations made it likely that sharply critical remarks such as these were the product of sex stereotyping—although Fiske admitted that she could not say with certainty whether any particular comment was the result of stereotyping. Fiske based her opinion on a review of the submitted comments, explaining that it was commonly accepted practice for social psychologists to reach this kind of conclusion without having met any of the people involved in the decisionmaking process.

In previous years, other female candidates for partnership also had been evaluated in sex-based terms. As a general matter, Judge Gesell concluded, "[c]andidates were viewed favorably if partners believed they maintained their femin[in]ity while becoming effective professional managers"; in this environment, "[t]o be identified as a 'women's lib[b]er' was regarded as [a] negative comment." 618 F. Supp., at 1117. In fact, the judge found that in previous years "[o]ne partner reportedly commented that he could not consider any woman seriously as a partnership candidate band and believed that women were not even capable of functioning as senior managers—yet the firm took no action to discourage his comments and recorded his vote in the overall summary of the evaluations." *Ibid.*

Judge Gesell found that Price Waterhouse legitimately emphasized interpersonal skills in its partnership decisions, and also found that the firm had not fabricated its complaints about Hopkins' interpersonal skills as a pretext for discrimination. Moreover, he concluded, the firm did not give decisive emphasis to such traits only because Hopkins was a woman; although there were male candidates who lacked these skills but who were admitted to partnership, the judge found that these candidates possessed other, positive traits that Hopkins lacked.

The judge went on to decide, however, that some of the partners' remarks about Hopkins stemmed from an impermissibly cabined view of the proper behavior of women, and that Price Waterhouse had done nothing to disavow reliance on such comments. He held that Price Waterhouse had unlawfully discriminated against Hopkins on the basis of sex by consciously giving credence and effect to the partners' comments that resulted from sex stereotyping. . . .

[*The Role of Stereotyping as Proof of Intentional Discrimination:*] . . . In saying that gender played a motivating part in an employment decision, we mean that, if we asked the employer at the moment of the decision what its reasons were and if we received a truthful response, one of those reasons would be that the applicant or employee was a woman.[13] In the specific context of sex stereotyping, an employer who acts on the basis of a belief that a woman cannot be aggressive, or that she must not be, has acted on the basis of gender.

Although the parties do not overtly dispute this last proposition, the placement by Price Waterhouse of "sex stereotyping" in quotation marks throughout its brief seems to us an insinuation either that such stereotyping was not present in this case or that it lacks legal relevance. We reject both possibilities. As to the existence of sex stereotyping in this case, we are not inclined to quarrel with the District Court's conclusion that a number of the partners' comments showed sex stereotyping at work. See *infra*, at 1793–1794. As for the legal relevance of sex stereotyping, we are beyond the day when an employer could evaluate employees by assuming or insisting that they matched the stereotype associated with their group, for "'[i]n forbidding employers to discriminate against individuals because of their sex, Congress intended to strike at the entire spectrum of disparate treatment of men and women resulting from sex stereotypes.'" *Los Angeles Dept. of Water and Power v. Manhart*, 435 U.S. 702, 707, n.13, (1978), quoting *Sprogis v. United Air Lines, Inc.*, 444 F.2d 1194, 1198 (CA7 1971). An employer who objects to aggressiveness in women but whose positions require this trait places women in an intolerable and impermissible catch 22: out of a job if they behave aggressively and out of a job if they do not. Title VII lifts women out of this bind.

Remarks at work that are based on sex stereotypes do not inevitably prove that gender played a part in a particular employment decision. The plaintiff must show that the employer actually relied on her gender in making its decision. In making this showing, stereotyped remarks can certainly be *evidence* that gender played a part. In any event, the stereotyping in this case did not simply consist of stray remarks. On the contrary, Hopkins proved that Price Waterhouse invited partners to submit comments; that some of the comments stemmed from sex stereotypes; that an important part of the Policy Board's decision on Hopkins was an assessment of the submitted comments; and that Price Waterhouse in no way disclaimed reliance on the sex-linked evaluations. This is not, as Price Waterhouse suggests, "discrimination in the air"; rather, it is, as Hopkins puts it, "discrimination brought to ground and visited upon" an employee. Brief for Respondent 30. By focusing on Hopkins' specific proof, however, we do not suggest a limitation on the possible ways of proving that stereotyping played a motivating role in an employment decision, and we refrain from deciding here which specific facts, "standing alone," would or would not establish a plaintiff's case, since such a decision is unnecessary in this case. But see *post*, at 1805 (O'CONNOR, J., concurring in judgment). . . .

The District Court found that sex stereotyping "was permitted to play a part" in the evaluation of Hopkins as a candidate for partnership. 618 F. Supp., at 1120. Price Waterhouse disputes both that stereotyping occurred and that it played any part in the decision to place Hopkins' candidacy on hold. In the firm's view, in other words, the District Court's factual conclusions are clearly erroneous. We do not agree.

In finding that some of the partners' comments reflected sex stereotyping, the District Court relied in part on Dr. Fiske's expert testimony. Without directly impugning Dr. Fiske's credentials or qualifications, Price Waterhouse insinuates that a social psychologist is unable to identify sex stereotyping in evaluations without investigating whether those evaluations have a basis in reality. This argument comes too late. At trial, counsel for Price Waterhouse twice assured the court that he did not question Dr. Fiske's expertise . . . and failed to challenge the legitimacy of her discipline. Without contradiction from Price Waterhouse, Fiske testified that she discerned sex stereotyping in the partners' evaluations of Hopkins and she further explained that it was part of her business to identify stereotyping in written documents. *Id.*, at 64. We are not inclined to accept petitioner's belated and unsubstantiated characterization of Dr. Fiske's testimony as "gossamer evidence" . . . based only on "intuitive hunches" (*id.*, at 44) and of her detection of

---

[13] After comparing this description of the plaintiff's proof to that offered by Justice O'Connor's opinion concurring in the judgment, we do not understand why the concurrence suggests that they are meaningfully different from each other. Nor do we see how the inquiry that we have described is "hypothetical." It seeks to determine the content of the entire set of reasons for a decision, rather than shaving off one reason in an attempt to determine what the decision would have been in the absence of that consideration. The inquiry that we describe thus strikes us as a distinctly nonhypothetical one.

sex stereotyping as "intuitively divined" (*id.*, at 43). Nor are we disposed to adopt the dissent's dismissive attitude toward Dr. Fiske's field of study and toward her own professional integrity, see *post*, at 1813, n.5.

Indeed, we are tempted to say that Dr. Fiske's expert testimony was merely icing on Hopkins' cake. It takes no special training to discern sex stereotyping in a description of an aggressive female employee as requiring "a course at charm school." Nor, turning to Thomas Beyer's memorable advice to Hopkins, does it require expertise in psychology to know that, if an employee's flawed "interpersonal skills" can be corrected by a soft-hued suit or a new shade of lipstick, perhaps it is the employee's sex and not her interpersonal skills that has drawn the criticism.[15]

Price Waterhouse also charges that Hopkins produced no evidence that sex stereotyping played a role in the decision to place her candidacy on hold. As we have stressed, however, Hopkins showed that the partnership solicited evaluations from all of the firm's partners; that it generally relied very heavily on such evaluations in making its decision; that some of the partners' comments were the product of stereotyping; and that the firm in no way disclaimed reliance on those particular comments, either in Hopkins' case or in the past. Certainly a plausible—and, one might say, inevitable—conclusion to draw from this set of circumstances is that the Policy Board in making its decision did in fact take into account all of the partners' comments, including the comments that were motivated by stereotypical notions about women's proper deportment.[16] . . .

Nor is the finding that sex stereotyping played a part in the Policy Board's decision undermined by the fact that many of the suspect comments were made by supporters rather than detractors of Hopkins. A negative comment, even when made in the context of a generally favorable review, nevertheless may influence the decisionmaker to think less highly of the candidate; the Policy Board, in fact, did not simply tally the "yeses" and "noes" regarding a candidate, but carefully reviewed the content of the submitted comments. The additional suggestion that the comments were made by "persons outside the decisionmaking chain" . . . and therefore could not have harmed Hopkins—simply ignores the critical role that partners' comments played in the Policy Board's partnership decisions.

Price Waterhouse appears to think that we cannot affirm the factual findings of the trial court without deciding that, instead of being overbearing and aggressive and curt, Hopkins is, in fact, kind and considerate and patient. If this is indeed its impression, petitioner misunderstands the theory on which Hopkins prevailed. The District Judge acknowledged that Hopkins' conduct justified complaints about her behavior as a senior manager. But he also concluded that the reactions of at least some of the partners were reactions to her as a *woman* manager. Where an evaluation is based on a subjective assessment of a person's strengths and weaknesses, it is simply not true that each evaluator will focus on, or even mention, the same weaknesses. Thus, even if we knew that Hopkins had "personality problems," this would not tell us that the partners who cast their evaluations of Hopkins in sex-based terms would have criticized her as sharply (or criticized her at all) if she had been a man. It is not our job to review the evidence and decide that the negative reactions to Hopkins were based on reality; our perception of Hopkins' character is irrelevant. We sit not to determine whether Ms. Hopkins is nice, but to decide whether the partners reacted negatively to her personality because she is a woman. . . .

[*The Legitimate Reason*:] . . . On too many occasions, however, Hopkins' aggressiveness apparently spilled over into abrasiveness. Staff members seem to have borne the brunt of Hopkins' brusqueness. Long before her bid for partnership, partners evaluating her work had counseled her to improve her relations with staff members. Although later evaluations indicate an improvement, Hopkins' perceived shortcomings in this important area eventually doomed her bid for partnership. Virtually all of the partners' negative remarks about Hopkins—even those of partners supporting her—had to do with her "interpersonal skills." Both "supporters and opponents of her candidacy," stressed Judge Gesell, "indicated that she was sometimes overly aggressive, unduly harsh, difficult to work with and impatient with staff." *Id.*, at 1113. . . .

---

[15] We reject the claim, advanced by Price Waterhouse here and by the dissenting judge below, that the District Court clearly erred in finding that Beyer was "responsible for telling [Hopkins] what problems the Policy Board had identified with her candidacy." 618 F. Supp., at 1117. This conclusion was reasonable in light of the testimony at trial of a member of both the Policy Board and the Admissions Committee, who stated that he had "no doubt" that Beyer would discuss with Hopkins the reasons for placing her candidacy on hold and that Beyer "knew exactly where the problems were" regarding Hopkins. Tr. 316.

[16] We do not understand the dissenters' dissatisfaction with the District Judge's statements regarding the failure of Price Waterhouse to "sensitize" partners to the dangers of sexism. *Post*, at 1813–1814. Made in the context of determining that Price Waterhouse had not disclaimed reliance on sex-based evaluations, and following the judge's description of the firm's history of condoning such evaluations, the judge's remarks seem to us justified.

[*The Standard to Apply When Both Legitimate and Illegitimate Reasons Exist*: The Supreme Court considered the problem of the appropriate burden to be placed on the parties in "mixed motives" cases. The Court explained why it disagreed with the rationale of the courts below.]

To say that an employer may not take gender into account is not, however, the end of the matter, for that describes only one aspect of Title VII. The other important aspect of the statute is its preservation of an employer's remaining freedom of choice. We conclude that the preservation of this freedom means that an employer shall not be liable if it can prove that, even if it had not taken gender into account, it would have come to the same decision regarding a particular person. The statute's maintenance of employer prerogatives is evident from the statute itself and from its history, both in Congress and in this Court. . . .

Price Waterhouse's claim that the employer does not bear any burden of proof (if it bears one at all) until the plaintiff has shown "substantial evidence that Price Waterhouse's explanation for failing to promote Hopkins was not the 'true reason' for its action" . . . merely restates its argument that the plaintiff in a mixed-motives case must squeeze her proof into *Burdine*'s framework. Where a decision was the product of a mixture of legitimate and illegitimate motives, however, it simply makes no sense to ask whether the legitimate reason was "the 'true reason'" . . . for the decision—which is the question asked by *Burdine*. . . .[12] Oblivious to this last point, the dissent would insist that *Burdine*'s

framework perform work that it was never intended to perform. It would require a plaintiff who challenges an adverse employment decision in which both legitimate and illegitimate considerations played a part to pretend that the decision, in fact, stemmed from a single source—for the premise of *Burdine* is that *either* a legitimate *or* an illegitimate set of considerations led to the challenged decision. To say that *Burdine*'s evidentiary scheme will not help us decide a case admittedly involving *both* kinds of considerations is not to cast aspersions on the utility of that scheme in the circumstances for which it was designed. . . .

As to the employer's proof, in most cases, the employer should be able to present some objective evidence as to its probable decision in the absence of an impermissible motive.[14] Moreover, proving "'that the same decision would have been justified . . . is not the same as proving that the same decision would have been made.'" Givhan, 439 U.S., at 416, quoting *Ayers v. Western Line Consolidated School District*, 555 F.2d 1309, 1315 (CA5 1977). An employer may not, in other words, prevail in a mixed-motives case by offering a legitimate and sufficient reason for its decision if that reason did not motivate it at the time of the decision. Finally, an employer may not meet its burden in such a case by merely showing that at the time of the decision it was motivated only in part by a legitimate reason. The very premise of a mixed-motives case is that a legitimate reason was present, and indeed, in this case, Price Waterhouse already has made this showing by convincing Judge Gesell that Hopkins' interpersonal problems were a legitimate concern. The employer instead must show that its legitimate reason, standing alone, would have induced it to make the same decision.

The courts below held that an employer who has allowed a discriminatory impulse to play a motivating part in an employment decision must prove by clear and convincing evidence that it would have made the same decision in the absence of discrimination. We are persuaded that the better rule is that the employer must make this showing by a preponderance of the evidence. . . .

Although Price Waterhouse does not concretely tell us how its proof was preponderant even if it was

[12] Nothing in this opinion should be taken to suggest that a case must be correctly labeled as either a "pretext" case or a "mixed-motives" case from the beginning in the District Court; indeed, we expect that plaintiffs often will allege, in the alternative, that their cases are both. Discovery often will be necessary before the plaintiff can know whether both legitimate and illegitimate considerations played a part in the decision against her. At some point in the proceedings, of course, the District Court must decide whether a particular case involves mixed motives. If the plaintiff fails to satisfy the factfinder that it is more likely than not that a forbidden characteristic played a part in the employment decision, then she may prevail only if she proves, following *Burdine*, that the employer's stated reason for its decision is pretextual. The dissent need not worry that this evidentiary scheme, if used during a jury trial, will be so impossibly confused and complex as it imagines Juries long have decided cases in which defendants raised affirmative defenses. The dissent fails, moreover, to explain why the evidentiary scheme that we endorsed over ten years ago in *Mt. Healthy City Bd. of Ed. v. Doyle*, 429 U.S. 274 (1977), has not proved unworkable in that context but would be hopelessly complicated in a case brought under federal antidiscrimination statutes.

[14] Justice WHITE's suggestion, post, at 1796, that the employer's own testimony as to the probable decision in the absence of discrimination is due special credence where the court has, contrary to the employer's testimony, found that an illegitimate factor played a part in the decision, is baffling.

not clear and convincing, this general claim is implicit in its request for the less stringent standard. Since the lower courts required Price Waterhouse to make its proof by clear and convincing evidence, they did not determine whether Price Waterhouse had proved by a *preponderance of the evidence* that it would have placed Hopkins' candidacy on hold even if it had not permitted sex-linked evaluations to play a part in the decision-making process. Thus, we shall remand this case so that that determination can be made. . . .

We hold that when a plaintiff in a Title VII case proves that her gender played a motivating part in an employment decision, the defendant may avoid a finding of liability only by proving by a preponderance of the evidence that it would have made the same decision even if it had not taken the plaintiff's gender into account. Because the courts below erred by deciding that the defendant must make this proof by clear and convincing evidence, we reverse the Court of Appeals' judgment against Price Waterhouse on liability and remand the case to that court for further proceedings.

It is so ordered.

Justice O'CONNOR, concurring in the judgment.

I agree with the plurality that, on the facts presented in this case, the burden of persuasion should shift to the employer to demonstrate by a preponderance of the evidence that it would have reached the same decision concerning Ann Hopkins' candidacy absent consideration of her gender. I further agree that this burden shift is properly part of the liability phase of the litigation. I thus concur in the judgment of the Court. My disagreement stems from the plurality's conclusions concerning the substantive requirement of causation under the statute and its broad statements regarding the applicability of the allocation of the burden of proof applied in this case. The evidentiary rule the Court adopts today should be viewed as a supplement to the careful framework established by our unanimous decisions in *McDonnell Douglas Corp. v. Green*, 411 U.S. 792 (1973) and *Texas Dept. of Community Affairs v. Burdine*, 450 U.S. 248 (1981), for use in cases such as this one where the employer has created uncertainty as to causation by knowingly giving substantial weight to an impermissible criterion. I write separately to explain why I believe such a departure from the *McDonnell Douglas* standard is justified in the circumstances presented by this and like cases, and to

express my views as to when and how the strong medicine of requiring the employer to bear the burden of persuasion on the issue of causation should be administered. . . .

Like the common law of torts, the statutory employment "tort" created by Title VII has two basic purposes. The first is to deter conduct which has been identified as contrary to public policy and harmful to society as a whole. As we have noted in the past, the award of backpay to a Title VII plaintiff provides "the spur or catalyst which causes employers and unions to self-examine and to self-evaluate their employment practices and to endeavor to eliminate, so far as possible, the last vestiges" of discrimination in employment. *Albermarle Paper Co. v. Moody*, 422 U.S. 405, 417–418 (1975) (citation omitted). The second goal of Title VII is "to make persons whole for injuries suffered on account of unlawful employment discrimination." *Id.* at 418.

Both these goals are reflected in the elements of a disparate treatment action. There is no doubt that Congress considered reliance on gender or race in making employment decisions an evil in itself. As Senator Clark puts it, "[t]he bill simply eliminates consideration of color [or other forbidden criteria] from the decision to hire or promote." 110 Cong. Rec. 7218 (1964). . . . Reliance on such factors is exactly what the threat of Title VII liability was meant to deter. While the main concern of the statute was with employment opportunity, Congress was certainly not blind to the stigmatic harm which comes from being evaluated by a process which treats one as an inferior by reason of one's race or sex. This Court's decisions under the Equal Protection Clause have long recognized that whatever the final outcome of a decisional process, the inclusion of race or sex as a consideration within it harms both society and the individual. . . . At the same time, Congress clearly conditioned legal liability on a determination that the consideration of an illegitimate factor caused a tangible employment injury of some kind.

Where an individual disparate treatment plaintiff has shown by a preponderance of the evidence that an illegitimate criterion was a *substantial* factor in an adverse employment decision, the deterrent purpose of the statute has clearly been triggered. More importantly, as an evidentiary matter, a reasonable factfinder could conclude that absent further explanation, the employer's discriminatory motivation "caused" the employment decision. The employer has not yet been shown to be a violator, but neither is it entitled to the same presumption of good faith concerning its employment decisions which is accorded employers facing only circumstantial evidence of discrimination. Both the policies behind the statute, and the evidentiary principles developed in the analogous area of causation in the law of torts, suggest that at this point the employer may be required to convince the factfinder that, despite the smoke, there is no fire. . . .

The facts of this case, and a growing number like it decided by the Courts of Appeals, convince me that the evidentiary standard I propose is necessary to make real the promise of *McDonnell Douglas* that "[I]n the implementation of [employment] decisions, it is abundantly clear that Title VII tolerates no . . . discrimination, subtle or otherwise." 411 U.S., at 801. In this case, the District Court found that a number of evaluations of Ann Hopkins submitted by partners in the firm overtly referred to her failure to conform to certain gender stereotypes as a factor militating against her election to the partnership. 618 F. Supp. 1109, 1116–1117 (DC 1985). The District Court further found that these evaluations were given "great weight" by the decisonmakers at Price Waterhouse. *Id*, at 1118. In addition, the District Court found that the partner responsible for informing Hopkins of the factors which caused her candidacy to be placed on hold, indicated that her "professional" problems would be solved if she would "walk more femininely, talk more femininely, wear make-up, have her hair styled, and wear jewelry." *Id.* at 1117 (footnote omitted). As the Court of Appeals characterized it, Ann Hopkins proved that Price Waterhouse "permitt[ed] stereotypical attitudes towards women to play a significant, though unquantifiable, role in its decision not to invite her to become a partner." 263 U.S. App. D.C., at 324, 825 F. 2d, at 461.

At this point Ann Hopkins had taken her proof as far as it could go. She had proved discriminatory input into the decisional process, and had proved that participants in the process considered her failure to conform to the stereotypes credited by a number of the decisionmakers had been a substantial factor in the decision. It is as if Ann Hopkins were sitting in the hall outside the room where the partnership decisions were being made. As the partners filed in to consider her candidacy, she heard several of them make sexist remarks in discussing her suitability for partnership. As the decisionmakers exited the room, she was *told* by one of those privy to the decisionmaking process that her gender was a major reason for the rejection of her partnership bid. If, as we noted in *Teamsters*, "[p]resumptions shifting the burden of proof are often created to reflect judicial evaluations of the prob-

abilities and to conform with a party's superior access to the proof," 431 U.S., at 359, n.45, one would be hard pressed to think of a situation where it would be more appropriate to require the defendant to show that its decision would have been justified by wholly legitimate concerns.

Moreover, there is mounting evidence in the decisions of the lower courts that the respondent here is not alone in her inability to pinpoint discrimination as the precise cause of her injury, despite having shown that it played a significant role in the decisional process. Many of these courts, which deal with evidentiary issues in Title VII cases on a regular basis, have concluded that placing the risk of nonpersuasion on the defendant in a situation where uncertainty as to causation has been created by its consideration of an illegitimate criterion makes sense as a rule of evidence and furthers the substantive command of Title VII. . . . Particularly in the context of the professional world, where decisions are often made by collegial bodies on the basis of largely subjective criteria, requiring the plaintiff to prove that *any* one factor was the definitive cause of the decisionmaker's action may be tantamount to declaring Title VII inapplicable to such decisions. . . .

Finally, I am convinced that a rule shifting the burden to the defendant where the plaintiff has shown that an illegitimate criterion was a "substantial factor" in the employment decision will not conflict with other congressional policies embodied in Title VII. Title VII expressly provides that an employer need not give preferential treatment to employees or applicants of any race, color, religion, sex, or national origin in order to maintain a work force in balance with the general population. . . . The interpretive memorandum, whose authoritative force is noted by the plurality . . . , specifically provides: "There is no requirement in Title VII that an employer maintain a racial balance in his work force. On the contrary, any deliberate attempt to maintain a racial balance, whatever such a balance may be, would involve a violation of Title VII because maintaining such a balance would require an employer to hire or refuse to hire on the basis of race." . . .

In my view, in order to justify shifting the burden on the issue of causation to the defendant, a disparate treatment plaintiff must show by direct evidence that an illegitimate criterion was a substantial factor in the decision. As the Court of Appeals noted below: "While most circuits have not confronted the question squarely, the consensus among those that have is that once a Title VII plaintiff has demonstrated by direct evidence that discriminatory animus played a significant or substantial role in the employment decision, the burden shifts to the employer to show that the decision would have been the same absent discrimination. . . . " Requiring that the plaintiff demonstrate that an illegitimate factor played a substantial role in the employment decision identifies those employment situations where the deterrent purpose of Title VII is most clearly implicated. . . .

Thus, stray remarks in the workplace, while perhaps probative of sexual harassment, see *Meritor Savings Bank v. Vinson*, 477 U.S. 57, 63–69 (1986), cannot justify requiring the employer to prove that its hiring or promotion decisions were based on legitimate criteria. Nor can statements by nondecisionmakers, or statements by decisionmakers unrelated to the decisional process itself, suffice to satisfy the plaintiff's burden in this regard. In addition, in my view testimony such as Dr. Fiske's in this case, standing alone, would not justify shifting the burden of persuasion to the employer. Race and gender always "play a role" in an employment decision in the benign sense that these are human characteristics of which decisionmakers are aware and about which they may comment in a perfectly neutral and nondiscriminatory fashion. For example, in the context of this case, a mere reference to "a lady candidate" might show that gender "played a role" in the decision, but by no means could support a rational factfinder's inference that the decision was made "because of" sex. What is required is what Ann Hopkins showed here: direct evidence that decisionmakers placed substantial negative reliance on an illegitimate criterion in reaching their decision.

It should be obvious that the threshold standard I would adopt for shifting the burden of persuasion to the defendant differs substantially from that proposed by the plurality, the plurality's suggestion to the contrary notwithstanding .. . . The plurality proceeds from the premise that the words "because of" in the statute do not embody any causal requirement at all. Under my approach, the plaintiff must produce evidence sufficient to show that an illegitimate criterion was a substantial factor in the particular employment decision such that a reasonable factfinder could draw an inference that the decision was made "because of" the plaintiff's protected status. Only then would the burden of proof shift to the defendant to prove that the decision would have been justified by other, wholly legitimate considerations. . . .

In sum, because of the concerns outlined above, and because I believe that the deterrent purposes of Title VII is disserved by a rule which places the burden of proof on plaintiffs on the issue of causation in all circumstances, I would retain but supplement the framework we established in *McDonnell Douglas'* subsequent cases. The structure of the presentation of evidence in an individual disparate treatment case should conform to the general outlines we established in *McDonnell Douglas* and *Burdine*. First, the plaintiff must establish the *McDonnell Douglas* prima facie case by showing membership in a protected group, qualification for the job, rejection for the position, and that after rejection the employer continued to seek applicants of complainant's general qualifications. . . . The plaintiff should also present any direct evidence of discriminatory animus in the decisional process. The defendant should then present its case, including its evidence as to legitimate, nondiscriminatory reasons for the employment decision. As the dissent notes, under this framework, the employer "has every incentive to convince the trier of fact that the decision was lawful." *Post*, at 1813, citing *Burdine*. . . . Once all the evidence has been received, the court should determine whether the *McDonnell Douglas* or *Price Waterhouse* framework properly applies to the evidence before it. If the plaintiff has failed to satisfy the *Price Waterhouse* threshold, the case should be decided under the principles enunciated in *McDonnell Douglas* and *Burdine*, with the plaintiff bearing the burden of persuasion on the ultimate issue whether the employment action was taken because of discrimination. In my view, such a system is both fair and workable, and it calibrates the evidentiary requirements demanded of the parties to the goals behind the statute itself. . . .

Questions

1. Should Problem 7 be evaluated as a *McDonnell Douglas* case, which must show that the employer's reasons for terminating Alicia were not true and that the real reason for the termination was discrimination based on her race and sex? Is this a *Price Waterhouse* mixed motives case, and if so, how should that be analyzed?

2. What should the employer do here? Should it focus on trying to show that discrimination did not exist as a factor in her treatment, or should it try to show that it would have fired her anyway? What difference does it make? How do 42 U.S.C. § 2000e(m) and § 2000e(5)(2)(B) affect the *Price Waterhouse* directions for proving a mixed motive case? 42 U.S.C. § 2000e(m) states: "Except as otherwise provided in this title, an unlawful employment practice is established when the complaining party demonstrates that

race, color, religion, sex, or national origin was a motivating factor for any employment practice, even though other factors also motivated the practice." 42 U.S.C. § 2000e(5)(2)(B) states:

> On a claim in which an individual proves a violation under section 703(m) and a respondent demonstrates that the respondent would have taken the same action in the absence of the impermissible motivating factor, the court —
>
> i. may grant declaratory relief, injunctive relief except as provided in clause (ii), and attorney's fees and costs demonstrated to be directly attributable only to the pursuit of a claim under section 703(m); and
> ii. shall not award damages or issue an order requiring any admission, reinstatement, hiring, promotion, or payment, described in subparagraph (A).

Discussion Notes

1. The relationship between *Price Waterhouse* mixed motives cases and *McDonnell Douglas* pretext cases has caused massive confusion in the litigation of disparate treatment claims since *Price Waterhouse* was decided in 1989 and after the Civil Rights Act of 1991 directly addressed mixed motives cases. Litigants have been unsure how to proceed. Proof of whether the claim is based on mixed motives or a single illegitimate motive may not be apparent at the onset of the case. Courts have allowed plaintiffs to proceed on the *McDonnell Douglas* model but have had to come to terms with the problem of mixed motives as they are developed in the course of litigation. Some courts have relied on the language of Justice O'Connor's concurring opinion in *Price Waterhouse* as if it reflects the plurality opinion of the Court, providing a requirement that the plaintiff show "direct evidence" of discrimination before the employer assumes the burden of showing that it is more likely than not that it would have fired the employee even without the discriminatory reason. Much discussion has occurred about the meaning of "direct evidence," and thus some courts have made

an important distinction between *McDonnell Douglas* ways of proving discrimination through inferences and this idea of "direct evidence" sufficient to impose a burden on the employer.

2. In the case on which Problem 7 is based, the U.S. Court of Appeals for the Ninth Circuit, sitting en banc, described the confusion as follows: "Within circuits, and often within opinions, different approaches are conflated, mixing burden of persuasion with the burden to establish an affirmative defense, and declining to acknowledge the role of circumstantial evidence." *Costa v. Desert Palace, Inc.*, 299 F.3d 838 (9th Cir. 2002), *cert. granted*, 537 U.S. 1099 (January 10, 2003). The court decided it did not need to decide whether Justice O'Connor's concurring opinion in *Price Waterhouse* was controlling on the need to show direct evidence of mixed motives because her references to direct evidence were "wholly abrogated" by the 1991 Act. It said that the statute "imposes no special [evidentiary] requirement and does not reference 'direct evidence'" The court of appeals concluded that the "plaintiff . . . may establish a violation through a preponderance of the evidence (whether direct or circumstantial) that a protected characteristic played 'a motivating factor.' *Costa v. Desert Palace, Inc.*, 299 F.3d 838 (9th Cir. 2002), *cert. granted*, 537 U.S. 1099 (January 10, 2003)." The U.S. Supreme Court viewed this case as its first opportunity "to consider the effects of the 1991 Act on jury instructions in mixed motive cases." The Supreme Court recognized that both the statute and the general rules in civil litigation require a plaintiff to prove the case by a preponderance of the evidence using direct or circumstantial evidence. Referring to their decision in 2002 in *Reeves*, the member of the Court reaffirmed the utility of circumstantial evidence. "In order to obtain an instruction under § 2000e-2(m), a plaintiff need only present sufficient evidence for a reasonable jury to conclude, by a preponderance of the evidence, that "race, color, religion, sex, or national origin was a motivating factor for any employment practice." *Desert Palace, Inc. v. Costa*, 539 U.S. 90 (2003).

chapter
3
Proving the Substance of a Disparate Treatment Claim of Discrimination

---

Problem 8

Alia Fezri works as an accountant in the firm of Peabody and Rusk in the big city. She was hired five years ago and has received two major promotions to the position of senior accountant. Last year she received several negative criticisms on her performance evaluation from her immediate supervisor. One involved a minor math error that she had not caught before a document was printed and sent to her supervisor. Another was a complaint that she had received two personal telephone calls at work. The two negative criticisms were used to explain why she was not given a promotion to "senior executive accountant" and the merit increase attached to that promotion. Later Alia discovered that Anthony Backstrom had received a promotion to senior executive accountant. Anthony had similar job experience and qualifications, and he, too, had received two negative criticisms on his most recent evaluations. Despite these negative criticisms, he was offered the promotion.

A. Introduction

Whether the employee is opposing a motion for summary judgment or proving the case at the trial stage, there must be some evidence that gives rise to inferences that intentional discrimination (disparate treatment) occurred. In order to show that a prima facie case of intentional discrimination has been established, a plaintiff may have direct proof by way of the "smoking gun" evidence or must follow the *McDonnell Douglas* model of proving a case by inferences. Proof of discrimination will occur in multiple ways, which we consider here. Section B of this chapter focuses on proof of discrimination by demonstrating that there has been different treatment of "similarly situated employees" where the only difference seems to be the status of membership in a protected Title VII class. As presented in material in Chapter 2 similar treatment is an essential component of one version of equality. Section C briefly presents the use of statistics as a way of supporting an inference of intentional discrimination. Section D examines the problem that occurs when the employer discovers legitimate reasons for the action after the employee has already been terminated; this is called "after-acquired evidence." Section E focuses on proof of intentional discrimination by use of inferences based on stereotypes. This section is divided into three parts: (1) stereotypes based on race, color, sex, religion, or national origin; (2) a new analysis that focuses on the way employees are expected to perform; and (3) gender stereotyping and sexual orientation discrimination. The chapter concludes with materials in Section F that address other ways that sexual orientation discrimination may be prohibited. The courts have, for the most part, ruled that discrimination on the basis of sexual orientation is not covered by Title VII, but local city ordinances, state laws, or state constitutions have expanded the scope of protection to include prohibitions against discrimination on the basis of sexual orientation. In Chapter 4, the issue of same-sex harrassment will be considered in conjunction with the development of the interpretation of Title VII to include charges of harassment on the basis of race, color, sex, religion, or national origin.

B. Proving an Inference of Discrimination by Comparing "Similarly Situated" Employees

Alia and Anthony may be employees who are "similarly situated" for purposes of comparison of their job responsibilities and the treatment that they should receive on the job. Inferences of intentional discrimination may be supported by proof that similarly situated employees were treated more favorably than an employee who is complaining of discrimination. This becomes an important basis for an inference of discrimination when the employees who received favorable treatment did not share the same race or color or sex or religion or national origin as the plaintiff, and no one who did belong to plaintiff's protected class received similar favorable treatment. It is possible for a trier of fact to infer intentional discrimination from that comparison.

The analysis of whether other employees are "similarly situated" to the plaintiff has become very complicated. Courts have differed on what facts are essential to the comparison. Plaintiffs have won or lost disparate treatment claims based on decisions about the comparisons of their duties and those of other employees. Although most courts recognized that the duties and situations did not have to be "identical," they differed on the degree to which the situations could vary. In the following case, the U.S. Court of Appeals for the Second Circuit provided a good example of the kind of inquiry that shapes a circumstantial evidence case of disparate treatment when there is a comparison of so-called similarly situated employees.

MCGUINNESS
v.
LINCOLN HALL
263 F.3d 49 (2d Cir. 2001)

LEVAL, Circuit Judge

[The Employment Problem]

[Sheila McGuinness, a white woman, was hired as the Director of Human Resources for Lincoln Hall, a residential program for troubled youth in Lincolndale, New York. Several others were hired, including Carlton Mitchell, an African-American male, as Deputy Director of Programs and Anthony J. Mohammed Dobbins, an African-American male, as Campus Ministry Coordinator. Both McGuinness and Mitchell served on the Executive Cabinet of top administrators of Lincoln Hall. In 1998, McGuinness, Mitchell, and Paul Turnley, a Caucasian-American male, who was Deputy Director of Development, were all terminated. McGuinness was given a two-week severance allowance. Mitchell was given 12 weeks of pay in return for a waiver of any claims arising from his employment. Turnley was not given a severance package. Neither Turnley nor McGuinness was asked to sign a release or waiver. A month and a half later, Dobbins, who had only worked for four months at Lincoln Hall, was terminated and given an amount slightly in excess of the amount provided to McGuinness, who had worked there for two years, in exchange for a release or waiver. McGuinness filed a lawsuit claiming that she had been discriminated against on the basis of both her sex and her race.]

[The Legal Issue]

[McGuinness had two separate claims to prove: (1) that she was discriminated against based on her gender and (2) that she was discriminated against based on her race. For each of these claims, the court had to decide whether she could establish a prima facie case. She attempted to demonstrate that she met this requirement in both situations because of the comparison between her and similarly situated employees.]

[The Decision and Rationale of the U.S. Court of Appeals for the Second Circuit]

[The Court of Appeals for the Second Circuit decided that McGuinness had properly met the requirements

for a prima facie case of discrimination on the basis of race.] A showing that the employer treated a similarly situated employee differently is "a common and especially effective method" of establishing a prima facie case of discrimination, but it "is only one way to discharge that burden." Where a plaintiff in a severance pay case seeks to establish her prima facie case in this manner, she may make out a prima facie case of employment discrimination by showing that she is within the protected group; that she is qualified for the position; that she was subject to an adverse employment action involving severance pay; and that a similarly situated employee not in the relevant protected group received better treatment. See *McDonnell Douglas Corp. v. Green,* 411 U.S. 792 (1973). As we have often emphasized, the burden of establishing this prima facie case in employment discrimination cases is "minimal". E.g., *St. Mary's Honor Center v. Hicks,* 509 U.S. 502, 506 (1993) See also, *Texas Dept. of Cmty. Affairs v. Burdine,* 450 U.S. 248, 253 (1981) ("not onerous"). Moreover, because the facts inevitably vary in different employment discrimination cases, both the Supreme Court and this Court have explained that the "prima facie proof required" in a given case will depend on the specific facts in question. *McDonnell Douglas,* 411 U.S. at 802 n.13.

It is not contested that plaintiff is a white woman and that she was qualified for the position. Furthermore, plaintiff has proffered evidence sufficient to allow a trier of fact to find that defendant offered her a different and less desirable severance package (one which involved less money) than it offered to plaintiff's colleague Carlton Mitchell, a black man who like plaintiff was an executive-level employee, and who was discharged two days after plaintiff. Under the circumstances of this case, this evidence alone satisfied plaintiff's "minimal" burden to establish a prima facie case that she was treated differently on the basis of her race and gender.

In *Shumway* we ruled where a plaintiff seeks to make out her prima facie case by pointing to the disparate treatment of a purportedly similarly situated employee, the plaintiff must show that she shared sufficient employment characteristics with that comparator so that they could be considered similarly situated. 118 F.3d at 64. The magistrate judge interpreted *Shumway* to mean that another employee cannot be similarly situated to a plaintiff unless the other employee had the same supervisor, worked under the same standards, and engaged in the same conduct. This was a misreading of *Shumway*. In *Shumway*, we explained that such an employee "must be similarly situated in all material respects"—not in all respects.[1] 118 F.3d at 64. . . . A plaintiff is not obligated to show disparate treatment of an identically situated employee. To the contrary, *Shumway* holds that in those cases in which a plaintiff seeks to establish her minimal prima facie case by pointing to disparate treatment of a similarly situated employee, it is sufficient that the employee to whom plaintiff points be similarly situated in all material respects. In other words, where a plaintiff seeks to establish the minimal prima facie case by making reference to the disparate treatment of other employees, those employees must have a situation sufficiently similar to plaintiff's to support at least a minimal inference that the difference of treatment may be attributable to discrimination.

In *Shumway*, plaintiff was forced to resign because of her violation of a rule against intracompany dating. Plaintiff proffered evidence that other male employees had not been forced to resign even though they also violated the rule against intracompany dating. We held that the employees to whom the plaintiff pointed were not similarly situated in material respect because there were so many distinctions between the plaintiff's situation and theirs that the defendant's treatment of those employees had no logical relevance to the plaintiff's claims. . . .

Here, by contrast, plaintiff has established that Mitchell was far more similarly situated to plaintiff McGuinness, so as to give at least minimal support to her claims that the severance differentials may have been based on race or gender discrimination. In the broadest outlines, plaintiff has established that she and Mitchell held positions of roughly equivalent rank (both in the Executive Cabinet), that she and Mitchell were fired at roughly the same time, that the decisions with respect to the severance were both made at the highest levels of the company, and that Mitchell received considerably more money in sever-

ance. The differences between plaintiff and Mitchell are not nearly as significant as those separating the plaintiff in *Shumway* from her comparators, and are not so significant as a matter of logic as to render defendant's disparate treatment of Mitchell irrelevant to plaintiff's claims of discrimination. We conclude that plaintiff's proffer of evidence that defendant treated Mitchell differently satisfies the minimal requirements to state a prima facie case of disparate treatment under the *McDonnell Douglas* framework.

Discrimination on the Basis of Gender

Plaintiff's Evidence of Disparate Treatment . . .

On the record in this case, no reasonable trier of fact could determine that defendant treated plaintiff differently on the basis of her gender. Plaintiff has proffered absolutely no evidence of statements or conduct by defendant or its agents evincing hostile animus toward women. Nor does plaintiff point to any history or past practice of providing female employees with smaller severance packages than male employees. Indeed, it is undisputed that at least one additional male executive-level employee was discharged at the same time as plaintiff, and under proximately the same terms. Finally, in the months prior to defendant's discharge of plaintiff, defendant discharged its Executive Director, who was also a woman, and offered her a generous severance package. Though plaintiff contends that this severance package resulted from the fact that the Executive Director had an unexpired employment contract for a term, unlike defendant's other employees who were employees at-will, defendant's offer of a high severance payment in this instance nonetheless cuts against plaintiff's claims of gender discrimination in the provision of severance packages.

Discrimination on the Basis of Race

Plaintiff has presented considerably more evidence, however, on her claim that she was treated differently on the basis of her race. To be sure, plaintiff has proffered no evidence of statements by defendant's animus against white employees. Nor has plaintiff presented any evidence of a history or past practice of discrimination against white employees by defendant. Nonetheless, the record is susceptible to a reasonable determination that the defendant offered employees different severance packages on the basis of their race. Turnley, who like plaintiff is white, was also offered a smaller severance package. And, in addition to plaintiff's evidence relating to Mitchell,

---

[1] We have already noted that because a Title VII plaintiff may establish a prima facie case of discrimination in a number of different ways depending on the specific facts of a given case, *Shumway* does not require that a plaintiff always be able to show disparate treatment of an otherwise similarly situated employee as a necessary prerequisite to a prima facie case under Title VII.

plaintiff also proffered similar evidence of a severance package involving more cash offered to Dobbins, a high-level black employee discharged a month and a half after plaintiff.

A trier of fact could reasonably determine on the basis of these facts that defendant decided on the basis of race to offer black employees more significant severance payments. Accordingly, the district court erred in ruling that plaintiff had proffered insufficient evidence to establish that she was treated differently on the basis of her race. We therefore remand for further proceedings on plaintiff's race discrimination claim.

Questions

1. How would you use the information about Anthony to argue that Alia could demonstrate a prima facie case of sex discrimination under Title VII? Would it make a difference if you had to argue that Alia could meet her ultimate burden of persuasion that sex discrimination occurred based on this evidence alone? Is the evidence that demonstrates the two employees were similarly situated utilized in different ways depending on the stage of litigation? How?

2. What if the two negative comments received by Anthony were different from the negative comments she received? For example, what if Anthony's criticisms focused on his arrival at work five minutes late on two occasions? Would that make a difference? Should it?

3. What if the two positions were not identical but similar? For example, what if Anthony was not a senior accountant at the time but a junior accountant and the promotion he received was to senior accountant rank? What if everything else was identical but the supervisors were different?

C. Statistics as Proof of Intentional Discrimination

Early cases of intentional discrimination were often termed "pattern and practice" cases—that is, the employee could show that there was a pattern and practice of discrimination in the employer's workplace by taking a look at what happened to other employees. Sometimes that evidence depended almost entirely on a statistical analysis of the workplace. Other times the case was supplemented with the testimony of witnesses, other employees who had been treated in the same discriminatory manner.

Statistics by themselves do not prove a case of intentional discrimination. In *Hazelwood School District v. United States*, 433 U.S. 299 (1977), the Supreme Court recognized that it was possible to meet the prima facie requirement of a disparate treatment case by introducing evidence of "gross statistical disparities" between the hiring numbers of the class of employees claiming that they had been discriminated against and those hired. In that case, statistics were used to show that there was a pattern and practice of discrimination in the hiring of teachers for the suburban schools in St. Louis County, Missouri. In order to demonstrate the discrimination, the plaintiffs tried to introduce evidence that the number of black teachers hired was significantly lower than the number of black teachers available in the labor pool of qualified teachers in the City of St. Louis as well as in the county. The decision required selecting the labor pool that accurately reflected the qualified public school teacher population of the relevant labor market. The Court had to decide whether it was fair to exclude or include the city statistics. The county argued that because the city had made a vigorous effort to maintain a 50 percent black teacher staff, the inclusion of those figures distorted the comparison.

The Supreme Court reversed the lower court's ruling and sent the case back for further fact finding as to the relevant labor pool for the comparison. The

Court cited its earlier decision in *Teamsters v. United States*, 431 U.S. 324 (1977), which described the role of statistics in proving intentional discrimination: "[A]bsent explanation, it is ordinarily to be expected that nondiscriminatory hiring practices will in time result in a work force more or less representative of the racial and ethnic composition of the population in the community from which employees are hired. Evidence of longlasting and gross disparity between the composition of a work force and that of the general population thus may be significant even though section 703(j) makes clear that Title VII imposes no requirement that a work force mirror the general population." *Id*. at 340 n.20.

In the *Teamsters* case, the Court noted, "the comparison between the percentage of Negroes on the employer's work force and the percentage in the general areawide population was highly probative, because the job skill there involved—the ability to drive a truck—is one that many persons possess or can fairly readily acquire. When special qualifications are required to fill particular jobs, comparisons to the general population (rather than to the smaller group of individuals who possess the necessary qualifications) may have little probative value. . . . " *Id*.

Questions

1. Consider the difficulties for both the employee and the employer in dealing with statistics and the choice of the relevant labor pool to compare. As you can see from the cases discussed above, the Court gets involved in a decision as to which statistical comparison is the right one. What are the costs involved in relying on statistical proof? Who is better able to bear this cost? What if there are no published statistics in the relevant labor market?
2. Why do statistics tend to prove that the employer acted intentionally? Is this fair to the employer? Refer to Chapter Nine for the *Sears* case. It is a good example of a failed use of statistics.

D. Use of Evidence Acquired After the Employer's Adverse Employment Action: Mixed Motives

MCKENNON
v.
NASHVILLE BANNER PUBLISHING CO.
513 U.S. 352 (1995)

Justice KENNEDY delivered the opinion of the Court.

[The Employment Problem]

[Christine McKennon worked for the Nashville Banner Publishing Company for 30 years. The employer claimed she was discharged during a cost-cutting reduction in force. McKennon, who was 62 years old at the time of her discharge, claimed that she was discharged based on age discrimination in violation of the Age Discrimination in Employment Act of 1967. During her deposition in the discovery part of the case, the employer learned that during her final year of employment, she had copied several confidential documents bearing on the company's financial condition. She had access to these records as secretary to the Banner's comptroller. McKennon took the copies home and showed them to her husband. Her motivation, she averred, was an apprehension she was about to be fired because of her age. When she became concerned about her job, she removed and copied the documents for "insurance" and "protection." A few days after these deposition disclosures, the Banner sent McKennon a letter declaring that removal and copying of the records was in violation of her job responsibilities and advising her (again) that she was terminated. The Banner's letter also recited that, had it known of McKennon's misconduct, it would have discharged her at once for that reason.

[The Decision and Rationale of the U.S. District Court]

For purposes of summary judgment, the Banner conceded its discrimination against McKennon. The district court granted summary judgment for the Banner, holding that McKennon's misconduct was grounds for her termination and that neither back pay nor any other remedy was available to her under the ADEA. The U.S. Court of Appeals for the Sixth Circuit affirmed on the same rationale.

[The Legal Issue]

The question before the Court was whether an employee discharged in violation of the Age Discrimination in Employment Act of 1967 is barred from all relief when, after her discharge, the employer discovers evidence of wrongdoing that, in any event, would have led to the employee's termination on lawful and legitimate grounds. . . . [The Supreme Court] granted certiorari to resolve conflicting views among the Courts of Appeals on the question whether all relief must be denied when an employee has been discharged in violation of the ADEA and the employer later discovers some wrongful conduct that would have led to discharge if it had been discovered earlier. [The Supreme Court reversed the decision below.]

[The Decision and Rationale of the U.S. Supreme Court]

The objectives of the ADEA are furthered when even a single employee establishes that an employer has discriminated against him or her. The disclosure through litigation of incidents or practices that violate national policies respecting nondiscrimination in the workforce is itself important, for the occurrence of violations may disclose patterns of noncompliance resulting from a misappreciation of the Act's operation or entrenched resistance to its commands, either of which can be of industry-wide significance. The efficacy of its enforcement mechanisms becomes one measure of the success of the Act. . . .

. . . As we have said, the case comes to us on the express assumption that an unlawful motive was the sole basis for the firing. McKennon's misconduct was not discovered until after she had been fired. The employer could not have been motivated by knowledge it did not have and it cannot now claim that the employee was fired for the nondiscriminatory reason. Mixed motive cases are inapposite here, except to the important extent they underscore the necessity of determining the employer's motives in ordering the discharge, an essential element in determining whether the employer violated the federal antidiscrimination law. . . .

The proper boundaries of remedial relief in the general class of cases where, after termination, it is discovered that the employee has engaged in wrongdoing must be addressed by the judicial system in the ordinary course of further decisions, for the factual permutations and the equitable considerations they raise will vary from case to case. We do conclude that here, and as a general rule in cases of this type, neither reinstatement nor front pay is an appropriate remedy. It would be both inequitable and pointless to order the reinstatement of someone the employer would have terminated, and will terminate, in any event and upon lawful grounds.

The proper measure of backpay presents a more difficult problem. Resolution of this question must give proper recognition to the fact that an ADEA violation has occurred which must be deterred and compensated without undue infringement upon the employer's rights and prerogatives. The object of compensation is to restore the employee to the position he or she would have been in absent the discrimination, but that principle is difficult to apply with precision where there is after-acquired evidence of wrongdoing that would have led to termination on legitimate grounds had the employer known about it. Once an employer learns about employee wrongdoing that would lead to a legitimate discharge, we cannot require the employer to ignore the information, even if it is acquired during the course of discovery in a suit against the employer and even if the information might have gone undiscovered absent the suit. The beginning point in the trial court's formulation of a remedy should be calculation of backpay from the date of the unlawful discharge to the date the new information was discovered. In determining the appropriate order for relief, the court can consider taking into further account extraordinary equitable circumstances that affect the legitimate interests of either party. An absolute rule barring any recovery of backpay, however, would undermine the ADEA's objective of forcing employers to consider and examine their motivations, and of penalizing them for employment decisions that spring from age discrimination.

Where an employer seeks to rely upon after-acquired evidence of wrongdoing, it must first establish that the wrongdoing was of such severity that the employee in fact would have been terminated on those grounds alone if the employer had known of it at the time of the discharge. The concern that the employers might as a routine matter undertake extensive discovery into an employee's background or performance on the job to resist claims under the Act is not an insubstantial one, but we think the authority of the courts to award attorney's fees, mandated under the statute, 29 U.S.C. §§ 216(b), 626(b), and in appropriate cases to invoke the provisions of Rule 11 of the Federal Rules of Civil Procedure will deter most abuses.

Questions

1. Should this case be evaluated as a *McDonnell Douglas* case to show that the employer's reasons for terminating Alicia were not true and that the real reason for the termination was discrimination based on her race and sex? Is this a *Price Waterhouse* mixed motives case, and if so, how should that be analyzed?
2. Should the employer focus on trying to show that discrimination did not exist as a factor in her treatment or on trying to show that it would have fired her anyway? What difference does it make? How do 42 U.S.C. § 2000e(m) & 42 U.S.C. § 2000e(5)(2)(B) affect *Price Waterhouse* directions for proving a mixed motives case?
3. Do you agree with the Supreme Court in *McKennon* that there has to be some damage award when there is a violation of Title VII even when the employer would have fired the employee anyway if the employer had known of the employee's unlawful actions?

Discussion Notes

1. The relationship between *Price Waterhouse* mixed motives cases and *McDonnell Douglas* pretext cases has caused massive confusion for the litigation of disparate treatment claims since *Price Waterhouse* was decided in 1989 and after the Civil Rights Act of 1991 directly addressed mixed motives cases. Litigants have been unsure how to proceed. Proof whether the claim is based on mixed motives or on a single illegitimate motive may not be apparent at the onset of the case. Courts have allowed plaintiffs to proceed on the *McDonnell Douglas* model but have had to come to terms with the problem of mixed motives as they are developed in the course of litigation. Some courts have relied on the language of Justice O'Connor's concurring opinion in *Price Waterhouse* as if it reflects the plurality opinion of the Court, providing a requirement that the plaintiff show "direct evidence" of discrimination before the employer assumes the burden of showing that it is more likely than not that it would have fired the employee even without the discriminatory reason. Much discussion has occurred about the meaning of direct evidence, and thus some courts have made an important distinction between *McDonnell Douglas* approach to proving discrimination through inferences and this idea of "direct evidence" sufficient to impose a burden on the employer.

E. Use of Stereotypes

> ### Problem 9
>
> Kathleen Cilra, from Problem 4, complained that her employer was utilizing stereotypes about women in its assessment of her work. One of the criticisms made by her supervisor was that "she talked too much on the phone at work." This supervisor admitted that all of the "talk on the phone" was business related. Kathleen felt that the employer's criticism was a stereotype about women talking too much even when it was a business-related exercise. She supervised the health and safety of over 7,000 employees and felt that the use of the phone was an absolute necessity to get her work done. No such criticism was leveled at her male counterparts who conducted business on the telephone.

> ### Problem 10
>
> Mary's supervisor complained that she was too aggressive on the job. Mary worked in a factory that made air conditioners. Her job involved making sure that all of the safety features on the line met OSHA regulations. When she found something that was not in compliance or that threatened workers' safety, she would continue to remind the supervisor that the item needed to be fixed. The line supervisors got irritated because they did not like a woman telling them what to do, and they did not appreciate her aggressive manner in getting the job done.

1. Stereotypes Based on Sex, Race, Color, Religion, or National Origin

Another way to prove disparate treatment is to demonstrate that the employer relied on impermissible stereotypes to make adverse employment decisions. The law has evolved slowly in this area of disparate treatment. The U.S. Supreme Court in the *Price Waterhouse v. Hopkins* case, which is discussed as a mixed motives case in Chapter 2, recognized the important role of gender stereotyping in the proof of disparate treatment. In that case, the focus seemed to be on direct statements that reflected gender stereotyping with respect to a candidate for partnership in the firm.

The U.S. Supreme Court implicitly recognized the role of stereotyping as one kind of evidence of intentional discrimination prohibited by Title VII. It can be shown either by direct evidence that stereotypes were relied on by decision makers in taking an adverse employment action or by circumstantial evidence of the use of stereotypes. Ann Hopkins used evidence of stereotypical expectations of women that was considered and relied on in making the adverse decision. Hopkins introduced evidence of statements that she should wear jewelry, walk more femininely, and go to charm school in order to improve her partnership prospects. In considering this evidence, the trier of fact had to decide (1) whether these statements were made; (2) whether they were, indeed, stereotypical statements; (3) whether they were made in the context of deciding her partnership status; and (4) whether they were relied on by the decision makers. The Supreme Court's language in this case is the most frequently cited authority where decisions based on stereotypes are alleged to have been used by the employer. This reliance is carried over to other kinds of discrimination cases that involve a traditional *McDonnell Douglas* circumstantial evidence analysis rather than a mixed motives analysis. Actions by the employer that may constitute stereotypical assumptions about the employee can be used to support an inference of discrimination along with other evidence. The Supreme Court has not squarely addressed the way that stereotypical assumptions may contribute to the circumstantial case, and the cases in the lower courts are "few and far between."

The Court did not address the more difficult situation of stereotypical beliefs that form the basis for certain employment decisions. Since that decision, however, courts have relied on *Price Waterhouse v. Hopkins* to find proof of decisions based on stereotypes. Notice how the court of appeals relies on the language of the Supreme Court to support a finding of gender stereotyping in the following case, where the owners of Joe's Stone Crab hired men as wait staff instead of women in order to create a "high class" establishment on the European model. Consider how the court explores the role of gender stereotyping in this case and how this might be applied to situations less explicit than this example.

EQUAL EMPLOYMENT OPPORTUNITY COMMISSION
v.
JOE'S STONE CRAB, INC.
220 F.3d 1263 (11th Cir. 2000)

MARCUS, Circuit Judge:

[The Employment Problem]

[Joe's Stone Crab, Inc., is a landmark restaurant in Miami Beach, Florida. The restaurant is known for hiring only male servers. From 1986 until 1990, it hired 108 male food servers and 0 female food servers. Several females who wanted to work at Joe's Stone Crab, Inc., complained to the EEOC, which filed suit on their behalf.]

[The Decision of the Trial Court]

[The district court concluded that Joe's Stone Crab was not liable for intentional discrimination but determined that it was liable for disparate impact discrimination based on the hiring statistics. The court of appeals overturned the disparate impact finding, reinstated the disparate treatment claim, and remanded

for further trial to include gender stereotyping as proof of intentional discrimination.] The facts of this case are reasonably straightforward and are fully outlined by the district court in *EEOC v. Joe's Stone Crab, Inc.*, 969 F. Supp. 727 (S.D. Fla. 1997). Joe's Stone Crab, Inc. is a fourth-generation, family-owned seafood restaurant and Miami Beach landmark. During the stone crab season, which lasts from October to May, the restaurant is extremely busy—serving up to 1450 patrons each weeknight and up to 1800 patrons each weekend night. Today, the restaurant employs between 230 and 260 employees; of those, approximately 70 are food servers. Throughout its history, Joe's has experienced extremely low food server turnover—a result of Joe's family ethos, generous salary and benefits package, and its seven-month employment season. From 1950 onward, however, the food servers have been almost exclusively male. . . .

To hire new food servers, Joe's conducts a "roll call" every year on the second Tuesday in October. Although Joe's rarely advertises significantly, the district court found that the roll call is "widely known throughout the local food server community," and typically attracts over 100 applicants for only a limited number of slots. *Joe's Stone Crab*, 969 F. Supp. at 733. At a typical roll call, each applicant completes a written application and an individual interview. Selected applicants then enter a three-day training program where they shadow experienced servers. Upon successful completion of the program, they then become permanent hires. See *id.* . . .

. . . The district court observed that while "women have predominated as owner/managers," "most of Joe's female employees have worked in positions traditionally viewed as 'women's jobs,' e.g., as cashiers or laundry workers. Food servers generally have been male." *Id.* at 731. Although Joe's hired female food servers during World War II, most of these positions "reverted to men at the conclusion of the war." *Id.* Further, the district court found that, "[f]rom 1950 on, the food serving staff has been almost exclusively male. Indeed, one striking exception proves the rule. Dotty Malone worked as a food server at Joe's for seventeen years, and for most of this time she was the lone female on a serving staff that ranged between twenty-four and thirty-two." *Id.*

In explaining this historical dearth of female food servers, the district court found that Joe's maintained an "Old World" European tradition, in which the highest level of food service is performed by men, in order to create an ambience of "fine dining" for its customers. *Id.* at 733. . . .

. . . [T]he district court pointed to the testimony of Grace Weiss, Joe's owner, who stated, "I cannot explain the predominance of male servers, but perhaps it has to do with the very heavy trays to be carried, *the ambience of the restaurant*, and the extremely low turnover in servers." *Id.* at 731–732. (emphasis added by the district court). Second, the district court highlighted the testimony of Roy Garrett, a long-time maitre d' of Joe's with hiring authority, who explained that Joe's had a "tradition" that food server positions were "a male server type of job":

As I said before, we had very few female applicants over the years. It was sort of a tradition. . . . *It was always tradition* from the time I arrived there *that it was a male server type* of job. And until just recently when we became aware that we had to do other things, . . . originally, *it was traditionally a male place. We always had women that were qualified*

women. . . . Traditionally, I mean, it's just some restaurants, when you walk in, you know there are going to be women waitresses, other restaurants you know its going to be male waiters.

Id. at 732 (emphasis added).[4] Finally, the district court referred to the testimony of Joe's own restaurant industry expert, Karen McNeil, for a historical explanation of the "male-only" server tradition.

It has been an attitude and standard, it comes from Europe. In all of Europe you will find in all of the grade three restaurants in Europe, there is an impression that service at that high level is the environment of men, and that it ought to be that way. And I think that that attitude a few decades ago came and was felt a little bit here in this country. . . . Those [European] opinions and those sensibilities, I think were in fact carried here by restauranteurs [sic] who hoped to create something serious. If you wanted to create a serious restaurant that would become known in the community, that would become one of the community's great restaurants, you did what they did in Europe, you modeled yourself after them. I don't think anybody thought about it. They said, well, men did it there. It tended to be men here, too, who had those skill sets, and so men were [sic] automatically became the labor pool. *Id.*

The district court added that "Joe's [had] sought to emulate Old World traditions by creating an ambience in which tuxedo-clad men served its distinctive menu." *Id.*

[Discussion of disparate impact reversal omitted.]

[The Decision and Rationale of the U.S. Court of Appeals for the 11th Circuit]

. . . [A]fter carefully reading the trial transcript, we believe the district court's conclusion that the EEOC has not met its burden of proving intentional discrimination may have been based on an erroneous view of Title VII case law. . . . In light of the district court's seemingly unambiguous findings that "Joe's has been a 'male server type' establishment for the better part of the century" and that "women have systematically been excluded from the most lucrative entry level position, that of server," *Joe's Stone Crab*, 969 F. Supp. at 740, we emphasize that a finding of disparate treat-

---

[4] Similarly, Anthony Arneson, the maitre d' in charge of hiring beginning in 1987, testified that gender was never mentioned by Joe's managers or employees because of a "perception that people didn't even think about . . . that many fine dining establishments throughout the world have an all male staff."

ment requires no more than a finding that women were intentionally treated differently by Joe's because of or on account of their gender. To prove discriminatory intent necessary for a disparate treatment or pattern or practice claim, a plaintiff need not prove that a defendant harbored some special "animus" or "malice" towards the protected group to which she belongs.[19] In the race discrimination context, we recently have explained that "ill will, enmity, or hostility are not prerequisites of intentional discrimination." *Ferrill v. Parker Group, Inc.*, 168 F.3d 468, 473 n.7 (11th Cir. 1999). In *Ferrill*, for example, we held a defendant, who acted without racial animus but consciously and intentionally made job assignments based on racial stereotypes, liable for intentional discrimination. See *id.* The Supreme Court reached a similar conclusion in *Goodman v. Lukens Steel Co.*, 482 U.S. 656 (1987). . . . While *Goodman* and *Ferrill* both involved § 1981 claims, there is no difference in the substantive doctrine of intentional discrimination under Title VII and § 1981.

Simply put, Title VII prohibits "the entire spectrum of disparate treatment of men and women resulting from sex stereotypes," *Los Angeles Dept. of Water & Power v. Manhart*, 435 U.S. 702, 708 n.13 (quoting *Sprogis v. United Air Lines Inc.*, 444 F.2d 1194, 1198 (7th Cir. 1971)), even where the stereotypes are benign or not grounded in group animus. Therefore, if Joe's deliberately and systematically excluded women from food server positions based on a sexual stereotype which simply associated "fine-dining ambience" with all-male food service, it then could be found liable under Title VII for intentional discrimination regardless of whether it also was motivated by ill-will or malice toward women.[20]

---

[19] Several ambiguous phrases in the district court's opinion suggest that the district court may have been operating under this erroneous view. For instance, in finding that Joe's did not have an express policy of excluding women from food server positions, the district court observed that the evidence only proved that "management acquiesced in and gave silent approbation to the notion that male food servers were preferable to female food servers." *Joe's Stone Crab*, 969 F. Supp. at 731. Of course, the district court's summary dispatch of the EEOC's intentional discrimination claims precludes us from knowing for certain whether it thought the EEOC had to prove that Joe's hiring policies emanated from some special "animus" or "malice" towards women.

[20] Perhaps the seminal case in this context is *Price Waterhouse v. Hopkins*, 490 U.S. 228 (1989). [See *infra* at p. 51 for edited segments of this case in the mixed motives context.] In *Price Waterhouse*, the district court found that the employer, an accounting firm, had discriminated against Ann Hopkins by permitting stereotypical attitudes about women (Hopkins had been found "too acerbic" in her tone for a woman) to play a role in its decision to deny her partnership in the firm. . . . On appeal, the employer contended that it could not be liable for disparate treatment because "Hopkins did not prove 'intentional' discrimination on the part of the [decision-making] Board, but only 'unconscious' sexual stereotyping by unidentified partners who participated in the selection process." *Hopkins v. Price Waterhouse*, 825 F.2d 458, 468 (D.C. Cir. 1987), *aff'g in part and rev'g in part, Hopkins*, 618 F. Supp. at 1113–21. This argument was squarely rejected by the court of appeals: In keeping with [Title VII's remedial] purpose, the Supreme Court has never applied the concept of intent so as to excuse an artificial, gender-based employment barrier.

---

2. Identity Performance

Recent scholarship has attempted to elaborate on the complex problem of gender and race identity. Interesting work by Professors Carbado and Gulati suggests a new way of looking at the problems of stereotyping and individual ways of expressing race and gender identity.

Devon W. Carbado, Mitu Gulati, *The Fifth Black Woman*,
11 J. Contemp. Legal Issues 701 (2001)

(This is an edited version of the article and footnotes are deleted.)

. . . In a nutshell, the theory of identity performance is that a person's experiences with and vulnerability to discrimination are based not just on a status marker of difference (call this a person's status identity) but also on the choices that person makes about how to present her difference (call this a person's performance identity). For example, take a person with the status of a male. This person makes choices (dress, hair style, accent, etc.) about how to present that maleness. These choices may be highly constrained by societal and other pressures, but they are nevertheless choices about performance. Understanding the relationship between discrimination and performance, we argue, is crucial to developing a plausible and coherent theory of discrimination. The insights of intersectionality theory provide a useful point of departure for the development of identity performance theory.

Among other things, intersectionality pushes for the legal recognition and delineation of specific status identities. The notion is that particular social groups (e.g., black people) are constituted by multiple status identities (e.g., black lesbians, black heterosexual women, and black heterosexual men). According to intersectionality theory, the different status identity holders within any given social group are differently situated with respect to how much, and the form of, discrimination they are likely to face. Intersectionality argues that, in ascertaining whether a particular individual is the victim of discrimination, courts should pay attention to the specific status identity that the person occupies. For example, if the plaintiff bringing a discrimination suit is a heterosexual Asian American female attorney, courts should adjudicate her discrimination claim with that status identity in mind. More specifically, the fact that the employer in question treated Asian American men (or white or other women) well should not be taken as dispositive evidence that the employer did not either exhibit animus towards or harbor negative impressions of Asian American women.

The significance of paying attention to the plaintiff's specific status identity is that it allows courts to consider or allow discovery on the question of whether the plaintiff's discrimination derives from an intra-group distinction. Typically, courts conceptualize racial discrimination as an inter-group distinction, a distinction, for example, between whites and Asian Americans. Under this conceptualization, an Asian American plaintiff will typically be required to demonstrate that she was treated differently (disparately) from a similarly situated non–Asian American (usually a white) employee. But our hypothetical plaintiff might not be the victim of this form of discrimination. As noted in the prior paragraph, it is possible that her firm prefers Asian American men to Asian American women, discriminating against the latter but not the former. Framing the discrimination question solely in terms of the plaintiff's Asian American identity ignores the fact that the plaintiff's discrimination could be a function of her more specific status identity, her identity as an Asian American female.

Consider the following hypothetical. Mary, a black woman, works in an elite corporate firm. There are eighty attorneys at the firm, twenty of whom are partners. Only two of the partners are black, and both are men. The firm has three female partners, and all three are white. There are no Asian American, Native American, or Latina/o partners. The firm is slightly more diverse at the associate rank. There are fifteen female associates: three, including Mary, are black, two are Asian American, and

one is Latina. The remaining female associates are white. Of the forty-five male associates, two are black, two are Latino, three are Asian American, and the rest are white.

Mary is a seventh-year associate at the firm. She, along with five other associates, is up for partnership this year. Her annual reviews have been consistently strong. The partners for whom she has worked praise her intellectual creativity, her ability to perform well under pressure, her strong work ethic, her client-serving skills, and her commitment to the firm. She has not brought in many new clients, but, as one of the senior partners puts it, "that is not unusual for a person on the cusp of partnership."

For the past three years, the Chair of the Associate's Committee, the committee charged with making partnership recommendations to the entire partnership, has indicated to Mary that she is "on track." Being "on track" was important to Mary because, were she not on track, she would have seriously explored the option of moving either to another firm with better partnership prospects for her or in-house to an investment bank that provided greater job security. It was generally understood, however, and the Chair made sure to make it clear that "being on track is not a guarantee that you will ultimately make partner."

Recall that Mary and five other associates are up for partnership. The Associate Committee recommends that the firm promote all six. However, the partners vote only four into the partnership: one black man, one Asian American male, one white man, and one white woman. They deny partnership to Mary and a white male associate. The partnership's decision to depart from the Associate Committee's recommendation is not unusual. While the partnership almost always accepts the Associate Committee's negative recommendation (i.e., a recommendation that an offer of partnership not be extended to a particular associate), it accepts the committee's positive recommendation only half of the time.

Subsequently Mary brings a disparate treatment discrimination suit under Title VII. She advances three separate theories: race discrimination, sex discrimination, and race and sex discrimination. She does not, however, have any direct evidence of animus against her on the part of the employer. In other words, Mary can point to no explicit statements such as "We don't like you because you are a woman," or "We think that you are incompetent; all blacks are." The evidence is all circumstantial: Mary was highly qualified, but was rejected for a position that was arguably open. . . .

The foregoing hypothetical articulates the classic intersectionality problem wherein black women fall through an anti-discrimination gap constituted by black male and white female experiences. The problem can be framed in terms of essentialism. Consider first the court's response to Mary's race discrimination claim. In determining whether Mary experienced race discrimination, the court assumes that there is an essential black experience that is unmodified by gender. The court's adjudication of Mary's race discrimination claim conveys the idea that racism is necessarily total. It is a particular kind of animus that reaches across gender, and affects men and women in the same way. It is about race—a hostility against all black people. This conception of discrimination suggests that it is unlikely that institutions possessing this animus will make intraracial distinctions, or that if such distinctions are made (i.e., a firm promotes and hires some black people but does not promote and hire others), what is at play is not racial animus. With this conception of anti-discrimination law, it is not surprising that the court would have difficulty with Mary's race discrimination claim. After all, this claim emerges out of a factual context in which there is no allegation that the firm discriminated against black men. Yet this is precisely what Mary is arguing. The intra-racial distinction argument is that the firm distinguishes between black women and black men, that it prefers the latter, and that this preference is discriminatory. However, to the extent that a court essentializes race (by, for example, conceptualizing race without gender specificity), it makes it likely that the court will not view the preference Mary identifies as racially discriminatory. Put another way, if, as in our hypothetical case, a court's anti-discrimination starting point is buttressed by an essential conception of race, that court may have difficulty understanding that a racist firm might promote some black people (e.g., men) but not others (e.g., women).

Consider now the court's adjudication of Mary's sex discrimination. Here, too, the court's analysis reflects essentialism. The essentialism in this context conveys the idea that women's experiences are unmodified by race. The court assumes that if a firm engages in sex discrimination, such discrimination will negatively affect all women—and in the same way. Thus, the possibility that an institution might make intra-gender distinctions does not occur to the court. The intra-gender distinction argument is that the firm distinguishes between black women and white women, that it prefers the latter, and that this preference is discriminatory. However, to the extent that a court essentializes gender (by, for example, conceptualizing gender without racial specificity), likely that court will not view the preference Mary identifies as gender discrimination. In other words, if, as in our hypothetical case, a court's anti-discrimination starting point is buttressed by an essential conception of gender, that court may have difficulty understanding that a sexist firm might promote some women (e.g., whites) and not others (e.g., blacks).

Finally, consider the court's rejection of Mary's compound discrimination claim. Here, the court doctrinally erases black women's status identity as black women. Its conclusion that this identity status is not cognizable means that, for purposes of Title VII, black women exist only to the extent that their experiences comport with the experiences of black men or white women. Under the

court's view, and in the absence of explicit race/gender animus, black women's discriminatory experiences as black women are beyond the remedial reach of Title VII.

The Identity Performance Problem

To appreciate the identity performance problem, assume again that Mary is an African American female in a predominantly white elite corporate law firm. As before, Mary is up for partnership and her evaluations have been consistently strong. Stipulate now that four other black women are up for partnership, as are two white women and two white men. The Associate's Committee recommends that the firm extends partnership to all nine associates. The members of the partnership, however, decide to depart from this recommendation. They grant partnership to four of the black women. The fifth black woman, Mary, does not make partner. Of the four white associates, the firm extends partnership to one of the men and one of the women.

The partnership's decision creates a buzz around the firm. The firm had never before granted partnership to so many non-white attorneys. Moreover, in the firm's fifty year history, it had only ever promoted two black people to partnership. Both of these partners are men, and the firm promoted both of them in the mid-1980s, a period during which the firm, along with many others, had enjoyed a high level of prosperity.

Prior to 1980, the firm had never hired a black female associate. Furthermore, most of those who were hired after that date left within two to three years of their arrival. Given the history of black women at the firm—low hiring rate, high attrition rate, low promotion rate—associates at the firm dubbed this year the "year of the black woman."

Mary, however, does not agree. Subsequent to the partnership decision, she files a Title VII discrimination suit, alleging (1) race and sex compound discrimination, i.e., discrimination against her on account of her being a black woman, and (2) discrimination based on identity performance. . . .

With respect to the first issue, the court agrees with Mary that a discrimination claim combining race and sex is, under Title VII, legally cognizable. The court has read, and understood, and it agrees with the literature on intersectionality. Under the court's view, black women should be permitted to ground their discrimination claims on their specific status identity as black women. According to the court, failing to do so would be to ignore the complex ways in which race and gender interact to create social disadvantage: a result that would be inconsistent with the goals of Title VII.

With respect to the second issue, the court agrees with the firm. The court reasons that recognizing Mary's status identity does not prove that the firm discriminated against her because of that identity. It explains that the firm promoted four associates with Mary's precise status identity—that is, four black women. Why, the court rhetorically asks, would a racist/sexist firm extend partnership to these women? The court suggests that when there is clear evidence of non-discrimination against the identity group within which the plaintiff is situated, that produces an inference that the plaintiff was not the victim of discrimination.

. . . The problem with the court's approach is that it fails to consider whether Mary was the victim of an intra-racial (or intra-gender) distinction based not simply on her identity status as a black woman but on her performance of that identity. In effect, the court's approach essentializes the identity status "black female." More specifically, the court assumes that Mary and the other four black women are similarly situated with respect to their vulnerability to discrimination. However, this might not be the case. The social meaning of being a black woman is not monolithic and static but contextual and dynamic. An important way in which it is shaped is by performance. In other words, how black women present their identity can (and often does) affect whether and how they are discriminated against.

Consider, for example, the extent to which the following performance issues might help to explain why Mary was not promoted, but the other black women were.

Dress. While Mary wears her hair in dreadlocks, the other black women relax their hair. On Casual Fridays, Mary sometimes wears West African influenced attire. The other black women typically wear khaki trousers or blue jeans with white cotton blouses.

Institutional Identity. Mary was the driving force behind two controversial committees: the committee for the Recruitment and Retention of Women and Minorities and the committee on Staff/Attorney Relations. She has been critical of the firm's hiring and work allocation practices. Finally, she has repeatedly raised concerns about the number of hours the firm allocates to pro bono work. None of the other four black women have ever participated on identity-related or employee relations–related committees. Nor have any of them commented on either the racial/gender demographics of the firm or the number of hours the firm allocates for pro bono work. [*Editor's Note:* The article also describes several other factors that could be considered here: "social identity," "educational affiliations," "marital status," "residence," and "professional affiliation."]

Because the court conceptualizes Mary's discrimination case solely in terms of her identity status as a black female, it does not consider any of the foregoing

performance dynamics. Yet any one of them could (and certainly all of them together would) explain the firm's decision not to promote Mary. In other words, it is possible that the partnership's promotion decisions reflect an identity preference based on performance.

Intersectionality does not capture this form of preferential treatment. While intersectionality recognizes that institutions make intra-group distinctions, that understanding is situated in an anti-discrimination context that is buttressed by a status conception of identity.

Assuming the foregoing performance issues obtain in Mary's case, do they reflect impermissible discrimination? The answer is not obviously yes. . . . Given our claim that this line of reasoning is flawed, the question is: What exactly is the relationship between identity performance and workplace discrimination?

Why Identity Performance Is Workplace Discrimination

Broadly speaking, there are two ways to make the point that intra-group distinctions based on identity performance implicate workplace discrimination. The first is to focus on the preferred group members. In our hypothetical, they are the four black women. The second way is to focus on the disfavored group members. Mary, the fifth black woman, falls into this category.

The Preferred Group Members: The Four Black Women

The question here is whether the firm's institutional norms (e.g., collegiality) and hard-to-measure criteria (e.g., social effort) created a workplace context within which the four black women were disadvantaged because of their status identity. This could come about because of a perception on the part of the firm that black women are likely to be both uncollegial and lazy. Within such an institutional context, black women might be said to have what we call "negative workplace standing."

In a prior article, *Working Identity*, we argued that an employee's awareness that identity-based assumptions about her are at odds with the institutional norms and criteria of a firm creates an incentive for that employee to work her identity.[32] There are a number of ways an employee might do this. The employee might laugh in response to, or engage in racist humor (signaling collegiality). She might socialize with her colleagues after work (signaling that she can fit in; is one of the boys). She might avoid contact with other employees with negative

[32] Carbado & Gulati, *Working Identity*, 85 Cornell L. Rev. 1259 (2000).

workplace standing (signaling that she is not really "one of them"). The list goes on. The point is that whatever particular strategy the employee deploys, her aim will likely be to comfort her supervisors/colleagues about her negative workplace standing. Specifically, the employee will attempt to signal that she can fit in, that she is not going to make her supervisors/colleagues uncomfortable about her identity—or theirs—and, at bottom, that the negative stereotypes that exist about her status identity are inapplicable to her. *Working Identity* refers to these strategies collectively as "comfort strategies." These strategies are constituted by identity performances.

Stipulate that the four black women in the hypothetical performed comfort strategies. The claim that the performance of such strategies constitutes discrimination is based on the idea that people with negative workplace standing (e.g., people of color) have a greater incentive to perform comfort strategies than people with positive workplace standing. This means that identity performances burden some employees (e.g., blacks) more than others (e.g., whites). Without more, this racial distribution of identity performances is problematic. The problem is compounded by the fact that identity performances constitute work, a kind of "shadow work." This work is simultaneously expected and unacknowledged. Plus, it is work that is often risky. Finally, this work can be at odds with the employee's sense of her identity. That is, the employee may perceive that she has to disassociate from or disidentify with her identity in order to fit in. To the extent the employee's continued existence and success in the workplace is contingent upon her behaving in ways that operate as a denial of self, there is a continual harm to that employee's dignity.

The Disfavored Group Member:
The Fifth Black Woman

Recall that the claim is that the firm's discrimination against Mary derives from an intra-group distinction based on Mary's dress, institutional identity, marital status, professional and educational affiliations, and residence. The question becomes, why is this discrimination impermissible? The short answer is that the distinction creates an intra-racial and an interracial problem. The problem is that the firm draws a line between black people who do (or whom the firm perceives as performing) identity work to fit in at the firm and black people who do not perform (or whom the firm perceives as not performing) such work. The interracial problem is that white people are not subject to this subcategorization. There are three ways to make the point that this subcategorization of black people but not white people violates Title VII: (1) it constitutes a racial term and condition of employment; (2) it is a form of race-plus discrimination; and (3) it reflects racial stereotyping. We do not present

these arguments as fully worked-out theories. Instead, we introduce them as possible approaches courts can develop to address the identity performance problem.

Racial Terms and Conditions of Employment

The terms and conditions of employment argument is this: Subcategorizing black people based on those who do identity work and those who do not constitutes the imposition of a race-based term and condition of employment. In effect, an institution that draws such a distinction vis-à-vis black people is saying:

> We hire only black people of a certain kind at our firm: black people who have a weak sense of racial identity and who eschew identity politics, black people who are assimilationist in political and social orientation, black people who are comfortable around, and who will not cause discomfort to, white people. In short, if you want a job at, or expect to do well within, this firm, you have to present yourself as a "good black."

The claim is that drawing intra-racial distinctions based on identity performances is tantamount to establishing the racial (identity) terms upon which people will be hired and/or promoted. This alone would seem to violate Title VII. The problem is compounded by the fact that white people are not subcategorized based on their performance of (white) racial identity. In other words, they are not subject to racial terms and conditions of employment. [*Editor's Note:* The authors also discuss factors such as race-plus discrimination and terms and conditions of employment as other ways of analyzing this problem.]

Stereotyping on the Basis of Performance

The set of cases that perhaps most clearly illustrate the judicial hostility towards performance claims are the transsexual cases. Typically, the case would involve a biological man who was performing in the workplace as a woman. These cases were easy losers, as one court explained, because Title VII protected biological sex and not social sex (i.e., gender). In other words, there was no room for claims based on gender performance. All of this changed recently.

A series of recent cases out of the First, Second, and Ninth Circuits, however, suggest that these claims are no longer easy losers.[42] The rationale is that these cases can be conceptualized as stereotyping claims. Stereotyping as related to Title VII's protected categories, everyone

---

[42] *See Higgins v. New Balance Athletic Shoe*, 194 F. 3d 252 (1st Cir. 1999) (Selya, J.); *Schwenk v. Hartford* 204 F. 3d 1187 (9th Cir. 2000) (Reinhardt, J.); *Rosa v. Park West Bank & Trust Co.*, 214 F. 3d 213 (1st Cir. 2000) (Lynch, J.); and *Simonton v. Runyon*, 2000 WL 1190195 (2d Cir. 2000) (Walker, J.).

agrees, is covered under Title VII. Take then the case of Brian, a biological man who is terminated by an employer because he is performing his identity as a woman (for example, by wearing a dress, lipstick, and affecting an effeminate manner). In terms of stereotyping, one could argue that Brian was fired because he did not behave in stereotypically masculine ways. If phrased in these terms, all four of the opinions agreed, there was an actionable claim. The notion is that Title VII protects employees from impermissible stereotyping: in Brian's case, sex-based stereotyping. Because sex-based stereotyping is conceptualized as discrimination "based on sex," there is no need to address the issue of immutability or fundamental rights.

As articulated above, the doctrine requires little expansion to encompass Mary's claim. Brian was terminated because he did not engage in what his employer perceived to be stereotypically masculine behavior. Mary was denied partnership because she did engage in what her employer perceived to be stereotypically black female behavior. The essence of both claims is the same, that is, an employer penalizing an employee for behavior that activated negative stereotypes.

Of course, things are never that simple.

Conclusion

The logical applicability of the doctrine is but the tip of the iceberg.

Question

1. Is identity performance feasible as a way of identifying discrimination? What would change in the employer's responsibility in the workplace? Is this possible? If not possible, then how do you solve the problem for the fifth black woman?

3. Gender Stereotyping and Sexual Orientation Discrimination

> **Problem 11**
>
> Gary Simon quit his job as an installer for the local cable company because his co-workers kept up a constant barrage of derogatory comments about him. The other men on the job assumed that he was gay because he never joined them after work at the local bar and he never joined in their discussions about their latest girlfriends. They made fun of the way he walked, talked, and combed his hair. On several occasions, they taped photographs of male strippers onto his locker at work. Although Gary went to the EEOC to file a charge, he was told that Title VII does not cover discrimination on the basis of sexual orientation.

The Supreme Court's recognition of gender stereotyping in *Price Waterhouse* has been used in recent years as the linchpin of a wave of cases that address the argument that the gender stereotyping of gay men and lesbians in employment situations is covered by Title VII. Ann Hopkins failed to meet the stereotypical expectations of women as "feminine"; gay men claim that they suffer the same kind of discrimination when their employers view them as failing to meet the stereotypical expectations of men. Given that sexual orientation has not been recognized as a protected class under Title VII, this is a significant interpretation of the nature of discrimination on the basis of "sex." The U.S. Supreme Court has not decided this question, and there is no case on its current docket that places this matter before the Court.

The development of this analysis of stereotyping as sex discrimination prohibited by Title VII has been the focus of a renewed effort by scholars and activists concerned about discrimination based on sexual orientation. Arguments that sexual orientation discrimination is prohibited by Title VII have been rejected by many courts. In the area of sexual harassment discrimination, discussed in the next chapter, the Supreme Court did recognize that same-sex harassment was covered by Title VII. Recent scholarship, as well as a few courts, have recognized that gender stereotyping prohibited by Title VII is not limited to questions of stereotypical expectations of women but may include stereotypical assumptions about the proper characteristics and mannerisms of men as men. Some courts reject this argument as a ruse to recognize "sexual orientation" as a protected class.

CENTOLA
v.
POTTER
183 F. Supp. 2d 403 (D. Mass. 2002)

Memorandum and Order Re: Defendants' Motion for Summary Judgment

GERTNER, *District Judge.*

[The Employment Problem]

[Stephen Centola worked for the United States Postal Service for over seven years. He claimed that his co-workers tormented him continuously by making comments and leaving photographs which mocked his masculinity, portrayed him as effeminate, and implied that he was a homosexual.] Although Centola is homosexual, he never disclosed his sexual orientation to any of his co-workers or managers. On one occasion, Centola's co-workers placed a sign stating "Heterosexual replacement on duty" at his [desk]. They taped pictures of Richard Simmons "in pink hot pants" to his [desk]. Fellow carriers asked Centola if he would be marching in the gay parade and asked him if he had gotten AIDS yet. At other times, his co-workers called him a "sword swallower" and anti-gay epithets. His co-workers also placed cartoons mocking gay men near him. Centola testified that this was a "constant thing."

Centola's supervisors and managers also would treat Centola differently from other male and female letter carriers. They would follow him into the bathroom to check on him. They permitted others to leave to get coffee but not Centola, and they disciplined him more severely than others for minor conduct and attendance infractions. His supervisors fired him when he complained to them about this conduct. He filed a lawsuit in federal court in Massachusetts after first filing a charge with the EEOC. The lawyers for the U.S. Post Office filed a motion for summary judgment claiming that the judge should dismiss the lawsuit before trial because, as a matter of law, Title VII does not protect against discrimination based on sexual orientation.

[The Legal Issue]

[Judge Nancy Gertner considered the issue to be] the extent to which Title VII of the Civil Rights Act of 1964 ... reaches allegations of employment-related discrimination on the basis of sex and sexual orientation.

[The Decision by the Trial Court: The U.S. District Court for the Eastern District of Massachusetts]

[Judge Gertner decided that Mr. Centola provided sufficient evidence to support the inference that he was harassed and retaliated against because of his sex and his failure to conform to his co-workers' sexual stereotypes. She denied the employer's motion for summary judgment. The role of sex stereotyping figured prominently in Judge Gertner's analysis.]

... [T]he law is relatively clear that discrimination on the basis of sexual orientation is not barred under Title VII so long as the persons discriminating are not also discriminating on the basis of another prohibited characteristic, such as race or sex. See *Higgins v. New Balance Athletic Shoe, Inc.*, 194 F.3d 252, 259 (1st Cir. 1999) (regarding "as settled law that, as drafted and authoritatively construed, Title VII does not proscribe harassment *simply* because of sexual orientation") (emphasis added); *Simonton v. Runyon,* 232 F.3d 33, 35–36 (2d Cir. 2000) (finding claim that plaintiff was discriminated against because of his sexual orientation alone was not cognizable under Title VII). By itself, Centola's claim that he was discriminated against on the basis of his sexual orientation cannot provide a cause of action under Title VII.

However, Centola does not only allege that he was discriminated against because of his sexual orientation. He also claims that he was discriminated against because of his sex. And harassment of a man by other men is actionable under Title VII so long as there has been "discriminat[ion] . . . because of . . . sex in the terms or conditions of employment." *Oncale v. Sundowner Offshore Serv., Inc.,* 523 U.S. 75, 79–80 (1988) (internal quotation marks omitted).

But the line between discrimination because of sexual orientation and discrimination because of sex is hardly clear. Sex stereotyping is central to all discrimination: Discrimination involves generalizing from the characteristics of a group to those of an individual, making assumptions about an individual because of that person's gender, assumptions that may or may not be true. In *Price Waterhouse v. Hopkins,* 490 U.S. 228, 250 (1989)[5], for example, the Court held that "an employer who acts on the basis of a belief that a woman cannot be aggressive, or that she must not be, has acted on the basis of gender." And that principle applies whether the plaintiff is a man or a woman. As the First Circuit noted, "just as a woman can ground an action on a claim that men discriminated against her because she did not meet stereotyped expectations of femininity, see *Price Waterhouse,* 490 U.S. at 250–251, a man can ground a claim on evidence that other men discriminated against him because he did not meet stereotyped expectations of masculinity." *Higgins,* 194 F.3d at 261 n.4. See also *Simonton,* 232 F.3d at 38 (recognizing that "a suit [by a man] alleging harassment or disparate treatment based upon nonconformity with sexual stereotypes is cognizable under Title VII as discrimination because of sex"); *Ianetta v. Putnam In-*

vestments, Inc., 142 F. Supp. 2d 131 (D. Mass. 2001) (finding that plaintiff had stated cause of action under Title VII where he alleged that he was discriminated against because he did not conform to the male gender stereotype).[6] Cf. *Rosa v. Park West Bank & Trust Co.,* 214 F.3d 213, 215–216 (1st Cir. 2000) (using Title VII case law to find that cause of action existed under the Equal Credit Opportunity Act if defendant refused to give a loan application to a cross-dressing male because his dress "did not accord with his male gender.") Stated in a gender neutral way, the rule is: If an employer acts upon stereotypes about sexual roles in making employment decisions, or allows the use of these stereotypes in the creation of a hostile or abusive work environment, then the employer opens itself up to liability under Title VII's prohibition of discrimination on the basis of sex.

This is the nub of Centola's complaint: Coworkers and supervisors, he claims, discriminated against him because he failed to meet their gender stereotypes of what a man should look like, or act like. In so doing, they created an objectively hostile and abusive work environment in violation of Title VII.

Centola does not need to allege that he suffered discrimination on the basis of his sex alone or that sexual orientation played no part in his treatment. Section 107 of the 1991 Civil Rights Act allows recovery based on proof of a "mixed motive," a combination of a lawful and an unlawful motive.[7] See also *Hopkins,* 490 U.S. at 240. ("Title VII meant to condemn even those decisions based on a mixture of legitimate and illegitimate considerations.") Thus, if Centola can demonstrate that he was discriminated against "because of . . . sex" as a result of sex stereotyping, the fact that he was also discriminated against on the basis of his sexual orientation has no legal significance under Title VII.

---

[5] In *Hopkins,* Price Waterhouse failed to promote Ann Hopkins, the only woman out of 88 candidates in her partnership class, after partners suggested that she take a "course in charm school" and "walk more femininely, talk more femininely, dress more femininely, wear make-up, have her hair styled, and wear jewelry." *Id.* at 235.

[6] In both *Higgins* and *Simonton,* the Circuit Courts refused to consider arguments based upon a sexual stereotyping theory at the appellate level because the plaintiffs had not properly raised these arguments first with the trial courts below. Here, however, Centola properly has alleged in his Complaint that the discrimination was "on account of Centola's sex—male" and raised this argument with supporting factual evidence in his summary judgment papers and at oral argument. Thus, I may properly decide on the merits whether his claim should survive summary judgment after examining the relevant factual record before me.

[7] It states, in pertinent part: "[A]n unlawful employment practice is established when the complaining party demonstrates that race, color, religion, sex, or national origin was a motivating factor for any employment practice, even though other factors also motivated the practice." 42 U.S.C. § 2000e–2(m).

A mixed motive approach is important here, precisely because of the difficulty in differentiating behavior that is prohibited (discrimination on the basis of sex) from behavior that is not prohibited (discrimination on the basis of sexual orientation). Sexual orientation harassment is often, if not always, motivated by a desire to enforce heterosexually defined gender norms. In fact, stereotypes about homosexuality are directly related to our stereotypes about the proper roles of men and women. While one paradigmatic form of stereotyping occurs when co-workers single out an effeminate man for scorn, in fact, the issue is far more complex. The harasser may discriminate against an openly gay co-worker, or a co-worker that he perceives to be gay, whether effeminate or not, because he thinks, "real men don't date men." The gender stereotype at work here is that "real" men should date women, and not other men.[8] Conceivably, a plaintiff who is perceived by his harassers as stereotypically masculine in every way except for his actual or perceived sexual orientation could maintain a Title VII cause of action alleging sexual harassment because of his sex due to his failure to conform with sexual stereotypes about what "real" men do or don't do.

In this case, however, I need not go so far. Centola never disclosed his sexual orientation to anyone at work. His co-workers made certain assumptions about him, assumptions informed by gender stereotypes. For example, they placed a picture of Richard Simmons "in pink hot pants" in Centola's work area. Without placing too fine a point on it, Richard Simmons "in pink hot pants" is hardly what most people in our society would consider to be a masculine icon. Certainly, a reasonable jury could interpret this picture, unaccompanied by any text, as evidence that Centola's co-workers harassed him because Centola did not conform with their ideas about what "real" men should look or act like. Just as Ann Hopkins was vilified for not being "feminine" enough, Centola was vilified for not being more "manly."

Although Centola never disclosed his sexual orientation to anyone at work, if Centola's co-workers leapt to the conclusion that Centola "must" be gay because they found him to be effeminate, Title VII's protections should not disappear. For the purposes of summary judgment, there is sufficient evidence to support the claim that Centola's co-workers punished him because they perceived him to be impermissibly feminine for a man. . . .

Because Centola has carried his summary judgment burden of proving that his co-workers and supervisors discriminated against him because of his sex by using impermissible sexual stereotypes against him, the Defendants' motion for summary judgment on Centola's Title VII sexual harassment claim is DENIED. . . .

Questions

1. In both the *Joe's Stone Crab* and the *Centola* cases, the evidence that supported an inference of intentional discrimination was based on statements or actions of gender stereotyping. What would happen if there were no direct statements or actions but there were statements and actions based on beliefs that were stereotypical? Since many people use stereotypes to form their basic beliefs about how the world operates, do you think the court should be able to find intentional discrimination based on these unstated stereotypical beliefs?

2. What is the difference between discrimination on the basis of sexual orientation and discrimination on the basis of gender stereotyping? This seems to be a critical distinction to the court in *Centola*. How do you explain the difference?

3. How should the problems in this chapter be solved?

Discussion Notes

1. An adverse employment action does not have to be a termination or a denial of a job or a promotion. Negative changes in the "terms and conditions of employment" can be the basis of a claim of discriminatory treatment. 42 U.S.C. § 2000e-2(a). In the *Centola* case, the claim is that the conditions under which Mr. Centola worked were hostile and abusive because of gender stereotyping. The definition of hostile and abusive conditions are discussed more fully as sexual harassment in Chapter 4. As noted by the judge in *Centola*, such harassment must be severe and pervasive in order to constitute actionable discrimination under Title VII.

2. Claims like Mr. Centola's have been rejected in other jurisdictions where the courts view it as one of sexual orientation discrimination, which is not covered by Title VII. The gender

---

[8] See Sylvia A. Law, *Homosexuality and the Social Meaning of Gender*, 1988 Wis. L. Rev. 187 (1988). Professor Law argues that disapprobation of homosexual behavior is a reaction to the violation of gender norms, i.e., traditional concepts of masculinity and femininity, rather than merely scorn for homosexual practices.

stereotyping argument accepted in *Centola* is the most recent attempt to address this type of discrimination under Title VII.

Recent scholarship has attempted to elaborate on the complex problem of gender identity. Interesting work by Professors Carbado and Gulati referred to in this chapter suggest a new way of looking at the problems of stereotyping and individual ways of expressing gender identity. What problems are being addressed by these scholars that are not presently addressed by Title VII?

3. The courts have, for the most part, ruled that discrimination on the basis of sexual orientation is not covered by Title VII, but city ordinances and state laws or constitutions have expanded the scope of protection to include prohibitions against discrimination on the basis of sexual orientation. In Chapter 4, the issue of same-sex harrassment will be considered in conjunction with the development of the interpretation of Title VII to include charges of harassment on the basis of race, color, sex, religion, or national origin. Chapter 9 addresses some of the issues for same-sex partner employment benefits, and Chapter 13 addresses issues related to sexual orientation and disability law.

F. Sources of Protection Other than Title VII

1. The Federal Constitution's Equal Protection Clause

Since Title VII does not provide protection against discrimination based on sexual orientation or gender identity, the scope of protections for gay, lesbian, and transgender persons rests somewhat, but not exclusively, on geography. A significant minority of states and municipalities have enacted statutes and ordinances that treat sexual orientation and gender identity as protected classes. These statutes offer protections against discrimination in employment, public accommodations, and credit. Although there is no federal Title VII protection based on sexual orientation or gender identity, the equal protection clause may under certain circumstances proscribe discrimination. Unlike Title VII, which requires an employment relationship, the equal protection clause operates when government, acting under color of law, draws discriminatory classifications among citizens that it cannot justify.

The analysis for an equal protection claim is different than one pursuant to Title VII. Although all are entitled to the equal protection of the laws, the courts have interpreted the clause with differing standards depending on the classifications made by the state. For example, classifications based on race are examined with strict scrutiny—that is, the state must demonstrate a compelling state interest, and the means chosen by the state to accomplish that compelling interest must be narrowly tailored to accomplishing the result. Classifications based on sex are examined with an intermediate scrutiny—that is, the state must demonstrate an important governmental interest and the means chosen by the state must be substantially related to that important interest. Most other classifications fall into a general category, which utilizes the rational basis test—that is, the state need only show a legitimate interest and means that are rationally related to that interest. This standard is far easier for the state to meet than the higher standards accorded to strict scrutiny or intermediate scrutiny.

Classifications based on sexual orientation have been treated as classifications in the general category. However, as the Supreme Court indicated in *Romer v. Evans*, 517 U.S. 620 (1996), a classification based on sexual orientation may sometimes fail to be justified even under the lenient rational basis test. In *Romer*, the Supreme Court considered the constitutionality of a Colorado amendment, passed by referendum, to the state constitution to require that local ordinances passed to protect individuals based on sexual orientation be approved by the legislature. No other local ordinances were required to submit to this extra legislative approval. The Court found that the classification did not survive the rational basis test because the state action was targeted animus against a particular group and that the effect of the hurdles created by the amendment interfered with the ability of certain citizens to engage in full civil participation. Some scholars have labeled this approach a "heightened rational basis review." *Romer* does not create a new classification to protect people from discrimination based on their sexual orientation, but it indicates that the Court is willing to use the rational basis test in a more comprehensive manner when the circumstances warranted.

The Court did not declare in *Romer* that gay men, lesbians, and bisexuals are entitled to heightened scrutiny. Instead, it applied rational basis review, asking whether the classification drawn by Colorado's Amendment 2 was a reasonable measure to address a subject of legitimate governmental concern. Rational basis review is the most lenient of constitutional standards. If science someday proves that sexual orientation is immutable, as the law has assumed race to be, should homosexuals and lesbians be treated as a suspect class deserving of a higher level of judicial scrutiny, like race and gender? What about bisexuals? Some local ordinances protect "bisexuals" or "heterosexuals" and extend protection to "perceptions" about sexual orientation. If heterosexual males are not discriminated against based on heterosexuality, should a bisexual male who is currently in a sexual relationship with a female, but who has been involved in sexual relationships with men in the past, be allowed to claim discrimination if his employer fires him for cohabiting with his female companion? Should bisexuality be protected at all until it intersects with a same-sex relationship, since heterosexuality has never been subjected to social censure in America? If homosexuality is not immutable, or lacks a genetic component, is Justice Scalia who wrote a dissent in *Romer*, correct to equate homosexuals with other persons who "choose" to wear animal fur or to vote Republican? One might wonder whether any PETA members or Republicans have been thrown out of their apartments or fired when their employer discovers these affiliations?

Colorado argued that protecting against discrimination based on sexual orientation detracted from resources necessary to combat other types of discrimination. Yet only three municipalities in Colorado would have faced the decision about where to apply civil rights enforcement resources because of local antidiscrimination ordinances. Do you think that Denver, Boulder, and Aspen have the right to make this decision about resource allocation locally? Does Colorado have an interest in local decisions about enforcement priorities? This argument is intimately related to Justice Scalia's seeming acceptance of the proposition that there is a "market" for civil rights and that homosexuals move to areas where they can exercise bloc voting power and political influence. He expressed both views in his dissent. In Justice Scalia's view, since homosexuals and lesbians seek protections based on sexual orientation, they seek a species of "special rights" not accorded the heterosexual population. (Some ordinances do purport to outlaw discrimination against heterosexuals because of their hetero-sexuality.) One could question whether civil rights are finite, so that enforcing a gay man's employment rights necessarily detracts from enforcing an African American's employment rights. Or one could question whether there is a scarcity of civil rights protections such that only the most "deserving" (however that criterion may be determined) plaintiffs may make a claim on them. If so, should women have a Title VII cause of action, assuming that their claims may consume judicial resources that could be applied to race claims, which have been accorded a higher level of scrutiny? The notion of "special rights" that per-meates Justice Scalia's dissent may be a way of delineating "deserving" from "undeserving" claimants.

Justice Scalia's dissent in *Romer* evokes a salient legal debate. There are those who believe that citizens who have enough "clout" to obtain fair treat-ment from the legislature are not in need of judicial redress. For adherents of this view, the courts are a default mechanism that come into operation only when the political process consistently fails to protect a minority group be-cause of its stereotypes about the minority group or its desire to retain exclu-sively the advantages it enjoys over the minority group. *See* J. Ely, Democracy and Distrust (1980). Justice Scalia appears to be arguing that homosexuals are such a powerful political force in certain locales that their influence has to be diluted by statewide forces. In Justice Scalia's schema, homosexuals who are "insiders" in their local legislative bodies—as evidenced by their success in ob-taining municipal protections—are not deserving of the local protections pre-cisely because they were powerful enough politically to secure them. In Justice Scalia's schema, the people of Colorado functioned as a sort of superlegislative check on the concentrated political power of homosexuals in three cities. In Professor John Hart Ely's schema, however, the action of the Colorado citizenry in overturning the municipal ordinances and preventing future enactment of antidiscrimination laws protecting gay men and lesbians is the sort of majori-tarian tyranny that justifies resort to the courts, since it indicates that the leg-islative process has failed to keep majorities from trammeling minority rights:

> The Constitution has [proceeded] from the quite sensible assumption that an effective majority will not inordinately threaten its own rights, and has sought to assure that such a majority will not systematically treat others less well than it treats [its own members]. Malfunction occurs when [the in group is] choking off the channels of political change to ensure that they will stay in and the outs will stay out. [Unclogging] stoppages in the democratic process is what judicial review ought preeminently to be about. . . . [We] cannot trust the [insiders] to decide who stays out, and it is therefore incumbent on the courts to ensure not only that no one is denied the vote for no reason, but also that where there is a reason [it] had better be a very convincing one.

Ely, Democracy and Distrust at 101–03 (1980).

Discussion Notes

1. Justice Scalia's *Romer* dissent accuses the majority of an elitist "law school" viewpoint that is out of step with the presumably more traditional majority of Americans. But the Court's members throughout recent American history have generally been drawn from the "elite of

the elite" subclass of law schools such as Harvard, Stanford, Columbia, and Virginia, and the Justices tend to hire law clerks at the top of their classes from such schools. The same "elitist" Supreme Court with the same "elitist" brand of law clerks had some ten years earlier written *Bowers v. Hardwick*, 478 U.S. 186 (1986), holding by a 5–4 vote that there is no substantive due process (privacy) right protecting consensual homosexual sodomy in one's home. (Justice Powell, incidentally, near the time of his death, publicly stated that he had "made a mistake" in casting the deciding vote in the case. *See* John C. Jeffries, Jr., Justice Lewis F. Powell, Jr. 530 (1994).)

The *Bowers* Court did not apply the privacy rights precedents from the line of cases involving the right to contraception or family association but instead used only descriptive language from two of its precedents, the facts of which it did not discuss. The Court applied the language of *Palko v. Connecticut*, 302 U.S. 319, 325 (1937), defining "fundamental" constitutional rights as those that are "implicit in the concept of ordered liberty" such that "neither liberty nor justice would exist if [they] were sacrificed," and the language of *Moore v. East Cleveland*, 431 U.S. 494, 503 (1977) defining fundamental rights as those that are "deeply rooted in this Nation's history and tradition." The *Bowers* majority did not consider any equal protection issue in the case, such as enforcement of the sodomy law against homosexuals but not heterosexuals. Notably, the majority's reasoning in *Bowers* rested on traditional morality:

> Proscriptions against [sodomy] have ancient roots. . . . Sodomy was a criminal offense at common law and was forbidden by the laws of the original 13 States when they ratified the Bill of Rights. In 1868, when the Fourteenth Amendment was ratified, all but 5 of the 37 States in the Union had criminal sodomy laws. In fact, until 1961, all 50 States outlawed sodomy, and today, 24 States and the District of Columbia continue to provide criminal penalties for sodomy performed in private and between consenting adults. . . . Against this background, to claim that a right to engage in such conduct is "deeply rooted in this Nation's history and tradition" or "implicit in the concept of ordered liberty" is, at best, facetious.

478 U.S. at 193–94.

Moreover, the majority opinion in *Bowers* stated:

> Even if the conduct at issue here is not a fundamental right, respondent asserts that there must be a rational basis for the law and that there is none in this case other than the presumed belief of a majority of the electorate in Georgia that homosexual sodomy is immoral and unacceptable. This is said to be an inadequate rationale to support the law. The law, however, is constantly based on notions of morality, and if all laws representing essentially moral choices are to be invalidated under the Due Process Clause, the courts will be very busy indeed. Even respondent makes no such claim, but insists that majority sentiments about the morality of homosexuality should be declared inadequate. We do not agree, and are unpersuaded that the sodomy laws of some 25 States should be invalidated on this basis.

Id. at 196.

Chief Justice Burger's concurring opinion in *Bowers* rests explicitly on "Judeao-Christian moral and ethical standards." *Id.* at 197. "Blackstone described 'the infamous crime against nature' as an offense of 'deeper malignity' than rape, a heinous act 'the very mention of which is a disgrace to human nature' and 'a crime not fit to be named.' " *Id*. Chief Justice Burger concluded, "To hold that the act of homosexual sodomy is somehow protected as a fundamental right would be to cast aside millennia of moral teaching." *Id*.

Justice Blackmun's dissent in *Bowers* was joined by Justices Brennan, Marshall, and Stevens:

> This case is no more about "a fundamental right to engage in homosexual sodomy," as the Court purports to declare, . . . than *Stanley v. Georgia*, 394 U.S. 557 (1969), was about a fundamental right to watch obscene movies. . . . Rather, this is a case about "the most comprehensive of rights and the right most valued by civilized men," namely, "the right to be let alone." *Olmstead v. United States*, 277 U.S. 438, 478 (Brandeis, J., dissenting).
>
> . . . Like Justice Holmes, I believe that "[i]t is revolting to have no better reason for a rule of law than that so it was laid down at the time of Henry IV. It is still more revolting if the grounds upon which it was laid down have vanished long since, and the rule simply persists from blind imitation of the past. . . ." I believe we must analyze respondent Hardwick's claim in the light of the values that underlie the constitutional right to privacy. If that right means anything, it means that, before Georgia can prosecute its citizens for making choices about the most intimate aspects of their lives, it must do more than assert that the choice they have made is an "abominable crime not fit to be named among Christians. . . ."

Id. at 199 (*Blackmun*, J., dissenting). The Supreme Court, in the summer of 2003, decided the case of *Lawrence v. Texas*, 539 U.S. 558 (2003), which overruled the *Bowers v. Hardwick* case and raises important questions for future courts about the right to privacy for homosexuals, including the right to marriage. That case tested a Texas criminal statute directed specifically at homosexuals who engaged in prohibited sexual acts in the privacy of their own homes. The Supreme Court determined that homosexuals were free as adults to engage in the private conduct in the exercise of their liberty under the due process clause of the Fourteenth Amendment to the Constitution. The *Bowers* decision, according to the *Lawrence* Court, "misapprehended the claim of liberty there presented to it." Although Justice O'Connor, in her concurring opinion, agreed with the judgment, she would have decided the case on equal protection grounds without overruling *Bowers*.

Questions

1. Besides the fact that *Bowers* and *Lawrence* were due process privacy cases and *Romer* was an equal protection case, what factors may explain the difference in judicial attitude reflected in the three opinions, released within a decade of each other? Does the right to be free of discrimination in employment "matter" more than the right to intimate association? Can you think of a legitimate reason that a case like *Romer*, involving employment rights at least in a general sense, should discuss sodomy laws at issue in *Bowers*? Do recent cases about racial discrimination

discuss Supreme Court precedents overturning state antimiscegenation laws? Is Justice Scalia onto something in observing a change in the attitudes toward homosexuals in academic halls and larger cities?

2. Is it appropriate to invoke specifically sectarian doctrines and moral precepts in judicial opinions, identifying certain principles as "Judeo-Christian" when laws themselves must be secular? Justice Blackmun, dissenting in *Bowers*, clearly thought it is not: "The assertion that 'traditional Judeo-Christian values proscribe' the conduct involved . . . cannot provide an adequate justification for [Georgia's sodomy law]. That certain, but by no means all, religious groups condemn the behavior at issue gives the State no license to impose their judgments on the entire citizenry. The legitimacy of secular legislation depends instead on whether the State can advance some justification for its law beyond its conformity to religious doctrine." 478 U.S. at 210 (Blackmun, J., dissenting). Is it appropriate in a judicial opinion to employ a phrase such as "culture war" somewhat gratuitously when that phrase is incendiary and has been identified with the far-right end of the American political spectrum? The phrase recurs in Justice Scalia's dissent and was used particularly forcefully in *Lawrence*. Does such language enhance or retard civil debate? No Justice in *Romer* criticized the use of those color words as Justice Blackmun had seized on the "Judeo-Christian" language in *Bowers*.

2. State and Local Antidiscrimination Laws

a. Legislation

Increasingly, since Title VII does not forbid employment discrimination based on sexual orientation, states and municipalities are extending it, just as did Denver, Aspen, and Boulder. Generally these local laws protect against sexual orientation discrimination in housing, credit, public accommodations, and employment. Typical among them is the ordinance of the Town of Normal, Illinois, one of 15 Illinois jurisdictions with antidiscrimination ordinances. Normal is a small college town that abuts Bloomington; these "twin cities" are about 125 miles from the outer limits of Chicago, Illinois' largest city and one of the nation's largest cities. The ordinance sets up a seven-member Human Relations Commission to investigate claims of discrimination and to conduct hearings and conciliations. Normal Mun. Code § 10–2–2, as amended. Excerpts from the Normal ordinance are representative of local antidiscrimination laws.

SEC. 10.2–5. Prohibited Practices in Employment, Public Accommodations, and Financing.

1. Definitions. As used herein, unless a different meaning appears from the context, the following words or phrases shall have the meanings provided in this section:
   a. "Age" as used in the Ordinance shall be limited to individuals who are at least forty (40) years of age or over.
   b. "Commission" means the Town of Normal Human Relations Commission.
   c. "Lawfully Discriminate" and "Unlawful Discrimination" mean any differences in treatment based on race, color, religion, sex (including sexual harassment), marital status, ancestry, national origin, age, disability (unrelated to ability), matriculation, or sexual orientation.

d. "Employee" includes any and all persons who perform services under the direction and control of and for any employer for compensation, whether in the form of wages, salary, commission, or otherwise, excluding the parents, spouses or children of the employer and excluding independent contractors, although they may be subject to the Ordinance as employers or in any other capacity covered hereunder.

e. "Employer" includes any person within the Town of Normal including but not limited to owners, managers, supervisors, and others who serve a supervisory function who hire [ ] or employ [ ] any employee, and any person wherever situated who hires or employs any employees whose services are to be partly or wholly performed in the Town of Normal, but excluding any religious or fraternal corporation, association, society or organization with respect to the hiring or employment of individuals from their membership.

f. "Employment Agency" means any person regularly undertaking, with or without compensation, to procure employees for any employer, or to procure for employees opportunities to work for an employer or to recruit, refer or place employees.

g. "Disability" means any physical or mental impairment resulting from or manifested by anatomical, physiological, neurological or psychological conditions, demonstrable by medically accepted clinical or laboratory diagnostic techniques, and which constitutes or is regarded as constituting a substantial limitation to one or more of a person's major life activities. A disabled person is one who has a physical or mental disability as defined above, has a record of such disability or is regarded as having such a disability.

h. "Matriculation." The condition of being enrolled in a college or university or other postsecondary educational institution. It is the intent of this provision to give standing and protection only to persons enrolled in a college, university or other postsecondary educational institution.

i. "Person" includes an individual, partnerships, associations, organizations, corporations, legal representatives, joint stock companies, mutual companies, trustees in bankruptcy, receivers, labor unions, or union labor organizations, and any other incorporated or unincorporated organized group. The term includes, but is not limited to, any real estate owner, lessor, assignor, builder, manager, broker, salesman or agent, any lending institution, the Town of Normal, and any department, unit, officer, or employee of any of the above. Other governmental entities are excluded from this definition.

j. "Public Accommodation" means any business, enterprise or activity consisting of or involving furnishing, providing or making available to the public any goods, services, restaurants, eating houses, soda fountains, soft drink parlors, taverns, hotels, roadhouses, barber shops, department stores, clothing stores, hat stores, shoe stores, restrooms, theaters, skating rinks, swimming pools, public golf courses, public golf driving ranges, concerts, crematories, cemeteries, airplanes, boats, and any other public conveyances on land, water, or air, and other places of public accommodation and/or amusement. This paragraph shall not apply to any public school system.

    k. "Sexual Harassment" means any sexual discrimination which involves unwelcome sexual advances, requests for sexual favors and other verbal or physical conduct of a sexual nature when:

        1. Submission to such conduct is made either explicitly or implicitly a term or condition of employment; or

        2. Submission to or rejection of such conduct by an individual is used as the basis for employment decisions affecting such individual; or

        3. Such conduct has the purpose or effect of unreasonably interfering with an individual's work performance or creates an intimidating, hostile or offensive working environment.

    l. "Contractor" means a person who contracts with or proposes to contract with the Town to provide, goods and/or services for the current fiscal year or who has contracted with the Town during the last preceding fiscal year.

    m. "Vendor" means a person who sells or has sold goods to the Town during the current or last preceding fiscal year.

    n. "Marital Status" means the legal status of being married, single, separated, divorced or widowed.

    o. "Sexual Orientation" means the status or expression, whether actual or perceived, of heterosexuality, homosexuality, or bisexuality.

2. Prohibited discriminatory practices in employment, public accommodations and financing. It shall be unlawful for any person to commit any of the following acts of "discrimination":

    a. to permit or take action which unlawfully discriminates in a person's selection, status, or eligibility for employment, promotion or transfer, or for apprenticeship, membership, or conditions and privileges or benefits directly or indirectly related to one's employment, except for a bona fide occupational qualification;

    b. to cause or permit to be permitted, posted or circulated, any notice, advertisement, job order, requisition or request for applicants for employment or apprenticeship for the referral thereof which makes or has the effect of making unlawful discrimination a condition of applying for employment of or referral thereof or indicates the existence of such a condition except for a bona fide occupational qualification;

    c. (omitted)

    d. to unlawfully discriminate against any person in the full enjoyment of goods, services, facilities, advantages or privileges of any public accommodation;

    e. to unlawfully discriminate or to participate directly or indirectly in unlawful discrimination in connection with the terms of loans, guaranteeing loans, accepting mortgages or otherwise making available funds for loans, provided that lending money is one of the principal aspects of the person's business or is incidental to the person's principal business.

3. Citizen Protection. It shall be unlawful for any person to aid, incite, coerce or participate directly or indirectly in the doing of any act or practice declared in this Section to be prohibited or to unlawfully discriminate or to take retaliatory action against any other person because such person has opposed any practice forbidden by this Section or because such person has made a charge, filed a complaint, testified or assisted in any manner in any investigation, proceeding, or hearing under this Section.

4. Equal Employment Opportunity Compliance. All vendors, contractors or financial institutions who conduct business with the Town of Normal and have unlawfully discriminated may, upon the recommendation of the Commission and approval of the Town Council, be prohibited from doing business with the Town for a period of at least one (1) year. . . .

5. Nothing in this [chapter] shall prohibit a religious organization, association or society, or any other not-for-profit institution or organization operated, supervised or controlled by or in conjunction with a religious organization, association or society from engaging in unlawful discrimination while carrying out or furthering the religious activities of such organization.

6. Nothing in this [chapter] shall prohibit an employer from using marital status as a factor in determining eligibility for participation in employee benefit programs.

[The remainder of the ordinance enumerates the 180-day charge-filing limit, the powers and duties of the Commission, the conciliation process, the preponderance of the evidence standard for liability, provision of attorney fees and costs and limitations of damages to $2,500 per violation, $1,000 fines for failure to comply with the Commission's discovery orders, procedures for hearings, and specific fair housing provisions.]

The Normal ordinance's exemption for fraternal and religious organizations engaged in noncommercial or governance-related conduct that is essential to their missions is standard fare. *See, e.g.*, Chicago Mun. Code § 2–160–080 ("Nothing in this chapter shall apply to the decisions of a religious society, association, organization or institution affecting the definition, promulgating or advancement of the mission, practices or beliefs of the society, association, organization or institution"). Note that the ordinance covers contractors with the Town of Normal and that, unlike Title VII, the ordinance does not exempt small employers.

The ordinance of Davenport, Iowa, identifies the same protected classes as Normal's except for university students and uses substantially the same definition of sexual orientation except for extending protection as well to those who have a "record of" being homosexual, heterosexual, or bisexual. *See* Davenport Civil Rights Ordinance, ch. 2.58.030 (1999). The Davenport ordinance has been used as a model by citizens' groups in East Moline, Illinois, seeking to have that city enact a comprehensive human relations statute, but the East Moline group seeks to add protections based on gender identity as well. Gender identity is a protected class in the town of DeKalb, Illinois, which has a permanent population of around 30,000. *See* DeKalb Mun. Code, ch. 49, § 49.02(i).

Both sexual orientation and gender identity provisions, where a state or municipality chooses to include them, engender controversy. Sometimes the controversy is about the breadth of the language used, and this controversy often divides even strong proponents of extending the statutory protection to these groups. For example, the Normal ordinance prevents discrimination based on "actual or perceived" heterosexuality, homosexuality, or bisexuality. Thus, it purports to prevent homosexuals from discriminating against heterosexuals and also to protect, for example, heterosexuals who are "perceived" as being homosexual. Some find enforcing a law that forbids discrimination based on "perception" to be problematic, although the Americans with Disabilities Act forbids discrimination on the basis of being "regarded as" having a disability.

The language proposed by Quad Citians Affirming Diversity, a citizens' group seeking passage of a comprehensive human rights ordinance for East Moline, would extend transgender protection as well as sexual orientation protection:

> "Gender" means a person's actual or perceived sex, and includes a person's gender identity, appearance or behavior, whether or not that gender identity, appearance or behavior is different from that traditionally associated with the person's sex at birth.

The language proposed for East Moline is the language of the DeKalb Municipal Code. *See* DeKalb Mun. Code, ch. 42, § 49.02(I).

The language of the Minnesota statute is even broader:

> "Sexual orientation" means having or being perceived as having an emotional, physical, or sexual attachment to another person without regard to the sex of that person or having or being perceived as having an orientation for such attachment, or having or being perceived as having a self-image or identity not traditionally associated with one's biological maleness or femaleness.

Minn. Stat. Ann. § 363.01, subd. 41b (2001).

As observed in the Discussion Notes on Religious Discrimination in Chapter 11, the courts usually defer to state or local antidiscrimination laws when the plaintiff has been denied employment or a public accommodation based on sexual orientation and the discriminator is a commercial actor. On occasion, however, the right of a private, nonprofit membership organization to freedom of association guaranteed by the First Amendment to the federal Constitution might come into conflict with a local jurisdiction's commitment to outlawing discrimination. This was the case in *Boy Scouts of America v. Dale*, 530 U.S. 640 (2000). *Dale* involved a clash between two important interests: New Jersey's commitment to antidiscrimination principles and a private, nonprofit organization's right to determine standards for selecting those persons with whom it will associate. As the Supreme Court described the facts of the case:

> Petitioners are the Boy Scouts of America and the Monmouth Council, a division of the Boy Scouts of America. . . . the Boy Scouts is a private, not-for-profit organization engaged in instilling its values in young people. The Boy Scouts asserts that homosexual conduct is inconsistent with the values it seeks to instill. Respondent is James Dale, a former Eagle Scout whose adult membership in the Boy Scouts was revoked when the Boy Scouts learned that he is an avowed homosexual and gay rights activist. The New Jersey Supreme Court held that New Jersey's public accommodations law requires that the Boy Scouts admit Dale. . . .
>
> James Dale entered scouting in 1978 at the age of eight by joining Monmouth Council's Cub Scout Pack 142. Dale became a Boy Scout in 1981 and remained a Scout until he turned 18. By all accounts, Dale was an exemplary Scout. In 1988, he achieved the rank of eagle Scout, one of Scouting's highest honors.
>
> Dale applied for adult membership in the Boy Scouts in 1989. The Boy Scouts approved his application for the position of assistant scoutmaster of Troop 73. Around the same time, Dale left home to attend Rutgers University. . . . He quickly became involved with, and eventually became the copresident of, the Rutgers University Lesbian/Gay Alliance. In 1990, Dale attended a seminar addressing the psychological and health needs of lesbian and gay teenagers. A

newspaper covering the event interviewed Dale about his advocacy of homo-sexual teenagers' need for gay role models. In early July 1990, the newspaper published the interview and Dale's photograph over a caption identifying him as the copresident of the Lesbian/Gay Alliance.

Later that month, Dale received a letter from Monmouth Council Executive James Key revoking his adult membership [because] the "Boy Scouts specifically forbid membership to homosexuals."

In 1992, Dale filed a complaint against the Boy Scouts . . . [alleging] that the Boy Scouts had violated New Jersey's public accommodations statute . . . [which] prohibits . . . discrimination on the basis of sexual orientation. . . .

[Ultimately, the] New Jersey Supreme Court . . . held that the Boy Scouts was a place of public accommodation subject to the public accommodations law, that it was not exempt from the law [under the express exemption for a distinctly private entity], and that the Boy Scouts violated the state's public accommodations law by revoking Dale's membership based on his avowed homosexuality.

Id. 645–46.

The Supreme Court rejected New Jersey's conclusion that the Boy Scouts was such a large and nonselective organization as to make it quasi-public rather than a private membership organization and thus obliged to comply with New Jersey's nondiscrimination law. It held that the Boy Scouts, as a private organization engaged in expressive association, had the First Amendment right not to associate with a person whose presence in a position involving role-modeling for youth would send the message that the Boy Scouts condoned homosexuality:

The Boy Scouts seeks to instill [its] values by having its adult leaders spend time with the youth members. . . . During the time spent with the youth members, the scoutmasters and assistant scoutmasters inculcate them with the Boy Scouts' values—both expressly and by example. It seems indisputable that an association that seeks to transmit such a system of values engages in expressive activity. . . .

Id. at 649–50.

The Court held that a private membership organization could not be forced to accept a person whose "presence . . . would, at the very least, force the organization to send a message, both to the youth members and the world," that it accepted homosexuality. *Id.* at 653. Because of the unique structure of the Boy Scouts and the way in which it treats its adult volunteers as similar to employees, however, the Boy Scouts may be *sui generis*. Because of this, courts may be cautious about reading *Dale* broadly.

Lower courts applying *Dale* in the employment context have noted that *Dale* stressed the "role modeling" and expressive aspects of adult Scout leaders' roles, leaving unresolved the question of whether those with less contact with an audience, who are unlikely to be regarded as conduits of an organizational message, would be protected under a municipal ordinance prohibiting employment discrimination based on sexual orientation. An Illinois appellate court has read *Dale* to allow the Boy Scouts to refuse to hire a homosexual as a Scout leader or in a similar role-modeling capacity without violating the employment discrimination proscription of the Chicago Human Relations Act but not to refuse to hire a homosexual for a janitorial or clerical position. *See Chicago Area Council of BSA v. City of Chicago Comm'n on Hum. Rel.*, No. 99–3018 (Ill. Ct.

App., 1st Cir. 2001). This position is consistent with the position taken by the Chicago Area Council of the Boy Scouts in its appellate briefs in the case.

Discussion Notes

1. Examining the human relations ordinance of Normal, Illinois, how would you assess the accuracy of Justice Scalia's assertion in dissent in *Romer* that homosexuals achieve legislative success because they have reached critical urban mass, which confers political power on them? Normal, Illinois, is a city with less than 100,000 permanent residents. It is located more than 100 miles from Illinois' largest city, Chicago, which has a substantial and vocal gay and lesbian population as well as a number of transgender-rights activists. Illinois itself has no provision in its statewide Human Rights Act for sexual orientation or gender identity, although it is likely that one will be enacted within a few years. In 2001, the City of Normal amended its citywide ordinance to include sexual orientation, a move that had been proposed two times after Normal's more general ordinance, which excluded sexual orientation, was passed.

   Normal, Illinois, is so close to Bloomington that the two cities are often referred to as Bloomington-Normal, although they have different city governments. Normal passed an amendment to its ordinance outlawing sexual orientation discrimination without a great deal of community rancor. A few months after the amendment passed in Normal, the Human Relations Commission in twin-city Bloomington held hearings on amending Bloomington's ordinance to include sexual orientation. The subject language was drafted by the Human Relations Commission on its own initiative. However, the language drafted by Bloomington's city attorney pleased neither those with religious objections to homosexuality nor those who sought to protect sexual orientation by amending the statute. Religious conservatives opposed adding sexual orientation to the ordinance, and gay-rights activists and their allies opposed the city attorney's attempts to include language that incorporated portions of the Illinois Religious Freedom Restoration Act and exemptions for organizations engaged in expressive association, language crafted on the basis of the *Dale* decision. The language proposed by the city attorney was as follows:

   > Sexual orientation. The prohibition of discrimination on the basis of sexual orientation shall not apply to a person or organization if such application would be a substantial burden on the exercise of the sincerely held religious beliefs of such person or organization or if such application would significantly burden the ability of an organization engaged in expressive association to advocate public or private viewpoints relating to sexual orientation.

   The city attorney's proposed language was ultimately rejected by the Bloomington Human Relations Commission, which recommended to the City Council instead the exact language of the Bloomington and Chicago ordinances exempting religious institutions and nonprofits where discrimination is inherent in promulgating their mission. However, the

Bloomington controversy perfectly illustrates the current status of the debate over extending municipal protections based on sexual orientation. Opponents of extending such protection often make the claim that complying with antidiscrimination ordinances abridges their religious liberty, as did the landlords in *Thomas v. Anchorage Equal Rights Commission*, 220 F.3d 1134 (9th Cir.) (en banc), *cert. denied*, 531 U.S. 1143 (2001), discussed in the religious discrimination section in Chapter 11.

In 1997, the Supreme Court struck down the Religious Freedom Restoration Act as unconstitutional because it exceeded Congress's powers as applied to the states. *See City of Boerne v. Flores*, 521 U.S. 507, 536 (1997). In the wake of this ruling, many states moved to enact their own Religious Freedom Restoration Acts (RFRAs). The Illinois RFRA is typical of these state laws. Like the laws of other states that rushed to enact them following the Supreme Court's striking down of the federal version of the law, it purports to exempt persons from complying with laws of neutral application (such as local antidiscrimination laws) if complying would place a "substantial burden" on the individual's free exercise of religion and if the noncompliance is "substantially motivated" by the individual's religious belief. Even if the proponent of a RFRA justification for discrimination can meet both of these threshold requirements, the government can still enforce its nondiscrimination law if it can show that it has a compelling interest served by the law and if it has not drafted a law that restricts more religious freedom than is necessary to serve its compelling interest. *See* 775 Ill. Comp. Stat. 35/1 *et seq.* (Illinois Religious Freedom Restoration Act). *See also City of Chicago Heights v. Living Word Outreach Full Gospel Church & Ministries*, 196 Ill. 2d 1, 749 N.E.2d 916 (2001) (explaining test under Illinois RFRA).

Courts generally have not been sympathetic to claims that individual persons who own secular businesses may opt out of complying with local antidiscrimination ordinances based on their religious beliefs. RFRA may be an overly broad basis for an individual's claim to a free-exercise right to discriminate against a class protected by a local law. Some scholars, nonetheless, have viewed the compelling-interest prong of state RFRAs as a standard that compromises the state's commitment to assuring equality for all citizens. *See* Vaitayanota, Note, *In State Legislatures We Trust? The "Compelling Interest" Presumption and Religious Free Exercise Challenges to State Civil Rights Laws,* 101 Colum. L. Rev. 886 (2001); Lin, Note, *Sexual Orientation Antidiscrimination Laws and the Religious Liberty Protection Act: The Pitfalls of the Compelling State Interest Inquiry,* 89 Geo. L.J. 719 (2001); Cordish, Comment, *A Proposal for the Reconciliation of Free Exercise Rights and Anti-Discrimination Law,* 43 UCLA L. Rev. 2113 (1996). A possibility exists, with such a standard, that a particular court could find that the state has no compelling interest in eradicating discrimination based on sexual orientation.

While it is true that homosexuals and lesbians have not been held to be protected classes under federal civil rights provisions, that does not necessarily mean that the state lacks a compelling interest in prohibiting discrimination against them. *See, e.g., Gay Rights Coal. of Geo. Univ. Law Center v. Geo. Univ. Law Center,* 536 A.2d 1, 37 (D.C. 1987) (Washington, D.C., has a compelling interest "in eradicating discrimination against the homosexually or bisexually oriented" that includes "the fostering of individual dignity, the creation of a climate and environment in which each individual can utilize his or her potential to contribute to and benefit from society, and equal protection of the life, liberty and property that the Founding Fathers guaranteed to us all.")

The Supreme Court, in cases predating *Dale*, has generally observed that the state has a definite interest in prohibiting "invidious discrimination" that trumps an alleged constitutional right to discriminate: "[A]cts of invidious discrimination in the distribution of goods, services, and other advantages cause unique evils that government has a compelling interest to prevent[,] wholly apart from the point of view such conduct may transmit. . . . Such practices are entitled to no constitutional protection." *Roberts v. United States Jaycees*, 468 U.S. 609, 628 (1984) (rejecting Jaycees' free-association right to discriminate against women in upholding a state law outlawing gender discrimination in public accommodations). *See also Bob Jones Univ. v. United States*, 461 U.S. 574 (1983) (government's interest in eradicating discrimination is sufficiently compelling to defeat university's claim that denying it tax-exempt status due to racial discrimination interferes with its free-exercise right).

Questions

1. Do you think that the Supreme Court may find a compelling interest only in prohibiting discrimination against classes that it has accorded heightened scrutiny, such as gender and race, and not to those classes to which it has accorded intermediate or only rational-basis scrutiny?
2. Compare the Bloomington city attorney's proposed language with the exemption that appears in the Normal ordinance excerpted above. Which do you think is least likely to provoke litigation? Does a system of exemptions for religious organizations and their associated nonprofits, and for fraternal associations, strike you as more carefully crafted than the language the Bloomington city attorney had proposed? Would the Bloomington city attorney's language create an exception that swallows the rule, totally defeating the objective of protecting against sexual orientation discrimination?

   Plain-text exemptions in an ordinance may help the municipality to show that its language is narrowly drawn so as to restrict religion as minimally as possible without sacrificing the goal of nondiscrimination. If this is true, does crafting exemptions for religious organizations satisfy a state RFRA's requirement that government employ the least restrictive means of achieving its interest in prohibiting discrimination? *See Sherbert v. Verner*, 374 U.S. 398, 406–07 (1963) (suggesting the system of exemptions is pertinent to establishing that the state's interest is compelling and that the action it has taken is appropriate to serve that interest). *See also Swanner v. Anchorage Equal Rights Comm'n*, 874 P.2d 274, 283 n.9 (Alaska 1994) ("The most effective tool the state has for combatting discrimination is to prohibit discrimination; these laws do exactly that. Consequently, the means are narrowly tailored and there is no less restrictive alternative.").

3. Proposed Federal Legislation: Employment Non-Discrimination Act (ENDA):

During the last decade of the twentieth century, members of the U.S. Congress attempted to pass legislation that was directed at prohibiting discrimination in employment based on sexual orientation. The legislation, although similar to Title VII, was not an amendment to that law. The legislation would have prohibited real and perceived discrimination on the basis of sexual orientation. The various versions of this legislation did not allow for affirmative action plans, nor did they allow for separate disparate impact claims, as in Title VII. The 1996 version was defeated by a 50–49 vote in the Senate. Although it seemed, for a time, as if the necessary votes could be mustered to pass this legislation, the bill failed to reach the House or Senate for a vote.

chapter

4

Workplace Harassment

Problem 12

Joan Chan was recently hired by a shipping company as an accountant. Her supervisor is Jake, the Vice-President of Corporate Operations. She works with one other accountant, Pete. Soon after she began work, Pete asked her out on a date. She refused, but he persisted. He went so far as to suggest that if she dated him, she would get better treatment at the company because he was friends with Jake. This was not true, as Jake and Pete did not get along. Meanwhile, Jake began to hit on Joan. She refused his advances as well, and he began to give her less interesting job assignments after she refused his advances. She is very concerned about what she should do. The job market in her area is not very good, and she needs the job to support herself and her mother. Should employment discrimination laws protect her from this kind of behavior?

Problem 13

Anne Barker is a waitress at a bar and restaurant. Her boss, Steve, has made lewd remarks to her since she began work. He has also made repeated sexual propositions to her. He has implied that her job would be affected if she did not have sex with him. She has refused so far, but is concerned because she is a single mother and needs the job to support her kids. Steve has taken no adverse action against her yet, but he continues his threats, and he has also threatened to not give her a good recommendation for other jobs unless she dates him. Thus, she is afraid that she might not be able to get another job even if she leaves to get away from his harassment. Do you think this is a common problem? How can the law help her in this situation?

> ### Problem 14
>
> Cindy Johanssen works as a police officer for a local police department. Her co-worker, Ted Oliver, has continuously propositioned her. He is not her superior, but he is best friends with Mark Adams, the local Chief of Police. Each time she has refused one of Ted's propositions, something happens to her job assignments. Either she gets a terrible shift schedule, or she is given undesirable duties. She has not been demoted or terminated, but her shift assignments and duties have become more onerous than those of any other officer in the department. Some of her fellow officers have even complained on her behalf, but to no avail. Mark simply tells them that she needs to be "nicer" to Ted and to be a "team player." How can Cindy prove what is going on? Whom can she alert to this problem and will it help?

A. Introduction and Overview

This chapter and Chapter 5 explore the issues involved in workplace harassment cases—issues that are at the forefront of modern employment discrimination law. The law relating to workplace harassment is complex and still evolving. Yet it is poorly understood by the media and the public at large, and it is subject to misinterpretations and oversimplifications. One oversimplification that is quite common in modern parlance is referring to this area of the law as sexual harassment. Sexual harassment is certainly a major facet of the law relating to workplace harassment, and sexual harassment cases have given rise to much of the legal development and all of the Supreme Court decisions in this area, but harassment based on race, national origin, religion, disability, age, and gender (i.e., nonsexualized misogyny, etc.) also raise significant legal issues. Fortunately, much of the analysis developed in the sexual harassment context is relevant to other actionable forms of workplace harassment. This greatly simplifies our task, because it enables us to explore the law relating to workplace harassment as a unitary theme. Most of the cases included in this chapter and Chapter 5 involve sexual harassment. When there are significant differences based on the class protected, those differences will be set forth and explained.

This chapter begins with a section providing a brief overview of workplace harassment law. Section 3 is broken into two parts, each addressing a key facet of the law of workplace harassment. The first of these subsections is devoted to *quid pro quo* harassment. The second focuses on hostile work environment harassment, and Chapter 5 explores an issue relevant to both *quid pro quo* and hostile work environment harassment—namely, employer liability. It is essential for the student of employment discrimination law to understand at the outset that workplace harassment is a dynamic and exceptionally fact sensitive area of the law. Once you have learned the key elements for each cause of action, the hypotheticals provided help you understand the importance of both the facts in a given case and the perspective of the decision maker. As you will see, factors such as the "severity or pervasiveness" of harassing conduct are often the focus of legal battles over workplace harassment claims, and a small change in the facts or a variation in the viewpoint of the judge or jury can have an impact on the results in a given case.

Title VII provides

 a. It shall be an unlawful employment practice for an employer—

 1. to fail or refuse to hire or to discharge any individual, or otherwise to discriminate against any individual with respect to his compensation, terms, conditions, or privileges of employment, because of such individual's race, color, religion, sex, or national origin. . . .

Similar language appears in the Americans with Disabilities Act (ADA) and the Age Discrimination in Employment Act (ADEA).

As a general matter, workplace harassment violates Title VII's prohibition of discrimination in the terms and conditions of employment when it is aimed at an employee or group of employees based on membership in a protected class. Thus, harassment aimed at an employee because of his or her sex, race, color, religion, or national origin is actionable under Title VII, and harassment based on disability and age is actionable under the ADA and ADEA, respectively. There are two causes of action generally associated with workplace harassment: (1) *quid pro quo* and (2) hostile work environment. *Quid pro quo* is generally relevant only in sexual harassment cases. Claims of *quid pro quo* harassment, while still large in number, are less common than hostile work environment claims.

Hostile work environment was initially recognized by the Fifth Circuit Court of Appeals in *Rogers v. EEOC*, 454 F.2d 234 (5th Cir. 1971), a case brought under Title VII involving race discrimination aimed at a Hispanic employee. Since then, the cause of action has been developed significantly by the courts, legal scholarship, and the Equal Employment Opportunity Commission (EEOC). The Supreme Court addressed the hostile work environment issue for the first time in 1986 in *Meritor Savings Bank v. Vinson*, a case involving sexual harassment. In that same case, the Court also recognized the *quid pro quo* cause of action, which had roots in academic literature and earlier lower court decisions.

In harassment cases, it is the totality of the harassing conduct that determines whether harassment is actionable or not. For example, in hostile work environment cases, each incident of harassment is considered in light of the other incidents of harassment to determine whether the work environment is hostile or abusive.

A determination that harassment has occurred is not the end of the analysis, however. Employer liability is another significant issue. Individual employees are not generally liable in their personal capacities under Title VII. It is the employer who is potentially liable, and therefore proving employer liability is central to a successful workplace harassment suit. In this regard, the Supreme Court has clarified the test for employer liability in two supervisory harassment cases, *Burlington Industries, Inc. v. Ellerth*, 524 U.S. 742 (1998), and *Faragher v. City of Boca Raton*, 524 U.S. 775 (1998). That test will be discussed in detail in Chapter 5. It is important to understand, however, that co-worker and third-party harassment claims are not governed by the test set forth in *Faragher* and *Ellerth*. The tests utilized in co-worker and third-party harassment cases also will be explored in Chapter 5.

B. Actionable Forms of Workplace Harassment

As noted above, there are two causes of action recognized in regard to workplace harassment. Quid pro quo harassment generally involves sexual harassment. Hostile work environment applies not only to sexual harassment, but also to harassment aimed at other classes protected by antidiscrimination laws. As will be seen below, some cases involve both types of harassment, and in many sexual harassment cases, the border between *quid pro quo* and hostile work environment is not clear. Significantly, in *Burlington Industries, Inc. v. Ellerth*, the Supreme Court held that for purposes of employer liability in supervisory harassment cases, the line between the causes of action is unimportant except in regard to the availability of affirmative defenses. The Court held that the difference between the two causes of action revolves around whether tangible employment action was actually taken. Yet the Court did recognize that the distinction between the two causes of action is still relevant when determining whether harassment is actionable in the first place.

Workplace harassment is an evolving area of law, and for lawyers, employees, and corporations, it is an exceptionally important one. Workplace harassment claims, which were not even recognized 35 years ago, have become one of the major issues in modern employment discrimination law. Thus, it is essential for the student of employment discrimination law to have a firm grasp of the legal concepts in this dynamic area of the law.

1. Quid Pro Quo Harassment

Quid pro quo harassment involves the conditioning of terms or conditions of employment, such as hiring, raises, promotions, and continuation of employment, on sexual favors. In some cases, the threat has actually been carried out. In others, the employee succumbed to the threat but later brought suit. In still other cases, the threat was made, and the employee brought suit before it could be carried out. The threat that job benefits would be conditioned on sexual favors is the key.

This form of harassment is most insidious. Imagine a single parent who works as a waitress to support her family. The manager of the restaurant threatens to fire her if she does not date him. The job is her only source of income in an area where there are few jobs available. She is thus presented with a Hobson's Choice: date and/or have sex with a person she is not interested in or risk the health and welfare of her children. Even if she chooses the latter and the threat is not carried out, she might be treated more poorly by the manager than before she turned him down, and the psychological impact of the situation might be great.

At what point a claim is no longer *quid pro quo* but rather a hostile work environment claim was a point of great interest until 1998. Many courts held that if there was no tangible job detriment, one could not make a *quid pro quo* claim, and the employer's threats would be relevant only to a possible hostile work environment claim. This was especially important to the issue of employer liability because employers were generally held automatically liable for *quid pro quo* harassment. However, in 1998, the Supreme Court decided two cases that addressed this employer liability question: *Burlington Industries v. Ellerth*, 524

U.S. 742 (1998), and *Faragher v. City of Boca Raton*, 524 U.S. 775 (1998). These cases are presented in much greater detail in Chapter 5. For present purposes, the key is that they suggest that the difference between *quid pro quo* and hostile work environment claims might be important for purposes of establishing a cause of action, but that those differences are less relevant for purposes of employer liability.

This was an important aspect of the holdings in those cases, because many plaintiffs tried to fit their claims into the *quid pro quo* cause of action in order to establish employer liability. After *Ellerth* and *Faragher*, this is no longer necessary. In *Ellerth*, the Court wrote:

> Cases based on threats which are carried out are referred to often as *quid pro quo* cases, as distinct from bothersome attentions or sexual remarks that are sufficiently severe or pervasive to create a hostile work environment. The terms *quid pro quo* and hostile work environment are helpful, perhaps, in making a rough demarcation between cases in which threats are carried out and those where they are not or are absent altogether, but beyond this are of limited utility.
>
> . . . We do not suggest the terms *quid pro quo* and hostile work environment are irrelevant to Title VII litigation. To the extent they illustrate the distinction between cases involving a threat which is carried out and offensive conduct in general, the terms are relevant when there is a threshold question whether a plaintiff can prove discrimination in violation of Title VII. When a plaintiff proves that a tangible employment action resulted from a refusal to submit to a supervisor's sexual demands, he or she establishes that the employment decision itself constitutes a change in the terms and conditions of employment that is actionable under Title VII. For any sexual harassment preceding the employment decision to be actionable, however, the conduct must be severe or pervasive."

As suggested in the excerpt above, quid pro claims are still actionable, and a valid *quid pro quo* claim requires that threats be carried out. What constitutes a threat, what evidence is needed to establish the nexus between the threat and a request for sexual favors, and how one proves that the threat was actually carried out (as opposed to the possibility that the alteration in the terms or conditions of employment was based on factors unrelated to sexual harassment) are matters of some interest. The following case addresses some of these questions.

FARRELL
v.
PLANTERS LIFESAVERS COMPANY
206 F.3d 271 (3d Cir. 2000)

RENDELL, Circuit Judge.

[The Employment Problem]

. . . In 1992, Planters, then located in Winston-Salem, North Carolina, hired Douglas DeLong as its Director of Materials Management. One of DeLong's central tasks involved formulating a plan to cut operating costs in Planters' Materials Management Department.

Beginning in the early 1990s and continuing through 1997, Planters sought to cut its operating costs by consolidating its workforce. DeLong quickly reorganized the Materials Management Department, bringing together the Purchasing, Packaging Services, Graphic Design and Production Planning Departments within the Materials Management Department and placing them all under his direct authority. In August 1993, DeLong wrote a memorandum to Norm Jungman, his supervisor, suggesting Planters merge the Packaging Services and Graphic Design Departments as part of its consolidation. DeLong explained that he hoped to merge the two departments by late 1994 or early 1995.

In late 1993, Planters decided to discharge the Director of Packaging Services, Ronald Yonker. Almost contemporaneously, Planters approached Susan Farrell, through a recruiter, to become a Packaging Engineer in the Packaging Services Department. Based on her qualifications, and DeLong's recommendation, Planters subsequently considered Farrell as a candidate to replace Yonker as Director of the Packaging Services Department. At the time, Farrell was a packaging engineer at McCormick & Company in Hunt Valley, Maryland.

In January of 1994, Farrell traveled to Winston-Salem to interview. By mistake, Planters had Farrell interview with Yonker, who did not know of the decision to fire him and believed Farrell to be interviewing for another position. Concerned about her own job security by virtue of Planters' treatment of Yonker, Farrell sought assurances during the recruitment process. DeLong assured her that she would only be fired for poor performance. A number of individuals told her that Yonker had been repeatedly warned about his performance before the decision was made to terminate him.

Planters formally offered Farrell Yonker's position, re-titled as Senior Manager of Packaging Services, by letter dated February 4, 1994. Planters also promised to purchase Farrell's home in Maryland for $240,000 and pay for Farrell's relocation back to Maryland if her employment with Planters ended within two years because of "performance concerns or position elimination." Farrell accepted the offer on February 11, 1994 and relocated to North Carolina. She began work at Planters on March 28, 1994. Farrell's husband remained in Maryland.

In mid-November 1994, Farrell traveled to Chicago to attend Pack Expo, an annual packaging exposition, with a number of Planters and Nabisco, Inc. managers. While attending the show, DeLong told Farrell that his supervisor, Norm Jungmann, was about to be fired and that he would assume Jungmann's position shortly. DeLong then praised Farrell's work performance, told her that he felt her style complemented his, and asked her if she would be interested in becoming the head of the Industrial Engineering Department in addition to her duties as manager of the Packaging Engineering Department once he replaced Jungmann.

A few hours later, DeLong asked Farrell to accompany him the next day on a planned business trip to Puerto Rico to tour a Planters' facility. DeLong instructed Farrell to book tickets on the same flight as his, with seats together. Farrell made the arrangements. DeLong and Farrell had traveled on business trips together on two prior occasions.

During the flight to Puerto Rico on November 16, 1994, DeLong placed his hand just above Farrell's knee while telling Farrell that his wife became jealous when he traveled with Farrell. He asked Farrell whether her husband became jealous when she traveled with DeLong. Farrell responded by removing his hand from her leg and firmly telling him, "no, I don't give him a reason to and I suggest you do the same." Farrell says DeLong's demeanor changed when she rejected his advance: he turned away, curled up and slept or pretended to sleep. . . . Farrell and DeLong engaged in little or no further conversation for the rest of the flight. The next day, DeLong flew back to Winston-Salem, informing Farrell that he was leaving a day early in order to find out more about Jungman's termination.

Farrell also says that DeLong often commented when she wore a skirt, and states that in October, DeLong told her that she was pretty calm considering she was living apart from her husband and that he would be "bitchier" if he were her. However, after the November flight, DeLong never made reference to the advance on the plane, nor made a second advance.

On December 13, 1994, less than a month after the trip to Puerto Rico and less than two weeks after Planters paid for her possessions to be moved to North Carolina and purchased her home in Maryland, Gary Eckenroth, Planters' Vice President for Human Resources, went to Farrell's office and asked her to come up to his office. On the way, Eckenroth told her that Planters was going to eliminate her position. Once inside his office where DeLong was waiting, Farrell says Eckenroth told her Planters would call her termination a position elimination, in order to allow Farrell to retain benefits and give her a severance package, but that she was actually being terminated because of interpersonal problems with other members of Planters' management. When Farrell asked for specifics, DeLong mentioned Suzanne Jabbour and Ed Lyons. He also made general reference to some others whom he did not name. After Farrell protested, questioning why Planters had just paid for movers and purchased her house in Maryland if they were terminating her, Eckenroth said that he did not know that Planters had just moved her. Eckenroth then asked DeLong to leave the room. Once DeLong left, Farrell says that Eckenroth told her that he had not checked DeLong's report of complaints and he promised he would do so.

The next day, Farrell spoke with Jabbour and Lyons and they both denied making negative comments to DeLong, but confirmed that DeLong had asked them about her. Lyons also told Farrell that he had told DeLong that he felt DeLong had a personal problem with Farrell. That same day, Farrell says Eckenroth told her that Jabbour and Lyons came to him and confirmed that they had not made negative comments about her to DeLong. In fact, DeLong's own internal memorandum, dated December 8, 1994 states "Ed Lyons said she was helpful with his group." Eckenroth also apologized for not having investigated DeLong's claim, but told Farrell that she would have to leave because rumors of her termination had begun to circulate. A few days later, Eckenroth talked to her about accepting the severance package in return for releasing her claims. Farrell did not agree to any terms of separation and left her position on December 28, 1994.

DeLong's memorandum, dated December 8, describes the events leading up to Farrell's termination. The memorandum refers to three conversations he had on December 7 and 8 with various Planters' managers who came to DeLong and complained about Farrell. The memorandum then refers to a meeting between DeLong and Eckenroth, spurred by these conversations, where they "discussed the option of eliminating" Farrell's position and merging the Packaging and Graphics Departments as DeLong had suggested in 1993.

DeLong notes that he spoke with Planters' managers, including Jabbour and Lyons, "to gather feedback about Farrell." DeLong summarizes their comments: "The most common response received was, 'I don't know what she does.' 'A lot of talk but no results.' 'Nice suit, but nothing in it.' Ed Lyons said she was helpful with his group." DeLong then detailed his subsequent conclusions, including:

> When all the issues with her peers were discussed and other feedback received discussed, it was clear that I had to deal with Susan. I could not run an area with the type of conflict that existed between Susan and the rest of my staff. . . .
>
> [B]ased on these discussion and conversations with people over the last several months who found Susan very difficult to work with, i.e., Phil, Mike, Peggy and Rob, I made the decision to eliminate her job and combine Graphics and Packaging under Peggy as per earlier recommendation and hire another Packaging Engineer.

Farrell alleges that her rejection of DeLong's advance resulted in her termination, forming the basis of her federal claims. . . .

Planters disputes many of the facts alleged by Farrell, and the inferences that might be drawn from them, and describes different reasons for Farrell's termination. According to Planters, Farrell was terminated because upper management made the decision to consolidate the Graphics and Packaging Departments and Planters determined that Peggy Bryan, the head of the Graphics Department, would better serve Planters than Farrell in the consolidated position. According to Planters, Eckenroth met with Sandy Putnam, Vice President of Planters, to discuss cost containment and reduction measures in November of 1994 and specifically discussed the possibility of implementing DeLong's 1993 proposal that Planters should consolidate the Packaging Services and Graphic Design Departments in late 1994 or early 1995.

Planters explains that DeLong and Eckenroth met on December 8 to discuss the consolidation. At that meeting, Eckenroth asked DeLong to make a recommendation about whether they should keep Farrell or Bryan, which he did. Planters contends that DeLong's December 8 memorandum is materially consistent with their explanation for Farrell's termination, since it describes a discussion about consolidating departments, efforts by DeLong to canvass opinion about Farrell, and the decision to retain Bryan.

Furthermore, in his certification and deposition testimony, DeLong denied ever having suggested to Farrell the possibility of a promotion or making the advance on the plane. Eckenroth and DeLong also denied that they told Farrell that the decision was a position elimination in name only during their meeting with Farrell. In their certifications and deposition testimony, DeLong and Eckenroth also support the choice to retain Bryan by stating that they received complaints about Farrell's availability, ability and attitude throughout her employment. Planters points out that in the summer of 1994, a peer group gave Farrell the mock award title of "phantom leader," and in October, DeLong wrote a memorandum to Farrell telling her to increase her visibility at Planters.

[The Decision by the Trial Court]

After her termination, Farrell filed suit. The District Court granted Planters summary judgment on all of Farrell's claims. Farrell appeals and argues that the

District Court erred in dismissing her Title VII *quid pro quo* sexual harassment and retaliation claims as well as her North Carolina contract law claims. We discuss each in turn, beginning with Farrell's Title VII claims. . . .

The District Court determined that Farrell failed to produce evidence showing a causal link between the rejection and her termination, as is required to establish a prima facie case for each claim. . . . Relying heavily upon *Lynch v. New Deal Delivery Serv., Inc.*, 974 F. Supp. 441 (D. N.J.1997), the Court dismissed Farrell's [*quid pro quo*] claim because there was no evidence that DeLong either acted hostilely towards Farrell after she rejected his advance or pressed the issue again.

The District Court granted summary judgment in favor of defendants Planters Lifesavers Company and Nabisco, Inc., on all of Farrell's claims. *See Farrell v. Planters Lifesavers Co.*, 22 F. Supp. 2d 372 (D. N.J.1998).

[The Legal Issues]

Farrell claims that Planters and Nabisco violated Title VII in two separate ways and presents her discrimination claim as two different causes of action. She alleges that her termination was both an impermissible act of retaliation and an act of *quid pro quo* sexual harassment. In this case, it is clear that both of Farrell's claims rely upon the same essential facts: DeLong's sexual advance, her rejection of the advance and her subsequent termination.

This appeal raises a number of employment law issues relating to the recruitment, hiring and later firing of appellant, Susan Farrell. . . . Farrell appeals the dismissal of her retaliation and *quid pro quo* sexual harassment claims under Title VII and the dismissal of her North Carolina contract law claim. Acting as Amicus Curiae, the Equal Employment Opportunity Commission supports Farrell's appeal from the dismissal of her federal claims.

[The Decision and Rationale of the U.S. Court of Appeals for the Third Circuit]

For the reasons described below, we conclude that the District Court erred by requiring that the causal connection for both claims be supported by a pattern of antagonism, retaliation or hostility and, thereby, engaged in too narrow a review of the plaintiff's evidence. Considering the record before us, we find ample evidence from which to infer a causal connection between Farrell's rejection of DeLong's advance and her subsequent termination that enables Farrell to make out a

prima facie case for both her claim of retaliation and her claim of *quid pro quo* sexual harassment. Since we find that Farrell makes out a prima facie case on all the evidence before us, we need not decide whether the three to four week period between the advance and termination would be sufficient, if considered alone. . . .

Farrell's companion claim of *quid pro quo* sexual harassment contains a similar . . . requirement of cause and effect. *See Robinson v. City of Pittsburgh*, 120 F.3d 1286, 1296 (3d Cir. 1997). In *Robinson*—one of the few cases in which we have shed light on this issue—we stated that a plaintiff may prove a claim of *quid pro quo* sexual harassment by showing that "his or her response to unwelcome advances was subsequently used as a basis for a decision about compensation, [terms, conditions, or privileges or employment]." *Id.* at 1297. We further explained that "the plaintiff need not show that the submission was linked to compensation, etc., at or before the time when the advances occurred. But the employee must show that his or her response was in fact used thereafter as a basis for a decision affecting his or her compensation, etc." *Id.* . . .

. . . [O]ur law contains no requirement that the plaintiff show that the employer implicitly or explicitly threatened retaliation when making the advance. We explained in *Robinson* that "the plaintiff must show that his or her response to unwelcome advances was subsequently used as a basis for a decision about compensation, etc. Thus, the plaintiff *need not show that the submission was linked to compensation etc., at or before the time when the advances occurred.*" *Robinson*, 120 F.3d at 1297 (emphasis added). While evidence of hostility or repeated demands for sexual favors would strengthen any plaintiff's case, the lack of such evidence does not render it fatally flawed. By following the reasoning of *Lynch*, the District Court narrowed its analysis of Farrell's evidence of causation by effectively engrafting an element onto the cause of action that is not required under our jurisprudence. . . .

Robinson, however, as the District Court noted, does require the plaintiff to "show that his or her response was in fact used thereafter as a basis for a decision affecting his or her compensation, etc." *Id.; Farrell*, 22 F. Supp. 2d at 387. As with Farrell's retaliation claim, the question becomes what evidence may the court consider in deciding whether that nexus is sufficiently proven to establish a prima facie case. While we recognize that a retaliation claim under Title VII and an adverse job discrimination claim are separately codified, compare 42 U.S.C. § 2000e-3(a), *with* 42 U.S.C. § 2000e-2(a), we see no reason to conclude that Farrell's burden should be higher, or the scope of evidence permissibly considered narrower, in this cause of action for *quid pro quo* sexual harassment than in a retaliation claim.

Our decision in *Robinson*, where we reversed the grant of judgment as a matter of law in favor of the defendants, leads us to conclude that the analysis can be, in fact, quite broad. See *Robinson*, 120 F.3d at 1298–99. . . . In *Robinson*, the plaintiff alleged that her supervisor blocked her transfer because she rejected his advance. *See id.* at 1298. At trial, the plaintiff testified that her supervisor had repeatedly promised her that he would recommend her for transfer but that after a party where he pulled her into a compromising position for a picture, he told her that after talking to others in the department, they said she had a bad attitude. *See id.* The plaintiff also testified that a coworker confirmed that her supervisor blocked her transfer, had made negative comments about her to others, and had a romantic interest in her. *See id.*

We conclude that the inquiry into whether a plaintiff has shown that a rejection of certain conduct was "used as the basis for employment decisions affecting such individual" should not be constrained; rather, the court can consider circumstantial evidence and draw inferences in favor of the non-moving party in reaching this determination on summary judgment.

Thus, in cases where a plaintiff must . . . show that certain conduct was "used" as a basis for employment decisions, a plaintiff may rely upon a broad array of evidence to do so. We will now review Farrell's evidence, which we find, when considered as a whole, and reviewed in the light most favorable to Farrell, adequately establishes the necessary connection to substantiate . . . her prima facie case of *quid pro quo* sexual harassment. . . .

As a preliminary matter, we disagree with the District Court's rejection of certain evidence regarding DeLong's reaction to Farrell's rejection of his advance on the flight to Puerto Rico. . . . In her certification in opposition to Planters' motion for summary judgment, Farrell explained that after she rejected DeLong's advance:

> DeLong's demeanor changed, he turned to face away from me, curled up and either slept or pretended to sleep. We had little or no further conversation on the flight, and I worked alone for the rest of the flight. The following day DeLong abruptly left Puerto Rico and returned to Winston-Salem without me. . . .

Farrell, obviously, places great significance upon the relatively close timing between her rejection of DeLong's advance and her termination. The District Court found the timing to be suggestive in its analysis of Farrell's retaliation claim but did not find it sufficient on its own. [*See Farrell*, 22 F. Supp. 2d at 393 (finding the timing not to be "unusually suggestive").] We view the timing of Farrell's termination as suggestive for both of Farrell's claims. The timing evidence is also enhanced by the occurrence of two other events. Although DeLong states that he recommended Bryan over Farrell based upon meetings with other members of Planters' management, and Planters points to complaints raised about Farrell's performance during her employment, his decision to terminate her came only three or four weeks after DeLong praised Farrell and asked her about her interest in a promotion. Further, although Planters justifies Farrell's termination in part because of economic concerns and management discussions that took place in November 1994, her termination occurred less than two weeks after Planters purchased her house in Maryland and moved all of her possessions to Winston-Salem. . . .

[Planters . . .] urges that we should draw no inference from the timing of DeLong's suggestion of a promotion because Farrell was not terminated because she was incompetent, but because of a required consolidation and the determination that Bryan was a better choice than Farrell. Further, Planters points out that DeLong explained in his deposition that he discounted complaints about Farrell until late November and December because Farrell was new. Planters argues that nothing should be read into the trip to Puerto Rico because the trip was planned for DeLong before he asked her to join him and Farrell had been required to tour other facilities with DeLong. Planters disagrees that Farrell establishes any inconsistencies, arguing that the memorandum supports the view that DeLong responded to his meeting with Eckenroth by interviewing other managers and by subsequently choosing Bryan.

We recognize that different inferences might be drawn from the evidence presented in the record. On summary judgment, however, when viewing the sufficiency of the prima facie case, our role is not to act as factfinder. Instead, we must consider the evidence taken in the light most favorable to the non-movant and determine whether Farrell can show the causation required for a prima facie case of . . . *quid pro quo* harassment. We believe that, taken as a whole, the behavior of DeLong, the timing of Farrell's termination and the inconsistencies she raised in Planters' explanation for her termination are sufficient to create the required inference. . . .

Accordingly, we will reverse the District Court's order granting summary judgment in favor of Planters on Farrell's federal claims, and remand for further proceedings. We will, however, affirm the District Court's ruling precluding Farrell's state law breach of contract claim.

Questions

1. What is the difference between *quid pro quo* harassment and hostile work environment harassment? Does the difference depend on whether there is a direct, tangible job threat tied to a request for sexual favors? In the next chapter, you will read the *Burlington Industries, Inc. v. Ellerth* and *Faragher v. City of Boca Raton* cases mentioned in the materials presented earlier. After reading those cases, which primarily deal with employer liability, come back to these questions.

2. Under what circumstances does a request for a date, or even sex, support a *quid pro quo* claim? What other factors must be present? How would you analyze the three problems at the beginning of this chapter?

3. How can a plaintiff demonstrate a nexus between sexual overtures or comments and tangible job action? How did the court treat Farrell's evidence in this regard?

4. What would happen if an employee without any power to deprive a victim of a tangible job benefit threatens to do so if the victim does not become romantically involved with him and the victim erroneously believes he does have such power (not because of any apparent authority implied by the employer)? What if such action is later taken by a friend of the harasser who does have such authority?

2. Hostile Work Environment Harassment

The general test applied to hostile work environment claims has three elements, each with its own subelements. For present purposes, we will refer to the key elements as the objective standard, the subjective standard, and employer liability. Employer liability will be discussed in Chapter 5. This section will focus on the first two elements. It is the objective standard that has led to the greatest amount of controversy. Perhaps this is because the test must be both flexible and restrictive in order to be useful in the fact-sensitive area of hostile work environment. As we will see, however, both the flexibility and the restrictiveness of the test have led to disparate results in the hands of courts with different views of the world.

a. The Objective Standard—Terms and Conditions/Severe or Pervasive

Problem 15

Michelle Johnson works in a large precinct of a major city police department. She is the supervising dispatcher. She works the day shift, and she is responsible for overseeing the other dispatchers with whom she works. Most of the dispatchers are female, and all of them treat Michelle with respect. She is generally liked by her dispatcher coworkers. Some of the officers and other staff members, however, treat all the dispatchers poorly. They are generally rude to dispatchers unless they are dealing with them on official business, such as when a dispatcher is communicating with them in the field. Sometimes officers, or other staff members, play pranks on dispatchers. For example, they hide dispatchers' jackets and car keys. Michelle has complained several times to the Chief of Police about the conduct.

Michelle has had to face a different level of conduct. Several officers have propositioned her for dates or sex. Many officers have made lewd comments to her. Some of the clerical staff have e-mailed her sexual photographs and have made lewd comments to her. Sexual jokes are regularly made around the office. One officer, Lieutenant Noclass, has repeatedly made sexual comments to her, such as, "You have one hot butt" and "I would like to get you alone and screw you all night." Michelle has told Noclass to stop making those comments, but his behavior gets worse after her rebukes. The day after Michelle complained about the treatment of the other dispatchers, sex toys were left on her seat with a note saying, "You better lighten up, maybe these will help."

Problem 16

Daniel Ferrigno is a mid-level management employee at the southeast regional office of a major manufacturer. He is African American and is one of the few management-level African-American employees in his regional office. One other managerial employee has called him Sambo on one occasion. On Martin Luther King Day in 2000, a noose was hung from a lighting fixture above his desk, along with a note saying, "To celebrate black history. Oh by the way, I know where you live." Nothing was ever done to Daniel's house, but his son reported that a dark car with tinted windows often drives by the home with no apparent destination in the neighborhood. *See Vance v. Southern Bell Telephone & Telegraph Co.*, 863 F.2d 1503 (11th Cir. 1989), for a case with similar facts.

Problem 17

Stephanie Williams works as a secretary in the office of a feed and grain company in a rural town. It is a small company with 15 employees. She works for the President of the company, George Neanderthal. He regularly refers to her as "that dumb blonde" and has said on numerous occasions that "women should be at home taking care of the kids." When Stephanie's husband stopped by the office one day to take her to lunch, Neanderthal asked, in Stephanie's presence, why he didn't keep her at home barefoot and pregnant. On other occasions, he has told Stephanie and other female employees that women are only good for bringing men beer and having sex. Neanderthal has always given Stephanie good job evaluations, and he pays all his employees, including Stephanie, generous salaries and good benefits.

> ### Problem 18
>
> Fred Allen works as a delivery person for a freight delivery company. Fred has a severe speech impediment, which causes him to mispronounce words. Co-workers have nicknamed him "Quasimodo" and regularly call him "dumb-ass retard." Radio dispatchers often try to imitate him over the radio when communicating with him from the main office. When he complained of the conduct to his supervisor, he was told: "They're just fooling with you. Don't take it personally."

When one speaks of the objective standard (sometimes referred to as the objective reasonableness standard) in hostile work environment cases, one is generally referring to the severity or pervasiveness of the conduct giving rise to the claim of workplace harassment. Severity or pervasiveness can also be relevant to the subjective standard. It is in the context of the objective standard that the issues surrounding severity and pervasiveness are most complex. There are issues that immediately jump to mind: When is conduct severe or pervasive enough to create an actionable hostile work environment? What is the difference between "severity" and "pervasiveness" in this context, and how do these concepts interact?

However, there are also less obvious issues of equal, if not greater, importance. For example, from what vantage point do we examine the severity and pervasiveness of the conduct? Do we use the victim's perspective, and if so, what is that perspective? Do we use the perspective of a "reasonable person," and if so, who is that reasonable person in this context? Would using a reasonable person standard serve the purposes of Title VII, or would it simply reinforce the prevailing norms in a work environment affected by animus against a class protected under that statute? Think about the issues raised above as you examine the following materials.

MERITOR SAVINGS BANK, FSB
v.
VINSON
477 U.S. 57 (1986)

Justice REHNQUIST delivered the opinion of the Court.

[The Employment Problem]

In 1974, [the employee] Mechelle Vinson met Sidney Taylor, a vice president of what is now petitioner Meritor Savings Bank (bank) and manager of one of its branch offices. When [the employee] asked whether she might obtain employment at the bank, Taylor gave her an application, which she completed and returned the next day; later that same day Taylor called her to say that she had been hired. With Taylor as her supervisor, [the employee] started as a teller-trainee, and thereafter was promoted to teller, head teller, and assistant branch manager. She worked at the same branch for four years, and it is undisputed that her advancement there was based on merit alone. In September 1978, [the employee] notified Taylor that she was taking sick leave for an indefinite period. On November 1, 1978, the bank discharged her for excessive use of that leave.

[The employee] brought this action against Taylor and the bank, claiming that during her four years at the bank she had "constantly been subjected to sexual harassment" by Taylor in violation of Title VII. . . .

At the 11-day bench trial, the parties presented conflicting testimony about Taylor's behavior during [the employee's] employment. . . . [The employee] testified that during her probationary period as a teller-trainee, Taylor treated her in a fatherly way and made no sexual advances. Shortly thereafter, however, he invited her out to dinner and, during the course of the meal, suggested that they go to a motel to have sexual relations. At first she refused, but out of what she described as fear of losing her job she eventually agreed. According to [the employee], Taylor thereafter made repeated demands upon her for sexual favors, usually at the branch, both during and after business hours; she estimated that over the next several years she had intercourse with him some 40 or 50 times. In addition, [the employee] testified that Taylor fondled her in front of other employees, followed her into the women's restroom when she went there alone, exposed himself to her, and even forcibly raped her on several occasions. These activities ceased after 1977, [the employee] stated, when she started going with a steady boyfriend.

. . . Finally, [the employee] testified that because she was afraid of Taylor she never reported his harassment to any of his supervisors and never attempted to use the bank's complaint procedure.

Taylor denied [the employee's] allegations of sexual activity, testifying that he never fondled her, never made suggestive remarks to her, never engaged in sexual intercourse with her, and never asked her to do so. He contended instead that [the employee] made her accusations in response to a business-related dispute. The bank also denied [the employee's] allegations and asserted that any sexual harassment by Taylor was unknown to the bank and engaged in without its consent or approval.

[The Decision of the Trial Court and the U.S. Court of Appeals for the District of Columbia Circuit]

The District Court denied relief. . . .

The Court of Appeals for the District of Columbia Circuit reversed. . . . 753 F.2d 141 ([D.C. Cir.] 1985). Relying on its earlier holding in *Bundy v. Jackson* . . . 641 F.2d 934 ([D.C. Cir] 1981), decided after the trial in this case, the court stated that a violation of Title VII may be predicated on either of two types of sexual harassment: harassment that involves the conditioning of concrete employment benefits on sexual favors, and harassment that, while not affect-

ing economic benefits, creates a hostile or offensive working environment. The court drew additional support for this position from the Equal Employment Opportunity Commission's Guidelines on Discrimination Because of Sex, 29 CFR § 1604.11(a) (1985), which set out these two types of sexual harassment claims. Believing that "Vinson's grievance was clearly of the [hostile environment] type," . . . 753 F.2d, at 145, and that the District Court had not considered whether a violation of this type had occurred, the court concluded that a remand was necessary. . . .

As to the bank's liability, the Court of Appeals held that an employer is absolutely liable for sexual harassment practiced by supervisory personnel, whether or not the employer knew or should have known about the misconduct. The court relied chiefly on Title VII's definition of "employer" to include "any agent of such a person," 42 U.S.C. § 2000e(b), as well as on the EEOC Guidelines. The court held that a supervisor is an "agent" of his employer for Title VII purposes, even if he lacks authority to hire, fire, or promote, since "the mere existence—or even the appearance—of a significant degree of influence in vital job decisions gives any supervisor the opportunity to impose on employees. . . ." 753 F.2d, at 150.

In accordance with the foregoing, the Court of Appeals reversed the judgment of the District Court and remanded the case for further proceedings. . . .

[The Legal Issues]

. . . This case presents important questions concerning claims of workplace "sexual harassment" brought under Title VII of the Civil Rights Act of 1964, 78 Stat. 253, as amended, 42 U.S.C. § 2000e *et seq.* . . .

[The Decision and Rationale of the U.S. Supreme Court]

. . . We granted certiorari, and now affirm but for different reasons. . . .

. . . The prohibition against discrimination based on sex was added to Title VII at the last minute on the floor of the House of Representatives. 110 Cong. Rec. 2577–2584 (1964). The principal argument in opposition to the amendment was that "sex discrimination" was sufficiently different from other types of discrimination that it ought to receive separate legislative treatment. *See id.*, at 2577 (statement of Rep. Celler quoting letter from United States Department of

Labor); *id.*, at 2584 (statement of Rep. Green). This argument was defeated, the bill quickly passed as amended, and we are left with little legislative history to guide us in interpreting the Act's prohibition against discrimination based on "sex."

[The employee] argues, and the Court of Appeals held, that unwelcome sexual advances that create an offensive or hostile working environment violate Title VII. Without question, when a supervisor sexually harasses a subordinate because of the subordinate's sex, that supervisor "discriminate[s]" on the basis of sex. [The Bank] apparently does not challenge this proposition. It contends instead that in prohibiting discrimination with respect to "compensation, terms, conditions, or privileges" of employment, Congress was concerned with what [the employee] describes as "tangible loss" of "an economic character," not "purely psychological aspects of the workplace environment." Brief for Petitioner 30–31, 34. In support of this claim [the employee] observes that in both the legislative history of Title VII and this Court's Title VII decisions, the focus has been on tangible, economic barriers erected by discrimination.

We reject [the employee's] view. First, the language of Title VII is not limited to "economic" or "tangible" discrimination. The phrase "terms, conditions, or privileges of employment" evinces a congressional intent "'to strike at the entire spectrum of disparate treatment of men and women'" in employment. *Los Angeles Dept. of Water and Power v. Manhart*, 435 U.S. 702, 707, n.13 (1978), quoting *Sprogis v. United Air Lines, Inc.*, 444 F.2d 1194, 1198 (CA7 1971). [The Employee] has pointed to nothing in the Act to suggest that Congress contemplated the limitation urged here.

Second, in 1980 the EEOC issued Guidelines specifying that "sexual harassment," as there defined, is a form of sex discrimination prohibited by Title VII. As an "administrative interpretation of the Act by the enforcing agency," *Griggs v. Duke Power Co.*, 401 U.S. 424, 433–434 (1971), these Guidelines, "'while not controlling upon the courts by reason of their authority, do constitute a body of experience and informed judgment to which courts and litigants may properly resort for guidance,'" *General Electric Co. v. Gilbert*, 429 U.S. 125, 141–142 (1976), quoting *Skidmore v. Swift & Co.*, 323 U.S. 134, 140 (1944). The EEOC Guidelines fully support the view that harassment leading to noneconomic injury can violate Title VII.

In defining "sexual harassment," the Guidelines first describe the kinds of workplace conduct that may be actionable under Title VII. These include

"[u]nwelcome sexual advances, requests for sexual favors, and other verbal or physical conduct of a sexual nature." 29 CFR. § 1604.11(a) (1985). Relevant to the charges at issue in this case, the Guidelines provide that such sexual misconduct constitutes prohibited "sexual harassment," whether or not it is directly linked to the grant or denial of an economic *quid pro quo*, where "such conduct has the purpose or effect of unreasonably interfering with an individual's work performance or creating an intimidating, hostile, or offensive working environment." § 1604.11(a)(3).

In concluding that so-called "hostile environment" (i.e., non *quid pro quo*) harassment violates Title VII, the EEOC drew upon a substantial body of judicial decisions and EEOC precedent holding that Title VII affords employees the right to work in an environment free from discriminatory intimidation, ridicule, and insult. *See generally* 45 Fed. Reg. 74676 (1980). *Rogers v. EEOC*, 454 F.2d 234 (CA5 1971), *cert. denied*, 406 U.S. 957 (1972), was apparently the first case to recognize a cause of action based upon a discriminatory work environment. In *Rogers*, the Court of Appeals for the Fifth Circuit held that a Hispanic complainant could establish a Title VII violation by demonstrating that her employer created an offensive work environment for employees by giving discriminatory service to its Hispanic clientele. The court explained that an employee's protections under Title VII extend beyond the economic aspects of employment:

> [T]he phrase "terms, conditions or privileges of employment" in [Title VII] is an expansive concept which sweeps within its protective ambit the practice of creating a working environment heavily charged with ethnic or racial discrimination. . . . One can readily envision working environments so heavily polluted with discrimination as to destroy completely the emotional and psychological stability of minority group workers. . . . 454 F.2d, at 238. . . .

Since the Guidelines were issued, courts have uniformly held, and we agree, that a plaintiff may establish a violation of Title VII by proving that discrimination based on sex has created a hostile or abusive work environment. As the Court of Appeals for the Eleventh Circuit wrote in *Henson v. Dundee*, 682 F.2d 897, 902 (1982):

> Sexual harassment which creates a hostile or offensive environment for members of one sex is every bit the arbitrary barrier to sexual equality at the workplace that racial harassment is to racial

equality. Surely, a requirement that a man or woman run a gauntlet of sexual abuse in return for the privilege of being allowed to work and make a living can be as demeaning and disconcerting as the harshest of racial epithets. . . .

. . . For sexual harassment to be actionable, it must be sufficiently severe or pervasive "to alter the conditions of [the victim's] employment and create an abusive working environment." *Ibid.* [The employee's] allegations in this case—which include not only pervasive harassment but also criminal conduct of the most serious nature—are plainly sufficient to state a claim for "hostile environment" sexual harassment. . . .

. . . [T]he District Court's conclusion that no actionable harassment occurred might have rested on its earlier "finding" that "[i]f [the employee] and Taylor did engage in an intimate or sexual relationship . . . , that relationship was a voluntary one." 23 FEP Cases, at 42. But the fact that sex-related conduct was "voluntary," in the sense that [the employee] was not forced to participate against her will, is not a defense to a sexual harassment suit brought under Title VII. The gravamen of any sexual harassment claim is that the alleged sexual advances were "unwelcome." 29 CFR § 1604.11(a) (1985). While the question whether particular conduct was indeed unwelcome presents difficult problems of proof and turns largely on credibility determinations committed to the trier of fact, the District Court in this case erroneously focused on the "voluntariness" of [the employee's] participation in the claimed sexual episodes. The correct inquiry is whether [the employee] by her conduct indicated that the alleged sexual advances were unwelcome, not whether her actual participation in sexual intercourse was voluntary.

[The Bank] contends that even if this case must be remanded to the District Court, the Court of Appeals erred in one of the terms of its remand. Specifically, the Court of Appeals stated that testimony about [the employee's] "dress and personal fantasies," 753 F.2d, at 146, n.36, which the District Court apparently admitted into evidence, "had no place in this litigation." *Ibid.* The apparent ground for this conclusion was that [the employee's] voluntariness *vel non* in submitting to Taylor's advances was immaterial to her sexual harassment claim. While "voluntariness" in the sense of consent is not a defense to such a claim, it does not follow that a[n] [employee's] sexually provocative speech or dress is irrelevant as a matter of law in determining whether he or she found particular sexual

advances unwelcome. To the contrary, such evidence is obviously relevant. The EEOC Guidelines emphasize that the trier of fact must determine the existence of sexual harassment in light of "the record as a whole" and "the totality of circumstances, such as the nature of the sexual advances and the context in which the alleged incidents occurred." 29 CFR § 1604.11(b) (1985). [The employee's] claim that any marginal relevance of the evidence in question was outweighed by the potential for unfair prejudice is the sort of argument properly addressed to the District Court. In this case, the District Court concluded that the evidence should be admitted, and the Court of Appeals' contrary conclusion was based upon the erroneous, categorical view that testimony about provocative dress and publicly expressed sexual fantasies "had no place in this litigation." 753 F.2d, at 146, n.36. While the District Court must carefully weigh the applicable considerations in deciding whether to admit evidence of this kind, there is no *per se* rule against its admissibility. . . .

We . . . decline the parties' invitation to issue a definitive rule on employer liability, but we do agree with the EEOC that Congress wanted courts to look to agency principles for guidance in this area. While such common-law principles may not be transferable in all their particulars to Title VII, Congress' decision to define "employer" to include any "agent" of an employer, 42 U.S.C. § 2000e(b), surely evinces an intent to place some limits on the acts of employees for which employers under Title VII are to be held responsible. For this reason, we hold that the Court of Appeals erred in concluding that employers are always automatically liable for sexual harassment by their supervisors. See generally Restatement (Second) of Agency §§ 219–237 (1958). For the same reason, absence of notice to an employer does not necessarily insulate that employer from liability. *Ibid.*

Finally, we reject [the Bank's] view that the mere existence of a grievance procedure and a policy against discrimination, coupled with [the employee's] failure to invoke that procedure, must insulate [the Bank] from liability. While those facts are plainly relevant, the situation before us demonstrates why they are not necessarily dispositive. [The Bank's] general nondiscrimination policy did not address sexual harassment in particular, and thus did not alert employees to their employer's interest in correcting that form of discrimination. App. 25. Moreover, the bank's grievance procedure apparently required an employee to complain first to her supervisor, in this case Taylor. Since Taylor was the alleged perpetrator, it is not altogether surprising that [the employee] failed to invoke the procedure and report her grievance to him. [The Bank's] contention that [the employee's] failure should insulate it from liability might be substantially stronger if its procedures were better calculated to encourage victims of harassment to come forward.

In sum, we hold that a claim of "hostile environment" sex discrimination is actionable under Title VII, that the District Court's findings were insufficient to dispose of [the employee's] hostile environment claim, and that the District Court did not err in admitting testimony about [the employee's] sexually provocative speech and dress. As to employer liability, we conclude that the Court of Appeals was wrong to entirely disregard agency principles and impose absolute liability on employers for the acts of their supervisors, regardless of the circumstances of a particular case.

Accordingly, the judgment of the Court of Appeals reversing the judgment of the District Court is affirmed, and the case is remanded for further proceedings consistent with this opinion.

[Justice STEVENS filed a concurring opinion stating that he joined both the majority opinion and Justice Marshall's concurring opinion since he saw them as consistent with each other but believed the question of statutory construction answered in Justice Marshall's concurrence was "fairly presented by the record."

Justice MARSHALL filed a concurring opinion that was joined by Justice BRENNAN, Justice BLACKMUN, and Justice STEVENS. Justice Marshall would have addressed the employer liability issue and would have adopted the EEOC standard for employer liability in supervisory harassment cases—i.e., "that an employer is liable if a supervisor or an agent violates Title VII, regardless of knowledge or any other mitigating factor."]

HARRIS
v.
FORKLIFT SYSTEMS, INC.
510 U.S. 17, (1993)

Justice O'CONNOR delivered the opinion of the Court.

[The Employment Problem]

Teresa Harris worked as a manager at Forklift Systems, Inc., an equipment rental company, from April, 1985, until October, 1987. Charles Hardy was Forklift's president.

The Magistrate found that, throughout Harris' time at Forklift, Hardy often insulted her because of her gender and often made her the target of unwanted sexual innuendos. Hardy told Harris on several occasions, in the presence of other employees, "You're a woman, what do you know" and "We need a man as the rental manager"; at least once, he told her she was "a dumb ass woman." App. to Pet. for Cert. A-13. Again in front of others, he suggested that the two of them "go to the Holiday Inn to negotiate [Harris'] raise." *Id.,* at A-14. Hardy occasionally asked Harris and other female employees to get coins from his front pants pocket. *Ibid.* He

threw objects on the ground in front of Harris and other women, and asked them to pick the objects up. *Id.,* at A-14 to A-15. He made sexual innuendos about Harris' and other women's clothing. *Id.,* at A-15.

In mid-August 1987, Harris complained to Hardy about his conduct. Hardy said he was surprised that Harris was offended, claimed he was only joking, and apologized. *Id.,* at A-16. He also promised he would stop, and based on this assurance Harris stayed on the job. *Ibid.* But in early September, Hardy began anew: While Harris was arranging a deal with one of Forklift's customers, he asked her, again in front of other employees, "What did you do, promise the guy . . . some [sex] Saturday night?" *Id.,* at A-17. On October 1, Harris collected her paycheck and quit.

Harris then sued Forklift, claiming that Hardy's conduct had created an abusive work environment for her because of her gender.

[The Decision of the Trial Court and the U.S. Court of Appeals for the Sixth Circuit]

The United States District Court for the Middle District of Tennessee, adopting the report and recommendation of the Magistrate, found this to be "a close case," *id.*, at A-31, but held that Hardy's conduct did not create an abusive environment. The court found that some of Hardy's comments "offended [Harris], and would offend the reasonable woman," *id.*, at A-33, but that they were not

> so severe as to be expected to seriously affect [Harris'] psychological well-being. A reasonable woman manager under like circumstances would have been offended by Hardy, but his conduct would not have risen to the level of interfering with that person's work performance.
>   Neither do I believe that [Harris] was subjectively so offended that she suffered injury. . . . Although Hardy may at times have genuinely offended [Harris], I do not believe that he created a working environment so poisoned as to be intimidating or abusive to [Harris]. *Id.*, at A-34 to A-35.

In focusing on the employee's psychological well-being, the District Court was following Circuit precedent. *See Rabidue v. Osceola Refining Co.*, 805 F.2d 611, 620 (6th Cir. 1986), *cert. denied*, 481 U.S. 1041, (1987). The United States Court of Appeals for the Sixth Circuit affirmed in a brief unpublished decision, 976 F.2d 733 (1992).

[The Legal Issue]

In this case, we consider the definition of a discriminatorily "abusive work environment" (also known as a "hostile work environment") under Title VII of the Civil Rights Act of 1964, 78 Stat. 253, as amended, 42 U.S.C. § 2000e *et seq.* (1988 ed., Supp. III). . . .

We granted certiorari to resolve a conflict among the Circuits on whether conduct, to be actionable as "abusive work environment" harassment (no *quid pro quo* harassment issue is present here), must "seriously affect [an employee's] psychological well-being" or lead the plaintiff to "suffe[r] injury." Compare *Rabidue* (requiring serious effect on psychological well-being); *Vance v. Southern Bell Telephone & Telegraph Co.*, 863 F.2d 1503, 1510 (11th Cir. 1989) (same); and *Downes v. FAA*, 775 F.2d 288, 292 (Fed. Cir. 1985) (same), with *Ellison v. Brady*, 924 F.2d 872, 877–878 (9th Cir. 1991) (rejecting such a requirement).

[The Decision and Rationale of the U.S. Supreme Court]

. . . As we made clear in *Meritor Savings Bank, FSB v. Vinson*, 477 U.S. 57, (1986), [the language of Title VII] "is not limited to 'economic' or 'tangible' discrimination. The phrase 'terms, conditions, or privileges of employment' evinces a congressional intent 'to strike at the entire spectrum of disparate treatment of men and women' in employment," which includes requiring people to work in a discriminatorily hostile or abusive environment. . . . When the workplace is permeated with "discriminatory intimidation, ridicule, and insult," 477 U.S., at 65, that is "sufficiently severe or pervasive to alter the conditions of the victim's employment and create an abusive working environment," *id.*, at 67, Title VII is violated.

This standard, which we reaffirm today, takes a middle path between making actionable any conduct that is merely offensive and requiring the conduct to cause a tangible psychological injury. As we pointed out in *Meritor*, "mere utterance of an . . . epithet which engenders offensive feelings in a employee," *ibid.* . . . does not sufficiently affect the conditions of employment to implicate Title VII. Conduct that is not severe or pervasive enough to create an objectively hostile or abusive work environment—an environment that a reasonable person would find hostile or abusive—is beyond Title VII's purview. Likewise, if the victim does not subjectively perceive the environment to be abusive, the conduct has not actually altered the conditions of the victim's employment, and there is no Title VII violation.

But Title VII comes into play before the harassing conduct leads to a nervous breakdown. A discriminatorily abusive work environment, even one that does not seriously affect employees' psychological well-being, can and often will detract from employees' job performance, discourage employees from remaining on the job, or keep them from advancing in their careers. Moreover, even without regard to these tangible effects, the very fact that the discriminatory conduct was so severe or pervasive that it created a work environment abusive to employees because of their race, gender, religion, or national origin offends Title VII's broad rule of workplace equality. The appalling conduct alleged in *Meritor*, and the reference in that case to environments "'so heavily polluted with discrimination as to destroy completely the emotional and psychological stability of minority group workers,'" *id.*, at 66, quoting *Rogers v. EEOC*, 454 F.2d 234, 238 (CA 5.

1971), *cert. denied*, 406 U.S. 957, (1972), merely present some especially egregious examples of harassment. They do not mark the boundary of what is actionable.

We therefore believe the District Court erred in relying on whether the conduct "seriously affect[ed] plaintiff's psychological well-being" or led her to "suffe[r] injury." Such an inquiry may needlessly focus the factfinder's attention on concrete psychological harm, an element Title VII does not require. Certainly Title VII bars conduct that would seriously affect a reasonable person's psychological well-being, but the statute is not limited to such conduct. So long as the environment would reasonably be perceived, and is perceived, as hostile or abusive, *Meritor, supra*, 477 U.S., at 67, there is no need for it also to be psychologically injurious.

This is not, and by its nature cannot be, a mathematically precise test. We need not answer today all the potential questions it raises. . . . But we can say that whether an environment is "hostile" or "abusive" can be determined only by looking at all the circumstances. These may include the frequency of the discriminatory conduct; its severity; whether it is physically threatening or humiliating, or a mere offensive utterance; and whether it unreasonably interferes with an employee's work performance. The effect on the employee's psychological well-being is, of course, relevant to determining whether the plaintiff actually found the environment abusive. But while psychological harm, like any other relevant factor, may be taken into account, no single factor is required.

Questions

1. What are the elements of a hostile work environment claim according to the Court in *Meritor*? *Harris*? Does *Harris* alter the test set forth in *Meritor* or simply expand on it? If it expands on it, does it add sufficient clarity to the test? Could it? Is such clarity possible given the concerns expressed by Justice Scalia? What would clarity mean in such a fact sensitive area of the law? Would a rigid line-drawing test be desirable according to Justice O'Connor's opinion for the majority in *Harris*? Justice Rehnquist's opinion for the majority in *Meritor*?

2. What provision of Title VII is violated by a hostile work environment?

3. How does a trier of fact determine whether conduct is "sufficiently severe or pervasive to alter the conditions of the victim's employment and create an abusive working environment"? What factors should be considered?

4. As noted above, the hostile work environment cause of action applies not only to cases of sexual harassment, but also to harassment based on race, national origin, religion, gender (such as nonsexualized harassment based on gender role stereotypes), disability, and age. How would the test set forth in *Harris* apply in cases of harassment based on these other protected classes?

5. Why does the Court require an objective reasonableness standard? Why not simply base a determination of the severity or pervasiveness on the subjective perceptions of the victim who is alleging the harassment? Might the objective and subjective perspectives be the same in many cases?

6. Does the use of the objective standard suggest that the subjective perceptions of most victims of hostile work environment harassment are unreasonable? Or is it simply an attempt to prevent liability in the case of hypersensitive employees? If it is the latter, is the reason for this that the employer is able to recognize and remedy conduct that a reasonable person would consider sufficiently severe or pervasive, and if it does not, liability should attach, but it is much harder for the employer to address an environment that is hostile only to a hypersensitive employee and not to others within that individual's protected class? What if a supervisor or co-worker intentionally harasses based on a known hypersensitivity of the victim?

7. What should the perspective of the reasonable person be? Does it matter whether it is the perspective of a reasonable person of the victim's protected class i.e., a reasonable woman if the victim is female? A reasonable person from the harasser's background? A reasonable person from that work environment regardless of protected class? A reasonable person in society generally? What would be the implications of the various choices?

8. How would you analyze problems 15–18 presented at the beginning of this section?

b. The Objective Standard—The Victim's Perspective?

Problem 19

Janice McDougal works as a sales associate for a major clothing manufacturer. Her office consists of her, two other sales associates, her manager, Mike, and a secretary. Until her arrival, the secretary was the only female employee. Early on, Janice became offended by the frequent sexual banter in the workplace. The male employees constantly made lewd remarks about female customers and other women. They rarely made such remarks about Janice or the secretary but often made the remarks in their presence. The remarks were brazenly sexual, often describing in explicit detail hardcore pornography or referencing the perceived sexual abilities of customers and others. Some of the comments were very demeaning toward less attractive customers. When Janice initially complained to Mike, he said it is just "boys being boys." He did offer to "tone it down," but he seemed aggravated about the complaint, so Janice did not push the issue. The secretary never complained about the behavior and participated frequently, but she did tell Janice privately that "sometimes they go too far with the jokes." Eventually Janice sued for sexual harassment based on hostile work environment.

Problem 20

Amy Seligman is a lawyer in a mid-sized law firm. She is extremely conservative (personally, not politically). She works exceptionally hard and does not engage in office conversation of any kind, except for professional discussions. Several of her colleagues (male and female) refer to her as "old frosty." On a few occasions, a male co-worker called her a "hotty." She sues for sexual harassment based on a hostile work environment.

The cases discussed in the previous section demonstrate that the severity or pervasiveness of the conduct is a central element of the objective (or objective reasonableness) standard in hostile work environment claims. The key is whether the conduct is so severe or pervasive that a reasonable person would objectively find the work environment to be hostile or abusive. As noted in the introduction to the preceding section, this necessarily raises issues about the vantage point from which the "reasonable person" is to evaluate the conduct. Is it the victim's perspective? The harasser's? Is the reasonable person to view the conduct from the perspective of the dominant group within a work environment or from the perspective of a reasonable member of the victim's gender, race, etc.? The answers to these questions can have an impact on the outcome of a case. For example, from a reasonable male's perspective, some sexually harassing conduct might simply be horseplay, albeit tasteless horseplay, while at the same time a reasonable female employee might find the same conduct hostile or abusive.

In the wake of *Harris*, courts have taken varied approaches to this issue. Significantly, in regard to the objective reasonableness standard, the *Harris* Court may have created more questions than it answered. As set forth above, the Court held that conduct is sufficiently severe or pervasive to create an objectively hostile work environment when a reasonable person would find the working environment to be hostile or abusive. However, the meaning of "reasonable person" under this standard is unclear. Other parts of the *Harris* opinion might provide some insight into the question, but the case provides no clear answer.

The Court noted that its test for hostile work environment cannot by its nature be mathematically precise. Thus, the Court implicitly acknowledged that given the nature of hostile work environment claims, there must be some flexibility in the structure applied to those claims to account for the wide variety of situations with which courts will be presented. Such flexibility could include consideration of the perspective of a reasonable member of the victim's protected class.

The Court also held that "whether an environment is hostile or abusive can be determined only by looking at all the circumstances." Such circumstances may include the severity and frequency of the conduct alleged, whether it involves physical threats or humiliation as opposed to a mere offensive utterance, and whether it "unreasonably interferes with" the victim's work performance. The Court's mandate to consider the totality of the circumstances in a hostile work environment case reinforces the flexibility of the hostile work environment standard and possibly lends support to the position that the perspective of the victim may be a factor that should be considered among all of the circumstances.

Finally, the Court expressly refused to consider the EEOC Proposed Guidelines on Harassment Based on Race, Color, Religion, Gender, National Origin, Age, or Disability, which were issued in October 1993 and have since been withdrawn, and noted, "We need not answer today all the potential questions [the Court's test] raises." The Court's refusal to consider the Proposed Guidelines is relevant because the Proposed Guidelines applied a reasonable person under the same or similar circumstances standard, which included consideration of the perspective of members of the alleged victim's protected class. By refusing to consider the EEOC Proposed Guidelines in light of the objective reasonableness standard the guidelines proposed, the Court left open the possibility that it would support an interpretation of the reasonable person standard that means a reasonable woman when the victim is female, a reasonable African American when the victim is black, and so on.

Moreover, the EEOC's interpretive guidance regarding *Harris* and its effect on the EEOC Guidelines applicable to sexual harassment, EEOC Enforcement Guidance on Harris v. Forklift Systems, 405 Fair Empl. Prac. Man. (BNA) 7165 (discussing *Harris* and noting it is consistent with the EEOC Guidelines dealing with sexual harassment as augmented by EEOC Policy Guidance) suggests that the victim's perspective be applied in hostile work environment cases. That guidance takes the position that the reasonable person standard set forth in *Harris* does allow for consideration of the perspectives of members of the victim's class.

In *Oncale* v. *Sundowner Offshore Services, Inc.*, 523 U.S. 75(1998), the Court shed some additional light on this issue. The Court wrote:

> We have emphasized, moreover, that the objective severity of harassment should be judged from the perspective of a reasonable person in the plaintiff's position, considering "all the circumstances." *Harris, supra*, at 23. . . . [T]hat inquiry requires careful consideration of the social context in which particular behavior occurs and is experienced by its target. . . . The real social impact of workplace behavior often depends on a constellation of surrounding circumstances, expectations, and relationships which are not fully captured by a simple recitation of the words used or the physical acts performed. Common sense, and an appropriate sensitivity to social context, will enable courts and juries to distinguish between simple teasing or roughhousing among members of the same sex, and conduct which a reasonable person in the plaintiff's position would find severely hostile or abusive. 523 U.S. 75, 81–82.

This language strongly hints that the victim's perspective should be considered, but there is also language that suggests that the nature of the work environment matters as well. As the following cases suggest, the latter suggestion may undermine the former. Thus, *Oncale*, while strongly suggesting a focus on the victim's perspective, does not clearly answer that question and may raise a new issue that could make application of that standard more confusing: By focusing on the nature of the work environment, is the Court suggesting that a woman might reasonably feel a given pattern of conduct is harassing in an office setting but not in a factory setting?

Those who argue for using the victim's perspective often suggest that this is essential to carrying out the purposes of Title VII because a strict reasonable person standard could lead to the perpetuation of the prevailing level of discriminatory attitudes and conduct in the workplace. Those opposed often suggest that it creates an unnecessary double standard and actually undermines Title VII's focus on equal treatment. While the *Harris* opinion did set forth an objective reasonableness standard in the sexual harassment context, it did little to clarify the issue because the application of that standard is subject to a variety of interpretations.

The case that follows was decided prior to *Harris*, but the opinions do an excellent job of addressing both sides of this issue. Since the Supreme Court's decisions in *Harris* and *Oncale* do not clearly answer the question of whose perspective should be used in analyzing the objective reasonableness standard, the following case should prove useful in understanding what is at stake in the debate. It is followed by some excerpts from post-*Harris* cases that address this issue.

ELLISON
v.
BRADY
924 F.2d 872 (9th Cir. 1991)

BEEZER, Circuit Judge:

[The Employment Problem]

Kerry Ellison worked as a revenue agent for the Internal Revenue Service in San Mateo, California. During her initial training in 1984, she met Sterling Gray, another trainee, who was also assigned to the San Mateo office. The two co-workers never became friends, and they did not work closely together.

Gray's desk was twenty feet from Ellison's desk, two rows behind and one row over. Revenue agents in the San Mateo office often went to lunch in groups. In June of 1986 when no one else was in the office, Gray asked Ellison to lunch. She accepted. Gray had to pick up his son's forgotten lunch, so they stopped by Gray's house. He gave Ellison a tour of his house.

Ellison alleges that after the June lunch Gray started to pester her with unnecessary questions and hang around her desk. On October 9, 1986, Gray asked Ellison out for a drink after work. She declined, but she suggested that they have lunch the following week. She did not want to have lunch alone with him, and she tried to stay away from the office during lunch time. One day during the following week, Gray uncharacteristically dressed in a three-piece suit and asked Ellison out for lunch. Again, she did not accept.

On October 22, 1986 Gray handed Ellison a note he wrote on a telephone message slip which read:

> I cried over you last night and I'm totally drained today. I have never been in such constant term oil (sic). Thank you for talking with me. I could not stand to feel your hatred for another day.

When Ellison realized that Gray wrote the note, she became shocked and frightened and left the room. Gray followed her into the hallway and demanded that she talk to him, but she left the building.

Ellison later showed the note to Bonnie Miller, who supervised both Ellison and Gray. Miller said "this is sexual harassment." Ellison asked Miller not to do anything about it. She wanted to try to handle it herself. Ellison asked a male co-worker to talk to Gray, to tell him that she was not interested in him and to leave her alone. The next day, Thursday, Gray called in sick.

Ellison did not work on Friday, and on the following Monday, she started four weeks of training in St. Louis, Missouri. Gray mailed her a card and a typed, single-spaced, three-page letter. She describes this letter as "twenty times, a hundred times weirder" than the prior note. Gray wrote, in part:

> I know that you are worth knowing with or without sex. . . . Leaving aside the hassles and disasters of recent weeks. I have enjoyed you so much over these past few months. Watching you. Experiencing you from O so far away. Admiring your style and elan. . . . Don't you think it odd that two people who have never even talked together, alone, are striking off such intense sparks . . . I will [write] another letter in the near future.[1]

Explaining her reaction, Ellison stated: "I just thought he was crazy. I thought he was nuts. I didn't know what he would do next. I was frightened."

She immediately telephoned Miller. Ellison told her supervisor that she was frightened and really upset. She requested that Miller transfer either her or Gray because she would not be comfortable working in the same office with him. Miller asked Ellison to send a copy of the card and letter to San Mateo.

Miller then telephoned her supervisor, Joe Benton, and discussed the problem. That same day she had a counseling session with Gray. She informed him that he was entitled to union representation. During this meeting, she told Gray to leave Ellison alone.

At Benton's request, Miller apprised the labor relations department of the situation. She also reminded Gray many times over the next few weeks that he must not contact Ellison in any way. Gray subsequently transferred to the San Francisco office on November 24, 1986. Ellison returned from St. Louis in late November and did not discuss the matter further with Miller.

After three weeks in San Francisco, Gray filed union grievances requesting a return to the San Mateo office. The IRS and the union settled the grievances in Gray's favor, agreeing to allow him to

---

[1] In the middle of the long letter Gray did say "I am obligated to you so much that if you want me to leave you alone I will. . . . If you want me to forget you entirely, I can not do that."

transfer back to the San Mateo office provided that he spend four more months in San Francisco and promise not to bother Ellison. On January 28, 1987, Ellison first learned of Gray's request in a letter from Miller explaining that Gray would return to the San Mateo office. The letter indicated that management decided to resolve Ellison's problem with a six-month separation, and that it would take additional action if the problem recurred.

After receiving the letter, Ellison was "frantic." She filed a formal complaint alleging sexual harassment on January 30, 1987 with the IRS. She also obtained permission to transfer to San Francisco temporarily when Gray returned.

Gray sought joint counseling. He wrote Ellison another letter which still sought to maintain the idea that he and Ellison had some type of relationship.[2]

The IRS employee investigating the allegation agreed with Ellison's supervisor that Gray's conduct constituted sexual harassment. In its final decision, however, the Treasury Department rejected Ellison's complaint because it believed that the complaint did not describe a pattern or practice of sexual harassment covered by the EEOC regulations. After an appeal, the EEOC affirmed the Treasury Department's decision on a different ground. It concluded that the agency took adequate action to prevent the repetition of Gray's conduct.

[The Decision of the Trial Court]

Ellison filed a complaint in September of 1987 in federal district court. The court granted the government's motion for summary judgment on the ground that Ellison had failed to state a prima facie case of sexual harassment due to a hostile working environment. Ellison appeals.

[The Legal Issues]

Kerry Ellison appeals the district court's order granting summary judgment to the Secretary of the Treasury on her sexual harassment action brought under Title VII of the Civil Rights Act of 1964. 42 U.S.C. § 2000e (1982). This appeal presents two important issues: (1) what test should be applied to determine whether conduct is sufficiently severe or pervasive to alter the conditions of employment and create a hostile working environment, and (2) what remedial actions can shield employers from liability for sexual

harassment by co-workers. The district court held that Ellison did not state a prima facie case of hostile environment sexual harassment.

[The Decision and Rationale of the U.S. Court of Appeals for the Ninth Circuit]

We reverse and remand. . . .

Since *Meritor*, we have not often reached the merits of a hostile environment sexual harassment claim. In *Jordan v. Clark*, 847 F.2d 1368, 1373 (9th Cir. 1988), *cert. denied sub nom., Jordan v. Hodel*, 488 U.S. 1006, (1989), we explained that a hostile environment exists when an employee can show (1) that he or she was subjected to sexual advances, requests for sexual favors, or other verbal or physical conduct of a sexual nature,[5] (2) that this conduct was unwelcome, and (3) that the conduct was sufficiently severe or pervasive to alter the conditions of the victim's employment and create an abusive working environment. . . .

We had another opportunity to examine a hostile working environment claim of sexual harassment in *E.E.O.C. v. Hacienda Hotel*, 881 F.2d 1504 (9th Cir. 1989). In that case, the district court found a hostile working environment where the hotel's male chief of engineering frequently made sexual comments and sexual advances to the maids, and where a female supervisor called her female employees "dog[s]" and "whore[s]." *Id.* at 1508. Upon a de novo review of the facts found by the district court, we agreed that the conduct was sufficiently severe and pervasive to alter the conditions of employment and create a hostile working environment.

The parties ask us to determine if Gray's conduct, as alleged by Ellison, was sufficiently severe or pervasive to alter the conditions of Ellison's employment and create an abusive working environment. The district court, with little Ninth Circuit case law to look to for guidance, held that Ellison did not state a prima facie case of sexual harassment due to a hostile working environment. It believed that Gray's

[2] It is unclear from the record on appeal whether Ellison received the third letter.

[5] Here, the government argues that Gray's conduct was not of a sexual nature. The three-page letter, however, makes several references to sex and constitutes verbal conduct of a sexual nature. We need not and do not decide whether a party can state a cause of action for a sexually discriminatory working environment under Title VII when the conduct in question is not sexual. *See Andrews v. City of Philadelphia*, 895 F.2d 1469, 1485 (3d Cir.1990) (conduct need not be sexual); *Hall v. Gus Construction Co.*, 842 F.2d 1010, 1014 (8th Cir.1988) (conduct need not be sexual).

conduct was "isolated and genuinely trivial." We disagree. . . .

Although *Meritor* and our previous cases establish the framework for the resolution of hostile environment cases, they do not dictate the outcome of this case. Gray's conduct falls somewhere between forcible rape and the mere utterance of an epithet. 477 U.S. at 60, 67. His conduct was not as pervasive as the sexual comments and sexual advances in *Hacienda Hotel*, which we held created an unlawfully hostile working environment. 881 F.2d 1504.

The government asks us to apply the reasoning of other courts which have declined to find Title VII violations on more egregious facts. In *Scott v. Sears, Roebuck & Co.*, 798 F.2d 210, 212 (7th Cir. 1986), the Seventh Circuit analyzed a female employee's working conditions for sexual harassment. It noted that she was repeatedly propositioned and winked at by her supervisor. When she asked for assistance, he asked "what will I get for it?" Co-workers slapped her buttocks and commented that she must moan and groan during sex. The court examined the evidence to see if "the demeaning conduct and sexual stereotyping cause[d] such anxiety and debilitation to the plaintiff that working conditions were 'poisoned' within the meaning of Title VII." *Id.* at 213. The court did not consider the environment sufficiently hostile. *Id.* at 214.

Similarly, in *Rabidue v. Osceola Refining Co.*, 805 F.2d 611 (6th Cir. 1986), *cert. denied*, 481 U.S. 1041 (1987), the Sixth Circuit refused to find a hostile environment where the workplace contained posters of naked and partially dressed women, and where a male employee customarily called women "whores," "cunt," "pussy," and "tits," referred to plaintiff as "fat ass," and specifically stated, "All that bitch needs is a good lay." Over a strong dissent, the majority held that the sexist remarks and the pin-up posters had only a de minimis effect and did not seriously affect the plaintiff's psychological well-being.

We do not agree with the standards set forth in *Scott* and *Rabidue*,[6] and we choose not to follow those

[6] We note that the Sixth Circuit has called *Rabidue* into question in at least two subsequent opinions. In *Yates v. Avco Corp.*, 819 F.2d 630, 637 (6th Cir. 1987), a panel of the Sixth Circuit expressly adopted one of the main arguments in the *Rabidue* dissent, that sexual harassment actions should be viewed from the victim's perspective. In *Davis v. Monsanto Chemical Co.*, 858 F.2d 345, 350 (6th Cir.1988), *cert. denied*, 490 U.S. 1110, (1989), the Sixth Circuit once again criticized *Rabidue*'s limited reading of Title VII. *See also Andrews v. City of Philadelphia*, 895 F.2d 1469, 1485 (3d Cir.1990) (explicitly rejecting *Rabidue* and holding that derogatory language directed at women and pornographic pictures of women serve as evidence of a hostile working environment).

decisions. . . . Neither *Scott's* search for "anxiety and debilitation" sufficient to "poison" a working environment nor *Rabidue's* requirement that a plaintiff's psychological well-being be "seriously affected" follows directly from language in *Meritor.* . . . It is the harasser's conduct which must be pervasive or severe, not the alteration in the conditions of employment. Surely, employees need not endure sexual harassment until their psychological well-being is seriously affected to the extent that they suffer anxiety and debilitation. *Accord, EEOC Policy Guidance on Sexual Harassment*, 8 Fair Employment Practices Manual (BNA) 405:6681, 6690, n.20 (March 19, 1990). Although an isolated epithet by itself fails to support a cause of action for a hostile environment, Title VII's protection of employees from sex discrimination comes into play long before the point where victims of sexual harassment require psychiatric assistance.

We have closely examined *Meritor* and our previous cases, and we believe that Gray's conduct was sufficiently severe and pervasive to alter the conditions of Ellison's employment and create an abusive working environment. We first note that the required showing of severity or seriousness of the harassing conduct varies inversely with the pervasiveness or frequency of the conduct. . . . For example, in *Vance v. Southern Bell Telephone and Telegraph Co.*, 863 F.2d 1503, 1510 (11th Cir. 1989), the court held that two incidents in which a noose was found hung over an employee's work station were sufficiently severe to constitute a jury question on a racially hostile environment.

Next, we believe that in evaluating the severity and pervasiveness of sexual harassment, we should focus on the perspective of the victim. *King*, 898 F.2d at 537; EEOC Compliance Manual (CCH) § 615, ¶ 3112, C at 3242 (1988) (courts "should consider the victim's perspective and not stereotyped notions of acceptable behavior.") If we only examined whether a reasonable person would engage in allegedly harassing conduct, we would run the risk of reinforcing the prevailing level of discrimination. Harassers could continue to harass merely because a particular discriminatory practice was common, and victims of harassment would have no remedy.

We therefore prefer to analyze harassment from the victim's perspective. A complete understanding of the victim's view requires, among other things, an analysis of the different perspectives of men and women. Conduct that many men consider unobjectionable may offend many women. *See, e.g., Lipsett v. University of Puerto Rico*, 864 F.2d 881, 898 (1st Cir. 1988) ("A male supervisor might believe, for example, that it is legitimate for him to tell a female subordinate that she has a 'great figure' or 'nice legs.' The female subordinate, however, may find such comments offensive"); *Yates*, 819 F.2d at 637, n.2 ("men and women are vulnerable in different ways and offended by different behavior"). *See also* Ehrenreich, *Pluralist Myths and Powerless Men: The Ideology of Reasonableness in Sexual Harassment Law*, 99 Yale L. J. 1177, 1207–1208 (1990) (men tend to view some forms of sexual harassment as "harmless social interactions to which only overly-sensitive women would object"); Abrams, *Gender Discrimination and the Transformation of Workplace Norms*, 42 Vand. L. Rev. 1183, 1203 (1989) (the characteristically male view depicts sexual harassment as comparatively harmless amusement).

We realize that there is a broad range of viewpoints among women as a group, but we believe that many women share common concerns which men do not necessarily share.[9] For example, because women are disproportionately victims of rape and sexual assault, women have a stronger incentive to be concerned with sexual behavior.[10] Women who are victims of mild forms of sexual harassment may understandably worry whether a harasser's conduct is merely a prelude to violent sexual assault. Men, who are rarely victims of sexual assault, may view sexual conduct in a vacuum without a full appreciation of the social setting or the underlying threat of violence that a woman may perceive.

In order to shield employers from having to accommodate the idiosyncratic concerns of the rare hyper-sensitive employee, we hold that a female plaintiff states a prima facie case of hostile environment sexual harassment when she alleges conduct which a reasonable woman[11] would consider sufficiently severe or pervasive to alter the conditions of employment and create an abusive working environment.[12] *Andrews*, 895 F.2d at 1482 (sexual harassment must detrimentally affect a reasonable person of the same sex as the victim); *Yates*, 819 F.2d at 637 (adopting "reasonable woman" standard set out in *Rabidue*, 805 F.2d 611, 626 (Keith, J. dissenting)); *Comment, Sexual Harassment Claims of Abusive Work Environment Under Title VII*, 97 Harv. L. Rev. 1449, 1459 (1984); cf. *State v. Wanrow*, 88 Wash. 2d 221, 239–241, (1977) (en banc) (adopting reasonable woman standard for self defense).

We adopt the perspective of a reasonable woman primarily because we believe that a sex-blind reasonable person standard tends to be male-biased and tends to systematically ignore the experiences of women. The reasonable woman standard does not establish a higher level of protection for women than men. *Cf. Rosenfeld v. Southern Pacific Co.*, 444 F.2d 1219, 1225–1227 (9th Cir. 1971) (invalidating under Title VII paternalistic state labor laws restricting employment opportunities for women). Instead, a gender-conscious examination of sexual harassment enables women to participate in the workplace on an equal footing with men. By acknowledging and not trivializing the effects of sexual harassment on reasonable women, courts can work towards ensuring that neither men nor women will have to "run a gauntlet of sexual abuse in return for the privilege of being allowed to work and make a living." *Henson v. Dundee*, 682 F.2d 897, 902 (11th Cir. 1982).

We note that the reasonable victim standard we adopt today classifies conduct as unlawful sexual harassment even when harassers do not realize that their conduct creates a hostile working environment. Well-intentioned compliments by co-workers or supervisors can form the basis of a sexual harassment cause of action if a reasonable victim of the same sex as the plaintiff would consider the comments sufficiently severe or pervasive to alter a condition of employment and create an abusive

---

[9] One writer explains: "While many women hold positive attitudes about uncoerced sex, their greater physical and social vulnerability to sexual coercion can make women wary of sexual encounters. Moreover, American women have been raised in a society where rape and sex-related violence have reached unprecedented levels, and a vast pornography industry creates continuous images of sexual coercion, objectification and violence. Finally, women as a group tend to hold more restrictive views of both the situation and type of relationship in which sexual conduct is appropriate. Because of the inequality and coercion with which it is so frequently associated in the minds of women, the appearance of sexuality in an unexpected context or a setting of ostensible equality can be an anguishing experience." Abrams, *Gender Discrimination and the Transformation of Workplace Norms*, 42 Vand. L. Rev. 1183, 1205 (1989).

[10] United States Department of Justice, Office of Justice Programs, Bureau of Justice Statistics, Sourcebook of Criminal Justice Statistics 1988 at 299, table 3.19 (1989). In 1988, an estimated 73 of every 100,000 females in the country were reported rape victims. Federal Bureau of Investigation, Uniform Crime Reports for 1988 at 16 (1989).

[11] Of course, where male employees allege that co-workers engage in conduct which creates a hostile environment, the appropriate victim's perspective would be that of a reasonable man.

[12] We realize that the reasonable woman standard will not address conduct which some women find offensive. Conduct considered harmless by many today may be considered discriminatory in the future. *Rogers*, 454 F.2d at 238. Fortunately, the reasonableness inquiry which we adopt today is not static. As the views of reasonable women change, so too does the Title VII standard of acceptable behavior.

working environment.[13] That is because Title VII is not a fault-based tort scheme. "Title VII is aimed at the consequences or effects of an employment practice and not at the . . . motivation" of co-workers or employers. *Rogers*, 454 F.2d at 239; see also *Griggs v. Duke Power Co.*, 401 U.S. 424, 432, (1971) (the absence of discriminatory intent does not redeem an otherwise unlawful employment practice). To avoid liability under Title VII, employers may have to educate and sensitize their workforce to eliminate conduct which a reasonable victim would consider unlawful sexual harassment. *See* 29 C.F.R. § 1604.11(f) ("Prevention is the best tool for the elimination of sexual harassment.")

The facts of this case illustrate the importance of considering the victim's perspective. Analyzing the facts from the alleged harasser's viewpoint, Gray could be portrayed as a modern-day Cyrano de Bergerac wishing no more than to woo Ellison with his words. . . . There is no evidence that Gray harbored ill will toward Ellison. He even offered in his "love letter" to leave her alone if she wished. Examined in this light, it is not difficult to see why the district court characterized Gray's conduct as isolated and trivial.

Ellison, however, did not consider the acts to be trivial. Gray's first note shocked and frightened her. After receiving the three-page letter, she became really upset and frightened again. She immediately requested that she or Gray be transferred. Her supervisor's prompt response suggests that she, too, did not consider the conduct trivial. When Ellison learned that Gray arranged to return to San Mateo, she immediately asked to transfer, and she immediately filed an official complaint.

We cannot say as a matter of law that Ellison's reaction was idiosyncratic or hyper-sensitive. We believe that a reasonable woman could have had a similar reaction. After receiving the first bizarre note from Gray, a person she barely knew, Ellison asked a co-worker to tell Gray to leave her alone. Despite her request, Gray sent her a long, passionate, disturbing letter. He told her he had been "watching" and "experiencing" her; he made repeated references to sex; he said he would write again. Ellison had no way of knowing what Gray would do next. A reasonable woman could consider Gray's conduct, as alleged by

Ellison, sufficiently severe and pervasive to alter a condition of employment and create an abusive working environment.

Sexual harassment is a major problem in the workplace.[15] Adopting the victim's perspective ensures that courts will not "sustain ingrained notions of reasonable behavior fashioned by the offenders." *Lipsett*, 864 F.2d at 898, quoting, *Rabidue*, 805 F.2d at 626 (Keith, J., dissenting). Congress did not enact Title VII to codify prevailing sexist prejudices. To the contrary, "Congress designed Title VII to prevent the perpetuation of stereotypes and a sense of degradation which serve to close or discourage employment opportunities for women." *Andrews*, 895 F.2d at 1483. We hope that over time both men and women will learn what conduct offends reasonable members of the other sex. When employers and employees internalize the standard of workplace conduct we establish today, the current gap in perception between the sexes will be bridged.

We next must determine what remedial actions by employers shield them from liability under Title VII for sexual harassment by co-workers. The Supreme Court in *Meritor* did not address employer liability for sexual harassment by co-workers. In that case, the Court discussed employer liability for a hostile environment created by a supervisor.

[The section of the opinion addressing employer liability and appropriate remedial measures is omitted. For analysis of those issues, see Chapter 5.]

. . . We reverse the district court's decision that Ellison did not allege a prima facie case of sexual harassment due to a hostile working environment, and we remand for further proceedings consistent with this opinion. Although we have considered the evidence

---

[13] If sexual comments or sexual advances are in fact welcomed by the recipient, they, of course, do not constitute sexual harassment. Title VII's prohibition of sex discrimination in employment does not require a totally desexualized work place.

[15] Over 40 percent of female federal employees reported incidents of sexual harassment in 1987, roughly the same number as in 1980. United States Merit Systems Protection Board, Sexual Harassment in the Federal Government: An Update 11 (1988). Victims of sexual harassment "pay all the intangible emotional costs inflicted by anger, humiliation, frustration, withdrawal, dysfunction in family life," as well as medical expenses, litigation expenses, job search expenses, and the loss of valuable sick leave and annual leave. *Id.* at 42. Sexual harassment cost the federal government $267 million from May 1985 to May 1987 for losses in productivity, sick leave costs, and employee replacement costs. *Id.* at 39.

in the light most favorable to Ellison because the district court granted the government's motion for summary judgment, we, of course, reserve for the district court the resolution of all factual issues.

REVERSED and REMANDED.

STEPHENS, District Judge, dissenting:

This case comes to us on appeal in the wake of the granting of a summary judgment motion. There was no trial, therefore no opportunities for cross examination of the witnesses. In addition, there are factual gaps in the record that can only lead by speculation. Consequently, I believe that it is an inappropriate case with which to establish a new legal precedent which will be binding in all subsequent cases of like nature in the Ninth Circuit. I refer to the majority's use of the term "reasonable woman," a term I find ambiguous and therefore inadequate.

Nowhere in section 2000e of Title VII, the section under which the plaintiff in this case brought suit, is there any indication that Congress intended to provide for any other than equal treatment in the area of civil rights. The legislation is designed to achieve a balanced and generally gender neutral and harmonious workplace which would improve production and the quality of the employees' lives. In fact, the Supreme Court has shown a preference against systems that are not gender or race neutral, such as hiring quotas. *See City of Richmond v. J. A. Croson Co.*, 488 U.S. 469, (1989). While women may be the most frequent targets of this type of conduct that is at issue in this case, they are not the only targets. I believe that it is incumbent upon the court in this case to use terminology that will meet the needs of all who seek recourse under this section of Title VII. Possible alternatives that are more in line with a gender neutral approach include "victim," "target," or "person."

The term "reasonable man" as it is used in the law of torts, traditionally refers to the average adult person, regardless of gender, and the conduct that can reasonably be expected of him or her. For the purposes of the legal issues that are being addressed, such a term assumes that it is applicable to all persons. Section 2000e of Title VII presupposes the use of a legal term that can apply to all persons and the impossibility of a more individually tailored standard. It is clear that the authors of the majority opinion intend a difference between the "reasonable woman" and the "reasonable man" in Title VII cases on the assumption that men do not have the same sensibilities as women. This is not necessarily true. A man's re-

sponse to circumstances faced by women and their effect upon women can be and in given circumstances may be expected to be understood by men.

It takes no stretch of the imagination to envision two complaints emanating from the same workplace regarding the same conditions, one brought by a woman and the other by a man. Application of the "new standard" presents a puzzlement which is born of the assumption that men's eyes do not see what a woman sees through her eyes. I find it surprising that the majority finds no need for evidence on any of these subjects. I am not sure whether the majority also concludes that the woman and the man in question are also reasonable without evidence on this subject. I am irresistibly drawn to the view that the conditions of the workplace itself should be examined as affected, among other things, by the conduct of the people working there as to whether the workplace as existing is conducive to fulfilling the goals of Title VII. In any event, these are unresolved factual issues which preclude summary judgment.

The focus on the victim of the sexually discriminatory conduct has its parallel in rape trials in the focus put by the defense on the victim's conduct rather than on the unlawful conduct of the person accused. Modern feminists have pointed out that concentration by the defense upon evidence concerning the background, appearance and conduct of women claiming to have been raped must be carefully controlled by the court to avoid effectively shifting the burden of proof to the victim. It is the accused, not the victim who is on trial, and it is therefore the conduct of the accused, not that of the victim, that should be subjected to scrutiny. . . . Many state legislatures have responded to this viewpoint, and rules governing the presentation of evidence in rape cases have evolved accordingly. . . . *See generally*, Galvin, *Shielding Rape Victims in the State and Federal Courts: A Proposal for the Second Decade*, 70 Minn. L. Rev. 763 (April 1986).

It is my opinion that the case should be reversed with instructions to proceed to trial. This would certainly lead to filling in the factual gaps left by the scanty record, such as what happened at the time of or after the visit of Ellison to Gray's house to cause her to be subsequently fearful of his presence. The circumstances existing in the workplace where only men are employed are different than they are where there are both male and female employees. The existence of the differences is readily recognizable and the conduct of employees can be changed appropriately. This is what Title VII requires. Whether a man or a woman has sensibilities peculiar to the person and what they are is not necessarily known. Until they become known by manifesting themselves in an obvious way, they do not become part of the circumstances of the work place. Consequently, the governing element in the equation is the workplace itself, not concepts or viewpoints of individual employees. This does not conflict with existing legal concepts.

The creation of the proposed "new standard" which applies only to women will not necessarily come to the aid of all potential victims of the type of misconduct that is at issue in this case. I believe that a gender neutral standard would greatly contribute to the clarity of this and future cases in the same area.

Summary judgment is not appropriate in this case.

c. Post-*Harris* Cases

The following are brief excerpts from post-*Harris* cases that have addressed the objective reasonableness standard. There is no clear agreement among the circuits about whether the perspective of a reasonable person or a reasonable woman/member of the victim's class should be used. The first case suggests the use of the reasonable woman standard and the second the use of the reasonable person standard. Both cases cite to *Harris* in laying out the overall objective reasonableness test. (The first case, which was decided by the ninth Circuit, cites to *Ellison* on the specific issue of the reasonable woman standard, implying that this is consistent with *Harris*.)

BROOKS
v.
CITY OF SAN MATEO
229 F.3d 917 (9th Cir. 2000)

KOZINSKI, Circuit Judge. . . .

[The Decision and Rationale of the U.S. Court of Appeals for the Ninth Circuit]

In order to prevail on her hostile work environment claim, Brooks must show that her "workplace [was] permeated with discriminatory intimidation . . . that [was] sufficiently severe or pervasive to alter the conditions of [her] employment and create an abusive working environment." *Harris*, 510 U.S. at 21. . . . "The working environment must both subjectively and objectively be perceived as abusive." *Fuller v. City of Oakland*, 47 F.3d 1522, 1527 (9th Cir. 1995) (citing *Harris*, 510 U.S. at 21–22). We use a totality of the circumstances test to determine whether a plaintiff's allegations make out a colorable claim of hostile work environment. *See Harris*, 510 U.S. at 23. *Harris* lists frequency, severity and level of interference with work performance among the factors particularly relevant to the inquiry. When assessing the objective portion of a plaintiff's claim, we assume the perspective of the reasonable victim. *See Ellison v. Brady*, 924 F.2d 872, 879 (9th Cir. 1991) ("[A] female plaintiff states a prima facie case of hostile environment sexual harassment when she alleges conduct which a reasonable woman would consider sufficiently severe or pervasive to alter the conditions of employment and create an abusive working environment. . . . ")

Brooks claims the incident pervaded her work environment to such a degree that she required psychological help and even then was unable to successfully return to her job. She has alleged sufficient facts to support the subjective portion of her hostile work environment claim. The question remains whether her apprehension was objectively reasonable. . . .

Which is why Selvaggio's conduct, while relevant, is not the primary focus of our inquiry. No one could reasonably dispute that what Selvaggio did was egregious; he was, after all, immediately removed from his job and prosecuted. He spent time in jail. But it is the city, and not Selvaggio, who is the defendant here. To hold her employer liable for sexual harassment under Title VII, Brooks must show that she reasonably feared she would be subject to such misconduct in the future because the city encouraged or tolerated Selvaggio's harassment. . . .

Brooks next attempts to morph Selvaggio's single assault into a course of conduct by claiming that each of his improper touchings constituted a separate incident. While Selvaggio did touch Brooks inappropriately on her stomach and breast, this happened within the course of a few minutes and was part of a single episode. Additionally, Selvaggio had no chance to become bolder because the city removed him from the workplace once his actions were uncovered. No reasonable woman in Brooks's position would believe that Selvaggio's misconduct had permanently altered the terms or conditions of her employment. . . .

We need not decide whether a single instance of sexual harassment can ever be sufficient to establish a hostile work environment. . . . As we have previously held, "the required showing of severity or seriousness of the harassing conduct varies inversely with the pervasiveness or frequency of the conduct." *Ellison,* 924 F.2d at 878 (citing *King v. Board of Regents,* 898 F.2d 533, 537 (7th Cir. 1990)). If a single incident can ever suffice to support a hostile work environment claim, the incident must be extremely severe. *See* EEOC Policy Guide, page 6 *supra,* at 405:6690–91 ("[A] single unusually severe incident of harassment may be sufficient to constitute a Title VII violation; the more severe the harassment, the less need to show a repetitive series of incidents. This is particularly true when the harassment is physical.") . . .

. . . Utilizing the *Harris* factors of frequency, severity and intensity of interference with working conditions, we cannot say that a reasonable woman in Brooks's position would consider the terms and conditions of her employment altered by Selvaggio's actions. . . . Brooks was harassed on a single occasion for a matter of minutes in a way that did not impair her ability to do her job in the long-term, especially given that the city took prompt steps to remove Selvaggio from the workplace. . . .

. . . Our holding in no way condones Selvaggio's actions. Quite the opposite: The conduct of which Brooks complains was highly reprehensible. But, while Selvaggio clearly harassed Brooks as she tried to do her job, "not all workplace conduct that may be described as harassment affects a term, condition, or privilege of employment within the meaning of Title VII." *Meritor Sav. Bank v. Vinson,* 477 U.S. 57, 67, 49 (1986). The harassment here was an entirely isolated incident. It had no precursors, and it was never repeated. In no sense can it be said that the city imposed upon Brooks the onerous terms of employment for which Title VII offers a remedy. . . . *See Faragher v. City of Boca Raton,* 524 U.S. 775, 788, (1998) ("[T]hese standards for judging hostility are sufficiently demanding to ensure that Title VII does not become a 'general civility code.'") (quoting *Oncale v. Sundowner Offshore Servs., Inc.,* 523 U.S. 75, 80, (1998)). We therefore affirm the district court's grant of summary judgment with respect to Brooks's hostile work environment claims under Title VII and FEHA. . . .

GILLMING
v.
SIMMONS INDUSTRIES
91 F.3d 1168 (8th Cir. 1996)

WOLLMAN, Circuit Judge. . . .

[The Decision and Rationale of the U.S. Court of Appeals for the 8th Circuit]

Gillming argues that the district court erroneously used a "reasonable person" rather than a "reasonable woman" standard in determining whether her reactions to the incidents were reasonable. We have found that the "reasonable woman" standard should be used in hostile environment litigation based on sex.

Burns v. McGregor Elec. Indus., 989 F.2d 959, 962 n.3 (8th Cir. 1993) ("[B]ehavior a reasonable woman would find objectionable may be actionable 'even if many people deem it to be harmless or insignificant.'"). Post-*Burns,* however, the Supreme Court has employed the "reasonable person" standard in a hostile work environment case. *Harris,* 510 U.S. at —, 114 S. Ct. at 370 ("Conduct that is not severe or pervasive enough to create an objectively hostile or abusive work environment—an environment that a reasonable person would find hostile or abusive—is beyond Title VII's purview.").

Courts of appeals addressing the issue after *Harris* have used a "reasonable person" standard. *See DeAngelis v. El Paso Mun. Police Officers Ass'n*, 51 F.3d 591, 594 (5th Cir.), *cert. denied*, — U.S —, (1995); *Fuller v. City of Oakland, Cal.*, 47 F.3d 1522, 1527 (9th Cir. 1995); *Dey v. Colt Constr. & Dev. Co.*, 28 F.3d 1446, 1454 (7th Cir. 1994); *King v. Hillen*, 21 F.3d 1572, 1582 (Fed. Cir. 1994). Given the Supreme Court's use of the "reasonable person" standard, we cannot find that the district court abused its discretion in using that standard in its jury instruction. . . .

The judgment is affirmed.

Questions

1. How would Janice's case come out under the different views of the objective reasonableness standard set forth above? What about Amy's case?
2. Is the reasonable person or reasonable woman (member of the same protected class) standard more consistent with the *Harris* case?
3. Is there any significant difference between the two standards, considering that courts will consider the totality of the circumstances in hostile work environment cases? If so, what is that difference?
4. How would the reasonable member of the protected class standard function in the context of harassment based on race, ethnicity, religion, disability, or age?
5. If the prevailing standard is that of a reasonable person without regard to the victim's protected class and the victim is a member of a group that has historically been subordinated by the majority, would that standard reinforce the prevailing level of discrimination and/or discriminatory attitudes?

d. The Subjective Standard

Problem 21

Stacy Carpenter works as a day trader at a mid-sized investment banking company. She works in a 52-person office. Her colleagues are predominantly male, and the support staff is mixed. Sexual banter and innuendo are common at the office, and Stacy has participated in some of it. Two employees, however, go beyond what Stacy can tolerate. They have used extremely crude language to refer to women, including women in the office. They have left sex toys in public places around the office (but not where customers have access). Additionally, their jokes are far cruder than the other comments. She does, however, giggle and stay around because she has noticed that female employees who demonstrate aversion to the banter are often made the brunt of jokes by the two. She is constantly afraid that they will find out that she once worked as a stripper to put herself through business school. Eventually, she and several other female employees bring a sexual harassment lawsuit. The employer moves to dismiss Stacy's complaint because the employer argues she did not find the conduct alleged hostile (the other plaintiffs avoided the offending employees when they engaged in their sexualized conduct). What is Stacy's argument? How should the law treat her situation?

The subjective prong of the hostile work environment test has not received the attention that the objective prong has received. *Meritor*, through its requirement that the conduct complained of be "unwelcome," demonstrated that the victim of harassment must subjectively perceive the offending conduct as hostile. *Harris* is quite explicit in its holding that the conduct giving rise to a hostile work environment must be perceived by the victim as hostile or abusive: "[I]f the victim does not subjectively perceive the environment to be abusive, the conduct has not actually altered the conditions of employment, and there is no Title VII violation."

One obvious reason that this element of the test is rarely at issue is that if someone has filed a complaint, it is quite likely that person found the environment to be hostile. Moreover, in many cases, the evidence demonstrates that the victim found the work environment to be hostile, and the primary issue is whether a reasonable person/woman would also have found the environment to be hostile. Still, issues arise as to whether a complainant actually felt her work environment to be hostile. Two of the more common issues that arise in this context are these: (1) Does it matter if the complainant participated in some way in the sexualized environment so long as she/he has complained about it? (2) Does it matter if a complainant's non-work-related behavior suggests that she/he has a more open view regarding sexualized activity away from the workplace? The following case provides an excellent discussion of the subjective prong of the hostile work environment framework, and it also addresses the issues noted above. Although the case was decided before *Harris*, and thus it focuses on the "unwelcome" language of *Meritor*, the reasoning remains sound. In fact, the unwelcome element set forth in *Meritor* is the underlying basis for the brief discussion of the subjective prong in subsequent cases, including *Harris*.

BURNS

v.

MCGREGOR ELECTRONIC INDUSTRIES, INC.
989 F.2d 959 (8th Cir. 1993)

LAY, Senior Circuit Judge.

[The Employment Problem and the Decision by the Trial Court]

The grisly and shocking facts supporting a finding of unwelcome sexual harassment are contained in our earlier opinion and need not be repeated here. *See Burns v. McGregor Elec. Indus., Inc.*, 955 F.2d 559, 560–63 (8th Cir. 1992).

In its first opinion, issued in July 1990, the district court found that there is "no doubt" that Paul Oslac, the owner of McGregor Electronic, made unwelcome sexual advances toward Burns during two periods when she was previously employed at the McGregor, Iowa company. . . . However, the district court found that plaintiff exaggerated the severity and pervasiveness of the sexual harassment and its effect on her. The trial court observed that Burns had previously appeared in provocative poses in a lewd magazine called *Easyriders*. Some employees brought the magazine to work and circulated it. Oslac and other male workers repeatedly made harassing comments to Burns about the photographs.

Based on Burns's past behavior and the district judge's observation of her at trial, the trial court found that although the sexual advances at work were considered by Burns to be unwelcome, she would not have been offended by these advances and by the sexual innuendo from other employees and supervisors. The court also found that the sexual harassment subsided after Burns returned to work the third time, and that the primary reason she terminated her employment in 1984 was a work-related argument with one of her co-workers, Eugene Ottaway. On this basis, the court found that plaintiff failed to prove by a preponderance of evidence that "the harassment affected a term, condition, or privilege of employment."

Although acknowledging the trial court's finding of fact must be sustained unless clearly erroneous, this court, in its earlier opinion, reversed on the ground that the district court erred, as a matter of law, because its factual finding that the sexual advances by her employer were unwelcome was inconsistent with the finding that the plaintiff was not offended by the conduct of her employer. 955 F.2d at 965. This court also reasoned that the district court erred in compartmentalizing the question of harassment into the three work periods. We held the district court must look at the totality of circumstances of the entire hostile work environment without dividing the "work environment into a series of discrete incidents and then measur[ing] the harm occurring in each episode." *Id.* at 564.

On remand, the district court, quoting from our opinion, found "that a reasonable person would consider the conduct of Oslac and his supervisors sufficiently severe or persuasive [SIC] to alter the conditions of employment and create an abusive working environment." . . . However, the court once again entered judgment in favor of the employer for the identical reasons set forth in its earlier opinion: (1) the employer's behavior did not offend the plaintiff because she had earlier posed nude for *Easyriders*; (2) the cause of termination was not related to the earlier sexual harassment.

[The Legal Issue]

. . . This is a sexual harassment case brought under Title VII of the Civil Rights Act of 1964, as amended, 42 U.S.C. § 2000e *et seq.* It comes to this court on appeal for the second time. The district court originally found in favor of the employer, McGregor Electronic Industries, Inc., on the ground that the plaintiff failed to prove sexual harassment under Title VII

and that her termination was unrelated to any harassment. This court reversed. In an unanimous opinion authored by Judge Wollman, we remanded the case for further consideration by the trial court. On April 7, 1992, the trial court reaffirmed its earlier findings. *Burns v. McGregor Elec. Indus., Inc.,* 807 F. Supp. 506 (N.D. Iowa 1992). [The Court of Appeals had to determine whether the trial correctly interpreted the meaning of the requirement that the conduct be subjectively unwelcome and offensive to the employee.]

[The Decision and Rationale of the U.S. Court of Appeals for the Eighth Circuit]

Based upon the undisputed facts, the district court's new determination that a reasonable person would find the employer's behavior sufficiently severe to alter the conditions of employment and create an abusive work environment, and the law of the case as determined in our earlier appeal, we now reverse with directions that the district court compute plaintiff's economic loss and enter judgment in favor of the plaintiff against the employer . . . .

On further review, we now reverse the trial court's order; based on the district court's latest opinion and the law of the case, as determined in our earlier review, we remand and direct that judgment be entered for the plaintiff, Lisa Ann Burns. . . .

In the decision now before us, the trial court explained that it believes there are two elements necessary for establishing sexual harassment: (1) whether the conduct was unwelcome because it was not solicited or invited, and (2) whether the conduct was offensive to the plaintiff.

We believe the trial court erred in requiring proof that the conduct at issue was unwelcome and offensive. Our statement in our prior opinion that the trial court's earlier findings were internally inconsistent was intended to convey this understanding. "The gravamen of any sexual harassment claim is that the alleged sexual advances were 'unwelcome.'" *Meritor Savs. Bank v. Vinson,* 477 U.S. 57, 68 (1986). On remand, the trial court overlooked this court's earlier direction that "the threshold for determining that conduct is *unwelcome*" is whether it was uninvited and offensive. 955 F.2d at 565 (emphasis added). Thus, as we earlier held, for the court to find that the conduct was unwelcome but not offensive was internally inconsistent as a matter of law. Whether the behavior is unwelcomed is to be determined by weighing whether the conduct was uninvited and offensive.

The Supreme Court in *Meritor* makes this clear. Whether a plaintiff acquiesces in the employer's conduct is relevant not as a separate defense to a claim of sexual harassment, but is relevant to whether the sexual advances were "unwelcome." *Meritor*, 477 U.S. at 68. Thus, the Court observed: "The correct inquiry is whether respondent by her conduct indicated that the alleged sexual advances were unwelcome, not whether the actual participation in sexual intercourse was voluntary." *Id.*

The district court found that notwithstanding the fact that the employer's conduct was unwelcome and created a hostile work environment, the plaintiff was not an "affected" individual in that she did not regard the conduct of her employer as undesirable or offensive. This finding was premised on the fact that plaintiff had appeared in non–work related nude poses in lewd magazines. We rejected this reasoning in our earlier opinion. We observed:

The district court's finding that Oslac's advances were unwelcome necessarily required the district court to believe Burns' testimony that Oslac's behavior was offensive to her. Thus, the district court's finding that Oslac made unwelcome advances toward Burns and its finding that Burns was not credible when she stated that Oslac's behavior was offensive appear on their face to be internally inconsistent.

955 F.2d at 565. We added:

The district court reasoned that a person who would appear nude in a national magazine could not be offended by the behavior which took place at the McGregor plant. It also believed that Burns had exaggerated the severity and pervasiveness of the harassment and its effect on her. Again, these findings are at odds with the district court's finding that Oslac's advances were unwelcome.

Id. at 566. The plaintiff's choice to pose for a nude magazine outside work hours is not material to the issue of whether plaintiff found her employer's work-related conduct offensive. This is not a case where Burns posed in provocative and suggestive ways at work. Her private life, regardless how reprehensible the trier of fact might find it to be, did not provide lawful acquiescence to unwanted sexual advances at her workplace by her employer. To hold otherwise would be contrary to Title VII's goal of ridding the workplace of any kind of unwelcome sexual harassment. In *Swentek v. USAIR, Inc.*, 830 F.2d 552 (4th Cir. 1987), the court rejected identical reasoning as used by the district court here. Even

though the plaintiff had used foul language in the past, the court reversed the district court and observed:

We note at the outset that the trial court misconstrued what constitutes unwelcome sexual harassment. It held that Swentek's own past conduct and use of foul language meant that Ludlam's comments were "not unwelcome" even though she told Ludlam to leave her alone. In his oral opinion, the judge determined, not that Swentek welcomed Ludlam's comments in particular, but that she was the kind of person who could not be offended by such comments and therefore welcomed them generally. We think that was error. Plaintiff's use of foul language or sexual innuendo in a consensual setting does not waive "her legal protections against unwelcome harassment." *Katz* [*v. Dole*] [251], 709 F.2d, at 254 n.3. The trial judge must determine whether plaintiff welcomed the particular conduct in question from the alleged harasser. . . .

The trial court made explicit findings that the conduct was not invited or solicited despite her posing naked for a magazine distributed nationally. The court believed, however, that because of her outside conduct, including her "interest in having her nude pictures appear in a magazine containing much lewd and crude sexually explicit material," the uninvited sexual advances of her employer were not "in and of itself offensive to her." The court explained that Burns "would not have been offended if someone she was attracted to did or said the same thing."

We hold that such a view is unsupported in law. If the court intended this as a standard or rationale for a standard, it is clearly in error. This rationale would allow a complete stranger to pursue sexual behavior at work that a female worker would accept from her husband or boyfriend. This standard would allow a male employee to kiss or fondle a female worker at the workplace. None of the plaintiff's conduct, which the court found relevant to bar her action, was work related. Burns did not tell sexual stories or engage in sexual gestures at work. She did not initiate sexual talk or solicit sexual encounters with co-employees. Under the trial court's rationale, if a woman taught part-time sexual education at a high school or college, a court would be compelled to find that sexual language, even though uninvited when directed at her in the workplace, would not offend her as it might someone else who was not as accustomed to public usage of the terms. . . .

We need not remand for reconsideration since we find that it is undisputed that the trial court has determined that the respondent's conduct was unwelcomed by the plaintiff and was such that a hypothetical reasonable woman would consider the conduct sufficiently severe or pervasive to alter the conditions of employment and create an abusive work environment. The evidence that plaintiff had engaged in posing for nude pictures in *Easyriders* magazine, although relevant to the totality of the events that ensued, cannot constitute a defense to her claim of a hostile sexual harassment environment at the workplace when, as here, the trial court has determined that it did not constitute an invitation to engage in sexual discourse. . . .

. . . [W]e find the district court erred in finding for the employer; we reverse and remand and direct that judgment be entered for the plaintiff. . . .

Questions:

1. Given the requirement that a work environment be objectively hostile in order to be actionable, what policy might underlie the subjective element of the test?

2. Should an employee's private conduct away from the workplace play any role in determining whether she/he found a work environment to be hostile? If so, why? If not, why not?

3. If an employee participates in office banter of a sexual nature, does that participation mean that she/he cannot find the environment hostile? What if an employee participates only because of a fear that she might become the focus of the banter if she excludes herself from the conversations? What if the banter she has participated in is mild and not offensive to her, but other comments in the same environment are offensive to her? What if she participates only because she is afraid that she will be treated poorly by her supervisors and/or co-workers if she does not? How can a trier of fact ever determine what the real reasons are for an employee's participation? Should the trier of fact try to do so?

4. Could conduct be considered unwelcome but not subjectively offensive or hostile?

e. Other Protected Classes: Race, National Origin, Religion, Disability

As mentioned in the introduction to this chapter, workplace harassment does not simply arise in the context of sexual harassment. Harassment claims based on race, ethnicity, religion, nonsexualized gender (i.e., misogyny/misandrony), disability, or age are all potentially actionable. For example, there are numerous racial harassment cases. In *Meritor*, the Supreme Court directly acknowledged that workplace harassment claims based on the other classes protected under Title VII are cognizable. Recent articles have pointed out that the same is true under the Americans with Disabilities Act and Age Discrimination in Employment Act. Of course, much of the law (and all of the Supreme Court cases) has developed in the context of sexual harassment.

The general test is the same regardless of the protected classes involved, although it would be hard to bring a *quid pro quo* claim based on anything other than sexual harassment and perhaps religion (i.e., job benefits somehow tied to conversion or religious practice/belief). One issue that may vary depending on the protected class involved is the perspective used for the objective reasonableness standard. After all, if the standard is a reasonable woman in sexual harassment cases, the standard in a race discrimination case would be a reasonable person of the plaintiff's race, and so forth.

Even if the standard in a sexual harassment case is the reasonable person standard, the result might be the same under the totality of the circumstances approach mandated by *Harris*. For example, in a disability case, how would a nondisabled person determine what would offend a person with a given disability without some understanding of the perspective of someone with that disability or with a disability that affects the same major life function? In a race case, a white person might not fully appreciate how a course of conduct might offend an African American without some discussion of how certain comments or acts would be perceived by a reasonable African American. The requirement under *Harris* that the trier of fact consider the totality of the circumstances would seem to mandate at least this indirect view of the victim's perspective. Thus, the class affected might matter in the context of the objective reasonableness test. Given the introductory nature of this text, we will not explore this issue further. It is important to consider it, however, when one is dealing with a workplace harassment case involving discrimination not based on sex.

One practical note worth adding at this point is that employer liability might be more of an issue in this area because some employers fail to recognize that harassment based on classifications other than sex are actionable, and thus these employers do not have adequate policies and/or procedures in place to address such claims. As a result, plaintiffs can have an easier time establishing employer liability. Of course, many employers are fully aware of this issue and have established broader workplace harassment policies to address it.

C. Same-Sex Harassment

ONCALE
v.
SUNDOWNER OFFSHORE SERVICES, INC.
523 U.S. 75 (1998)

Justice SCALIA delivered the opinion of the Court.

[The Employment Problem]

In late October 1991, Oncale was working for respondent Sundowner Offshore Services on a Chevron U.S.A., Inc., oil platform in the Gulf of Mexico. He was employed as a roustabout on an eight-man crew which included respondents John Lyons, Danny Pippen, and Brandon Johnson. Lyons, the crane operator, and Pippen, the driller, had supervisory authority, App. 41, 77, 43. On several occasions, Oncale was forcibly subjected to sex-related, humiliating actions against him by Lyons, Pippen and Johnson in the presence of the rest of the crew. Pippen and Lyons also physically assaulted Oncale in a sexual manner, and Lyons threatened him with rape.

Oncale's complaints to supervisory personnel produced no remedial action; in fact, the company's Safety Compliance Clerk, Valent Hohen, told Oncale that Lyons and Pippen "picked [on] him all the time too," and called him a name suggesting homosexual-

ity. *Id.*, at 77. Oncale eventually quit—asking that his pink slip reflect that he "voluntarily left due to sexual harassment and verbal abuse." *Id.*, at 79. When asked at his deposition why he left Sundowner, Oncale stated "I felt that if I didn't leave my job, that I would be raped or forced to have sex." *Id.*, at 71.

[The Decision of the Trial Court and the U.S. Court of Appeals for the Fifth Circuit]

Oncale filed a complaint against Sundowner in the United States District Court for the Eastern District of Louisiana, alleging that he was discriminated against in his employment because of his sex. Relying on the Fifth Circuit's decision in *Garcia v. Elf Atochem North America*, 28 F.3d 446, 451–452 [5Cir.] (1994), the district court held that "Mr. Oncale, a male, has no cause of action under Title VII for harassment by male co-workers." App. 106. On appeal, a panel of the Fifth Circuit concluded that *Garcia* was binding Circuit precedent, and affirmed. 83 F.3d 118 (1996). . . .

[The Legal Issue]

This case presents the question whether workplace harassment can violate Title VII's prohibition against "discriminat[ion] . . . because of . . . sex," 42 U.S.C. § 2000e-2(a)(1), when the harasser and the harassed employee are of the same sex. . . .

[The Decision and Rationale of the U.S. Supreme Court]

Title VII of the Civil Rights Act of 1964 provides, in relevant part, that "[i]t shall be an unlawful employment practice for an employer . . . to discriminate against any individual with respect to his compensation, terms, conditions, or privileges of employment, because of such individual's race, color, religion, sex, or national origin." 78 Stat. 255, as amended, 42 U.S.C. § 2000e-2(a)(1). We have held that this not only covers "terms" and "conditions" in the narrow contractual sense, but "evinces a congressional intent to strike at the entire spectrum of disparate treatment of men and women in employment." *Meritor Savings Bank, FSB v. Vinson*, 477 U.S. 57, 64 (1986). . . . "When the workplace is permeated with discriminatory intimidation, ridicule, and insult that is sufficiently severe or pervasive to alter the conditions of the victim's employment and create an abusive working environment, Title VII is violated." *Harris v. Forklift Systems, Inc.*, 510 U.S. 17, 21 (1993). . . .

Title VII's prohibition of discrimination "because of . . . sex" protects men as well as women, *Newport News Shipbuilding & Dry Dock Co. v. EEOC*, 462 U.S. 669, 682 (1983), and in the related context of racial discrimination in the workplace we have rejected any conclusive presumption that an employer will not discriminate against members of his own race. "Because of the many facets of human motivation, it would be unwise to presume as a matter of law that human beings of one definable group will not discriminate against other members of that group." *Castaneda v. Partida*, 430 U.S. 482, 499 (1977). See also *id.*, at 514 n.6 (Powell, J., joined by Burger, C.J., and REHNQUIST, J., dissenting). In *JOHNSON v. Transportation Agency, Santa Clara Cty.*, 480 U.S. 616, (1987), a male employee claimed that his employer discriminated against him because of his sex when it preferred a female employee for promotion. Although we ultimately rejected the claim on other grounds, we did not consider it significant that the supervisor who made that decision was also a man. See *id.*, at 624–625.

If our precedents leave any doubt on the question, we hold today that nothing in Title VII necessarily bars a claim of discrimination "because of . . . sex" merely because the plaintiff and the defendant (or the person charged with acting on behalf of the defendant) are of the same sex.

Courts have had little trouble with that principle in cases like *Johnson*, where an employee claims to have been passed over for a job or promotion. But when the issue arises in the context of a "hostile environment" sexual harassment claim, the state and federal courts have taken a bewildering variety of stances. Some, like the Fifth Circuit in this case, have held that same-sex sexual harassment claims are never cognizable under Title VII. *See also, e.g., Goluszek v. H.P. Smith*, 697 F. Supp. 1452 (N.D. Ill.1988). Other decisions say that such claims are actionable only if the plaintiff can prove that the harasser is homosexual (and thus presumably motivated by sexual desire). Compare *McWilliams v. Fairfax County Board of Supervisors*, 72 F.3d 1191 (C.A.4. 1996), with *Wrightson v. Pizza Hut of America*, 99 F.3d 138 (C.A.4. 1996). Still others suggest that workplace harassment that is sexual in content is always actionable, regardless of the harasser's sex, sexual orientation, or motivations. See *Doe v. Belleville*, 119 F.3d 563 (C.A.7. 1997).

We see no justification in the statutory language or our precedents for a categorical rule excluding same-sex harassment claims from the coverage of Title VII. As some courts have observed, male-on-male sexual harassment in the workplace was assuredly not the principal evil Congress was concerned with when it enacted Title VII. But statutory prohibitions often go beyond the principal evil to cover reasonably comparable evils, and it is ultimately the provisions of our laws rather than the principal concerns of our legislators by which we are governed. Title VII prohibits "discriminat [ion] . . . because of . . . sex" in the "terms" or "conditions" of employment. Our holding that this includes sexual harassment must extend to sexual harassment of any kind that meets the statutory requirements.

Respondents and their amici contend that recognizing liability for same-sex harassment will transform Title VII into a general civility code for the American workplace. But that risk is no greater for same-sex than for opposite-sex harassment and is adequately met by careful attention to the requirements of the statute. Title VII does not prohibit all verbal or physical harassment in the workplace; it is directed only at "discriminat [ion] . . . because of . . . sex." We have never held that workplace harassment, even harassment between men and women, is automatically discrimination because of sex merely because the words used have sexual content or connotations. "The critical issue, Title VII's text indicates, is whether members of one sex are exposed to disadvantageous terms or conditions of employment to which members of the other sex are not exposed." *Harris, supra*, at 25 (Ginsburg, J., concurring).

Courts and juries have found the inference of discrimination easy to draw in most male-female sexual harassment situations, because the challenged conduct typically involves explicit or implicit proposals of sexual activity; it is reasonable to assume those proposals would not have been made to someone of the same sex. The same chain of inference would be available to a plaintiff alleging same-sex harassment, if there were credible evidence that the harasser was homosexual. But harassing conduct need not be motivated by sexual desire to support an inference of discrimination on the basis of sex. A trier of fact might reasonably find such discrimination, for example, if a female victim is harassed in such sex-specific and derogatory terms by another woman as to make it clear that the harasser is motivated by general hostility to the presence of women in the workplace. A same-sex harassment plaintiff may also, of course, offer direct comparative evidence about how the alleged harasser treated members of both sexes in a mixed-sex workplace. Whatever evidentiary route the plaintiff chooses to follow, he or she must always prove that the conduct at issue was not merely tinged with offensive sexual connotations, but actually constituted "discrimina[tion] . . . because of . . . sex."

And there is another requirement that prevents Title VII from expanding into a general civility code: As we emphasized in *Meritor* and *Harris*, the statute does not reach genuine but innocuous differences in the ways men and women routinely interact with members of the same sex and of the opposite sex. The prohibition of harassment on the basis of sex requires neither asexuality nor androgyny in the workplace; it forbids only behavior so objectively offensive as to alter the "conditions" of the victim's employment. "Conduct that is not severe or pervasive enough to create an objectively hostile or abusive work environment—an environment that a reasonable person would find hostile or abusive—is beyond Title VII's purview."

Harris, 510 U.S., at 21, citing *Meritor*, 477 U.S., at 67. We have always regarded that requirement as crucial, and as sufficient to ensure that courts and juries do not mistake ordinary socializing in the workplace—such as male-on-male horseplay or intersexual flirtation—for discriminatory "conditions of employment."

We have emphasized, moreover, that the objective severity of harassment should be judged from the perspective of a reasonable person in the plaintiff's position, considering "all the circumstances." *Harris, supra*, at 23. In same-sex (as in all) harassment cases, that inquiry requires careful consideration of the social context in which particular behavior occurs and is experienced by its target. A professional football player's working environment is not severely or pervasively abusive, for example, if the coach smacks him on the buttocks as he heads onto the field—even if the same behavior would reasonably be experienced as abusive by the coach's secretary (male or female) back at the office. The real social impact of workplace behavior often depends on a constellation of surrounding circumstances, expectations, and relationships which are not fully captured by a simple recitation of the words used or the physical acts performed. Common sense, and an appropriate sensitivity to social context, will enable courts and juries to distinguish between simple teasing or roughhousing among members of the same sex, and conduct which a reasonable person in the plaintiff's position would find severely hostile or abusive.

Because we conclude that sex discrimination consisting of same-sex sexual harassment is actionable under Title VII, the judgment of the Court of Appeals for the Fifth Circuit is reversed, and the case is remanded for further proceedings consistent with this opinion.

It is so ordered.

Justice THOMAS, concurring:

I concur because the Court stresses that in every sexual harassment case, the plaintiff must plead and ultimately prove Title VII's statutory requirement that there be discrimination "because of . . . sex."

D. Sexual Orientation and Gender Identity

> ### Problem 22
>
> Assume that George Merit, a gay hotel butler, is sexually harassed by his co-workers and his supervisor. His co-workers whistle at him, blow kisses, call him "sweetheart," show him homosexual pornography, give him crude sexually themed gifts, tell ribald jokes, grab his genital area, and even simulate anal sex with the plaintiff. His supervisor participates in all these sorts of activities. Is this harassment because of homosexuality, or is it actionable sexual harassment? Suppose that the same-sex harasser is homosexual. If he makes advances to male subordinates, is there a Title VII claim?

> ### Problem 23
>
> Suppose that a school district is notified that Doreen Olinsky, a male-to-female transgender employee, presents as a female and that she wants to use the women's restrooms, and the school district notes no problem with this. However, another employee has a grave problem with this and verbally objects, without stating any particular grounds other than revulsion based on gender norms. The school board does not back down, and the objecting employee resorts to using a student bathroom or a single-stall, unisex bathroom to avoid being offended. She sues, alleging a hostile work environment based on gender, and also religious discrimination. What is the result?

DESANTIS
v.
PACIFIC TELEPHONE & TELEGRAPH CO.
608 F.2d 327 (9th Cir. 1979)

CHOY, Circuit Judge.

[The Employment Problem]

[Four] homosexuals brought three separate federal district court actions claiming that their employers or former employers discriminated against them in employment decisions because of their homosexuality. . . .

Appellant Strailey, a male, was fired by the Happy Times Nursery School after two years' service as a teacher. He alleged that he was fired because he wore a small gold ear-loop to school prior to the commencement of the school year. . . .

DeSantis, Boyle, and Simard, all males, claimed that Pacific Telephone & Telegraph Co. (PT&T) impermissibly discriminated against them because of their homosexuality. DeSantis alleged that he was not hired when a PT&T supervisor concluded that he was a homosexual. According to appellants' brief, "Boyle was continually harassed by his co-workers and had to quit to preserve his health after only three months because his supervisors did nothing to alleviate this condition." "Finally," [according to appellants' brief], "Simard was forced to quit under similar conditions after almost four years of employment with PT&T, but he was harassed by his supervisors as well [as co-workers].". . .

[The Legal Issues]

[The plaintiffs] alleged that such discrimination violated Title VII of the Civil Rights Act of 1964, 42 U.S.C. § 2000e *et seq.*, and 42 U.S.C. § 1985(3). The district courts dismissed the complaints as failing to state claims under either statute. Plaintiffs below appealed. Because of the similarity of issues involved, this court consolidated the appeals at the request of counsel for appellants. We affirm. . . .

[The Decision and Rationale of the U.S. Court of Appeals for the Ninth Circuit]

Title VII Claim

Appellants argue first that the district courts erred in holding that Title VII does not prohibit discrimination on the basis of sexual preference. They claim that in prohibiting . . . employment discrimination on the basis of "sex," Congress meant to include discrimination on the basis of sexual orientation. They add that in a trial they could establish that discrimination against homosexuals disproportionately affects men and that this disproportionate impact and correlation between discrimination on the basis of sexual preference and discrimination on the basis of "sex" requires that sexual preference be considered a subcategory of the "sex" category of Title VII. . . .

In *Holloway v. Arthur Anderson & Co.*, 566 F.2d 659, (9th Cir. 1977), plaintiff argued that her employer had discriminated against her because she was undergoing a sex transformation and that this discrimination violated Title VII's prohibition on sex discrimination. This court rejected that claim, writing:

> . . . Giving the statute its plain meaning, this court concludes that Congress had only the traditional notions of "sex" in mind. Later legislative activity makes this narrow definition even more evident. Several bills have been introduced to amend the Civil Rights Act to prohibit discrimination against "sexual preference." None [has] been enacted into law.
>
> Congress has not shown any intent other than to restrict the term "sex" to its traditional meaning.

Therefore, the court will not expand Title VII's application in the absence of Congressional mandate. The manifest purpose of Title VII's prohibition against sex discrimination in employment is to ensure that men and women are treated equally, absent a bona fide relationship between the qualifications for the job and the person's sex. . . .

Following *Holloway*, we conclude that Title VII's prohibition of "sex" discrimination applies only to discrimination on the basis of gender and should not be judicially extended to include sexual preference such as homosexuality. . . .

The *Holloway* court noted that in passing Title VII, Congress did not intend to protect sexual orientation and has repeatedly refused to extend such protection. . . . Appellants now ask us to employ the [disparate] impact decisions as an artifice to "bootstrap" Title VII protection for homosexuals under the guise of protecting men generally.

This we are not free to do. Adoption of this bootstrap device would frustrate congressional objectives as explicated in *Holloway*, not effectuate congressional goals as in *Griggs*. It would achieve by judicial "construction" what Congress did not do and has consistently refused to do on many occasions. It would violate the rule that our duty in construing a statute is to "ascertain . . . and give effect to the legislative will." . . .

Appellants next contend that recent decisions have held that an employer generally may not use different employment criteria for men and women. They claim that if a male employee prefers males as sexual partners, he will be treated differently from a female employee who prefers male partners. They conclude that the employer thus uses different employment criteria for men and women and [thus violates Supreme Court precedent].

We must again reject appellants' efforts to "bootstrap" Title VII protection for homosexuals. While we do not express approval of an employment policy that differentiates according to sexual preference, we note that whether dealing with men or women the employer is using the same criterion: it will not hire or promote a person who prefers sexual partners of the same sex. Thus this policy does not involve different decisional criteria for the sexes.

Interference with Association [Section 1985(3) Claim]

Appellants argue that the EEOC has held that discrimination against an employee because of the race of the employee's friends may violate discrimination based on race in violation of Title VII. . . . They contend that analogously, discrimination because of the sex of the employees' sexual partner should constitute discrimination based on sex.

Appellants, however, have not alleged that appellees have policies of discriminating against employees because of the gender of their friends. That is, they do not claim that the appellees will terminate anyone with a male (or female) friend. They claim instead that the appellees discriminate against employees who have a certain type of relationship—i.e., homosexual relationship—with certain friends. As noted earlier, that relationship is not protected by Title VII. . . . Thus, assuming it would violate Title VII for an employer to discriminate against employees because of the gender of their friends, appellants' claims do not fall within this purported rule.

[The court went on to reject appellant Strailey's claims that he was discriminated against because he wore an earring and that discrimination based on "effeminacy" was impermissible because it was premised on a gender role stereotype.]

SIMONTON
v.
RUNYON
232 F.3d 33 (2d Cir. 2000)

WALKER, Chief Judge, SACK and KATZMANN, Circuit Judges

[The Employment Problem]

Simonton was employed as a postal worker in Farmingdale, New York for approximately twelve years. He repeatedly received satisfactory to excellent performance evaluations. He was, however, subjected to an abusive and hostile environment by reason of his sexual orientation. The abuse he allegedly endured was so severe that he ultimately suffered a heart attack.

For the sake of decency and judicial propriety, we hesitate before reciting in detail the incidents of Simonton's abuse. Nevertheless, we think it is important both to acknowledge the appalling persecution Simonton allegedly endured and to identify the precise nature of the abuse so as to distinguish this case from future cases as they arise. We therefore relate some, but not all, of the alleged harassment that forms the basis for this suit.

Simonton's sexual orientation was known to his co-workers who repeatedly assaulted him with such comments as "go fuck yourself, fag," "suck my dick," and "so you like it up the ass?" Notes were placed on the wall of the employees' bathroom with Simonton's name and the names of celebrities who had died of AIDS. Pornographic photographs were taped to his work area, male dolls were placed in his vehicle, and copies of *Playgirl* magazine were sent to his home. Pictures of an erect penis were posted in his workplace, as were posters stating that Simonton suffered from a mental illness as a result of "bung hole disorder." There were repeated statements that Simonton was a "fucking faggot. . . . "

[The Legal Issues]

Plaintiff-appellant Dwayne Simonton sued the Postmaster General and the United States Postal Service . . . for abuse and harassment he suffered by reason of his sexual orientation. The United States District Court for the Eastern District of New York . . . dismissed Simonton's complaint pursuant to Fed. R. Civ. P. 12(b)(6) for failure to state a claim, reasoning that Title VII does not prohibit discrimination based on sexual orientation. . . .

[Decision and Rationale of the U.S. Court of Appeals for the Second Circuit]

We agree. . . . There can be no doubt that the conduct allegedly engaged in by Simonton's co-workers is morally reprehensible whenever and in whatever context it occurs, particularly in the modern workplace. Nevertheless, as the First Circuit recently explained in a similar context, "we are called upon here to construe a statute as glossed by the Supreme Court, not to make a moral judgment." *Higgins v. New Balance Athletic Shoe, Inc.*, 194 F.3d 252, 259 (1st Cir. 1999). When interpreting a statute, the role of a court is limited to discerning and adhering to legislative meaning. The law is well-settled in this circuit and in all others to have reached the question that Simonton has no cause of action under Title VII because Title VII does not prohibit harassment or discrimination because of sexual orientation. . . .

The Equal Employment Opportunity Act of 1972 extended Title VII's protections to certain federal employees, including U.S. Postal Service employees. *See* 42 U.S.C. § 2000e-16(a). Section 2000e-16(a) provides, in part, that all personnel actions affecting covered employees "shall be made free from any discrimination based on race, color, religion, sex, or national origin." *Id.* Simonton argues that discrimination based on "sex" includes discrimination based on sexual orientation. We disagree.

Admittedly, we have "little legislative history to guide us in interpreting the Act's prohibition against discrimination based on 'sex.'" *Meritor Sav. Bank v. Vinson*, 477 U.S. 57, 64 (1986). But we are informed by Congress' rejection, on numerous occasions, of bills that would have extended Title VII's protection to people based on their sexual preferences. *See, e.g.,* Employment Discrimination Act of 1996, S. 2056, 104th Cong. (1996); Employment Discrimination Act of 1995, H.R. 1863, 104th Cong. (1995); Employment Discrimination Act of 1994, H.R.4636, 103d Cong. (1994); *See also Ulane v. Eastern Airlines, Inc.*, 742 F.2d 1081, 1085–86 (7th Cir. 1984) (noting that Congress has rejected a number of proposed amendments to Title VII to prohibit discrimination based on sexual orientation). Although congressional inaction subsequent to the enactment of a statute is not always a helpful guide, Congress' refusal to expand the reach of Title VII is strong evidence of congressional intent in the face of consistent judicial decisions refusing to interpret "sex" to include sexual orientation. *See, e.g., Wrightson v. Pizza Hut of Am., Inc.*, 99 F.3d 138, 143 (4th Cir. 1996) ("Title VII does not afford a cause of action for discrimination based upon sexual orientation"); *Williamson v. A.G. Edwards & Sons, Inc.*, 876 F.2d 69, 70 (8th Cir. 1999) ("Title VII does not prohibit discrimination against homosexuals"); *DeSantis v. Pacific Tel. & Tel. Co.*, 608 F.2d 327, 329–32 (9th Cir. 1979).

Moreover, we are not writing on a clean slate. In *DiCintio v. Westchester County Medical Center*, 807 F.2d 304 (2d Cir. 1986), we reversed a plaintiff's verdict in a Title VII suit alleging that a male employer had passed over several male applicants for a promotion in order to hire a woman with whom the employer had a romantic relationship. Interpreting the definition of "sex," we held that

> the other categories afforded protection under Title VII refer to a person's status as a member of a particular race, color, religion or nationality. "Sex," when read in this context, logically could only refer to membership in a class delineated by gender, rather than sexual activity regardless of gender. . . . The proscribed differentiation under Title VII, therefore, must be a distinction based on a person's sex, not on his or her sexual affiliations.

Id. at 306–07; *see also DeSantis*, 608 F.2d at 329–30. Because the term "sex" in Title VII refers only to membership in a class delineated by gender, and not to sexual affiliation, Title VII does not proscribe discrimination because of sexual orientation.

Simonton argues that *Oncale v. Sundowner Offshore Services, Inc.*, 523 U.S. 75 (1998), permits us to revisit our holding in *DiCintio*. We disagree that such an opportunity presents itself here. In *Oncale*, the Supreme Court rejected a *per se* rule that same-sex sexual harassment was non-cognizable under Title VII. The Court reasoned that "nothing in Title VII necessarily bars a claim of discrimination 'because of . . . sex' merely because the plaintiff and the defendant (or person charged with acting on behalf of the defendant) are of the same sex." *Id.* at 79. *Oncale* did not suggest, however, that male harassment of other males always violates Title VII. *Oncale* emphasized that every victim of such harassment must show that he was harassed because he was male. *See id.* at 80–81.

Subsequent to the Supreme Court's decision in *Oncale*, the First Circuit reaffirmed the inapplicability of Title VII to discrimination based on sexual orientation. *See Higgins*, 194 F.3d at 259 ("[W]e regard it as settled law that, as drafted and authoritatively construed, Title VII does not proscribe harassment simply because of sexual orientation") (citing *Hopkins v. Baltimore Gas & Elec. Co.*, 77 F.3d 745, 751–52 (4th Cir. 1996), and *Williamson*, 876 F.2d at 70). We likewise do not see how *Oncale* changes our well-settled precedent that "sex" refers to membership in a class delineated by gender. The critical issue, as stated in *Oncale*, "is whether members of one sex are exposed to disadvantageous terms or conditions of employment to which members of the other sex are not exposed." *Oncale*, 523 U.S. at 80. Simonton has alleged that he was discriminated against not because he was a man, but because of his sexual orientation. Such a claim remains non-cognizable under Title VII.

Simonton argues . . . that the harassment he suffered could be construed as discrimination based on sex rather than sexual orientation. . . . Simonton first argues that . . . he has pled facts [sufficient to withstand a motion to dismiss under Rule 12 (b) (6).] We disagree.

. . . "[G]enerally a complaint that gives full notice of the circumstances giving rise to the plaintiff's claim for relief need not also correctly plead the legal theory or theories and statutory basis supporting the claim." . . . Nevertheless, there is no basis to infer from the complaint that the harassment Simonton suffered was because of his sex and not, as he urges throughout his complaint, because of his sexual orientation. In the context of male-female sexual harassment, involving more or less explicit sexual proposals, it is easy to infer discrimination because of sex since "it is reasonable to assume those proposals would not have been made to someone of the same sex." *Oncale*, 523 U.S. at 80. And, as the Supreme Court stated, "[t]he same chain of inference would be available to a plaintiff alleging same-sex harassment, if there were credible evidence that the harasser was homosexual." *Id.* But since Simonton does not offer "direct comparative evidence about how the alleged harasser treated members of both sexes in [his] mixed-sex workplace," *id.* at 80–81, and does not allege a basis for inferring gender-based animus, we are unable to infer that the alleged conduct would not have been directed at a woman. Accepting as true all the facts that Simonton has pled, the only inference we can draw is that he was harassed because of his sexual orientation. As we have explained, such harassment is not cognizable under Title VII.

Simonton also argues that discrimination because of sexual orientation is discrimination based on sex because it disproportionately affects men. We decline to adopt a reading of Title VII that would . . . "achieve by judicial 'construction'" what Congress did not do and has consistently refused to do on many occasions," *DeSantis*, 608 F.2d at 330. Therefore, this argument is unavailing.

Simonton next relies on *Price Waterhouse v. Hopkins*, 490 U.S. 228 (1989), to argue that the abuse he suffered was discrimination based on sexual stereotypes, which may be cognizable as discrimination based on sex. We find this argument more substantial than Simonton's previous two arguments, but not sufficiently pled in this case. We express no opinion as to how this issue would be decided in a future case in which it is squarely presented and sufficiently pled.

The plaintiff in *Price Waterhouse* filed suit after having been denied partnership in an accounting firm, in part because she was "macho." *Id.* at 235. She was advised that she could improve her chances for partnership if she would "walk more femininely, talk more femininely, dress more femininely, wear make-up, have her hair styled, and wear jewelry." *Id.* Justice Brennan, writing for the plurality, held that this was impermissible sex discrimination, and that "[i]n the specific context of sex stereotyping, an employer who acts on the basis of a belief that a woman canot be aggressive, or that she must not be, has acted on the basis of gender." *Id.* at 250. Other courts have suggested that gender discrimination—discrimination based on a failure to conform to gender norms—might be cognizable under Title VII. *See Schwenk v. Hartford*, 204 F.3d 1187, 1202 (9th Cir. 2000) (stating, in dicta, that Title VII encompasses instances in which "the perpetrator's actions stem from the fact that he believed that the victim was a man who 'failed to act like' one" and that "'sex' under Title VII encompasses both sex—that is, the biological differences between men and women—and gender"); *Higgins*, 194 F.3d at 261 n.4 ("[J]ust as a woman can ground an action on a claim that men discriminated against her because she did not meet stereotyped expectations of femininity, a man can ground a claim on evidence that other men discriminated against him because he did not meet stereotypical expectations of masculinity.")

Simonton argues that the same theory of sexual stereotyping could apply here, as the harassment he endured was based on his failure to conform to gender norms, regardless of his sexual orientation. The Court in *Price Waterhouse* implied that a suit alleging harassment or disparate treatment based upon nonconformity with sexual stereotypes is cognizable under Title VII as discrimination because of sex. This theory would not bootstrap protection for sexual orientation into Title VII because not all homosexual men are stereotypically feminine, and not all heterosexual men are stereotypically masculine. But, under this theory, relief would be available for discrimination based upon sexual stereotypes.

We do not reach the merits of this issue, however, as Simonton has failed to plead sufficient facts for our consideration of this issue. . . . [W]e have no basis in the record to surmise that Simonton behaved in a stereotypically feminine manner and that the harassment he endured was, in fact, based on his nonconformity with gender norms instead of his sexual orientation. Moreover, because this theory was not presented to the district court, we are without the benefit of lower court consideration. In the circumstances, we think the wisest course is to defer consideration of the merits of such an argument to another case in which it comes to us after being properly pled and presented to the district court.

Discussion Note

1. Recall the discussion in Chapter 2 regarding the proof of inferences of discrimination under Title VII disparate treatment by use of stereotypes. The First Circuit in *Higgins*, cited in the above case, did not consider the analogous argument about gender stereotyping based on expectations of what a male norm or standard might be because the issues were not sufficiently raised in that case. The Second Circuit Court of Appeals also declined to decide this issue, which it found as a stronger argument, because the plaintiff had not raised the issue properly below. However, in the *Centola* case, discussed in Chapter 3, a federal district court judge found that discrimination based on deviations from male stereotypes was a violation of Title VII disiparate treatment.

ULANE
v.
EASTERN AIRLINES, INC.
742 F.2d 1081 (7th Cir. 1984)

Harlington WOOD, Jr., Circuit Judge:

[The Employment Problem]

Plaintiff, as Kenneth Ulane, was hired in 1968 as a pilot for defendant, Eastern Air Lines Inc., but was fired as Karen Frances Ulane in 1981. . . .

Ulane became a licensed pilot in 1964, serving in the United States Army from that time until 1968 with a record of combat missions in Vietnam for which Ulane received the Air Medal with eight clusters. Upon discharge in 1968, Ulane began flying for Eastern. With Eastern, Ulane progressed from Second to First Officer, and also served as a flight instructor, logging over 8,000 flight hours.

Ulane was diagnosed a transsexual in 1979.[3] She explains although embodied as a male, from early childhood she felt like a female. Ulane first sought psychiatric and medical assistance in 1968 while in the military. Later, Ulane began taking female hormones as part of her treatment, and eventually developed breasts from the hormones. In 1980, she underwent "sex reassignment surgery. . . . " After the surgery, Illinois issued a revised birth certificate indicating Ulane was female, and the FAA certified her for flight status as a female. Ulane's own physician explained, however, that the operation would not create a biological female in the sense that Ulane would "have a uterus and ovaries and be able to bear babies." Ulane's chromosomes, all concede, are unaffected by the hormones and surgery. . . . Ulane, however, claims that the lack of change in her chromosomes is irrelevant. . . . Eastern was not aware of Ulane's transsexuality, her hormone treatments, or her psychiatric counseling until she attempted to return to work after her reassignment surgery. Eastern knew Ulane only as one of its male pilots. . . .

[The Legal Issue]

. . . Ulane filed a timely charge of sex discrimination with the Equal Employment Opportunity Commission, which subsequently issued a right to sue letter. This suit followed. Counts I and II allege that Ulane's discharge violated Title VII of the Civil Rights Act of 1964. . . . : Count I alleges that Ulane was discriminated against as a female; Count II alleges that Ulane was discriminated against as a transsexual. The judge ruled in favor of Ulane on both counts after a bench trial. . . .

[The Decision by the Trial Court]

The district judge first found under Count II that Eastern discharged Ulane because she was a transsexual, and that Title VII prohibits discrimination on this basis . . .

---

[3] [The preferred term at this time is "transgender."]

[The Decision and Rationale of the U.S. Court of Appeals for the Seventh Circuit]

While we do not condone discrimination in any form . . . we are constrained to hold that Title VII does not protect transsexuals, and that the district court's order on this count therefore must be reversed for lack of jurisdiction. . . .

Other courts have held that the term "sex" as used in the statute is not synonymous with "sexual preference." *See, e.g., Sommers v. Budget Marketing, Inc.*, 667 F.2d 748, 750 (8th Cir. 1982) (per curiam); *DeSantis v. Pacific Tel. & Tel. Co.*, 608 F.2d 327, 329–30 (9th Cir. 1979); *Smith v. Liberty Mutual Insurance Co.*, 569 F.2d 325, 326–27 (5th Cir. 1978); *Holloway v. Arthur Andersen & Co.*, 566 F.2d 659, 662 (9th Cir. 1977); *Voyles v. Ralph K. Davies Medical Center*, 403 F. Supp. 456, 457 (N.D. Cal. 1975), *aff'd mem.*, 570 F.2d 354 (9th Cir. 1978). The district court recognized this, and agreed that homosexuals and transvestites do not enjoy Title VII protection, but distinguished transsexuals as persons who, unlike homosexuals and transvestites, have sexual identity problems; the judge agreed that the term "sex" does not comprehend "sexual preference," but held that it does comprehend "sexual identity." The district judge based this holding on his finding that "sex is not a cut-and-dried matter of chromosomes," but is in part a psychological question—a question of self-perception; and is in part a social matter—a question of how society perceives the individual. . . . The district judge further supported his broad view of Title VII's coverage by recognizing Title VII as a remedial statute to be liberally construed. He concluded that it is reasonable to hold that the statutory word "sex" literally and scientifically applies to transsexuals even if it does not apply to homosexuals or transvestites. . . . We must disagree.

Even though Title VII is a remedial statute, and even though some may define "sex" in such a way as to mean an individual's "sexual identity," our responsibility is to interpret this congressional legislation and determine what Congress intended when it decided to outlaw discrimination based on sex. . . . The district judge did recognize that Congress manifested an intention to exclude homosexuals from Title VII coverage. Nonetheless, the judge defended his conclusion that Ulane's broad interpretation of the term "sex" was reasonable and could therefore be applied to the statute by noting that transsexuals are different than homosexuals, and that Congress never considered whether it should include or exclude transsexuals. While we recognize distinctions among homosexuals, transvestites, and transsexuals, we believe that the same reasons for holding that the first two groups do not enjoy Title VII coverage apply with equal force to deny protection for transsexuals.

It is a maxim of statutory construction that, unless otherwise defined, words should be given their ordinary, common meaning. . . . The phrase in Title VII prohibiting discrimination based on sex, in its plain meaning, implies that it is unlawful to discriminate against women because they are women and against men because they are men. The words of Title VII do not outlaw discrimination against a person who has a sexual identity disorder, *i.e.*, a person born with a male body who believes herself to be female, or a person born with a female body who believes herself to be male; a prohibition against discrimination based on an individual's sex is not synonymous with a prohibition against discrimination based on an individual's sexual identity disorder or discontent with the sex into which they were born. . . .

When Congress enacted the Civil Rights Act of 1964, it was primarily concerned with race discrimination. "Sex as a basis of discrimination was added as a floor amendment one day before the House approved Title VII, without prior hearing or debate." *Holloway v. Arthur Andersen & Co.*, 566 F.2d 659, 662 (9th Cir. 1977). . . . omitted; *Developments in the Law–Employment Discrimination and Title VII of the Civil Rights Act of 1964*, 84 Harv. L. Rev. 1109, 1167 (1971). This sex amendment was the gambit of a congressman seeking to scuttle adoption of the Civil Rights Act. The ploy failed and sex discrimination was abruptly added to the statute's prohibition against race discrimination. *See Bradford v. Peoples Natural Gas Co.*, 60 F.R.D. 432, 434–35 & n.1 (W.D. Pa. 1973).

The total lack of legislative history supporting the sex amendment, coupled with the circumstances of the amendment's adoption, clearly indicates that Congress never considered nor intended that this 1964 legislation apply to anything other than the traditional concept of sex. Had Congress intended more, surely the legislative history would have at least mentioned its intended broad coverage of homosexuals, transvestites, or transsexuals, and would no doubt have sparked an interesting debate. There is not the slightest suggestion in the legislative record to support an all-encompassing interpretation.

Members of Congress have, moreover, on a number of occasions, attempted to amend Title VII to prohibit discrimination based upon "affectional or sexual orientation. . . . " Each of these attempts has failed. While the proposed amendments were directed toward homosexuals, see, e.g., Civil Rights Act Amendments of 1981: Hearings on H.R. 1454 Before the Subcomm. on Employment Opportunities of the House Comm. on Education and Labor, 97th Cong., 2d Sess. 1–2 (1982) (statements of Rep. Hawkins, chairman of subcommittee, and Rep. Weiss, N. Y., author of bill); Civil Rights Amendments Act of 1979: Hearings on H.R. 2074 Before the Subcomm. on Employment Opportunities of the House Comm'n on Education and Labor, 96th Cong., 2d Sess. 6 (1980) (statements of Rep. Hawkins, chairman of subcommittee, and Rep. Weiss, N. Y., coauthor of bill), their rejection strongly indicates that the phrase in the Civil Rights Act prohibiting discrimination on the basis of sex should be given a narrow, traditional interpretation, which would also exclude transsexuals. Furthermore, Congress has continued to reject these amendments even after courts have specifically held that Title VII does not protect transsexuals from discrimination [leading to the inference that Congress could have "corrected" the judiciary's interpretation had it intended to]. . . .

Although the maxim that remedial statutes should be liberally construed is well recognized, that concept has reasonable bounds beyond which a court cannot go without transgressing the prerogatives of Congress. In our view, to include transsexuals within the reach of Title VII far exceeds mere statutory interpretation. . . . *See Gunnison v. Commissioner*, 461 F.2d 496, 499 (7th Cir. 1972) (it is for the legislature, not the courts, to expand the class of people protected by a statute). This we must not and will not do.

Congress has a right to deliberate on whether it wants such a broad sweeping of the untraditional and unusual within the term "sex" as used in Title VII. Only Congress can consider all the ramifications to society of such a broad view. We do not believe that the interpretation of the word "sex" is a mere matter of expert medical testimony or the credibility of witnesses produced in court. Congress may, at some future time, have an interest in testimony of that type, but it does not control our interpretation of Title VII based on the legislative history or lack thereof. If Congress believes that transsexuals should enjoy the protection of Title VII, it may so provide. Until that time, however, we decline in behalf of the Congress to judicially expand the definition of sex as used in Title VII beyond its common and traditional interpretation.

Our view of the application of Title VII to this type of case is not an original one. *Sommers v. Budget Marketing, Inc.*, 667 F.2d 748, 750 (8th Cir. 1982) (per curiam), and *Holloway v. Arthur Andersen & Co.*, 566 F.2d 659, 662–63 (9th Cir. 1977), the only two circuit court cases we found that have specifically addressed the issue, both held that discrimination against transsexuals does not fall within the ambit of Title VII. . . . In *Sommers*, Budget Marketing fired an anatomical male who claimed to be female once Budget discovered that he had misrepresented himself as female when he applied for the job. In *Holloway*, Arthur Andersen, an accounting firm, dismissed the plaintiff after he informed his superior that he was undergoing treatment in preparation for sex change surgery. We agree with the Eighth and Ninth Circuits that if the term "sex" as it is used in Title VII is to mean more than biological male or biological female, the new definition must come from Congress.

Title VII and Ulane as a Female.

The trial judge originally found only that Eastern had discriminated against Ulane under Count II as a transsexual. The judge subsequently amended his findings to hold that Ulane is also female and has been discriminated against on this basis. Even if we accept the district judge's holding that Ulane is female, he made no factual findings necessary to support his conclusion that Eastern discriminated against her on this basis. All the district judge said was that his previous "findings and conclusions concerning sexual discrimination against the plaintiff by Eastern Airlines, Inc. apply with equal force whether plaintiff be regarded as a transsexual or a female." This is insufficient to support a finding that Ulane was discriminated against because she is a female, since the district judge's previous findings all centered around his conclusion that Eastern did not want "[a] transsexual in the cockpit. . . . "

Ulane is entitled to any personal belief about her sexual identity she desires. After the surgery, hormones, appearance changes, and a new Illinois birth certificate and FAA pilot's certificate, it may be that society, as the trial judge found, considers Ulane to be female. But even if one believes that a woman can be so easily created from what remains of a man, that does not decide this case. If Eastern had considered Ulane to be female and had discriminated against her because she was female (*i.e.*, Eastern treated females less favorably than males), then the argument might be made that Title VII applied, *cf. Holloway v. Arthur Andersen*, 566 F.2d at 664 (although Title VII does not prohibit discrimination against transsexuals, "transsexuals claiming discrimination because of their sex, male or female, would clearly state a cause of action under Title VII") (dicta), but that is not this case. It is clear from the evidence that if Eastern did discriminate against Ulane, it was not because she is female, but because

Ulane is a transsexual . . . a biological male who takes female hormones, cross-dresses, and has surgically altered parts of her body to make it appear to be female.

Since Ulane was not discriminated against as a female, and since Title VII is not so expansive in scope as to prohibit discrimination against transsexuals, we reverse the order of the trial court and remand for entry of judgment in favor of Eastern on Count I and dismissal of Count II.

Discussion Notes:

1. The *Ulane* court relied heavily on legislative history. Generally, where the text of a provision is clear, courts should stick to the text and should not stretch the plain meaning of ordinary terms. *See Alexander v. Sandoval*, 532 U.S. 275 284-85 & n.7 (2001); *Oncale v. Sundowner Offshore Servs., Inc.*, 523 U.S. 75, 79 (1998). ("[It is] ultimately the provisions of our laws rather than the principal concerns of our legislators by which we are governed.") Only where the text is not plain should courts wade into what the Supreme Court has termed "the thicket" of legislative history. *United States v. Gonzales*, 510 U.S. 1, 4 (1997). The mere fact that the parties may disagree about the meaning of a statute's text does not render the text unclear. *Miller v. French*, 530 U.S. 327, 336 (2000).

   The Supreme Court has offered a number of cautions about reliance on legislative history for statutory construction. It has observed that legislative history is particularly unhelpful when it consists of "snippets" that might support either party's position. *Associates Comm. Corp. v. Rash*, 520 U.S. 953 (1997). The Court has also warned that where the legislative history consists only of inaction—the failure to enact a bill or amendment—it is a dubious tool for statutory construction. *PBGC v. LTV Corp.*, 496 U.S. 633, 650 (1990) ("Congressional inaction lacks persuasive significance because several equally tenable inferences may be drawn from such inaction, including an inference that the statute already incorporates the offered change."); *United States v. Estate of Romani*, 523 U.S. 517 (1998) (SCALIA, J., concurring) ("Congress can no more express its will by not legislating than an individual member can express his will by not voting."). It has been particularly concerned about lower courts' reliance on legislative history that takes place

after a bill's enactment. *See Central Bank of Denver*, 511 U.S. 164, 187 (1994) ("[F]ailed legislative proposals are 'a particularly dangerous ground on which to rest an interpretation of a prior statute.'") (internal citations omitted).

Bearing in mind these principles, should the Seventh Circuit in *Ulane* have looked to the legislative history at all as to whether transsexuals are a protected class when Title VII does not enumerate them in its text? Is the Seventh Circuit's reliance on legislative history on better ground in determining the question of whether Ulane was discriminated against as a female—a more traditional gender-discrimination claim? Is legislative history merely a handy way for courts to supply content to their own opinions, particularly where the legislative history is a failure to enact a bill or amendment? In view of the fact that the Fourteenth Amendment was enacted solely to prevent race discrimination and it was the Supreme Court that extended its protections to women although the legislative history makes plain that women were not the intended object of the Fourteenth Amendment's protections, is the *Ulane* court's extended discussion of legislative history persuasive? *See Reed v. Reed*, 404 U.S. 71 (1971) (extending Fourteenth Amendment's equal protection clause to gender classifications). What about the remedial purposes of the statute and Congress's intent to eliminate what the *Rabidue* court termed the "poison" of workplace discrimination?

The *Ulane* decision predates the existence of the Americans with Disabilities Act, which explicitly excludes transsexualism per se as a protected class. See 42 U.S.C.A. § 12211 (excluding from definition of "disability" homosexuality, bisexuality, transvestism, transsexualism, pedophilia, exhibitionism, voyeurism, "gender identity disorders not resulting from physical impairments," "other sexual behavior disorders," compulsive gambling, kleptomania, pyromania, and psychoactive substance use disorders resulting from current illegal use of drugs). Had the ADA's specific exclusion been around at the time *Ulane* was decided, could the Court have relied on Congress's decision to exclude "transsexuals" from ADA coverage as a statement of congressional intent for Title VII purposes?

2. Is sex-reassignment surgery really a fraud on the employer, as the *Ulane* court implies in describing the Eighth Circuit's decision in *Sommers* as one about termination following a "misrepresentation" about the employee's gender? Is it the same as failing to disclose that one was fired from one's last job for brawling in the workplace and therefore fairly subject to the after-acquired evidence strictures?

3. Compare the legal theories used in the *DeSantis* and *Ulane* cases. Did the lawyers in *DeSantis* push the envelope too far with their "disparate impact" theory? Their approach certainly was not one calculated to make lesbians feel that they had any reason to support the male homosexual plaintiffs, whose theory effectively would have excluded lesbians from the protections of any victory had the plaintiffs won. Is it surprising that the same claim would be made with a plaintiff who presented much more compelling facts, more than 20 years later, in *Simonton*?

4. Is *Simonton* correct in drawing a distinction between cases that attempt to "bootstrap into Title VII," such as those involving the unprotected classes of transgender employees and homosexual employees, and a subclass of a protected class—those whom Title VII protects on the basis of gender, and among them, those who do not conform to gender-based stereotypes? *Simonton* indicated that the latter class, given proper presentation of the claim and sufficient evidence, was indeed a viable class under Title VII. Do you find the *Simonton* court's reasoning based on *Price Waterhouse* persuasive? *See also Frontiero v. Richardson*, 411 U.S. 677 (1973) (legislature may not draw a classification based on antiquated gender stereotypes that operates to perpetuate discrimination). Did the *Simonton* court read *Oncale* correctly in rejecting the plaintiff's argument based on *Oncale*? Reconsider the discussion in Chapter 2 on the development of a stereotype claim of sex discrimination under Title VII for cases where expectations of gender stereotyping may overlap with discrimination against someone for their sexual orientation.

5. Consider "bootstrapping" and the theory apparent in *Schroeder v. Hamilton School District*,

282 F. 3d 946, cert. denied 537 U.S. 974 (2002). Plaintiff Schroeder, a teacher, sued the school district under 42 U.S.C. § 1983 for his students' harassment of him and the administration's alleged failure to remediate the harassment. It is well settled that student-on-student sexual harassment is actionable under Section 1983 if it is so severe as to interfere with the plaintiff's ability to get an education and school officials, although aware of the harassment, exhibit deliberate indifference toward the victim of the harassment in their treatment of the matter. *See Davis v. Monroe County Bd. of Educ.*, 526 U.S. 629 (1999) (Title IX). This includes peer sexual harassment that creates a hostile learning environment for a gay or lesbian student. *Nabozny v. Podlesny*, 92 F.3d 446 (7th Cir. 1996). The ordinary equal protection standard that is applied to classifications based on homosexuality, however, is rational basis review. The Seventh Circuit rejected the novel theory that the teacher could state an equal protection violation because the administration responded to his complaints about student conduct with less vigor than they responded to complaints of other teachers involving students' racial harassment, but its decision was heavily fact intensive. It is possible that a teacher who presented much more compelling evidence could state a claim based on the equal protection clause, but the proof would have to be overwhelming.

6. Assuming that *Simonton* would countenance a gender stereotyping claim by an effeminate male, does the earring-wearing plaintiff in *DeSantis* state a claim? Is a male's wearing of an earring to work an indication of effeminacy? Bearing in mind the requirements of severe or pervasive, recurrent conduct, would the earring-wearing male employee ever state a claim if he were reprimanded one time for wearing an earring to work? Doesn't an employer have the right to prescribe a workplace dress code? If so, does the employer have the right to enforce different jewelry or hair-length requirements for male and female employees?

5 Employer Liability for Harassment by Supervisors or Co-workers

Problem 24

Marianne is a dispatcher for a taxi company. Her supervisor, Mark, has consistently made sexual comments to her, and he has also brushed up against her body on numerous occasions. The company has a sexual harassment policy, which she follows. The harassment does not stop even after the company warns Mark to cease his conduct.

Problem 25

Stephania is a teller at a local bank. Her co-workers regularly make crude sexual comments in the office, leave sexually explicit pictures around the office, and make sexual jokes about employees, including Stephania. Moreover, several male co-workers have sexually propositioned her. When she turned down one co-worker named John, he loudly referred to her as a "tight-ass" who doesn't "put out," in front of several other employees. Another co-worker regularly referred to her as that "tight little piece of ass." She complained to her supervisor about the conduct, and the supervisor told the employees involved to stop the behavior. The behavior stopped for a few days but then began again.

Problem 26

Mark is an African-American engineer at a large construction company. Other employees regularly make racially derogatory comments to him. They have also left on his desk pictures demeaning African Americans. Racist e-mails are often sent via the office list to all employees in the office, including Mark. The company has no policy governing racial harassment. Assuming the conduct is sufficiently severe or pervasive to create a hostile work environment and Mark complains to his supervisor, should the company be liable if it fails to stop the harassment? What if there is a policy in place and Mark complains, but the company does nothing more than send a memorandum reminding employees that racial discrimination violates company policy? What if there is no policy, but Mark complains to his supervisor, who promptly ends the harassment? What if the supervisor knows of the harassment but ends it only after Mark complains? Would the existence of an adequate policy make a difference in the latter situation? What if the supervisor instigates the harassment, and when Mark complains to higher-level management, nothing is done? What if Mark complains to higher-level management, and the harassment is stopped and the supervisor disciplined? What if there is no policy in the latter situation?

A. Introduction: Employer Liability for Harassment by Supervisors or Co-workers

Employer liability is a major issue in the law of workplace harassment. As you have already learned, the employer is liable for violations of Title VII and the Americans with Disabilities Act. Thus, while individual employees may perpetrate the harassment, it is necessary to prove employer liability in order to prevail on a workplace harassment claim. The individual employees who engaged in the harassment are often sued under state law tort theories, such as intentional infliction of emotional distress. These tort claims are frequently very hard to prove, and even when proven, the harasser(s) often do not have the resources to pay a large judgement. Some statutes, such as 42 U.S.C. § 1981 in the race discrimination context, might also allow a claimant to sue the discriminating employee(s) in appropriate circumstances.

Early on, the issue of employer liability for workplace harassment became a point of major interest. Courts took a variety of approaches that often conflicted. Three distinct issues caused a great deal of confusion: (1) the test for employer liability for the conduct of supervisory personnel, (2) the test for employer liability for the conduct of co-workers (and, to a lesser extent, customers and other nonemployees), and (3) the nature and scope of corrective action required when an employer learns of a harassment situation. The Equal Employment Opportunity Commission (EEOC) issued guidelines that set forth standards regarding all three issues mentioned above, but courts did not always follow the EEOC Guidelines, and even when they did, there were differences in the application and interpretation of those guidelines. In *Meritor*, the Supreme Court noted that courts should use agency principles to determine employer liability for supervisory harassment, but the Court did not specify which ones or how those principles should be applied. That issue became a particularly tricky and controversial one.

It was not until 1998 that the Court directly confronted the issue of employer liability for workplace harassment, and even then, the Court focused primarily on the issue of liability for the acts of supervisors. The Court did so through the two cases that follow. As you read those cases, consider the various paths that the Court did not choose to take, whether the Court had other options, and whether those options would have been as prudent as the path chosen by the Court. Following the section on employer liability for the conduct of officers and supervisory personnel is a section on employer liability for the conduct of co-workers and the corrective action required of the employer when it learns of workplace harassment. The discussion of appropriate corrective action in the co-worker section may also be relevant to supervisory harassment under the standards set forth in the two cases that follow. Questions and hypotheticals on employer liability for workplace harassment generally are presented after the second section.

B. Officers and Supervisory Personnel

BURLINGTON INDUSTRIES, INC.
v.
ELLERTH
524 U.S. 742 (1998)

Justice KENNEDY delivered the opinion of the Court.

[The Employment Problem]

Summary judgment was granted for the employer, so we must take the facts alleged by the employee to be true. *United States v. Diebold, Inc.*, 369 U.S. 654, 655 (1962) (per curiam). The employer is Burlington Industries, the petitioner. The employee is Kimberly Ellerth, the respondent. From March 1993 until May 1994, Ellerth worked as a salesperson in one of Burlington's divisions in Chicago, Illinois. During her employment, she alleges, she was subjected to constant sexual harassment by her supervisor, one Ted Slowik.

In the hierarchy of Burlington's management structure, Slowik was a mid-level manager. Burlington has eight divisions, employing more than 22,000 people in some 50 plants around the United States. Slowik was a vice president in one of five business units within one of the divisions. He had authority to make hiring and promotion decisions subject to the approval of his supervisor, who signed the paperwork. See 912 F. Supp. 1101, 1119, n.14 (N.D. Ill.1996). According to Slowik's supervisor, his position was "not considered an upper-level management position," and he was "not amongst the decision-making

or policy-making hierarchy." *Ibid.* Slowik was not Ellerth's immediate supervisor. Ellerth worked in a two-person office in Chicago, and she answered to her office colleague, who in turn answered to Slowik in New York.

Against a background of repeated boorish and offensive remarks and gestures which Slowik allegedly made, Ellerth places particular emphasis on three alleged incidents where Slowik's comments could be construed as threats to deny her tangible job benefits. In the summer of 1993, while on a business trip, Slowik invited Ellerth to the hotel lounge, an invitation Ellerth felt compelled to accept because Slowik was her boss. App. 155. When Ellerth gave no encouragement to remarks Slowik made about her breasts, he told her to "loosen up" and warned, "You know, Kim, I could make your life very hard or very easy at Burlington." *Id.*, at 156.

In March 1994, when Ellerth was being considered for a promotion, Slowik expressed reservations during the promotion interview because she was not "loose enough." *Id.*, at 159. The comment was followed by his reaching over and rubbing her knee. *Ibid.* Ellerth did receive the promotion; but when

Slowik called to announce it, he told Ellerth, "you're gonna be out there with men who work in factories, and they certainly like women with pretty butts/legs." *Id.*, at 159–160.

In May 1994, Ellerth called Slowik, asking permission to insert a customer's logo into a fabric sample. Slowik responded, "I don't have time for you right now, Kim—unless you want to tell me what you're wearing." *Id.*, at 78. Ellerth told Slowik she had to go and ended the call. *Ibid*. A day or two later, Ellerth called Slowik to ask permission again. This time he denied her request, but added something along the lines of, "are you wearing shorter skirts yet, Kim, because it would make your job a whole heck of a lot easier." *Id.*, at 79.

A short time later, Ellerth's immediate supervisor cautioned her about returning telephone calls to customers in a prompt fashion. 912 F. Supp., at 1109. In response, Ellerth quit. She faxed a letter giving reasons unrelated to the alleged sexual harassment we have described. *Ibid*. About three weeks later, however, she sent a letter explaining she quit because of Slowik's behavior. *Ibid*.

During her tenure at Burlington, Ellerth did not inform anyone in authority about Slowik's conduct, despite knowing Burlington had a policy against sexual harassment. *Ibid*. In fact, she chose not to inform her immediate supervisor (not Slowik) because "'it would be his duty as my supervisor to report any incidents of sexual harassment.'" *Ibid*. On one occasion, she told Slowik a comment he made was inappropriate. *Ibid*.

In October 1994, after receiving a right-to-sue letter from the Equal Employment Opportunity Commission (EEOC), Ellerth filed suit in the United States District Court for the Northern District of Illinois, alleging Burlington engaged in sexual harassment and forced her constructive discharge, in violation of Title VII.

[The Decision by the Trial Court and the U.S. Court of Appeals for the Seventh Circuit]

The District Court granted summary judgment to Burlington. The court found Slowik's behavior, as described by Ellerth, severe and pervasive enough to create a hostile work environment, but found Burlington neither knew nor should have known about the conduct. There was no triable issue of fact on the latter point, and the court noted Ellerth had not used Burlington's internal complaint procedures. *Id.*, at 1118. Although Ellerth's claim was framed as a hostile work environment complaint, the District Court

observed there was a *quid pro quo* "component" to the hostile environment. *Id.*, at 1121. Proceeding from the premise that an employer faces vicarious liability for *quid pro quo* harassment, the District Court thought it necessary to apply a negligence standard because the *quid pro quo* merely contributed to the hostile work environment. *See id.*, at 1123. The District Court also dismissed Ellerth's constructive discharge claim.

The Court of Appeals en banc reversed in a decision which produced eight separate opinions and no consensus for a controlling rationale. The judges were able to agree on the problem they confronted: Vicarious liability, not failure to comply with a duty of care, was the essence of Ellerth's case against Burlington on appeal. The judges seemed to agree Ellerth could recover if Slowik's unfulfilled threats to deny her tangible job benefits was sufficient to impose vicarious liability on Burlington. *Jansen v. Packaging Corp. of America*, 123 F.3d 490, 494 (C.A. 7 1997) (per curiam). With the exception of Judges Coffey and Easterbrook, the judges also agreed Ellerth's claim could be categorized as one of *quid pro quo* harassment, even though she had received the promotion and had suffered no other tangible retaliation. *Ibid*.

The consensus disintegrated on the standard for an employer's liability for such a claim. . . .

The disagreement revealed in the careful opinions of the judges of the Court of Appeals reflects the fact that Congress has left it to the courts to determine controlling agency law principles in a new and difficult area of federal law. We granted certiorari to assist in defining the relevant standards of employer liability. 522 U.S. 1086 (1998). . . .

[The Legal Issues]

We decide whether, under Title VII of the Civil Rights Act of 1964, 78 Stat. 253, as amended, 42 U.S.C. § 2000e *et seq.*, an employee who refuses the unwelcome and threatening sexual advances of a supervisor, yet suffers no adverse, tangible job consequences, can recover against the employer without showing the employer is negligent or otherwise at fault for the supervisor's actions. . . .

[The Decision and Rationale of the U.S. Supreme Court]

At the outset, we assume an important proposition yet to be established before a trier of fact. It is a premise assumed as well, in explicit or implicit terms, in the various opinions by the judges of the Court of

Appeals. The premise is: a trier of fact could find in Slowik's remarks numerous threats to retaliate against Ellerth if she denied some sexual liberties. The threats, however, were not carried out or fulfilled. Cases based on threats which are carried out are referred to often as *quid pro quo* cases, as distinct from bothersome attentions or sexual remarks that are sufficiently severe or pervasive to create a hostile work environment. The terms *quid pro quo* and hostile work environment are helpful, perhaps, in making a rough demarcation between cases in which threats are carried out and those where they are not or are absent altogether, but beyond this are of limited utility.

Section 703(a) of Title VII forbids

an employer "(1) to fail or refuse to hire or to discharge any individual, or otherwise to discriminate against any individual with respect to his compensation, terms, conditions, or privileges of employment, because of such individual's . . . sex." 42 U.S.C. § 2000e-2(a)(1).

"Quid pro quo " and "hostile work environment" do not appear in the statutory text. The terms appeared first in the academic literature, *see* C. MacKinnon, Sexual Harassment of Working Women (1979); found their way into decisions of the Courts of Appeals, *see, e.g.,* *Henson v. Dundee*, 682 F.2d 897, 909 (C.A.11 1982); and were mentioned in this Court's decision in *Meritor Savings Bank, FSB v. Vinson*, 477 U.S. 57 (1986). *See generally* E. Scalia, *The Strange Career of Quid Pro Quo Sexual Harassment*, 21 Harv. J.L. & Pub. Policy 307 (1998).

In *Meritor*, the terms served a specific and limited purpose. There we considered whether the conduct in question constituted discrimination in the terms or conditions of employment in violation of Title VII. We assumed, and with adequate reason, that if an employer demanded sexual favors from an employee in return for a job benefit, discrimination with respect to terms or conditions of employment was explicit. Less obvious was whether an employer's sexually demeaning behavior altered terms or conditions of employment in violation of Title VII. We distinguished between *quid pro quo* claims and hostile environment claims, see 477 U.S., at 65, and said both were cognizable under Title VII, though the latter requires harassment that is severe or pervasive. *Ibid.* The principal significance of the distinction is to instruct that Title VII is violated by either explicit or constructive alterations in the terms or conditions of employ-

ment and to explain the latter must be severe or pervasive. The distinction was not discussed for its bearing upon an employer's liability for an employee's discrimination. On this question, *Meritor* held, with no further specifics, that agency principles controlled. *Id.*, at 72.

Nevertheless, as use of the terms grew in the wake of *Meritor*, they acquired their own significance. The standard of employer responsibility turned on which type of harassment occurred. If the plaintiff established a *quid pro quo* claim, the Courts of Appeals held, the employer was subject to vicarious liability. See *Davis v. Sioux City*, 115 F.3d 1365, 1367 (C.A.8 1997); *Nichols v. Frank*, 42 F.3d 503, 513–514 (C.A.9 1994); *Bouton v. BMW of North America, Inc.*, 29 F.3d 103, 106–107 (C.A.3 1994); *Sauers v. Salt Lake County*, 1 F.3d 1122, 1127 (C.A.10 1993); *Kauffman v. Allied Signal, Inc.*, 970 F.2d 178, 185–186 (C.A.6), cert. denied, 506 U.S. 1041 (1992); *Steele v. Offshore Shipbuilding, Inc.*, 867 F.2d 1311, 1316 (C.A.11 1989). The rule encouraged Title VII plaintiffs to state their claims as *quid pro quo* claims, which in turn put expansive pressure on the definition. The equivalence of the *quid pro quo* label and vicarious liability is illustrated by this case. The question presented on certiorari is whether Ellerth can state a claim of *quid pro quo* harassment, but the issue of real concern to the parties is whether Burlington has vicarious liability for Slowik's alleged misconduct, rather than liability limited to its own negligence. The question presented for certiorari asks:

Whether a claim of *quid pro quo* sexual harassment may be stated under Title VII. . . where the plaintiff employee has neither submitted to the sexual advances of the alleged harasser nor suffered any tangible effects on the compensation, terms, conditions or privileges of employment as a consequence of a refusal to submit to those advances?

Pet. for Cert. i.

We do not suggest the terms *quid pro quo* and hostile work environment are irrelevant to Title VII litigation. To the extent they illustrate the distinction between cases involving a threat which is carried out and offensive conduct in general, the terms are relevant when there is a threshold question whether a plaintiff can prove discrimination in violation of Title VII. When a plaintiff proves that a tangible employment action resulted from a refusal to submit to a supervisor's sexual demands, he or she establishes that the employment decision itself constitutes a change in the terms and conditions of employment that is actionable under Title VII. For any sexual harassment preceding the employment decision to be actionable, however, the conduct must be severe or pervasive. Because Ellerth's claim involves only unfulfilled threats, it should be categorized as a hostile work environment claim which requires a showing of severe or pervasive conduct. See *Oncale v. Sundowner Offshore Services, Inc.*, 523 U.S. 75, 81, (1998); *Harris v. Forklift Systems, Inc.*, 510 U.S. 17, 21, (1993). For purposes of this case, we accept the District Court's finding that the alleged conduct was severe or pervasive. See *supra*, at 2262–2263. The case before us involves numerous alleged threats, and we express no opinion as to whether a single unfulfilled threat is sufficient to constitute discrimination in the terms or conditions of employment.

When we assume discrimination can be proved, however, the factors we discuss below, and not the categories *quid pro quo* and hostile work environment, will be controlling on the issue of vicarious liability. That is the question we must resolve.

We must decide, then, whether an employer has vicarious liability when a supervisor creates a hostile work environment by making explicit threats to alter a subordinate's terms or conditions of employment, based on sex, but does not fulfill the threat. We turn to principles of agency law, for the term "employer" is defined under Title VII to include "agents." 42 U.S.C. § 2000e(b); see *Meritor, supra*, at 72. In express terms, Congress has directed federal courts to interpret Title VII based on agency principles. Given such an explicit instruction, we conclude a uniform and predictable standard must be established as a matter of federal law. We rely "on the general common law of agency, rather than on the law of any particular State, to give meaning to these terms." *Community for Creative Non-Violence v. Reid*, 490 U.S. 730, 740, (1989). . . .

As *Meritor* acknowledged, the Restatement (Second) of Agency (1957) (hereinafter Restatement), is a useful beginning point for a discussion of general agency principles. 477 U.S., at 72. Since our decision in *Meritor*, federal courts have explored agency principles, and we find useful instruction in their decisions, noting that "common-law principles may not be transferable in all their particulars to Title VII." *Ibid*. The EEOC has issued Guidelines governing

sexual harassment claims under Title VII, but they provide little guidance on the issue of employer liability for supervisor harassment. See 29 CFR § 1604.11(c) (1997) (vicarious liability for supervisor harassment turns on "the particular employment relationship and the job functions performed by the individual").

A.

Section 219(1) of the Restatement sets out a central principle of agency law:

A master is subject to liability for the torts of his servants committed while acting in the scope of their employment.

An employer may be liable for both negligent and intentional torts committed by an employee within the scope of his or her employment. Sexual harassment under Title VII presupposes intentional conduct. While early decisions absolved employers of liability for the intentional torts of their employees, the law now imposes liability where the employee's "purpose, however misguided, is wholly or in part to further the master's business." W. Keeton, D. Dobbs, R. Keeton, & D. Owen, Prosser and Keeton on Law of Torts § 70, p. 505 (5th ed. 1984) (hereinafter Prosser and Keeton on Torts). In applying scope of employment principles to intentional torts, however, it is accepted that "it is less likely that a willful tort will properly be held to be in the course of employment and that the liability of the master for such torts will naturally be more limited." F. Mechem, Outlines of the Law of Agency § 394, p. 266 (P. Mechem 4th ed., 1952). The Restatement defines conduct, including an intentional tort, to be within the scope of employment when "actuated, at least in part, by a purpose to serve the [employer]," even if it is forbidden by the employer. Restatement §§ 228(1)(c), 230. For example, when a salesperson lies to a customer to make a sale, the tortious conduct is within the scope of employment because it benefits the employer by increasing sales, even though it may violate the employer's policies. See Prosser and Keeton on Torts § 70, at 505–506.

As Courts of Appeals have recognized, a supervisor acting out of gender-based animus or a desire to fulfill sexual urges may not be actuated by a purpose to serve the employer. See, *e.g.*, *Harrison v. Eddy Potash, Inc.*, 112 F.3d 1437, 1444 (C.A.10 1997), vacated on other grounds, 524 U.S. 947 (1998); *Torres v. Pisano*, 116 F.3d 625, 634, n.10 (C.A.2 1997). But see *Kauffman v. Allied Signal, Inc.*, 970 F.2d, at 184–185 (holding harassing supervisor acted within scope of employment, but employer was not liable because of its quick and effective remediation). The harassing supervisor often acts for personal motives, motives unrelated and even antithetical to the objectives of the employer. . . . There are instances, of course, where a supervisor engages in unlawful discrimination with the purpose, mistaken or otherwise, to serve the employer. *E.g., Sims v. Montgomery County Comm'n*, 766 F. Supp. 1052, 1075 (M.D. Ala. 1990) (supervisor acting in scope of employment where employer has a policy of discouraging women from seeking advancement and "sexual harassment was simply a way of furthering that policy").

The concept of scope of employment has not always been construed to require a motive to serve the employer. *E.g., Ira S. Bushey & Sons, Inc. v. United States*, 398 F.2d 167, 172 (C.A.2 1968). Federal courts have nonetheless found similar limitations on employer liability when applying the agency laws of the States under the Federal Tort Claims Act, which makes the Federal Government liable for torts committed by employees within the scope of employment. . . .

The general rule is that sexual harassment by a supervisor is not conduct within the scope of employment.

Scope of employment does not define the only basis for employer liability under agency principles. In limited circumstances, agency principles impose liability on employers even where employees commit torts outside the scope of employment. The principles are set forth in the much-cited § 219(2) of the Restatement:

> (2) A master is not subject to liability for the torts of his servants acting outside the scope of their employment, unless: (a) the master intended the conduct or the consequences, or (b) the master was negligent or reckless, or (c) the conduct violated a non-delegable duty of the master, or (d) the servant purported to act or to speak on behalf of the principal and there was reliance upon apparent authority, or he was aided in accomplishing the tort by the existence of the agency relation.

See also § 219, Comment e (Section 219(2) "enumerates the situations in which a master may be liable for torts of servants acting solely for their own purposes and hence not in the scope of employment").

Subsection (a) addresses direct liability, where the employer acts with tortious intent, and indirect liability, where the agent's high rank in the company makes him or her the employer's alter ego. None of the parties contend Slowik's rank imputes liability under this principle. There is no contention, furthermore, that a nondelegable duty is involved. See § 219(2)(c). So, for our purposes here, subsections (a) and (c) can be put aside.

Subsections (b) and (d) are possible grounds for imposing employer liability on account of a supervisor's acts and must be considered. Under subsection (b), an employer is liable when the tort is attributable to the employer's own negligence. § 219(2)(b). Thus, although a supervisor's sexual harassment is outside the scope of employment because the conduct was for personal motives, an employer can be liable, nonetheless, where its own negligence is a cause of the harassment. An employer is negligent with respect to sexual harassment if it knew or should have known about the conduct and failed to stop it. Negligence sets a minimum standard for employer liability under Title VII; but Ellerth seeks to invoke the more stringent standard of vicarious liability.

Section 219(2)(d) concerns vicarious liability for intentional torts committed by an employee when the employee uses apparent authority (the apparent authority standard), or when the employee "was aided in accomplishing the tort by the existence of the agency relation" (the aided in the agency relation standard). . . .

As a general rule, apparent authority is relevant where the agent purports to exercise a power which he or she does not have, as distinct from where the agent threatens to misuse actual power. Compare Restatement § 6 (defining "power") with § 8 (defining "apparent authority"). In the usual case, a supervisor's harassment involves misuse of actual power, not the false impression of its existence. Apparent authority analysis therefore is inappropriate in this context. If, in the unusual case, it is alleged there is a false impression that the actor was a supervisor, when he in fact was not, the victim's mistaken conclusion must be a reasonable one. Restatement § 8, Comment *c* ("Apparent authority exists only to the extent it is reasonable for the third person dealing with the agent to believe that the agent is authorized"). When a party seeks to impose vicarious liability based on an agent's misuse of delegated authority, the Restatement's aided in the agency relation rule, rather than the apparent authority rule, appears to be the appropriate form of analysis.

We turn to the aided in the agency relation standard. In a sense, most workplace tortfeasors are aided in accomplishing their tortious objective by the existence of the agency relation: Proximity and regular contact may afford a captive pool of potential victims. See *Gary v. Long*, 59 F.3d 1391, 1397 (C.A.D.C. 1995). Were this to satisfy the aided in the agency relation standard, an employer would be subject to vicarious liability not only for all supervisor harassment, but also for all co-worker harassment, a result enforced by neither the EEOC nor any court of appeals to have considered the issue. . . . The aided in the agency relation standard, therefore, requires the existence of something more than the employment relation itself.

At the outset, we can identify a class of cases where, beyond question, more than the mere existence of the employment relation aids in commission of the harassment: when a supervisor takes a tangible employment action against the subordinate. Every Federal Court of Appeals to have considered the question has found vicarious liability when a discriminatory act results in a tangible employment action. . . . In *Meritor*, we acknowledged this consensus. See 477 U.S., at 70–71. Although few courts have elaborated how agency principles support this rule, we think it reflects a correct application of the aided in the agency relation standard.

In the context of this case, a tangible employment action would have taken the form of a denial of a raise or a promotion. The concept of a tangible employment action appears in numerous cases in the Courts of Appeals discussing claims involving race, age, and national origin discrimination, as well as sex discrimination. Without endorsing the specific results of those decisions, we think it prudent to import the concept of a tangible employment action for resolution of the vicarious liability issue we consider here. A tangible employment action constitutes a significant change in employment status, such as hiring, firing, failing to promote, reassignment with significantly different responsibilities, or a decision causing a significant change in benefits. Compare *Crady v. Liberty Nat. Bank & Trust Co. of Ind.*, 993 F.2d 132, 136 (C.A.7 1993) ("A materially adverse change might be indicated by a termination of employment, a demotion evidenced by a decrease in wage or salary, a less distinguished title, a material loss of benefits, significantly diminished material responsibilities, or other indices that might be unique to a particular situation"), with *Flaherty v. Gas Research Institute*, 31 F.3d 451, 456 (C.A.7 1994) (a "bruised ego" is not enough); *Kocsis v. Multi-Care Management, Inc.*, 97 F.3d 876, 887

(C.A.6 1996) (demotion without change in pay, benefits, duties, or prestige insufficient) and *Harlston v. McDonnell Douglas Corp.*, 37 F.3d 379, 382 (C.A.8 1994) (reassignment to more inconvenient job insufficient).

When a supervisor makes a tangible employment decision, there is assurance the injury could not have been inflicted absent the agency relation. A tangible employment action in most cases inflicts direct economic harm. As a general proposition, only a supervisor, or other person acting with the authority of the company, can cause this sort of injury. A co-worker can break a co-worker's arm as easily as a supervisor, and anyone who has regular contact with an employee can inflict psychological injuries by his or her offensive conduct. . . . But one co-worker (absent some elaborate scheme) cannot dock another's pay, nor can one co-worker demote another. Tangible employment actions fall within the special province of the supervisor. The supervisor has been empowered by the company as a distinct class of agent to make economic decisions affecting other employees under his or her control.

Tangible employment actions are the means by which the supervisor brings the official power of the enterprise to bear on subordinates. A tangible employment decision requires an official act of the enterprise, a company act. The decision in most cases is documented in official company records and may be subject to review by higher level supervisors. . . . The supervisor often must obtain the imprimatur of the enterprise and use its internal processes. *See Kotcher v. Rosa & Sullivan Appliance Center, Inc.*, 957 F.2d 59, 62 (C.A.2 1992) ("From the perspective of the employee, the supervisor and the employer merge into a single entity").

For these reasons, a tangible employment action taken by the supervisor becomes for Title VII purposes the act of the employer. Whatever the exact contours of the aided in the agency relation standard, its requirements will always be met when a supervisor takes a tangible employment action against a subordinate. In that instance, it would be implausible to interpret agency principles to allow an employer to escape liability, as *Meritor* itself appeared to acknowledge. . . .

Whether the agency relation aids in commission of supervisor harassment which does not culminate in a tangible employment action is less obvious. Application of the standard is made difficult by its malleable terminology, which can be read to either expand or limit liability in the context of supervisor harassment. On the one hand, a supervisor's power and authority invests his or her harassing conduct with a particular threatening character, and in this sense, a supervisor always is aided by the agency relation. See *Meritor*, 477 U.S., at 77 (Marshall, J., concurring in judgment) ("[I]t is precisely because the supervisor is understood to be clothed with the employer's authority that he is able to impose unwelcome sexual conduct on subordinates"). On the other hand, there are acts of harassment a supervisor might commit which might be the same acts a co-employee would commit, and there may be some circumstances where the supervisor's status makes little difference.

It is this tension which, we think, has caused so much confusion among the Courts of Appeals which have sought to apply the aided in the agency relation standard to Title VII cases. The aided in the agency relation standard, however, is a developing feature of agency law, and we hesitate to render a definitive explanation of our understanding of the standard in an area where other important considerations must affect our judgment. In particular, we are bound by our holding in *Meritor* that agency principles constrain the imposition of vicarious liability in cases of supervisory harassment. . . . Congress has not altered *Meritor's rule even though it has made significant amendments to Title VII in the interim.* See *Illinois Brick Co. v. Illinois*, 431 U.S. 720, 736, (1977) ("[W]e must bear in mind that considerations of *stare decisis* weigh heavily in the area of statutory construction, where Congress is free to change this Court's interpretation of its legislation"). . . .

In order to accommodate the agency principles of vicarious liability for harm caused by misuse of supervisory authority, as well as Title VII's equally basic policies of encouraging forethought by employers and saving action by objecting employees, we adopt the following holding in this case and in *Faragher v. Boca Raton*, 524 U.S. 775 (1998), also decided today. An employer is subject to vicarious liability to a victimized employee for an actionable hostile environment created by a supervisor with immediate (or successively higher) authority over the employee. When no tangible employment action is taken, a defending employer may raise an affirmative defense to liability or damages, subject to proof by a preponderance of the evidence, see Fed. Rule Civ. Proc. 8(c). The defense comprises two necessary elements: (a) that the employer exercised reasonable care to prevent and correct promptly any sexually harassing behavior, and (b) that the plaintiff employee unreasonably failed to take advantage of any preventive or corrective opportunities provided by the employer or to avoid harm otherwise. While proof that an employer had promulgated an anti-harassment policy with complaint procedure is not necessary in every instance as a matter of law, the need for a stated policy suitable to the employment circumstances may appropriately be addressed in any case when litigating the first element of the defense. And while proof that an employee failed to fulfill the corresponding obligation of reasonable care to avoid harm is not limited to showing any unreasonable failure to use any complaint procedure provided by the employer, a demonstration of such failure will normally suffice to satisfy the employer's burden under the second element of the defense. No affirmative defense is available, however, when the supervisor's harassment culminates in a tangible employment action, such as discharge, demotion, or undesirable reassignment.

Relying on existing case law which held out the promise of vicarious liability for all *quid pro quo* claims. . . . Ellerth focused all her attention in the Court of Appeals on proving her claim fit within that category. Given our explanation that the labels *quid pro quo* and hostile work environment are not controlling for purposes of establishing employer liability. . . . Ellerth should have an adequate opportunity to prove she has a claim for which Burlington is liable.

Although Ellerth has not alleged she suffered a tangible employment action at the hands of Slowik, which would deprive Burlington of the availability of the affirmative defense, this is not dispositive. In light of our decision, Burlington is still subject to vicarious liability for Slowik's activity, but Burlington should have an opportunity to assert and prove the affirmative defense to liability. . . .

For these reasons, we will affirm the judgment of the Court of Appeals, reversing the grant of summary judgment against Ellerth. On remand, the District Court will have the opportunity to decide whether it would be appropriate to allow Ellerth to amend her pleading or supplement her discovery.

The judgment of the Court of Appeals is affirmed. *It is so ordered.*

[Justice GINSBURG'S opinion concurring in the judgment is omitted.

Justice THOMAS'S dissenting opinion, which was joined by Justice SCALIA, is omitted.]

FARAGHER
v.
CITY OF BOCA RATON
524 U.S. 775 (1998)

Justice SOUTER delivered the opinion of the Court.

[The Employment Problem]

Between 1985 and 1990, while attending college, petitioner Beth Ann Faragher worked part time and during the summers as an ocean lifeguard for the Marine Safety Section of the Parks and Recreation Department of respondent, the City of Boca Raton, Florida (City). During this period, Faragher's immediate supervisors were Bill Terry, David Silverman, and Robert Gordon. In June 1990, Faragher resigned.

In 1992, Faragher brought an action against Terry, Silverman, and the City, asserting claims under Title VII, Rev. Stat. § 1979, 42 U.S.C. § 1983, and Florida law. So far as it concerns the Title VII claim, the complaint alleged that Terry and Silverman created a "sexually hostile atmosphere" at the beach by repeatedly subjecting Faragher and other female lifeguards to "uninvited and offensive touching," by making lewd remarks, and by speaking of women in offensive terms. The complaint contained specific allegations that Terry once said that he would never promote a woman to the rank of lieutenant, and that Silverman had said to Faragher, "Date me or clean the toilets for a year." Asserting that Terry and Silverman were agents of the City, and that their conduct amounted to discrimination in the "terms, conditions, and privileges" of her employment, 42 U.S.C. § 2000e-2(a)(1) Faragher sought a judgement against the City for nominal damages, costs, and attorney's fees.

[The Decision of the Trial Court and the U.S. Court of Appeals for the Eleventh Circuit]

Following a bench trial, the United States District Court for the Southern District of Florida found that throughout Faragher's employment with the City, Terry served as Chief of the Marine Safety Division, with authority to hire new lifeguards (subject to the approval of higher management), to supervise all aspects of the lifeguards' work assignments, to engage in counseling, to deliver oral reprimands, and to make a record of any such discipline. 864 F. Supp. 1552, 1563–1564 (1994). Silverman was a Marine Safety lieutenant from 1985 until June 1989, when he

became a captain. *Id.*, at 1555. Gordon began the employment period as a lieutenant and at some point was promoted to the position of training captain. In these positions, Silverman and Gordon were responsible for making the lifeguards' daily assignments, and for supervising their work and fitness training. *Id.*, at 1564.

The lifeguards and supervisors were stationed at the city beach and worked out of the Marine Safety Headquarters, a small one-story building containing an office, a meeting room, and a single, unisex locker room with a shower. *Id.*, at 1556. Their work routine was structured in a "paramilitary configuration," *Id.*, at 1564, with a clear chain of command. Lifeguards reported to lieutenants and captains, who reported to Terry. He was supervised by the Recreation Superintendent, who in turn reported to a Director of Parks and Recreation, answerable to the City Manager. *Id.*, at 1555. The lifeguards had no significant contact with higher city officials like the Recreation Superintendent. *Id.*, at 1564.

In February 1986, the City adopted a sexual harassment policy, which it stated in a memorandum from the City Manager addressed to all employees. *Id.*, at 1560. In May 1990, the City revised the policy and reissued a statement of it. *Ibid.* Although the City may actually have circulated the memos and statements to some employees, it completely failed to disseminate its policy among employees of the Marine Safety Section, with the result that Terry, Silverman, Gordon, and many lifeguards were unaware of it. *Ibid.*

From time to time over the course of Faragher's tenure at the Marine Safety Section, between 4 and 6 of the 40 to 50 lifeguards were women. *Id.*, at 1556. During that 5-year period, Terry repeatedly touched the bodies of female employees without invitation, *ibid.*, would put his arm around Faragher, with his hand on her buttocks, *id.*, at 1557, and once made contact with another female lifeguard in a motion of sexual simulation, *id.*, at 1556. He made crudely demeaning references to women generally, *id.*, at 1557, and once commented disparagingly on Faragher's shape, *ibid*. During a job interview with a woman he hired as a lifeguard, Terry said that the female life-guards had sex with their male counterparts and asked whether she would do the same. *Ibid*.

Silverman behaved in similar ways. He once tackled Faragher and remarked that, but for a physical characteristic he found unattractive, he would readily have had sexual relations with her. *Ibid*. Another time, he pantomimed an act of oral sex. *Ibid*. Within earshot of the female lifeguards, Silverman made frequent, vulgar references to women and sexual matters, commented on the bodies of female lifeguards and beachgoers, and at least twice told female lifeguards that he would like to engage in sex with them. *Id.*, at 1557–1558.

Faragher did not complain to higher management about Terry or Silverman. Although she spoke of their behavior to Gordon, she did not regard these discussions as formal complaints to a supervisor but as conversations with a person she held in high esteem. *Id.*, at 1559. Other female lifeguards had similarly informal talks with Gordon, but because Gordon did not feel that it was his place to do so, he did not report these complaints to Terry, his own supervisor, or to any other city official. *Id.*, at 1559–1560. Gordon responded to the complaints of one lifeguard by saying that "the City just [doesn't] care." *Id.*, at 1561.

In April 1990, however, two months before Faragher's resignation, Nancy Ewanchew, a former lifeguard, wrote to Richard Bender, the City's Personnel Director, complaining that Terry and Silverman had harassed her and other female lifeguards. *Id.*, at 1559. Following investigation of this complaint, the City found that Terry and Silverman had behaved improperly, reprimanded them, and required them to choose between a suspension without pay or the forfeiture of annual leave. *Ibid*.

On the basis of these findings, the District Court concluded that the conduct of Terry and Silverman was discriminatory harassment sufficiently serious to alter the conditions of Faragher's employment and constitute an abusive working environment. *Id.*, at 1562–1563. The District Court then ruled that there were three justifications for holding the City liable for the harassment of its supervisory employees. First, the court noted that the harassment was pervasive enough to support an inference that the City had "knowledge, or constructive knowledge," of it. *Id.*, at 1563. Next, it ruled that the City was liable under traditional agency principles because Terry and Silverman were acting as its agents when they committed the harassing acts. *Id.*, at 1563–1564. Finally, the court observed that Gordon's knowledge of the harassment, combined with his inaction, "provides a further

basis for imputing liability on [sic] the City." *Id.*, at 1564. The District Court then awarded Faragher one dollar in nominal damages on her Title VII claim. *Id.*, at 1564–1565. . . .

A panel of the Court of Appeals for the Eleventh Circuit reversed the judgment against the City. 76 F.3d 1155 (1996). Although the panel had "no trouble concluding that Terry's and Silverman's conduct . . . was severe and pervasive enough to create an objectively abusive work environment," *id.*, at 1162, it overturned the District Court's conclusion that the City was liable. The panel ruled that Terry and Silverman were not acting within the scope of their employment when they engaged in the harassment, *id.*, at 1166, that they were not aided in their actions by the agency relationship, *id.*, at 1166, n.14, and that the City had no constructive knowledge of the harassment by virtue of its pervasiveness or Gordon's actual knowledge, *id.*, at 1167, and n.16.

In a 7-to-5 decision, the full Court of Appeals, sitting en banc, adopted the panel's conclusion. 111 F.3d 1530 (1997). Relying on our decision in *Meritor Savings Bank, FSB v. Vinson*, 477 U.S. 57 (1986), and on the Restatement (Second) of Agency § 219 (1957) (hereinafter Restatement), the court held that "an employer may be indirectly liable for hostile environment sexual harassment by a superior: (1) if the harassment occurs within the scope of the superior's employment; (2) if the employer assigns performance of a nondelegable duty to a supervisor and an employee is injured because of the supervisor's failure to carry out that duty; or (3) if there is an agency relationship which aids the supervisor's ability or opportunity to harass his subordinate." 111 F.3d, at 1534–1535.

Applying these principles, the court rejected Faragher's Title VII claim against the City. First, invoking standard agency language to classify the harassment by each supervisor as a "frolic" unrelated to his authorized tasks, the court found that in harassing Faragher, Terry and Silverman were acting outside of the scope of their employment and solely to further their own personal ends. *Id.*, at 1536–1537. Next, the court determined that the supervisors' agency relationship with the City did not assist them in perpetrating their harassment. *Id.*, at 1537. Though noting that "a supervisor is always aided in accomplishing hostile environment sexual harassment by the existence of the agency relationship with his employer because his responsibilities include close proximity to and regular contact with the victim," the court held that traditional agency law does not employ so broad a concept of aid as a predicate of employer liability, but requires something more than a mere combination of agency relationship and improper conduct by the agent. *Ibid*. Because neither Terry nor Silverman threatened to fire or demote Faragher, the court concluded that their agency relationship did not facilitate their harassment. *Ibid*.

The en banc court also affirmed the panel's ruling that the City lacked constructive knowledge of the supervisors' harassment. The court read the District Court's opinion to rest on an erroneous legal conclusion that any harassment pervasive enough to create a hostile environment must *a fortiori* also suffice to charge the employer with constructive knowledge. *Id.*, at 1538. Rejecting this approach, the court reviewed the record and found no adequate factual basis to conclude that the harassment was so pervasive that the City should have known of it, relying on the facts that the harassment occurred intermittently, over a long period of time, and at a remote location. *Ibid*. In footnotes, the court also rejected the arguments that the City should be deemed to have known of the harassment through Gordon, *id.*, at 1538, n.9, or charged with constructive knowledge because of its failure to disseminate its sexual harassment policy among the lifeguards, *id.*, at 1539, n.11.

[The Legal Issue]

This case calls for identification of the circumstances under which an employer may be held liable under Title VII of the Civil Rights Act of 1964, 78 Stat. 253, as amended, 42 U.S.C. § 2000e *et seq.*, for the acts of a supervisory employee whose sexual harassment of subordinates has created a hostile work environment amounting to employment discrimination.

[The Decision and Rationale of the U.S. Supreme Court]

We hold that an employer is vicariously liable for actionable discrimination caused by a supervisor, but subject to an affirmative defense looking to the reasonableness of the employer's conduct as well as that of a plaintiff victim. . . .

Since our decision in *Meritor*, Courts of Appeals have struggled to derive manageable standards to govern employer liability for hostile environment harassment perpetrated by supervisory employees. While following our admonition to find guidance in the common law of agency, as embodied in the Restatement, the Courts of Appeals have adopted different approaches. . . .

While indicating the substantive contours of the hostile environments forbidden by Title VII, our cases have established few definite rules for determining when an employer will be liable for a discriminatory environment that is otherwise actionably abusive. Given the circumstances of many of the litigated cases, including some that have come to us, it is not surprising that in many of them, the issue has been joined over the sufficiency of the abusive conditions, not the standards for determining an employer's liability for them. There have, for example, been myriad cases in which District Courts and Courts of Appeals have held employers liable on account of actual knowledge by the employer, or high-echelon officials of an employer organization, of sufficiently harassing action by subordinates, which the employer or its informed officers have done nothing to stop. See, *e.g.*, *Katz v. Dole*, 709 F.2d 251, 256 (C.A. 1983) (upholding employer liability because the "employer's supervisory personnel manifested unmistakable acquiescence in or approval of the harassment"); *EEOC v. Hacienda Hotel*, 881 F.2d 1504, 1516 (C.A.9 1989) (employer liable where hotel manager did not respond to complaints about supervisors' harassment); *Hall v. Gus Constr. Co.*, 842 F.2d 1010, 1016 (C.A.8 1988) (holding employer liable for harassment by co-workers because supervisor knew of the harassment but did nothing). In such instances, the combined knowledge and inaction may be seen as demonstrable negligence, or as the employer's adoption of the offending conduct and its results, quite as if they had been authorized affirmatively as the employer's policy. Cf. *Oncale, supra*, at 77, (victim reported his grounds for fearing rape to company's safety supervisor, who turned him away with no action on complaint).

Nor was it exceptional that standards for binding the employer were not in issue in *Harris, supra*. In that case of discrimination by hostile environment, the individual charged with creating the abusive atmosphere was the president of the corporate employer, 510 U.S., at 19, who was indisputably within that class of an employer organization's officials who may be treated as the organization's proxy. *Burns v. McGregor Electronic Industries, Inc.*, 955 F.2d 559, 564 (C.A.8 1992) (employer-company liable where harassment was perpetrated by its owner); see *Torres v. Pisano*, 116 F.3d 625, 634–635, and n.11 (C.A.2) (noting that a supervisor may hold a sufficiently high position "in the management hierarchy of the company for his actions to be imputed automatically to the employer"), cert. denied, 522 U.S. 997 (1997); cf. *Katz, supra*, at 255 ("Except in situations where a proprietor, partner or corporate officer participates personally in the harassing behavior," an employee must "demonstrat[e] the propriety of holding the employer liable").

Finally, there is nothing remarkable in the fact that claims against employers for discriminatory employment actions with tangible results, like hiring, firing, promotion, compensation, and work assignment, have resulted in employer liability once the discrimination was shown. . . .

A variety of reasons have been invoked for this apparently unanimous rule. Some courts explain, in a variation of the "proxy" theory discussed above, that when a supervisor makes such decisions, he "merges" with the employer, and his act becomes that of the employer. See, *e.g., Kotcher v. Rosa and Sullivan Appliance Ctr., Inc.,* 957 F.2d 59, 62 (C.A.2 1992) ("The supervisor is deemed to act on behalf of the employer when making decisions that affect the economic status of the employee. From the perspective of the employee, the supervisor and the employer merge into a single entity"); *Steele v. Offshore Shipbuilding, Inc.,* 867 F.2d 1311, 1316 (C.A.11 1989) ("When a supervisor requires sexual favors as a *quid pro quo* for job benefits, the supervisor, by definition, acts as the company"); see also Lindemann & Grossman 776 (noting that courts hold employers "automatically liable" in *quid pro quo* cases because the "supervisor's actions, in conferring or withholding employment benefits, are deemed as a matter of law to be those of the employer"). Other courts have suggested that vicarious liability is proper because the supervisor acts within the scope of his authority when he makes discriminatory decisions in hiring, firing, promotion, and the like. See, *e.g., Shager v. Upjohn Co.,* 913 F.2d 398, 405 (C.A.7 1990) ("[A] supervisory employee who fires a subordinate is doing the kind of thing that he is authorized to do, and the wrongful intent with which he does it does not carry his behavior so far beyond the orbit of his responsibilities as to excuse the employer" (citing Restatement § 228)). Others have suggested that vicarious liability is appropriate because the supervisor who discriminates in this manner is aided by the agency relation. See, *e.g., Nichols v. Frank,* 42 F.3d 503, 514 (C.A.9 1994). Finally, still other courts have endorsed both of the latter two theories. See, *e.g., Harrison,* 112 F.3d, at 1443; *Henson,* 682 F.2d, at 910.

The soundness of the results in these cases (and their continuing vitality), in light of basic agency principles, was confirmed by this Court's only discussion to date of standards of employer liability, in *Meritor, supra,* which involved a claim of discrimination by a supervisor's sexual harassment of a subordinate over an extended period. In affirming the Court of Appeals's holding that a hostile atmosphere resulting from sex discrimination is actionable under Title VII, we also anticipated proceedings on remand by holding agency principles relevant in assigning employer liability and by rejecting three per se rules of liability or immunity. . . . We observed that the very definition of employer in Title VII, as including an "agent. . . " expressed Congress's intent that courts look to traditional principles of the law of agency in devising standards of employer liability in those instances where liability for the actions of a supervisory employee was not otherwise obvious . . . ibid., and although we cautioned that "common-law principles may not be transferable in all their particulars to Title VII," we cited the Restatement §§ 219–237, with general approval. . . .

We then proceeded to reject two limitations on employer liability, while establishing the rule that some limitation was intended. We held that neither the existence of a company grievance procedure nor the absence of actual notice of the harassment on the part of upper management would be dispositive of such a claim; while either might be relevant to the liability, neither would result automatically in employer immunity. . . . Conversely, we held that Title VII placed some limit on employer responsibility for the creation of a discriminatory environment by a supervisor, and we held that Title VII does not make employers "always automatically liable for sexual harassment by their supervisors. . . contrary to the view of the Court of Appeals, which had held that "an employer is strictly liable for a hostile environment created by a supervisor's sexual advances, even though the employer neither knew nor reasonably could have known of the alleged misconduct. . . .

The Court of Appeals identified, and rejected, three possible grounds drawn from agency law for holding the City vicariously liable for the hostile environment created by the supervisors. It considered whether the two supervisors were acting within the scope of their employment when they engaged in the harassing conduct. The court then inquired whether they were significantly aided by the agency relationship in committing the harassment, and also considered the possibility of imputing Gordon's knowledge of the harassment to the City. Finally, the Court of Appeals ruled out liability for negligence in failing to prevent the harassment. Faragher relies principally on the latter three theories of liability.

. . . The proper analysis here, then, calls not for a mechanical application of indefinite and malleable factors set forth in the Restatement, see, *e.g.*, §§ 219, 228, 229, but rather an inquiry into the reasons that would support a conclusion that harassing behavior ought to be held within the scope of a supervisor's employment, and the reasons for the opposite view. The Restatement itself points to such an approach, as in the commentary that the "ultimate question" in determining the scope of employment is "whether or not it is just that the loss resulting from the servant's acts should be considered as one of the normal risks to be borne by the business in which the servant is employed." *Id.*, § 229, Comment *a*. See generally *Taber v. Maine*, 67 F.3d 1029, 1037 (C.A.2 1995) ("As the leading Torts treatise has put it, 'the integrating principle' of *respondeat superior* is 'that the employer should be liable for those faults that may be fairly regarded as risks of his business, whether they are committed in furthering it or not'") (quoting 5 F. Harper, F. James & O. Gray, Law of Torts § 26.8, pp. 40–41 (2d ed.1986)).

In the case before us, a justification for holding the offensive behavior within the scope of Terry's and Silverman's employment was well put in Judge Barkett's dissent: "[A] pervasively hostile work environment of sexual harassment is never (one would hope) authorized, but the supervisor is clearly charged with maintaining a productive, safe work environment. The supervisor directs and controls the conduct of the employees, and the manner of doing so may inure to the employer's benefit or detriment, including subjecting the employer to Title VII liability." 111 F.3d, at 1542 (opinion dissenting in part and concurring in part). It is by now well recognized that hostile environment sexual harassment by supervisors (and, for that matter, coemployees) is a persistent problem in the workplace. . . . An employer can, in a general sense, reasonably anticipate the possibility of such conduct occurring in its workplace, and one might justify the assignment of the burden of the untoward behavior to the employer as one of the costs of doing business, to be charged to the enterprise rather than the victim. . . .

[D]evelopments like this occur from time to time in the law of agency.

Two things counsel us to draw the contrary conclusion. First, there is no reason to suppose that Congress wished courts to ignore the traditional distinction between acts falling within the scope and acts amounting to what the older law called frolics or detours from the course of employment. Such a distinction can readily be applied to the spectrum of possible harassing conduct by supervisors, as the following examples show. First, a supervisor might discriminate racially in job assignments in order to placate the prejudice pervasive in the labor force. Instances of this variety of the heckler's veto would be consciously intended to further the employer's interests by preserving peace in the workplace. Next, supervisors might reprimand male employees for workplace failings with banter, but respond to women's shortcomings in harsh or vulgar terms. A third example might be the supervisor who, as here, expresses his sexual interests in ways having no apparent object whatever of serving an interest of the employer. If a line is to be drawn between scope and frolic, it would lie between the first two examples and the third, and it thus makes sense in terms of traditional agency law to analyze the scope issue, in cases like the third example, just as most federal courts addressing that issue have done, classifying the harassment as beyond the scope of employment.

The second reason goes to an even broader unanimity of views among the holdings of District Courts and Courts of Appeals thus far. Those courts have held not only that the sort of harassment at issue here was outside the scope of supervisors' authority, but, by uniformly judging employer liability for coworker harassment under a negligence standard, they have also implicitly treated such harassment as outside the scope of common employees' duties as well. . . . If, indeed, the cases did not rest, at least implicitly, on the notion that such harassment falls outside the scope of employment, their liability issues would have turned simply on the application of the scope-of-employment rule. . . .

It is quite unlikely that these cases would escape efforts to render them obsolete if we were to hold that supervisors who engage in discriminatory harassment are necessarily acting within the scope of their employment. The rationale for placing harassment within the scope of supervisory authority would be the fairness of requiring the employer to bear the burden of foreseeable social behavior, and the same rationale would apply when the behavior was that of co-employees. The employer generally benefits just as obviously from the work of common employees as from the work of supervisors; they simply have different jobs to do, all aimed at the success of the enterprise. As between an innocent employer and an innocent employee, if we use scope-of-employment reasoning to require the employer to bear the cost of an actionably hostile workplace created by one class of employees (i.e., supervisors), it could appear just as appropriate to do the same when the environment was created by another class (i.e., co-workers).

The answer to this argument might well be to point out that the scope of supervisory employment may be treated separately by recognizing that supervisors have special authority enhancing their capacity to harass, and that the employer can guard against their misbehavior more easily because their numbers are by definition fewer than the numbers of regular employees. But this answer happens to implicate an entirely separate category of agency law (to be considered in the next section), which imposes vicarious liability on employers for tortious acts committed by use of particular authority conferred as an element of an employee's agency relationship with the employer. Since the virtue of categorical clarity is obvious, it is better to reject reliance on misuse of supervisory authority (without more) as irrelevant to scope-of-employment analysis.

The Court of Appeals also rejected vicarious liability on the part of the City insofar as it might rest on the concluding principle set forth in § 219(2)(d) of the Restatement, that an employer "is not subject to liability for the torts of his servants acting outside the scope of their employment unless . . . the servant purported to act or speak on behalf of the principal and there was reliance on apparent authority, or he was aided in accomplishing the tort by the existence of the agency relation." Faragher points to several ways in which the agency relationship aided Terry and Silverman in carrying out their harassment. She argues that in general, offending supervisors can abuse their authority to keep subordinates in their presence while they make offensive statements, and that they implicitly threaten to misuse their supervisory powers to deter any resistance or complaint. Thus, she maintains that power conferred on Terry and Silverman by the City enabled them to act for so long without provoking defiance or complaint.

The City, however, contends that § 219(2)(d) has no application here. It argues that the second qualification of the subsection, referring to a servant "aided in accomplishing the tort by the existence of the agency relation," merely "refines" the one preceding it, which holds the employer vicariously liable for its servant's abuse of apparent authority. Brief for Respondent 30–31, and n.24. But this narrow reading is untenable; it would render the second qualification of § 219(2)(d) almost entirely superfluous (and would seem to ask us to shut our eyes to the potential effects

of supervisory authority, even when not explicitly invoked). The illustrations accompanying this subsection make clear that it covers not only cases involving the abuse of apparent authority, but also cases in which tortious conduct is made possible or facilitated by the existence of the actual agency relationship. See Restatement § 219 Comment *e* (noting employer liability where "the servant may be able to cause harm because of his position as agent, as where a telegraph operator sends false messages purporting to come from third persons" and where the manager who operates a store "for an undisclosed principal is enabled to cheat the customers because of his position"); id., § 247, Illustration 1 (noting a newspaper's liability for a libelous editorial published by an editor acting for his own purposes).

We therefore agree with Faragher that in implementing Title VII it makes sense to hold an employer vicariously liable for some tortious conduct of a supervisor made possible by abuse of his supervisory authority, and that the aided-by-agency-relation principle embodied in § 219(2)(d) of the Restatement provides an appropriate starting point for determining liability for the kind of harassment presented here.[3]

Several courts, indeed, have noted what Faragher has argued, that there is a sense in which a harassing supervisor is always assisted in his misconduct by the supervisory relationship. . . . The agency relationship affords contact with an employee subjected to a supervisor's sexual harassment, and the victim may well be reluctant to accept the risks of blowing the whistle on a superior. When a person with supervisory authority discriminates in the terms and conditions of subordinates' employment, his actions necessarily draw upon his superior position over the people who report to him, or those under them, whereas an employee generally cannot check a supervisor's abusive conduct the same way that she might deal with abuse from a co-worker. When a fellow employee harasses, the victim can walk away or tell the offender where to go, but it may be difficult to offer such responses to a supervisor, whose "power to supervise—[which may be] to hire and fire, and to set work schedules and pay rates—does not disappear . . .

---

[3] We say "starting point" because our obligation here is not to make a pronouncement of agency law in general or to transplant § 219(2)(d) into Title VII. Rather, it is to adapt agency concepts to the practical objectives of Title VII. As we said in *Meritor Savings Bank, FSB v. Vinson*, 477 U.S. 57, 72 (1986), "common-law principles may not be transferable in all their particulars to Title VII."

when he chooses to harass through insults and offensive gestures rather than directly with threats of firing or promises of promotion." Estrich, Sex at Work, 43 Stan. L. Rev. 813, 854 (1991). Recognition of employer liability when discriminatory misuse of supervisory authority alters the terms and conditions of a victim's employment is underscored by the fact that the employer has a greater opportunity to guard against misconduct by supervisors than by common workers; employers have greater opportunity and incentive to screen them, train them, and monitor their performance.

In sum, there are good reasons for vicarious liability for misuse of supervisory authority. That rationale must, however, satisfy one more condition. We are not entitled to recognize this theory under Title VII unless we can square it with *Meritor's* holding that an employer is not "automatically" liable for harassment by a supervisor who creates the requisite degree of discrimination . . . and there is obviously some tension between that holding and the position that a supervisor's misconduct aided by supervisory authority subjects the employer to liability vicariously; if the "aid" may be the unspoken suggestion of retaliation by misuse of supervisory authority, the risk of automatic liability is high. To counter it, we think there are two basic alternatives, one being to require proof of some affirmative invocation of that authority by the harassing supervisor, the other to recognize an affirmative defense to liability in some circumstances, even when a supervisor has created the actionable environment.

There is certainly some authority for requiring active or affirmative, as distinct from passive or implicit, misuse of supervisory authority before liability may be imputed. That is the way some courts have viewed the familiar cases holding the employer liable for discriminatory employment action with tangible consequences, like firing and demotion. . . . And we have already noted some examples of liability provided by the Restatement itself, which suggests that an affirmative misuse of power might be required. . . .

But neat examples illustrating the line between the affirmative and merely implicit uses of power are not easy to come by in considering management behavior. Supervisors do not make speeches threatening sanctions whenever they make requests in the legitimate exercise of managerial authority, and yet every subordinate employee knows the sanctions exist; this is the reason that courts have consistently held that acts of supervisors have greater power to alter the environment than acts of co-employees generally. How far from the course of ostensible supervisory behavior would a company officer have to step before his orders would not reasonably be seen as actively using authority? Judgment calls would often be close, the results would often seem disparate even if not demonstrably contradictory, and the temptation to litigate would be hard to resist. We think plaintiffs and defendants alike would be poorly served by an active-use rule.

The other basic alternative to automatic liability would avoid this particular temptation to litigate but would allow an employer to show as an affirmative defense to liability that the employer had exercised reasonable care to avoid harassment and to eliminate it when it might occur, and that the complaining employee had failed to act with like reasonable care to take advantage of the employer's safeguards and otherwise to prevent harm that could have been avoided. This composite defense would, we think, implement the statute sensibly, for reasons that are not hard to fathom.

As long ago as 1980, the EEOC, charged with the enforcement of Title VII, 42 U.S.C. § 2000e-4, adopted regulations advising employers to "take all steps necessary to prevent sexual harassment from occurring, such as . . . informing employees of their right to raise and how to raise the issue of harassment." 29 CFR § 1604.11(f) (1997), and in 1990, the EEOC issued a policy statement enjoining employers to establish a complaint procedure "designed to encourage victims of harassment to come forward [without requiring] a victim to complain first to the offending supervisor." EEOC Policy Guidance on Sexual Harassment, 8 FEP Manual 405:6699 (Mar. 19, 1990). . . . It would therefore implement clear statutory policy and complement the Government's Title VII enforcement efforts to recognize the employer's affirmative obligation to prevent violations and give credit here to employers who make reasonable efforts to discharge their duty. Indeed, a theory of vicarious liability for misuse of supervisory power would be at odds with the statutory policy if it failed to provide employers with some such incentive.

The requirement to show that the employee has failed in a coordinate duty to avoid or mitigate harm reflects an equally obvious policy imported from the general theory of damages, that a victim has a duty "to use such means as are reasonable under the circumstances to avoid or minimize the damages" that result from violations of the statute. *Ford Motor Co. v. EEOC*, 458 U.S. 219, 231, n.15 (1982) (quoting C. McCormick, Law of Damages 127 (1935). . . . An employer may, for example, have provided a proven, effective mechanism for reporting and resolving complaints of sexual harassment, available to the employee without undue risk or expense. If the plaintiff unreasonably failed to avail herself of the employer's preventive or remedial apparatus, she should not recover damages that could have been avoided if she had done so. If the victim could have avoided harm, no liability should be found against the employer who had taken reasonable care, and if damages could reasonably have been mitigated, no award against a liable employer should reward a plaintiff for what her own efforts could have avoided.

In order to accommodate the principle of vicarious liability for harm caused by misuse of supervisory authority, as well as Title VII's equally basic policies of encouraging forethought by employers and saving action by objecting employees, we adopt the following holding in this case and in *Burlington Industries, Inc. v. Ellerth* . . . ante also decided today. An employer is subject to vicarious liability to a victimized employee for an actionable hostile environment created by a supervisor with immediate (or successively higher) authority over the employee. When no tangible employment action is taken, a defending employer may raise an affirmative defense to liability or damages, subject to proof by a preponderance of the evidence, see Fed. Rule Civ. Proc. 8(c). The defense comprises two necessary elements: (a) that the employer exercised reasonable care to prevent and correct promptly any sexually harassing behavior, and (b) that the plaintiff employee unreasonably failed to take advantage of any preventive or corrective opportunities provided by the employer or to avoid harm otherwise. While proof that an employer had promulgated an antiharassment policy with complaint procedure is not necessary in every instance as a matter of law, the need for a stated policy suitable to the employment circumstances may appropriately be addressed in any case when litigating the first element of the defense. And while proof that an employee failed to fulfill the corresponding obligation of reasonable care to avoid harm is not limited to showing an unreasonable failure to use any complaint procedure provided by the employer, a demonstration of such failure will normally suffice to satisfy the employer's burden under the second element of the defense. No affirmative defense is available, however, when the supervisor's harassment culminates in a tangible employment action, such as discharge, demotion, or undesirable reassignment. . . .

Applying these rules here, we believe that the judgment of the Court of Appeals must be reversed. The District Court found that the degree of hostility in the work environment rose to the actionable level and was attributable to Silverman and Terry. It is undisputed that these supervisors "were granted virtually unchecked authority" over their subordinates, "directly controll[ing] and supervis[ing] all aspects of [Faragher's] day-to-day activities. . . . It is also clear that Faragher and her colleagues were "completely isolated from the City's higher management. . . . The City did not seek review of these findings.

While the City would have an opportunity to raise an affirmative defense if there were any serious prospect of its presenting one, it appears from the record that any such avenue is closed. The District Court found that the City had entirely failed to disseminate its policy against sexual harassment among the beach employees and that its officials made no attempt to keep track of the conduct of supervisors like Terry and Silverman. The record also makes clear that the City's policy did not include any assurance that the harassing supervisors could be bypassed in registering complaints. App. 274. Under such circumstances, we hold as a matter of law that the City could not be found to have exercised reasonable care to prevent the supervisors' harassing conduct. Unlike the employer of a small work force, who might expect that sufficient care to prevent tortious behavior could be exercised informally, those responsible for city operations could not reasonably have thought that precautions against hostile environments in any one of many departments in far-flung locations could be effective without communicating some formal policy against harassment, with a sensible complaint procedure.

We have drawn this conclusion without overlooking two possible grounds upon which the City might argue for the opportunity to litigate further. There is, first, the Court of Appeals's indulgent gloss on the relevant evidence: "There is some evidence that the City did not effectively disseminate among Marine Safety employees its sexual harassment policy. . . . " But, in contrast to the Court of Appeals's characterization, the District Court made an explicit finding of a "complete failure on the part of the City to disseminate said policy among Marine Safety Section employees." 864 F. Supp., at 1560. The evidence supports the District Court's finding and there is no contrary claim before us.

The second possible ground for pursuing a defense was asserted by the City in its argument addressing the possibility of negligence liability in this case. It said that it should not be held liable for failing to promulgate an antiharassment policy, because there was no apparent duty to do so in the 1985–1990 period. The City purports to rest this argument on the position of the EEOC during the period mentioned, but it turns out that the record on this point is quite against the City's position. Although the EEOC issued regulations dealing with promulgating a statement of policy and providing a complaint mechanism in 1990... ever since 1980, its regulations have called for steps to prevent violations, such as informing employees of their rights and the means to assert them, *Ibid.* The City, after all, adopted an antiharassment policy in 1986.

The City points to nothing that might justify a conclusion by the District Court on remand that the City had exercised reasonable care. Nor is there any reason to remand for consideration of Faragher's efforts to mitigate her own damages, since the award to her was solely nominal.

The Court of Appeals also rejected the possibility that it could hold the City liable for the reason that it knew of the harassment vicariously through the knowledge of its supervisors. We have no occasion to consider whether this was error, however. We are satisfied that liability on the ground of vicarious knowledge could not be determined without further factfinding on remand, whereas the reversal necessary on the theory of supervisory harassment renders any remand for consideration of imputed knowledge entirely unjustifiable (as would be any consideration of negligence as an alternative to a theory of vicarious liability here).

The judgment of the Court of Appeals for the Eleventh Circuit is reversed, and the case is remanded for reinstatement of the judgment of the District Court. It is so ordered.

Justice THOMAS, with whom Justice SCALIA joins, dissenting.

[A]bsent an adverse employment consequence, an employer cannot be held vicariously liable if a supervisor creates a hostile work environment. Petitioner suffered no adverse employment consequence; thus the Court of Appeals was correct to hold that the City of Boca Raton (City) is not vicariously liable for the conduct of Chief Terry and Lieutenant Silverman. Because the Court reverses this judgment, I dissent.

As for petitioner's negligence claim, the District Court made no finding as to the City's negligence, and the Court of Appeals did not directly consider the issue. I would therefore remand the case to the District Court for further proceedings on this question alone. I disagree with the Court's conclusion that merely because the City did not disseminate its sexual harassment policy, it should be liable as a matter of law....

The City should be allowed to show either that: (1) there was a reasonably available avenue through which petitioner could have complained to a City official who supervised both Chief Terry and Lieutenant Silverman[2] ... or (2) it would not have learned of the harassment even if the policy had been distributed.... Petitioner, as the plaintiff, would of course bear the burden of proving the City's negligence.

Questions

1. In Problem 24, should the company be liable for Mark's conduct if a court determines that it otherwise rises to the level of a hostile work environment? What if the company has a policy in place, but Marianne never reported the conduct pursuant to that policy, and therefore the company is unaware of the conduct? What if the policy requires her to report that conduct to her supervisor— i.e., Mark? What if she reports the conduct pursuant to a policy that provides appropriate channels for her to report the incident, and the company quickly acts to end the harassment?

2. Assuming the conduct is sufficiently severe or pervasive in Problem 25 to establish a hostile work environment, is the bank liable for the harassment? What if Stephania never complained to the supervisor, and no one in management knew of the conduct? What if she did not complain, but the supervisor regularly witnessed the conduct? What if she did not complain because the supervisor regularly participated in the conduct? What if she complained of the conduct and the supervisor quickly acted to end the conduct? What if she did not complain, but the supervisor began to notice the conduct on her own and eventually acted to end the conduct? What if she did not complain, but the supervisor noticed the conduct and quickly acted to end the conduct? Would the existence of an appropriate workplace harassment policy, combined with Stephania's failure to follow it, affect your answer to any of the above questions? What if she followed the policy?

[2]The City's Employment Handbook stated that employees with "complaints or grievances" could speak to the City's Personnel and Labor Relations Director about problems at work. See App. 280. The District Court found that the City's Personnel Director, Richard Bender, moved quickly to investigate the harassment charges against Terry and Silverman once they were brought to his attention. See App. to Pet. for Cert. 80a.

C. Co-workers

It is evident after *Farragher* and *Ellerth* that a negligence-type standard applies to determine employer liability for the conduct of co-workers, but the Supreme Court did not directly address that standard in those cases. What that standard is, how it functions, and how it relates to the standard for harassment by supervisors are the focus of the following cases. The cases included were all decided after *Farragher* and *Ellerth*.

WILLIAMS
v.
GENERAL MOTORS CORPORATION
187 F.3d 553 (6th Cir. 1999)

DAUGHTREY, Circuit Judge.

[The Employment Problem]

The plaintiff, Marilyn Williams, began working at General Motors Corporation's Delphi-Packard Plant in Warren, Ohio, in 1965 or 1966. Over the years, she worked in various departments. From September 1994 until May 1996 . . . Williams worked in the tool crib, a warehouse used to store materials and components used at the plant, from which materials were distributed by an attendant to assemblers who requested them. In May 1995, Williams was transferred to the third, or "midnight shift," to fill a vacancy caused by another employee's retirement.

While working the midnight shift in the crib, Williams alleges that she was subjected to sexual harassment in the form of a hostile working environment. As summarized by the district court in its memorandum opinion, she alleged the following:

1. Don Giovannoe, an hourly tool crib employee, constantly used the "F-word" as part of his vocabulary.
2. In June of 1995, as Giovannoe approached the window at the counter of the tool crib, Appellant heard him say, "Hey slut."
3. In July of 1995, Pat Ryan, her general supervisor, while talking to Williams' co-worker, Dodie, looked at Williams' breasts and said something to the effect of, "You can rub up against me anytime." He also said, "You would kill me, Marilyn. I don't know if I can handle it, but I'd die with a smile on my face."

4. A few days after the incident alleged in No. 3, Williams was bending over and Ryan came up behind her and said, "Back up; just back up," or "You can back right up to me," or words to that effect.
5. On another occasion, in July of 1995, Williams was sitting at her desk writing the name "Hancock Furniture Company" on a piece of paper. Ryan came up behind her, put his arm around her neck and leaned his face against hers, and said, "You left the dick out of the hand."
6. Workers conspired against her: she was forced to take the midnight shift when Steve Bivolesky retired, even though Don Giovannoe had originally agreed to take the job.
7. In September of 1995, when she came in for her midnight shift, she discovered a box of tool crib release forms glued to the top of her desk.
8. Later on the same day she discovered the box glued to her desk, Williams claims to have heard Giovannoe say, "I'm sick and tired of these fucking women." As Williams waited on people at the crib window, Giovannoe came over to the desk and threw a box on it. Williams and Giovannoe had a verbal altercation ending with Giovannoe throwing another couple boxes, the last of which grazed Williams' [sic] hip, but did not hurt her.
9. Williams claims that she was denied overtime.
10. She complained that she was the only person who did not have a key to the office.

11. Williams stated that she was the only person denied a break.
12. She was not allowed to sit at the table at the window of the crib, but had to go in the back instead.
13. One night when Williams came to work, she found a buggy (a motorized cart used to haul supplies) sitting on a wooden skid and blocking the other buggies. She had to find a co-worker to help her move it.
14. On one occasion, a female hourly worker, Shalimar Kufchak, padlocked the crib's main entrance while Williams was inside.
15. On a couple of occasions, materials were stacked in front of the alternate exit, blocking access in and out.

In May 1996, she filed suit against General Motors, alleging sexual harassment under Title VII of the Civil Rights Act, 42 U.S.C. §§ 2000e *et seq.*, and under Ohio state law. She also alleged retaliation under Title VII for having filed sex and race discrimination charges with the Ohio Civil Rights Commission in 1995.

[The Decision by the Trial Court]

The district court granted summary judgment to General Motors on both the federal and state claims, finding that the incidents of alleged sexual harassment, while offensive, were not so severe or pervasive as to constitute a hostile work environment under the standard set out in *Harris v. Forklift Systems, Inc.,* 510 U.S. at 21, 1 and also that Williams had failed to meet the subjective test under *Harris.* . . .

[The Decison and Rationale of the U.S. Court of Appeals for the Sixth Circuit]

The Supreme Court has recently reaffirmed the "severe or pervasive" test—*Harris's* core holding—in *Faragher v. City of Boca Raton,* 524 U.S. 775 (1998), and *Burlington Industries, Inc. v. Ellerth,* 524 U.S. 742 (1998). Moreover, these cases invalidate a portion of prior caselaw in this circuit and require that we recast the analytical framework for a hostile-work-environment claim based on a supervisor's actions. Previously, to establish such a claim, a plaintiff had to show not only that (1) she was a member of a protected class; (2) she was subject to unwelcomed sexual harassment; (3) the harassment was based on her sex; and (4) the harassment created a hostile

work environment; but also that (5) the supervisor's harassing actions were foreseeable or fell within his or her scope of employment, and the employer failed to respond adequately and effectively. See *Kauffman v. Allied Signal, Inc.,* 970 F.2d 178, 183–184 (6th Cir.1992). After *Faragher* and *Burlington Industries,* however, it is no longer enough for an employer to take corrective action; employers now have an *affirmative duty* to prevent sexual harassment by supervisors. Once an employee has established actionable discrimination involving "no tangible employment action," *Faragher.* . . . an employer can escape liability only if it took reasonable care to *prevent and correct* any sexually harassing behavior. *Id.* . . .

The Supreme Court has not ruled on the appropriate requirements for a hostile-work-environment claim stemming from a co-worker's actions. . . . to establish employer liability for harassment by a co-worker, a plaintiff must show that the employer "knew or should have known of the charged sexual harassment and failed to implement prompt and appropriate corrective action." *Hafford v. Seidner,* 183 F.3d 506, 513 (6th Cir. 1999). . . . (explaining employer liability for both co-worker and supervisor harassment). *See also, Blankenship v. Parke Care Centers, Inc.,* 123 F.3d 868, 872 (6th Cir. 1997), *cert. denied,* 522 U.S. 1110 (1998); *Fleenor v. Hewitt Soap Co.,* 81 F.3d 48, 50 (6th Cir. 1996) (the standard "is one of failure-to-correct-after-notice or duty to act after knowledge of harm").

Without addressing the differing standards for employer liability based on the perpetrator of the harassment, the district court granted summary judgment on the hostile environment claim on two grounds: first, that Williams had not alleged conduct that met the "severe or pervasive" threshold test enunciated in *Harris* and, second, that Williams had not "met the subjective test for a sexually hostile work environment because she herself admits that she did not feel threatened or harassed when these various incidents occurred." We conclude, however, that the evidence presented by Williams does raise a genuine issue of material fact as to whether she was subjected to "severe or pervasive" conduct constituting a hostile work environment, and we also conclude that she has adequately alleged the subjective component of the claim. In deciding otherwise, the district court committed several errors in its analysis, en route to dismissing the incidents as "infrequent, not severe, not threatening or humiliating, but merely offensive."

First, the district court disaggregated the plaintiff's claims, contrary to the Supreme Court's "totality of circumstances" directives, which robbed the incidents of their cumulative effect.[3] Second, the district court improperly concluded that the conduct alleged to have created a hostile work environment must be explicitly sexual. Finally, the court misconstrued the requirements of the subjective test.

Totality of Circumstances

In determining whether the alleged harassment is sufficiently severe or pervasive to constitute a hostile work environment under the *Harris* standard, it is well-established that the court must consider the totality of circumstances. *Harris*, 510 U.S. at 23 ("whether an environment is 'hostile' or 'abusive' can be determined only by looking at all the circumstances"); *Oncale v. Sundowner Offshore Servs., Inc.*, 523 U.S. 75 (1998). . . .

In this case, however, the district court divided and categorized the reported incidents, divorcing them from their context and depriving them of their full force. The court's analysis is clearly premised on an impermissible disaggregation of the incidents: "Williams' complaints can be separated into four types: (1) foul language in the workplace; (2) mean or annoying treatment by co-workers; (3) perceived inequities of treatment; and (4) sexually related remarks directed toward [Williams]. The court shall examine each group of complaints below." From this point, the district court proceeded to analyze each allegation within the narrow categories the court had defined.

Of course, when the complaints are broken into their theoretical component parts, each claim is more easily dismissed. For example, after discussing "the first group of complaints," which it termed "foul language in the workplace," the district court stated, "This use of foul language, although not condoned by the Court and though certainly well beyond the boundaries of polite behavior, does not satisfy the test enunciated in *Harris*." On reviewing Williams's "second class of complaints," characterized as "mean or annoying treatment by co-workers," the district court found that "mean behavior, without more, does not equate to a sexually hostile work environment." Obviously, however, there was more, i.e., the other cate-

gories of incidents similarly dismissed. Thus, the issue is not whether each incident of harassment *standing alone* is sufficient to sustain the cause of action in a hostile environment case, but whether—taken together—the reported incidents make out such a case.

We recognize that district courts are required to separate conduct by a supervisor from conduct by co-workers in order to apply the appropriate standards for employer liability, the fifth element in a hostile-work-environment-claim. However, the totality-of-the-circumstances test mandates that district courts consider harassment by all perpetrators combined when analyzing whether a plaintiff has alleged the existence of a hostile work environment, the fourth element of a hostile-work-environment claim. The totality of the circumstances, of necessity, includes all incidents of alleged harassment; as such, district courts must not conduct separate analyses based on the identity of the harasser unless and until considering employer liability.[4]

Moreover, the totality-of-circumstances test must be construed to mean that even where individual instances of sexual harassment do not on their own create a hostile environment, the accumulated effect of such incidents may result in a Title VII violation. This totality-of-circumstances examination should be viewed as the most basic tenet of the hostile-work-environment cause of action. Hence, courts must be mindful of the need to review the work environment as a whole, rather than focusing single-mindedly on individual acts of alleged hostility. . . .

The district court in this case concluded that the conduct alleged was "infrequent, not severe, not threatening or humiliating, but merely offensive." We cannot agree. Under the facts as alleged in this case, viewed in their entirety and in their proper context, we believe a rational trier of fact could conclude that Williams was subjected to a hostile work environment. Certainly, at minimum, the allegations raise a

[3]As mentioned above, the district court did not separate Williams's allegations of harassment according to the perpetrators in order to apply the distinct standards for liability. Instead, as discussed *infra*, the court categorized the harassment by the type of harassing action when determining the existence of a hostile environment.

[4]Because the first four elements of hostile-work-environment claim are identical regardless of the harasser, in most circumstances, a court addressing a claim involving both harassment by co-workers and harassment by supervisors can and should conduct a single, unified analysis of the first four elements. At the very least, however, all allegations of harassment must be considered when determining whether the harassment created a hostile work environment. Each incident of harassment contributes to the context in which every other incident occurs; the totality-of-the-circumstances test set forth in *Harris* requires consideration of all incidents, regardless of the perpetrator, when determining the existence of a hostile work environment.

question of fact for the jury and were not properly summarily dismissed. . . .

Even though a plaintiff's failure to report alleged harassment is not relevant to our analysis of the threshold question—whether the plaintiff in this case has established a hostile work environment—it may, of course, be relevant to the affirmative defense to employer liability in cases of harassment by a supervisor recently adopted by the Supreme Court in *Faragher* and *Burlington Industries,* and to the establishment of employer liability in co-worker harassment cases under *Blankenship.* . . . The district court in this case did not address the issue of employer liability, and neither will we, except to note the Supreme Court's recent expansion of employer liability for harassment by a supervisor in cases not involving tangible employment action and the importance of careful factfinding with regard to the raising of the affirmative defense. *See id.* Such careful factfinding is also required when determining employer liability for co-worker harassment. . . .

Conclusion

We cannot agree with the district court that, as a matter of law, the conduct alleged in this case was merely offensive and not so severe or pervasive as to constitute a hostile work environment. We find that the conduct alleged, taken as a whole and viewed in its appropriate context, creates a material question of disputed fact as to whether Williams was subjected to a hostile work environment. We also find that Williams sufficiently established that she subjectively perceived her work environment to be hostile. We therefore REVERSE the grant of summary judgment on this claim and remand the case for further proceedings.

However . . . we AFFIRM the grant of summary judgment on the retaliation claim.

COURTNEY
v.
LANDAIR TRANSPORT, INC.
227 F.3d 559 (6th Cir. 2000)

MERRITT, Circuit Judge.

[The Employment Problem]

Due to the parties' disagreement on what the record shows, we have included citations to sources in the record from which we compiled our statement of facts. . . . During her employment with Landair, plaintiff alleges that she was subjected to a hostile work environment based both upon the conduct of supervisors and the conduct of two other truck drivers, Virgil Mizner and James Jarrett, who were independent contractors for defendant Landair. Her problems began shortly after she began working for Landair in March 1996. She alleges that on several occasions James Jarrett stuck his tongue out at her making sexual gestures and suggested that plaintiff should ride with him in his truck. If she did so, Jarrett remarked that he would hire someone else to do the driving because he and Courtney would be "busy in the back" of the truck. . . . In addition, defendant's Columbus terminal manager approached plaintiff early in her employment to inform her that she was not appropriately dressed and that she was distracting other employees by showing too much cleavage. . . .

In response to these incidents, plaintiff wrote a letter dated May 5, 1996, to Gerald Howard, one of Landair's vice-presidents, and Craig Zeroski, who ran the Columbus terminal, complaining to them about the reprimand she received and a "double standard" she believed existed in the treatment of men and women at work. . . . In this letter, she complained that office personnel copied offensive and lewd pictures as jokes for male drivers and also complained about Jarrett's offensive tongue gestures and remarks that she should be his driving partner so that they could have a sexual relationship. . . . Plaintiff ended her letter by stating, "I'm not going to take the harassment from drivers, etc. anymore. . . . I'm a good asset to this company and have a good reputation as far as my job performance! . . . " No action was taken by defendant Landair at this time.

Plaintiff also alleges that she experienced harassment from Virgil Mizner. In her deposition, she describes an occasion, although no date is given, when she was walking with Mizner and her partner, Sam Helber, in a parking lot and Mizner allegedly bumped his whole body into plaintiff, continually bumping her breast. . . . It was not until later that plaintiff felt that his actions were intentional. . . . She describes another incident that occurred in July 1996, in which Mizner approached plaintiff from behind and tried to touch her left breast. . . . After plaintiff backed away, Mizner asked, "What's the matter? You're not going to let me touch it? . . . " She further alleges that in October 1996, when plaintiff was alone in the break room, Mizner tugged on her shirt and asked if she was mad at him. . . . Finally, plaintiff also alleges that in November 1996, at the Columbus terminal, in the break room, Mizner crept up behind her, blew air in her ear, and laughed at her. Plaintiff responded by yelling, "Virgil, leave me the f—k alone!" Other drivers in the room laughed and remarked aloud, "Getting kind of testy, aren't we? . . . "

Due to the incidents of harassment and management's alleged refusal to address plaintiff's complaints, plaintiff hired a lawyer. On December 4, 1996, plaintiff's counsel wrote a letter to the defendant management in Columbus asking it to stop the harassment of her client. That same day, the terminal manager of defendant's Indianapolis terminal, Dave Blevins, wrote plaintiff a letter. . . . The letter stated:

. . . As I told you, [defendant] is committed to maintaining an environment that is free from all forms of harassment, including sexual harassment. This is not always easy to do in the trucking business.

As we discussed, it is my intention to confront the individuals that you identified in your letter and make certain that they understand that this type of behavior will not be tolerated by [defendant]. During today's telephone conversation, I asked you if there were any other individuals and you indicated that there were not. After I have the opportunity to talk to these individuals, I will be back in touch with you. In the meantime, please contact me immediately if there are any other issues related to this situation that you wish to bring to our attention. . . .

On December 11, 1996, defendant Landair released a memorandum to all owner-operators about Landair's commitment to a harassment-free environment. . . . Defendant states that the timing of the memorandum was designed to address plaintiff's complaints of sexual harassment. . . .

From the record, it appears that further harassment from Mizner or Jarrett ceased. Then on January 3, 1997, while plaintiff and Helber were in Columbus waiting to make their run, defendant Landair informed plaintiff and Helber that they were not to return to Seattle because management had decided that another driver should take their route. Plaintiff charges that the assignment change was retaliation for her sexual harassment complaints. Defendant claims it did not pull plaintiff and Helber from their route because of a retaliatory motive, but rather pulled them because of normal holiday interruptions that occur in the trucking business. Because of her route change, plaintiff sent two communications to N. Jeffrey Woods, vice president of operations for Landair, complaining of the change. Woods responded by a telephone conference with plaintiff and Helber in which he gave them the option of becoming Indianapolis-based drivers and keeping the route to Seattle.

On January 12, 1997, plaintiff wrote a letter to Dave Blevins, the Indianapolis terminal manager, protesting the treatment she and Helber received the week earlier and indicated that she believed the treatment by defendant was retaliatory in nature. . . . After detailing the route change, plaintiff wrote in part:

Makes you wonder if all the so called misunderstandings weren't retaliation or pay back. . . .

The[re] is no way you could understand, or that I could beg[i]n to convey the Anger, Rage, or Hostility, along with the Headaches, upset stomachs I've been dealing with [sic].

Not to mention the Resentment I feel towards Landair Management.

You all keep saying your [sic] glad they drive for owner-op[erator]s.

Well there's one important thing you all seem to forget. I'm a Company Driver. And as a Company Driver, I depended on the Management of LandAir [sic] to protect me from the unwanted actions from the 2 old men I reported. Who by the way are old enough to be my father [sic]. The thought of them is sickening and disgusting. Instead, my complaints went unanswered. So for nine months I endured the crap. Yes, I'm angry. . . .

I need to have this problem taken care of be for [sic] it gets out of hand and I end up hurting someone.

Sincerely, Janice Courtney. . . .

I've held my tongue for almost a year. NO More. . . .

Blevins forwarded the letter to Woods and after reading the letter, Woods terminated plaintiff's employment. Woods stated in an affidavit that he "became concerned about [plaintiff's] competence to drive [defendant]'s trucks. . . . " Plaintiff operated semi-trucks weighing 80,000 pounds on public roadways and Woods concluded that plaintiff posed a potential risk to the general public. Additionally, Woods stated that he became concerned that even if plaintiff did not pose a risk to the general public, any accident involving the plaintiff could result in liability if an injured party obtained the January 12 letter in plaintiff's personal file. . . . Woods telephoned plaintiff and informed her that based upon her letter, her "competency as a driver to the company and the public were at risk. . . . " Woods contended that plaintiff's earlier complaints of sexual harassment and retaliation had no bearing on his decision. . . . Following her termination, plaintiff filed this lawsuit.

[The Legal Issues]

In this sexual harassment case brought by plaintiff Janice Courtney in diversity under Ohio law, there are four issues on appeal: [the first issue is]: whether her employer, Landair Transport, Inc., a trucking corporation, discriminated against her by creating a hostile work environment. . . . [The other three issues decided by the court are excluded here.] The court below granted summary judgment for defendant on all issues. We conclude that there is a material dispute of fact . . . and therefore reverse and remand for further proceedings. . . .

[The Decision and Rationale of the U.S. Court of Appeals for the Sixth Circuit]

Plaintiff brings her claim for sexual harassment due to hostile work environment under Ohio Revised Code § 4112.02. . . . Sexual harassment claims under Ohio Revised Code § 4112.02 are subject to the same standards applicable to federal harassment claims brought under Title VII. . . . For hostile work environment cases, courts distinguish between harassment by supervisors or management and harassment by co-workers. *See Fenton v. HISAN*, 174 F.3d 827, 829 (6th Cir. 1999); *Pierce v, Commonwealth Life Ins. Co.*, 40 F.3d 796, 803–04 (6th Cir. 1994). Plaintiff Courtney alleges both kinds in this case.

First, we will address plaintiff's claim of sexual harassment due to a hostile work environment created by supervisors. Plaintiff claims that management discriminated against her because a terminal manager cautioned her as to her inappropriate attire in the workplace. A manager's warning, without more, that plaintiff's clothing is inappropriate in the workplace is not sexual harassment. Plaintiff fails to show that the terminal manager's comments were anything more than a legitimate concern regarding appropriate dress in the workplace.

Plaintiff also errs in claiming that management's failure to end the co-worker harassment in May 1996

constitutes sexual harassment. In *Fenton v. HISAN*, 174 F.3d 827 (6th Cir. 1999), a case in which the harassment was committed by a co-worker, we confronted the same issue as presented by the plaintiff in this case. In *Fenton*, the plaintiff brought a Title VII action against her former employer alleging liability for hostile work environment sexual harassment by a coworker. We concluded:

> . . . In *Burlington Industries v. Ellerth*, 524 U.S. 742 (1998), the Supreme Court again held that an employer's liability in sexual harassment cases is governed by common law agency principles and specifically adopted section 219(2) of the Restatement (Second) of Agency as setting out the governing principles [*See* discussion of this Restatement section in the *Burlington Industries v. Ellerth* case at the beginning of this chapter.]
>
> In *Ellerth*, the Supreme Court concluded that subsection (d)—and specifically the last clause thereof ("or he was aided in accomplishing the tort by the existence of the agency relation")—applies in supervisor harassment cases and therefore does not require a showing of negligence or reckless conduct under subsection (b) in order to bring the case within the supervisor's "scope of employment." Hence the Court concluded that employers may be held, subject to certain affirmative defenses, vicariously liable in supervisor sexual harassment cases. . . . But under the Supreme Court's reasoning in *Ellerth*, unlike a supervisor, a coworker does not have power or authority emanating from the employer over the victim. Therefore, since the "master" does not normally intend or abet the coworker's conduct (subsection (a)) or have a nondelegable duty to prevent it in all circumstances (subsection (c)), the liability of the employer in coworker cases is governed by subsection (b) of section 219(2) of the Restatement (Second) of Agency. The victim of coworker sexual harassment must therefore prove negligence by the employer. *See id*. This standard is consistent with the negligence standard we have previously employed in coworker harassment cases. In *Blankenship v. Parke Care Centers, Inc.*, 123 F.3d 868, 872–73 (6th Cir. 1997), cert. denied, 522 U.S. 1110 (1998), we stated that in coworker cases the standard is based on a "reasonableness" standard: "when an employer responds to charges of coworker sexual harassment, the employer can be liable only if its response manifests indifference or unreasonableness in light of the facts the employer knew or should have known.

"*Fenton*, 174 F.3d at 829. In this case, just as in *Fenton* and *Blankenship*, plaintiff must show that the defendant knew or should have known of the harassment and failed to take appropriate remedial action. *See id*. The record shows that defendant took remedial action in December 1996 to address plaintiff's allegations by issuing a memorandum to all owner-operators reiterating Landair's harassment free work environment policy, at which point all harassment towards plaintiff ceased. Plaintiff does not dispute this fact. Instead, plaintiff alleges that defendant knew of the harassment as early as May 1996 but failed to do anything to stop it. She offers as evidence the letter she wrote on May 5, 1996, to Gerald Howard, a vice-president of the defendant, Craig Zeroski, the Columbus terminal manager, and others in which she aired several complaints.

The content of the May 5 letter does not place defendant on notice of Jarrett's and Mizner's harassment. Plaintiff begins her May 5 letter by defending herself and complaining about a double standard she perceived as a result of the reprimand she received regarding more appropriate work clothing. She then complains about several loose sexual references made around the terminal, some of which were directed towards her specifically, but she fails to name the harassers or ask the defendant to do anything in particular about her complaints. She ends her letter again defending her job performance. That was not sufficient to put management on notice that plaintiff wanted it to intervene to stop the co-worker harassment.

Plaintiff also offers as evidence another letter, dated August 10, 1996, sent to Zeroski, the Columbus terminal manager, in which she compiled three logged entries describing more sexual references directed towards her, but again never asked defendant to address the problem. Again, because this correspondence is less than clear as to its purpose, it does not constitute notice to defendant. It was not until December 4, 1996, when defendant received the lawyer's letter asking defendant to stop the harassment, that defendant had notice of the harassment. That same day, defendant telephoned plaintiff to discuss her complaints and sent a letter to her detailing their conversation. It was at this point that defendant issued the memorandum to all owner-operators reemphasizing Landair's anti-harassment policy. With this action, the record shows that all harassment ceased. We agree with the court below that, taking the evidence in the light most favorable to plaintiff, the defendant's conduct was not negligent or indifferent to plaintiff's situation.

[The sections of the opinion dealing with retaliation and state law tort claims are omitted.]

HOWLEY
v.
TOWN OF STRATFORD
217 F.3d 141 (2d Cir. 2000)

KEARSE, Circuit Judge.

[The Employment Problem]

. . . The Town's Fire Department consists of approximately 100 firefighting personnel. Howley, who attained the rank of lieutenant, was at all pertinent times the Department's only female firefighter. In the present action, Howley contends principally that the Town, in violation of Title VII, discriminated against her on the basis of gender in denying her a promotion to the position of assistant chief in the Department's fire suppression division, and that it tolerated a hostile work environment in which she was subjected to sexual harassment. Viewed in the light most favorable to Howley as the party challenging the grant of summary judgment, the affidavits, depositions, and documents in the record reveal the following events. . . .

Howley's claim that the Town tolerated a hostile work environment in which she was subjected to sexual harassment, along with her related claims against the Town and Holdsworth [a lieutenant with less seniority than Howley] for infliction of emotional distress, were based principally on the conduct of Holdsworth at a firefighters benevolent association meeting in April 1995. The issue at the meeting was whether to admit to membership in the benevolent association Cybart, who had been appointed assistant chief in September 1994, and Ronald Nattrass, who had become deputy chief in October 1994. The issue was controversial because Nattrass and Cybart had not come up through the ranks of the Department and were viewed by some as outsiders. Holdsworth supported their admission; Howley was opposed.

The events at the meeting, which do not appear to be materially in dispute, were summarized by the district court as follows:

> Holdsworth was off-duty at the time of the meeting, and Howley was asked to attend even though she was on duty because the membership needed a quorum.
>
> As she entered the meeting, Howley said that the members should "Just vote no" regarding one of the applicants with whom Holdsworth was friendly. Holdsworth responded by angrily telling Howley to "shut the fuck up, you fucking whining cunt." He thereafter made further inappropriate remarks concerning Howley's menstrual cycle.
>
> Neither of the gentlemen considered during the meeting [was] offered membership. After the meeting, in response to the admonitions of several other firefighters that he should apologize to Howley for his outburst, Holdsworth yelled in Howley's direction that "[t]here is no fucking way that I will fucking apologize to the fucking cunt down there." When Howley confronted him about his behavior, Holdsworth launched into an extended barrage of obscene verbal abuse, including at least one comment to the effect that the reason she did not make assistant chief was because she did not "suck cock good enough and only made lieutenant. . . . "

Howley reported the incident immediately and filed a written complaint the next day. The Department's investigation of the complaint was conducted by Nattrass. During the month following Howley's complaint, the Town asked Howley to agree that it was appropriate for Holdsworth to receive only a reprimand rather than a suspension. After Howley disagreed, the Town suspended Holdsworth for two days, stating, *in toto*, as follows:

> You are hereby suspended from 0700 hours May 20, 1995 through 1700 hours May 21, 1995 for conduct unbecoming an officer on the evening of April 12, 1995. It is further recommended that you apologize to Lt. Howley and "B" shift as soon as possible. . . .

Holdsworth served the suspension on the weekend of May 20–21. He did not apologize.

The Town moved to dismiss Howley's hostile-work-environment claim on the grounds that Holdsworth's verbal harassment was not sufficiently severe or pervasive to alter Howley's working environment and that the Town had taken suitable steps in re-

sponse to Howley's complaint. In opposition, Howley contended that the Town's response was inappropriate, beginning with the fact that the investigation had been assigned to Nattrass, whose unsuccessful candidacy for membership in the benevolent association (opposed by Howley) had sparked the April 12 confrontation. She argued further that the action taken by the Town was torpid and tepid. The Town took no action against Holdsworth until some five weeks after his obscene harangue—a tirade Holdsworth did not deny. And then it merely suspended him for two days and informed him that his conduct was "unbecoming." The Town never required Holdsworth to apologize. Further, some five months later, the Department relocated Holdsworth's work assignment to Department headquarters, where Howley worked. Although Howley and Holdsworth did not work the same shift, contact between the two was unavoidable because their shifts were contiguous and because of overtime scheduling.

In addition, Howley's affidavit stated that Holdsworth's harassment had continued after April 1995, albeit taking forms other than obscene verbal assault. Although Holdsworth too was a lieutenant, Howley was his superior by reason of seniority. Holdsworth's continued harassment took the form of insubordination, false statements undermining Howley's authority with other subordinates, and creating safety hazards for Howley. Howley stated that "Holdsworth refuses to acknowledge that I am a Lieutenant," and that although at a fire scene Howley would be entitled to give Holdsworth orders, "Holdsworth would not accept orders from me, thereby presenting a safety risk to myself and the rest of the Company. . . ." Further, she stated that on more than one occasion equipment for which Holdsworth was responsible, and which was to be used by Howley on the next shift, had been left in disrepair, both impairing Howley's performance and endangering her safety. In addition, Howley had received complaints from older firefighters resulting from Holdsworth's spreading untrue rumors that Howley sought to give them certain assignments that were likely to cause heart attacks. The Town rejected Howley's request that Holdsworth not be assigned to work at Department headquarters. Howley also presented medical evidence of psychiatric trauma caused by the April 12 incident.

The district court granted the Town's motion to dismiss Howley's hostile-work-environment claim, holding that the single incident of Holdsworth's verbal abuse was insufficient to create a hostile work environment:

> It is undisputed that Holdsworth was verbally abusive to Howley on the night of April 12, 1995,

and that such conduct is out of place in a civilized society. However, one instance of verbal harassment, standing alone, is insufficient to create a hostile work environment. While a single incident of physical sexual assault may warrant a finding of a hostile work environment . . . the same cannot be said for abusive language. The court does not condone, and indeed views with palpable distaste, the barrage of insults to which Howley was subjected but cannot find that, as a matter of law, Holdsworth's lack of tact created a hostile work environment. There is no evidence that Howley was ever harassed prior to the evening of April 12, 1995, nor that she has ever been harassed in the years since. Because the court finds that there was no hostile environment, it need not address the adequacy of the town's response and sanction of Holdsworth.

. . . This appeal followed. . . .

[The Legal Issues]

Plaintiff Ellen Howley appeals from so much of a final judgment of the United States District Court for the District of Connecticut, as (1) dismissed her complaint alleging that defendant Town of Stratford ("Town") failed to promote her to the position of assistant chief of its Fire Department ("Department" or "Fire Department"), and permitted a hostile work environment, in violation of Title VII of the Civil Rights Act of 1964. . . . , and (2) declined to exercise supplemental jurisdiction over her state-law claims against the Town and defendant William Holdsworth for intentional infliction of emotional distress through sexual harassment.

[The Decision by the Trial Court]

The district court granted summary judgment in favor of the Town, dismissing the Title VII claims on the ground that there was insufficient evidence to show . . . that Holdsworth's verbal abuse of Howley created a hostile work environment.

[The Decision and Rationale of the U.S. Court of Appeals for the Second Circuit]

On appeal, Howley contends principally that the court impermissibly . . . disregarded pertinent evidence in support of her hostile-work-environment claim. For the reasons that follow, we agree, and we vacate the judgment of the district court and remand for further proceedings. . . .

On appeal, Howley contends that the district court improperly invaded the province of the factfinder by accepting the Town's explanations for its refusal to promote her, and that it disregarded pertinent evidence in dismissing her claim of hostile work environment. For the reasons that follow, we agree that summary judgment was not properly granted. . . .

A Hostile-Work-Environment Claim

In order to prevail on a claim that sexual harassment has caused a hostile work environment in violation of Title VII, a plaintiff must establish two elements. The first relates principally to the environment itself and its effect on the plaintiff; the second relates to the employer's response to a complaint about the environment.

First, the plaintiff must show that the workplace is permeated with "discriminatory intimidation, ridicule, and insult . . . that is sufficiently severe or pervasive to alter the conditions of the victim's employment and create an abusive working environment." *Harris v. Forklift Systems, Inc.*, 510 U.S. 17, 21 (1993). . . . Usually, a single isolated instance of harassment will not suffice to establish a hostile work environment unless it was "extraordinarily severe." *Cruz v. Coach Stores, Inc.*, 202 F.3d at 570. . . . Thus, the plaintiff must demonstrate "either that a single incident was extraordinarily severe, or that a series of incidents were sufficiently continuous and concerted to have altered the conditions of her working environment." *Cruz v. Coach Stores, Inc.*, 202 F.3d at 570 . . . *see also Faragher v. City of Boca Raton*, 524 U.S. 775, 788 (1998) ("conduct must be extreme to amount to a change in the terms and conditions of employment"). . . .

However, "[t]here is neither a threshold magic number of harassing incidents that gives rise, without more, to liability as a matter of law, nor a number of incidents below which a plaintiff fails as a matter of law to state a claim." *Richardson v. New York State Department of Correctional Service*, 180 F.3d 426, 439 (2d Cir. 1999). . . .

[W]hether an environment is "hostile" or "abusive" can be determined only by looking at all the circumstances. These may include the frequency of the discriminatory conduct; its severity; whether it is physically threatening or humiliating, or a mere offensive utterance; and whether it unreasonably interferes with an employee's work performance. The effect on the employee's psychological well-being is, of course, relevant to determining whether the plaintiff actually found the environment abusive. But while psychological harm, like any other relevant factor, may be taken into account, no single factor is required.

Harris v. Forklift Systems, Inc., 510 U.S. at 23.

Second, the plaintiff must show that "a specific basis exists for imputing the conduct that created the hostile environment to the employer." *Perry v. Ethan Allen, Inc.*, 115 F.3d 143, 149 (2d Cir. 1997); *see also Murray v. New York University College of Dentistry*, 57 F.3d 243, 249 (2d Cir. 1995). When the source of the alleged harassment is a co-worker, the plaintiff must demonstrate that the employer "'failed to provide a reasonable avenue for complaint or [that] it knew, or in the exercise of reasonable care should have known, about the harassment yet failed to take appropriate remedial action.'" *Richardson v. New York State Department of Correctional Service*, 180 F.3d at 441 (quoting *Kracunas v. Iona College*, 119 F.3d 80, 89 (2d Cir. 1997)); *see* 29 C.F.R. § 1604.11(d) (1999) (employer is liable for co-worker harassment if "the employer (or its agents or supervisory employees) knows or should have known of the conduct, unless it can show that it took immediate and appropriate corrective action").

The district court here, in granting summary judgment dismissing Howley's hostile-work-environment claim, stated simply that a single incident of verbal harassment is not sufficient, apparently without considering the totality of the circumstances. Yet, considering all the circumstances, Holdsworth's conduct could reasonably be viewed as having intolerably altered Howley's work environment, for Holdsworth did not simply make a few offensive comments; nor did he air his views in private; nor were his comments merely obscene without an apparent connection to Howley's ability to perform her job. Although Holdsworth made his obscene comments only on one occasion, the evidence is that he did so at length, loudly, and in a large group in which Howley was the only female and many of the men were her subordinates. And his verbal assault included charges that Howley had gained her office of lieutenant only by performing fellatio. It cannot be concluded as a matter of law that no rational juror could view such a tirade as humiliating and resulting in an intolerable alteration of Howley's working conditions: In an occupation whose success in preserving life and property often depends on firefighters' unquestioning execution of line-of-command orders in emergency situations, the fomenting of gender-based skepticism as to the competence of a commanding officer may easily have the effect, among others, of diminishing the respect accorded the officer by subordinates

and thereby impairing her ability to lead in the life-threatening circumstances often faced by firefighters.

In addition, Howley presented evidence that Holdsworth had perpetrated repeated acts of harassment even after the April 1995 incident in order to undermine further her subordinates' respect for her, and hence to cast doubt on the degree of compliance and cooperation she could expect from them. . . .

Finally, although the Town takes the position that all of the alleged incidents between Howley and Holdsworth subsequent to April 12, 1995, are simply irrelevant, we disagree. Given the contents of Holdsworth's April 12 barrage, a factfinder would be entitled to infer that any harassment Holdsworth directed at Howley thereafter, with or without obscenities, was gender-based. Further, leaving aside any questions as to the form of evidence presented to show that such incidents occurred, the fact that they continued and were gender-based, if proven, is relevant to the question of the appropriateness of the Town's response to Howley's complaints.

Even without evidence as to the subsequent incidents, however, we are persuaded that Howley presented sufficient evidence to withstand summary judgment with respect to the second element of her hostile-work-environment claim, i.e., that the Town's response to her complaint about Holdsworth's harassment was inadequate. Howley complained to her superior officer on the night of Holdsworth's verbal assault and filed a written complaint the next day; the harangue was witnessed by a roomful of Howley's colleagues; and Holdsworth did not deny making any of the statements attributed to him. The Town took five weeks to mete out any discipline whatever. When the Town did act, it issued a two-day suspension and merely "recommended" that Holdsworth apologize to Howley and to the firefighter group. Holdsworth did not apologize, and the record does not suggest that the Town took any action to persuade him to do so. Because the ordinary dangers of the profession involve emergency situations in which firefighters must rely on each other and have confidence in their commanding officers, the Town's failure to take any remedial action, other than a weekend suspension and a "recommend[ation]" for apology, to remedy Holdsworth's public attempt to undermine Howley's authority may be viewed as an inappropriate response.

Further, we note that when Howley complained of Holdsworth's ensuing acts of harassment, the Town did not concede even that Holdsworth's April 12, 1995 conduct constituted sexual harassment. Notwithstanding Holdsworth's having repeatedly called Howley a slang term for the female sex organ, having repeatedly referred to her menstrual cycle, and having suggested that she had achieved her lieutenancy only by performing sexual favors, the Town stated that its position was that Holdsworth had merely engaged in "'conduct unbecoming' an officer, *not sexual harassment.*" (Memorandum of Town Manager Mark S. Barnhart to Howley dated December 24, 1997, at 1 (emphasis added).) Reasonable minds could draw the opposite inference.

We conclude that, although not all of the evidence cited by Howley in support of her hostile-work-environment claim was proffered in a form that would be admissible at trial, she presented sufficient admissible evidence to prevent the summary dismissal of that claim. Accordingly, we remand for trial of the hostile-work-environment claim.

CONCLUSION

We have considered all of the Town's contentions in support of summary judgment and have found them to be without merit. The judgment of the district court is vacated insofar as it dismissed Howley's claims under Title VII and state law; the matter is remanded to the district court for trial of the hostile-work-environment claim. . . .

Costs to plaintiff.

Questions

1. What policies might underlie the decision to hold an employer vicariously liable for harassment by supervisory employees but not co-workers?
2. When "should" an employer have known of harassment under the negligence standard for co-worker harassment? Is this issue adequately addressed by any of the cases included in this chapter? Given the numerous possible factual variations regarding such notice, could any one case ever adequately address this issue? Obviously, when an employee reports harassment to supervisory or management-level personnel pursuant to a harassment policy, the employer knows or should have known of the harassment, but what about when the conduct is going on in front of supervisory or management-level personnel and is not reported because the victims assume that management either is on notice or does not care?
3. What remedial action is appropriate when an employer learns of workplace harassment? How quickly must the remedial action be taken? What if the employer is investigating a harassment complaint, and the investigation is necessarily taking a good deal of time?
4. Must the remedial action actually end the harassment? If the employer takes significant remedial measures, but the harassment continues, should the employer fire the harassers? Would your answer be different depending on whether a supervisor or a co-worker was the harasser?

Discussion Notes

1. Significantly, sexual harassment, which is often the center of attention in this area of law, can take the form of overt sexual conduct, but conduct need not be overtly sexual to violate Title VII so long as it is aimed at an employee because of his or her gender. *See, e.g.,* Frank S. Ravitch, *Contextualizing Gender Harassment: Providing an Analytical Framework for an Emerging Concept in Discrimination Law,* 1995 DETROIT C. L. AT MICH. ST. L. REV. 853 (1995) (annual labor law issue).
2. One issue that is beyond the scope of this introductory text, but that arises often enough to be mentioned in this note, is the situation where an employee claims that he or she has been harassed because of the relationship between two employees (usually a supervisor and another employee). This situation can raise complex issues that are beyond the scope of this text. As a general matter, these claims, which are asserted on the basis of some sort of "sexual favoritism," are unsuccessful unless there is other conduct involved as well. For an example of this type of claim, *see Thompson v. Olsen,* 866 F. Supp. 1267 (D. N.D. 1994), *aff'd,* 56 F.3d 69 (8th Cir. 1995).

chapter

6

A Separate Claim
for Retaliation

Problem 27

Marisa Hernandez, an employee of the Sedgwick Manufacturing Company, complains to management of sexual harassment. Over the course of the following months, she is removed from a desirable assignment and reassigned to a less desirable one, with no diminution in pay; she receives a less favorable performance evaluation than she has ever received before; her company car is taken away; she is denied permission to attend professional seminars; she is singled out to provide special documentation of leave time that is not customary in the office; and she is placed on administrative leave while management investigates a consumer complaint against her. Marisa has amended her original charge with the Equal Employment Opportunity Commission (EEOC) to include a charge of retaliation against her. When should employers be held responsible for their reactions to a charge that they discriminated against an employee?

Problem 28

Suppose that Marisa Hernandez quits her job shortly after complaining about the supervisor's sexual harassment. Paul Owens, a secretary who remains employed by the company, secretly removes confidential personnel documents from the supervisor's office and mails copies of the documents to Marisa. Once the company discovers what Paul has done, he is fired. He wants to file a charge of retaliation with the EEOC. Should he be protected against retaliatory action by the employer?

A. Introduction: The Requirements of a Claim of Retaliation

Section 704(a) of Title VII, 42 U.S.C. § 2000e-3(a), outlaws retaliation against those who have either opposed an employer's discriminatory employment practices or participated in proceedings brought under Title VII:

> (a) It shall be an unlawful employment practice for an employer to discriminate against any of his employees or applicants for employment, for an employment agency . . . to discriminate against any individual, or for a labor organization to discriminate against any member thereof or applicant for membership, because he has opposed any practice made an unlawful employment practice by this title, or because he has made a charge, testified, assisted, or participated in any manner in an investigation, proceeding, or hearing under this title.

Section 704 thus protects applicants, employees, and (most courts agree in most circumstances) former employees against an employer's reprisals for opposing an action of the employer proscribed by Title VII and for filing a discrimination charge or lawsuit or assisting someone else in doing so.

In order to be successful, a claim of retaliation by an employee must demonstrate under Title VII, first, that the employee participated in a "protected activity," which may involve, for example, making a charge with the Equal Employment Opportunity Commission (EEOC), seeking advice from an attorney, serving as a witness for someone who has made a charge, or seeking assistance within the workplace in the face of discriminatory action. The courts get involved in many questions concerning the nature of a protected activity for purposes of a retaliation claim.

Second, an employee must demonstrate that he or she has suffered an adverse employment action. This is often an easy requirement if the employee claims that he or she was fired, but sometimes the adverse employment action is a more questionable kind of action by the employer. For example, a transfer to a less desirable location, a transfer to a different shift, and a change in nontangible benefits (like a move from one area of the office to another) may be more difficult for the courts when making a determination that the employee has suffered an adverse employment action.

Third, an employee must demonstrate a connection between the adverse employment action and the participation in the protected activity. This is often the most difficult part of a retaliation claim. The connection between the employer's decision to transfer someone to a different shift and the employee's participation as a witness in a co-employee's charge of employment discrimination may be difficult to show.

The courts also discuss both "opposition clause" and "participation clause" retaliation under Section 704 of Title VII. Opposition clause retaliation involves those situations where the alleged victim of retaliation has opposed some action of the employer, claiming that the employer violated Title VII provisions. The retaliation by the employer is claimed to be because of the opposition to the employer's violation of Title VII. Participation clause retaliation involves those situations where the alleged victim of retaliation by the employer has participated in some capacity in someone else's claim that the employer violated Title VII. This may be because the "victim" of retaliation was a witness to the claimed violation of Title VII or participated in some other capacity in the investigation of the claim.

Retaliation claims are also treated by many courts like other mixed-motives discrimination claims under Title VII. *See generally Wideman v. Wal-Mart Stores*, 141 F.3d 1453 (11th Cir. 1998). As discussed in Chapter 2, the Supreme Court has made it clear that, where the employer has mixed motives for its discriminatory action (e.g., its decision was motivated in part by illegal discrimination and in part by other factors), the plaintiff has proved a prima facie case. Under the Court's decision in *Price Waterhouse v. Hopkins*, 490 U.S. 228 (1989), once the plaintiff shows that the employer's discriminatory motive was a motivating factor in the adverse employment decision, the burden of persuasion (not production) shifts to the employer; the employer must show that even without the discriminatory factor, it would have taken the same action for legitimate, nondiscriminatory reasons.

The Civil Rights Act of 1991, 42 U.S.C. §§ 2000e-2(m), 2000e-5(g)(2)(B), arguably modifies *Price Waterhouse* for retaliation claims. While *Price Waterhouse* would dictate that the employee loses his case if the employer proves that notwithstanding the discriminatory motive, the nondiscriminatory motive would have led to the same employment action, the 1991 Act reduces the remedies available but does not defeat the plaintiff's claim entirely.

The courts are not unanimous on whether the 1991 Act's mixed motives provision applies to retaliation claims because it refers on its face only to "race, color, religion, sex, or national origin" and does not mention "retaliation" per se. *See* 42 U.S.C. § 2000e-2(m). While the majority of courts have applied the 1991 Act rather than the 1989 *Price Waterhouse* decision to retaliation claims, it is always advisable to ascertain circuit precedent.

Question

1. In Problem 28, Paul Owens, the secretary who sent the employer's documents to Marisa Hernandez after she was fired, is in a difficult situation. What role does the mixed motives analysis play in how his situation will be handled? Assume that sending company documents to anyone outside the company could constitute good grounds for firing someone. Even if the employer has independent grounds to punish Paul, is there any reason why a retaliation claim should still protect Paul? Watch for the problem of mixed motives in all of the cases discussed in this chapter. The problem of how to provide adequate protection against retaliation and still leave the employer free to deal with employees who break the rules is a difficult issue.

B. The First Requirement: Protected Activity

The courts have reached widely divergent conclusions about what kinds of activities are protected by Section 704. An important point to remember is that a retaliation claim can be successful even when the employee loses on his or her claim of a Title VII violation as a result of race, sex, color, religion, or national origin discrimination. As long as the employee had a good-faith belief that he or she was a victim of employment discrimination under the Act and suffered retaliation by the employer as defined by the Act, the employee can recover particular damages for that retaliation.

The courts have also differed widely in their analysis of the nexus between the date of the employer's notice of the employee's opposition or participation and the date on which the alleged retaliation occurred, as well as in their analysis of whether the protected conduct caused the retaliation. One thing is predictable about the law of retaliation: It is highly susceptible to judicial subjectivity.

One of the first questions the courts need to address is whether the complaint of retaliation is actually one that falls within the coverage of Title VII or one of the other antidiscrimination statutes.

LEARNED
v.
CITY OF BELLEVUE
860 F.2d 928 (9th Cir. 1988)

GEORGE, District Judge

[The Employment Problem]

Learned has been employed by the City of Bellevue in the Parks and Recreation Department since 1975. In 1977, Learned was promoted to "crew leader" where he supervised three to ten persons responsible for the maintenance of street trees. Learned enjoyed favorable employment evaluations and a positive working relationship with his superiors.

In May 1978, Learned was stabbed by a co-worker while in the course of his employment. Learned suffered serious injuries requiring hospitalization and plastic surgery, for which he received industrial insurance medical benefits from the State of Washington. Learned returned to work in June 1978, and in October 1980, his industrial insurance claim was closed. In September 1982, however, Learned sought to re-open his claim. . . . The action would have required proof of intentional injury on the part of Learned's employer, but the suit was ultimately dismissed as untimely.

Soon after filing suit, Learned experienced "problems" at work. Learned was assigned a new supervisor who was dissatisfied with Learned's work. Learned was allegedly harassed with charges of negligence and misconduct and given special rules regarding breaks. His responsibilities as crew leader were dramatically decreased. Learned developed an ulcer and began to see a psychiatrist. His employer thereafter allegedly harassed him about his medical appointments and made a special rule for Learned regarding notice and documentation of all medical appointments. In addition, Learned alleged that his supervisors referred to him as "crazy" or "sick" when conversing with co-workers.

In October 1982, Learned filed a complaint with the Washington Human Rights Commission (HRC) alleging discrimination on the basis of physical and mental limitations in violation of state law. He also charged retaliatory conduct, but later withdrew that charge. At the bottom of the complaint, Learned checked a box that said:

"I also allege a violation of Title VII of the Civil Rights Act of 1964 and request that this Complaint be filed with the U.S. Equal Employment Opportunity Commission."

When Learned's supervisors continued to "harass" him and treat him differently than they did other employees, Learned filed a second complaint with the state HRC alleging retaliatory conduct for Learned's having filed the first HRC complaint and [the earlier lawsuit]. Again, Learned checked the box with the provision quoted above. In November 1983, Learned filed a third complaint with the HRC alleging retaliatory conduct and checking the box with the provision quoted above. Three months later, Learned "voluntarily" transferred to the ballfield maintenance division where his title and salary have remained the same, but his responsibilities have diminished.

In April 1984, following an investigation of the matter, the HRC found reasonable cause to believe that Learned's allegations were true. . . . [The investigation revealed evidence that Bellevue was attempting to "build a case" against and "dump" him because he was "irrational" and had become a "liability" to Bellevue.] Learned did not pursue the matter by filing a charge with the . . . EEOC. . . . Nevertheless, Learned . . . filed this action in the United States District Court for the Western District of Washington. . . .

[The Legal Issue]

Learned contends that the district court erred in granting summary judgment on his "claim" under the anti-retaliation provision of Title VII, section 704(a), 42 U.S.C. 2000e-3.

[The Decision by the Trial Court and the U.S. Court of Appeals for the Ninth Circuit]

Section 704(a) provides in pertinent part:

(a) It shall be an unlawful employment practice for an employer to discriminate against any of his employees . . . because he has opposed any practice made an unlawful employment practice by this subchapter, or because he has made a charge, testified, assisted, or participated in any manner in an investigation, proceeding, or hearing under this subchapter. . . .

Learned contends that his employer's conduct violated both the "opposition clause" and the "participation clause" contained in section 704(a). . . .

The Opposition Clause

[T]he opposition clause, by its terms, protects only those employees who oppose what they reasonably perceive as discrimination *under the Act*. An employee need not establish that the opposed conduct in fact violated the Act in order to establish a valid claim of retaliation. *Id*. That is, an employee may fail to prove an "unlawful employment practice" and nevertheless prevail on his claim of unlawful retaliation.

However, the opposed conduct must fall within the protection of Title VII to sustain a claim of unlawful retaliation. . . .

Learned did not allege that he ever opposed any discrimination based upon race, color, religion, sex, or national origin. Any retaliation in this case related to Learned's having filed a . . . state industrial insurance [lawsuit] and Learned's opposition to what he believed was discrimination based upon physical and mental limitations only. Learned could not reasonably have believed that Bellevue discriminated against him in violation of Title VII, and therefore, he cannot claim that he was retaliated against for opposing discrimination prohibited by Title VII.

The Participation Clause

The participation clause is broadly construed to protect employees who utilize the tools provided by Congress to protect their rights. . . . As with the opposition clause, it is not necessary to prove that the underlying discrimination in fact violated Title VII in order to prevail in an action charging unlawful retaliation. *Id*. "If the availability of that protection were to turn on whether the employee's charge were ultimately found to be meritorious, resort to the remedies provided by the Act would be severely chilled. . . ."

The mere fact that an employee is participating in an investigation or proceeding involving charges of some sort of discrimination, however, does not automatically trigger the protection afforded under section 704(a); the underlying discrimination must be reasonably perceived as discrimination prohibited by Title VII. . . . Thus, even if the filing of Title VII charges with a state agency such as HRC could be construed as participation in an investigation, proceeding, or hearing under Title VII . . . , the HRC filing does not fall within the protection of 704(a) . . . because Learned did not allege discrimination prohibited by Title VII. Because Learned did not produce any evidence of, or even allege, a valid Title VII claim, we conclude that the district court properly granted summary judgment as to this claim.

The following case illustrates the way retaliation questions are considered in age discrimination claims. The requirement that the retaliation complained of be connected to activity that is protected by the employment discrimination act involved is even more difficult to analyze. Here the question focused on whether the Age Discrimination in Employment Act of 1967 covered the kind of retaliation claimed.

GRANT
v.
HAZELETT STRIP-CASTING CORP.
880 F.2d 1564 (2d Cir. 1989)

George C. PRATT, Circuit Judge

[The Employment Problem]

In the spring of 1974, Grant was hired as controller of HSCC, a position he retained until his dismissal from the company at the end of March 1987. . . . As controller, Grant was a member of HSCC's management committee and worked closely with R. William Hazelett, the company's founder, president, and chief executive officer. . . .

[In the months preceding Grant's discharge, Hazelett expressed a number of criticisms of Grant's performance, prompting other managers to suggest that Grant be given a lateral intracompany transfer that would remove him from daily contact with Hazelett. One of the options suggested was a long-term consulting arrangement for Grant, which would require HSCC to engage a new full-time controller to replace Grant in his current position. Hazelett asked Grant to assist in recruiting a new controller.] Grant first recommended Carolyn Antone, an HSCC employee who had worked closely with Grant, but Hazelett responded that "I don't want a woman in this job. A woman can't do the job." . . . There was also testimony . . . that no Jewish candidates would be considered because "many years ago the Hazelett family had a very unhappy experience with a group of Jewish financiers, and it left a very bitter taste in their mouth."

But of greater relevance to Grant's age discrimination suit, Hazelett also said that he wanted a younger person in the job. . . . At trial, Hazelett and other members of the management committee gave various reasons for preferring a younger controller, including their perceptions that (1) older candidates would demand a higher salary; (2) older employees "won't be able to be as productive"; and (3) "a person with a lot of experience wouldn't want Bill [Hazelett] telling him what to do."

. . . Grant approached Hazelett with a memo listing the qualifications desired in the new controller. Hazelett discussed these qualifications with Grant, filled in the salary range, and signed the memo. It reads . . .

Last week I discussed with [you] the additional qualifications you are looking for.

They are as follows:

A "hands-on" fellow who has enthusiasm and energy for a challenging position.

This young man will be between 30 and 40 years old, will have a CPA certificate, the ability to do tax returns, and hopefully a manufacturing background. (If he does not have manufacturing experience, Carolyn, as you pointed out, can train him.) . . .

A copy of this memo was given to the company's personnel director, Peter Rowan, who immediately told Grant "this is a no-no" because, as Rowan later testified, the document "was clearly in violation of EEO law." After Grant said that the memo reflected exactly what Hazelett was looking for in a new controller, Rowan replied that they must "protect Bill from himself." Later that day, Rowan and Regan edited the memo to remove any references to age and gender, and asked Grant to destroy all copies of the original memo. Grant refused. Before the day ended, Hazelett and Grant had an argument that the participants remembered as a "shouting match," resulting in a mutual decision that Grant would take the remainder of the week off as "a cooling off period." On March 30, 1987, the day Grant was to return to the office, Hazelett called Grant at home and told him he was no longer an employee of HSCC. The company replaced Grant with a 30-year-old man.

[The Legal Issue]

[Under 29 U.S.C. § 623(d) (the antiretaliation provision of the Age Discrimination in Employment Act, which mirrors Section 704), what kind of activities satisfy the participation clause where the employee is required to demonstrate a good-faith belief that the employer's actions violate the Act?]

[The Decision and Rationale of the U.S. Court of Appeals for the Second Circuit]

[It is plausible] that in asking Hazelett to approve the . . . memo, and in later refusing to destroy it, Grant was attempting to gather evidence for a future lawsuit and was therefore "participat[ing] in any manner in . . . litigation. . . ." Although the district court concluded that Grant's conduct "amounted to nothing more than a self-serving attempt to entrap his employer into the appearance of engaging in age discrimination, where no such discrimination existed," other inferences are equally plausible from the evidence presented. Based on testimony that Hazelett and others on the management committee had orally expressed their preference for a younger replacement, [a factfinder could conclude] that Grant's memo did not *create* the appearance of discrimination but, as Grant testified, merely documented a discriminatory practice that already existed.

The [district court was mistaken] to the extent it held, as a matter of law, that Grant's conduct was so unreasonable and disruptive that it could not receive protection under the act. We have not before addressed a claim such as this, but the first circuit did so in *Hochstadt v. Worcester Foundation for Experimental Biology* 545 F.2d 222(1st Cir. 1976), a case relied on by HSCC. There, the plaintiff interrupted staff meetings, misused secretarial services, ran up exorbitant telephone bills, invited a reporter to examine confidential salary information, was reprimanded several times for unsatisfactory work, caused two other employees to leave the company, and created numerous other disturbances in her efforts to protest allegedly discriminatory employment practices. These activities persisted over a period of three years before the plaintiff was ultimately terminated. Under these circumstances, and applying the principle that "the employer's right to run his business must be balanced against the rights of the employee to express his grievances and promote his own welfare," the court ruled that the plaintiff's actions, even though associated with a protected objective, were so extreme as to fall outside the ambit of Title VII. *Id.* at 230–34.

Hochstadt, however, is clearly an exceptional case, and we agree with the ninth circuit that it "must be read narrowly lest legitimate activism by employees asserting civil rights be chilled. . . ." Grant's activities fall far short of, indeed bear little resemblance to, the prolonged obstreperous acts and misconduct described in *Hochstadt*. Moreover, any disruption of HSCC's affairs seems less attributable to the actions of Grant than to the reactions of those around him. . . .

[T]he district court . . . expressed no opinion as to whether a sufficient causal link existed between Grant's activity and HSCC's decision to fire him. There is no need to remand on this issue, however, because . . .

Hazelett bluntly stated . . . that "we had to" fire Grant "[b]ecause he was in there getting evidence on me to do what's happening today. Simple." This corroborated his prior testimony that "having me sign this memo is the final main reason we decided that something had to be done." Other witnesses testified to the same effect. Such evidence of retaliatory motive is plainly sufficient to support [a] conclusion of a causal relation between Grant's protected activities and his discharge.

Discussion Notes

1. Note that Mr. Learned's case was brought before the Americans with Disabilities Act (ADA) was enacted. The ADA might have covered the retaliation against him based on his underlying worker's compensation claim. The ADA contains its own antiretaliation provision, which is substantially identical to Section 704. In the absence of a federally created right like the ADA protection, why should the federal court not take jurisdiction of independent state-law claims when they might be retaliatory under state worker's compensation laws?

2. Is *Learned* inconsistent with *Grant* concerning what an employee reasonably believed to be a violation of Title VII? *Grant* represents the majority rule that, if an employee reasonably believes that he has spoken out against or participated in redressing a Title VII violation, even if he is mistaken about the illegality of the employer's conduct, the employee is protected—so long as the action is based on a characteristic protected by federal antidiscrimination laws. The reasonableness of the employee's good-faith belief, however, has been subject to a great deal of disagreement among parties and the courts, as discussed in detail later in this chapter.

3. What is legitimate opposition to an unlawful employment practice? *See Cruz v. Coach Stores, Inc.*, 202 F.3d 560 (2d Cir. 2000) (male employee made extremely inappropriate comments to female employee; she slapped him; he then placed her in a headlock). Not surprisingly, the Second Circuit did not find slapping to be protected "opposition."

4. Do you think Marisa in Problem 27 and/or Paul in Problem 28 "opposed" an unlawful employment practice as defined by these cases?

1. Objective Reasonableness and the Opposition Clause

> ### Problem 29
>
> LaTonya Jones, an African-American attorney, is employed as in-house counsel for a government contractor. She mails to government officials a copy of a letter she has written to company officials detailing instances of racial and gender discrimination she has observed or experienced at the contracting company. The letter discusses matters she has handled as an attorney for the company that are subject to attorney-client privilege. As an attorney, she is not supposed to reveal this client information to anyone without the permission of her client. When she is fired for sending this letter, she files a retaliation claim against her employer.

In *Wideman v. Wal-Mart Stores*, 141 F.3d 1453 (11th Cir. 1998), the parties agreed that to establish a prima facie case of retaliation, the plaintiff must prove (1) she engaged in statutorily protected conduct, (2) she suffered an adverse employment action, and (3) the adverse employment action was causally related to the protected expression. They disagreed, however, about whether the plaintiff must prove as part of her prima facie case in a participation clause suit that her good-faith belief that the conduct violated Title VII was objectively reasonable. The Eleventh Circuit has made clear that, when the plaintiff brings a Section 704 claim based on the opposition clause rather than the participation clause, she must have a good-faith belief that the conduct she has opposed violates Title VII, and the belief must be objectively reasonable as measured against the legal standard. In other words, if the plaintiff thinks that she is opposing sexual harassment, the conduct she opposes had better be very close to what a court would determine to be sexual harassment, or she has no retaliation claim when her employer exacts reprisals for her opposition.

In *Clover v. Total System*, 176 F.3d 1346 (11th Cir. 1999), the Eleventh Circuit reversed a jury award of $160,000 in punitive damages and $25,000 in compensatory damages on an opposition clause retaliation claim. The plaintiff told internal investigators that she knew the supervisor lingered in the complainant's work area without any business purpose, called the complainant on her beeper during working hours, sequestered the complainant in a furtive way, and hung up the phone when other employees besides the complainant answered. The plaintiff told investigators that the complainant's response to the supervisor's actions was somewhat flirtatious. Within two days of providing this information, Ms. Clover was fired. The employer alleged that it terminated her for tardiness, including showing up late for her appointment with the human resources officer investigating the co-worker's sexual harassment charge. The Eleventh Circuit observed:

> The objective reasonableness of an employee's belief that her employer has engaged in an unlawful employment practice must be measured against existing substantive law.
>
> To establish a hostile environment claim premised on sexual harassment, a plaintiff must establish, among other things, that the harassment occurred be-

cause of her sex, and "that the harassment was sufficiently severe or pervasive to alter the conditions of her environment and create an abusive working environment." Clover contends that her belief that Pettis engaged in sexual harassment attributable to [the employer] was objectively reasonable "based on the nature of [Pettis'] conduct in connection [with the complainant Waters], a seventeen-year-old high school student[,] combined with Pettis' position within the company [as an assistant vice president]." However, the disparity between Pettis' and Waters' ages and positions in the company does not make Clover's belief objectively reasonable. None of the conduct that Clover described comes anywhere near constituting sexual harassment, regardless of the relative positions of the employees involved. As the Supreme Court recently stated:

> [T]he statute does not reach genuine but innocuous differences in the ways men and women routinely interact with members of the opposite sex. The prohibition of harassment on the basis of sex requires neither asexuality nor androgyny in the workplace; it forbids only behavior so objectively offensive as to alter the "conditions" of the victim's employment.

Oncale v. Sundowner Offshore Servs., Inc., 523 U.S. 75, 79–80 (1998). The Supreme Court has held that the conduct in question must be severe or pervasive enough that a reasonable person would find it hostile or abusive. That requirement is crucial "to ensur[ing] that courts and juries do not mistake ordinary socializing in the workplace—such as . . . intersexual flirtation–for discriminatory 'conditions of employment.' " *Id.* at 80.

We do not mean to hold that the conduct opposed must actually be sexual harassment, but it must be close enough to support an objectively reasonable belief that it is. The conduct Clover described misses the mark by a country mile. It follows that Clover's belief [that] the conduct created a sexually hostile environment for Waters was not objectively reasonable. . . .

Nor does the fact that Pettis engaged in conduct which led Waters to file an EEOC complaint and for the company to initiate an in-house investigation alter our conclusion. . . .

[F]or purposes of determining whether Clover satisfied the objective reasonableness component of the test it is critical to distinguish between the conduct that Clover opposed, i.e., what she saw or heard and then reported during the in-house interview, and the actual conduct Waters experienced and reported in her complaint to the EEOC. . . . For opposition clause purposes, the relevant conduct does not include conduct that actually occurred—or that was averred in an EEOC complaint by the alleged victim—but was unknown to the person claiming protection under the clause. Instead, what counts is only the conduct the person opposed, which cannot be more than she was aware of.

Id. at 1352. *See also Byers v. Dallas Morning News*, 209 F.3d 419 (5th Cir. 2000) (to satisfy opposition clause, plaintiff need not prove that employer's practices were actually unlawful, but his belief that they were unlawful must be reasonable based on existing substantive law).

The Fifth, Ninth, and Eleventh Circuits may be vindicated in their "objective reasonableness" standard by a more recent Supreme Court decision. In *Clark County School District v. Breeden*, 532 U.S. 268 (2001), the Court did not directly rule on the question of whether a plaintiff in an opposition clause suit must have an objectively reasonable belief that the conduct challenged actually violated Title VII; however, it did assume for purposes of argument that the plaintiff in an opposition clause case must have a reasonable belief that the conduct violated Title VII. Because the plaintiff herself was not offended by the supervisor's comment, she could not have assumed that it violated Title VII.

Plaintiff Breeden had made an internal complaint of sexual harassment based on one sexually explicit comment that her male supervisor repeated in her presence, which had actually been initially made by a job applicant to a woman he had once worked with: "I hear making love to you is like making love to the Grand Canyon." 532 U.S. at 269. The male supervisor and another male employee were in a meeting with the plaintiff at the time, discussing whether to hire this applicant and reviewing a written report in which the offensive comment appeared. The male supervisor, after repeating this applicant's comment, turned to the other male present and stated, "I don't know what that means." *Id.* The male employee responded, "Well, I'll tell you later," and the supervisor and the male employee laughed. *Id.* The plaintiff reported this incident to management.

In her deposition conducted after she had filed suit, she testified that she was not offended by the remark, even though she had reported it to management. She was transferred two years after reporting the comment to management to a position that had the same pay and benefits but that was regarded as having less advancement potential. The Court held that her internal complaint about this one comment did not trigger Section 704(a) opposition clause protection because the plaintiff could not reasonably have believed that this one comment could constitute sexual harassment, since nothing in this one remark was so severe as to alter the material terms and conditions of her employment and she herself testified that she was not offended.

The fact that the Breeden opinion was per curiam (without a specific justice identified with the writing of the opinion) and discussed the reasonableness issue less than definitively may make employers and lower courts hesitant to rely on it. The singularity of the facts—involving a plaintiff who herself disavows a belief that what she "opposed" was sexual harassment—also counsels caution in relying on the decision.

Question

1. Does LaTonya Jones have a retaliation claim? How should her claim be analyzed? What mixed motives does the employer have here, and how should they be handled? Do you think she has "opposed" an unlawful employment practice such that she should receive protection from retaliation?

2. Scope of the Participation Clause

Problem 30

A union official employed by Company 1 investigated Alice Abromsky's charge of sexual harassment against the union's president. Alice is employed by Company 2. The union official is subsequently subjected to a series of reprisals by Company 1.

a. Objective Reasonableness and the Participation Clause

GLOVER
v.
SOUTH CAROLINA LAW ENFORCEMENT DIVISION
170 F.3d 411 (4th Cir. 1999)

WILKINSON, Chief Judge.

[The Employment Problem]

SLED [South Carolina Law Enforcement Division] hired Lydia Glover as a police captain in June 1994. . . .

Glover and Martin spent much of Glover's probationary period at daggers drawn. Martin criticized Glover for inferior work, for missing deadlines, and for failing to learn the operational aspects of CJICS. In March 1995 Glover wrote a memorandum to SLED Chief Robert Stewart criticizing Martin's management style and suggesting that he be moved to a different work location. Glover's memorandum described Martin as "moody, unpredictable, and overly critical" as well as "authoritarian and dictatorial." Sensing that their relationship had badly deteriorated, Chief Stewart asked Glover and Martin to enter mediation.

At about the same time, Glover received a notice of deposition for a Title VII action that had been filed in the United States District Court for the District of South Dakota. Jane Koball, a deputy marshal in South Dakota, had sued the United States Marshals Service for gender discrimination. Glover's connection to the case came from her own years in the Marshals Service—immediately before SLED hired her, Glover had been the United States Marshal for the District of South Carolina. During her nine-year career in that office, she had served as chair of the Marshals Service Equal Opportunity Advisory Committee and had met and counseled Koball.

Glover's deposition lasted the entire day of April 3, 1995. Her testimony was open and wide-ranging. With minimal prompting from the government's deposing attorney, Glover freely offered facts directly related to Koball's problems with the South Dakota marshal's office but also her impressions of the operations of the South Carolina marshal's office. In particular, Glover perorated upon the perceived failings of her successor as the South Carolina U.S. Marshal, Israel Brooks. During the course of her testimony, Glover accused Brooks of mismanagement, destruction of office documents, wasting funds, inappropriate behavior, dishonesty, and discrimination.

The parties offer different explanations for Glover's testimonial attack on Marshal Brooks. Glover asserts that she was merely responding to the questions of the deposing attorney. SLED, on the other hand, argues that Glover went out of her way (through irrelevant and unresponsive answers) to malign and disparage Brooks and other members of his office. In any event, the subject of Brooks and the state of the South Carolina marshals office occupies nearly one hundred pages of the 268-page deposition transcript.

Brooks eventually learned of Glover's deposition testimony and complained to SLED Chief Stewart. After reading the deposition testimony, Stewart reprimanded Glover for her testimony.

On June 16, 1995, Stewart informed Glover that he would not be retaining her after the expiration of her probationary period. Stewart cited three reasons for his decision. Two stemmed from the quality of her work during the first ten months of her tenure: first, that she had not developed an appropriate level of knowledge for her position, and second, that her priorities were inconsistent with those of the organization. Stewart's third criticism was that Glover's performance in her deposition had demonstrated poor judgment.

Stewart later admitted that he did not fire Glover solely for her job performance. Instead, he acknowledged that "the deposition caused [him] to go back and rethink the whole issue," that he "took the deposition into consideration" and that the deposition testimony "tipped the balance in favor of firing."

Glover filed discrimination and retaliation charges against SLED with the South Carolina Human Affairs Commission and with the Equal Employment Opportunity Commission (EEOC). Both agencies issued right-to-sue letters. Glover then filed this retaliatory discharge claim. . . .

[The Decision by the Trial Court]

On SLED's motion for summary judgment, the district court found that Glover had been terminated because of her deposition testimony. The court also found, however, that the specific testimony that led to Glover's termination was not protected "participation" under section 704(a), since it was "unresponsive, uncompelled, and gratuitous."

[The Legal Issue]

[The Fourth Circuit considered whether the district correctly granted summary judgment to SLED, based on its reasoning that Glover's conduct was not within the participation clause of section 704(a) because she testified unreasonably in her deposition.]

[The Decision and Rationale of the U.S. Court of Appeals for the Fourth Circuit]

We hold that the participation clause shields even allegedly unreasonable testimony from employer retaliation, and we therefore reverse the judgment of the district court. . . .

A plaintiff makes out a prima facie case of retaliation by showing that she engaged in a protected activity, that she suffered an adverse employment action, and that the two were causally related. . . . It is plain from the record that Glover suffered an adverse employment action and that there was a causal connection between that action and her deposition testimony. It is also plain that testifying in a deposition in a Title VII case generally constitutes protected activity under section 704(a)'s participation clause. . . . In the absence of a legitimate, nondiscriminatory explanation for Glover's termination, our inquiry would normally be at an end.

SLED contends, however, that an employee's conduct is only protected if that conduct is "reasonable." To determine reasonableness, SLED asks us to import a balancing test into the participation clause. SLED finds guidance in our application of section 704(a)'s opposition clause. To determine whether conduct is protected opposition activity, "[w]e balance the purpose of the Act to protect persons engaging reasonably in activities opposing . . . discrimination, against Congress' equally manifest desire not to tie the hands of employers in the objective selection and control of personnel. . . ." Because Glover's attacks on Marshal Brooks and his team were irrelevant to Koball's Title VII claim, SLED con-

tends that her behavior was unreasonable and that it fails this balancing test. Under SLED's rationale, Glover's testimony thus does not constitute protected "participation."

We are willing to assume for the purposes of this case that Glover's testimony was unreasonable. SLED still cannot prevail. Reading a reasonableness test into section 704(a)'s participation clause would do violence to the text of that provision and would undermine the objectives of Title VII.

The plain language of the participation clause itself forecloses us from improvising such a reasonableness test. The clause forbids retaliation against an employee who "has made a charge, testified, assisted, or participated in any manner" in a protected proceeding. 42 U.S.C. § 2000e-3(a). Glover was fired because she "testified" in a Title VII deposition. The term "testify" has a plain meaning: "[t]o bear witness" or "to give evidence as a witness." Black's Law Dictionary 1476 (6th ed. 1990).

Moreover, those who testify in Title VII proceedings are endowed with "exceedingly broad protection." *Pettway v. American Cast Iron Pipe Co.*, 411 F.2d 998, 1006 n.18 (5th Cir. 1969). "The word 'testified' is not preceded or followed by any restrictive language that limits its reach." *Merritt v. Dillard Paper Co.*, 120 F.3d 1181, 1186 (11th Cir. 1997). In fact, it is followed by the phrase "in any manner"–a clear signal that the provision is meant to sweep broadly. . . . Congress could not have carved out in clearer terms this safe harbor from employer retaliation. A straightforward reading of the statute's unrestrictive language leads inexorably to the conclusion that all testimony in a Title VII proceeding is protected against punitive employer action.

This conclusion is consistent with the purpose of the participation clause: "Maintaining unfettered access to statutory remedial mechanisms." *Robinson v. Shell Oil Co.*, 519 U.S. 337 (1997). . . . If a witness in a Title VII proceeding were secure from retaliation only when her testimony met some slippery reasonableness standard, she would surely be less than forthcoming. . . . [S]ee also Ross [v. Communications Satellite Corp., 759 F.2d 355, 357 n.1 (4th Cir. 1985)] (antiretaliation provision applies even where underlying discrimination claim is not meritorious). . . . Congress has determined that some irrelevant and even provocative testimony must be immunized so that Title VII proceedings will not be chilled. It is not for this court to overturn that judgment.

b. Meaning of "Proceeding" Under Participation Clause

Recall the *Clover* case cited in the earlier discussion of the opposition clause. Plaintiff Clover, in addition to her opposition claim, brought a claim under Section 704(a)'s participation clause. She contended that her participation in the company's internal investigation of the sexual harassment complaint of her coworker was participation entitled to Section 704's protection. The company countered that "Clover did not engage in protected conduct because she simply participated in an internal employer investigation, which [it contends is not] 'participat[ion] in any manner in an investigation. . . .' Clover, 176 F.3d 1352. The Eleventh Circuit rejected this position:

> [The employer] relies upon *dicta* from *Silver v. KCA, Inc.*, 586 F.2d 138, 141 (9th Cir. 1978), that participation conduct is "participation in the machinery set up by Title VII to enforce its provisions." Thus, the issue we must resolve is whether an employee's participation in an investigation conducted by her employer in response to an EEOC notice of charge of discrimination is 'participat[ion] in any manner in an investigation . . . under this subchapter."
>
> [A]lthough subchapter VI of chapter 21 of title 42 does not define the term "investigation . . . under this subchapter," it is clear that, at a minimum, the term encompasses EEOC investigations of alleged unlawful discrimination. *See* 42 U.S.C. § 2000e-5(b) ("Whenever a charge is filed by . . . a person . . . alleging that an employer . . . has engaged in an unlawful employment practice, the [EEOC] . . . shall make an investigation thereof."). . . .
>
> Thus, an employer receiving a form notice of charge of discrimination knows that any evidence it gathers after that point and submits to the EEOC will be considered by the EEOC as part of the EEOC investigation. . . . [T]he EEOC considers employer-submitted evidence on an equal footing with any evidence it gathers from other sources. Because the information the employer gathers as part of its investigation in response to the notice of charge of discrimination will be utilized by the EEOC, it follows that an employee who participates in the employer's process of gathering such information is participating, in some manner, in the EEOC's investigation.
>
> . . . Congress chose to protect employees who "participate[d] in *any* manner" in an EEOC investigation. 42 U.S.C. § 2000e-3(a) (emphasis added). The words "participate in any manner" express Congress's intent to confer "exceptionally broad protection" upon employees covered by Title VII. As we pointed out in *Merritt v. Dillard Paper Co.*, 120 F.3d 1181, 1186 (11th Cir. 1997), "the adjective 'any' is not ambiguous. . . . [I]t has an expansive meaning, that is, one or some indiscriminately of whatever kind. . . . [A]ny means all." Because participation in an employer's investigation conducted in response to a notice of charge of discrimination is a form of participation, indirect as it is, in an EEOC investigation, such participation is sufficient to bring the employee within the protection of the participation clause.

The court went on to hold that, even so, the plaintiff's participation claim failed for other reasons. 176 F.3d 1346, 1356.

Questions

1. Does the union official in Problem 30 have a retaliation claim even though the female employee whose charge he investigated works for Company 2? In what way does the participation clause apply to him?

2. Why have the courts refrained from engrafting the judge-made "objectively reasonable" requirement onto the participation clause? Is this explained by the *Glover* majority's sensitivity to the potential chilling effect such a requirement might have? Does the fact that employees can be subpoenaed to testify, on pain of contempt, justify the special solicitude for employees who "participate" rather than "oppose" a practice they think is unlawful? Does the subjectivity involved in determining what testimony is "reasonable" demonstrate the correctness of the *Glover* majority's reasoning?

3. Does the "objectively reasonable" test for opposition clause claims require laypeople to be lawyers? How well does the proponent of an opposition clause claim have to know the law?

4. Why does the antiretaliation provision use a "motivating factor" standard rather than a sole reason or "but for" standard? In *Glover*, suppose that Chief Stewart had identified only two reasons for the plaintiff's termination, both of which were legitimate and nondiscriminatory and had not mentioned her deposition testimony at all, even if it privately motivated him? Wouldn't the plaintiff then have had a harder time proving her case, having only the circumstantial evidence of a call from Israel Brooks about the deposition testimony and a termination shortly thereafter?

5. Does it seem odd that Glover's testimony is protected when she was testifying about events that did not involve herself or a co-worker? Glover was not called to testify against her employer, but against Koball's. That being the case, did Glover run the same risk of retaliation that a person testifying in a co-worker's Title VII case would run? Did Congress intend to protect employees who testify for co-workers against their mutual employer? Did Congress intend to protect employees as broadly as the Glover majority decided to protect them?

6. If the employer claims a good-faith belief that the employee lied in his deposition or in investigative proceedings, what effect does that have on the legitimate, nondiscriminatory motive inquiry? Does the employer have to show that its belief is objectively reasonable? Interestingly, the Eleventh Circuit has held that an employer's good-faith belief that an employee lied in an in-house Title VII investigation—even if the employer does not prove that the employee lied—is a legitimate, nondiscriminatory reason to fire the employee, over a participation clause objection. *See EEOC v. Total Sys. Serv.*, 221 F.3d 1171 (11th Cir. 2000), *reh'g en banc denied*, 240 F.3d 899 (11th Cir. 2001). Is this result consistent with the remedial purposes of Title VII? Does it encourage employers to call employees liars, regardless of whether they are truthful, to avoid liability?

C. The Second Requirement: Adverse Employment Action

Problem 31

Kim Soo, a physical education teacher, complained of discrimination on the basis of his Korean national origin in violation of Title VII. For 10 days after his complaint, he was deprived of his additional title of Coordinator of Sports Studies, and his name was omitted from a publication by the state school where he worked. He suffered no diminution in income, and the title was restored. Kim filed a charge of retaliation.

Problem 32

Elena Druzina resists her supervisor's sexual advances and reports him to management. Her disciplinary record is not spotless at the time she makes the report. She and other cashiers at the store are later instructed by the supervisor to clean the restrooms. The plaintiff, however, is reprimanded when she refuses to clean the toilets without a brush, and she is later fired. She files a charge of sexual harassment and retaliation against her employer.

Problem 33

Elena Druzina's co-workers hear that she has complained about her supervisor's sexual advances. She is the only woman on the staff. The men are outraged that she has made these accusations against the supervisor. Thereafter, dead squirrels begin showing up in the plaintiff's truck, graffiti is scrawled on her possessions, the crew ostracizes her, and no one helps her with two-person jobs. Elena quits because she cannot stand the negativity of these co-workers. She files a charge of sexual harassment and retaliation against the employer for the actions of the supervisor and the co-workers.

A prima facie case requires the plaintiff to show an adverse employment action. Often, the question of whether the plaintiff has suffered such an adverse employment action proceeds hand-in-glove with the timing of the alleged retaliation in relation to the underlying participation or opposition, but not invariably. Employers often contend that nothing short of an "ultimate employment decision"—firing or not hiring—constitutes an adverse employment action for purposes of Section 704(a).

WIDEMAN
v.
WAL-MART STORES INC. 141
F.3d 1453 (11th Cir. 1998)

[The Employment Problem]

The plaintiff filed an EEOC race discrimination charge after she was passed over for a promotion. She alleged that supervisors told her that the position would not go to a black person. On February 9, 1995, the plaintiff filed an EEOC race discrimination charge. On February 10, she informed management that she had filed the charge. On February 11, she was told she would be charged with an unexcused absence even though the "absence" was on a day she had previously been given permission to be off. When she reported to work in order to avoid being charged with the absence, her supervisor told her to work anyway and did not give her a lunch break. On February 13, one of the supervisors against whom she had complained of race discrimination gave her a written reprimand, followed by a reprimand on February 22. In the 11 months she had worked at Wal-Mart prior to filing her charge, she had not received any reprimands. Around February 13, the supervisor who had issued the written reprimand began seeking negative comments from co-workers about the plaintiff, ignoring positive comments.

When the plaintiff reported to work on April 3, she learned that she had not been scheduled for this expected and customary shift. She threatened to call Wal-Mart headquarters and inquire, whereupon the assistant manager on duty threatened to shoot her in the head. One month later, the plaintiff suffered an allergic reaction that required medical treatment. Although the assistant manager on duty was aware of the plaintiff's need, she needlessly delayed authorizing the medical treatment.

[The Decision and Rationale of the U.S. Court of Appeals for the Eleventh Circuit]

Wal-Mart contends that none of those acts [is] sufficient to constitute an adverse employment action for purposes of a retaliation claim. Relying principally on the Fifth Circuit's holding in *Mattern v. Eastman Kodak Co.*, 104 F.3d 702 (5th Cir. 1997), Wal-Mart argues that unless the alleged act of retaliation was an "ultimate employment action" such as discharge or failure to hire, it does not qualify as an adverse employment action for purposes of an unlawful retaliation claim. . . .

There is a circuit split on this issue. While the Eighth Circuit has sided with the Fifth Circuit, *see Ledergerber v. Stangler*, 122 F.3d 1142, 1144 (8th Cir. 1997) (only adverse employment decisions that "rise to the level of an ultimate employment decision [are] intended to be actionable under Title VII."), the First, Ninth, and Tenth Circuits have all held that Title VII's protection against retaliatory discrimination extends to adverse actions which fall short of ultimate employment decisions. *See Wyatt v. City of Boston*, 35 F.3d 13, 15–16 (1st Cir. 1994) (stating that actions other than discharge are covered by Title VII's anti-retaliation provision and listing as examples, "employer actions such as demotions, disadvantageous transfers or assignments, refusals to promote, unwarranted negative job evaluations and toleration of harassment by other employees."); *Yartzoff v. Thomas*, 809 F.2d 1371, 1375 (9th Cir. 1987) (holding that such non-ultimate employment decisions as "[t]ransfers of job duties and undeserved performance ratings, if proven, would constitute 'adverse employment decisions' cognizable under" Title VII's antiretaliation provision); *Berry v. Stevinson Chevrolet*, 74 F.3d 980, 984–86 (10th Cir. 1996) (construing Title VII's antiretaliation provision to reach beyond ultimate employment decisions and [to] protect an employee from a malicious prosecution action brought by former employer). In addition, the D.C. Circuit has held that the Age Discrimination in Employment Act's anti-retaliation clause, which is identical to Title VII's, "does not limit its reach only to acts of retaliation that take the form of cognizable employment actions such as discharge, transfer or demotion." *Passer v. American Chem. Soc'y*, 935 F.2d 322, 331 (D.C. Cir. 1991). *See also Welsh v. Derwinski*, 14 F.3d 85, 86 (1st Cir. 1994) (stating that the ADEA's anti-retaliation provision covers more than discharge, demotion, or failure to promote and that a "case-by-case review" is necessary to determine whether an employer's actions rise to the level of adverse employment actions for purposes of stating a prima case of retaliation).

We join the majority of circuits which have addressed the issue and hold that Title VII's protection against retaliatory discrimination extends to adverse actions which fall short of ultimate employment decisions. The Fifth and Eighth Circuits' contrary position is inconsistent with the plain language of 42 U.S.C. § 2000e-3 (a), which makes it "unlawful to *discriminate* against any of his employees . . . because he has made a charge . . . " (emphasis added). Read in the light of ordinary understanding, the term "discriminate" is not limited to "ultimate employment decisions." Moreover, our plain language interpretation of 42 U.S.C. § 2000e-3(a) is consistent with Title VII's remedial purpose. Permitting employers to discriminate against an employee who files a charge of discrimination so long as the retaliatory discrimination does not constitute an ultimate employment action could stifle employees' willingness to file charges of discrimination.

Although we do not doubt that there is some threshold level of substantiality that must be met for unlawful discrimination to be cognizable under the anti-retaliation clause, we need not determine in this case the exact notch into which the bar should be placed. It is enough to conclude, as we do, that the actions about which [plaintiff] Wideman complains considered collectively are sufficient. . . .

To establish the causal relation element of her prima facie case of retaliation, [the plaintiff] need only show "that the protected activity and the adverse action are not completely unrelated. . . ." [Plaintiff Wideman] has done that by presenting evidence that Wal-Mart knew of her EEOC charge—she testified that she informed her Wal-Mart managers on February 10, 1995 that she had filed an EEOC charge of discrimination the day before—and that the series of adverse employment actions commenced almost immediately after management learned she had filed the charge. *See Donnellon v. Fruehauf Corp.*, 794 F.2d 598, 601 (11th Cir. 1986) ("The short period of time [one month] between the filing of the discrimination complaint and the [adverse employment action] belies any assertion by the defendant that the plaintiff failed to prove causation.").

Thus, we conclude that Wideman presented sufficient evidence to establish a prima facie case of retaliation. Because of that and because Wal-Mart did not assert in the district court any non-discriminatory reasons for the adverse employment actions Wideman allegedly suffered in retaliation for filing her charge, she was not required to present additional evidence in order to survive Wal-Mart's motion for judgment as a matter of law. . . . (14 F.3d at 86; *accord, Ray v. Henderson*, 217 F.3d 1234 (9th Cir. 2000).)

Discussion Notes

1. The Eighth Circuit has not retrenched on its "ultimate adverse employment action" rule. In *LaCroix v. Sears, Roebuck & Co.*, 240 F.3d 688 (8th Cir. 2001), it reaffirmed its rule. In that case, the plaintiff's attorney had written a letter to managers complaining about his client's harassment and retaliation at the hands of managers. The plaintiff contended that the employer used the attorney's letter as a basis to reduce pay and to threaten firing. The Eighth Circuit found no evidence that the attorney's letter resulted in a material employment disadvantage, since the employee was not fired.

2. The Seventh Circuit appears to be adopting a restrictive concept of employer reprisals without wholly embracing the minority "ultimate adverse employment action" position. In *Krause v. City of LaCrosse*, 246 F.3d 995 (7th Cir. 2001), the court held that a written reprimand and a transfer to an undesirable location within the same office were not actionable retaliation for a complaint of sex discrimination: "[A] materially adverse change in employment conditions must be more disruptive than a mere inconvenience or an alteration of job responsibilities." *Id.* at 1001.

3. The Supreme Court has indicated that a former employer's interference with the ex-employee's ability to find a new job by giving him a bad reference can state a retaliation claim. *Robinson v. Shell Oil Co.*, 519 U.S. 337 (1997).

4. The EEOC has issued some guidance on the meaning of a tangible adverse employment action. The EEOC would apply these criteria:

   a. A tangible [adverse] employment action is the means by which the supervisor brings the official power of the employer to bear on subordinates, as demonstrated by the following:

      - it requires an official act of the enterprise;
      - it usually is documented in official company records;
      - it may be subject to review by higher level supervisors; and
      - it often requires the formal approval of the enterprise and use of its internal processes.

   b. A tangible employment action usually inflicts direct economic harm.

   c. A tangible employment action, in most instances, can only be caused by a supervisor or other person acting with the authority of the company.

   Examples of tangible employment actions include:

      - hiring and firing;
      - promotion and failure to promote;
      - demotion;
      - undesirable reassignment;
      - a decision causing a significant change in benefits;
      - compensation decisions; and
      - work assignment.

   EEOC Enforcement Guidance 915.002 (6/18/99), *reprinted in* EEOC COMPLIANCE MANUAL (BNA) N:4078. While this guidance is more useful in answering the questions that arise under the *Faragher/Ellerth* regime, *see infra* Chapter 5, these criteria might be imported into the retaliation inquiry by a court.

Questions

1. In Problem 27, Marisa Hernandez was removed from a desirable assignment and reassigned to a less desirable one, with no loss of pay; also she received a less favorable performance evaluation, her company car was taken away, and she was denied permission to attend professional seminars. If she loses her claim of sexual harassment, does she still have a good claim of retaliation? What if she is in an "ultimate employment decision" rule state? What if she is in a jurisdiction that does not subscribe to the "ultimate employment decision" rule?

2. In Problem 31, Kim Soo did not suffer any loss of pay, but his title was taken away from him for 10 days and his name was omitted from a school publication. Is this an adverse employment action sufficient to meet the requirement for a retaliation charge?

3. What is the difference between Elena Druzina's situation in Problems 32 and 33 regarding the adverse action requirement? In Problem 32, may Elena Druzina succeed on her retaliation claim if her claim of sexual harassment does not prevail? Under what circumstances does she have a viable claim? In Problem 33, Elena quit because she could not stand the negative actions of her co-workers. Should this count as an adverse employment action when she took matters into her own hands and quit?

In one situation, Elena is asked to clean the bathrooms, but so are the other employees; can this be considered an adverse employment action? What about the negative treatment of Elena in Problem 33, where her co-workers are angry about her complaints of sexual harassment against their supervisor? Can their negative and sometimes ugly treatment of her constitute an adverse action by the employer?

D. The Third Requirement: Causal Nexus and Temporal Factors

Problem 34

Judith Gray complained of sexual harassment following some ribald remarks by her supervisors, and she is later fired for reasons of deficient performance. The company's investigation disclosed that the plaintiff herself frequently engaged in sexual banter, told crude jokes, and touched the alleged harasser in a sexually suggestive manner. She is fired within 12 days of her complaint of sexual harassment.

Closeness in time between the opposition or participation and the adverse action is helpful in establishing that the employer's action is retaliatory. In *Clark County School District v. Breeden*, 532 U.S. 268 (2001) *(per curiam)*, the Supreme Court rejected the plaintiff's claim that her transfer to a position with the same pay and benefits but on a worse career track than she had occupied before filing her EEOC charge was retaliatory. The plaintiff was transferred three months after the EEOC issued the right-to-sue letter and one month after the plaintiff filed her suit. *Breeden*, however, turned on other factors, including the apparent frivolity of the suit. *See* subpart B, *supra*.

The courts are sensitive to the fact that employees whose futures are precarious may launch a preemptive strike, claiming discrimination as a cover for inadequate performance, and then, when fired for performance-related reasons, claim retaliation for having filed an EEOC charge of discrimination. For this reason, the courts have found temporal proximity to be relevant but not to constitute a prima facie case standing alone. *See Slattery v. Swiss Reins. Am. Corp.*, 248 F.3d 87 (2d Cir. 2001) (while temporal proximity between plaintiff's EEOC filing and subsequent firing can demonstrate a causal nexus between the two, here the plaintiff's graduated discipline was commenced five months before plaintiff filed the EEOC charge and thus cannot give rise to an inference of retaliation); *Contreras v. Suncast Corp.*, 237 F.3d 756 (7th Cir. 2001) (plaintiff who falsified documents, was tardy, and was insubordinate did not establish retaliation case even though he was fired one month after filing an ADA charge); *Nyugen v. City of Cleveland*, 229 F.3d 559, 566 (6th Cir. 2000) (plaintiff denied a promotion soon after complaint of discrimination could not rely on temporal proximity alone; "temporal proximity in the absence of other evidence of causation is not sufficient to raise an inference of a causal link"); *Figgous v. Allied/Bendix*, 906 F.2d 360 (8th Cir. 1990) (plaintiff filed charges of discrimination in 1982 and in 1983 and was fired for poor performance, but in 1984, he was rehired pursuant to a grievance settlement between his union and the employer, with the proviso that if plaintiff transgressed any employer rules, he would be fired; his termination for violating attendance rules was upheld against retaliation challenge).

The cases below show the interplay of closeness in time between the alleged discrimination and the alleged retaliation in making a plaintiff's Section 704(a) case.

JACKSON
v.
ST. JOSEPH STATE HOSPITAL
840 F.2d 1387 (8th Cir. 1988)

GIBSON, Senior Circuit Judge

[The Employment Problem]

In May 1975, Jackson was hired by St. Joseph State Hospital as its chief accountant to correct problems which had developed in the preparation of Medicare cost reports. As early as 1977, the hospital administration began receiving complaints about Jackson and the low morale in the accounting department. Jackson's subordinates complained that he would discuss one employee's private life with other employees. One employee filed a grievance claiming that Jackson was disruptive, agitated one employee against another, and created a stressful work environment. Complaints about Jackson were also made to state legislators.

In May 1978, a meeting was held to discuss changes to be made in the accounting department. . . . Jackson declined to attend. Hospital superintendent Dr. Nicholas Bartulica continued to receive complaints about Jackson, so a second meeting was held in late May. Jackson preferred not to attend and stated that further complaints should be put in writing. Jackson's request was communicated to his subordinates, but no further complaints were received by the administration.

In July 1978, the accounting department was audited by the Department of Mental Health. The chief auditor found that Jackson's managerial style was causing morale problems in the accounting department. Jackson was informed that disciplinary actions would be taken if he did not correct the problems in his department.

In October 1978, Jackson's secretary filed a grievance against him stating that he frequently discussed employees' personal lives, that he had problems communicating, and that he frequently called her into his office on Friday afternoons to criticize and demean her. At a meeting between Jackson, the secretary, and Dave Farrar, the assistant superintendent for administration, Jackson became angry and stated that he would run the secretary out of his department. As a result of Jackson's conduct, Farrar informed him that if he did not change his ways, he would risk losing his position as department head.

Complaints about Jackson abated until January 1982, when Roxanne Kuhn filed an internal complaint against him alleging harassment. Several months before the complaint was filed, Jackson had begun inquiring into Kuhn's personal life. He told Kuhn that he did not approve of her black boyfriend and that she should not expect any promotions while the relationship continued. Also, Jackson stated that he disapproved of the fact that Kuhn's children lived with her ex-husband. Kuhn's complaint also alleged that Jackson frequently touched or grabbed her.

On the same day that Kuhn filed her complaint, Jackson requested that she be suspended for one day with pay for failing to complete certain reports. Dr. Bartulica met individually with Kuhn and Jackson to discuss a compromise. Kuhn agreed to withdraw her complaint subject to reinstatement if the harassment continued, and Jackson agreed to withdraw his request for suspension after being told that the request would not be supported by the hospital administration.

On June 4, 1982 Jackson went to Kuhn's office to discuss work-related matters, but she was not there. He eventually found her sitting in Rhonda Mahoney's office with her back to the door. Jackson approached Kuhn from behind and placed his hands on her shoulders and did not remove them until she stood up and left the room. On June 9, Jackson called Kuhn into his office to discuss her drinking habits.

On June 10 Kuhn filed another complaint against Jackson citing the June 4 and June 9 incidents. On July 14, Jackson was issued a reprimand and directed not to place his hands on female employees, make inquiries into or discuss employees' private lives, or counsel or discipline female employees without a witness present. In response, Jackson filed an internal complaint alleging sex discrimination. The division director found against him on October 1, 1982 and on November 17, Jackson filed complaints with the Equal Employment Opportunity Commission (EEOC) and the Missouri Commission on Human Rights. Jackson was advised by the hospital administration that suspension was being considered if he did not cooperate, and shortly thereafter, he was suspended for three days without pay.

On January 10, 1983, Jackson was notified by the EEOC that a fact finding conference had been scheduled for January 27. In preparation for the conference, Jackson approached Rhonda Mahoney regarding the June 4 incident in her office. Jackson wanted proof that his touching of Roxanne Kuhn was not sexual in nature. During a forty-five minute conversation, Mahoney repeatedly told Jackson that she had already given a statement and that she did not think it was proper to discuss the incident further. Later that day, Jackson again approached Mahoney and requested a statement. Mahoney became so upset that she left work for the remainder of the day.

On January 26, two days later, Jackson gave Mahoney a prepared statement and asked her to review it, make any changes necessary, and sign it. It stated that Mahoney did not remember what happened in her of-

fice on June 4; Mahoney refused to sign the statement and complained to Jackson's supervisor that if Jackson did not leave her alone, she would lodge a formal complaint of harassment. Later that day, Jackson was put on administrative leave with pay pending investigation of the incident with Mahoney.

[On February 17, 1983, Jackson was terminated following the company's internal investigation. The hospital issued him a letter stating the reasons for dismissal as inadequate and ineffective job performance, disruption of the workplace, and his treatment of Ms. Mahoney, which the hospital had determined was harassment. Jackson was accorded the opportunity to file a written response and did so. The hospital affirmed its decision to terminate Jackson.]

[The Legal Issue]

Whether district court correctly determined that Jackson failed to establish a prima facie case of retaliatory discharge when they found that his conduct was not reasonable protected activities. . . .

In order to establish a prima facie case of retaliatory discharge, Jackson must prove that 1) he was engaged in statutorily protected activity, 2) he suffered adverse employment action, and 3) a causal connection between the two exists.

[The Decision by the Trial Court]

The district court found for the hospital on all three claims. . . .

The district court found that Jackson failed to establish a prima facie case because his conduct in pursuing a statement from Mahoney was not protected activity as it was "bizarre." Jackson argues that the cases cited by the district court, *Garrett v. Mobil Oil Corp.* 531 F.2d 892 (8th Cir.),. *Cert. denied* 429 U.S. 848 (1976), and *EEOC v. Shoney's, Inc,* 536 F. Supp. 875 (N.D. Ala. 1982), are inapplicable because the conduct of the plaintiffs in those cases was unreasonable whereas his own conduct was reasonable.

[The Decision and Rationale of the U.S. Court of Appeals for the Eighth Circuit]

In *Garrett,* an employee pursuing an EEOC complaint refused direct orders, left her work station, and barged in on meetings of managerial personnel. In *Shoney's* an employee neglected his job for three days while pursuing an EEOC complaint. Jackson argues that the time he spent pursuing a statement is reasonable when compared to *Shoney's*, and his "polite efforts" cannot be compared to those in *Garrett*. This argument, however, overlooks several important facts.

First, although Jackson's efforts did not take more than a few hours, additional work time was lost when he had his secretary typing and copying documents for him on hospital time and when he disturbed Mahoney so greatly that she left work early on January 24, 1983. Second, Jackson's pursuit of a statement cannot be characterized as polite. Once Mahoney stated that she did not want to make a statement to him, Jackson should have left her alone. Mahoney had already given a statement to the EEOC. Furthermore, since the EEOC has subpoena power, Jackson had other less objectionable and disruptive avenues open for obtaining Mahoney's testimony. Also, Jackson's repeated assertions to Mahoney that her memory of the June 4 incident was incorrect was entirely out of line and was aptly perceived by the district court to be "bizarre," and was an abusive attempt to have Mahoney change her views of the incident in her office.

Further, Jackson had a long string of complaints and reprimands preceding his termination. The mere act of filing an EEOC complaint does not render illegal all subsequent disciplinary actions taken by the hospital. As the district court noted, Jackson's conduct in pursuing a statement from Mahoney was the "last straw." He was fired for pursuing a statement in a highly offensive and disruptive manner after repeated warnings that he needed to change the way in which he dealt with subordinates. To require the hospital to overlook Jackson's past simply because he filed an EEOC complaint would unduly hamper the hospital's right to make employment decisions. Likewise, it would be unreasonable to hold that while on the state payroll Jackson had a federally protected right to harass Mahoney to the point that she had to leave work. . . .

Title VII protection from retaliation for filing a complaint does not clothe the complainant with immunity for past and present inadequacies, unsatisfactory performance, and uncivil conduct in dealing with subordinates and with his peers. The public and the state should not have to suffer waste of public funds in countenancing the arrogant and bizarre conduct exhibited by Jackson. Department heads should strive to create harmonious relationships amongst subordinates and working personnel rather than discord, personal humiliation, and chaos. Jackson's record of performance was not only inferior but atrocious in making unreasonable demands on subordinates, creating inefficiency in department operations, wasting state resources, and in his personal harassment of Mahoney. The aforementioned conduct is not protected nor should it be countenanced by the statutory purposes set forth in Title VII.

[Discussion of the due process violation claim is omitted.]

Because we hold that Jackson established neither a prima facie case of retaliatory discharge nor a due process violation, the order of the district court entering judgment in favor of the defendants is affirmed.

Questions

1. Can Judith Gray, in Problem 34, raise an inference of retaliatory action based on the timing of her discharge based on the court analysis in Jackson? What if she was not discharged for two months? A year? Does she have a claim based on complaining and being fired in a circuit with a lenient "good-faith belief" construction of the law? What other circumstances would help to show that a connection exists between the timing of her complaints and her discharge?

2. Retaliation aside, does Mr. Jackson state a prima facie case of gender discrimination against St. Joseph Hospital? If Mr. Jackson had been able to compare his treatment with the treatment of a female employee who was not disciplined for similarly harassing behavior, would he have had a viable Title VII gender claim? (Courts sometimes refer to persons who are accused of sexual harassment and who then file a discrimination suit based on a claim that the employer treated the investigation into their guilt or innocence differently than it treated investigations against more favored classes as proponents of "whipsaw liability.")

   Did the hospital fire Mr. Jackson for sexually harassing Ms. Mahoney? Was Jackson's action toward Ms. Mahoney sexually harassing or merely harassing? Does one instance of placing his hands on Ms. Kuhn rise to the level of sexual harassment by Jackson? Does the touching of her shoulders, combined with a history of discussing Kuhn's and other employees' personal lives, constitute conduct that is severe, repetitive, and pervasive, so as to be proscribed as sexual harassment under Title VII? What about when Jackson's conduct is combined with his statements to Kuhn about a boyfriend who we are to assume was of another race than Jackson and Kuhn? Does Jackson's additional intrusive questioning about Kuhn's custodial arrangements for her children shed any light on the question of whether Jackson acted out of gender bias himself? Could the hospital reasonably have feared that Kuhn might file a sexual harassment action if Jackson was not removed from the workplace? Would such a fear be reasonable? Could the hospital have feared that Mahoney would file a sexual harassment suit?

3. Does the *Jackson* court's discussion give one the impression that "harassment" is independently actionable when the employer is a public employer? Would you suspect a bias toward employers in discrimination suits if the discussion of wasted time and resources had appeared in an opinion in which the employer was private rather than public? Should public employers be given more leeway by the courts? Don't private employers suffer losses and have to pay their lawyers to defend against baseless suits as well?

4. Who really has a retaliation claim here, given Jackson's role as a supervisor when he accosted Mahoney? What about Jackson's disciplinary action toward Kuhn?

5. If Jackson's conversations with Mahoney were made in the context of preparation for an EEOC fact-finding conference, why should they not be considered protected activity? Is it a satisfactory response to exclude "bizarre" behavior from Section 704 protection? Should the reasonableness, or lack thereof, of actions be a question for a judge to resolve, or is this a question of fact for the jury?

6. Would Jackson's behavior toward Mahoney have resulted in discharge if his EEOC charge was not pending? Considering his history of counterproductive dealings with employees that did not result in termination, is it too convenient that the "bizarre" actions toward Mahoney coincided with his EEOC proceedings? Why wasn't he fired for the earlier spate of incidents the court describes? Does an employer's prior reluctance to fire an employee like Jackson undermine its defense to a retaliation claim? In describing Jackson's behavior as "bizarre" or unreasonable, is the court gauging reasonableness through Mahoney's eyes, and if so, should it? Is the court's emphasis of Jackson's composite work history a smokescreen for the close proximity between the EEOC proceedings and the termination?

ROBINSON
v.
SOUTHEASTERN PENNSYLVANIA TRANSPORTATION AUTHORITY, RED ARROW DIVISION
982 F.2d 892 (3d Cir. 1993)

[The Employment Problem]

[The Southeastern Pennsylvania Transportation Authority (SEPTA)] employed David Robinson, a black male, from February 28, 1983 through December 24, 1985. . . . After about seven months of employment, Robinson began experiencing on-the-job problems which he claims were race related. He attempted to halt the discrimination through several mechanisms.

[The Legal Issue]

SEPTA initially asserts that events occurring in early 1984 were too remote from his December 24, 1985 dismissal to be considered a cause of his termination. Al-

though almost two years passed between these events and Robinson's termination from employment, we cannot say the trial judge was clearly erroneous in including these events in his determination that retaliation occurred. The mere passage of time is not legally conclusive proof against retaliation. . . .

[The Decision by the Trial Court]

The trial judge determined that SEPTA ultimately dismissed Robinson in retaliation for these efforts, which the court grouped into three clusters of events. The first series of events relates to Robinson's union grievance and Pennsylvania Human Relations Commission (PHRC) complaint in February 1984. The second involves Robinson's letter to his congressman, Rep. Robert Edgar, in mid-1985. The third concerns Robinson's note of complaint to a supervisor in November 1985, shortly before his termination.

The trial judge determined that Robinson's troubles began with discussions about race between Robinson and Charles Berridge, the general superintendent of the garage, in September 1983 and February 1984. On September 21, Robinson and another black employee complained to Berridge about a racially offensive remark made by a fellow employee. In mid-February, Robinson again complained to Berridge about racial discrimination, this time concerning a shift change that resulted in Robinson being bumped to the night shift by a less senior black employee. The trial judge found that during this discussion Berridge became verbally abusive. Robinson filed a grievance on February 18, 1984 with his union concerning the incident, and two days later filed a complaint with the Pennsylvania Human Relations Commission (PHRC), alleging his [shift change] was retaliation for his September 21, 1983 complaint. On February 24, 1984, Robinson, Berridge and various union officials met to discuss Robinson's complaint. Robinson testified that his concerns about racism at the garage were a subject of discussion.

Following the union grievance, Robinson's relationship with his supervisors deteriorated sharply. The trial judge determined that Robinson's direct supervisors, all of whom reported to Berridge, began a pattern of harassing Robinson by repeatedly disciplining him for minor matters, miscalculating his points for absences from work, and generally trying to provoke Robinson to unsubordination. . . .

[The Decision and Rationale of the U.S. Court of Appeals for the Third Circuit]

The evidence supporting a finding of retaliation for the February, 1984 events is substantial. The issue here, however, is whether there is sufficient evidence to support the trial judge's conclusion that this series of events [is] causally linked to his termination. The temporal proximity noted in other cases . . . is missing here and we might be hard pressed to uphold the trial judge's finding were it not for the intervening pattern of antagonism that SEPTA demonstrated. As the trial judge found, SEPTA subjected Robinson to a "constant barrage of written and verbal warnings, inaccurate point totalings, and disciplinary action, all of which occurred soon after plaintiff's initial complaints and continued until his discharge." The court could reasonably find that the initial series of events thus caused Robinson's and SEPTA's relationship to deteriorate, and set a pattern of behavior that SEPTA followed in retaliating against Robinson's later efforts at opposing Title VII violations he perceived. . . . ("A play cannot be understood on the basis of some of its scenes but only on its entire performance, and similarly, a discrimination analysis must concentrate, not on individual incidents, but on the overall scenario"). Because these events do not stand alone in this case, we cannot say that the trial court's finding of a causal link is clearly erroneous. . . .

Questions

1. Now that you are aware of the Supreme Court's construction of the word "employee" in *Robinson v. Shell Oil Co.*, does that change your opinion about the breadth of protection the *Glover* court afforded?

2. What about other types of misconduct besides coercion of co-workers that have a negative impact on Title VII proceedings? What if an employee had lied to the EEOC during its investigation of his charge of race discrimination, and the employer disciplined him for this? Is the discipline retaliation, or is it justifiable in order to punish a misstatement? *See EEOC v. Snyder Doors*, 844 F. Supp. 1020, 1029 (E.D. Pa. 1994):

   > . . . [T]he premise . . . that [the employer] was retaliating not against the filing of the EEOC complaint, but against the untruths told in carrying it out, carves out a distinction too fine to be meaningfully justiciable. Except in the most blatant instances, it is probably the case that most employers accused of improper treatment of and discrimination against their workers will perceive events differently than the worker. To treat as dispositive the distinction between the employer's view of the procedural act of filing a complaint, and his or her views of the allegations made within it, would elevate form over substance to an unwarranted degree. . . .

   Does the *Snyder Doors* language make sense? Is it desirable for the legal system to subsidize untruths by allowing the case to go forward despite them? Can a lie to a government agency be characterized as "form" rather than "substance" in any just investigation? Is *Jackson v. St. Joseph State Hospital* consistent with *Snyder Doors?* On the other hand, does the Eleventh Circuit go too far in holding that an employer's mere belief, without proof, that an employee lied defeats a retaliation claim? *Cf. EEOC v. Total Sys. Serv.*, 221 F.3d 1171 (11th Cir. 2000), *reh'g en banc denied*, 240 F.3d 899 (11th Cir. 2001).

3. Is there a balance that can be reached between the employee's right to call attention to discriminatory conduct and the employer's need and desire to have the employee at work, productive, and not inciting other employees to dissatisfaction? The Seventh Circuit has suggested such a balancing test. In *Mozee v. Jeffboat, Inc.*, 746 F.2d 365 (7th Cir. 1984), African-American employees missed work to protest what they believed was workplace discrimination. The Seventh Circuit held that once an employee has stated a prima facie case of retaliation, the court must balance the inconvenience to the employer's business caused by the disruption against the goal of eliminating employment discrimination. The Court of Appeals reversed the district court and remanded to the trial court for trial. Is this a workable test, or does it invite excessive subjectivity?

4. Do *Figgous* (cited in the introductory text) and *Robinson* suggest that a court will read evidence of temporal proximity in whatever way it wishes? The approach of each suggests the breadth of authority that exists on the causal nexus. The *Robinson* approach has a sophistication that more bright-line analyses lack, even though it involves more judicial resources. Do cases like *Figgous* encourage the shrewd employer to wait a while before exacting a reprisal against the employee in order to defeat the employee's proof of a temporal connection between his protected activity and the adverse employment action? Is the lesson the employer should take from cases like *Figgous* that revenge is a dish best served cold?

E. Miscellaneous Issues

1. Former Employees

In *Robinson v. Shell Oil Co.*, 519 U.S. 337 (1997), the Supreme Court held that a former employee of a company was protected from retaliation. The plaintiff's former employer, against which the plaintiff had filed an EEOC charge, gave the plaintiff a bad reference, and the plaintiff alleged that the bad reference was retaliatory. Noting that the term "employee" is not restrictively defined in the statute, the Court looked to the policy underlying Title VII for guidance. Allowing former employees to sue would deter discrimination and take away the employer's incentive to simply fire employees who file Title VII claims against it. Any other construction, the Court held, would encourage employers to retaliate against anyone who had charged them with discrimination.

Employers, of course, retain any qualified privileges regarding the giving of candid references that they may have under state law. The employer against whom the former employee once filed any charge or litigation, however, might be well advised to provide only a neutral reference that states the rate of pay, job title, and dates of employment in order to minimize exposure to retaliation and state-law claims.

2. Filing of a Separate Retaliation Charge with Pending EEOC Charge

Most courts hold that, when the plaintiff has already filed an EEOC charge and subsequently encounters employer retaliation, she need not file a separate charge alleging retaliation if the retaliation would likely have been uncovered by the EEOC in the course of investigating the underlying discrimination charge. *See, e.g., Clockledile v. New Hampshire Dep't of Corr.*, 245 F.3d 1 (1st Cir. 2001). However, the more cautious practice would be to amend the initial charge to allege specific acts of retaliation, labeling the retaliation charge with the charge number the EEOC assigned to the underlying discrimination charge and clearly marking the new charge "Amended" in order to avoid questions about what reasonably might have been discovered within the scope of the investigation.

Question

1. Do you think the courts should award damages for a retaliation action even though the employee was not able to prove her claim of discrimination on the basis of sex, race, national origin, or religion? What is the purpose of a separate retaliation claim?

chapter

7

Affirmative Action Plans Under Title VII

Problem 35

The executives of Ace Software Company recognize that their company has a history of excluding persons of Mexican ancestry from employment with the company. In the past, many of the executives were outspoken about those "Mexicans who were invading our country." The company has changed management, and the new executives would like to take affirmative steps to remedy the current makeup of the company by instituting a plan to hire 50 new employees nationwide in the next six months. The goal is to hire as many qualified employees of Mexican ancestry as possible. If the qualifications of two employees are deemed to be equal, the hiring supervisors will be instructed to hire the one who is Mexican. This plan will be in force for only the six-month period.

A. Provisions of Title VII Regarding Affirmative Action Plans

Efforts to remedy past or current discrimination by implementation of voluntary employer affirmative action plans can be problematic because of Title VII's general prohibition against intentional discrimination. The effort to affirmatively redress past discrimination may involve decisions to deliberately distinguish applicants or present employees on the basis of their race, color, religion, sex, or national origin. Section 703(a) seems to directly prohibit this. There are, however, definite references to affirmative action as an acceptable method under some circumstances identified in Title VII. For example, Section 706(g) of the Act provides that a court may order remedies when it finds intentional discriminatory practices have occurred in the past, and these remedies may include any affirmative action necessary:

> If the court finds that the respondent has intentionally engaged in or is intentionally engaging in an unlawful employment practice charged in the complaint, the court may enjoin the respondent from engaging in such unlawful employment practice, and order such affirmative action as may be appropriate. . . .

The affirmative action may include, but is not limited to

> reinstatement or hiring of employees, with or without back pay . . . or any other equitable relief as the court deems appropriate.

Further, in the 1991 Civil Rights Act amendments to Title VII, Section 703(n)(1)(a) added specific recognition that court-ordered remedies could not be challenged by anyone who had notice of the court's proposed judgment and a reasonable opportunity to object in a timely manner.

The Nondiscrimination in Federal Government Employment Act of 1972, which became Section 717 of Title VII, includes directions to the Equal Employment Opportunity Commission (EEOC) to "be responsible for the annual review and approval of a national and regional equal employment opportunity plan which each department and agency and each appropriate unit referred to . . . shall submit in order to maintain an affirmative program of equal employment opportunity for all such employees and applicants for employment." Further, the EEOC is responsible for reviewing and evaluating "the operation of all agency equal employment opportunity programs."

Section 718, which was an amendment made to Title VII in 1972, specifically addresses the requirement that

> [n]o Government contract . . . with any employer, shall be denied, withheld, terminated, or suspended, by any agency or officer of the United States under any equal eployment opportunity law or order, where such employer has an affirmative action plan which has previously been accepted by the Government for the same facility within the past twelve months without first according such employer full hearing and adjudication. . . : Provided, that if such employer has deviated substantially from such previously agreed to affirmative action plan, this section shall not apply. . . .

To clear up disputes by the courts following the 1972 amendments, Congress added the following language to the Civil Rights Act of 1991:

> Sec. 116. Lawful Court-Ordered Remedies, Affirmative Action, and Conciliation Agreements Not Affected
> Nothing in the amendments made by this title shall be construed to affect court-ordered remedies, affirmative action, or conciliation agreements, that are in accordance with the law.

Several sections of Title VII specifically prohibit preferences and attempts to achieve racial balance in the workplace. For example, Section 703(j) states

> Nothing contained in this title shall be interpreted to require any employer, employment agency, labor organization, or joint labor-management committee . . . to grant preferential treatment to any individual or to any group because of the race, color, religion, sex, or national origin of such individual or group on account of an imbalance which may exist with respect to the total number or percentage of persons of any race, color, religion, sex, or national origin employed by any employer . . . or employed in any apprenticeship or other training program, in comparison with the total number or percentage of persons of such race, color, religion, sex, or national origin in any community, State, section, or other area, or in the available work force in any community, State, section, or other area.

The Civil Rights Act of 1991 amended Title VII to add Section 703(*l*) in order to make clear that adjustment of test scores is not a way to achieve equal opportunities. It provides that

[i]t shall be an unlawful employment practice for a respondent, in connection with the selection or referral of applicants or candidates for employment or promotion, to adjust the scores of, use different cutoff scores for, or otherwise alter the results of, employment related tests on the basis of race, color, religion, sex, or national origin.

Section 703(m), also added as a result of the Civil Rights Act of 1991, provides

Except as otherwise provided in this title, an unlawful employment practice is established when the complaining party demonstrates that race, color, religion, sex, or national origin was a motivating factor for any employment practice, even though other factors also motivated the practice.

There is an internal tension between various sections of Title VII that reflects the ambiguous way in which affirmative action is treated as a legitimate method to remediate when there are current or past practices of discrimination. The following case provides some insight into the way in which these tensions play out in the adjudication of tough employment claims.

B. Voluntary Affirmative Action Plans: Discrimination or an Accepted Method of Achieving the Goals of Title VII?

The following case describes the various Supreme Court cases that have considered whether voluntary employer affirmative action plans violate either Title VII of the Civil Rights Act of 1964 or the U.S. Constitution. The courts have approved voluntary affirmative action plans in the employment context when the employer can show (1) that the plan is designed to eliminate work force imbalances in traditionally segregated job categories, (2) the plan does not unnecessarily trammel the rights of other employees, and (3) the plan is temporary. Generally these plans survive judicial scrutiny when they require merely that consideration be given to affirmative action concerns and the factor is only one of several criteria used to make a decision between equally qualified applicants or employees.

TAXMAN
v.
BOARD OF EDUCATION OF THE TOWNSHIP OF PISCATAWAY
91 F.3d 1547 (3d Cir. 1996)

MANSMANN, Circuit Judge.

[The Employment Problem]

[Sharon Taxman, who is white, and Debra Williams, who is Black, were both teachers in the Business Department at Piscataway High School. They had equal seniority in terms of time at the position.] Williams was the only minority teacher among the faculty of the Business Department. In May 1989, the School Board accepted a recommendation from the Superin-

tendent of Schools to reduce the teaching staff in the Business Department by one.

. . . The Superintendent recommended . . . that the affirmative action plan [adopted by the Board of Education in 1975] be invoked in order to determine which teacher to retain. The purpose of the [affirmative action] program is "to provide equal educational opportunity for students and equal employment opportunity for employees and prospective employees" and "to make a concentrated effort to attract . . . minority personnel for all positions so that their qualifications can be evaluated along with other candidates." . . . The operative language is . . . , "In all cases, the most qualified candidate will be recommended for appointment. However, when candidates appear to be of equal qualification, candidates meeting the criteria of the affirmative action program will be recommended." The phrase "candidates meeting the criteria of the affirmative action program," refers to members of racial, national origin, or gender groups identified as minorities for statistical reporting purposes by the New Jersey State Department of Education, including Blacks. [The program specifically included "layoffs."]

[The Superintendent recommended that the affirmative action plan be invoked and that, because the two teachers were tied in seniority and were equally qualified and because Ms. Williams was the only Black teacher in the Business Education Department, she be retained.]

[The Legal Issue]

In this Title VII matter, [the court had to] determine whether the Board of Education of the Township of Piscataway violated that statute when it made race a factor in selecting which of two equally qualified employees to lay off. Specifically, [the court had to] decide whether Title VII permits an employer with a racially balanced work force to grant a non-remedial racial preference in order to promote "racial diversity."

[The Decision and Rationale of the U.S. Court of Appeals for the Third Circuit]

It is clear that the language of Title VII is violated when an employer makes an employment decision based upon an employee's race. The Supreme Court determined in *United Steelworkers v. Weber*, 443 U.S. 193 (1979), however, that Title VII's prohibition against racial discrimination is not violated by affirmative action plans which first, "have purposes that mirror those of the statute" and second, do not "unnecessarily trammel the interests of the [non-minority] employees," *id.* at 208.

We hold that Piscataway's affirmative action policy is unlawful because it fails to satisfy either prong of *Weber*. Given the clear antidiscrimination mandate of Title VII, a non-remedial affirmative action plan, even one with a laudable purpose, cannot pass muster. We will affirm the district court's grant of summary judgment to Sharon Taxman. . . .

The 1975 document states that the purpose of the Program is "to provide equal educational opportunity for students and equal employment opportunity for employees and prospective employees," and "to make a concentrated effort to attract . . . minority personnel for all positions so that their qualifications can be evaluated along with other candidates." The 1983 document states that its purpose is to "ensure[ ] equal employment opportunity . . . and prohibit [ ] discrimination in employment because of [, *inter alia*,] race. . . . "

The Board's affirmative action policy did not have "any remedial purpose"; it was not adopted "with the intention of remedying the results of any prior discrimination or identified underrepresentation of minorities within the Piscataway Public School System." At all relevant times, Black teachers were neither "underrepresented" nor "underutilized" in the Piscataway School District work force.[3] Indeed, statistics in 1976 and 1985 showed that the percentage of Black employees in the job category which included teachers exceeded the percentage of Blacks in the available work force. . . .

. . . In relevant part, Title VII makes it unlawful for an employer "to discriminate against any individual with respect to his compensation, terms, conditions, or privileges of employment" or "to limit, segregate, or classify his employees . . . in any way which would deprive or tend to deprive any individual of employment opportunities or otherwise affect his status as an employee" on the basis of "race, color, religion, sex, or national origin. . . . 42 U.S.C. § 2000e-2(a). For a time, the Supreme Court construed this language as absolutely prohibiting discrimination in employment, neither requiring nor permitting any preference for any group. *Johnson v. Transportation Agency, Santa Clara County*, 480 U.S.616, 643 (1987) (*Stevens*, J. concurring) (citing, *inter alia, Griggs v. Duke Power Co.*, 401 U.S. 424, 431 (1971), and *McDonald v. Santa Fe Trail Transp. Co.*, 427 U.S. 273, 280 (1976)).

In 1979, however, the Court interpreted the statute's "antidiscriminatory strategy" in a "fundamentally different way", *id.* at 644, holding in the seminal case of *United Steelworkers v. Weber*, 443 U.S.

---

[3] In the use of designations such as "Black," "White," and "Minority," we adopt the terms used by both the district court and the parties in their stipulated facts.

193 (1979), that Title VII's prohibition against racial discrimination does not condemn all voluntary race-conscious affirmative action plans. In *Weber,* the Court considered a plan implemented by Kaiser Aluminum & Chemical Corporation. Prior to 1974, Kaiser hired as craftworkers only those with prior craft experience. *Id.* at 198. Because they had long been excluded from craft unions, Blacks were unable to present the credentials required for craft positions. *Id.* Moreover, Kaiser's hiring practices, although not admittedly discriminatory with regard to minorities, were questionable. *Id.* at 210. As a consequence, while the local labor force was about 39% Black, Kaiser's labor force was less than 15% Black and its crafts-work force was less than 2% Black. *Id.* at 198. In 1974, Kaiser entered into a collective bargaining agreement which contained an affirmative action plan. The plan reserved 50% of the openings in an in-plant, craft-training program for Black employees until the percentage of Black craft-workers in the plant reached a level commensurate with the percentage of Blacks in the local labor force. *Id.* at 198. During the first year of the plan's operation, 13 craft-trainees were selected, seven of whom were Black and six of whom were White. *Id.* at 199.

Thereafter, Brian Weber, a White production worker, filed a class action suit, alleging that the plan unlawfully discriminated against White employees under Title VII. Relying upon a literal reading of subsections 703(a) and (d)[7] of the Act, 42 U.S.C. § 2000e-2(a), (d), and upon the Court's decision in *McDonald*

---

[7] Subsection 2000e-2(a) provides:

(a) Employer practices

It shall be an unlawful employment practice for an employer—

(1) to fail or refuse to hire or to discharge any individual, or otherwise to discriminate against any individual with respect to his compensation, terms, conditions, or privileges of employment, because of such individual's race, color, religion, sex, or national origin; or

(2) to limit, segregate, or classify his employees or applicants for employment in any way which would deprive or tend to deprive any individual of employment opportunities or otherwise adversely affect his status as an employee, because of such individual's race, color, religion, sex, or national origin.]

Subsection 2000e-2 (d) of the act provides:

(d) Training program

It shall be an unlawful employment practice for any employer, labor organization, or joint labor-management committee controlling apprenticeship or other training or retraining, including on-the-job training programs to discriminate against any individual because of his race, color, religion, sex, or national origin in admission to, or employment in, any program established to provide apprenticeship or other training. 42 U.S.C. § 2000e-2(d).

v. Santa Fe Trail Transp. Co., 427 U.S. at 273, where the Court held that Title VII forbids discrimination against Whites as well as Blacks, the plaintiffs argued that it necessarily followed that the Kaiser plan, which resulted in junior Black employees receiving craft training in preference to senior White employees, violated Title VII. *Id.* at 199. The district court agreed and entered a judgment in favor of the plaintiffs; the Court of Appeals for the Fifth Circuit affirmed. *Id.* at 200.

The Supreme Court, however, reversed, noting initially that although the plaintiffs' argument was not "without force", it disregarded "the significance of the fact that the Kaiser-USWA plan was an affirmative action plan voluntarily adopted by private parties to eliminate traditional patterns of racial segregation." *Id.* at 201. The Court then embarked upon an exhaustive review of Title VII's legislative history and identified Congress' concerns in enacting Title VII's prohibition against discrimination—the deplorable status of Blacks in the nation's economy, racial injustice, and the need to open employment opportunities for Blacks in traditionally closed occupations. *Id.* at 202–204. Against this background, the Court concluded that Congress could not have intended to prohibit private employers from implementing programs directed toward the very goal of Title VII—the eradication of discrimination and its effects from the workplace:

> It would be ironic indeed if a law triggered by a Nation's concern over centuries of racial injustice and intended to improve the lot of those who had "been excluded from the American dream for so long," 110 Cong. Rec. 6552 (1964) (remarks of Sen. Humphrey), constituted the first legislative prohibition of all voluntary, private, race-conscious efforts to abolish traditional patterns of racial segregation and hierarchy.

Id. at 204. . . .

In 1987, the Supreme Court decided a second Title VII affirmative action case, *Johnson v. Transportation Agency, Santa Clara County,* 480 U.S. at 616. There, the Santa Clara County Transit District Board of Supervisors implemented an affirmative action plan stating that "'mere prohibition of discriminatory practices [was] not enough to remedy the effects of past discriminatory practices and to permit attainment of an equitable representation of minorities, women and handicapped persons.'" *Id.* at 620. The plan noted that women were represented in numbers far less than their proportion of the available work force in the Agency as a whole and in the skilled craft-worker job category relevant to the case, and observed that a lack of motivation in women to seek training or employment where opportunities were limited partially explained the underrepresentation. *Id.* at 621. The plan authorized the Agency to consider as one factor the gender of a qualified candidate in making promotions to positions with a traditionally segregated job classification in which women were significantly underrepresented. *Id.* at 620–621. The plan did not set quotas, but had as its long-term goal the attainment of a work force whose composition reflected the proportion of women in the area labor force. *Id.* at 621–22. Acknowledging the practical difficulties in attaining the long-term goal, including the limited number of qualified women, the plan counseled that short range goals be established and annually adjusted to serve as realistic guides for actual employment decisions. *Id.* at 622. . . .

. . . Declaring its prior analysis in *Weber* controlling, the [Supreme] Court examined whether the employment decision at issue "was made pursuant to a plan prompted by concerns similar to those of the employer in *Weber*" and whether "the effect of the [p]lan on males and nonminorities [was] comparable to the effects of the plan in that case." *Id.* at 631. The first issue the Court addressed, therefore, was whether "consideration of the sex of applicants for Skilled Craft jobs was justified by the existence of a 'manifest imbalance' that reflected underrepresentation of women in 'traditionally segregated job categories.'" *Id.* at 631 (quoting *Weber*, 443 U.S. at 197. Although the Court did not set forth a quantitative measure for determining what degree of disproportionate representation in an employer's work force would be sufficient to justify affirmative action, it made clear that the terms "manifest imbalance" and "traditionally segregated job category" were not tantamount to a *prima facie* case of discrimination against an employer, since the constraints of Title VII and the Federal Constitution on voluntarily adopted affirmative action plans are not identical. *Johnson*, 480 U.S. at 632. In this regard, the Court further reasoned that requiring an employer in a Title VII affirmative action case to show that it had discriminated in the past "would be inconsistent with Weber's focus on statistical imbalance, and could inappropriately create a significant disincentive for employers to adopt an affirmative action plan." *Id.* at 633. . . .

Reviewing Agency statistics which showed that women were concentrated in traditionally female jobs and represented a lower percentage in other jobs than would be expected if traditional segregation had not occurred, the Court concluded that the decision to promote Joyce was made pursuant to a plan designed to eliminate work force imbalances in traditionally segregated job categories and thus satisfied *Weber's* first prong. *Id.* at 634. Moving to *Weber's* second prong, whether the plan unnecessarily trammeled the rights of male employees, the Court concluded that the plan passed muster because it authorized merely that consideration be given to affirmative action concerns when evaluating applicants; gender was a "plus" factor, only one of several criteria that the Agency Director considered in making his decision; no legitimate, firmly rooted expectation on the part of Johnson was denied since the Agency Director could have promoted any of the seven candidates classified as eligible; even though Johnson was refused a promotion, he retained his employment; and the plan was intended to attain a balanced work force, not to maintain one. *Id.* at 638–640. . . .

Having reviewed the analytical framework for assessing the validity of an affirmative action plan as established in *United Steelworkers v. Weber*, 443 U.S. 193 (1979), and refined in *Johnson*, 480 U.S. at 616, we turn to the facts of this case in order to determine whether the racial diversity purpose of the Board's policy mirrors the purposes of the statute. We look for the purposes of Title VII in the plain meaning of the Act's provisions and in its legislative history and historical context. *See Edwards v. Aguillard*, 482 U.S. 578, 594–95 (1987) (in determining a statute's purpose, courts look to the statute's words, legislative history, historical context and the sequence of events leading to its passage). . . .

Thus, based on our analysis of Title VII's two goals, we are convinced that unless an affirmative action plan has a remedial purpose, it cannot be said to mirror the purposes of the statute, and, therefore, cannot satisfy the first prong of the *Weber* test.

We see this case as one involving straightforward statutory interpretation controlled by the text and legislative history of Title VII as interpreted in *Weber* and *Johnson*. The statute on its face provides that race cannot be a factor in employer decisions about hires, promotions, and layoffs, and the legislative history demonstrates that barring considerations of race from the workplace was Congress' primary objective. If exceptions to this bar are to be made, they must be made on the basis of what Congress has said. The affirmative action plans at issue in *Weber* and *Johnson* were sustained only because the Supreme Court, examining those plans in light of congressional intent, found a secondary congressional objective in Title VII that had to be accommodated—i.e., the elimination of the effects of past discrimination in the workplace. Here, there is no congressional recognition of diversity as a Title VII objective requiring accommodation.[9]

Accordingly, it is beyond cavil that the Board, by invoking its affirmative action policy to lay off Sharon Taxman, violated the terms of Title VII. While the Court in *Weber* and *Johnson* permitted some deviation from the antidiscrimination mandate of the statute in order to erase the effects of past discrimination, these rulings do not open the door to additional non-remedial deviations. Here, as in *Weber* and *Johnson*, the Board must justify its deviation from the statutory mandate based on positive legislative history, not on its idea of what is appropriate[10]. . . .

[9]Our dissenting colleagues would have us substitute our judgment for that expressed by Congress and extend the reach of Title VII to encompass "means of combatting the attitudes that can lead to future patterns of discrimination." Such a dramatic rewriting of the goals underlying Title VII does not have support in the Title VII caselaw.

[10]Although no other reported case has addressed the precise question before us, we believe that the decision reached by the Court of Appeals for the Tenth Circuit in *Cunico v. Pueblo School Dist. No. 60,* 917 F.2d 431 (10th Cir. 1990), merits mention. There the plaintiff, a White social worker, who was laid off during a reduction in force, sued her employer, a Colorado school district, under Title VII and the Constitution for discriminating against her on the basis of race by retaining Wayne Hunter, a less senior Black social worker. The district asserted in its defense that even though there was no evidence of past discriminatory conduct on its part to justify remedial race-conscious affirmation action, its decision was lawful because it was made pursuant to an valid affirmative action plan and aimed at retaining the district's only Black administrator. *Id.* at 436, 439. The affirmative action plan at issue had two long-range goals: "to achieve a diverse, multi-racial faculty and staff capable of providing excellence in the education of its students and for the welfare and enrichment of the community" and "to achieve equity for all individuals through equal employment opportunity policies and practices." *Id.* at 437 n.3. . . . Affirming the district court's judgment in the plaintiff's favor, the court of appeals stated that "[t]he purpose of race-conscious affirmative action must be to remedy the effects of past discrimination against a disadvantaged group that itself has been the victim of discrimination." *Id.* at 437 (citing, *inter alia, United Steelworkers v. Weber,* 443 U.S. 193, (1979), and *Wygant v. Jackson Board of Education,* 476 U.S. 267 (1986)) (footnote omitted). Because the record did not contain evidence of past or present discrimination against Blacks by the district or proof of a statistical imbalance in the district's work force, the court held that the district's decision to lay off the plaintiff violated the first prong of either a Title VII or Equal Protection analysis. *Id.* at 438–39 & n. 5. Unfortunately, the court did not set forth its reasons for concluding that affirmative action must be remedial to be lawful.

[T]he Board's sole purpose in applying its affirmative action policy in this case was to obtain an educational benefit which it believed would result from a racially diverse faculty. While the benefits flowing from diversity in the educational context are significant indeed, we are constrained to hold, as did the district court, that inasmuch as "the Board does not even attempt to show that its affirmative action plan was adopted to remedy past discrimination or as the result of a manifest imbalance in the employment of minorities," 832 F. Supp. at 845, the Board has failed to satisfy the first prong of the *Weber* test. *United States v. Board of Educ. of Township of Piscataway,* 832 F. Supp. 836, 848 (D. N.J. 1993).

We turn next to the second prong of the *Weber* analysis. This second prong requires that we determine whether the Board's policy "unnecessarily trammel [s] . . . [nonminority] interests. . . ." *Weber,* 443 U.S. at 208. Under this requirement, too, the Board's policy is deficient.

We begin by noting the policy's utter lack of definition and structure.[15] While it is not for us to decide how much diversity in a high school facility is "enough," the Board cannot abdicate its responsibility to define "racial diversity" and to determine what degree of racial diversity in the Piscataway School is sufficient.

The affirmative action plans that have met with the Supreme Court's approval under Title VII had objectives, as well as benchmarks which served to evaluate progress, guide the employment decisions at issue and assure the grant of only those minority preferences necessary to further the plans' purpose. *Johnson,* 480 U.S. at 621–22, (setting forth long-range and short-term objectives to achieve "'a statistically measurable yearly improvement in hiring, training and promotion of minorities and women . . . in all major job classifications where they are underrepresented'"); *Weber,* 443 U.S. at 193 (reserving for Black employees 50% of the openings in craft-training programs until the percentage of Black craftworkers reflected the percentage of Blacks in the available labor force). By contrast, the Board's policy, devoid of goals and standards, is governed entirely by the Board's whim, leaving the Board free, if it so chooses, to grant

[15]Despite the suggestion in the dissent of Chief Judge SLOVITER to the contrary, we do not intend this statement to suggest that a policy, in order to pass muster, must set a "specific numerical goal." The absence of goals, while it may not have been fatal alone, is a factor contributing to the overall vagueness of the plan.

racial preferences that do not promote even the policy's claimed purpose. Indeed, under the terms of this policy, the Board, in pursuit of a "racially diverse" work force, could use affirmative action to discriminate against those whom Title VII was enacted to protect. Such a policy unnecessarily trammels the interests of nonminority employees.

Moreover, both *Weber* and *Johnson* unequivocally provide that valid affirmative action plans are "temporary" measures that seek to "'attain,'" not "maintain" a "permanent racial . . . balance." *Johnson*, 480 U.S. at 639–40. *See Weber*, 443 U.S. at 208. The Board's policy, adopted in 1975, is an established fixture of unlimited duration, to be resurrected from time to time whenever the Board believes that the ratio between Blacks and Whites in any Piscataway School is skewed. On this basis alone, the policy contravenes *Weber*'s teaching. *See Cunico v. Pueblo School Dist. No. 60*, 917 F.2d 431, 440 (10th Cir. 1990) (holding that the school district's layoff decision aimed at ensuring the employment of the district's only Black administrator was "outright racial balancing" in violation of *Weber*'s second prong).

Finally, we are convinced that the harm imposed upon a nonminority employee by the loss of his or her job is so substantial and the cost so severe that the Board's goal of racial diversity, even if legitimate under Title VII, may not be pursued in this particular fashion. This is especially true where, as here, the nonminority employee is tenured. In *Weber* and *Johnson* when considering whether nonminorities were unduly encumbered by affirmative action, the Court found it significant that they retained their employment. *Weber*, 443 U.S. at 208 (observing that the plan did not require the discharge of nonminority workers); *Johnson*, 480 U.S. at 638 (observing that the nonminority employee who was not promoted nonetheless kept his job). We, therefore, adopt the plurality's pronouncement in *Wygant* that "[w]hile hiring goals impose a diffuse burden, often foreclosing only one of several opportunities, layoffs impose the entire burden of achieving racial equality on particular individuals, often resulting in serious disruption of their lives. That burden is too intrusive." *Wygant*, 476 U.S. at 283. . . .

Accordingly, we conclude that under the second prong of the *Weber* test, the Board's affirmative action policy violates Title VII. In addition to containing an impermissible purpose, the policy "unnecessarily trammel[s] the interests of the [nonminority] employees." *Weber*, 443 U.S. at 208.

SLOVITER, Chief Judge, dissenting, with whom Judges LEWIS and MCKEE join.

In the law, as in other professions, it is often how the question is framed that determines the answer that is received. Although the divisive issue of affirmative action continues on this country's political agenda, I do not see this appeal as raising a broad legal referendum on affirmative action policies. Indeed, it is questionable whether this case is about affirmative action at all, as that term has come to be generally understood— i.e. preference based on race or gender of one deemed "less qualified" over one deemed "more qualified." Nor does this case even require us to examine the parameters of the affirmative action policy originally adopted in 1975 by the Board of Education of the Township of Piscataway (School Board or Board) in response to a state regulation requiring affirmative action programs or the Board's concise, 1983 one-page affirmative action policy.

Instead, the narrow question posed by this appeal can be restated as whether Title VII *requires* a New Jersey school or school board, which is faced with deciding which of two equally qualified teachers should be laid off, to make its decision through a coin toss or lottery, a solution that could be expected of the state's gaming tables, or whether Title VII *permits* the school board to factor into the decision its bona fide belief, based on its experience with secondary schools, that students derive educational benefit by having a Black faculty member in an otherwise all-White department. Because I believe that the area of discretion left to employers in educational institutions by Title VII encompasses the School Board's action in this case, I respectfully dissent. . . .

The majority presents *Weber* and *Johnson* as if their significance lies in the obstacle course they purportedly establish for any employer adopting an affirmative action program. But, as the Justices of the Supreme Court recognized, the significance of each of those cases is that the Supreme Court sustained the affirmative action plans presented, and in doing so deviated from the literal interpretation of Title VII precluding use of race or gender in any employment action. . . .

While the majority in this case views the Supreme Court's articulation of the factors that rationalized its upholding of the affirmative action plans in those cases as establishing boundaries, no language in either *Weber* or *Johnson* so states and, in fact, there is language to the contrary. The majority draws the line at the factors used in those cases. In both *Weber* and *Johnson*, the

Court inquired whether consideration of race in the employment decision was justified by a permissible purpose, and then it examined the effect on nonminorities to ascertain whether the action taken "unnecessarily trammel[ed] the interests of the white employees." *Weber,* 443 U.S. at 208; *Johnson,* 480 U.S. at 630.

However, it does not follow as a matter of logic that because of the two affirmative action plans in *Weber* and *Johnson,* which sought to remedy imbalances caused by past discrimination withstood Title VII scrutiny, every affirmative action plan that pursues some purpose other than correcting a manifest imbalance or remedying past discrimination will run afoul of Title VII. Indeed, the Court in *Weber* explicitly cautioned that its holding in that case should not be read to define the outer boundaries of the area of discretion left to employers by Title VII for the voluntary adoption of affirmative action measures. The Court stated:

> We need not today define in detail the line of demarcation between permissible and impermissible affirmative action plans. It suffices to hold that the challenged Kaiser-USWA affirmative action plan falls on the permissible side of the line. The purposes of the plan mirror those of the statute. Both were designed to break down old patterns of racial segregation and hierarchy. Both were structured to "open employment opportunities for Negroes in occupations which have been traditionally closed to them."

Weber, 443 U.S. at 208. *See also id.* at 215–216 (BLACKMUN, J., concurring) (noting that Kaiser plan "is a moderate one" and that "the Court's opinion does not foreclose other forms of affirmative action"). . . .

It is "ironic indeed" that the promotion of racial diversity in the classroom, which has formed so central a role in this country's struggle to eliminate the causes and consequences of racial discrimination, is today held to be at odds with the very Act that was triggered by our "Nation's concern over centuries of racial injustice." *Weber,* 443 U.S. at 204. Nor does it seem plausible that the drafters of Title VII intended it to be interpreted so as to require a local school district to resort to a lottery to determine which of two qualified teachers to retain, rather than employ the School Board's own educational policy undertaken to insure students an opportunity to learn from a teacher who was a member of the very group whose treatment motivated Congress to enact Title VII in the first place. In my view, the Board's purpose of obtaining the educational benefit to be derived from a racially diverse faculty is entirely consistent with the purposes animating Title VII and the Civil Rights Act of 1964. . . .

I therefore respectfully disagree with the majority, both in its construction of *Weber* and *Johnson* as leaving no doors open for any action that takes race into consideration in an employment situation other than to remedy past discrimination and the consequential racial imbalance in the workforce, and in what appears to be its limited view of the purposes of Title VII. I would hold that a school board's bona fide decision to obtain the educational benefit to be derived from a racially diverse faculty is a permissible basis for its voluntary affirmative action under Title VII scrutiny. . . .

SCIRICA, Circuit Judge, dissenting, with whom Chief Judge SLOVITER joins.

While I find much with which I agree in the majority's opinion, I am constrained to express my disagreement because I believe education presents unique concerns.

In *University of California Regents v. Bakke,* 438 U.S. 265 (1978), Justice Powell recognized that "the 'nation's future depends upon leaders trained through wide exposure' to the ideas and mores of students as diverse as this Nation of many peoples." *Id.* at 313 (citation omitted). As he noted, in the university: "[A] great deal of learning occurs . . . through interactions among students of both sexes, of different races, religions, and backgrounds. . . ." *Id.* at 312–13 n.48 (citation omitted). Eighteen years later, the wisdom of this statement resonates as strongly as ever. When added to a university's high academic standards, this exposure constitutes a formidable educational experience. . . .

Questions

1. What are the key factors the court relies on to decide that this voluntary affirmative action decision violates Title VII? Does the Supreme Court decision in *Weber* require this result? What are the important points of difference between the majority decision and the various dissenting opinions?

2. How would an employer attempt to address societal problems of underrepresentation of various minority populations in the work force if not by voluntary affirmative action plans? What else might an employer do to address this problem in his or her work force?

3. Consider this problem as you read the article below. How is the affirmative action debate in employment influenced by the perspective adopted concerning the goals of Title VII, the role of unconscious or willful blindness in

discriminatory practices, or the debate about remediation or color-blind equality?

Discussion Note

1. Civil rights groups became very concerned about the fate of this case on appeal. Many civil rights activists felt that further erosion of affirmative action would occur if the U.S. Supreme Court granted certiorari on this case. Efforts were made to dissuade the school board from appealing, and assistance was provided to support a settlement instead of an appeal. *See, e.g.*, Lisa Estrada, *Buying the Status Quo on Affirmative Action: The Piscataway Settlement and Its Lessons About Group Path Manipulation*, 9 Geo. Mason U. Cir. Rts. L.J. 207 (Summer, 1999); Katrina Patterson, Note, *What May Have Become a New Title VII Precedent on Affirmative Action in the Workplace*: Piscataway Township Board of Education v. Taxman—*Permissible or Impermissible?"*, 15 N.Y.L. Sch. J. Hum. Rts. 355 (Winter, 1999).

C. Note on Public-Sector Affirmative Action

The previous section addressed affirmative action under Title VII. While this book is primarily focused on employment discrimination statutes such as Title VII, a brief discussion of public-sector affirmative action is useful at this point. That discussion could logically fit here or in Part II of the Additional Materials, which deals with public employees. We have chosen to include it here, however, because it is useful to include public-sector affirmative action near the discussion of private-sector affirmative action.

The issue of public-sector affirmative action is highly complex, and much of the debate is well beyond the scope of this book. Thus, this note is meant to simply highlight the basic framework for public-sector affirmative action. Two cases are central to this framework: *City of Richmond v. J.A. Croson Co.*, 488 U.S. 469 (1989), which addresses state and local government programs, and *Adarand Constructors, Inc. v. Pena*, 515 U.S. 200 (1995), which addresses federal programs. Both are government contracting cases, and thus they do not directly address affirmative action in employment, but the holdings in both cases would seem to apply to all government affirmative action programs, except perhaps in education.

State and local public-sector affirmative action programs are generally challenged under the equal protection clause of the Fourteenth Amendment to the U.S. Constitution, *see, e.g.*, *Croson*, 488 U.S. 469 (City of Richmond program challenged under the Fourteenth Amendment), and federal programs under the implicit equal protection mandate of the Fifth Amendment. *See, e.g.*, *Adarand*, 515 U.S. 200 (federal program challenged under the Fifth Amendment). *Croson* and *Adarand* set forth the current standard, which requires that government affirmative action programs based on race meet strict scrutiny. This means that the government must have a compelling interest in maintaining the program, and the program must be narrowly tailored to meet that compelling government interest. The Court has held, however, that remedying broad societal discrimination is not a compelling interest, and thus to survive a challenge under the equal protection clause, a government affirmative action program based on race must be meant to remedy specific past discrimination by the government entity, or at least specific past discrimination that was furthered by the government entity. *Croson*, 488 U.S. at 496–99, 505–06.

Many people initially thought the reasoning in *Croson* would be limited to state and local governments because Congress has a special power in the civil rights area, *see* U.S. Const. amend. XIV, § 5, but in *Adarand,* the Court extended the reasoning of *Croson* to federal programs. *Adarand,* 515 U.S. 200. Thus, most government-run, race-based affirmative action programs (except perhaps in the education context) are now unconstitutional, whether the program is a federal, state, or local program. Programs that meet the strict scrutiny requirement, however, are constitutional.

In the education context, the U.S. Supreme Court recently decided important cases including a state university and affirmative action. *See Grutter v. Bollinger,* 539 U.S. 306 (2003) (and its sister case, *Gratz v. Bollinger,* 539 U.S. 244 (2003)). Justice O'CONNOR, writing for the majority in *Grutter,* applied strict scrutiny in reviewing the admissions policies of the University of Michigan Law School. The Court determined that the University had a compelling interest in diversity as essential to its educational mission. The admissions policies, which considered race as one of many relevant factors in the admissions procedure, were "narrowly tailored" to that compelling state interest because, unlike a quota, the racial consideration was only one of a number of criteria considered to achieve diversity. In *Gratz v. Bollinger,* however, the Supreme Court determined that the affirmative action plan utilized in undergraduate admissions at the University of Michigan violated the equal protection clause of the fourteenth Amendment to the U.S. Constitution. The Court felt that the plan lacked the individualized consideration of all relevant factors and made the award of points for "race" decisive for "virtually every minimally qualified underrepresented minority applicant."

A strange result of the *Croson/Adarand* line of cases is that gender- and disability-based affirmative action would seem to be subject to a lower level of constitutional scrutiny than race-based affirmative action. A program based on gender would be subject to intermediate scrutiny and a program based on disability would be subject to rational basis scrutiny. Thus, affirmative action programs based on gender would seem to have a better chance of being upheld than those based on race, and disability-based affirmative action programs would have a better chance of surviving constitutional challenge than either gender- or race-based affirmative action. *See* Frank S. Ravitch, *Creating Chaos in the Name of Consistency: Affirmative Action and the Odd Legacy of* Adarand Constructors, Inc. v. Pena, 101 Dick. L. Rev. 281 (1997). This is a result of the "consistency" principle in *Croson/Adarand.* Those cases demand consistency within each tier of equal protection scrutiny. Thus, racial classifications receive strict scrutiny whether they are based on invidious discrimination aimed at African Americans or are used as part of a race-based, affirmative action program, gender classifications are subject to intermediate scrutiny whether they favor men or women, and so forth. *Adarand,* 515 U.S. at 224. Lower courts have grappled with this issue and have found this to be the case. *See, e.g., Contractors Association v. City of Philadelphia,* 6 F.3d 990 (3rd Cir. 1990) (applying strict scrutiny to race-based aspects of city affirmative action program, intermediate scrutiny to gender-based aspects of the program, and rational basis scrutiny to disability-based aspects of the program); *Coral Construction Co. v. King County,* 941 F.2d 910 (9th Cir. 1991) (applying strict scrutiny to race-based aspects of the program and intermediate scrutiny to gender-based aspects of the program).

At this point, a government entity might have a hard time defending against a constitutional challenge to a race-based (and probably a gender-based) affirmative action program. Thus, fewer government employers will be able to maintain race- and gender-based affirmative action programs in the absence of specific proof of past discrimination by the specific government employer involved. In the absence of such proof, it would be virtually impossible for a government-run affirmative action program based on race or gender to survive an equal protection challenge.

Significantly, court-ordered remedial affirmative action also involves state action (i.e., constitutional limitations apply) even when applied to private-sector employees and employers and thus would seemingly have to meet the *Croson/Adarand* standard, but as will be seen, most court-ordered affirmative action is meant to remedy specific past discrimination at a specific entity, and courts frequently try to narrow the scope of such remedies to address the specific problem at a given entity. Thus, court-ordered affirmative action could be more likely to survive a constitutional challenge, although such court orders may be susceptible to challenge on narrow tailoring grounds.

D. The Future of Affirmative Action

Deborah C. Malamud, *Values, Symbols, and Facts in the Affirmative Action Debate*, 95 Mich. L. Rev. 1668 (1997)

(This is an edited version of the article and footnotes are deleted.)

. . . My generation of decisionmakers—professionals who came of age in the 1980s and 1990s—inherited affirmative action as part of the status quo. But affirmative action has lost its just-so quality. The common sense of its continued existence has been pierced by courts. . . , by long-pioneering institutions . . . and by a bellwether electorate. . . . To make matters worse, the controversy has broken the polite silence that had for so long made it possible simultaneously to support affirmative action and deny how white our institutions would look without it. . . .

On what basis are we to decide? On the basis of core values? Of political symbolism? Of an empirical evaluation of the continuing need for, and effectiveness of, affirmative action? Is the answer to these questions different now than it would have been in the 1960s (the legal peak of the civil rights movement) or in the 1970s (when affirmative action first became a central part of government and corporate policy), and, if so, why? Are we in fact free to ask these questions, or does asking them place us outside the boundaries of the civil rights community? . . .

. . . I . . . turn to six key questions I have asked myself about affirmative action. . . . The questions are:

1. What is affirmative action? How much of current antidiscrimination policy should be seen as "affirmative action"?
2. Why was affirmative action adopted in the first place? Should we defer to our original decision to adopt affirmative action on the assumption that it represents a careful analysis of the issues? Is that assumption borne out by the history of affirmative action as a policy?
3. Why do opponents of affirmative action object to it? Is there any validity and/or moral stature to their views?
4. What are the justifications for doing affirmative action? Are they valid, both as to their ends and their means?
5. Does affirmative action succeed in meeting its goals? Can it be eliminated and its legitimate goals met in other, less controversial ways?
6. Ought a person even be asking these questions? Ought we, at this stage, assess affirmative action based on its success or failure as a social policy? Or is the current symbolic significance of affirmative action such that one simply must take a political stand for it or against it based on one's general support for the goals of the civil rights community? . . .

What is Affirmative Action? . . .

. . . Except for some on the fringe, the real battle line in the war for affirmative action is not being drawn at pure colorblindness. . . . It is being drawn at the voluntary and court-ordered use of racial (and kindred) preferences. It is true that the argument can be made that the actual political divide is incoherent, that preferences are not meaningfully different from the accepted uses of race consciousness, and that one must therefore go either to the far right or the far left of the debate. That is, of course, the strategic purpose of drawing the connections among all forms of race consciousness—precisely to make those of us in the middle take sides. But I remain convinced that there is a meaningful difference, for example, between using disparate impact theory to invalidate a test at the behest of members of a minority group who are disadvantaged by it (the usual result of which is that the test remains in use for no one) and, in contrast, continuing to use the test as the sole hiring criterion for whites (thereby proclaiming its validity) but using preferences to select lower minority scorers over higher white scorers. Preferences are, and are perceived as, the use of a different set of selection criteria for whites than for minorities. That, it seems to me, distinguishes them from the mere employer consciousness of race as a prophylactic against discrimination. To say otherwise is to make hard questions far too easy. . . .

Why do Opponents of Affirmative Action Object to It? . . .

[The Problem of Veterans' Preferences]

. . . Veterans' preferences are a . . . complex story. . . . [V]eterans' preferences in employment arose as a compromise measure, to compensate for eliminating schemes of veterans' bonuses and pensions that were widely seen as unduly expensive and corrupt. . . . Veterans' preferences reached a height of public acceptability after World War II. Thanks to the draft, the popularity of the war, and the sheer size of the war effort, eligibility for preferences was spread widely throughout the United States. Not everyone was a veteran or the survivor of a veteran, but everyone knew someone who was. Yet even these factors did not place veterans' preferences beyond question. . . . [T]he courts that were upholding veterans' preferences were able to find the moral space from which to question them as unwise. . . . They did so despite the fact that it was women who were least likely to be veterans and who therefore disproportionately suffered because of veterans' preferences—and women's claim to a place in the workforce was at its weakest in the post-war years. . . .

Whether because of the resonances of Hitler or the resonances of Plessy . . . race stands on a different moral plane than kinship . . . , veterans' status, or most of the other bases on which government decisionmakers reach their pragmatic accommodations. The moral lessons of Nazism and slavery are not beyond contestation. For the Right, the lesson is the moral superiority of colorblindness. For the Left, it is the moral superiority of a commitment to benign and efficacious intervention on behalf of the disadvantaged. But to say that the colorblind po-

sition loses its claim to the moral high ground because the abstract individualism upon which it stands has been breached in the cases of nepotism and veterans' preferences does not take the moral and historical argument for colorblindness sufficiently seriously. . . .

In sum, the colorblind position is built not only on an imperfect abstract individualism. It is also built on the historical lesson that race consciousness is a morally and politically dangerous business. Some supporters of colorblindness are absolutists and believe racial preferences should not be used, whatever the costs. The absolutist position is not, in my view, morally bankrupt—although it approaches moral bankruptcy when its adherents either insist that discrimination no longer exists or when they refuse to commit the economic resources necessary to combat discrimination without using affirmative action as a tool. . . . [M]ost opponents of affirmative action are not absolutists. They believe instead, that the moral costs of the use of racial preferences are sufficiently high that they should only be used for the most important of reasons, and then only if they can be proven to have powerfully positive results.

What Are the Justifications for Doing Affirmative Action?

Beyond the use of affirmative action as a court-ordered remedy for proven instances of judicially cognizable discrimination, affirmative action has two broad rationales: removing barriers to equal economic opportunity and creating diversity. . . .

Supporters of affirmative action must face the fact that affirmative action disproportionately benefits the best-off members of the eligible group and that it is rarely the best-off members of the ineligible group who are hurt by it. . . . [For some, this is] a compelling case for using class rather than race as the criterion for affirmative action eligibility. . . .

[I]t is possible to defend race-based affirmative action as based upon socioeconomic disadvantage, even for the black middle class. . . . Whether we should also explore class-based affirmative action as a supplementary program is a complex matter of moral, political, and practical judgment. There is no doubt that the question would not be on the agenda had it not been presented as an alternative to race-based affirmative action. . . .

As a rationale for affirmative action, diversity—or inclusion . . . —has become a popular alternative to the remediation of socioeconomic disadvantage, for three reasons. The first reason is that the Supreme Court rejects "societal discrimination" as a constitutional rationale for affirmative action but has accepted the rationale of diversity when that issue has come before it. . . . The second reason is that the diversity rationale solves the (perceived) problem of affirmative action for the black middle class. . . . The third reason . . . is that the goals of diversity and inclusion resonate with those of integration . . . and, as embattled in daily practice as it is, integration still carries a legitimacy that the concept of preferences does not. . . .

It is a mistake . . . to rely on the diversity as a completely independent rationale for affirmative action. The question must be, at all times, why it is that institutions are so dependent upon affirmative action for meeting their diversity goals. Affirmative action has far greater moral legitimacy if the reason we use it is that past and present discrimination impede the ability of minorities to compete in a nonpreference marketplace. Only then is the entitlement of affirmative action beneficiaries to be present in the institution rooted at least in part on their own moral worthiness—their demonstrated performance in the face of obstacles—rather than purely on the instrumental need of empowered institutions for the diversification services members of minority groups provide.

Does Affirmative Action Succeed in Meetings Its Goals?

. . . [W]e know very little about whether redistributive and antidiscrimination mechanisms other than affirmative action, had they been vigorously pursued, could have resulted in the same level of progress for minorities that we have achieved through affirmative action. . . . Labor economists have drawn some tentative conclusions from comparing minority hiring inside and outside the federal contracting sector, relying on the fact that the Office of Federal Contract Compliance insisted on affirmative action before it became the vogue in the noncontracting sector. But their data are difficult to interpret, in large part because affirmative action heightened employer recruiting efforts within the federal contracting sector and the competition may have suppressed what would otherwise have been the employment of minorities outside of government contracting, where employer incentives came from the enforcement of antidiscrimination laws rather than from affirmative action. . . . In later years, affirmative action was so prevalent in the business community that comparative data are unavailable.

Our situation, then, is that supporters of affirmative action cannot tell a compelling empirical story about the need for it, either in the early years or in the present. To the extent that the underfunding of the EEOC and kindred agencies is due in part to the political unpopularity that flows from their pursuit of affirmative action, one cannot even take present underfunding as a hard fact independent of context. Nor, of course, can affirmative ac-

tion's opponents give us any assurances that alternative methods of antidiscrimination enforcement would work. How does one make decisions in a condition of empirical stalemate—particularly where, as here, so little weight can be placed on the presumed rationality of the original decisionmaking process?

But perhaps we are not at empirical stalemate. Although we cannot retrace where we would be as a society had we not begun using affirmative action in the 1970s, we can learn what would happen if we stopped race-based affirmative action right now. We are beginning to find out the answer to this question, and it is not pretty. Data are now available that suggest that African-Americans and Latinos remain heavily dependent on affirmative action for admission to law school. This is what the data that emerged from the Hopwood litigation and the aggregate data Linda Wightman has compiled on the use of race-based affirmative action in law school admissions show. Without race-based affirmative action, according to Wightman, law schools would be as white now as they were thirty years ago. [*The Threat to Diversity in Legal Education: An Empirical Analysis of the Consequences of Abandoning Race as a Factor in Law School Admission Decisions*, 72 N.Y.U.L. Rev. 1, 50 (1997).] The University of California's ban on affirmative action has already caused a "dramatic drop in the number of black and Latino students offered admission this fall to the university system's prestigious law schools," despite the use of low socioeconomic status as a plus factor in admissions. [Kenneth R. Weiss, *U.C. Law Schools' New Rules Cost Minorities Spots*, L.A. Times, May 15, 1997, at A1.] In this sense, for these institutions, we do know what affirmative action now does, and what would immediately go undone if we abandoned it. This is exceedingly important information, and similar studies need to be done of other institutions—however disturbing the news. One cannot defend affirmative action in a time of crisis without admitting how much we have relied on it for the integration of our institutions.

We do not know for sure, then, what our society would look like today if vigorous antidiscrimination enforcement rather than affirmative action had been the policy thrust of the past two decades. We do know—or at least we are beginning to know—that for at least some institutions, eliminating affirmative action now would eliminate most of our progress in race relations. That is a frightening prospect—far more akin to shock therapy than to cold turkey.

But it is an equally frightening prospect that so much of the progress we thought we had made depends on the continued use of affirmative action. The fact that affirmative action is being challenged should not merely lead to defenses of affirmative action. The challenge should lead to a realization that the use of affirmative action has been masking a disturbing lack of underlying change in the ability of African Americans to compete in the nonpreference marketplace. If we continue to use affirmative action after the realizations made possible by the current debate, we must also redouble our efforts to get at root causes of race-based economic inequality. Calling them culture, as Kahlenberg does, is not satisfactory. But neither is ignoring them. If that was what affirmative action permitted us to do, it was a mistake.

Ought a Person Even Be Asking These Questions?

Ought we, at this stage, assess affirmative action based on its success or failure as a social policy? Or is the current symbolic significance of affirmative action such that one must simply take a political stand for it or against it based on one's general support for the goals of the civil rights community?

  The arguments for retaining affirmative action because of its symbolic importance are strong. . . . [A]ffirmative action has meant racial progress to two generations of African Americans. That is its symbolic significance. The dramatic act of eliminating it now carries with it an undeniably negative message to and about its potential beneficiaries. Our original decision to adopt affirmative action as the lynchpin of American race policy may have been wrong. It may have been right, but for reasons that were not the basis for the original decision. But too much time has gone by, too many reasonable expectations have been built upon it, to change courses now. For affirmative action has become to the African-American community what abortion rights have become for the feminist community—the constitutive issue, the program because of which we find ourselves a part of the debate rather than the disempowered outsiders.

  . . . For some feminists abortion rights freed women from unwanted childbearing. But for others, by diminishing the risk of unwanted pregnancy, abortion rights took from women their most respected defense to unwanted sex. It is important that abortion rights exist, the argument goes, but it is equally important to understand the harm they cause when they exist within patriarchy. . . . The feminist community is strong enough to harbor this debate. . . . So needs to be the case for affirmative action. It must be made possible, within the civil rights community, to argue that race-based affirmative action cannot be "the remedy," that imposing progress from the top down is not the same as achieving it from the ground up. Why, when blatant discrimination rears its head at Texaco or at Denny's, is the solution more affirmative action? Why is it not something more profound and harder to achieve—like challenging and eradicating the underlying causes of the bigotry itself? A symbolic commitment to the continued use of affirmative action must not blind us to the real opportunity costs of satisfying ourselves with something less than a true solution to the continuing problem of race discrimination in America.

  Where does this leave me? I find it relatively easy to conclude that on both the practical and symbolic level, the significance of a wholesale eradication of race-based affirmative action would be devastating—too devastating to contemplate. But I am concerned that because we must now advocate for affirmative action, we will oversell it to ourselves. . . . My hope is that there is room inside the circle of the civil rights community for the asking of fundamental questions about whether our long-standing dependency on affirmative action has become intrinsically problematic. I deeply believe that even now, in a time of peril, this is not the question of a wicked child—at least not if it is asked passionately and from the inside.

Question

1. The Ace Software executives in Problem 35 (at the beginning of this chapter) were trying to do the right thing by hiring more persons of Mexican ancestry given the company's history of discrimination. Please refer also to articles by Professor Iglesias in chapter 10 and Professors Sturm and Guinier in chapter fifteen for further analysis of this problem.

TWO

Allocating Responsibility for Unintentional Discrimination

chapter

8

Title VII and Disparate Impact

Problem 36

Dante Thomas applied and was appointed to a position as a firefighter with the Zander Town Fire Department. Dirk Jones, his captain, informed him that he would have to shave his beard in order to start working. Captain Jones explained that the beard would interfere with the respirator, otherwise known as a positive pressure self-contained breathing apparatus (SCBA). The SCBA works properly and safely only if the edges are able to seal securely to the wearer's face.

Firefighter Thomas suffers from a condition called pseudofolliculitis barbae (PFB), a skin disorder that causes men's faces to become infected if they shave. It is generally known that African-American men suffer from this condition at a much higher rate than Caucasian men. Firefighter Thomas is African American. He was informed by other firefighters that there used to be a policy that allowed those suffering from this skin condition to wear a "shadow beard" if they kept it short enough to ensure safety. The Fire Department abandoned that policy, even though there were no instances of safety problems while firefighters had short shadow beards. The Captain refused to allow Thomas to wear a shadow beard, and he terminated Thomas.

A. The Road to Disparate Impact

In a unanimous opinion in 1971, the U.S. Supreme Court recognized that the discriminatory effects of a "neutral" employment practice or policy could constitute discrimination in violation of Title VII of the Civil Rights Act of 1964. *Griggs v. Duke Power Co.*, 401 U.S. 424 (1971). The Court relied on language in Title VII that reflected the purpose of the Act to remove barriers to equal employment opportunities. *Id.* at 432. According to the Court, "practices, procedures, or tests neutral on their face, and even neutral in terms of intent, cannot be maintained if they operate to 'freeze' the status quo of prior discriminatory practices." *Id*. at 430–31. The popular name for the claim is a "disparate impact" claim.

The Court interpreted Title VII language to allow claims where the plaintiffs could not prove intentional discrimination if they could show that an employment practice or policy resulted in a disproportionate negative effect on a protected class of employees. In *Griggs*, black employees brought a class action lawsuit against Duke Power Company's Dan River facility, alleging discrimination based on race resulting from the employer's imposition of new educational qualifications, including general intelligence tests and proof of high school graduation as minimal screening devices for new hires and transfers to higher-paid departments. The company had participated in discriminatory hiring practices prior to the enactment of Title VII by assigning black employees to the lowest-paid department without possibility of transfer to higher-paid departments. Although the company no longer continued this practice, it allowed former employees to waive the new testing and educational requirements and retain their previously held positions.

Chief Justice BURGER, writing the opinion for the Court, stated that "[t]he Act proscribes not only overt discrimination but also practices that are fair in form, but discriminatory in operation. The touchstone is business necessity. If an employment practice which operates to exclude Negroes cannot be shown to be related to job performance, the practice is prohibited." *Id*. at 431. Both the high school graduation and the general intelligence test requirements were held to be unrelated to successful job performance as evidenced by the successful job performance of those who were allowed to waive the requirements. *Id*. Only those requirements that are job related could be sufficient to justify the negative effects on a protected class of employees. *Id*.

GRIGGS
v.
DUKE POWER CO.
401 U.S. 424 (1971)

Mr. Chief Justice BURGER delivered the opinion of the Court.

[The Employment Problem]

All the petitioners are employed at the Company's Dan River Steam Station, a power generating facility located at Draper, North Carolina. At the time this action was instituted, the Company had 95 employees at the Dan River Station, 14 of whom were Negroes; 13 of these are petitioners here.

The District Court found that prior to July 2, 1965, the effective date of the Civil Rights Act of 1964, the Company openly discriminated on the basis of race in the hiring and assigning of employees at its Dan River plant. The plant was organized into five operating de-partments: (1) Labor, (2) Coal Handling, (3) Operations, (4) Maintenance, and (5) Laboratory and Test. Negroes were employed only in the Labor Department where the highest paying jobs paid less than the lowest paying jobs in the other four "operating" departments in which only whites were employed. [2] . . . Promotions were normally made within each department on the

---

[2] A Negro was first assigned to a job in an operating department in August 1966, five months after charges had been filed with the Equal Employment Opportunity Commission. The employee, a high school graduate who had begun in the Labor Department in 1953, was promoted to a job in the Coal Handling Department.

basis of job seniority. Transferees into a department usually began in the lowest position.

In 1955, the Company instituted a policy of requiring a high school education for initial assignment to any department except Labor, and for transfer from the Coal Handling to any "inside" department (Operations, Maintenance, or Laboratory). When the Company abandoned its policy of restricting Negroes to the Labor Department in 1965, completion of high school also was made a prerequisite to transfer from Labor to any other department. From the time the high school requirement was instituted to the time of trial, however, white employees hired before the time of the high school education requirement continued to perform satisfactorily and achieve promotions in the "operating" departments. Findings on this score are not challenged.

The Company added a further requirement for new employees on July 2, 1965, the date on which Title VII became effective. To qualify for placement in any but the Labor Department, it became necessary to register satisfactory scores on two professionally prepared aptitude tests, as well as to have a high school education. Completion of high school alone continued to render employees eligible for transfer to the four desirable departments from which Negroes had been excluded if the incumbent had been employed prior to the time of the new requirement. In September 1965, the Company began to permit incumbent employees who lacked a high school education to qualify for transfer from Labor or Coal Handling to an "inside" job by passing two tests—the Wonderlic Personnel Test, which purports to measure general intelligence, and the Bennett Mechanical Comprehension Test. Neither was directed or intended to measure the ability to learn to perform a particular job or category of jobs. The requisite scores used for both initial hiring and transfer approximated the national median for high school graduates.[3]

[The Decisions by the Trial Court and the U.S. Court of Appeals for the Fourth Circuit]

The District Court had found that while the Company previously followed a policy of overt racial discrimination in a period prior to the Act, such conduct had

ceased. The District Court also concluded that Title VII was intended to be prospective only and, consequently, the impact of prior inequities was beyond the reach of corrective action authorized by the Act.

The Court of Appeals was confronted with a question of first impression, as are we, concerning the meaning of Title VII. After careful analysis, a majority of that court concluded that a subjective test of the employer's intent should govern, particularly in a close case, and that in this case there was no showing of a discriminatory purpose in the adoption of the diploma and test requirements. On this basis, the Court of Appeals concluded there was no violation of the Act.

The Court of Appeals reversed the District Court in part, rejecting the holding that residual discrimination arising from prior employment practices was insulated from remedial action.[4] The Court of Appeals noted, however, that the District Court was correct in its conclusion that there was no showing of a racial purpose or invidious intent in the adoption of the high school diploma requirement or general intelligence test and that these standards had been applied fairly to whites and Negroes alike. It held that, in the absence of a discriminatory purpose, use of such requirements was permitted by the Act. In so doing, the Court of Appeals rejected the claim that because these two requirements operated to render ineligible a markedly disproportionate number of Negroes, they were unlawful under Title VII unless shown to be job related.[5]

[The Legal Issue]

[The Supreme Court] granted the writ in this case to resolve the question whether an employer is prohibited by the Civil Rights Act of 1964, Title VII, from re-

---

[3]The test standards are thus more stringent than the high school requirement, since they would screen out approximately half of all high school graduates.

[4]The Court of Appeals ruled that Negroes employed in the Labor Department at a time when there was no high school or test requirement for entrance into the higher paying departments could not now be made subject to those requirements, since whites hired contemporaneously into those departments were never subject to them. The Court of Appeals also required that the seniority rights of those Negroes be measured on a plantwide, rather than a departmental, basis. However, the Court of Appeals denied relief to the Negro employees without a high school education or its equivalent who were hired into the Labor Department after institution of the educational requirement.

[5]One member of that court disagreed with this aspect of the decision, maintaining, as do the petitioners in this Court, that Title VII prohibits the use of employment criteria that operate in a racially exclusionary fashion and do not measure skills or abilities necessary to performance of the jobs for which those criteria are used.

quiring a high school education or passing of a standardized general intelligence test as a condition of employment in or transfer to jobs when (a) neither standard is shown to be significantly related to successful job performance, (b) both requirements operate to disqualify Negroes at a substantially higher rate than white applicants, and (c) the jobs in question formerly had been filled only by white employees as part of a longstanding practice of giving preference to whites.[1]

[The Decision and Rationale of the U.S. Supreme Court]

. . . The objective of Congress in the enactment of Title VII is plain from the language of the statute. It was to achieve equality of employment opportunities and remove barriers that have operated in the past to favor an identifiable group of white employees over other employees. Under the Act, practices, procedures, or tests neutral on their face, and even neutral in terms of intent, cannot be maintained if they operate to "freeze" the status quo of prior discriminatory employment practices.

The Court of Appeals' opinion, and the partial dissent, agreed that, on the record in the present case, "whites register far better on the Company's alternative requirements" than Negroes.[6] 420 F.2d 1225, 1239

---

[1]The Act Provides:

Sec. 703. (a) It shall be an unlawful employment practice for an employer— . . .

(2) to limit, segregate, or classify his employees in any way which would deprive or tend to deprive any individual of employment opportunities or otherwise adversely affect his status as an employee, because of such individual's race, color, religion, sex, or national origin. . . .

(h) Notwithstanding any other provision of this title, it shall not be an unlawful employment practice for an employer . . . to give and to act upon the results of any professionally developed ability test provided that such test, its administration or action upon the results is not designed, intended or used to discriminate because of race, color, religion, sex or national origin. . . . "78 Stat. 255, 42 U.S.C. § 2000e-2.

[6]In North Carolina, 1960 census statistics show that while 34% of white males had completed high school, only 12% of Negro males had done so. U.S. Bureau of the Census, U.S. Census of Population: 1960, Vol. 1, Characteristics of the Population, pt. 35, Table 47.

Similarly, with respect to standardized tests, the EEOC in one case found that use of a battery of tests, including the Wonderlic and Bennett tests used by the Company in the instant case, resulted in 58% of whites passing the tests, as compared with only 6% of the blacks. Decision of EEOC, CCH Empl. Prac. Guide, 17,304.53 (Dec. 2, 1966). See also Decision of EEOC 70-552, CCH Empl. Prac. Guide, 6139 (Feb. 19, 1970).

n.6. This consequence would appear to be directly traceable to race. Basic intelligence must have the means of articulation to manifest itself fairly in a testing process. Because they are Negroes, petitioners have long received inferior education in segregated schools, and this Court expressly recognized these differences in *Gaston County v. United States*, 395 U.S. 285 (1969). There, because of the inferior education received by Negroes in North Carolina, this Court barred the institution of a literacy test for voter registration on the ground that the test would abridge the right to vote indirectly on account of race. Congress did not intend by Title VII, however, to guarantee a job to every person regardless of qualifications. In short, the Act does not command that any person be hired simply because he was formerly the subject of discrimination, or because he is a member of a minority group. Discriminatory preference for any group, minority or majority, is precisely and only what Congress has proscribed. What is required by Congress is the removal of artificial, arbitrary, and unnecessary barriers to employment when the barriers operate invidiously to discriminate on the basis of racial or other impermissible classification.

Congress has now provided that tests or criteria for employment or promotion may not provide equality of opportunity merely in the sense of the fabled offer of milk to the stork and the fox. On the contrary, Congress has now required that the posture and condition of the job-seeker be taken into account. It has—to resort again to the fable—provided that the vessel in which the milk is proffered be one all seekers can use. The Act proscribes not only overt discrimination but also practices that are fair in form, but discriminatory in operation. The touchstone is business necessity. If an employment practice which operates to exclude Negroes cannot be shown to be related to job performance, the practice is prohibited.

On the record before us, neither the high school completion requirement nor the general intelligence test is shown to bear a demonstrable relationship to successful performance of the jobs for which it was used. Both were adopted, as the Court of Appeals noted, without meaningful study of their relationship to job-performance ability. Rather, a vice president of the Company testified, the requirements were instituted on the Company's judgment that they generally would improve the overall quality of the work force.

The evidence, however, shows that employees who have not completed high school or taken the tests have continued to perform satisfactorily and make progress in departments for which the high school and test criteria are now used.[7] The promotion record of present employees who would not be able to meet the new criteria thus suggests the possibility that the requirements may not be needed even for the limited purpose of preserving the avowed policy of advancement within the Company. In the context of this case, it is unnecessary to reach the question whether testing requirements that take into account capability for the next succeeding position or related future promotion might be utilized upon a showing that such long-range requirements fulfill a genuine business need. In the present case the Company has made no such showing. . . .

The facts of this case demonstrate the inadequacy of broad and general testing devices as well as the infirmity of using diplomas or degrees as fixed measures of capability. History is filled with examples of men and women who rendered highly effective per-

---

[7]For example, between July 2, 1965, and November 14, 1966, the percentage of white employees who were promoted but who were not high school graduates was nearly identical to the percentage of nongraduates in the entire white work force.

formance without the conventional badges of accomplishment in terms of certificates, diplomas, or degrees. Diplomas and tests are useful servants, but Congress has mandated the commonsense proposition that they are not to become masters of reality.

[Discussion is omitted on the application of Section 703(h), which permits job-related professionally developed testing, and on the legislative history regarding permissible testing.]

Nothing in the Act precludes the use of testing or measuring procedures; obviously they are useful. What Congress has forbidden is giving these devices and mechanisms controlling force unless they are demonstrably a reasonable measure of job performance. Congress has not commanded that the less qualified be preferred over the better qualified simply because of minority origins. . . . What Congress has commanded is that any tests used must measure the person for the job and not the person in the abstract.

The judgment of the Court of Appeals is, as to that portion of the judgment appealed from, reversed.

Mr. Justice BRENNAN took no part in the consideration or decision of this case.

Problem 37

Elvin Arroya, a Hispanic employee of the U.S. Postal Service, applied several times to be the Manager of Customer Services at one of the branches in Hartford, Connecticut. Each time he failed to receive a promotion, the successful candidate was not Hispanic. Mr. Arroya wants to file a federal lawsuit claiming discrimination based on his race, in violation of Title VII. He has proof that of the more than 1,000 Grade 15 and above positions that existed during the time he filed his applications for promotion, only eight were occupied by Hispanics, despite a large pool of professionally qualified individuals. He also has proof that "from a national perspective, roughly only 4.5% of the management employees within the Postal Service who are at grade levels from Grade 15 and above are Hispanic." Mr. Arroya has a report from the firm of Bobo, Jaynes & McKinney that analyzed data regarding the ethnic composition of Connecticut's Postal Service for the period from 2000 to 2002. In four out of five years, the difference between the actual number of Hispanics in the various groups and the expected number of Hispanics in the upper groups was statistically significant. Although Mr. Arroya cannot prove any intentional discrimination by the U.S. Postal Service, do you think he should be able to prove discrimination based on the statistical information provided?

Questions

1. How would you advise Firefighter Thomas or Mr. Arroya with respect to a disparate impact claim? In Problem 36, what is the employer's concern, and how should that affect the outcome of this case? In Problem 37, is there enough information here to show a disproportionate impact on Hispanics?

   Problem 36 is based on *Fitzpatrick v. City of Atlanta*, 2 F.3d 1112 (11th Cir. 1993); Problem 37 is based on *Malave v. Potter*, 320 F.3d 321 (2d Cir. 2003). In *Malave*, the court of appeals held that the trial court made an error of law when it determined that a lack of statistical data on an applicant pool always makes it impossible to establish a prima facie case of disparate impact. Where statistics are not available on Hispanics, other statistics may be used to support the finding. The court made suggestions of other ways that the trial court could consider relevant information.

2. Mr. Arroya does not have proof of intentional discrimination by his employer, but he does have examples where the decisions were made on the basis of subjective impressions of the candidates. Why would subjective decisions be included in a claim based on disparate impact analysis?

3. What is the Title VII source for the disparate impact claim that is found by the Supreme Court in the *Griggs* case?

B. *Wards Cove* and the Reaction of Congress

After almost two decades of controversy over the validity of this "disparate impact" basis for a Title VII claim, a more hostile Supreme Court revisited the issue. In *Wards Cove Packing Co. v. Atonio*, 490 U.S. 642 (1989), the Court expressed strong concern about the validity of this form of Title VII discrimination claim. In a five-to-four decision, the Court severely limited plaintiffs' ability to prove such a claim by requiring clear proof as to the contribution of each employment policy or practice to the discriminatory result as well as limiting the nature of the comparisons that might be made to show disparate impact at all.

Congress reacted to the decision in *Wards Cove* by adding language to the Civil Rights Act of 1991 amending Title VII of the Civil Rights Act of 1964 to specifically include "disparate impact" claims of employment discrimination. Congress passed specific language in the amendment allowing plaintiffs to merge different employment practices rather than requiring an impossible separation of cause and effect for each practice. Further, Congress reaffirmed the requirement that the employer demonstrate that the employment practice is "job related and consistent with business necessity" in order to withstand the employee showing of a disparate impact from that practice.

WARDS COVE PACKING CO.
v.
ATONIO
490 U.S. 642 (1989)

Justice WHITE delivered the opinion of the Court.

[The Employment Problem]

The claims before us are disparate-impact claims, involving the employment practices of petitioners, two companies that operate salmon canneries in remote and widely separated areas of Alaska. The canneries operate only during the salmon runs in the summer months. They are inoperative and vacant for the rest of the year. In May or June of each year, a few weeks before the salmon runs begin, workers arrive and prepare the equipment and facilities for the canning operation. Most of these workers possess a variety of skills. . . .

Jobs at the canneries are of two general types: "cannery jobs" on the cannery line, which are unskilled positions; and "noncannery jobs," which fall into a variety of classifications. Most noncannery jobs are classified as skilled positions.[3] Cannery jobs are filled predominantly by nonwhites: Filipinos and Alaska Natives. The Filipinos are hired through, and dispatched by, Local 37 of the International Longshoremen's and Warehousemen's Union pursuant to a hiring hall agreement with the local. The Alaska Natives primarily reside in villages near the remote cannery locations. Noncannery jobs are filled with predominantly white workers, who are hired during the winter months from the companies' offices in Washington and Oregon. Virtually all of the noncannery jobs pay more than cannery positions. The predominantly white noncannery workers and the predominantly nonwhite cannery employees live in separate dormitories and eat in separate mess halls.

[Decisions by the Trial Court and the U.S. Court of Appeals for the Ninth Circuit]

In 1974, respondents, a class of nonwhite cannery workers who were (or had been) employed at the canneries, brought this Title VII action against petitioners. Respondents alleged that a variety of petitioners' hiring/promotion practices—e.g., nepotism, a rehire preference, a lack of objective hiring criteria, separate hiring channels, a practice of not promoting from within—were responsible for the racial stratification of the work force and had denied them and other nonwhites employment as noncannery workers on the basis of race. Respondents also complained of petitioners' racially segregated housing and dining facilities. All of respondents' claims were advanced under both the disparate-treatment and disparate-impact theories of Title VII liability. . . .

In holding that respondents had made out a prima facie case of disparate impact, the Court of Appeals relied solely on respondents' statistics showing a high percentage of nonwhite workers in the cannery jobs and a low percentage of such workers in the noncannery positions.[5]

[The Legal Issue]

Petitioners sought review of the Court of Appeals' decision in this Court, challenging it on several grounds. Because some of the issues raised by the decision below were matters on which this Court was evenly divided in *Watson v. Fort Worth Bank & Trust*, . . . we granted certiorari, 487 U.S. 1232 (1988), for the purpose of addressing these disputed questions of the proper application of Title VII's disparate-impact theory of liability.

---

[3]The noncannery jobs were described as follows by the Court of Appeals: "Machinists and engineers are hired to maintain the smooth and continuous operation of the canning equipment. Quality control personnel conduct the FDA-required inspections and recordkeeping. Tenders are staffed with a crew necessary to operate the vessel. A variety of support personnel are employed to operate the entire cannery community, including, for example, cooks, carpenters, store-keepers, bookkeepers, beach gangs for dock yard labor and construction, etc." 768 F.2d, at 1123.

[5]The parties dispute the extent to which there is a discrepancy between the percentage of nonwhites employed as cannery workers and those employed in noncannery positions. Compare, e.g., Brief for Petitioners 4–9 with Brief for Respondents 4–6. The District Court made no precise numerical findings in this regard but simply noted that there were "significant disparities between the at-issue jobs [i.e., noncannery jobs] and the total workforce at the canneries" which were explained by the fact that "nearly all employed in the 'cannery worker' department are non-white." *See* 34 EPD § 34,437, pp. 33,841, 33,829 (W.D. Wash.1983). . . .

[The Decision and Rationale of the U.S. Supreme Court]

[Establishing a Prima Facie Case for Disparate Impact]

. . . Although statistical proof can alone make out a prima facie case, *see Teamsters v. United States*, 431 U.S. 324, 339 (1977); *Hazelwood School Dist. v. United States*, 433 U.S. 299, 307–308 (1977), the Court of Appeals' ruling here misapprehends our precedents and the purposes of Title VII, and we therefore reverse. . . .

It is clear to us that the Court of Appeals' acceptance of the comparison between the racial composition of the cannery work force and that of the noncannery work force, as probative of a prima facie case of disparate impact in the selection of the latter group of workers, was flawed for several reasons. Most obviously, with respect to the skilled noncannery jobs at issue here, the cannery work force in no way reflected "the pool of *qualified* job applicants" or the "*qualified* population in the labor force." Measuring alleged discrimination in the selection of accountants, managers, boat captains, electricians, doctors, and engineers . . . by comparing the number of nonwhites occupying these jobs to the number of nonwhites filling cannery worker positions is nonsensical. If the absence of minorities holding such skilled positions is due to a dearth of qualified nonwhite applicants (for reasons that are not petitioners' fault),[7] petitioners' selection methods or employment practices cannot be said to have had a "disparate impact" on nonwhites. . . .

The Court of Appeals also erred with respect to the unskilled noncannery positions. Racial imbalance in one segment of an employer's work force does not, without more, establish a prima facie case of disparate impact with respect to the selection of workers for the employer's other positions, even where workers for the different positions may have somewhat fungible skills (as is arguably the case for cannery and unskilled noncannery workers). As long as there are no barriers or practices deterring qualified nonwhites from applying for noncannery positions, *see* n.6, *supra*, if the percentage of selected applicants who are nonwhite is not significantly less than the percentage of qualified applicants who are nonwhite, the employer's selection mechanism probably does not operate with a disparate impact on minorities.[8] Where

this is the case, the percentage of nonwhite workers found in other positions in the employer's labor force is irrelevant to the question of a prima facie statistical case of disparate impact. As noted above, a contrary ruling on this point would almost inexorably lead to the use of numerical quotas in the workplace, a result that Congress and this Court have rejected repeatedly in the past.

Moreover, isolating the cannery workers as the potential "labor force" for unskilled noncannery positions is at once both too broad and too narrow in its focus. It is too broad because the vast majority of these cannery workers did not seek jobs in unskilled noncannery positions; there is no showing that many of them would have done so even if none of the arguably "deterring" practices existed. Thus, the pool of cannery workers cannot be used as a surrogate for the class of qualified job applicants because it contains many persons who have not (and would not) be noncannery job applicants. Conversely, if respondents propose to use the cannery workers for comparison purposes because they represent the "qualified labor population" generally, the group is too narrow because there are obviously many qualified persons in the labor market for noncannery jobs who are not cannery workers. . . .

First is the question of causation in a disparate-impact case. . . .

Our disparate-impact cases have always focused on the impact of *particular* hiring practices on employment opportunities for minorities. Just as an employer cannot escape liability under Title VII by demonstrating that, "at the bottom line," his work force is racially balanced (where particular hiring practices may operate to deprive minorities of employment opportunities), *see Connecticut v. Teal*, 457 U.S., at 450, a Title VII plaintiff does not make out a case of disparate impact simply by showing that, "at the bottom line," there is racial *imbalance* in the work force. As a general matter, a plaintiff must demonstrate that it is the application

[7]Obviously, the analysis would be different if it were found that the dearth of qualified nonwhite applicants was due to practices on petitioners' part which—expressly or implicitly—deterred minority group members from applying for noncannery positions. *See*, e.g., *Teamsters v. United States, supra*, 431 U.S., at 365.

[8]We qualify this conclusion—observing that it is only "probable" that there has been no disparate impact on minorities in such circumstances—because bottom-line racial balance is not a defense under Title VII. See *Connecticut v. Teal*, 457 U.S. 440 (1982). Thus, even if petitioners could show that the percentage of selected applicants who are nonwhite is not significantly less than the percentage of qualified applicants who are nonwhite, respondents would still have a case under Title VII, if they could prove that some particular hiring practice has a disparate impact on minorities, notwithstanding the bottom-line racial balance in petitioners' workforce. See *Teal, supra*, at 450.

of a specific or particular employment practice that has created the disparate impact under attack. Such a showing is an integral part of the plaintiff's prima facie case in a disparate-impact suit under Title VII.

Here, respondents have alleged that several "objective" employment practices (e.g., nepotism, separate hiring channels, rehire preferences), as well as the use of "subjective decision making" to select noncannery workers, have had a disparate impact on nonwhites. Respondents base this claim on statistics that allegedly show a disproportionately low percentage of nonwhites in the at-issue positions. . . .

Consequently, on remand, the courts below are instructed to require, as part of respondents' prima facie case, a demonstration that specific elements of the petitioners' hiring process have a significantly disparate impact on nonwhites.

[Employer's Need to Demonstrate Business Necessity if a Prima Facie Case of Disparate Impact Is Established]

If, on remand, respondents meet the proof burdens outlined above, and establish a prima facie case of disparate impact with respect to any of petitioners' employment practices, the case will shift to any business justification petitioners offer for their use of these practices. This phase of the disparate-impact case contains two components: first, a consideration of the justifications an employer offers for his use of these practices; and second, the availability of alternative practices to achieve the same business ends, with less racial impact. See, *e.g., Albemarle Paper Co. v. Moody*, 422 U.S., at 425. We consider these two components in turn.

Though we have phrased the query differently in different cases, it is generally well established that at the justification stage of such a disparate-impact case, the dispositive issue is whether a challenged practice serves, in a significant way, the legitimate employment goals of the employer. See, *e.g., Watson v. Fort Worth Bank & Trust*, 487 U.S. at 997–999; *New York City Transit Authority v. Beazer*, 440 U.S., at 587, n.31; *Griggs v. Duke Power Co.*, 401 U.S., at 432. The touchstone of this inquiry is a reasoned review of the employer's justification for his use of the challenged practice. A mere insubstantial justification in this regard will not suffice, because such a low standard of review would permit discrimination to be practiced through the use

of spurious, seemingly neutral employment practices. At the same time, though, there is no requirement that the challenged practice be "essential" or "indispensable" to the employer's business for it to pass muster: this degree of scrutiny would be almost impossible for most employers to meet and would result in a host of evils we have identified above. See *supra*, at 2122.

In this phase, the employer carries the burden of producing evidence of a business justification for his employment practice. The burden of persuasion, however, remains with the disparate-impact plaintiff. . . . The persuasion burden here must remain with the plaintiff, for it is he who must prove that it was "because of such individual's race, color," etc., that he was denied a desired employment opportunity. See 42 U.S.C. § 2000e-2(a).

Finally, if on remand the case reaches this point, and respondents cannot persuade the trier of fact on the question of petitioners' business necessity defense, respondents may still be able to prevail. To do so, respondents will have to persuade the factfinder that "other tests or selection devices, without a similarly undesirable racial effect, would also serve the employer's legitimate [hiring] interest[s]"; by so demonstrating, respondents would prove that "[petitioners were] using [their] tests merely as a 'pretext' for discrimination." *Albermarle Paper Co., supra*, 422 U.S. at 425; see also *Watson*, 487 U.S., at 998 (O'CONNOR, J.); *id.*, at 1005–1006 (BLACKMUN, J., concurring in part and concurring in judgment). If respondents, having established a prima facie case, come forward with alternatives to petitioners' hiring practices that reduce the racially disparate impact of practices currently being used, and petitioners refuse to adopt these alternatives, such a refusal would belie a claim by petitioners that their incumbent practices are being employed for nondiscriminatory reasons.

Of course, any alternative practices which respondents offer up in this respect must be equally effective as petitioners' chosen hiring procedures in achieving petitioners' legitimate employment goals. Moreover, "[f]actors such as the cost or other burdens of proposed alternative selection devices are relevant in determining whether they would be equally as effective as the challenged practice in serving the employer's legitimate business goals." *Watson, supra*, at 998 (O'CONNOR, J.). "Courts are generally less competent than employers to restructure business practices," *Furnco Construction Corp. v. Waters*, 438 U.S.

567, 578 (1978); consequently, the judiciary should proceed with care before mandating that an employer must adopt a plaintiff's alternative selection or hiring practice in response to a Title VII suit.

For the reasons given above, the judgment of the Court of Appeals is reversed, and the case is remanded for further proceedings consistent with this opinion.

It is so ordered.

Justice STEVENS, with whom Justice BRENNAN, Justice MARSHALL, and Justice BLACKMUN join, dissenting. [other dissenting opinions are omitted.]

Fully 18 years ago, this Court unanimously held that Title VII of the Civil Rights Act of 1964 . . . prohibits employment practices that have discriminatory effects as well as those that are intended to discriminate. *Griggs v. Duke Power Co.*, 401 U.S. 424 (1971). Federal courts and agencies consistently have enforced that interpretation, thus promoting our national goal of eliminating barriers that define economic opportunity not by aptitude and ability but by race, color, national origin, and other traits that are easily identified but utterly irrelevant to one's qualification for a particular job. . . . Regrettably, the Court retreats from these efforts in its review of an interlocutory judgment respecting the "peculiar facts" of this lawsuit. . . . Turning a blind eye to the meaning and purpose of Title VII, the majority's opinion perfunctorily rejects a longstanding rule of law and underestimates the probative value of evidence of a racially stratified work force.[4] I cannot join this latest sojourn into judicial activism. . . .

[4]. . . Some characteristics of the Alaska salmon industry described in this litigation—in particular, the segregation of housing and dining facilities and the stratification of jobs along racial and ethnic lines—bear an unsettling resemblance to aspects of a plantation economy. *See generally* Plantation, Town, and County, Essays on the Local History of American Slave Society 163–334 (E. Miller & E. Genovese eds. 1974). Indeed the maintenance of inferior, segregated facilities for housing and feeding nonwhite employees, *see* 34 EPD ¶ 34,437, pp. 33,836, 33,843–33,844, strikes me as a form of discrimination that, although it does not necessarily fit neatly into a disparate-impact or disparate-treatment mold, nonetheless violates Title VII. *See generally* Brief for National Association for the Advancement of Colored People as Amicus Curiae. Respondents, however, do not press this theory before us.

[I]ntent plays no role in the disparate-impact inquiry. The question, rather, is whether an employment practice has a significant, adverse effect on an identifiable class of workers—regardless of the cause or motive for the practice. The employer may attempt to contradict the factual basis for this effect; that is, to prevent the employee from establishing a prima facie case. But when an employer is faced with sufficient proof of disparate impact, its only recourse is to justify the practice by explaining why it is necessary to the operation of business. Such a justification is a classic example of an affirmative defense. . . .

The majority's opinion begins with recognition of the settled rule that "a facially neutral employment practice may be deemed violative of Title VII without evidence of the employer's subjective intent to discriminate that is required in a 'disparate-treatment' case." *Ante*, at 2119. It then departs from the body of law engendered by this disparate-impact theory, reformulating the order of proof and the weight of the parties' burdens. Why the Court undertakes these unwise changes in elementary and eminently fair rules is a mystery to me.

I respectfully dissent.

Discussion Notes

1. In response to the Supreme Court's opinion in *Ward's Cove*, Congress included the following language as part of the Civil Rights Act of 1991:
   (1)(A) An unlawful employment practice based on disparate impact is established under this title only if—
   (i) a complaining party demonstrates that a respondent uses a particular employment practice that causes a disparate impact on the basis of race, color, religion, sex, or national origin and the respondent fails to demonstrate that the challenged practice is job related for the position in question and consistent with business necessity; or
   (ii) the complaining party makes the demonstration described in subparagraph (C) with respect to an alternative employment practice and the respondent refuses to adopt such alternative employment practice.
   (B) (i) With respect to demonstrating that a particular employment practice

causes a disparate impact as described in subparagraph (A)(i), the complaining party shall demonstrate that each particular challenged employment practice causes a disparate impact, except that if the complaining party can demonstrate to the court that the elements of a respondent's decision making process are not capable of separation for analysis, the decision making process may be analyzed as one employment practice.

(ii) If the respondent demonstrates that a specific employment practice does not cause the disparate impact, the respondent shall not be required to demonstrate that such practice is required by business necessity.

(C) The demonstration referred to by subparagraph (A)(ii) shall be in accordance with law as it existed on June 4, 1989, with respect to the concept of "alternative employment practice."

(2) A demonstration that an employment practice is required by business necessity may not be used as a defense against a claim of intentional discrimination under this title.... Section 703(k), 42 U.S.C. § 2000e-2(k).

2. *Albemarle Paper Co. v. Moody*, 422 U.S. 405 (1975), further clarified the steps necessary to prove a disparate impact claim. The plaintiff had to demonstrate the existence of a statistically significant impact on a protected class (by identification of the particular practices, the disparate impact, and a connection between the two). The defendant then had to demonstrate a business necessity for the practice, and the plaintiff had a final opportunity to prove that the business interests could be met by alternative practices that would not result in the disparate impact on the class. *Id.*

3. The Supreme Court directly addressed whether discrimination claims based on subjective decision making could be considered under disparate impact analysis. In *Watson v. Fort Worth Bank & Trust*, 487 U.S. 977 (1988), the Court allowed such claims when there were no structured guidelines for employment decisions.

4. "Bottom line" defenses were also rejected by the Supreme Court in *Connecticut v. Teal*, 457 U.S. 440 (1982). The Court refused to allow the employer to introduce its final statistics on employee hires to defend against claims of disparate impact where the employer used a test to disqualify a statistically significant number of minority employees. *Id.*

5. Section 703(h) of Title VII of the Civil Rights Act of 1964 specifically allows an employer to use "professionally developed tests" that are based on business necessity. The section also refers to "bona fide seniority systems," which are exempt from claims of discrimination unless they are discriminatory facially or as applied or were adopted for a discriminatory reason even if there is a disparate impact. *Id.*

6. Often the claims for intentional discrimination and disparate impact are brought in the same lawsuit. For example, when the women employees of DaimlerChrysler Corporation recently complained that their health insurance policy violated Title VII, their suit contained both a disparate treatment claim and a disparate impact claim. The policy excluded coverage for prescription contraceptives. They made their claim on behalf of all female employees of DaimlerChrysler who used prescription contraceptives and were denied coverage. They asserted that it was intentional discrimination because Title VII as amended by the Pregnancy Discrimination Act of 1978 prohibits intentionally treating pregnancy-related medical conditions differently from any other conditions covered by an employer. They also asserted that the plan had an adverse disparate impact on women. The federal court in Missouri rejected motions by the employer to dismiss both claims. The court found that the women had made a prima facie case of both intentional discrimination and disparate impact. The case can be found at *Cooley v. DaimlerChrysler Corp.*, 281 F. Supp. 2d 979 (E.D. Mo. 2003).

Questions

1. After *Wards Cove*, how would the Supreme Court have approached the problems presented by the women employees of DaimlerChrysler?

2. What changes does the 1991 Civil Rights Act accomplish with respect to the way that this claim against DaimlerChrysler would be treated? Why?

C. Developments Since the Civil Rights Act of 1991: The Demise of Disparate Impact?

Disparate Impact claims remain difficult to prove. In the years since Congress amended Title VII to specifically address disparate impact, the focus has shifted to age- and disability-related claims, which are covered by different statutes. Chapters 13 & 14 will address the recent Supreme Court decision on disability and disparate impact. Chapter 12 will address the question of whether an age discrimination claim can be proven without intentional discrimination on the part of the employer. Disparate impact claims have not fared well under the Age Discrimination in Employment Act as interpreted by the courts.

Disparate impact claims have also been used to challenge English-only requirements in the workplace. These claims treat the English-only policy as a "neutral" policy because of the difficulty of proving intentional discrimination under a disparate treatment theory. The Equal Employment Opportunity Commission (EEOC) has issued guidelines that make recommendations about how to address this problem. The issue will be discussed further in Chapter 10.

The debate about disparate impact has been intense. The potential of disparate impact to challenge the institutional structures of the workplace has not been ignored by advocates and proponents of the concept. Disciplines such as economics and psychology have contributed widely varying insights that illuminate the ramifications of expanding or contracting the scope of antidiscrimination laws to reach neutral, unconscious, or cognitively formed stereotypes about people and institutions.

John J. Donohue III, *Employment Discrimination Law in Perspective:
Three Concepts of Equality*, 92 Mich. L. Rev. 2583 (1994)

(This is an edited version of the article and footnotes are deleted.)

Over the past fifty years, the body of law prohibiting discrimination in employment has grown enormously in terms of the extent of geographic coverage, the range of covered employers, the array of protected workers, and the spectrum of prohibited practices. . . .

Prior to 1971, employment discrimination laws had banned only intentional discrimination. But in the first Supreme Court case interpreting Title VII, *Griggs v. Duke Power Co* . . . Chief Justice Burger, writing for a unanimous Court, extended the reach of the law through the novel formulation of the disparate impact doctrine— which prohibited the application of neutral employment practices that generated adverse effects upon the protected classes specified in Title VII, absent a showing that the practices were justified by business necessity. Since then, subsequent decisions and legislative enactments have banned an array of diverse practices—ranging from actuarially based pension plans . . . and exclusions of childbirth expenses from employer health insurance

plans . . . to sexual harassment . . . —that were not at first seen as discriminatory. In addition, the passage of the Age Discrimination in Employment Act . . . , the Americans with Disabilities Act . . . , and a large array of state and local employment discrimination laws that are more expansive than Title VII has greatly broadened the number of workers falling into some protected category.

One might suppose that the burgeoning corpus of employment discrimination law reflects a consensus that this form of regulation has been working well and should be expanded. But the contentious and protracted struggle among the Supreme Court, Congress, and the Bush administration that culminated in the passage of the Civil Rights Act of 1991 . . . , as well as the growing academic debate over the appropriate scope of employment discrimination law, belie this view. There are deep disagreements about whether the country would be best served by a reduction or an intensification of the legal attack on employment discrimination. This essay attempts to provide a conceptual framework with which one can assess both the enormous transformations of employment discrimination law and the continuing disagreements over its proper scope. The thrust of the argument is that the initial creation and subsequent growth of employment discrimination law has been generated by the development over time of a richer conception of the demands of equality, while the antagonism between the contending parties is at least in part explained by differences concerning which version of equality best describes the modern labor market. . . .

Over time, three different conceptions of equality have influenced the development of employment discrimination law. Before World War II, the nation's willingness to accept the outcomes generated by competitive labor markets was premised on an implicit conception of equality—namely, that a worker's wage should equal the market-determined value of the individual's labor. I refer to this concept of equality as "contingent equality" because a worker's value often depended on the degree of discrimination against a particular group of workers—and therefore was contingent on attitudes about the worker and not just on his work. . . . [T]here is a distinction between the equality one can expect from a competitive labor market and the greater degree of equality that is generated by a more perfectly competitive market such as an efficient capital market. Capital markets ensure that the price of assets will equal their value even in the presence of severe bias or discriminatory attitudes on the part of investors. The capital market equates price not with mere contingent value but with intrinsic value and in this sense guarantees "intrinsic equality." The initial goal of employment discrimination law was to provide intrinsic equality, which the free labor market could not deliver, to the enumerated protected classes. But while a consensus has emerged that intrinsic equality is a desirable goal for protected workers, there is significant disagreement regarding both the extent to which intrinsic equality has already been achieved and the degree to which the goal itself is adequate. A richer notion of equality, which I refer to as "constructed equality," has motivated much of the growth of employment discrimination law in an effort to go beyond the protections that even a perfectly competitive market would afford.

. . . [T]he early civil rights movement sought to achieve the equivalent of intrinsic equality for black workers; the goal was to have black workers receive what would be the true value of their labor in a nondiscriminatory environment. Some of the principled opponents of antidiscrimination law in the early 1960s based their opposition on the view that intrinsic equality already existed. Many of the principled opponents of today believe that intrinsic equality has now been achieved and thereby deny the continued need for legal intervention in labor markets to protect female and minority workers. Yet, while the labor market has tendencies pushing in the direction of intrinsic equality, there is likely to be a significant difference between contingent equality—which is all that workers can hope for without government intervention—and intrinsic equality. . . .

. . . [A]lthough women, the elderly, and the disabled at first embraced the quest for intrinsic equality, the closer they have come to achieving it the more they have sought to reject it as the goal of employment discrimination law. Law increasingly seeks and requires a higher degree of equality—"constructed equality." Rather than compelling employers to pay protected workers the true value of their productivity by equating wages and intrinsic value, the demand is to have employers make workers equal. Although the market was often an ally—albeit at times an inconsistent one—of the quest for intrinsic equality for protected workers, the market cannot achieve constructed equality. In fact, the market relentlessly opposes it. . . .

Because southern blacks in the early 1960s earned dramatically less than the benchmark group of otherwise identical southern white workers . . . , one can conclude that southern blacks were earning less than their "true value." But because wages are simply the price paid to labor, and because one of the hallmarks—indeed the very defining characteristic—of a competitive market is that price equals value, we are confronted with something of an anomaly. . . . Either the southern labor market was not competitive, in which case it is not particularly surprising that the price paid to black labor did not equal its value, . . . or, more plausibly, it was broadly competitive but the "value" of black workers did not equal the "value" of the otherwise identical white workers.

In order to address this apparent anomaly, it may be helpful to elaborate on the concept of a perfectly competitive market. As I noted above, a perfectly competitive market is one in which the value of an asset equals its price. Perhaps the best illustration of such a market is the market for financial securities. Here the hallmarks of perfect competition are most in evidence: all the shares of a given company's stock are perfectly fungible, and millions of investors and money managers spend much time and effort trying to ascertain the true value of these shares. Moreover, when investors perceive any divergence between value and price, they can buy or sell the under- or overvalued security very quickly in a trading market that has very low transaction costs. . . .

These features of modern capital markets imply that there will be a strong tendency for price and value to be equal. If the price of a capital asset, such as a financial security, is below its true value, a host of offers to purchase will tend to elevate the price to the point at which the price-value discrepancy is eliminated. Conversely, if the price of an asset lingers above the true value, the downward pressures on price operate quickly as owners of the asset try to sell it. Even nonowners can facilitate the rapid price drop toward the true value through the use of short sales. With so much at stake in discerning whether price equates with value, with only a few thousand stocks that need to be valued, with tens of thousands of analysts spending all their time trying to ascertain this value, and with the fantastic volume of stock trading that provides at very low cost virtually constant updates on the latest assessment of value by knowledgeable market participants, the stock market is unparalleled in the degree to which it approximates the perfectly competitive market. . . .

One point in particular should be underscored. The existence of irrational biases or prejudices on the part of investors does not prevent capital markets from ensuring that price equals value. . . .

. . . [B]ecause there are enough investors who care only about maximizing profits and who can quickly and cheaply purchase any undervalued securities, prejudice against a security owner or a company simply cannot cause the price of a security to diverge from its value. These biases do not pose a concern to issuers of stock or to those who own stock, because millions of investors are trying to ascertain the value of a security, and others who do not carry biases against the particular stock will be happy to step in to fill the void if the stock can be purchased at a price below its value.

But confidence that the market will assure the equality of value and price does not extend to all markets. Indeed, the very existence of employment discrimination law would seem to reflect the enormous concern over precisely this question in labor markets. Consequently, one of the major goals of the civil rights movement and the women's movement was to achieve a federal guarantee that the wages of workers in certain protected classes equaled the value of what those workers would produce in a perfectly competitive—and nondiscriminatory—market.

Note that the appended qualification that the market be nondiscriminatory was deemed superfluous in the case of capital markets. Price equaled value in that context even if many investors were highly prejudiced. But this statement cannot always be made in less efficient markets. . . . [F]or a very extended period of time, blacks and women felt that they could not rely on the protections of the market to ensure that they would be hired and paid their true value. This fundamental fact explains much of the focus of the civil rights movement on securing the passage of legislation prohibiting discrimination in employment: the goal was to assure that the price that protected workers received for their labor was equal to the value of their labor in the American economy, so long as value was determined only with respect to intrinsic productivity and was not distorted by discriminatory preferences of employers, fellow workers, or customers.

When employers, fellow workers, or customers shun certain protected workers for certain jobs, they impose social costs even apart from the depressing of wages of the dispreferred group. Such slights can in themselves cause psychological pain; indeed, the very reason members of one group might discriminate is to secure some gain in self-esteem at the expense of the other group. . . . But for now, I want to leave this issue aside and focus only on the question of the equality of price and value, or the lack thereof. Why do labor markets fall so short of what capital markets seem to deliver?

There are two reasons. First, labor markets are far less efficient markets than capital markets, and as one departs from the features of a perfectly competitive market, the forces that equate price and value weaken. Persistent and substantial divergences between price and value can exist in imperfect markets. Second, at best, labor markets can only be expected to equate price with the value of labor as determined not simply by the intrinsic value of the assets as in capital markets but also by the contingent assessment that will be influenced by an array of discriminatory participants. Put differently, labor markets can only hope to achieve contingent equality, while capital markets can deliver the higher ideal of intrinsic equality. . . .

The many differences between the two markets reveal that the success of capital markets in equating price and value is an ideal that labor markets might approach but never reach. In capital markets, the high profits that are attainable through identifying divergences between price and value ensure that correct pricing of individual securities will be the norm. In labor markets, by contrast, the relatively small value and high cost of determining worker productivity ensures that employers will frequently find it profitable not to determine the correct prices for individual workers. Instead, employers often use cheap proxies such as race and sex to approximate true worker value. In other words, statistical discrimination cannot exist in capital markets, but it can thrive in labor markets.

Unlike capital assets, labor assets—that is, workers—are not mere passive investments; therefore, statistical discrimination will likely distort workers' decisions with regard to investment in human capital. If a member of a group knows that he will be treated as though he possesses the average traits of all group members, he will have no incentive to make investments that would increase his productivity. Thus, there may be an efficiency rationale for prohibiting statistical discrimination against protected workers in labor markets. . . , which Title VII clearly does. . . .

. . . [M]odern capital markets ensure that the price of an actively traded security will equal its value. Most importantly, this statement is true regardless of whether or not many investors are biased against holding the particular security. The security will trade at the same price as if no investors were biased against it. Although there are tendencies, perhaps even strong ones, pushing the price of labor toward the value of labor, in every dimension capital markets will necessarily do a better job of equating price and value than labor markets will. . . .

. . . [I]f one considers the criticisms of employment discrimination laws by their primary principled opponents, it becomes clear that those opponents think of the labor market as being as perfectly competitive as modern capital markets. . . .

. . . [D]escriptions of how employers will quickly take advantage of discrepancies between the value of workers and their price focus only on the intrinsic productivity of the workers and ignore the contingent value. In other words, this analysis much more aptly describes how an investor would quickly buy up any undervalued stock than how an employer would contemplate hiring when productivity is not clearly known and certain workers are dispreferred. . . . [I]ntense discrimination may prevent the employment of any worker from the less desirable pool, regardless of intrinsic productivity. For example, it was not that long ago that only whites could play major league baseball. Certainly, there was a highly talented pool of labor that the market had contrived to ignore, and no governmental restriction prevented black players from being hired. Moreover, this problem is exacerbated when productivity is not easily measured and the dispreferred group has some apparent shortcomings, such as lower-quality education. . . .

The recent story of discrimination at the Shoney's restaurant chain is instructive. The cofounder and longtime chief executive officer of Shoney's, Ray Danner, was clearly a highly prejudiced individual. . . . Several high-ranking Shoney's executives testified to the effect that "Danner would say that no one would want to eat at a restaurant where 'a bunch of niggers' were working. . . . " At one point, Danner wrote a letter complaining about the performance of one restaurant in Jacksonville, Florida, and noting that it had more blacks—some of whom were subsequently fired—than other fast-food restaurants that Danner had visited in the area. . . . Indeed, judging from Shoney's success with 1800 stores in thirty-six states . . . , Danner's business instincts about what southern white customers would want from a low-budget restaurant may, regrettably, not have been without substance. Unrestrained profit-maximizing firms would in fact avoid hiring blacks in positions where they could be seen by diners if that were the preference of their customers. Indeed, the fact that Denny's and Wendy's restaurants have been charged with similar discriminatory conduct may reveal that the tendencies toward efficiency in the labor market are not always the ally of black workers.

Moreover, Danner in all likelihood did not apply racist business theories with the laserlike precision of a profit-maximizer—that is, he did not shun blacks for visible positions to please the customers but at the same time

welcome them in jobs where the customers would not see them. Only one out of sixty-eight division directors and none of the higher-level corporate managers at Shoney's were black. . . . It would seem that the hiring policies at Shoney's reflected deference not only to the discriminatory attitudes of its customers but also to those of its CEO and largest stockholder. But the market penalties for this behavior did not seem to be strong, and it was only a huge settlement in excess of $100 million in damages coupled with a substantial stock-price drop when Danner showed signs of resisting the remedial measures designed to increase the number of black managerial employees that led to Danner's departure from Shoney's. . . .

A number of lessons emerge from the Shoney's case. No one contended that the black workers that Danner did not want customers to see were less able. They were considered to be less valuable because certain customers appeared to dislike seeing them. Thus, the value that was being equated to price was not the intrinsic value of these workers but their contingent value in light of racist customer preferences. It would not be surprising to learn that this apparently widespread racist attitude would depress the demand for black labor. As a result, black wages would be lower than the wages of otherwise identical white workers. This underscores the difference between labor markets—in which prices are determined by supply and demand, with discriminatory attitudes of employers, fellow employees, and customers influencing the demand—and capital markets—in which an arbitrage model of pricing is appropriate and price will be determined only by the intrinsic value of the asset. . . . While the demand for stocks is perfectly elastic, no study of labor demand has ever found it to be highly elastic, let alone horizontal. . . .

Moreover, the market penalty for the full array of Shoney's discriminatory practices, some of which enhanced and some of which diminished profits, was not particularly powerful. Indeed, only the intervention of antidiscrimination law established the costliness of the racist policy, at which point the market did encourage the departure of a severely discriminatory owner. Although Danner's racist policy of not hiring visible black employees might have been profit-maximizing to the extent it accorded with customer preference, his general antipathy to hiring any black supervisory workers even in nonvisible positions would not be consistent with profit maximization. Thus, although the market penalty for such non-profit-maximizing discrimination did not seem to be capable of driving Danner from the market, the introduction of a sizable legal penalty enabled the market to achieve the desired social outcome. It is precisely this mechanism that might render Title VII efficient, as I have suggested elsewhere. . . . But the important point here is that the value of black workers to Shoney's was not simply based on their intrinsic productivity but rather depended on the discriminatory tastes of customers and the employer. This is the distinction between what the labor market achieves in terms of equating price and contingent value and what would be achieved if the labor market functioned in the same fashion as the capital market.

. . . Those who find intrinsic equality to be insufficient believe that a higher level of what I call "constructed equality" should be the aim of the law. Interestingly, while the first success in the law of employment discrimination was the acknowledgement, if not the attainment, of the right to intrinsic equality, over time this demand for equality has come to be overshadowed in much the same way that the early demands of blacks for the equal protection of the laws subsequently came to be seen as wholly inadequate. . . .

. . . [T]he civil rights movement sought to achieve what the market had yet to offer to black Americans— wages equal to the true value of their labor in a nondiscriminatory environment. This aspect of the civil rights movement was virtually a complete success, at least at the doctrinal and aspirational levels. At one point, the idea that the government could coerce private employers to hire individuals that they did not wish to have as employees had little widespread support; today there is a staunch consensus that such coercion is appropriate to guarantee to protected workers what they would secure in a nondiscriminatory free market. . . . As the goal of eradicating the appalling mistreatment of black Americans provided the battering ram against the doctrine of freedom of contract in employment, other disadvantaged groups—initially women and then the elderly and the disabled—attached themselves to this quest for legal equality in the workplace. Once this initial version of equality became widely accepted, the demands for a more aggressive employment discrimination policy began to grow.

In the same way that the doctrine of "separate but equal" came to be seen as the embodiment of inequality— even though for decades it was the basis of a legal strategy to advance the status of blacks—the initial phase of employment discrimination law that tried to confer what a perfectly competitive market would provide has come to be seen by many as a stunted form of equality that represents an impediment to needed change. These claims to go beyond the protections of an idealized market are seen in the argument that the special burdens of childbirth and childrearing require preferential treatment of female employees. . . . Women are not to be given only what a pure profit-maximizing, nonmisogynistic employer would offer them; instead they should receive what the modern conception of gender equality demands.

The Age Discrimination in Employment Act . . . emerged in 1967 from the combined support of those who sought to guarantee the intrinsic notion of equality—that is, what a non-ageist, idealized free market would yield to workers who were over the age of forty—and those who thought older workers needed to be protected from the market. . . . The latter group was uncomfortable with the relentless logic of disregarding the surface attributes of race, color, religion, sex, or age and focusing exclusively on those traits purely related to productivity. In their opinion, the single-minded focus on worker productivity, which is the very essence of the intrinsic notion of equality, could itself be the enemy of female and older workers.

The requirement that employers shift their focus away from what an idealized market would offer to what fairness requires was taken a step further with the passage of the Americans with Disabilities Act (ADA). . . . Like the Age Discrimination in Employment Act before it, the ADA incorporates a component of the market protection conception of antidiscrimination in that it prohibits employers from irrationally discriminating on the basis of a disability. A disabled worker who can perform the essential functions of a job may not be rejected because of an employer's irrational aversion to the worker's disability. This conforms precisely to the intrinsic notion of equality—workers should receive what they would get in a nondiscriminatory free market. But, at the same time, the ADA is not content with this notion of equality. The Act goes much further by requiring employers to make reasonable accommodations that would enable disabled workers to perform adequately on the job. . . . Clearly, given a choice between two equally productive workers, one requiring the expenditure of significant sums in order to accommodate him and one requiring no such expenditures, the profit-maximizing firm would prefer the worker who is less costly to hire. Thus, the transformation that has occurred in the realm of civil rights is that the ideal nondiscriminatory market solution, which previously was both the benchmark of intrinsic equality and what the law demanded, is now regarded as the obstacle to social justice. . . .

The framework of contingent, intrinsic, and constructed equality offers insights into some of the major issues of employment discrimination law. For example, some have argued that the Supreme Court's creation of the disparate impact doctrine represented a departure from the congressional intent to prohibit only intentional discrimination. . . . The claim is that the disparate impact standard represents an unwarranted shift in Title VII's purpose from guaranteeing equality of opportunity to ensuring equality of result. But the move to a disparate impact standard, which was ultimately endorsed by Congress in the Civil Rights Act of 1991, is consistent with the goal of trying to guarantee intrinsic equality. Neutral rules that adversely affect protected workers without being tightly tied to their productivity are obstacles to the attainment of intrinsic equality, because the use of such neutral rules reflects the existence of statistical discrimination. As we saw above, intrinsic equality, which is defined by what would exist in a market that was as perfectly competitive as the capital market, cannot coincide with statistical discrimination. . . .

In addition, the tripartite equality framework can also be used to focus discussion concerning the likely success of various legal interventions. Intrinsic equality will necessarily be easier to generate than constructed equality because the pressures of the market at least push in the direction of intrinsic equality, but they steadfastly resist the attainment of constructed equality. This is not to say that the attainment of intrinsic equality is relentlessly encouraged by the market. For example, pure market forces do not encourage the hiring of groups that are disfavored by the employer, fellow employees, or customers, nor do they dictate the disregard of low-cost statistical proxies that generate a reasonably productive work force. Still, if workers could be properly sorted throughout the economy, a market equilibrium could exist in which every worker was being paid precisely his or her intrinsic value. . . . This could not happen with respect to constructed equality, because any employer who was paying a worker more than the worker's intrinsic value would find it advantageous to replace the worker. . . . This implies that intrinsic equality is at least in theory a goal that is attainable for all workers. Conversely, ambitious efforts to extend the enlarged demands of constructed equality to a growing array of protected workers moves society away from a conceptually attainable goal to an amorphous objective, which can only be defined through wrangling among conflicting interests in the political process. This fact in no way undermines the desirability of certain objectives, but it does suggest that political power may play a greater role than principled discourse in determining the future contours of constructed equality.

Conclusion

. . . Primarily through litigative efforts on behalf of female and elderly employees, the courts began to broaden the notion of equality beyond what a perfect market could give to what a perfect market would negate. Advocates of affirmative action began not only to seek the idealized market solution but to push for broader social justice. In this vision of constructed equality, the dictates of law are defined no longer through some abstract market paradigm but rather through considering what steps would be necessary to define a fair society. Releasing the law and its goals from the theoretical confines of a market paradigm has the advantage of freeing it to promote a more refined notion of justice, especially in light of the nonmarket roles of women as childbearers and caretakers, than would otherwise have been possible. On the other hand, freed from the theoretical mooring that the market paradigm provided, the malleable claims for constructed equality began to proliferate in ways that have weakened the moral force of antidiscrimination law. Employment discrimination law began to provide avenues for windfall gains rather than opportunities for promoting corrective justice, and the moral imperative that impelled the civil rights movement has been blunted to the extent that employment discrimination protections have been extended by special interest legislation to groups, such as smokers, with little to commend their legislative demands other than the political power of tobacco companies.

The ADA has imposed perhaps the greatest demands of constructed equality by explicitly requiring that employers take reasonable measures to make the disabled equal. Rather than the early Title VII insistence that employers disregard the traits of protected workers, the ADA requires employers to identify the traits of the disabled that undermine their productivity and to seek whenever possible to overcome these traits. The ADA has paved the way for the possibility that economically disadvantaged minorities such as blacks, whose position as the central focus of employment discrimination law has gradually diminished, will employ the ADA's rationale to argue that the effects of the factors that have undermined their productivity—including very poor schooling and broken families—are now to be corrected by employers. Although the conceptual groundwork for this step has been laid, the fracturing of the consensus forged by the civil rights movement may render this next step unattainable in the current political environment.

D. The Relationship Between Neutral Policies and Unconscious Discrimination

The Civil Rights Act of 1991 ensured that disparate impact would remain a viable approach under Title VII. In addition to the debate about the viability of disparate impact analysis, there has been much consideration about the meaning of disparate treatment discrimination and whether unconscious gender stereotyping can be considered disparate treatment under Title VII.

All of these questions force one to consider the issue of responsibility for discrimination. Is one relieved of discrimination claims if one acted in a way that created discriminatory results as long as the person didn't understand the nature of the discrimination? What then of the way that affects the victim of that discrimination? If we recognize that the harm has occurred, does it make a difference in the degree of discrimination, or is it discrimination at all? In criminal law, a similar problem is resolved by distinguishing between the more serious crimes and lesser crimes when the level of "mens rea," or conscious intent to do the act, varies. The punishment is less for the lack of a motive or intent to cause the harm, but society recognizes that reckless or negligent behavior can also cause serious harm. Society imposes some measure of responsibility on the one who caused the harm.

Consider the questions raised by Professor Charles Lawrence regarding the role of unconscious discrimination. In what ways does his analysis question underlying assumptions about your understanding of the nature of discrimination?

Charles R. Lawrence III, *The Id, the Ego, and Equal Protection*: *Reckoning with Unconscious Racism*, 39 Stan. L. Rev. 317 (1987)

(This is an edited version of this article and footnotes have been deleted.)

Prologue

It is 1948. I am sitting in a kindergarten classroom at the Dalton School, a fashionable and progressive New York City private school. My parents, both products of a segregated Mississippi school system, have come to New York to attend graduate and professional school. They have enrolled me and my sisters here at Dalton to avoid sending us to the public school in our neighborhood where the vast majority of the students are black and poor. They want us to escape the ravages of segregation, New York style.

It is circle time in the five-year old group, and the teacher is reading us a book. As she reads, she passes the book around the circle so that each of us can see the illustrations. The book's title is *Little Black Sambo.* Looking back, I remember only one part of the story, one illustration: Little Black Sambo is running around a stack of pancakes with a tiger chasing him. He is very black and has a minstrel's white mouth. His hair is tied up in many pigtails, each pigtail tied with a different color ribbon. I have seen the picture before the book reaches my place in the circle. I have heard the teacher read the 'comical' text describing Sambo's plight and have heard the laughter of my classmates. There is a knot in the pit of my stomach. I feel panic and shame. I do not have the words to articulate my feelings—words like 'stereotype' and 'stigma' that might help cathart the shame and place it outside of me where it began. But I am slowly realizing that, as the only black child in the circle, I have some kinship with the tragic and ugly hero of this story—that my classmates are laughing at me as well as at him. I

wish I could laugh along with my friends. I wish I could disappear.

I am in a vacant lot next to my house with black friends from the neighborhood. We are listening to *Amos and Andy* on a small radio and laughing uproariously. My father comes out and turns off the radio. He reminds me that he disapproves of this show that pokes fun at Negroes. I feel bad—less from my father's reprimand than from a sense that I have betrayed him and myself, that I have joined my classmates in laughing at us.

I am certain that my kindergarten teacher was not intentionally racist in choosing *Little Black Sambo.* I knew even then, from a child's intuitive sense, that she was a good, well-meaning person. A less benign combination of racial mockery and profit motivated the white men who produced the radio show and played the roles of Amos and Andy. But we who had joined their conspiracy by our laughter had not intended to demean our race.

A dozen years later I am a student at Haverford College. Again, I am a token black presence in a white world. A companion whose face and name I can't remember seeks to compliment me by saying, "I don't think of you as a Negro." I understand his benign intention and accept the compliment. But the knot is in my stomach again. Once again, I have betrayed myself.

This happened to me more than a few times. Each time my interlocutor was a good, liberal, white person who intended to express feelings of shared humanity. I did not yet understand the racist implications of the way in which the feelings were conceptualized. I am certain that my white friends did not either. We had not yet grasped the compliment's underlying premise: To be thought of as a Negro is to be thought of as less than human. We were all victims of our culture's racism. We had all grown up on *Little Black Sambo* and *Amos and Andy.*

Another ten years pass. I am thirty-three. My daughter, Maia, is three. I greet a pink-faced, four-year old boy on the steps of her nursery school. He proudly presents me with a book he has brought for his teacher to read to the class. 'It's my favorite,' he says. The book is a new edition of *Little Black Sambo.*

Introduction

Much of one's inability to know racial discrimination when one sees it results from a failure to recognize that racism is both a crime and a disease. . . . This failure is compounded by a reluctance to admit that the illness of racism infects almost everyone. . . . Acknowledging and understanding the malignancy are prerequisites to the discovery of an appropriate cure. But the diagnosis is difficult, because our own contamination with the very illness for which a cure is sought impairs our comprehension of the disorder.

1. "Thy Speech Maketh Thee Manifest": A Primer on the Unconscious and Race

We have found—that is we have been obliged to assume—that very powerful mental processes or ideas exist which can produce all the effects in mental life that ordinary ideas do (including effects that can in their turn become conscious as ideas), though they themselves do not become conscious. . . .

A. Racism: A Public Health Problem

Not every student of the human mind has agreed with Sigmund Freud's description of the unconscious, but few today would quarrel with the assertion that there is an unconscious—that there are mental processes of which we have no awareness that affect our actions and the ideas of which we are aware. There is a considerable, and by now well respected, body of knowledge and empirical research concerning the workings of the human psyche and the unconscious. . . . Common sense tells us that we all act unwittingly on occasion. We have experienced slips of the tongue and said things we fully intended not to say, . . . and we have had dreams in which we experienced such feelings as fear, desire, and anger that we did not know we had.

The law has, for the most part, refused to acknowledge what we have learned about the unconscious. Psychiatrists and psychologists are called to court to discuss the mental state of the criminal defendant or the suspected incompetent or to report on the mental pathology produced by an alleged tort, a neglectful parent, or the deprivation of a civil right. . . . But in most other legal matters, students of the unconscious are excluded, and we pretend that what they have learned is unknown.

It is hardly surprising that lawyers resist recognizing theories that describe the effects of unknown forces on our lives. For the most part, this reluctance is appropriate. The law is our effort to rationalize our relationships with the other. It is a system through which we attempt to define obligations and responsibilities. Denial of the irrational is part of that system, as is our notion that one should not be held responsible for any thoughts or motives of which one is unaware. . . .

. . . Racism is irrational in the sense that we are not fully aware of the meanings we attach to race or why we have made race significant. It is also arguably dysfunctional to the extent that its irrationality prevents the optimal use of human resources. In this light it seems an appropriate candidate for study and/or treatment by the psychoanalyst as well as for exclusion from law, the discipline that attempts to govern or influence the actions of rational people. But unlike other forms of irrational and dysfunctional behavior, which we think of as deviant or abnormal, racism is "normal." It is a malady that we all share, because we have all been scarred by a common history. Racism's universality renders it normal. . . .

Racism's ubiquity underscores the importance of incorporating our knowledge of the unconscious into the legal theory of equal protection. The law has traditionally used psychological theory to define abnormality in order to exclude the irrational from the law's protection or sanction. But where the law's purpose is to eradicate racial discrimination, it must recognize that racism is both irrational and normal. We must understand that our entire culture is afflicted, and we must take cognizance of psychological theory in order to frame a legal theory that can address that affliction . . .

Whatever our preferred theoretical analysis, there is considerable commonsense evidence from our everyday experience to confirm that we all harbor prejudiced attitudes that are kept from our consciousness.

. . . Another manifestation of unconscious racism is akin to the slip of the tongue. One might call it a slip of the mind: While one says what one intends, one fails to grasp the racist implications of one's benignly motivated words or behavior. For example, in the late 1950s and early 1960s, when integration and assimilation were unquestioned ideals among those who consciously rejected the ideology of racism, white liberals often expressed their acceptance of and friendship with blacks by telling them that they "did not think of them as Negroes." Their conscious intent was complimentary. The speaker was saying, "I think of you as normal human beings, just like me." But he was not conscious of the underlying implication of his words. What did this mean about most Negroes? Were they not normal human beings? If the white liberal were asked if this was his inference, he would doubtless have protested that his words were being misconstrued and that he only intended to state that he did not think of anyone in racial terms. But to say that one does not think of a Negro as a Negro is to say that one thinks of him as something else. The statement is made in the context of the real world, and implicit in it is a comparison to some norm. In this case, the norm is whiteness. . . . The white liberal's unconscious thought, his slip of the mind, is, "I think of you as different from other Negroes, as more like white people."

One indication of the nonneutrality of the statement, "I don't think of you as a Negro," when spoken as a compliment by a white is the incongruity of the response, "I don't think of you as white." This could also be a complimentary remark coming from a black, conveying the fact that she does not think of her friend in the usual negative terms she associates with whiteness. But this statement does not make sense coming from an individual who would accept as complimentary a statement characterizing her as unlike other Negroes. If anything, the response only makes sense as a light-hearted but cautionary retort. It conveys the following message: "I understand that your conscious intent was benign. But let me tell you something, friend. I think being black is just fine. If anything, our friendship is possible because you are unlike most white folks."

Of course, the statements of both these interlocutors are ethnocentric. But it is the white who has made the slip of the mind. He was unmindful of the ethnocentric premise upon which his "compliment" was based. He would find it painful to know that it is a premise in which he believes. His black friend's ethnocentrism is self-conscious and self-affirming. She is well aware of the impact of her reply. It is a defensive parry against the dominant society's racism.

A crucial factor in the process that produces unconscious racism is the tacitly transmitted cultural stereotype. If an individual has never known a black doctor or lawyer or is exposed to blacks only through a mass media where they are portrayed in the stereotyped roles of comedian, criminal, musician, or athlete, he is likely to deduce that blacks as a group are naturally inclined toward certain behavior and unfit for certain roles. . . . But the lesson is not explicit: It is learned, internalized, and used without an awareness of its source. Thus, an individual may select a white job applicant over an equally qualified black and honestly believe that this decision was based on observed intangibles unrelated to race. The employer perceives the white candidate as "more articu-

late," "more collegial," "more thoughtful," or "more charismatic." He is unaware of the learned stereotype that influenced his decision. Moreover, he has probably also learned an explicit lesson of which he is very much aware: Good, law-abiding people do not judge others on the basis of race. Even the most thorough investigation of conscious motive will not uncover the race-based stereotype that has influenced his decision.

This same process operates in the case of more far-reaching policy decisions that come to judicial attention because of their discriminatory impact. For example, when an employer or academic administrator discovers that a written examination rejects blacks at a disproportionate rate, she can draw several possible conclusions: that blacks are less qualified than others; that the test is an inaccurate measure of ability; or that the testers have chosen the wrong skills or attributes to measure. . . . When decisionmakers reach the first conclusion, a predisposition to select those data that conform with a racial stereotype may well have influenced them. Because this stereotype has been tacitly transmitted and unconsciously learned, they will be unaware of its influence on their decision.

If the purpose of the law's search for racial animus or discriminatory intent is to identify a morally culpable perpetrator, the existing intent requirement fails to achieve that purpose. There will be no evidence of self-conscious racism where the actors have internalized the relatively new American cultural morality which holds racism wrong or have learned racist attitudes and beliefs through tacit rather than explicit lessons. The actor himself will be unaware that his actions, or the racially neutral feelings and ideas that accompany them, have racist origins.

Of course, one can argue that the law should govern only consciously motivated actions—that societal sanctions can do no more than attempt to require that the individual's ego act as society's agent in censoring out those unconscious drives that society has defined as immoral. Under this view, the law can sanction a defective ego that has not fully internalized current societal morality and has, therefore, allowed illegal racist wishes to reach consciousness and fruition in an illegal act. But the law should not hold an individual responsible for wishes that never reach consciousness, even if they also come to fruition in discriminatory acts.

The problem is that this argument does not tell us why the law should hold the individual responsible for racial injury that results from one form of ego disguise but not the other. I believe the law should be equally concerned when the mind's censor successfully disguises a socially repugnant wish like racism if that motive produces behavior that has a discriminatory result as injurious as if it flowed from a consciously held motive.

Barbara Flagg, *"Was Blind, But Now I See:" White Race Consciousness and the Requirement of Discriminatory Intent*, 91 Mich. L. Rev. 953 (1993)

(This is an edited version of this article and footnotes are deleted.)

A Reformist Disparate Impact Rule

The thoroughly skeptical white decisionmaker regards all facially neutral criteria of decision as presumptively white-specific; the existence of racially disparate effects only confirms what his skepticism already counsels. Thus, the individual decisionmaker who takes transparency seriously has no need for a rule that treats facially neutral criteria of decision with racially disparate effects differently from facially neutral criteria in general. . . . A rule that requires a showing of disparate effects as a predicate for heightened scrutiny is a satisfactory alternative because it provides for judicial intervention whenever the presumed transparency phenomenon has produced concrete racial consequences. . . .

. . . [T]he proposed rule anticipates the need for evidentiary guidelines concerning proof of adverse effects, and it permits the constitutional challenger to make such a demonstration by relying on a statistical disparity between the racial composition of the group selected by the challenged criteria of decision and that of the general population. . . . The difference in techniques of proof reflects the distinction between blame and responsibility. . . . [A] rule designed to require government to take responsibility for racial justice regardless of who or what caused a given disparity would afford the constitutional challenger greater latitude on the question of the existence of disparate effects. . . .

Once the challenger has proved the existence of racially disparate effects . . . government should have to articulate the purpose or goal the challenged criteria are designed to accomplish. Initially this is simply a burden of production, so that challenger need not guess at government's policies or purposes. However, transparency can infect government's purposes as readily as it can affect chosen means, so the interpretation of government's articulated purpose is critical. . . .

Under the disparate impact analysis proposed here, a reviewing court ought to construe government's purpose, if possible, in a manner that would not advantage whites. . . . Once the question of purpose has been settled . . . the burden of production shifts to the challenger . . . to introduce means of achieving that purpose that do not disproportionately disadvantage nonwhites. . . .

Finally, government has the burden of persuasion on the question of means. Government must show that challenger's proposed alternative(s) will be less effective in achieving its purpose, as interpreted by the court, than the criteria of decision employed by the government. If government fails to carry its burden here, it will be required to employ challenger's criteria of decision either as a substitute for, or in parallel with, the criteria previously in use. . . .

The deeper design of the proposed rule is to foster constructive dialogue concerning the necessity and appropriateness of assimilationist governmental purposes and means. The transparency phenomenon means that blacks evaluated under "facially neutral" norms in fact often face a choice between assimilation and exclusion. The proposed rule is intended to counteract the assimilationist force of transparency and to require government to confront the possibility of greater openness to cultural diversity in the formulation of public policy and the exercise of governmental power. At the same time, the constitutional challenger becomes responsible for proposing alternative means of achieving government's articulated goals. . . . This requirement operates to relieve a white-controlled government of some of the burden of diversification; it does not require whites suddenly to be able to envision remedies for a phenomenon that has too often escaped our awareness altogether. . . . Nonwhites who challenge transparently white- specific governmental criteria of decision must take an active role in reformulating them. . . .

E. Cognitive Foundations and the Debate About Responsibility

Gary Blasi, *Advocacy Against the Stereotype: Lessons from Cognitive Social Psychology*, 49 U.C.L.A. L. Rev. 1241 (2002)

(This is an edited version of this article and footnotes are deleted.)

The current "colorblind" jurisprudence of the U.S. Supreme Court rests on an implicit theory of stereotyping and prejudice, the central premise of which is that prejudice is a matter of motivation and intent. Borrowing from quite different traditions in psychology, Charles

Lawrence and Linda Kreiger demonstrate in two seminal articles that this implicit theory is wrong: The behavior of real human beings is often guided by racial and other stereotypes of which they are completely unaware. . . . Since these articles were published, scientific knowledge of how stereotypes operate in the human mind has accumulated steadily. Striking recent experimental results have required science to build new models of human thinking and behavior. New theories explain—and sophisticated computer models now simulate—a broad range of experimental findings. Researchers in the new field of social cognitive neuroscience have developed techniques for illuminating not only how but where in the brain race is processed.[9] Many of the most recent scientific discoveries have significant implications for how lawyers and legal scholars should think about stereotypes and prejudice. With a handful of exceptions, however, legal scholars and practicing lawyers have generally ignored these developments.[10] As a result, advocates are often operating on the basis of an implicit theory of prejudice that is as flawed as the theory guiding the evolution of constitutional doctrine. Indeed, as I explain, it is in some ways the same theory. Persisting inequality and discrimination may therefore partially reflect, in addition to unsound legal principles and political failure, the results of antidiscrimination advocacy conducted on the basis of incorrect assumptions about people and prejudice. . . .

What would it mean to take these scientific findings seriously? More particularly, if lawyers and public policy advocates rigorously engaged in this scientific literature, how might lawyering and policy advocacy be reshaped? In addition to unrealized potential benefits, would the approaches suggested by science entail certain costs? Although my intended audience is advocates and lawyers, scholars and law teachers have an especially important role to play in exploring these questions, as potential intermediaries between psychological science and adversary practice. Just as engineers constructing bridges need access to the best metallurgical science, so too must lawyers and advocates understand as accurately as possible the cognitive and motivational processes of judges, jurors, policymakers, and voters. Unfortunately, both legal scholarship and practice too often rest on implicit theories of prejudice and stereotyping that are, if not entirely wrong, now known to be seriously incomplete. . . .

[9]See Allen J. Hart et al., Differential Response in the Human Amygdala to Racial Outgroup vs. Ingroup Face Stimuli, 11 Neuroreport 2351 (2000); Kevin N. Ochsner & Matthew D. Lieberrman, The Emergence of Social Cognitive Neuroscience, 56 Am. Psychologist 717 (2001); Elizabeth A. Phelps et al., Performance on Indirect Measures of Race Evaluation Predicts Amygdala Activation, 12 J. Cognitive Neuroscience 729 (2000).
[10]One exception is Professor Krieger, who updated the science in her earlier piece. See Linda Hamilton Krieger, Civil Rights Perestroika: Intergroup Relations after Affirmative Action, 86 Cal. L. Rev. 1251 (1998); see also Jerry Kang, Cyber-Race, 113 Harv. L. Rev. 1130 (2000); Dan Simon, A Psychological Model of Judicial Decision Making, 30 Rutgers L.J. 1 (1998); Amy L. Wax, Discrimination as Accident, 74 Ind . L.J. 1129 (1999).

To the extent that there is good news in the current science about stereotypes, it is that while we may be unable to do much about their automatic activation, we can nevertheless behave in substantially nonprejudiced ways if we are so motivated. The effects of motivation can be introduced in many different ways. What seems to matter most is whether antidiscrimination norms are activated, either directly or indirectly.

I do not mean to argue here that scientific findings about stereotyping and prejudice provide a definitive approach to legal arguments or to public policy advocacy. The science does suggest why common current strategies are flawed and suggests alternatives. There are normative implications for social change agendas as well. For example, part of the CRT project has been to negotiate between short-term and long-term antiracist strategies. Taking the science seriously might, at least in some contexts, privilege short-term strategies or alter the calculation of tradeoffs. In the end, the questions of what advocacy strategies are likely to be most effective in which situations raises empirical questions that cannot be entirely answered by extrapolation from scientific research conducted in more controlled circumstances. Much more research is required, focused specifically on the implications of the recent science for the effectiveness of advocacy. There is already, however, enough directly applicable science to suggest that ignoring it guarantees that antidiscrimination advocacy will be less effective than it might be. . . .

The implications of these experimental results are distressing. If racism and other stereotype-driven phenomena are located so deeply in human cognition, if we are all affected by stereotypes of which we have no conscious awareness, stereotypes about others as well as ourselves, what can we do to control stereotyping and to reduce prejudice? To be sure, people do display differences in these effects. Stereotypes are more easily activated in people who display more conscious prejudice. Stereotype activation also varies according to the parts of the stereotype that are used to prime activation. Words associated with the negative features of a stereotype will activate the stereotype in persons of both low and high prejudice. Associated words that are positive or neutral will activate the stereotype only in more prejudiced people. . . . All people are less likely to activate stereotypes during periods in which exceptional demands are placed on cognitive resources and people are being kept "cognitively busy.". . .

Despite these variations, however, all of us behave in ways that demonstrate that we are subject to the effects of stereotypes, including those we expressly disavow. Many readers will believe otherwise. Most of us would prefer to believe that we do not, for example, differentially associate "good" and "bad" with members of stereotyped groups, including racial groups. I encourage skeptical readers to spend the few minutes on the Internet necessary to take the extensively validated Implicit Association Test, which uses reaction times to measure implicitly held stereotypes and attitudes toward stereotyped groups. . . .

On a more hopeful note, it is also possible for motivational processes to lead to the inhibition of stereotypes. . . . Under circumstances in which activating or applying a negative stereotype would tend to diminish our self-concept—as when White males react to praise from a Black doctor or a female teacher—we are less likely to do so. These effects raise the question of whether egalitarian norms themselves can inhibit stereotype activation and application. For if part of our self-concept is that we are unprejudiced, fair, and egalitarian, then knowing that we have acted on the basis of a stereotype may diminish our view of ourselves. That connection may tend to inhibit the effects of stereotypes among people who adhere consciously to egalitarian norms norms—provided they are aware of their reliance on stereotypes. In part, this means that we must accept that it is not only anonymous subjects described in psychology journals who suffer from the irrational processes described above. These processes are universal, and they apply to each of us.

A general awareness of our frail rationality, however, is not sufficient. In order to inhibit judgments and behavior based on stereotypes, we must be aware of the specific stereotype at the time it is activated. The entire thrust of the research reported above is that stereotype activation often takes place at a preconscious or subconscious level. Assuming we do have some specific and timely awareness, we must also have both the motivation and the ability to control stereotype activation and application. Motivation can be supplied by social norms or our own moral values and personal will. The ability to control these otherwise automatic processes means devoting time and cognitive resources to focusing on individuating information. One of the reasons stereotypes persist is that they are easy to maintain; overcoming them requires significant effort. Whether all these conditions can obtain is, ultimately, an empirical matter. . . .

This is but one of many studies that demonstrate a "rebound effect," in which the active suppression of stereotypes leads to increased stereotyping at the next opportunity. Of course, even people who have prejudiced thoughts may still be able to control their behavior, at least in terms of what would appear blatantly prejudiced, either to themselves or others. As noted above,

Sommers and Ellsworth demonstrated that White jurors behaved as if they were "on guard" against racism in race-salient cases, but not in cases in which race was not so apparently at issue. Apparently, controlling more subtle expressions of prejudice requires conscious awareness that behavior may be affected by stereotypes.

Finally, one line of recent experiments suggests that people can develop habits of mind that work to suppress stereotyping. Having and frequently expressing the chronic goal of egalitarianism can suppress the degree to which we automatically activate stereotypes. . . . Results suggest that priming subjects with fairness or egalitarian goals might activate unconscious cognitions that would counter the effects of the automatic activation of stereotypes, leaving the entire battle between fairness and prejudice to be played out at a subconscious level. . . .

Discussion Notes

1. Disparate impact claims often do not survive preliminary efforts by employers to get the courts to dismiss the claims before trial. Employees often fail to introduce enough solid evidence in the record at early stages of the process to convince the court that a prima facie claim exists. It is often impossible for the employee to obtain the information necessary to prove a causal connection between any disparate impact statistics and the neutral employment practices.

Questions

1. What difference does it make whether the court views a policy as neutral or as a product of unconscious stereotypes? What difficulties would need to be addressed if the law tried to remedy the problems created by unconscious or cognitively formed stereotypes?
2. How could the law make someone responsible for acts motivated by unconscious stereotypes? Is this fair? Can you think of any analogous situations where we hold a person accountable for something they don't understand? Who bears the burden when we refuse to hold persons accountable for their unconscious stereotypes? How is this similar to different from the doctrine of disparate impact discussed above?

THREE

Who and What Should Be Protected?

9

Sexonomics, the Glass Ceiling, and the Family and Medical Leave Act

Problem 38

Erin McCaffrey is a controller at the World Widget Company and has been rejected for a promotion by an all-male hiring committee. The committee members admit they "did not want to work with an emotional woman." McCaffrey served the company with a demand letter delineating her discrimination complaints, and the company responded by ousting her from meetings, circumventing her in the chain of command, removing her hiring and firing authority, and denying her a raise until right before her case went to trial. She is joined in her lawsuit by Alia Jackson, who took over a man's job but was paid about half what he had earned to do the job; she was not promoted incident to the increased responsibilities, however, because, as the company told her, "the men would run right over you." In pursuing her complaint, she also discovered that men were being paid more than women for the same job.

A. The Equal Pay Act

Section 206(d) of 29 U.S.C. provides:

No employer having employees subject to any provisions of this section shall discriminate, within any establishment in which such employees are employed, between employees on the basis of sex by paying wages to employees in such establishment at a rate less than the rate at which he pays wages to employees of the opposite sex in such establishment for equal work on jobs the performance of which requires equal skill, effort, and responsibility, and which are performed under similar working conditions except where such payment is made pursuant to

  i. a seniority system;
  ii. a merit system;

iii. a system which measures earnings by quantity or quality of production; or

iv. a differential based on any other factor other than sex:

Provided, that an employer who is paying a wage rate differential in violation of this subsection shall not, in order to comply with the provision of this subsection, reduce the wage rate of any employee.

HOUCK
v.
VIRGINIA POLYTECHNIC INSTITUTE
10 F.3d 204 (4th Cir. 1993)

HILTON, Senior District Judge

[The Employment Problem]

Appellant Cherry K. Houck is a Professor at Virginia Polytechnic Institute and State University in the College of Education's Curriculum and Instruction Division. She sued the appellee university for violating the Equal Pay Act for fiscal years 1988–89, 1989–90, and 1990–91. . . . [T]he District Court dismissed her suit under Rule 50 of the Federal Rules of Civil Procedure for failing to establish a *prima facie* case under the Equal Pay Act.

Appellant testified that men in her department received higher pay than she did despite having the same skill, effort, and responsibility and working conditions. Without identifying colleagues or reciting facts on which any specific job comparison could be made, Professor Houck testified that there were men in her division who both made more and less than she did. She testified that she considers her job to be of equal skill, effort and responsibility under the same working conditions as unspecified male comparators. This comparison was based solely on when she saw various men and women colleagues in their offices.

Appellant stipulated statistical testimony of Dr. Donald Gantz of George Mason University that there existed men of all ranks and equal ranks in the same division and college that received higher merit salary adjustments than Dr. Houck. Dr. Gantz made statistical charts that purported to adjust for factors such as calendar year versus academic year, cost of living adjustments for Northern Virginia faculty, and "equity" to conclude that Professor Houck received lower salary adjustments than males in her division.

Appellant stipulated testimony of fellow faculty members Dr. Terry Graham, Dr. Susan Asselin, and Dr. Larry Harris that Dr. Houck is isolated and disliked by many in her division. Finally, appellant stipulated testimony of various other faculty members to attack the university's merit pay system.

There are twenty males in the Curriculum and Instruction Division and fewer than ten females. University records indicate that during the years in question, Professor Houck received an average raise of 7.03% compared to the 6.23% raise males in her division received.

[The Decision of the Trial Court]

The District Court ruled against the plaintiff because she failed to compare herself to a particular male comparator. The court noted that she compared herself to a hypothetical male, not a male that exists. When the court asked appellant to identify her male comparator, she responded, "the comparators are any men who got any higher salary increases than she did, any and all of them." She could not identify a particular male comparator from the trial record when queried by this court, either.

[The Decision and Rationale of the U.S. Court of Appeals for the Fourth Circuit]

In order to establish a *prima facie* case under the Equal Pay Act, the plaintiff must show that she receives less pay than a male co-employee performing work substantially equal in skill, effort, and responsibility under similar working conditions. This comparison must be made factor by factor with the male comparator. The plaintiff may not compare herself to a hypothetical male with a composite average of the group's skill, effort, and responsibility, but must identify a particular male for the inquiry. . . .

The District Court properly found that appellant failed to make a *prima facie* case. Appellant failed to identify any individual comparators. The closest Dr. Houck got to establishing a comparator was in questioning by the court. The court inquired if a comparison was made with a person promoted simultaneously with appellant. Houck responded that two males were so promoted and that one received a greater and one a lesser percentage raise than she did. She presented no evidence as to their responsibilities. Without further evidence, as long as there were men receiving less pay than Professor Houck, it is just as likely that their jobs were comparable as the jobs of ones who may have made more.

Professor Houck's testimony merely stated her unsupported legal conclusion without any concrete comparison. She did not compare teaching loads other than to state that her load was low and that other faculty members taught more students. She did not reveal whether her hypothetical comparators taught on an academic or calendar year basis. Nor did she compare her research to anyone else's research or compare her level of service to that of other faculty members. Although nearly two thirds of her colleagues in her division are males, she failed to identify and compare herself in any way to any male receiving a higher level of compensation.

Dr. Gantz's testimony did not bolster appellant's case because he did not identify any relevant comparators either. It is impossible to determine whether Dr. Gantz compared assistant, associate, or full professors. Also, his charts did not compare salaries of Dr. Houck with specific males having similar jobs or levels of performance.

The stipulated testimony of the faculty members regarding Dr. Houck's purported isolation within the College of Education was irrelevant to establishing a *prima facie* case because it shed no light on the required comparisons.

In sum, the court correctly reasoned that appellant did not establish a *prima facie* Equal Pay Act case on the grounds that appellant did not single out an actual comparator instead of a hypothetical one. Yet, even if she had identified an individual comparator, that might not have been enough to establish a *prima facie* case. As this court has recently pointed out in the Title VII context, isolated incidents or random comparisons demonstrating disparities in treatment may be insufficient to draw a *prima facie* inference of discrimination without additional evidence that the alleged phenomenon of inequality also exists with respect to the entire relevant group of employees. . . .

Besides disputing whether appellant established a *prima facie* case, Professor Houck also argues that the District Court erred in failing to find as a matter of law that . . . Virginia Tech did not have a bona-fide merit system in the college of education. After the plaintiff establishes a *prima facie* Equal Pay Act case, the burden shifts to the employer to prove, by a preponderance of the evidence, that the pay differential is justified by one of the four statutory exemptions of a seniority system, a merit system, a system which measures earnings by quantity or quality of production or a differential based on any . . . factor other than sex. . . . Because the plaintiff failed to establish a prima facie case, the affirmative defense of a merit system was not before the court and no ruling on the issue was necessary. . . .

A Note on the EPA's Basic Contours

Note that the court termed the evidence of colleagues' animus toward Professor Houck irrelevant to her Equal Pay Act (EPA) claim. The same evidence, however, might have been relevant to a gender discrimination claim under Title VII. Although an Equal Pay Act violation may also be a violation of Title VII, the converse is not necessarily true. The Equal Pay Act reaches compensation, not discrimination in promotion, hiring, or material conditions of employment as Title VII does. In addition, Title VII generally requires a showing of discriminatory intent, whereas the EPA sets up a regime of strict liability if wage disparity based on sex is shown. *Tidwell v. Fort Howard Corp.*, 989 F.2d 406 (10th Cir. 1993) (EPA verdict does not necessarily establish a Title VII violation, since EPA verdict could have been reached without a showing of discriminatory intent and Title VII violation could not). Finally, the EPA claim lapses if not filed in court within two years of the violation (three in cases of willfulness); although the EPA charge can be filed with the Equal Employment Opportunity Commission (EEOC), the pendency of an EEOC charge will protect only Title VII statutes of limitations, not EPA statutes of limitations.

Note also that the court in *Houck* did not state that the jobs of male and female employees had to be identical in order to establish a claim under the Equal Pay Act. The standard is comparability.

The courts have interpreted "wages" generously, finding all forms of compensation to be subsumed by the term. *EEOC v. First Nat'l Bank,* 740 F. Supp. 1338 (N.D. Ill. 1990) (sex-based differential in pension benefits); *Colby v. J.C. Penney Co.,* 705 F. Supp. 425 (N.D. Ill. 1989) (medical benefits). They have generally construed the statutory language "any establishment" less liberally, however, finding "any establishment" to generally be a distinct, physical location rather than myriad locations in which a single employer might operate. *See Wetzel v. Liberty Mut. Ins. Co.,* 449 F. Supp. 397 (W.D. Pa. 1978). However, just as with Title VII claims, an "integrated" employer may be treated as one location for comparative purposes. Under the "integrated employer" test, the court examines the degree of shared management and resources, the sharing of key personnel, intracompany transfers, the line of business, and the degree to which the ostensibly separate enterprises share common personnel policies. *See Walker v. Toolpushers Sup. Co.,* 955 F. Supp. 1377 (D. Wyo. 1997).

The "equal work" definition and the exemptions and defenses have proved the most challenging aspects of the straightforward statute.

FALLON
v.
STATE OF ILLINOIS
882 F.2d 1206 (7th Cir. 1989)

MANION, Circuit Judge.

[The Employment Problem]

Linda Fallon sued the State of Illinois under the Equal Pay Act and Title VII of the Civil Rights Act of 1964. . . . Following a bench trial, the district court found that the jobs of Veterans Service Officer (VSO) and Veterans Service Officer Associate (VSOA) (currently all VSOs are males and all VSOAs are females) were substantially equal within the meaning of the Equal Pay Act, 29 U.S.C. § 206(d), that female VSOAs were paid less than the male VSOs, and that no factors other than sex justified the pay differential. . . .

[The Legal Issue]

The State appeals the Equal Pay Act claim, contending that the trial court's "substantially equal" finding was clearly erroneous, that there was a valid factor other than sex justifying the pay disparity (a require-

ment that VSOs be wartime veterans), and that, in any event, liquidated damages were inappropriate. . . .

[The Decision and the Rationale of the U.S. Court of Appeals for the Seventh Circuit]

By statute, VSOs must be wartime (our term) veterans. . . . The VSO job description provides that VSOs, under general supervision, are to manage the field office in preparing and presenting veterans' benefit claims, and perform other necessary services for veterans or their dependents. Most VSOs additionally have what is called itinerant field service duty (14 field offices have no such duties), which means they visit veterans hospitals and prisons, if they exist in the assigned area, and speak to veterans groups at those locations. VSOs are encouraged to actively participate in and join any veterans groups.

. . . The VSO in the Champaign field office was Ronald Menaugh.

Fallon was the VSOA in the Champaign field office. Initially, Fallon was hired as a Clerk Typist II in 1969. In 1975, she became a VSOA when the State created the VSOA position. The VSOA job description provides that VSOAs, under the "general supervision of the [VSO]" will assist in preparing and presenting veterans' benefit claims, are "responsible for serving veterans independently," and are to "work independently in offices located throughout the State."

Both the VSO and the VSOA are under the supervision of a Veterans Service Officer Supervisor (Supervisor). There are five such Supervisors throughout the State. They generally visit each field office in their respective regions every four to six weeks to answer questions and solve problems. Supervisors evaluate the work of both VSOs and VSOAs.

The district court found that VSOs and VSOAs "do virtually the same work." Both interview veterans and veterans' dependents regarding benefit claims. Both assist putative claimants in completing forms for assorted benefits (e.g., medical, disability). And both type and answer the telephone. . . . And although some VSOs were required to perform itinerant work, the trial court found that the work done outside the office was virtually identical to the work done in the office. The court also dismissed the State's arguments that VSOs had added responsibility and ultimately were accountable for their respective field office's operation. Relatedly, the court found that VSOs had no authority to hire, fire, or discipline or evaluate VSOAs. Based on these findings, the district court held the VSO and VSOA jobs were substantially equal, and that no factors other than sex (the State proffered wartime veteran status and education, but presses only the former), existed to warrant the salary disparity between the positions. Accordingly, the district court held the State violated . . . the Equal Pay Act. . . .

To establish a *prima facie* case under the Equal Pay Act, a plaintiff must show: (1) that different wages are paid to employees of the opposite sex; (2) that the employees do equal work which requires equal skill, effort, and responsibility; and (3) that the employees have similar working conditions. . . . To succeed, a plaintiff "must establish, based upon 'actual job performance and content—not job titles, classifications or descriptions that the work performed . . . is substantially equal'. . . . " The work need not be identical; it is sufficient if the duties are "substantially equal." . . .

"'The crucial finding on the equal work issue is whether the jobs to be compared have a "common core" of tasks, i.e., whether a significant portion of the two jobs is identical.'" . . . If a plaintiff establishes this "common core," the question then becomes whether any additional tasks make the jobs "'substantially different.'" . . . Significantly, the state in effect admits that the core functions performed by VSOs and VSOAs (e.g., interviews, completing forms, and clerical work) are the same. This is hardly surprising, though, given the fact that three VSOs, including Menaugh, testified that VSOs did exactly the same work as VSOAs—a probative fact in establishing a *prima facie* case. . . .

Nevertheless, the State claims the positions are not substantially equal because the VSOs perform itinerant work, and have greater responsibility and accountability. The State points to Menaugh's infrequent itinerant work, . . . his membership in various veterans' organizations, his additional "responsibilities," and differences in the way the two positions are evaluated. . . .

The district court rejected VSO itinerant work as a distinguishing factor, and we cannot say that was clearly erroneous. The district court acknowledged that VSOs, and occasionally Menaugh, did this work. Nonetheless, it found this slight difference unpersuasive as a distinction between the jobs. Several factors support this conclusion. First of all, not all VSOs were required to do itinerant work; Menaugh was among those not so required. Even more significant, the district court found that VSOs who did perform itinerant duties did virtually the same work outside the office as they did inside it. That is, itinerant work involved traveling to another location to do exactly the same work as that done in the field office—work which was substantially equal to that performed by VSOAs. The mere fact that some travel was required does not override the court's conclusion that the work was substantially the same. . . . Differences in responsibility must be substantial; to argue that *any* difference in supervisory responsibility renders jobs unequal" [for purposes of EPA application] "is manifestly incorrect as a matter of law." . . .

The State next points to what it contends are additional responsibilities required of VSOs. As an example, it says all complaints regarding the field office were channeled to the VSO. This, the State argues, shows the VSO was in charge of and accountable for the field office. It may show something along those lines, but the fact remains that the district court found (and the State doesn't challenge this finding), that the Supervisor actually managed the field office. The State's position is further undermined by Menaugh's testimony that he had no managerial role whatever. . . . Moreover, VSOs had no authority to hire, fire, discipline, or evaluate

VSOAs . . . Cf. *Hill v. J.C. Penney Co., Inc.,* 688 F.2d 370, 373–74 (5th Cir. 1982) (even when male "supervisor" had authority to hire and evaluate, his input on evaluations was minimal; thus supervisory designation held "illusory"). . . . Given the VSOs almost complete lack of control over VSOAs, it strains credibility to say VSOs were responsible or accountable for the field office's smooth operation.

The district court also noted that there was nothing to managing a two-person office, or at least this two-person office. . . . [T]he VSO virtually had no supervisory authority over the VSOA. Indeed, as the district court noted, the VSO and VSOA both were evaluated by the Supervisor who managed the office. And the fact that VSOs kept track of sparse office supplies (if indeed VSOs did that—Menaugh testified he had no authority to purchase additional supplies) is not a meaningful distinction.

The State also observes that VSOs and VSOAs were evaluated on different criteria; VSOs tend[ed] to be judged on supervisory ability, and VSOAs . . . on clerical acuity. . . . [But] the State in its zeal to discount as merely clerical Fallon's self-described job objectives (contained on her prior evaluations), overlooks the fact that Menaugh, on at least two prior evaluations, listed identical "clerical" objectives ("upgrading files"). . . .

Finally, the State contends that VSOs were required to join veterans groups for which the VSO was qualified. The testimony of this point was equivocal, however. Menaugh testified that he was not required to join such groups, although he did join on his own. Another VSO . . . stated that when initially hired, he did not join any of these groups. . . . The district court found that while membership in veterans groups was encouraged, it was not required. Given the divergent evidence and the district court's opportunity to observe the witnesses, we cannot say the district court's choice was clearly erroneous. . . .

Once a plaintiff establishes a *prima facie* case under the Equal Pay Act, the burden of proof shifts to the employer to show that the pay disparity is due to: (1) a seniority system; (2) a merit system; (3) a system which measures earnings by quantity or quality of production; or (4) any . . . factor other than sex. . . . These are affirmative defenses on which the employer bears the burden of proof (persuasion). . . .

The fourth affirmative defense . . . is a broad "catch-all" exception and embraces an almost limitless number of factors, so long as they do not involve sex. . . . [The catch-all exception] prevents courts and administrative agencies from substituting their judgment for the employer's judgment and avoids unnecessary disruption of bona fide job evaluation systems. . . .

The factor other than sex must . . . be bona fide. In other words, an employer cannot use a gender-neutral factor to avoid liability unless the factor is used and applied in good faith; it was not meant to provide a convenient escape from liability. . . .

The State asserted that the pay differential between VSOs and VSOAs was based on the VSO's wartime veteran status; that is, VSOs are required by statute to be wartime veterans, . . . and that accounts for the difference in pay. . . . The State argues that wartime veteran status is much like preferring (and rewarding) experience, which is perfectly permissible and a valid affirmative defense under the Equal Pay Act. . . . Employers may prefer and reward experience, believing it makes a more valuable employee, for whatever reason. . . . And it is not our province to second-guess employers' business judgment. . . . The State believes that wartime veterans will have a special comaraderie with other veterans, making it more likely that veterans needing the Department's aid will open up to the VSO, when they otherwise might not do so. The shared experience of military service during a time of war is thus critical, the state argues. This seems eminently reasonable. There can be few experiences even remotely similar to having served one's country during wartime. If applied in good faith and in a nondiscriminatory manner, we believe wartime veteran status can be a legitimate factor other than sex [within the meaning of the EPA exception].

The district court, however, flatly rejected this defense, apparently concluding that it failed as a matter of law. The court conclusively held that "[t]he single fact that [VSOs] are veterans and the [VSOAs] are not cannot justify the higher wages paid to the [VSOs]. *Grove v. Frostburg National Bank,* 549 F. Supp. 922, 940 (D. Md. 1982)." The trial court's citation to *Grove* is unilluminating. There, the district court held that the employer bank could not justify the higher salary it paid a male bank teller by claiming it was a reward for his prior military service. *Id.* at 934. Importantly, the court was willing to assume that a reward for veteran status could be a valid factor other than sex. *Id.* The problem though, according to the court, was that the male employee had been drafted into military service while the plaintiff women could not have been drafted. *Id.* This is the extent of the court's analysis; and we are left to guess at what it really means. If it meant that military service pursuant to the draft was not a valid factor other than sex because it caused a discriminatory consequence, the court's rationale is questionable. *Cf. County of Washington v. Gunther,* 452 U.S. at 171. . . .

But regardless of what was meant, *Grove* is inapplicable to this case, at least on the record before us. There is nothing in the record showing that VSOs were all beneficiaries of a draft excluding women, or that the wartime veteran status factor had a discriminatory effect. Even if there were a draft which excluded women, [legal under the rule of] *Rostker v. Goldberg,* 453 U.S. 57 (1981), though, that doesn't necessarily mean that women were excluded from military service altogether. The statute required only that VSOs be wartime veterans [which] could include women as well as men. *Cf. Personnel Administrator of Massachusetts v. Feeney,* 442 U.S. 256, 275 (1979). In fact, at one time there was a female VSO who was a veteran. . . . Moreover, large numbers of males (both nonveterans and peacetime veterans) are likely to be excluded by the statute's eligibility requirement. *Id.*

The district court prematurely rejected the state's asserted affirmative defense that the VSO's requisite wartime veteran status was a factor other than sex justifying the pay differential. Under proper circumstances, as outlined above, we believe this can be a valid factor other than sex. Accordingly, we must remand the case to the district court for appropriate findings on this issue. . . .

Discussion Notes

1. Could Ms. Fallon have succeeded in a claim of a sex-segregated work force under Title VII, as a result of disparate impact? Would it have been based on a male-only draft, or could it have been based simply on a 100% division of males and females into the VSO and VSOA classifications? Consider the distinction the Supreme Court has drawn between the mechanics of Title VII and the design of the fourth exception to the EPA:

   Title VII's prohibition of discriminatory employment practices was intended to be broadly inclusive, proscribing "not only overt discrimination but also practices that are fair in form, but discriminatory in operation." . . . The structure of Title VII litigation, including presumptions, burdens of proof, and defenses, has been designed to reflect this approach. The fourth affirmative defense of the Equal Pay Act, however, was designed differently, to confine the application of the Act to wage differentials attributable to sex discrimination. . . .

Equal Pay Act litigation, therefore, has been structured to permit employers to defend against charges of discrimination where their pay differentials are based on a bona fide use of "other factors other than sex.". . . .

County of Washington v. Gunther, 452 U.S. 161, 170 (1981).

Does this language add a gloss to the understanding of the Equal Pay Act as a strict-liability statute? If it is a strict-liability statute, and if intentional discrimination is not an element of an EPA violation, did the *Fallon* court wrongly impose a requirement of good faith on the employer's bona fide system? Or, conversely, could any system be considered bona fide if it was not applied in good faith? The employer's good faith is generally discussed not in terms of the employer's liability but in terms of damages after a finding of liability. The Equal Pay Act allows successful plaintiffs to recover lost wages as well as "liquidated damages" in an amount equal to lost wages but only where the court finds that the employer did not act on a good-faith belief that it was correctly applying the law. *See EEOC v. Altmeyer's Home Stores, Inc.,* 698 F. Supp. 594 (W.D. Pa. 1988). One other matter to which the employer's degree of scienter is relevant is the statute of limitations for EPA claims; a "willful" violation of the Act is subject to a three-year, rather than a two-year, statute of limitations. *See* 29 U.S.C. §§ 255. Finally, if willfulness is proved, a plaintiff can be awarded back pay for three years prior to the filing of the complaint rather than for only two years. 29 U.S.C. § 255(a).

2. The *Fallon* court cites *Rostker v. Goldberg,* 453 U.S. 57 (1981), which upheld a males-only military draft against an equal protection challenge. The *Fallon* court then suggests that women might have been wartime veterans in noncombat roles. Suppose that all the women VSOAs were noncombat Vietnam veterans. Couldn't the state then present as its affirmative defense that combat experience was necessary to "getting men to open up to the VSO, when they might not otherwise do so," *Fallon,* 822 F.2d at 1212, and that no other experience during wartime was the sort of crucible that would forge a link between VSOs and veterans? Does the court's remand on the "factor other than sex"

affirmative defense suggest that if Ms. Fallon shows that only males were drafted, she wins? Or does the court suggest that even the fact that only males were drafted will not show discrimination because (a) women could be veterans without having been drafted and (b) only male wartime veterans would qualify to be VSOs, so any discrimination was not based on sex? What does the latter issue have to do with discrimination in the particular job classification anyway? If Ms. Fallon proves on remand that the state already has a version of 38 U.S.C. § 2014, part of the Vietnam Era Veterans' Readjustment Assistance Act, that gives preference in hiring to both Vietnam veterans and Vietnam veterans with a Service-connected disability, would this have any relevance to Ms. Fallon's case? Could she then argue that the preference is already a "reward" and that enhanced pay is therefore double dipping? Or, since the EPA applies only to wages, would any special preferences be relevant to the EPA analysis? The Title VII analysis?

3. Recall what the *Fallon* court said about *Grove v. Frostburg National Bank*, 549 F. Supp. 922 (D. Md. 1982). In what way can prior military service be used to justify higher pay in a private-sector job that has no connection to the military? Is a state veterans' agency more justified than a bank in taking military service into account in fixing pay? Would a private-sector defense contractor be justified in doing so under the fourth exception to the EPA?

4. What about the case in which a female supervisor earns less than her male subordinates but does the same work they do apart from her supervisory duties? Compare *Riordan v. Kempiners*, 831 F.2d 690 (7th Cir. 1987) (EPA applies) with *Pajic v. CIGNA Corp.*, 56 Fair Empl. Prac. Cas. (BNA) 1624, 1990 WL 191939 (E.D. Pa. 1990) (EPA does not apply).

5. How does an employee of a law firm, stock brokerage house, accounting firm, or college faculty prove an Equal Pay Act claim against the affirmative defense that wages are set based on quantity or quality of the work? Is there any way that a court can review such a case without potentially "substituting [its] judgment for the employer's judgment"? *See Gunther*, 452 U.S. at 171. Courts have found seniority, merit- or productivity-based, and "factor other than sex" defenses meritorious when dealing with claims of professionals. *See, e.g., Byrd v. Ronayne*, 61 F.3d 1026 (1st Cir. 1995) (female lawyer failed to establish prima facie case where she was paid $62,500 yearly with two slight bonuses, whereas male attorney was paid $70,000 plus 15% of fees generated; court found that female attorney failed to prove that her work required substantially equal skill, responsibility, and effort, particularly in view of male attorney's bankruptcy practice and greater fee-generating caseload for firm); *Dey v. Colt Const. & Development. Co.*, 28 F.3d 1446 (7th Cir. 1994) (female controller was paid roughly $7,000 less at termination than successor male was paid on hire; however, male had MBA degree and female had only associate's degree, and male negotiated a salary commensurate with his salary in his previous job); *Bartges v. University of North Carolina at Charlotte*, 908 F. Supp. 1312, *aff'd*, 94 F.3d 641 (4th Cir. 1996) (university may compensate coaches based on revenue generated by their sports teams; this qualifies as factor other than sex within the meaning of the Act); *Schwartz v. Florida Bd. of Regents*, 954 F.2d 620 (11th Cir. 1991).

6. What about sales jobs, where commissions are explicitly based on productivity? *See Keziah v. W.M. Brown & Son, Inc.*, 888 F.2d 322 (4th Cir. 1989) (employer must establish that it does not discriminate in applying its draw-against-commissions policy so that it *de facto* pays males a higher "salary" without sufficient justification, such as proof of the male's superior sales experience).

B. Is There a Glass Ceiling? The Debate over Economics and Barriers to Management Positions

> **Problem 39**
>
> Allison Bridges is a 31-year-old executive manager at Bloomdale Incorporated, a high-end chain of home furnishing stores. Allison has been working with the company for 10 years and has risen to the level of Manager of Sales for her region, but she has been unsuccessful in achieving her goal of becoming a Regional Vice President or President. All of her references have been excellent, and she has been responsible for major sales in the company. Her boss, however, fears that she will be feeling the "biological clock" soon and doesn't want to take the risk that she will lower her work standards once she starts having a family. He doesn't tell Allison this because he knows that it would be problematic. Instead, he claims that the males who have been promoted are more qualified. Allison does want to start a family, but she is aware of the risks to her career.

1. The Creation of the Glass Ceiling Commission

The term "glass ceiling" became popular in the 1980s and 1990s to describe the artificial barriers to opportunity and advancement, based on stereotypes or other attitudinal and institutional bias, that prevented qualified minorities and nonminority women from advancing to top management positions.

Congress passed the Glass Ceiling Act (GCA) in 1991, Pub. L. N. 102–166, 105 Stat. 1081, 42 U.S.C. § 2000e (1994). Section 202(b) gives Congress the power to establish

1. a Glass Ceiling Commission to study—
   a. the manner in which business fills management and decisionmaking positions;
   b. the developmental and skill-enhancing practices used to foster the necessary qualifications for advancement into such positions; and
   c. the compensation programs and reward structures currently utilized in the workplace; . . .

Section 203 authorized the Commission

to conduct a study and prepare recommendations concerning—

1. eliminating artificial barriers to the advancement of women and minorities; and
2. increasing the opportunities and developmental experiences of women and minorities to foster advancement of women and minorities to management and decisionmaking positions in business.

When the Commission issued its report, *Good for Business: Making Full Use of the Nation's Human Capital: Fact Finding Report of the Federal Glass Ceiling*

Commission (March 16, 1995), it concluded that "95–97% of the senior managers of Fortune 1000 industrial and Fortune 500 companies are white males." *Id.* at 3. It identified at least three types of barriers to the advancement of women and minorities, including (1) social barriers, (2) internal structural barriers, and (3) government barriers. The Commission expired by a sunset provision that ended its mandate in 1995 after the issuance of the report. The Office of Federal Contract Compliance (OFCCP), the government agency charged with oversight of all businesses that obtain contracts with the government, developed Glass Ceiling Initiatives that apply to government contractors. The OFCCP has the power to investigate companies in order to determine whether they are following the federal nondiscrimination laws, including Title VII. The OFCCP can recommend to Congress that a particular company lose its contracts if the company is not in compliance. As a result of its Glass Ceiling Initiatives, the OFCCP has audited numerous corporations each year in order to review their policies and practices that affect the "glass ceiling" barriers for women and minorities.

Kingsley R. Browne, *Sex and Temperament in Modern Society: A Darwinian View of the Glass Ceiling and the Gender Gap*, 37 Ariz. L. Rev. 971 (1995)

(This is an edited version of the article and footnotes are deleted.)

The idea of a fundamental "human nature" is resisted by many, . . . apparently out of concern that recognition of biological roots of human nature would deny the autonomy and dignity of the individual. . . . But to say that there is an underlying "psychic unity of mankind" is not to deny individual difference or personal autonomy. Indeed, the concept of such a unity had its origins in liberal notions of fundamental human equality. Many also have political objections to the idea of a fundamental human nature, fearing that appeals to a biological human nature are merely a subterfuge to maintain the status quo. . . . Nonetheless, an understanding of why we are the way we are is a precondition to our becoming the way that we hope to be.

An understanding of human behavior and psychology may illuminate many public policy issues. One of the thorniest sets of issues facing our society today is the appropriate role of the sexes—in the workplace, in the home, and in the political arena. Although no one doubts that at the core of our distinction between males and females is a biological difference in reproductive biology, the legal and public-policy literature largely ignores other biological sex differences, differences that extend beyond reproductive biology to temperament and behavior. Yet it is at least conceivable—and as I attempt to show below, highly probable—that major aspects of sex roles in our society are strongly influenced by biological predispositions. . . .

The current debate over the respective roles of the sexes in the workplace proceeds on the basis of usually unstated assumptions about the nature of man and woman. A concrete application of such assumptions can be found in the literature on the "glass ceiling." The "glass ceiling" is a metaphor that is meant to reflect the fact that women tend to be substantially underrepresented in the upper reaches of management. . . . It is a clever metaphor for it not only captures an empirical observation—that women's progression up the hierarchy tends to "stall" at some point—but it also contains within it an assumption that the causes of this lack of progression are often-invisible forces that are external to women but internal to the organization.

The recently released report of the Federal Glass Ceiling Commission focuses on societal and corporate barriers to women in the work force. . . . However, if one were to begin without any preconceived notions about the reason for the empirical observation, one might cast a broader net searching for possible explanations. First, there might indeed be something about the institution—either outright discrimination or other barriers—that makes achievement by women more difficult than achievement by men. Second, there might be factors at work in society at large that lead to the observed circumstances. Third, there might be something intrinsic to men and women themselves—possibly differences in interest, ability, temperament, or qualifications—that leads to the result. The beauty of the "glass ceiling" metaphor is that it carries within it the assumption that it is the first reason that accounts for most of what we see, although proponents of the metaphor will readily concede that society-at-large is hardly blameless. The Glass Ceiling report hardly touches upon, and certainly does not address in any serious way, the third explanation, instead identifying the underlying cause as "white male anxiety. . . . "

The assumption that the primary blame lies within organizations focuses attention on the behavior of employers. If the problem is caused by employer behavior, then the problem can be fixed by modification of employer behavior. It is more difficult to change society, but if we create the proper role models for little boys and girls at school, then society may take care of itself. . . .

The common understanding of the "gender gap" in compensation typically is similar to the understanding of the glass ceiling. In its usual form, the gender gap is described as the difference between the average earnings of full-time male employees and full-time female employees, typically expressed as the ratio of women's earnings to men's. Although one still frequently hears the outdated fifty-nine cent figure . . . —that is, that a full-time female employee earns only fifty-nine cents for every dollar earned by a full-time male employee—the current figure is more like seventy-one or seventy-two cents, and for young women the figure is much higher. . . . Again, the term "gender gap" is a loaded one in that it implies the need for correction; whether a "gap" is a gender gap or a missile gap, it is something that presumptively needs to be closed.

Notwithstanding the shrinking of the compensation gap, the fact that the average full-time female employee earns only seventy-two cents for every dollar earned by the average full-time male employee is seen as a measure of inequality having its source in failings of both employers and society. Most students of the gender gap do not believe that it is primarily a consequence of employer discrimination in compensation, but rather a product of occupational segregation, differences in productivity-related traits, and perhaps a devaluation of the kinds of tasks at which women excel. . . . As with the glass ceiling, it is seldom considered that the gender gap may be a reflection of real differences between men and women.

The assumption that men and women are substantially identical in respects relevant to the workplace leads to a reflexive suspicion whenever differences in outcome exist between the sexes, at least when the comparison is viewed as unfavorable to women. Thus, we speak of a gender gap in compensation to characterize the lower income of women, although one seldom hears about a gender gap in occupational deaths, despite the fact that thirteen men die on the job for every woman who dies. . . . When viewed through the current lens of "gender equality," the former is a "problem" while the latter is merely a "fact." . . .

If a major cause of these differential outcomes is the nature of men and women themselves, our attitudes toward them might change. Suppose, for example, that by nature men and women differ temperamentally and that these temperamental differences are substantial causes of the differences in outcome. How would we, or should we, respond? That is an important question to ponder even if one doubts the existence of such differences, since it helps illuminate one's conception of sexual equality.

The clarity of our definition of equality is not seriously challenged as long as we assume that the "second class" status of women in the workplace is due to unfair actions of employers or society that create artificial distinctions between effectively identical people. If unfair behavior has caused inequality, then fair behavior will presumably cause equality. However, if the differential status of men and women in the workplace is caused by true and fundamental sex differences, the response is not as obvious. One could argue that if differential outcomes are reflections of real differences, they are not arbitrary and require no correction. On the other hand, one might hold that even real sex differences cannot justify differential outcomes, either because differential outcomes are inherently unfair whatever their cause or because the differential outcomes are a consequence of employers' and society's arbitrarily and unfairly overvaluing male traits and undervaluing female ones.

In order to evaluate the validity of the argument that it is unfair to structure a reward system in a way that tends to favor men, one must understand the workings of the system. One should also examine the underlying premise itself—that men are favored by current arrangements. Assume that for some reason men are more competitive than women and more inclined to expend effort to climb hierarchies. Would it be unfair if a disproportionate number of men achieved the highest positions in the hierarchy? One might respond that the outcome is appropriate; after all, those who achieved the status are those who were most inclined to work for it. On the other hand, one might respond that the outcome is inappropriate; we should not reward the competitive behavior of men but rather we should reward the cooperative behavior of women. The latter response, however, may misconceive what is meant by competitive behavior. In this context, competitive behavior means the sort of behavior that is necessary in order to achieve status. If one must demonstrate cooperation in order to progress up the ladder, that is what the competitive person will do. If one must dole out soup in a soup kitchen to get ahead, the competitive person will probably beat the compassionate person to the soup line. . . .

Suppose also that men are more inclined to take "career risks" than women. If men are more willing to put themselves into positions where there is substantial personal accountability and possibility of failure, one would expect more of the great successes—and great failures—to be men. Again, the question is whether it would be appropriate to structure workplace rewards in such a way as to equalize rewards between those who take risks for their success and those who do not.

Along the same lines, assume that men are more single-minded about acquiring resources than women. This is not to suggest that women are not interested in acquiring resources; almost everyone views resource acquisition positively and, all else being equal, would prefer more to less. The assumption that the reader is asked to indulge is that men place a higher priority on resource acquisition than women. Starting from this assumption, the question is whether it is arbitrary or unfair to have a system that leads to greater resource acquisition by those who are most willing to make sacrifices in other areas of their lives to obtain them.

Assume further that women are inclined to be more nurturant and oriented toward others, resulting in a greater attachment to their children and a lesser willingness to trade material resources for time spent with their children or in other activities. The psychic satisfaction they receive from devotion to family outweighs for them the reduced economic satisfaction that results from a lesser attachment to the workplace. If women work less because they have other forces in their lives that are as important as, or more important than, work, it is not obvious that social policy should be oriented toward ensuring that economic outcomes are nonetheless equivalent.

Consider also the "gender gap" in occupational deaths. The concentration of men in dangerous occupations has resulted in a substantial overrepresentation of men among those who die on the job. Should we be as concerned about this gender gap as we are about the gap in compensation? If not, why not? Some might argue that no one "forces" men to take dangerous jobs, but by equivalent reasoning one could say that no one forces women to take low-paying jobs. Others might argue that the wages of the dangerous jobs incorporate a "risk premium," so that men have been paid for taking such risks. However, one would then not be in a strong position to argue that women should earn as much as men. Life is full of trade-offs, and if men and women tend to make different ones, it is to be expected that both benefits and burdens will be different for the two sexes.

Would a showing that men are more inclined than women to take physical risks affect our view of the acceptability of the "death gap"? If we are prepared to accept the notion that men and women might tend to sort themselves on the basis of their own values, we should hardly be surprised if the group that is more risk averse tends to find itself more often in occupations that are less risky. Also, even if there were no sex difference in risk

preference per se, the fact that men assign higher priority than women to resource acquisition might make men disproportionately willing to trade safety for dollars.

No doubt this sounds terribly sexist to some. The reader is asked to assume that men are more competitive, more driven toward acquisition of status and resources, and more inclined to take risks; women are more nurturant, risk averse, less greedy, and less single-minded. These are familiar stereotypes to us and to people around the world. . . . Of course, stereotypes are not necessarily false; in fact, they usually contain some element, often a large one, of truth. . . . If these particular stereotypes are true as generalizations, as the evidence suggests, then they could go far toward explaining the face of the contemporary workplace. The fact that the generalizations do not hold true for all individuals is irrelevant, because the phenomena to be explained are themselves based upon group comparisons.

Even if these generalizations are the proximate cause of the various "gaps," however, the appropriate public policy response may vary depending upon their cause. It is probably fair to say that the overwhelming majority of legal scholars and others who write about these matters from a public-policy perspective believe either that the generalizations are not accurate or, perhaps more commonly, that they may be accurate but that they are a product of a sexist society with its accompanying sexist child-rearing practices; society causes these differences by treating functionally identical individuals differently. That is, men are competitive, acquisitive risk-takers and women are cooperative, risk-averse nurturers because they learned these traits as little boys and girls and have been reinforced in them ever since. Little attention is given to the possibility that there is something inherent in males and females that causes them to behave in different ways. Many are prepared to reject the notion that relevant biological sex differences exist without having even passing familiarity with the extensive literature to the contrary. Alternatively, the issue may not be one of evidence, for as Michael Levin has observed, "[a]ny veteran of adolescence and parenthood still able to believe that boys and girls are born alike has already withstood more evidence than any laboratory can provide."[34]

It is easy to view the question as entailing a choice between "nature" and "nurture," yet that is a false dichotomy. . . . Biology is the study of life and life processes, so in a sense everything that humans do is "biological"; everything that humans do is "allowed" by their biology. Not everything that is allowed by humans' physical makeup is allowed by their psychological

[34]Michael Levin, Feminism and Freedom 55 (1987).

makeup, however. Humans are quite capable physically of eating their young, as do some other species, yet that is not a behavioral pattern that humans generally express. . . .

I should at this point say exactly what I am arguing. It is my central thesis that much of what we call the glass ceiling and gender gap is the product of basic biological sex differences in personality and temperament. These differences have resulted from differential reproductive strategies that have been adopted by the two sexes during human history and are every bit as much a product of natural selection as our bipedal locomotion and opposable thumbs. Although these temperamental traits evolved in our hunting-and-gathering ancestral environment, they remain with us today whether or not they remain adaptive.

I should similarly emphasize what I am not arguing. It is not my position that biology is the exclusive cause of the glass ceiling or the gender gap. Indeed, such a claim would be specious, since all behavior involves the organism's interaction with its environment. But even beyond this truism, I do not doubt that some portion of these two phenomena are produced by social attitudes, some of them arbitrary, as well as by outright sex discrimination that may be based upon false assumptions about the relative capacities of the sexes. I also do not argue that social reinforcement of these differences is insignificant. It would be very strange if social institutions were oblivious to these differences.

Notwithstanding the above disclaimers, the position articulated in this article will no doubt be dismissed by some as "biological determinism." As Robert Wright has recently written, however, accusations of biological determinism are often born of ignorance of both biology and determinism.[43] No one argues that human behaviors are "hard wired" into the brain; if they were, there would be little room for individual responsibility, and our own experience (though perhaps an illusion) tells us that we are capable, within limits, of exercising free will. But some behaviors come more readily than others, and some "cultural values" are universal. It is these predispositions and universals that characterize us as humans. . . .

I write this article with some hesitation. Many who are familiar with the biological and psychological literature I discuss are likely to respond, "So what; everyone knows that." On the other hand, those who are not familiar with this literature, but who are committed to a social-constructionist view, may well respond, "That can't be true." The current trend—that the more science tells us about sex differences, the more the prevailing

ideology denies them . . . —must be reversed if we are to have any hope of formulating realistic public policy. . . .

Conclusion

Men and women are different; they have—on average—different temperaments, priorities, and definitions of success. These differences are produced in substantial measure by underlying biological differences that were adaptive in our evolutionary history. The sex differences we see in our society are replicated both in other societies and, in many cases, throughout the mammalian world. They are fundamentally products of the interaction of hormones and the brain, and they are not simply products of western civilization, capitalism, or industrialism. . . .

Given the undeniable differences between men and women, the nature of sex-discrimination litigation must change. If the goal is to prevent employers from improperly discriminating against women, then proof of actual discrimination should be required. . . . If the true goal is proportional representation of women at all levels of the work force irrespective of workforce commitment, then that goal should be candidly acknowledged and defended on its own terms.

Understanding of the origins of observed differences should also affect the way that we evaluate arguments for social change, even if it does not alter our conclusions. The feminist argument that sex roles are something that society has imposed upon female victims is inadequate; if current workplace arrangements are the products of choices made by men and women predisposed to make choices in a particular way, arguments that society must remedy the injustice that it has visited on women are based upon an erroneous premise of societal culpability. It may be that the same policy prescriptions will be forthcoming, but they must rest on an alternative rationale, a rationale that has not yet been offered. We may also conclude that the remedies advocated by many feminists, such as changes in the workplace and increased childcare, will not produce the results that they expect. . . .

One possible response would be to attempt to make the sexes more similar. One could, for example, attempt to increase women's preference for risk, although it is not clear why one would not also attempt to increase the risk preference of risk-averse males at the same time. . . .

Much of the disagreement over the status of women in the workplace is a philosophical one: is the appropriate focus of social policy on groups or on individuals? If current workplace arrangements are largely a result of individual choices of men and women guided by the male and female psyches, are the outcomes of those choices rendered suspect—if not illegitimate—by group differences in the choices made? The fact that some people prefer to focus their energies on their families while

[43]Robert Wright, The Moral Animal: The New Science of Evolutionary Psychology 137 (1994).

others prefer to concentrate on their careers does not seem to be the perceived problem. The demand for social intervention arises from the fact that the former group is disproportionately female, while the latter group is disproportionately male. Similarly, the fact that the business world rewards competitive risk-takers is not by itself a problem; the problem is that risk-takers tend to be men.

At bottom, the feminist case is based upon a normative vision of what women should want, rather than on what they do want. Many feminists are hostile to the process that allows women to make these decisions because they are hostile to the results. But to deny the effect of choice because of that which is chosen is ultimately an authoritarian response. . . . In a very real sense, the patterns we now see are in fact a product of female choice; over thousands of generations, women have chosen men who display the traits that feminists now claim to disdain. . . .

. . . the fact that women are not dissatisfied seems to be viewed as a problem. Proponents of social construction have been extremely successful in preventing the biological explanation of differences from affecting public-policy discussions. They have had this success only because of a gross asymmetry in burdens of proof. Without convincing evidence of their own, social constructionists have been permitted to shift the burden to those favoring a biological explanation simply by uttering the word "socialization." Yet broad arguments of social construction are fundamentally unscientific, because no specific predictions flow from a social constructionist view and its tenets are not falsifiable. Since "social construction" can provide a post hoc explanation for any conceivable pattern, it ultimately explains nothing. Unfortunately, for those who believe that biology is necessary for a full understanding of the differences, the standard of proof that is applied to biological explanations seems to be something approaching proof beyond a reasonable doubt. If social-construction explanations had faced the same skepticism that biological explanations face, they could not have persisted as they have. . . .

The belief that the sexes are effectively identical has led to a number of policies of doubtful wisdom and effec-

tiveness. Employers are pressured to eliminate statistical disparities in their work forces even at the cost of productivity; schools have been converted into organs of propaganda for the view of sexual sameness, without regard to the loss of credibility that may flow from propaganda so at variance with children's own experience; military readiness has been seriously compromised, according to many, by the admission of women into almost all positions and the changes in standards that have been necessary to accomplish that end. . . . A biological perspective cannot answer the normative question of whether these policies should be adopted, but it can provide insight into the correctness of the assumptions on which they are based, as well as into their costs and potential effectiveness. The Glass Ceiling Commission, in contrast, spent three million dollars examining the glass ceiling and apparently never considered that differences in work force outcome might be a consequence of inherent differences between the sexes. The Commission's response is characteristic of those believing that societal flaws are responsible for all disfavored conditions: failure of social intervention to yield the desired result is considered proof of the need for further intervention rather than an indication that their diagnosis is incorrect or that the conditions might not be susceptible of productive modification.

In evaluating competing claims concerning the origins of human behavior, the question should not be whether those finding answers in biology can prove their case to a moral certainty. No claim is made that the data and analysis presented in this article are the last word—the "truth" in some absolute sense. Some of the specifics will no doubt require future revision as our understanding of human behavior increases. The important question should be whether the explanation offered here—that genuine and deep-seated differences between the sexes are a substantial cause of current workplace arrangements—is a more plausible account than the social-constructionists have provided. It is hoped that those who still have doubts concerning the biological explanation will bring the same degree of skepticism, and the same demand for rigorous proof, to the purely sociological explanations.

Richard A. Posner, *An Economic Analysis of Sex Discrimination Laws,*
56 U. Chi. L. Rev. 1311 (1989)

(This is an edited version of the article and footnotes are deleted.)

There is now substantial economic literature on discrimination. The literature focuses on racial discrimination but has implications for other forms of discrimination as well, including sex discrimination.[1] There is also substantial economic literature on the extent and causes of disparities between men and women in wages, employment level, and other measures of professional attainment. . . . At the intersection of the two literatures one finds a number of studies of the economics of sex discrimination in employment. . . . There is also—it goes without saying—an enormous legal literature on sex discrimination law, again focused on employment. But there is relatively little writing on sex discrimination law from an economic standpoint. . . . My objective in this paper is to examine the economic properties of the laws and doctrines relating to sex discrimination in employment. Although I am unable on the basis of existing information and analysis to estimate either the efficiency or the distributive effects of these laws and doctrines, I believe it is a plausible hypothesis—no stronger statement is possible—that sex discrimination law has not increased, and it may even have reduced, the aggregate welfare of women. Underlying this conclusion are four general arguments supported by smatterings of empirical evidence: (1) the sheer variety of practices that cluster together under the law's label "sex discrimination"; (2) the distributive complexities arising from interdependent positive utilities and joint consumption between men and women; (3) the pervasive conflicts of interest between different groups of women (for example, nonworking housewives and unmarried working women); and (4) the probably substantial, and growing, costs of administering sex discrimination laws. Arguments (2) and (3) are related. . . . and together help explain why women, despite being a majority of voters, may not have succeeded in obtaining effective antidiscrimination legislation. . . .

Some Economics of Sex Discrimination

Before the economic effects of sex discrimination law can be evaluated, one must get a grip on the economics of sex discrimination. This section lists the basic assumptions of the analysis, then examines the causes of sex discrimination, and finally makes a stab at estimating what

our labor markets would be like today without any sex discrimination laws.

Assumptions

I assume that all people—men and women alike—are rational in the usual economic sense. That is, they consistently act to maximize the excess of their private benefits over their private costs. It is consistent with this model, as we shall see, that some—or, for that matter, many or even most—men are misogynistic, exploitative, or ill-informed. I further assume that even if there is no discrimination against women, women will, on average, invest less than men in human capital, both general and job-specific. The qualification that it is only on average that women will invest less is important. The characteristics that are related to productive employment are unevenly distributed within each sex, so that even if the means of the distributions differ, the distributions themselves overlap, with the result that many women invest more in their human capital than many men invest in their own human capital. Nevertheless, the average woman expects to take more time out of the work force than the average man to raise children, . . . which makes the expected lifetime earnings of the average woman, and hence return to human capital, lower than those of the average man. The average woman will therefore invest less in her human capital, causing her wage to be lower than the average man's, since a part of every wage is repayment of the worker's investment in human capital.

It is possible that the greater propensity of women than men to take time out of the labor force is itself a product of sex discrimination, but I am skeptical of that proposition—I think child-rearing is an area where nature dominates culture—and I do not accept it for purposes of my analysis. However, I will not try to defend this assumption. It is also possible that the propensity will in time disappear, but again I am skeptical, and for the same reason. Even if it does eventually disappear, there can be little doubt that women's current wages are depressed because today's working women did not invest heavily in their human capital when they were young. Table 7-3 in the 1987 Economic Report of the President . . . shows, for example, that while in 1968 only 27.5 percent of young white women expected to be working when they were 35 years old, in 1985 more than 70 percent of these women were working. The table also shows that, by 1979, young women had changed their expectations: almost exactly the same percentage of young women expected to be working at age 35 as were in fact

---

[1] See my book, Richard A. Posner, *Economic Analysis of Law* ch 27 (Little, Brown, 3d ed 1986), for an introduction to the economics of discrimination with references to some of the leading studies.

working at that age in 1985. Since women now have more realistic expectations concerning their labor force participation, we can expect them to invest more heavily in their human capital and therefore earn higher wages in the future. Thus, although the fact that the average woman earns substantially less than the average man is often taken to be prima facie evidence of sex discrimination, it is not, and in any case the differential is likely to decline for reasons unrelated to sex discrimination law.

Finally, I assume that men's and women's utility functions are interdependent, and specifically that women derive a benefit from an increase in the income of a husband or other male relative (son, father, brother, etc.), even if no part of the increased income is consumed by the woman. This qualification is necessary because of the importance of joint consumption in the household. Normally if one spouse's income rises, the other spouse will benefit because so much of the consumption in a household is joint. We thus have separate interdependencies: the "pure" interdependency that results from altruism (the satisfaction that most people experience from an increase in the happiness of a close relative), and the interdependency resulting from joint consumption within the household. For simplicity's sake I shall confine my attention to the interdependencies between wife and husband and ignore other relatives.

It is important to note that the interdependencies between spouses often persist after divorce or the death of a spouse. If a widow's or divorcee's standard of living is a function of her husband's income, increases in that income will increase the wife's welfare. This increase will persist even after a woman is widowed, since her standard of living remains tied to her husband's former income; similarly, a divorced woman's standard of living often remains tied to her former husband's current income. Thus the large percentage of women who are unmarried exaggerates the economic independence of women from men. The vast majority of women marry at some time during their lives, and this is all that is necessary to establish a pervasive economic interdependence between the sexes.[21]

---

[21]In 1986, of all white women 15 years and older, 20.9 percent had never been married, 56.4 percent were married and living with their husband, 2.7 percent were married but not living with their husband, 11.8 percent were widowed, and 8.2 percent were divorced. Rix, The American Woman at 354–55 fig. 2. For black women, the figures are 36.4 percent 32.4 percent, 8.9 percent, 11.6 percent, and 10.8 percent, respectively. . . . In 1986, among all women 55–64 years old, only 3.9 percent had never been married. Statistical Abstract of the United States at 40 table 49. . . . Of course, this figure may decline since fewer women are marrying nowadays. On the changing demographics of American women, see Heidi I. Hartmann, Changes in Women's Economic and Family Roles in Post-World War II United States, in Lourdes Beneria and Catharine R. Stimpson, eds, Women, Households, and the Economy 33 (Rutgers, 1987).

The relationship between majority and minority groups is not characterized by interdependence of either the joint-consumption or altruistic varieties, if only because racial intermarriage remains rare. . . . Interdependence gives the economics of sex discrimination a distinctive cast. To take the extreme case, suppose that all workers were married and that all consumption within the household were joint. Then discrimination against women in the labor force would be compensated for completely in the home, for while wives' wages would be lower than in a nondiscriminatory regime, wives would benefit dollar for dollar from the correspondingly higher wages of their husbands. Of course these assumptions are too strong, and they ignore the fact that a woman's earning power may affect her influence over household expenditure decisions, . . . but they point to an important difference between sex discrimination and the other forms of discrimination with which sex discrimination is often, but perhaps facilely, linked.

The Meaning and the Causes of Sex Discrimination

To avoid building a normative assessment into the word "discrimination," I shall follow the lead of Title VII and define sex discrimination as treating a woman differently from a man because she is a woman, without worrying at the definitional stage about whether the discrimination is invidious on the one hand, or justified or even beneficent on the other. . . . This definition is more problematic than it may appear to be, because it leaves unresolved the question whether it is discriminatory (in a sense pertinent to public policy) to treat a woman differently because of a characteristic that no men but only some women have, such as the capacity to bear children. The Supreme Court in *Gilbert* held that such differentiation was not discriminatory, . . . but the Court was overruled by Congress. I shall follow Congress's approach and assume that discrimination based on pregnancy is a form of sex discrimination—which is not to say, of course, that it necessarily is inefficient.

When discrimination is defined as broadly as I am defining it, the causes are multifarious. Here are the main ones, in (roughly) descending order of invidiousness. The discussion is confined to employment discrimination, the focus of this paper.

Misogyny

By this I mean an elemental distaste on the part of men for associating with women at work, not founded on any notions of productivity or efficiency. The misogynist, as I am using the word, is not someone misinformed about either the average or individual quality of female employees—he just doesn't like them in the workplace, maybe because he has traditional views of "the woman's place." Misogyny may appear to be a taste like any other, and therefore ethically neutral from an economic standpoint—a given. But this is not so clear. Insofar as it is expressed in hostile behavior, it may be more akin to a taste for assault than to a taste for chocolate ice cream. Perhaps misogyny is in between a harmless taste and an actual externality like rape or theft. But the precise status in economics of misogyny is not important to my analysis. To further complicate the picture, I note that a disinclination to associate with women in the workplace need not reflect a dislike of women and could in fact reflect something nearly opposite to dislike—a desire, not necessarily insincere, to protect women from the hardships of the workplace.

Physical or Psychological Aggression

A straightforward case of exploitation, more clearly akin to theft or rape than to misogynistic refusal to accept women workers, is sexual harassment—conduct designed to elicit sexual favors from women against their will. This phenomenon is related to the "conduit" type of discrimination discussed below, because ordinarily it is not the employer himself (more often, itself) who harasses women, but male employees. The employer merely doesn't want to go to the expense of preventing harassment by its employees. More precisely, the required expense would exceed the potential benefit to the employer from not having to compensate female employees for the disutility of being sexually harassed.

Ignorance About the Average Working Woman

A man who is not a misogynist may nevertheless labor under serious misconceptions concerning the abilities of working women. This is especially likely if there are few women in the workplaces with which the man is familiar. This ignorance may be rational, but that is not to say that it is admirable. Indeed, it may be rational for the entire market to be misinformed, because of the well-known externality problems with information. Whom would it pay to develop information about the working qualities of women in general? How would the social benefits of such information be translated into private benefits for the producer of the information? The pioneer in hiring women in a particular segment of the work force may simply be paving the way for his competitors to learn from his mistakes. Notice that in an era of minimum wage (and equal pay) laws, a woman cannot compensate her employer for taking a chance with an unknown quantity by accepting a lower wage. However, the minimum wage is not an important factor in professional and other well-paid employment or in periods such as the present when the minimum wage is far below the average wage.

Monopsony

Married women have high relocation costs when the husband earns more than the wife, as is usually the case. In areas where competition for labor among local employers is weak, these employers may be able to set a monopsonistic wage for female employees, so long as such women represent a large fraction of the female labor force or the employer is able to discriminate among women, paying less to those he believes would have difficulty relocating. Monopsony wage-setting is exploitation of female labor in a straightforward economic sense, although it is less invidious than certain other forms of discrimination because it does not rest on any premise that women are inferior workers to men.

Conduit of Discrimination

In many cases of discrimination the discriminator is merely reflecting the tastes of customers, employees, government agencies, or others with whom the discriminator has a commercial or regulatory relationship. If male employees don't like working with women, or if customers don't like female workers, the employer will perceive these aversions as additional costs of hiring women and will hire fewer of them, or will pay the women a lower wage to compensate the employer for their greater cost.

Statistical Discrimination

Even if employers and their male employees and customers have no discriminatory feelings and are perfectly well informed concerning the average characteristics of women in the various types of job, it may be rational for employers to discriminate against women because of the information costs of distinguishing a particular female employee from the average female employee. For example, the average woman may be physically or emotionally less suited for combat than the average man, even though the two distributions overlap. If it is too costly for the Department of Defense to identify women who are as well suited for combat as the minimally qualified male recruit, the Department may rationally, noninvidiously, decide to exclude all women from combat jobs.

Differentiation Infinitely Costly

Discussions of statistical discrimination normally assume that, while it would not be efficient to ascertain individual qualifications, it would be possible to do so—that is, the cost would not be infinite. But in the case of women, the cost sometimes would be infinite, because the uncertainty is inherent and ineradicable. For example, when an employer hires two 21-year-old workers, one male and one female, he knows that the former, being male, has a shorter life expectancy than the latter, but he doesn't know and ordinarily couldn't discover whether this female will outlive this male. Similarly, he knows that the man is likely to take less sick leave than the woman, . . . but this is just betting on the averages—he doesn't know whether these two workers will track the average experience of male and female workers. If differentiations are to be made, they must be made on a statistical basis.

Three things should be noted about my list of the causes of sex discrimination. The first is that it describes a world without sex discrimination laws; for example, we shall see that the problem of "rational ignorance" would be less serious if there were no Equal Pay Act. The second thing to note is the importance of information costs. Half the causes I have identified are based on such costs: ignorance of the average qualities of women workers, statistical discrimination, and inherent uncertainty. Third, only half the causes reflect market failure in a clear economic sense: monopsonistic exploitation of higher relocation costs, aggression against women, and ignorance of the average qualities of women due to information externalities. The other forms of discrimination are, or at least may be, efficient—which does not necessarily make them good from an ethical standpoint. Misogyny, for example, is a morally unattractive trait, but from an economic standpoint it may be no different in character from having an aversion to cabbage or rutabaga, though then again it may.

Of the three causes of sex discrimination in employment that clearly reflect a market failure, one has little or no contemporary importance: ignorance of the average qualities of women workers. So many women are employed in so many and diverse fields that few employers can be ignorant any longer concerning women's abilities as workers. The time when the law might have done something to eliminate this information externality is long gone. Another cause, high relocation costs conferring monopsony power on employers, has probably never been very important; I do not recall having seen it mentioned in the literature on female employment. The third cause, sexual harassment in the workplace, probably is largely self-correcting. As more and more women are employed, the employer's self-interest in curbing intrigue and harassment, which lower productivity, grows apace.

I conclude that there is no strong theoretical reason to believe that sex discrimination, even if not prohibited by law, would be a substantial source of inefficiency in American labor markets today. If I am correct, then the costs of administering that law will be largely a dead-weight loss, from an economic standpoint. That does not make the law immoral or unjust, but any deadweight losses from law enforcement must be considered in deciding whether a particular law or set of laws furthers the public interest.

Discrimination Trends, Ex Law

How much sex discrimination of any sort could we expect today if there were no sex discrimination laws or other pertinent governmental interventions (for example, subsidies for daycare)? Some, surely; for we have just seen that some, perhaps most, forms of differential treatment are efficient. But sex discrimination would probably be declining, perhaps steeply, even in the absence of any laws against sex discrimination. The engine of decline is the increasing participation of women in the work force. No one thinks that discrimination would keep all women from working, any more than racial discrimination keeps blacks from working. The main effect would be to depress the wages women were paid, lower their fringe benefits, and alter the distribution of women among jobs. There would, however, be some effect on the total number of women employed—more so, indeed, than on the number (as distinct from wages and working conditions) of blacks employed. This is because the elasticity of the supply of labor is higher for women than for men, a phenomenon especially pronounced when a higher percentage of women were married and raising children than is the case today. A married woman, especially with children at home, is in an economic sense "employed" in the home, and her household income will be less if she works in the market. Therefore a small reduction in market wages may keep many women out of the labor market, and conversely a small increase in those wages may draw many women into the labor market.

Women began working in large numbers long before sex discrimination in the workplace was widely criticized, let alone prohibited, and certainly long before sex discrimination ceased to be rampant (some believe it is still rampant). The percentage of the labor force that is female has grown steadily since 1947, . . . and the primary causes of this growth could not be anti-discrimination laws. The other causes of the increased female participation in the work force are by now well-known. With the decline in infant and child mortality, with improved techniques of contraception, and with the advent of inexpensive household labor-saving devices, women spent less time pregnant and raising children and doing household chores, so their opportunity costs of working in the market fell. At the same time, work was becoming less strenuous, in part because the entrance of large numbers of women into the work force increased the demand for services, hence for service workers, who do lighter work than industrial workers. So the demand for female workers rose, and hence their wages rose. As their wages rose, the opportunity costs of pregnancy and child raising rose too, reinforcing the trend toward fewer pregnancies. This in turn reduced the benefits of marriage to both men and women. The improvement in female job opportunities also reduced women's dependence on men. For both reasons, marriage rates fell and divorce rates soared: the former trend increased women's incentive to invest in their human capital, because they were working more; the latter increased the pressure on women to work, both as insurance against divorce and to maintain their standard of living after divorce.

Assuming that the increased female participation in the labor force is largely independent of the laws forbidding sex discrimination, one may ask what effect the increase is likely to have had on the incidence of sex discrimination (still ex law). It should reduce that incidence. First, as more women enter the work force, misconceptions concerning the average qualities of female workers should become less common. Of course, if the misconception consisted of exaggerated [sic] those qualities, women would be worse off by the elimination of the misconception. But the likelier misconception about a class of people not commonly encountered in the work force is that they are not as good as the existing workers, and this misconception would tend to dissipate with the entry of large numbers of that class into all kinds of jobs.

Second, as more wives and daughters enter the work force, we can expect misogyny to decline. Men who love their wives and daughters and empathize with their wives' and daughters' efforts to find work and to cope with misogynistic co-workers or supervisors are less likely to be misogynists in the workplace than if they lacked this family experience. Third, as more women enter the work force, misogynistic employers are placed at a competitive disadvantage: their labor costs are higher than nonmisogynists' because their employment decisions are constrained by misogyny. Fourth, with more and more women workers, sexual harassment becomes more costly. Apart from the impact on productivity noted earlier, a larger fraction of the work force is offended by it, so the total compensating differential that the employer must pay its female employees rises.

As discrimination falls, we can also expect the wage gap between men and women to fall. Another factor working in this direction is the growing value of women's work relative to men's as physical strength becomes a less important labor asset. The declining wage gap among current workers may be masked, however, by an influx of new women workers, since less-experienced workers are paid less than more experienced ones. Thus a reduction in discrimination can actually lower average female wages, rather than, as one would expect, raise them.

Because economic analysis predicts that sex discrimination would have declined and the wage gap between men and women narrowed since 1963, when the first federal sex discrimination law—the Equal Pay Act—was passed, these trends cannot automatically be attributed, even in part, to law. Law may have had little

or even nothing to do with improvements in women's status in the labor force. This suggestion may seem paradoxical: if the law penalizes certain conduct, the economist's "Law of Demand" implies that the conduct will become less frequent. This assumes, however, that the law is effective, and it may not be, for reasons to be examined in the next section.

The effect of sex discrimination laws on discrimination is ultimately an empirical question—and a difficult one. As argued above, discrimination would have declined without those laws—indeed was declining, before those laws were enacted—and it is difficult to isolate the effect of one variable from the others pushing in this direction.

. . . [T]he costs of administering the sex discrimination laws must be factored into any attempt at an overall evaluation of those laws. No laws are costless to enforce, not even ineffectual ones. The burdens that sex discrimination laws place on the courts are substantial and are growing even as discrimination is declining. John Donohue and Peter Siegelman have shown in a recent paper that declining discrimination may be associated with a rise rather than (as one might expect) a fall in the number of cases brought, because as more women are employed in better-paying jobs the gains from suit rise, and because women working side by side with men have a benchmark for proving unequal treatment.[34]

An Economic Examination of Specific Laws and Doctrines

Having sketched the basic sex discrimination laws and the basic economics of sex discrimination, I am prepared to analyze those laws from an economic standpoint. The highly tentative character of the analysis should be self-evident. . . .

Title VII

Two different types of Title VII sex discrimination cases should be distinguished. In a disparate impact case, the employee challenges a practice (for example, a height requirement, or a prohibition, as part of an "anti-nepotism" rule, on hiring employees' spouses) that has a disproportionate exclusionary effect on women, though it was not intended to exclude them. Traditionally, such a practice

[34] See John J. Donohue and Peter Siegelman, The Changing Nature of Employment Discrimination Litigation (Am Bar Found, unpublished April 1989). Their discussion covers racial as well as sexual discrimination and reaches the same conclusion: as blacks move into higher-paid positions and work in integrated jobs, the net expected gains from filing employment discrimination suits rise.

was unlawful unless the employer could show that it was a business necessity; in practice, such a showing was difficult to make. Disparate impact litigation has been important in eliminating personnel practices that tended to exclude blacks (i.e., requiring a high-school diploma), but has not been very important in the area of sex discrimination. Most practices challenged under disparate impact theories involve tests and credentials, and these are rarely sex-biased. Recently, the Supreme Court watered down the "business justification" defense and shifted the burden of proof to the plaintiff, so we can expect disparate impact cases to decline. . . .

The other, and more common, type of sex discrimination case is the disparate treatment case. This requires proof that the employer intentionally treated the female employee (or applicant) less favorably than it would have treated a similarly situated male employee. The practical difficulties in such litigation are great. First, it is difficult to prove a complex counterfactual (for example, what would have happened if the employee had been male rather than female). Second, it often does not pay the plaintiff to invest in the necessary proof—which involves looking at similarly situated males to show that the plaintiff's inadequacies were not responsible for her being fired or otherwise mistreated. . . . The stakes are small. They consist of back-pay minus whatever the plaintiff has earned in a substitute job (for the employee has a duty to mitigate her damages) plus reinstatement. But reinstatement will rarely be sought, since usually the plaintiff will have gotten another job while the litigation was pending and will be reluctant to go back to work for an employer who mistreated her and whom she sued. Finally, bringing an employment suit impairs the plaintiff's earning capacity: employers are reluctant to hire people who sue employers! . . .

Although the plaintiff's costs in bringing successful sex discrimination litigation under Title VII may well outweigh her gains, there is an important qualification. If class action treatment is possible, as where a large employer is alleged to be discriminating against all or most of its female employees, then plaintiffs will find safety in numbers and it will be feasible for them to develop statistical evidence of discrimination. Yet such evidence often is inconclusive. It usually comes down to an unexplained difference in the wages or number of men and women employed, and it is always possible for the employer to argue that the statistical methodology is insufficiently sensitive to identify all noninvidious explanatory variables.

To the extent that disparate treatment suits do succeed, it is uncertain whether they increase the net welfare of women. Since some forms of unlawful sex discrimination are efficient, Title VII litigation will reduce the efficiency with which employers use labor, and this will result in lower average wages and higher product prices. The direct costs of Title VII litigation—lawyers' fees, executive

time, and so forth—will work in the same direction. Full-time housewives will bear a disproportionate share of these costs, since their husbands' wages will fall and the prices they and their husbands pay for goods and services will rise. . . . Conversely, single working women will tend to benefit, except to the extent that employers are reluctant to hire women in the first place out of fear that Title VII will restrict their ability to fire an unsatisfactory female employee without inviting a lawsuit. . . .

Conclusion

What has been the net effect of the cascade of laws and lawsuits aimed at eliminating sex discrimination in employment? This is maddeningly difficult to say, but it is possible that women as a whole have not benefitted and have in fact suffered. Because of the heterogeneity of women as an economic class and their interdependence with men, laws aimed at combating sex discrimination are more likely to benefit particular groups of women at the expense of other groups rather than women as a whole. And to the extent that the overall effect of the law is to reduce aggregate social welfare because of the allocative and administrative costs of the law, women as a group are hurt along with men. Sex discrimination has long been on the decline, for reasons unrelated to law, and this makes it all the more likely that the principal effect of public intervention may have been to make women as a group worse off by reducing the efficiency of the economy. The case for ambitious extensions of sex discrimination law—for example in the direction of comparable worth—is therefore weak.

These suggestions should not be surprising, in light of the extensive, and largely negative, economic literature on regulation. There is a tendency to suppose that laws forbidding discrimination are somehow exempt from the critique of regulation. This position is difficult to sustain.

It is possible that the economic costs of sex discrimination law are offset by gains not measured in an economic analysis—gains in self-esteem, for example. But it is not clear that, if the canvass is broadened in this fashion, the picture brightens. For example, if by reducing the wages of men sex discrimination law propels more wives into the job market, with the result that (since they still bear the principal burden of household production) they work harder, have fewer children, and have less stable marriages, it is not clear that they are better off on balance than they were when their husbands had higher wages and they stayed home. The social, like the economic, consequences of sex discrimination law are murky and not necessarily positive. In any event, it is important to know what the sex discrimination laws cost; the price tag for an increase in women's self-esteem, if known, might be thought too high by society.

Margaret Chon, *Sex Stories—A Review of Sex and Reason by Richard A. Posner,*
62 Geo. Wash. U. L. Rev. 162 (1993) (book review)

(This is an edited version of the article and footnotes are deleted.)*

. . . Posner has a pragmatic goal—to engage in law and economics in order to generate testable hypotheses for the fine-tuning of laws, the consequences of which are judged "by their conformity to social or other human needs." . . . Thus he claims that he wants simply to help increase the sum of human happiness.

But, significantly, the relationship that he posits is that of conquest. Although reason powerfully explains sex, sex does not have much to say about reason. The stories that Posner tells are those of an unremittingly unself-conscious utopian rationalist, squarely within the Enlightenment-as-faith tradition of American social planners. They are inscribed with the Western need to define a "self"—an individual rational self—through the act of setting up the "other." These opposite poles are not simply opposites; they are fundamental to the structuring of knowledge within both the human and natural sciences. One pole of each dualism requires the other; one pole of each dualism dominates the other. Posner continually asserts that reason—specifically, bioeconomic theory—predicts sexual behavior. Thus he does not subvert the dualism of sex and reason (which is what he thinks he is doing) so much as reinforce it. What remains unexamined in his stories are the reasons for privileging reason over sex.

Posner introduces a new scientific tool in this book: bioeconomics. He marries the social scientific methods of law and economics to the evolutionary theory of the biological sciences. The consummation of the science of economics with the science of biology produces an offspring that is a superexplanatory paradigm, even more powerful than each of its parents, perhaps bionic. His decision to invoke the discourse and methods of sociobiology signals his commitment to a rigorous standard of reason as a basis for recommending legal programs.

. . . I want . . . to explore the implications of his exuberant faith in bioeconomic reasoning, unalloyed by any of the late modernist or postmodernist challenges to the nature and limits of science and its transformative potential. In doing so, I attempt three things. First, I discuss some of his sociobiological assertions in order to demonstrate that evolutionary biology consists of a much richer and more contradictory set of assertions than Posner would have us believe. Even within the empiricist framework, therefore, Posner leaves out many stories that could produce a less biased picture of human sexual behavior. Second, I examine these sociobiological "facts" about sex for what they tell us about reason. The stories that Posner tells about human sexual behavior fit into a typology of scientific narrative—one that depends upon the elucidation of an irreducible core of scientific "fact." Human sociobiology, however, is a field so free of fact constraints that a sociobiological "fact" tells us more about the scientist's standpoint than it does about the human social behavior that person is purporting to describe. . . . Posner's reliance upon sociobiology to distance himself from constructivist accounts of human sexuality is, therefore, misplaced. Finally, I analyze how Posner's scientific method defines and delimits the concept of "objectivity" in an unnecessarily constricting fashion. Although he employs the methods of a comparativist (comparing different cultures, different historical epochs, and even different disciplines), he is tied to a view of objectivity that fundamentally denies the possibility of a comparative perspective. His standpoint is that of a putatively detached, uninterested, scientific observer—a standpoint that disables him from appreciating, much less acknowledging, the different perspectives possible even within his native discipline of law and economics. . . . This is glaringly evident, for example, in his responses to various review essays already published. . . .

. . . I am specifically interested in showing the power of modernist thought to subvert itself through the application of reason to reason itself. Judge Posner's stories casually rely on the self-evident superiority of a particular form of scientific knowledge to other forms of knowledge in accounting for material phenomena, resting ironically on a scientific discipline—human sociobiology—that itself is suspect science. . . . Examining his methods exposes his foundational assumptions. Although scientific narratives are not inherently conservative, the particulars of Posner's narrative severely limit the possibilities of human change. More important, however, they deny the relevance and even the existence of any other stories, scientific or not. Posner's insistence that his brand of "reason" is superior to any other form raises the interesting question of why it is that an intelligent, rational, skeptical, secular humanist is unable to critique the logic or appreciate the limitations of his own rather enormous assumptions.

*Editors note: This article is a review of another book by Richard Posner and not a direct response to the article, *An Economic Analysis of Sex Discrimination Laws;* however, the author's critique is relevant to the ideas presented in that piece.

Bioeconomics After the Honeymoon

For those who are not trained as biologists, Carl Degler offers this explanation of how sociobiology approaches the question of sexual behavior:

Insofar as sex differences are concerned, the most relevant sociobiological principle is called differential reproductive strategies. Simply put, it states that males and females, especially among mammals, have different approaches to reproduction because of the nature of sexual reproduction. For females, the cost of reproduction is high, entailing a high investment of energy in the form of large eggs and, most important, long periods of gestation and lactation. For males, reproduction is quick, cheap, and easy. The distinction is the basis of Darwin's principle of sexual selection. . . .

Posner, uses this difference as the primary explanatory principle of human sexual behavior. Men have different sexual strategies from women, that is, different strategies for optimizing the appearance of their genes in the next generation's gene pool. Posner then claims that the cultural differences in sexual behavior can be attributed to just a few additional variables, most important of which is "the changing occupational role of women. . . . " He is an unapologetic determinist—for him, both biology and economics posit a view of human behavior driven by ends that are largely predetermined, although economics is slightly more constructivist than biology is and represents the cultural variation among biologically similar human beings. . . . In the case of biology, that end is the maximization of one's (or one's family's) genes in the gene pool; in the case of economics, that end is the maximization of benefits and minimization of costs to a rational individual. "Both analyze rational behavior in the sense of the fitting of means to ends. . . . "

Sociobiology aside, biological science has the very distinct purpose of attempting to provide explanations of natural, organic phenomena. It is not the primary purpose of biology to provide descriptions, explanations, or— significantly—prescriptions or justifications for human social practices. Even the leading proponent of sociobiology, Edward O. Wilson, cautions that sociobiology is mostly about animals other than humans . . . and that his work is not to be read "uncritically as a tested product of science. . . . " Economics, by contrast, is all about human social behavior, and law, of course, is all about human norms. The tension and incompatibility between the natural sciences and the social sciences, which Judge Posner fails to acknowledge in his use of bioeconomics, is one source of insight into his various methodological biases. Social science, as I will discuss below, is deeply implicated within human social practices in a way that biological science simply cannot be.

Judge Posner repeatedly commits the same basic mistake in his bioeconomic analysis of sex—that is, presuming too much from the "facts" about sex. Just as he errs in inferring scientific kinship from mere resemblance in characteristics, he similarly errs in confounding correlation with causality. Two examples should suffice. Early on, he contends:

[T]he male's promiscuity reduces the danger of incest. The male is not content with one sexual partner, who may happen to be a close relative; and the more sexual partners he has, the less likely are all or most of them to be his close relatives, since a person has only a limited number of close relatives. . . .

Assuming for the purposes of evolutionary theory that optimal male sexual strategies can include promiscuity, this assertion claims far too much. It is true that if a man impregnates women outside his immediate family, the quality, not just the quantity, of the gene pool will increase. The biological explanation for this is that incest is likely to lead to the pairing of recessive genes that carry harmful characteristics, and thus is more likely to lead to less fit individuals. But how does Judge Posner conclude that male promiscuity reduces the likelihood of incest? One could assert just as easily (perhaps even more easily) that male promiscuity is biologically maladaptive because it increases the likelihood of incest by having a male turn from an unrelated companion to kin. The ease with which this assertion can be turned on its head raises a suspicion of a biological apologia for the good old double standard: Male promiscuity is a biologically adaptive response to incest, a biologically maladaptive act. . . .

Another assertion that Posner makes repeatedly is that, "[i]n the economic analysis of sex, women surrender their sexual freedom to men not (or not only) out of altruism or biological predisposition, but in exchange for protection from men. . . . " This assertion underpins his detailed economic analysis of the effect of the American and Swedish welfare policies in discouraging companionate relationships. These programs, as well as the increase in job opportunities for women, have led to "a change in the female sexual strategy. No longer is the male offer of protection as valuable to the female, so women are less willing to provide the commodity used to purchase that protection—female chastity. . . . " Assuming for the purposes of evolutionary theory that optimal female sexual strategies can include ensuring that a man who impregnates her will stick around and take care of her (a distinctively mammalian need because of the relatively long period of gestation and lactation compared to other species), why does this compel a quid pro quo arrangement of sexual sequestration in exchange for protection? As biologists have observed, "among chimpanzees, our closest relatives, the females turn out to be highly promiscuous. . . . " Anthropologist Adrienne Zihlman's interpretation of chimpanzee behavior posits early human groups as matrilocal, mobile societies characterized by impermanent male-female pair bonds which were not dependent on a sharp sexual division of labor. . . . Female promiscuity therefore cannot be rejected out of hand as inconsistent with the goals of the gene to maximize its appearance in succeeding generations.

The prevailing sociobiological accounts of this sexual pact (male protection in return for female monogamy) rely heavily on the notion that a tribe of human beings can only be united through a common identifiable male ancestor. . . . But even as a matter of pure logic, this cannot be the case. A common female ancestor certainly is more readily identifiable than a male ancestor, because progeny issue from her body, and thus matrilineal ancestral claims are practically uncontrovertible. Thus, a common female ancestor could be just as strong a tribal icon as a male ancestor. Moreover, polygyny is not necessarily inconsistent with male care of the young. Sociobiologist Sarah Blaffer Hardy, for example, describes various studies of "male baboons and macaques which, in spite of female promiscuity (or more precisely, matings with multiple but selected partners), were protecting and carrying about selected infants, many of whom but not all were probably their own. . . . "

Both of these examples of Posner's sociobiological reasoning illustrate the tendency of sociobiological explanations of human behavior to prove too much, thus nullifying their persuasiveness. Moreover, these examples show that the large zone of explanatory discretion characteristic of bioeconomic accounts tends to be used to justify certain existing sexual practices, but not to justify equally legitimate opposite inferences that are not apparent in dominant social patterns.

The inferences that are typically left out in sociobiological accounts of human behavior are ones that relate to the sexual practices of a minority of human beings (such as lesbians) or those of a politically or physically less powerful majority (such as women) or those of politically powerless minorities (lesbian women). Posner is not troubled much by this because he believes that the dominant social practices reflect "durable adaptations to deep, though not necessarily innate or genetic, human capacities, drives, needs, and interests. . . . " But his lack of speculation over what isn't reveals a fatal reductionism. Despite his claims to neutrality and objectivity, Posner collapses the biological "fact" (male reproductive strategies, which are consistent with promiscuity) into the social "fact" (near-universal incest taboos), in a highly simplistic and logically questionable fashion. He also collapses the biological "fact" (long human female

lactation periods) into prevailing social norms (female chastity), although he claims to be motivated strictly by rational and not moral concerns.

The observation that a different scientist could take the same "facts" and construct a different theoretical explanation for them is hardly startling. . . . But another problem with Judge Posner's facts stems from the distinct logical weaknesses of sociobiology as a subset of evolutionary biology. There are many questionable links in the inferential chain, beginning with the difficulty in describing the relevant behavior that leads to evolutionary change. . . . By focusing on one set of behavioral facts to the exclusion of others, the scientist risks proposing an explanatory theory that has little, if anything at all, to do with the processes of evolution.

In Posner's sociobiological descriptions of human sexual behavior, for example, he relies on male competition rather than female choice as the significant behavior from an evolutionary standpoint. As explained succinctly by biologist Stephen Jay Gould:

> Darwin delineated two modes of sexual selection, called "male competition" and "female choice." In male competition—e.g., among antlered deer—males fight like hell and the winners get the females. In female choice males strut and preen, display and bellow, and females choose to mate with the individuals that impress them most. Peacocks, in other words, do not evolve their showy tails for direct victory in battle over other males, but to win a beauty contest run by females. . . .

Posner puts men in the driver's seat of evolution (much as some feminist legal scholars theorizing about sex from a purely constructivist stance do with respect to power relations between men and women). But if one decides to focus on female animal behavior—particularly in other primates—one may find that the sexual selection process may be explained just as adequately through a female choice model. . . . Whatever construct is more descriptive of human sexual behavior, it is nonetheless revealing that Posner chooses not to discuss women as active decisionmakers until the transition from what he calls stage two to stage three (from women who function primarily as childrearers in companionate marriages to women who participate in the wage labor market). An imprimatur of male competition throughout thousands of years of biological evolution and cultural development is thus stamped on Posner's bioeconomic history of sexuality. But this is only one possible story of human evolution, even within the parameters of biology itself. . . . And outside the parameters of sociobiology, others have documented the historical contingency of the male competition model. . . .

> ## Problem 40
>
> Maria Sanchez wants to be a successful salesperson at her department store. She knows that the Appliance Department salesmen make far more money on commissions than she can possibly make as a salesperson in the Linen or the Clothing Department. She also knows that she has a very slim chance of being accepted as a salesperson in the Appliance Department because the personnel director has actively discouraged her from applying for the position. He tells her that she would have to learn a lot about appliances and that she would be working on commission. He told her that commissions are a very risky way for a single parent like her to make a living since "you never know whether the money is going to come in this week."

2. The *Sears* Case

In a case that received national attention, the U.S. District Court for the Northern District of Illinois held that the Equal Employment Opportunity Commission failed to prove that Sears, Roebuck & Company discriminated against the women in its sales force. The EEOC claimed that Sears was involved in a pattern and practice of sex discrimination when it failed to hire or promote female applicants for commission selling jobs on the same basis as male applicants and when it paid female salaried employees less than similarly situated male employees. The case has been extensively edited; those particularly interested in the methodology used to analyze the statistical data presented should consult the full case. Most of the extensive footnotes from the case have been deleted.

EQUAL EMPLOYMENT OPPORTUNITY COMMISSION
v.
SEARS, ROEBUCK & CO.
628 F. Supp. 1264 (N.D. Ill. 1986)

[The Employment Problem]

Sears is the nation's largest retailer of general merchandise, employing approximately 380,000 persons in over 4,000 facilities across the country. During the relevant time period, Sears had approximately 920 retail stores. . . . Its corporate headquarters was located in Chicago, Illinois. Between 1973 and 1980, the relevant time period, Sears was divided into five territories: Eastern, Midwestern, Pacific Coast, Southern, and Southwestern.

General corporate policies at Sears are formulated at the corporate headquarters, communicated to the territorial organizations, and eventually disseminated to individual stores.

Commission Sales at Sears

During 1973–1980, Sears retail stores were divided into approximately 55 retail divisions. Salespersons in these divisions were paid either on a commission or noncommission basis. Merchandise sold on commission was usually much more expensive and complex than merchandise not sold on commission. Commission selling usually involved "big ticket" items, meaning high cost merchandise, such as major appliances, furnaces, air conditioners, roofing, tires, sewing machines, etc. Noncommission selling normally involved lower priced "small ticket" items, such as apparel, linens, toys, paint, and cosmetics. . . .

After 1977 . . . Sears changed its method of compensating commission salespersons to a "salary plus commission" basis. This change was implemented primarily to reduce the financial risk of selling on commission in an effort to attract more women to commission sales. Under this system, the salesperson earned a nominal salary plus a three percent commission. However, the salesperson's income was still substantially dependent on the amount of sales made, and failure to make sufficient sales could result in termination.

Noncommission salespeople were compensated on a straight hourly rate, except that a nominal 1% commission was earned by full-time salespersons on all sales until January 1979. Throughout the period from 1973 through 1980, full-time and part-time commission salespersons on average earned substantially more than full-time and part-time noncommission salespersons. . . .

Qualifications for Commission Sales Positions

No written document at Sears specifically identifies the qualifications for commission sales positions. Sears' Retail Testing Manual . . . contains the only written description of a desirable commission sales candidate. The commission salesperson is described as a "special breed of cat," with a sharper intellect and more powerful personality than most other retail personnel. According to the manual, a good commission salesperson possesses a lot of drive and physical vigor, is socially dominant, and has an outgoing personality and the ability to approach easily persons they do not know. A good commission salesperson needs the ability to react quickly to a customer's verbal suggestions and modify the approach accordingly. Thus, according to the Retail Testing Manual, a higher level of "salesmanship" is required of the commission salesperson than is required of the general salesperson.

However, the Retail Testing Manual generally was not relied on to any significant extent in selecting commission salespersons. Most managers and interviewers relied far more heavily on past experience with commission salespeople. Many managers and personnel employees involved in the hiring process testified about the qualities they sought in commission sales people based on their own experience and the experience of their superiors.

First, in reviewing applications to identify potential commission sales candidates, Sears managers and interviewers look for: prior commission selling experience, prior experience selling a product line sold on commission at Sears, any specific indication of interest in commission sales, knowledge or experience of any kind in a product line, availability during the hours required for a particular job, a work or personal background reflecting a history of achievement, prior experience involving significant public contact, and any special training, education, or experience indicating an active, outgoing personality. Previous product line experience was particularly important when there was a commission sales vacancy in an installed home improvements division, the automotive divisions, or custom draperies.

However, most of the essential qualities for commission selling could be determined only from an interview, not from a written application. As will be discussed below, all candidates were interviewed at least twice before being hired. During the interview, managers looked for a number of important qualities, including aggressiveness or assertiveness, competitiveness, the ability to communicate effectively, persuasiveness, an outgoing, social, or extroverted personality, self-confidence, personal dominance, a strong desire to earn a substantial income, resilience and the ability to deal with rejection, a high level of motivation and enthusiasm for the job, maturity, and a good personal appearance. The extent that each of these characteristics was required depended on the particular job opening. However, one critical prerequisite for all commission sales jobs was availability during the required hours. An otherwise qualified individual could be rejected if he was not available during the hours required for the particular job. Each manager and interviewer used his best judgment to choose applicants with the best combination of these qualities for each job. However, as with all hiring decisions at Sears, the qualifications sought in commission sales applicants were often modified or relaxed to comply with Sears' Affirmative Action Plan, described below. . . .

It was Sears' policy to extend an initial interview to each applicant as a courtesy, whether or not a position was available at the time. This initial interview was often conducted at the personnel counter when the applicant handed in a completed application. The interviewers were usually experienced personnel department employees. The great majority of Sears' interviewers were women.

The content of the initial interview varied from store to store, but often applicants were not informed of specific openings during this interview. The interviewer attempted to glean basic information from the applicant, such as availability for work and areas of interest. The interviewer often wrote comments on the applications regarding the applicant's personal interests, qualifications, or suitability for a particular position. In some cases, the interviewer would convey her comments to the personnel manager orally.

The second step of the hiring process involved a second interview and sometimes testing. Procedures for moving to this second step varied among stores. At some stores, the initial interviewer screened applications on the basis of factors such as availability, prior job experience, and affirmative action requirements before moving applicants to the second stage. At other stores, the store personnel manager reviewed all applications before deciding whether a second interview or testing was appropriate. At still other stores, applications were screened by various members of the personnel staff.

However, despite this variation in the mechanics of the process, at all stores, the most important part of the hiring process was the second interview. This interview was usually conducted by the store's personnel manager and normally lasted approximately one-half hour. The interviewer would evaluate the applicant's personal characteristics, such as appearance, manner, assertiveness, friendliness, ability to communicate, motivation, and overall potential. Various job openings might be discussed with the applicant at this time.

Following this interview, the applicant might also be interviewed by the appropriate division manager or merchandise manager and in some cases by the store manager. However, the personnel manager's recommendation was followed in most cases. . . .

Finally, all aspects of the hiring process, from the initial interview to the final selection of a candidate for commission sales, were highly influenced by the requirements of Sears' stringent affirmative action programs.

Affirmative Action at Sears

Sears has for many years had a far ranging and effectively enforced affirmative action program. Sears was the first major retail employer in the nation to institute an affirmative action program. Sears' program became a model plan followed by other corporations in the retail industry and in other industries as well. . . .

In February, 1973, A. Dean Swift became president of Sears. One of his first actions as president was to call a conference of Sears' top 250 executives, for

the first time in 23 years, to discuss affirmative action. The topic of the conference was the personal accountability of managers for affirmative action. . . . Out of this conference grew the Mandatory Achievement of Goals (MAG) Plan. The MAG Plan set long term goals for both timecard and checklist women. To meet these goals for timecard employees (including commission sales), the Plan required that managers fill one out of every two positions with women or minorities. When jobs were vacated by women or minorities, the Plan required replacement-in-kind. . . .

In 1977, Sears raised its long range goal for women from 38 percent to 40 percent for all jobs at Sears except craft-type jobs, for which the long range goal was 20 percent. In 1979, Sears added to its checklist affirmative action program the requirement that 50 percent of all openings be filled by women and minorities. Prior to that time, there were too few qualified female and minority candidates in line for checklist promotions to make this a realistic goal.

In addition to imposing these hiring and promotion goals, in 1972, Sears implemented an Equal Pay Affirmative Action Plan. Under the plan, a nationwide formula was established for setting timecard salary to ensure that male and female timecard employees received equal pay. Task forces, a majority of whose members were women, conducted audits in every store and had complete authority to make on-the-spot pay changes. In 1974, Sears also developed its "Equitable Pay Package," which consisted of administrative procedures designed to ensure uniform application of wage scales to male and female employees.

The sincere dedication and commitment of Sears management at all levels to affirmative action was evident from the testimony of the Sears' officials and employees, whom the court found to be highly credible witnesses. . . . Sears' program exceeded the requirements of Title VII or any other governmental regulation. Sears' specific efforts to place women in commission sales will be discussed below.

[The Decision by the Trial Court]

This opinion marks the culmination of a lengthy dispute between the Equal Employment Opportunity Commission (EEOC) and Sears, Roebuck & Co. (Sears), the world's largest retail seller of general merchandise. In 1973, an EEOC commissioner's charge was filed. After an extensive investigation and extensive conciliation discussions, EEOC filed this suit in 1979, alleging nationwide discrimination by Sears against women in virtually all aspects of its business, in violation of Title VII of the Civil Rights Act of 1964, as amended, 42 U.S.C. § 2000e et seq. (Title VII), and the Equal Pay Act, 29 U.S.C. § 206(d).

This is a case of claimed statistical disparities. As originally filed, this suit involved 42 distinct claims of nationwide sex discrimination by Sears. By the time of trial, EEOC had abandoned all of its Equal Pay Act claims, and all but two of its claims under Title VII. The two allegations EEOC sought to prove at trial were that Sears engaged in a nationwide pattern or practice of sex discrimination: (1) by failing to hire female applicants for commission selling on the same basis as male applicants, and by failing to promote female noncommission salespersons into commission sales on the same basis as it promoted male noncommission salespersons into commission sales (commission sales claim); and (2) by paying female checklist management employees in certain job categories lower compensation than similarly situated male checklist management employees (checklist compensation claim). . . . The allegations are limited to the time period beginning March 3, 1973 and ending December 31, 1980. A trial before the court was held lasting 10 months. The court observed each witness, made extensive contemporaneous trial notes of the testimony of each witness, and made specific determinations of the credibility of each witness and the weight to be given to the testimony as the witness testified. . . . The court has drawn what it believes to be the correct reasonable inferences from this evidence and has evaluated the legal principles presented by the parties and developed through legal research of the court.

Based on all of the testimony presented, the credibility of the witnesses and the weight to be given their testimony, the exhibits received in evidence, and the law governing this case, the court concludes that the EEOC has failed to prove its case on either claim of discrimination and finds that Sears has not discriminated against women in hiring, promotion, or pay, as claimed. . . .

Statistics

In General

Virtually all the proof offered by the EEOC in this case is statistical in nature, or related to the statistical evidence. Statistics are an accepted form of circumstantial evidence of discrimination. In some cases, where "gross disparities" are shown, statistics alone may constitute a *prima facie* case. . . . However, as the Court in *Teamsters* cautioned, "statistics are not irrefutable; they

come in an infinite variety and, like any other kind of evidence, they may be rebutted. In short, their usefulness depends on all of the surrounding facts and circumstances." 431 U.S. at 340.

Statistical evidence, like other evidence, must not be accepted uncritically. The usefulness of statistics depends to a large extent on "the existence of proper supportive facts and the absence of variables which would undermine the reasonableness of the inference of discrimination which is drawn. . . . " Inaccuracies or variations in data or in the formulae used to test such data may easily lead to different, contradictory, or even misleading conclusions by experts. Courts therefore must carefully evaluate all the assumptions and data underlying the statistical analyses to determine whether they are sufficiently related to reality to provide any useful information to the court.

As this case will demonstrate, the assumptions made by a statistician in formulating a model can be far more important than the numerical complexities and results of the analysis. Without a sound theoretical basis, which is carefully reasoned and closely tailored to the factual circumstances of the case, the statistical results can be meaningless. Close attention will therefore be paid in this case to the assumptions made by the experts and their relation to reality.

Statistical Significance

In view of the highly statistical nature of the EEOC's proof in this case, a short discussion of a few relevant statistical principles is necessary.

An important concept to bear in mind in evaluating any statistical analysis is that no statistical analysis can prove causation *per se*. Statistical experts on both sides of this case have readily admitted this. Rather than attempting to prove what caused the results obtained from their analyses, statisticians endeavor to estimate the likelihood that the results occurred merely by chance. In statistical terms, they attempt to measure the level of statistical significance of their results.

One commonly used measure of statistical significance, the likelihood that the result occurred by chance, is the standard deviation. The standard deviation measures how much a typical observation varies from the average of all observations. D. Barnes, *A Commonsense Approach to Understanding Statistical Evidence*, 21 San Diego L. Rev. 809 (1984). A standard deviation of 2 indicates that there is a .045 probability (that is, almost a 5% probability), that the results observed occurred due to chance. A standard deviation of 3 represents a .003 probability, and a standard deviation of 4 represents a .006 probability that the result occurred by chance.

Statisticians generally consider results to be statistically significant at two or three standard deviations. However, statistical significance merely indicates that chance is not likely to have caused the result. As EEOC's expert, Dr. Siskin, testified, statistical significance and practical significance are two completely different concepts. Statistical significance can be determined merely by calculating the standard deviation or some other test statistic. To determine the practical significance of statistical results, a court must look at the theories and assumptions underlying the analysis and apply common sense.

Courts have not blindly adopted any test of statistical or practical significance. In *Castaneda v. Partida*, 430 U.S. 482, 496 n.17 (1977), and *Hazelwood School District v. United States*, 433 U.S. at 308 n.14, 311 n.17, the Court indicated that, as a general rule, if the observed result is more than 2 or 3 standard deviations from the expected or average value, a hypothesis that the result occurred by chance is suspect. However, the Court has not laid down any hard and fast rules for evaluating statistical or practical significance in every case, and the Court's "2 or 3" standard deviation approach should be applied with caution. *See* D. Baldus and J. Cole, *Statistical Proof of Discrimination* 294–95 nn.12–13 (1980). The Seventh Circuit has recommended using "extreme caution" in drawing any conclusions from statistical significance at a two-to-three standard deviation level. *Coates*, 756 F.2d at 547 n.22. *See also EEOC v. American National Bank*, 652 F.2d 1176, 1198 (4th Cir. 1981), *cert. denied*, 459 U.S. 923 (1982). The *Coates* court recognized that courts are not required to conclude from low standard deviations that the statistics conclusively prove discrimination, particularly when the statistical model is not well adapted to the facts. *Coates*, 756 F.2d at 547 n.22. *See Teamsters*, 431 U.S. at 340 (the usefulness of statistics depends on surrounding facts and circumstances). The court will therefore carefully examine the models underlying the statistical analyses before attributing practical significance to standard deviations in the 2 to 3 range. As a guide for discussion, however, this court will generally consider that differences between actual and expected values that exceed 3 standard deviations may be statistically significant. However, it is important to emphasize that the standard deviation and other measures of statistical significance merely attempt to eliminate chance as the reason for the results. They do not prove what in fact caused the results. . . .

As discussed above, the assumptions underlying any statistics must be critically examined by the court. In a regression analysis, this requires a careful evaluation of the variables included in the model, the ability to accurately measure these variables, and the importance of variables not included in the model, including variables which cannot be measured on a mathematical scale. In short, the court must evaluate "the fit" of the model to the reality of the facts and circumstances. *See* T. J. Campbell, *Regression Analysis in Title VII Cases: Minimum Standards, Comparable Worth, and Other Issues Where Law and Statistics Meet*, 36 Stan. L. Rev. 1299, 1305–09 (1984). . . .

The court therefore will carefully examine the factors included and excluded from the regression analyses in this case, and the weight given to measures of statistical significance will depend upon the fit of the statistical model to the actual hiring and compensation practices of Sears.

Finally, it is important to recognize at the outset the limitations of statistical analyses when evaluating complex decision making processes. Although mathematical models such as those used in regression analyses can provide useful information in appropriate circumstances, the intricacies of human decision making often cannot be reduced to mathematical formulae. The more complex the decision making, the less accurate a regression model will generally be. Thus, statistical analyses can be quite accurate when used to analyze relatively simple fact situations, such as when a job requires only a small number of minimum objective job qualifications. However, as will be seen below, as more qualifications and subjective factors are required, mathematical models are less able to accurately analyze the decision making process.

Hiring and Promotion into Commission Sales

EEOC attempted to prove at trial that Sears intentionally discriminated against women in hiring and promotion into commission sales on a nationwide basis from 1973 until 1980. Both parties have analyzed separately those hired directly into commission sales and those promoted to commission sales from other jobs at Sears. Full-time and part-time positions in each category were also analyzed separately. The court will structure its analysis accordingly. . . .

EEOC's Evidence: Hiring into Commission Sales
Nonstatistical Evidence

Despite the comprehensive, nationwide scope of its lawsuit, EEOC did not produce any victims of discrimination by Sears, or any persons who claimed they witnessed discrimination against women by Sears. EEOC points, instead, to two aspects of Sears' selection process to support its statistical analyses: the subjective nature of Sears' selection process, and its testing practices. First, EEOC asserts that the absence of objective criteria for selection provides a ready mechanism for discrimination. It presented evidence showing a lack of written guidelines for selection of commission salespersons, and the lack of formal training of interviewers, both of which permitted subjective hiring decisions. The interviewers, most of whom were women, were formally trained primarily on nondirective interview techniques designed to encourage the applicant to "open up" during the interview. No formal instruction was provided regarding the qualities to look for in commission sales candidates. Interviewers were expected to learn the desirable characteristics for commission salespersons from observation of those persons presently selling on commission, and from managers' guidance as to the types of individuals who had been successful in the past.

EEOC also relies on Sears' Retail Testing Manual, discussed above, which apparently contains the only written descriptions of the desirable characteristics of a commission salesperson. EEOC focuses on the original version of the manual, issued in 1953, which describes a commission salesperson as a man who is "active," "has a lot of drive," possesses "considerable physical vigor," "likes work which requires physical energy," etc. References to males were eliminated in the 1960's. The present version is otherwise substantially similar in content to the original version.

EEOC also presented evidence of Sears' testing practices, EEOC focused its presentation on the Vigorous Dimension of the Thurstone Temperament Schedule. Some of the questions from which the vigor score is determined would more likely be answered affirmatively by males. . . .

Analysis of EEOC's Evidence: Hiring . . .

Faulty Basic Assumptions

Even more important than EEOC's errors in constructing its data base and adjusting for factors important to commission sales hires, EEOC's statistical analyses are based on two essential assumptions for which there is no credible support in the record. In designing all of his statistical analyses relating to commission sales, Dr. Siskin made the important assumptions that (1) all male and female sales applicants are equally likely to accept a job offer for all commission sales positions at Sears, and (2) all male and female sales applicants are equally qualified for all commission sales positions at Sears. Plaintiff's Siskin Exhibit 12; EEOC Commission Sales Report at 4. The court finds that both of these assumptions were proven untrue. Without these assumptions, EEOC's statistical analyses are virtually meaningless.[35]

Assumption of Equal Interest

EEOC has offered no credible evidence to support its assumption of equal interest by male and female applicants in all commission sales positions at Sears. Sears, on the other hand, has offered much credible evidence that employees' and applicants' interests, preferences and aspirations are extremely important in determining who applies for and accepts commission sales jobs at Sears. Sears has proven, with many forms of evidence, that men and women tend to have different interests and aspirations regarding work, and that these differences explain in large part the lower percentage of women in commission sales jobs in general at Sears, especially in the particular divisions with the lowest proportion of women selling on commission.

The most credible and convincing evidence offered at trial regarding women's interest in commission sales at Sears was the detailed, uncontradicted testimony of numerous men and women who were Sears store managers, personnel managers and other officials, regarding their efforts to recruit women into commission sales. As discussed above, attracting women to commission sales has been an important priority in Sears' affirmative action programs since the first affirmative action questionnaire was circulated in 1968. Sears managers and other witnesses with extensive store experience over the entire relevant time pe-

---

[35]In essence, EEOC's statistical case is based on the erroneous underlying presupposition that all relevant Sears employee applicants and hires, as well as the jobs involved, are fungible. It is assumed that, not only are all the jobs alike, but also all men and women are exactly alike except for a few specific simplified characteristics that have been somewhat quantified in a limited way. Since the attempt to differentiate between men and women applicants and hires is inadequate, and no attempt is made to distinguish between jobs, this results in misleading statistics that do not accurately reflect the considerations and decisions that actually go into the individual hiring process for each Sears employee for each job in each store and unit throughout the vast Sears organization. *See, e.g.*, Written Direct Testimony of Dr. David A. Wise. EEOC's pay analysis suffers from the same erroneous presupposition and analysis.

riod testified that far more men than women were interested in commission selling at Sears. Numerous managers described the difficulties they encountered in convincing women to sell on commission. . . . Sears managers continually attempted to persuade women to accept commission selling or other non-traditional jobs. Women who expressed an interest in commission selling were given priority over men when an opening occurred. Managers attempted to persuade even marginally qualified women to accept commission selling positions. They would sometimes guarantee a woman her former position if she would try commission selling for a certain period. Store managers reported that they had interviewed every woman in the store and none were willing to sell on commission. Managers often had to "sell" the job to reluctant women, even though enthusiasm and interest in the positions were qualities management valued highly in commission salespeople. Despite these unusual efforts, managers had only limited success in attracting women to commission sales.

Female applicants who indicated an interest in sales most often were interested in selling soft lines of merchandise, such as clothing, jewelry, and cosmetics, items generally not sold on commission at Sears. Male applicants were more likely to be interested in hard lines, such as hardware, automotive, sporting goods and the more technical goods, which are more likely to be sold on commission at Sears. These interests generally paralleled the interest of customers in these product lines. Men, for example, were usually not interested in fashions, cosmetics, linens, women's or children's clothing, and other household small ticket items. Women usually lacked interest in selling automotives and building supplies, men's clothing, furnaces, fencing and roofing. Women also were not as interested as men in outside sales in general, . . . and did not wish to invest the time and effort necessary to learn to sell in the home improvements divisions. . . .

Custom draperies, however, was one division in which women were willing to sell on a commission basis, even though it could require some outside selling. More women were willing to sell custom draperies on commission because they enjoyed the fashion and creative aspect of the job, most had past experience in the field, and it was a relatively low pressure commission division. Applicants expressing an interest in the division were almost all women. Very few men were willing to sell draperies.

The percentage of women hired in the various categories generally paralleled their interests and background in the product line involved. This illus-

trates how much an applicant's interest in the product sold can influence his willingness to accept a particular commission sales position. As is evident from the above discussion, interests of men and women often diverged along patterns of traditional male and female interest.

This lack of interest of women in commission sales was confirmed by the number of women who rejected commission sales positions. Although evidence was presented only for the Eastern territory, this evidence showed that many women turned down commission sales job offers or otherwise expressly indicated that they were not interested in commission selling at Sears.[39]

Women at Sears who were not interested in commission sales expressed a variety of reasons for their lack of interest. Some feared or disliked the perceived "dog-eat-dog" competition. Others were uncomfortable or unfamiliar with the products sold on commission. There was fear of being unable to compete, being unsuccessful, and of losing their jobs. Many expressed a preference for noncommission selling because it was more enjoyable and friendly. They believed that the increased earnings potential of commission sales was not worth the increased pressure, tension, and risk. . . .

Sears' evidence also demonstrated that women's attitudes toward work changed measurably between 1970 and 1980. During this time, significant changes occurred in the sexual compositions of the workforce. The number of females in many traditionally male-dominated fields doubled or tripled (e.g., securities and financial services salespeople, lawyers, hardware and building supplies). The female proportion of college students majoring in business subjects rose from 10 percent to nearly one-third in each category. Sears evidence also showed that, by the late 1970s, women were more open to commission sales positions than in the early 1970s, but it was still necessary to "sell" the job to them in many cases. Some reasons for the increased willingness of women to accept commission sales jobs were: (1) commission sales jobs changed from being almost exclusively full time to largely part time, and many more women preferred to work part time; (2) the change in compensation for commission

---

[39] . . . EEOC also argues that evidence of female job refusals is not helpful unless the number of male refusals is also known. However, even without data on male refusals, this evidence corroborates Sears' witnesses' testimony that sincere and extensive efforts were made to recruit women into commission sales, and that many women were not interested.

sales from draw versus commission to salary plus commission, which reduced the risk perceived by some women in commission selling; (3) a group of successful commission saleswomen that over time provided role models for other women; and (4) the increased availability of daycare, which increased the hours many women were available to work. Thus, female interest in and availability for commission sales increased during the period from 1973 through 1980.

In addition, specific surveys of the interests of Sears employees reveal that far more men than women are interested in commission sales. Sears has taken regular morale surveys of its employees in every retail store approximately once every three years since 1939. . . . Sears has also conducted a number of special surveys to ascertain employee opinions on particular subjects. . . .

Conclusions Regarding Commission Sales Claim: Hiring

Viewing all of this evidence together, considering the credibility of the witnesses and the reasonableness of their testimony, the court finds that EEOC has failed to carry its burden of persuasion on this claim. Its statistical evidence is wholly inadequate to support its allegations. The evidence is replete with flaws which, if any were considered alone, might invalidate the statistical conclusions. Together, all of these flaws leave the analysis with little probative value.

The most eggregious flaw is EEOC's failure to take into account the interests of applicants in commission sales and products sold on commission at Sears. EEOC turned a blind eye to reality in constructing its artificial, overinclusive "sales" pool, and assuming away important differences in interests and in qualifications. The court finds that, because of these errors, EEOC's highly inadequate coding of data available to it, and the other problems with the analyses discussed above, the results of EEOC's statistical analyses are entitled to little weight.

Moreover, evidence presented by Sears provided a more reasonable basis for evaluating Sears, and showed that Sears met all reasonable estimates of the proportion of qualified and interested women. Its evidence demonstrated that, when interest and qualifications are taken into account, EEOC's alleged disparities are virtually eliminated.

Equally important, EEOC has failed to counter Sears' highly convincing evidence of its affirmative action programs. Sears has proven that it has had a long and serious commitment to affirmative action, which applied to the recruitment of women for its commission sales force. Sears' affirmative action evidence established that, not only were women much less interested in commission sales at Sears than men, but also, more importantly, Sears did not have any intent to discriminate against women. Sears' affirmative action efforts to recruit women to commission sales went much further than is required by law. EEOC has not presented any credible evidence to cast doubt on the commitment of Sears to affirmative action. The court therefore finds that Sears' evidence of its strictly enforced affirmative action programs is strong evidence that it did not in fact intentionally discriminate against women.

Finally, notably absent from EEOC's presentation was the testimony of any witness who could credibly claim that Sears discriminated against women by refusing to hire or promote women into commission sales. It is almost inconceivable that, in a nationwide suit alleging a pattern and practice of intentional discrimination for at least eight years involving more than 900 stores, EEOC would be unable to produce even one witness who could credibly testify that Sears discriminated against her. . . . EEOC's total failure to produce any alleged victim of discrimination serves only to confirm the court's conclusion that no reasonable inference of sex discrimination can be drawn from EEOC's statistical evidence regarding hiring into commission sales.

Therefore, based on all of the evidence presented, the court concludes that EEOC has failed to prove that Sears had a pattern or practice of intentionally discriminating against women in hiring into commission sales. On the contrary, the court finds that Sears has proven that it did not have such a pattern or practice. Further, Sears has proven legitimate, non-discriminatory reasons for the alleged statistical disparities between the hiring of men and women into commission sales from 1973 until 1980, and EEOC has not proven them pretextual. . . .

[Discussion of Promotions Claim is Omitted]

Questions

1. The court found that the EEOC had made two faulty assumptions: (1) that all male and female sales applicants are equally likely to accept a job offer for all commission sales positions at Sears and (2) that all male and female sales applicants are equally qualified for all commission sales positions at Sears. What do you think of these assumptions? Are they important to the case? What are the costs of these assumptions?
2. Why do you think the EEOC presented only evidence based on statistics rather than evidence

from witnesses who wanted to be refrigerator saleswomen but had been denied the opportunity to be a commissioned salesperson? What is the significance of a court ruling that bases its finding on a statistical disparity like this?

3. How would Posner, Chon, and Browne analyze this case?

C. The Family and Medical Leave Act (FMLA)

Problem 41

George Anderson, a truck driver for a grocery store, takes four weeks' leave to care for his father, who is deeply depressed after a family member's murder. The father does not feel better after the four weeks' leave, and George and the employer agree that George should resign. Six months later he is rehired, but his seniority is not reinstated; he is probationary just as any new hire is. George sues, contending that the FMLA entitles him to reinstatement at the same level of benefits, including seniority.

Problem 42

Mary Allen, a factory employee, attempts suicide and thereafter is hospitalized for depression for a week. While she is hospitalized, she informs the plant manager of her suicide attempt and her hospitalization, and he places her on paid leave. On her return the following week, however, the personnel manager, who is aware of her hospitalization and the reasons for it, fires Mary. He tells her that the grounds are that her suicide attempt shows that she is too irresponsible to discharge her responsibilities at the plant.

The Family and Medical Leave Act (FMLA) requires covered employers to provide up to 12 weeks of unpaid leave per year to qualifying employees to attend to their own or family members' serious health condition. A serious health condition is defined as an illness, injury, impairment, or physical or mental condition that requires either (a) inpatient care at a hospital, hospice, or residential care facility and follow-up care from the same, including convalescence, or (b) continuing treatment by a health care provider if it involves one of the following five situations:

1. a period of incapacity exceeding three consecutive calendar days where treatment was required two or more times by a health care provider or practitioner, or where treatment occurred once but was followed by a regimen of continuing treatment on medical orders;
2. a period of incapacity due to pregnancy or for prenatal care;

3. a chronic condition requiring treatment that requires periodic visits or treatments by a health care provider, that continues for an extended period, and that may cause episodic rather than consistent incapacity (such as epilepsy or asthma);

4. a permanent or long-term period of incapacity because of a condition for which treatment may be ineffective (such as a stroke or terminal illness); or

5. a condition requiring multiple treatments, including convalescence from treatment, where treatment was required by a health care provider to restore function or to treat a condition that, if untreated, would likely result in more than three consecutive days' absence (such as chemotherapy or dialysis).

29 C.F.R. § 825.114(a)(1), (2). Routine physical examinations do not qualify as "treatments." 29 C.F.R. § 825.114(b). Neither do cosmetic measures. 29 C.F.R. § 825.114(c).

This leave may be taken on a sporadic or "intermittent" basis until it totals 12 weeks, or it may be taken in a block. The employee is entitled to reinstatement upon return from leave to the same or an equivalent position. 29 U.S.C. § 2614(a). If the employee is unable to perform an essential function of the job because of her serious health condition, however, the employer is not obliged to reinstate her. 29 C.F.R. § 825.214(b). *See also Tardie v. Rehabilitation Hosp.*, 168 F.3d 538 (1st Cir. 1999) (ability to work overtime can be an essential job function); *Williams v. Saad's Heatlhcare*, 2000 362038 not reported in F.Supp.2d (S.D. Ala. Mar. 16, 2000) (unlike ADA, FMLA does not contain a "reasonable accommodation" provision). The employer may also refuse to reinstate, and immediately replace, "key employees" whose absence would cause "substantial and grievous economic injury" to the employer. 29 U.S.C. § 2614(b). A key employee is defined as one whose salary is among the top 10% of all employees within 75 miles of the employee's worksite. Id.

1. The Duty to Provide Notice Under the FMLA

The notice requirements imposed on the employee by the FMLA are exceedingly light. An employee need not tell the employer that he is seeking FMLA leave specifically; there is no requirement that he mention the FMLA by name in order to evoke its protections. 29 C.F.R. §§ 825.302(c), .303(b). The employee has given sufficient notice if he merely states that he needs leave for a reason that potentially qualifies for FMLA protection. It is the employer's job to ascertain whether the reason for which the employee seeks leave is an FMLA-qualifying one. 29 C.F.R. §§ 825.302(c), .303(b). If the employer had no reason to know that the leave was for an FMLA-qualifying reason, the employee can retroactively designate the leave as FMLA leave within two business days after returning to work. 29 C.F.R. § 825.208(e)(1). An employee who knows that he will take leave, such as leave for a scheduled surgery, must give the employer 30 days' notice; for unforeseen leave, the employee must notify the employer "as soon as practicable" after the need for leave becomes known to him. 29 C.F.R. §§ 825.302(a), (b); 825.303(a).

The employer's duty to give the employee notice of whether his request qualifies for FMLA protection is far more rigorous. The employer from which

FMLA leave is requested must give notice to the employee within one to two business days of the request that the request is or is not qualified as FMLA leave. Department of Labor (DOL) regulations provide that an otherwise ineligible employee is treated as eligible if the employer fails to give this notice within two days of receiving the request. 29 C.F.R. § 825.110(d). The lower federal courts, however, have largely held this agency regulation contrary to the scope of the Act intended by Congress and to the text of the statute and have found the regulation unenforceable. *See Brungart v. BellSouth Telecomms., Inc.*, 231 F.3d 791 (11th Cir. 2000), *cert. denied*, 532 U.S. 1037 (2001) (DOL regulation elevates agency policy preference over Congress's express text); *Scheidecker v. Arvig Enterprises, Inc.*, 122 F. Supp. 2d 1031 (D. Minn. 2000); *McQuain v. Ebner Furnaces, Inc.*, 55 F. Supp. 2d 763 (N.D. Ohio 1999); *Seaman v. Downtown Partnership of Baltimore, Inc.*, 991 F. Supp. 751 (D. Md. 1998); *Wolke v. Dreadnought Marine, Inc.*, 954 F. Supp. 1133 (E.D. Va. 1997).

The Seventh and Second Circuits, while finding that the DOL regulation exceeds agency rule-making powers and is accordingly invalid, have nonetheless recognized that it may be appropriate to allow the ineligible employee to be treated as eligible where that is equitable. This might be the case where the employer's assurance of eligibility, later dishonored, had lulled the employee into relying on the employer's assurance to his detriment (the doctrine of equitable estoppel). *Dormeyer v. Comerica Bank-Illinois*, 226 F.3d 915 (7th Cir. 2000); *Woodford v. Community Action of Greene County, Inc.*, 268 F.3d 51 (2d Cir. 2001).

Also highly contentious has been DOL regulation regarding the employer's duty to formally designate FMLA-qualifying leave as FMLA leave—and no other sort of leave that the employer may provide. This DOL regulation had penalized employers that knew that the employee was taking leave for reasons that qualified for FMLA protection but that failed to designate that leave as FMLA leave. Where this had occurred, the DOL regulation provides that the employee's time off cannot be counted against her 12-week FMLA leave although the employee is entitled to FMLA-mandated benefits coverage and restoration to her job upon her return from leave. 29 C.F.R. § 825.208(c). Four circuits have refused to enforce this DOL regulation, while two have found it enforceable.

The Supreme Court resolved aspects of the notice and designation questions raised by the DOL regulations during its 2001 term. In *Ragsdale v. Wolverine Worldwide Inc.*, 535 U.S. 81 (2002), the Supreme Court struck down the DOL regulation's penalty on employers who fail to provide timely notice of the FMLA designation. The decision was five to four, and the Court left open the possibility that, where the employer's error caused prejudice to the employee, the employee might be able to invoke the DOL regulation. In other words, the regulation was not ruled invalid on its face. Thus, the Seventh and Second Circuits, with their case-by-case inquiry looking for prejudice to the employee, appear to have been on the right track. Since the regulations were not struck entirely, the prudent employer will continue to designate an employee's leave as FMLA-qualifying if the employer knows that it is.

2. The Requirement of Proof of Fitness to Return to Work Following Leave

If an employee takes FMLA leave for his own serious medical condition, the employer can require that he provide a certification of medical necessity for the leave as well as a fitness-for-duty certification and a return-to-work clearance from his physician after the leave. The employer can also use the certification procedures embodied in a collective bargaining agreement if those procedures are not more burdensome than the procedures prescribed by the FMLA. *Marrero v. Camden County Bd. of Soc. Servs.*, 164 F. Supp. 2d 455 (D.N.J. 2001); *Conroy v. Township of Lower Merion*, 2001 WL 894051 (E.D. Pa. Aug. 7, 2001); Dep't of Labor Adv. Op. No. 113 (Sept. 11, 2000). The employer must inform the employee in writing of any medical certification requirement it imposes; failure to do so may result in waiver of the employer's right to challenge the employee's leave rights. However, the employee must comply in good faith with any employer certification policy, and if she fails to do so, she cannot state an FMLA claim. *See Rager v. Dade Behring, Inc.*, 210 F.3d 776 (7th Cir. 2000) (employee did not comply with employer's policy requiring certification of medical necessity for leave). Courts may be less than sympathetic where the employee's personal physician's certification is perfunctory or unclear. *See Peterson v. Exide Corp.*, 123 F. Supp. 2d 1265 (D. Kan. 2000).

3. FMLA Eligibility Requirements

The eligibility rules for FMLA coverage are highly specific. To be FMLA-eligible,

1. The employee must be employed at a worksite that has 50 employees or by an employer that has 50 or more employees within 75 surface miles of his worksite. 29 U.S.C. § 2611(2)(B)(ii). An employee must be eligible for FMLA leave at the time he gives his employer notice of his request for leave. 29 C.F.R. § 825.110(f).
2. The employee must have worked for the employer for a minimum of 12 months, although the 12 months need not run consecutively. 29 C.F.R. § 825.110(b).
3. The employee must have worked for the employer for 1,250 hours, against which paid vacation, sick days, paid holidays, and paid FMLA leave may not be applied to reach the 1,250 hours. 29 C.F.R. § 825.110(c); Fair Labor Standards Act, 29 U.S.C. § 207(e)(2). If the employee takes intermittent leave rather than a block of leave for the same serious health condition of himself or a family member during the same 12-month FMLA leave year, the 1,250 hours is tested only once (not each time a new leave is taken); if the employee meets the 1,250-hour threshold the first time he takes leave, that hourly requirement is satisfied for the balance of the 12 weeks' eligibility time. *Barron v. Runyon*, 11 F. Supp. 2d 676 (E.D. Va. 1998), *aff'd*, 205 F.3d 1332 (4th Cir. 2000); Dep't of Labor Adv. Op. No. 112 (Sept. 11, 2000). The onus is on the employer to accurately record employee hours worked; if the employer has not kept accurate records, the Act puts the burden on the employer to prove that the employee is not eligible for leave because he does not meet the 1,250-hour threshold. 29 C.F.R. § 825.110(c).

4. Retaliation Under the FMLA

An employee cannot be retaliated against for exercising her FMLA rights. The FMLA's nonretaliation provision forbids such adverse actions as using the leave to downgrade evaluations or to discipline the employee or deny a promotion. 29 C.F.R. § 825.220(c). *See also Hodgens v. General Dynamics Corp.,* 144 F.3d 151 (1st Cir. 1998). In order to state a retaliation claim, the employee must show that the employer's challenged action was motivated by a desire to retaliate against her for exercising her rights under the Act. The retaliation analysis proceeds just as it would under a Title VII regime: The plaintiff makes a prima facie case; the employer articulates a legitimate, nondiscriminatory reason for taking the challenged action; and the plaintiff then must show that the employer's articulated reason is pretextual.

Questions

1. A single owner controls two companies. The company controller handles the fiscal accountability functions for both companies. She advises the employer of a medical condition and takes leave. After three days off work, she is fired. She sues both companies under the FMLA. Neither company, standing alone, employs more than 50 persons. What theory is available to the employee?
2. Suppose that an employer does not have 50 employees on its payroll, but it does employ three separate classes of contract employees. May the FMLA plaintiff count the contract employees toward her jurisdictional requirement?
3. Can former employees sue under the FMLA? Assume that an employee uses FMLA leave and that he subsequently resigns but reapplies a year later. If the supervisor has written on his personnel file that he is not eligible for rehire and the supervisor's basis for this determination is that the employee previously "took a lot of leave," does the former employee have an FMLA claim based on failure to hire?
4. What kind of notice and medical certification is required of the employee? Suppose that an employee has 72 absences in four years for which the employee occasionally provided doctor's notes that identify a variety of ailments at different times, such as sinusitis, bronchitis, gastroenteritis, a viral infection, and intermittent depression. For general edification on one occasion when the employee was being disciplined for general absenteeism, the employee's physician tendered a catchall explanation that the employee suffered from hyperthyroidism, which caused hypothyroidism and depressive episodes. This note did not link any particular absences to this underlying diagnosis, however. The employee ultimately was fired for absenteeism and sued under the FMLA. Can the employee survive summary judgment?
5. What result in George and Mary's situations in Problems 41 and 42? How would you analyze their cases? What are the concerns for the employer in implementing the FMLA? How can these concerns be addressed?

D. Employer-Provided Benefits: Domestic Partnerships

A small minority of employers provide domestic partner benefits to the same-sex partners of their employees. Although the substantive aspects of such policies may vary, they are generally designed to provide such baseline benefits as

274 Chapter 9

medical coverage. Employers are by no means required to provide such coverage. To date, only Vermont and California probate laws require the same treatment for surviving same-sex partners as for legally recognized spouses. *On the Road to Recovery: Ensuring That Gay Survivors of September 11 Attacks Find Equal Justice*, Hum. Rights Campaign Q., Spring 2002, at 9. Nebraska law, unless a court invalidates a 2000 constitutional amendment, forbids the state of Nebraska from recognizing any domestic partnership arrangement.

Gay and lesbian couples often find themselves unable to avail themselves of any survivors' benefits that the employer might provide to the spouse of a deceased employee. *See Id.* at 8–9 (at least 25 gay or lesbian couples lost a partner in September 11 attacks involving three commercial planes hijacked and used as weapons by terrorists on American soil; federal disaster relief fund did not explicitly include same-sex survivors, although ultimately benefits were not denied). Federal employees receive no domestic partner benefits. Following nine years of congressional scuttling of efforts by Washington, D.C., to enact domestic partner legislation for municipal employees, the full Congress in December 2001 passed legislation enabling the District of Columbia to fund the program. *Id.* at 7.

If a particular employer does provide domestic partner benefits to same-sex employees, must it provide them to heterosexuals who otherwise meet the employer's eligibility criteria?

IRIZARRY
v.
BOARD OF EDUCATION OF THE CITY OF CHICAGO
251 F.3d 604 (7th Cir. 2001)

Before POSNER, MANION, and KANNE, Circuit Judges.

POSNER, Circuit Judge

[The Employment Problem]

Although Milagross Irizarry has lived with the same man for more than two decades and they have two (now adult) children, they have never married. As an employee of the Chicago public school system, she receives health benefits but he does not, even though he is her "domestic partner" (the term for persons who are cohabiting with each other in a relationship similar to marriage), though he would if he were her husband. In July 1999, the Chicago Board of Education extended spousal health benefits to domestic partners—but only if the domestic partner was of the same sex as the employee, which excluded Irizarry's domestic partner, an exclusion that she contends is unconstitutional.

[The Legal Issue]

Besides being of the same sex, applicants for domestic-partner status must be unmarried, unrelated, at least 18 years old, and "each other's sole domestic partner, responsible for each other's common welfare." They must satisfy two of the following four additional conditions as well: that they have been living together for a year; that they jointly own their home; that they jointly own other property of specified kinds; that the domestic partner is the primary beneficiary named in the employee's will. Although the board's purpose in entitling domestic partners so defined to spousal benefits was to extend such benefits to homosexual employees, homosexual marriage not being recognized by Illinois, . . . entitlement to the benefits does not require proof of sexual orientation.

Irizarry's domestic partner satisfies all the conditions for domestic-partner benefits except being of the same sex. She argues that the board's policy denies equal protection and, secondarily, due process. The district court dismissed her suit for failure to state a claim.

[The Decision and Rationale of the U.S. Court of Appeals for the Seventh Circuit]

The board of education makes two arguments for treating homosexual couples differently from unmarried heterosexual couples. First, since homosexual marriage is not possible in Illinois (or anywhere else in the United States, although it is possible in the Netherlands), and heterosexual marriage of course is, the recognition of a domestic-partnership surrogate is more important for homosexual than for heterosexual couples, who can obtain the benefits simply by marrying. Second, the board wants to attract homosexual teachers in order to provide support for homosexual students.... According to its brief, the board "believes that lesbian and gay male school personnel who have a healthy acceptance of their own sexuality can act as role models and provide emotional support for lesbian and gay students.... They can support students who are questioning their sexual identities or who are feeling alienated due to their minority sexual orientation. They can also encourage all students to be tolerant and accepting of lesbians and gay males, and discourage violence directed at these groups."

This line of argument will shock many people even today; it was not that long ago when homosexual teachers were almost universally considered a public menace likely to seduce or recruit their students into homosexuality, then regarded with unmitigated horror. The plaintiff does not argue, however, that the Chicago Board of Education is irrational in having turned the traditional attitude toward homosexual teachers upside down. It is not for a federal court to decide whether a local government agency's policy of tolerating or even endorsing homosexuality is sound. Even if the judges consider such a policy morally repugnant—even dangerous—they may not interfere with it unless convinced that it lacks even minimum rationality, which is a permissive standard. It is a fact that some schoolchildren are homosexual, and the responsibility for dealing with that fact is lodged in the school authorities, and (if they are public schools), ultimately in the taxpaying public, rather than in the federal courts.

The efficacy of the policy may be doubted. Although it had been in effect for a year and a half when the appeal was argued, only nine employees out of some 45,000 had signed up for domestic-partner benefits and none of the nine indicated whether he or she was homosexual; they may not all have been, as we shall see—perhaps none were. Nor is there any indication that any of the nine are new employees attracted to teach in the Chicago public schools by the availability of health benefits for same-sex domestic partners.... No matter; limited efficacy does not make the policy irrational—not even if we think limited efficacy evidence that the policy is more in the nature of a political gesture than a serious effort to improve the lot of homosexual students—if only because with limited efficacy comes limited cost. Because homosexuals are a small fraction of the population, because the continuing stigma of homosexuality discourages many of them from revealing their sexual orientation, and because nowadays a significant number of heterosexuals substitute cohabitation for marriage in response to the diminishing stigma of cohabitation, extending domestic-partner benefits to mixed-sex couples would greatly increase the expense of the program.

Irizarry argues that the child of an unmarried couple ought equally to be entitled to the mentoring and role-model benefits of having teachers who live in the same way as the student's parents do. Cost considerations to one side, the argument collides with a nationwide policy in favor of marriage.... The Chicago Board of Education cannot be faulted, therefore, for not wishing to encourage heterosexual cohabitation; and, though we need not decide the point, the refusal to extend domestic-partner benefits to heterosexual cohabitors could be justified on the basis of the policy favoring marriage for heterosexuals quite apart from the reasons for wanting to extend the spousal fringe benefits to homosexual couples.

Of course, self-selection is important; people are more likely to marry who believe they have characteristics favorable to a long-term relationship.... But the Chicago Board of Education would not be irrational (though it might be incorrect) in assigning some causal role to the relationship itself. Linda J. Waite, "Does Marriage Matter?" 32 Demography 483, 498–99 (1995), finds that cohabitants are much less likely than married couples to pool financial resources, more likely to assume that each partner is responsible for supporting himself or herself financially, more likely to spend free time separately, and less likely to agree on the future of the relationship. This makes both investment in the relationship and specialization with this partner much riskier than in marriage, and so reduces them. Whereas marriage connects individuals to other important social institutions, such as organized religion, cohabitation seems to distance them from these institutions.

Irizarry and her domestic partner may, given the unusual duration of their relationship, be an exception to generalizations about the benefits of marriage. We are not aware of an extensive scholarly literature comparing marriage to long-term cohabitation. This may be due to the fact that long-term cohabitation is rare—only ten percent of such relationships last for five years or more, Pamela J. Smock, "Cohabitation in the United States: An Appraisal of Research Themes, Findings, and Implications," 26 Ann. Rev. Sociology 1 (2000). But there is evidence that the widespread substitution of cohabitation for marriage in Sweden has given that country the highest rate of family dissolution and single parenting in the developed world. David Popenoe, Disturbing the Nest: Family Change and Decline in Modern Societies 173–74 (1988). . . . True, Irizarry's cohabitation has not dissolved; but law and policy are based on the general rather than the idiosyncratic. . . . Nor is it entirely clear that this couple ought to be considered an exception to the general concern with heterosexuals who choose to have a family outside of marriage. For when asked at argument why the couple had never married, Irizarry's counsel replied that he had asked his client that question and she had told him that "it just never came up." There may be good reasons why a particular couple would not marry even after producing children, but that the thought of marriage would not even occur to them is disquieting.

The Lambda Legal Defense and Education Fund has filed an *amicus curiae* brief surprisingly urging reversal—surprisingly because Lambda is an organization for the promotion of homosexual rights, and if it is the law that domestic-partnership benefits must be extended to heterosexual couples, the benefits are quite likely to be terminated for everyone lest the extension to the heterosexual cohabitors impose excessive costs and invite criticism as encouraging heterosexual cohabitation and illegitimate births and discouraging marriage and legitimacy. But Lambda is concerned with the fact that state and national policy encourages (heterosexual) marriage in all sorts of ways that domestic-partner health benefits cannot begin to equalize. Lambda wants to knock marriage off its perch by requiring the board of education to treat unmarried heterosexual couples as well as it treats married ones, so that marriage will lose some of its luster.

This is further evidence of the essentially symbolic or political rather than practical significance of the board's policy. Lambda is not jeopardizing a substantial benefit for homosexuals because very few of them want or will seek the benefit. In any event, it would not be proper for judges to use the vague concept of "equal protection" to undermine marriage just because it is a heterosexual institution. . . .

. . . [W]e do not understand the plaintiff to be arguing that the board of education must have anything more than a rational basis for its action in order to defeat the plaintiff's equal protection claim. Only when the plaintiff in an equal protection case is complaining of a form of discrimination that is suspect because historically it was irrational or invidious is there a heavier burden of justifying a difference in treatment than merely showing that it is rational. . . . Heterosexuals cohabiting outside of marriage are not such a class. There is a history of disapproval of (nonmarital) cohabitation, and some states still criminalize it. . . . But the disapproval is not necessarily irrational or invidious, . . . given the benefits of marriage discussed earlier. It was rational for the board to refuse to extend domestic-partnership benefits to persons who can if they wish marry and by doing so spare the board from having to make a factual inquiry into the nature of their relationship.

The least rational feature of the board's policy, although not emphasized by the plaintiff, is that although domestic-partner benefits are confined to persons of the same sex, the partners need not be homosexual. They could be roommates who have lived together for a year and own some property jointly and for want of relatives are each other's sole "domestic partner," and if so they would be entitled to domestic-partner benefits under the board of education's policy. To distinguish between roommates of the same and of different sexes, as the policy implicitly does, cannot be justified on the ground that the latter but not the former could marry each other!

So the policy does not make a very close fit between end and means. But it doesn't have to, provided there is a rational basis for the loose fit. *See, e.g., Kimel v. Florida Bd. of Regents, supra*, 528 U.S. 62, 83–84. . . . This follows from our earlier point that cost is a rational basis for treating people differently. Economy is one of the principal reasons for using rules rather than standards to govern conduct. Rules single out one or a few facts from the welter of possibly relevant considerations and make that one or those few facts legally determinative, thus dispensing with inquiry into the other considerations. A standard that takes account of all relevant considerations will produce fewer arbitrary differences in outcome, but at a cost in uncertainty, administrative burden, and sometimes even—as here—in invading people's privacy. It is easy to see why the board of education does not want to put applicants to the proof of their sexual preference. That would be resented. The price of avoiding an inquiry that would be costly because it would be obnoxious is that a few roommates may end up with windfall benefits. We cannot say that the board is being irrational in deciding to pay that price rather than snoop into people's sex lives. . . .

Discussion Notes

1. Is Judge Posner's hymn to marriage as an institution relevant here? Is it "snooping into people's sex lives" to require them to get married to get benefits if they are heterosexual?
2. Do you think Judge Posner is correct in his surmise as to why Lambda Legal Defense took the position it did in this case? Does it seem odd that, at the same time Lambda Legal Defense has agitated for legalized same-sex marriage, it would be trying in this case to "knock marriage off of its perch"? What do you think should happen in the debate about constitutional amendments to reserve "marriage" for heterosexuals?

Questions

1. How do these theories of male and female behavior get reflected in the Equal Pay Act and in Title VII's prohibition against discrimination on the basis of sex? Do these laws do an adequate job of taking these factors into account? What would be different about the law if these views were dominantly reflected in the law? Which is the fundamental root of the problem: nature or nurture? What should we do about these differences?
2. How would these authors approach the problems faced by the employees and employers in Problem 38 and the cases presented in this chapter?

chapter

10 Discrimination Based on National Origin and Against Native Americans

The world has changed a great deal since the passage of the civil rights laws of 1964. From a global perspective, the rights of indigenous peoples have become an important human rights issue. As measures are utilized to combat terrorism across the globe and in the United States, U.S. employers will have to learn how to enforce the prohibitions against discrimination on the basis of national origin mandated by Title VII of the Civil Rights Act of 1964 and take measures to ensure that the fears and stereotypes held by some of their employees and customers are not used to discriminate against innocent victims of that bias.

This chapter will first present material on the prohibition against national origin discrimination and then deal specifically with the case of Native Americans. Excerpts from the scholarship of a number of authors have been added to help the reader think about the special circumstances of different ethnic minorities and the issues that are raised from their perspective.

A. Discrimination Based on National Origin

Problem 43

Chung Shin is a Korean-American man who is employed with the U.S. Department of Health and Human Services. He is currently a Management Analyst (Team Leader) GS-343-14. Since 1993, Shin has applied for three announced GS-15 vacancies. In the last instance, he applied for a position as Manager, Special Initiatives, Program Support Center. He was not promoted, and he claims that he is more qualified than Steven Seward, a white male, who was promoted to the position. Further, he can show that there is an absence of Asian employees at the GS-15 level and above. He claims that he was denied the promotion because of his race and his national origin.

1. Introduction

Title VII of the Civil Rights Act of 1964 did not define the term "national origin." The Equal Employment Opportunity Commission (EEOC) has recognized the difficulty of a rigid definition. Title VII's protection is available to any U.S. worker whether he or she was born in the United States or elsewhere. Congress recognized that ancestry, whether Mexican, Ukrainian, Filipino, Arab, Native American, or any other nationality, must not be a barrier to equal opportunity in employment. According to the EEOC, "today, about one in ten Americans is foreign-born. The largest numbers of recent immigrants have come from Asia, including China, India, and Vietnam, and from Latin America, including Mexico, El Salvador, and Cuba." EEOC Guidance on National Origin Discrimination (Dec. 2002) The EEOC has recognized that the population of the United States is changing dramatically, with a significant rise in the population of Asians, Hispanics, and Black Americans, including new immigrants from the Caribbean and sub-Saharan Africa. The EEOC recognized that the American work force has also changed in similar fashion; the *EEOC Compliance Manual* reports that, "[i]n 1999, immigrant workers numbered 15.7 million, accounting for 12 percent of the U.S. workers. Between 1990 and 1998, 12.7 million new jobs were created in the United States, and 38% (5.1 million) were filled by immigrants. In 2000, Hispanics, Asians and American Indians constituted 15.2% of the workforce employed by private employers with 100 or more employees. . . . "

Discrimination on the basis of national origin may include discrimination on the basis of ethnicity; of physical, linguistic, or cultural traits; or of the perception that someone is of a certain national origin. These differences can sometimes cause confusion and often overlap with discrimination on the basis of race.

The following case is a good illustration of the way that the courts have manipulated the meaning of race when dealing with minority populations at various times in the past.

2. The Meaning of Race in the National Origin Context

PEOPLE
v.
HALL[1]
4 Cal. 399 (1854)

Mr. Ch. J. MURRAY delivered the opinion of the Court.

The appellant, a free White citizen of this State, was convicted of murder upon the testimony of Chinese witnesses.

The point involved in this case, is the admissibility of such evidence.

The 394th section of the Act Concerning Civil Cases provides that no Indian or Negro shall be allowed to testify as a witness in any action or proceeding in which a White person is a party.

The 14th section of the Act of April 16th, 1850, regulating Criminal Proceedings, provides that "No Black, or Mulatto person, or Indian, shall be allowed to give evidence in favor of, or against a white man."

The true point at which we are anxious to arrive is the legal signification of the words, "Black, Mulatto,

[1]4 Cal. 399 (1854) See further discussion in Leslie Bender and Daan Braveman, Power Privilege and Law, A Civil Rights Reader 141–145 (1995).

Indian and White person," and whether the Legislature adopted them as generic terms, or intended to limit their application to specific types of the human species.

Before considering this question, it is proper to remark the difference between the two sections of our Statute, already quoted, the later being more broad and comprehensive in its exclusion, by use of the word "Black," instead of Negro.

Conceding, however, for the present, that the word "Black," as used in the 14th section, and "Negro," in 394th, are convertible terms, and that the former was intended to include the latter, let us proceed to inquire who are excluded from testifying as witnesses under the term "Indian." . . .

We have adverted to these speculations [on various meanings of the term as used in the past] of showing that the name of Indian, from the time of Columbus to the present day, has been used to designate, not alone the North American Indian, but the whole of the Mongolian race, and that the name, though first applied probably through mistake, was afterwards continued as appropriate on account of the supposed common origin. . . .

Again: the words of the Act must be construed in *pari materia*. It will not be disputed that "White" and "Negro," are generic terms, and refer to two of the great types of mankind. If these, as well as the word "Indian," are not to be regarded as generic terms, including the two great races which they were intended to designate, but only specific, and applying to those Whites and Negroes who were inhabitants of this Continent at the time of the passage of the Act, the most anomalous consequences would ensue. The European white man who comes here would not be shielded from the testimony of the degraded and demoralized caste, while the Negro, fresh from the coast of Africa, or the Indian of Patagonia, the Kanaka, South Sea Islander, or New Hollander, would be admitted, upon their arrival, to testify against white citizens in our courts of law.

To argue such a proposition would be an insult to the good sense of the Legislature. . . .

The evident intention of the Act was to throw around the citizen a protection for life and property, which could only be secured by removing him above the corrupting influences of degraded castes.

It can hardly be supposed that any Legislature would attempt this by excluding domestic Negroes and Indians, who not unfrequently have correct notions of their obligations to society, and turning loose upon the community the more degraded tribes of the same species, who have nothing in common with us, in language, country or laws. . . .

By use of [the term "Black"], we understand it to mean the opposite of "White," and that it should be taken as contradistinguished from all White persons. . . .

We are not disposed to leave this question in any doubt. The word "White" has a distinct signification, which *ex vi termini*, excludes black, yellow, and all other colors. . . .

If the term, "White," as used in the Constitution, was not understood in its generic sense as including the Caucasian race, and necessarily excluding all others, where was the necessity of providing for the admission of Indians to the privilege of voting, by special legislation? . . .

The same rule which would admit them to testify, would admit them to all the equal rights of citizenship, and we might soon see them at the polls, in the jury box, upon the bench, and in our legislative halls.

This is not a speculation which exists in the excited and over-heated imagination of the patriot and statesman, but it is an actual and present danger.

The anomalous spectacle of a distinct people, living in our community, recognizing no laws of this State except through necessity, bringing with them their prejudices and national feuds, in which they indulge in open violation of the law; whose mendacity is proverbial; a race of people whom nature has marked as inferior, and who are incapable of progress or intellectual development beyond a certain point, as their history has shown; differing in language, opinions, color, and physical conformation; between whom and ourselves nature has placed an impassable difference, is now presented, and for them is claimed, not only the right to swear away the life of a citizen, but the further privilege of participating with us in the administering of the affairs of our Government. . . .

For these reasons, we are of opinion that the testimony was inadmissible.

The judgment is reversed and the cause remanded. Mr. Justice WELLS dissented.

Questions

1. In *People v. Hall,* how does the court treat the problem of identifying the characteristics of race? What assumptions are made by the court in reaching its opinion? Should the law play a role in deciding who belongs in a particular racial category? To what extent is the definition of race an important element in the construction of what constitutes discrimination?

2. How has the law shaped the debate about discrimination in the experience of African Americans? Can you see any differences in the way that the law approaches the problem of race for Asian Americans or Latinas, for example?

---

3. Judicial Limitations on the Meaning of National Origin Discrimination

National origin discrimination cases have been comparatively rare, perhaps because of the rigorous limitations imposed by the U.S. Supreme Court in the case below.

ESPINOZA
v.
FARAH MANUFACTURING CO.
414 U.S. 86 (1973)

Justice MARSHALL delivered the opinion of the Court.

[The Employment Problem]

[Cecilia Espinoza was a citizen of Mexico but was a lawfully admitted resident alien in the United States. Her husband, an American citizen, lived with her in San Antonio, Texas. Ms. Espinoza applied for a job as a seamstress at Farah Manufacturing Company, which refused to hire her because of its policy against hiring aliens. Espinoza sued, alleging that Farah had violated Title VII's prohibition on discrimination based on national origin.]

[The Legal Issue]

The question posed in the present case . . . is not whether aliens are protected from illegal discrimination under the Act, but what kinds of discrimination the Act makes illegal. Certainly it would be unlawful for an employer to discriminate against aliens because of race, color, religion, sex, or national origin—for example, by hiring aliens of Anglo-Saxon background but refusing to hire those of Mexican or Spanish ancestry. Aliens are protected from illegal discrimination under the Act, but nothing in the Act makes it illegal to discriminate on the basis of citizenship or alienage.

[The Decision by the Trial Court and the U.S. Court of Appeals for the Fifth Circuit]

[The district court ruled for Ms. Espinoza; the court of appeals reversed, holding that "national origin" dis-

crimination does not include discrimination based on one's citizenship.]

[The Decision and Rationale of the U.S. Supreme Court]

[Title VII] makes it 'an unlawful employment practice for an employer . . . to fail or refuse to hire . . . any individual . . . because of such individual's race, color, religion, sex, or national origin.' Certainly the plain language of the statute supports the result reached by the Court of Appeals. The term 'national origin' on its face refers to the country where a person was born, or, more broadly, the country from which his or her ancestors came. . . .

The statute's legislative history . . . fully supports this construction. The only direct definition given the phrase 'national origin' is the following remark made on the floor of the House of Representatives by Congressman Roosevelt, Chairman of the House Subcommittee which reported the bill: 'It means the country from which you or your forebears came. . . . You may come from Poland, Czechoslovakia, England, France, or any other country.' 110 Cong. Rec. 2549 (1964). . . .

There are other compelling reasons to believe that Congress did not intend the term 'national origin' to embrace citizenship requirements. Since 1914, the Federal Government itself, through Civil Service Commission regulations, has engaged in what amounts to discrimination against aliens by denying them the right to enter competitive examination for federal employment. Exec. Order No. 1997 H.R. Doc. No. 1258, 63d Cong., 3d Sess. 118 (1914); see 5 U.S.C. § 3301; 5 CFR § 338.101 (1972). But it has never been suggested that the citizenship requirement for federal employment constitutes discrimination based on national origin, even though since 1943, various Executive Orders have expressly prohibited discrimination on the basis of national origin in Federal Government employment....

Moreover, Section 701(b) of Tit. VII ... makes it 'the policy of the United States to insure equal employment opportunities for Federal employees without discrimination because of ... national origin....' The legislative history of that section reveals no mention of any intent on Congress' part to reverse the longstanding practice of requiring federal employees to be United States citizens. To the contrary, there is every indication that no such reversal was intended. Congress itself has on several occasions since 1964 enacted statutes barring aliens from federal employment....

To interpret the term 'national origin' to embrace citizenship requirements would require us to conclude that Congress itself has repeatedly flouted its own declaration of policy. This Court cannot lightly find such a breach of faith....

... [W]e cannot conclude Congress would at once continue the practice of requiring citizenship as a condition of federal employment and, at the same time, prevent private employers from doing likewise....

The District Court drew primary support from its holding from an interpretative guideline issued by the Equal Employment Opportunity Commission which provides:

Because discrimination on the basis of citizenship has the effect of discriminating on the basis of national origin, a lawfully immigrated alien who is domiciled or residing in this country may not be discriminated against on the basis of his citizenship....

Like the Court of Appeals, we have no occasion here to question the general validity of this guideline insofar as it can be read as an expression of the Commission's belief that there may be situations where discrimination on the basis of citizenship would have the effect of discriminating on the basis of national origin. In some instances, for example, a citizenship requirement might be but one part of a wider scheme of unlawful national-origin discrimination.... Certainly Tit. VII prohibits discrimination on the basis of citizenship whenever it has the purpose or effect of discriminating on the basis of national origin....

It is equally clear, however, that these principles lend no support to petitioners in this case. There is no indication in the record that Farah's policy against employment of aliens had the purpose or effect of discriminating against persons of Mexican national origin.... It is conceded that Farah accepts employees of Mexican origin, provided the individual concerned has become an American citizen. Indeed, the District Court found that persons of Mexican ancestry make up more than 96% of the employees in the company's San Antonio division, and 97% of those doing the work for which Mrs. Espinoza applied....

Finally, petitioners seek to draw support from the fact that Title VII protects all individuals from unlawful discrimination, whether or not they are citizens of the United States. We agree that aliens are protected from discrimination under the Act....

---

4. Perspectives on Discrimination Against Asians and Asian Americans

Frank H. Wu, *Changing America: Three Arguments About Asian Americans and the Law*, 45 Am. U. L. Rev. 811 (1996)

(This is an edited version of the article and footnotes are omitted.)

... In what will be a famous or an infamous passage, depending on the course of later events, Justice Antonin SCALIA concurring in the result but implicitly dissenting in the reasoning in the Supreme Court's recent affirmative action case, wrote, "In the eyes of the government, we are just one race here. It is American."[8]

This simple statement in dicta exemplifies the color-blind view in contemporary constitutional discourse ... The color-blind philosophy fails when it is tested against the Asian American experiences. Color-blindness fails on all of its three conceptual levels with Asian Americans. First, at the level of private beliefs, mainstream society repeatedly refers to the race of Asian American individuals in making judgments. Second, at the level of government action, the United States has, in the past, relied on the race of Asians in establishing public policy that disfavors them, and might well do so again. Third,

---

[8]*Adarand Constructors, Inc. v. Pena*, 115 S. Ct. 2097, 2119 (1995) (SCALIA, J., concurring).

at the theoretical level, as a result of the racialized role of Asian Americans as individuals and as a group, they cannot find a "neutral" vantage point in race relations. These levels are analyzed in turn.

At the first level of private action, the myth of the model minority reveals the myth of color-blindness. Criticism of the model minority image of Asian Americans has become so familiar as to be taken for granted by many of us. But every generation should be reminded of the lies of the myth and their use for dubious purposes. The myth might never be debunked, no matter how thorough or objective the efforts to do so.

Anyone who studies Asian Americans knows about the model minority myth. Since the arrival of Asian immigrants in the nineteenth century, and most notably since the 1960s, this ubiquitous superminority image has suggested that Asian Americans achieve economic success and gain societal acceptance through conservative values and hard work.

The image is a myth because Asian Americans have not achieved economic success except in a superficial sense. Comparing equally educated individuals, Whites earn more money than Asian Americans. . . . Qualifications count less than race, in a pattern of regular discrimination, not so-called "reverse" discrimination. The discrimination which Asian Americans in fact face can be reinforced by the exaggerations of the myth. This reinforcement occurs, for example, when non–Asian Americans believe that Asian Americans should be subjected to maximum quotas in college admissions because they have done too well and represent unfair competition. . . .

Yet, the model minority myth ought to self-destruct. After all, to be able to see Asian Americans as a racial group, especially a racial group which can be contrasted with other racial groups, requires a highly developed sense of color-consciousness. If society was color-blind in the sense of blotting out race and all references to race, it would be impossible to point at Asian Americans, much less use them as an example. Ironically, when Asian Americans are used to attack affirmative action, the case for evaluating the merit of individuals focuses on the supposed success of a racial group.

At the second level of government action, the new attacks on immigration reveal the myth of color-blindness from a different angle. The historical restrictionist approach to immigration is articulated in the Supreme Court's late nineteenth century decisions upholding the Chinese Exclusion. . . . In precedent that has never been explicitly overruled, but, has repeatedly been expressly affirmed, the Court has abdicated its role. . . . It accepted the congressional finding that "the presence of foreigners of a different race in this country, who will not assimilate with us, [is] dangerous to [the country's] peace and security." . . . Since then, federal legislation in the immigration area has moved steadily, if slowly, toward what might be termed race-neutral standards, but recently a counter-reaction has emerged. . . .

At the third level of theory, it is impossible to be neutral in race relations. Everyone has a vested interest. Color-blindness has been promoted as an idea of neutrality. Asian Americans sometimes have been portrayed as living between black and white and, accordingly, neutral. The most famous Asian American of late, Los Angeles Judge Lance ITO, while presiding over the O. J. Simpson trial in 1994 and 1995, was described as "neutral" in the racialized "trial of the century." . . . Even Judge ITO could not maintain his "neutral" place racially. Despite his judicial role and corresponding neutrality in the symbolism of the trial process, and even though his racial status may have seemed irrelevant, it became relevant to observers. One revealing episode was Senator Alfonse D'Amato's appearance on a radio show mid-way through the trial. . . . In his remarks, Senator D'Amato mocked Judge ITO as having a heavy Asian accent, later explaining that he was using the racial reference as a means of criticizing the conduct of the trial. . . . Numerous other racial references to Judge ITO and Asian American witnesses occurred within the trial itself and in the extensive media coverage. . . .

It would be a cliche but for the denials, that for many people, race remains important. Justice SCALIA's facile remark that we are all Americans effectively obscures the legal construction of that category. . . . Not everyone can become an American. Those people who cannot become Americans, regardless of their consent to the ideals of the community, have been excluded in the past because of their race and may again be excluded in the future because of their race. Even as citizens, Asian Americans can be treated as outsiders to their own society, as demonstrated most vividly by the wartime internment decisions. . . . Even as full members within their own society, Asian Americans may be used as a model minority to criticize other racial minorities. Throughout the spectrum of possibilities, race is relevant.

If the Stereotype Fits, Wear It?

The recurring debate over the use of social science in the law has concentrated on empirical data that has been used to reach results that are "liberal," most notably in *Brown v. Board of Education.* . . . The latest version of this debate, which is only starting to become apparent, will turn on empirical data that is used to reach results that are "conservative," most likely arguments along the lines of "it can't be racism if it's true." It is only a matter of time before politicians seeking to rationalize official discrimination rely on *The Bell Curve*, or parties involved in litigation defend private prejudice based on similar studies.

With only rudimentary guidelines from the Supreme Court in *Adarand Constructors, Inc. v. Pena,* . . .

that strict scrutiny is not always fatal, and that lower courts should consider "evidence," it is unclear whether social science as a means will support liberal ends. In any event, the model minority myth will be an important exhibit. Needless to say, the model minority myth has some truth to it. There is a credible and possibly persuasive argument that Asian American family income is, on the average, higher than white family income. . . . Like all good social science, such data presents as many questions as it provides answers. It is as problematic as it is polemic.

While one can respond to the critique of the model minority myth, such a defense of the model minority myth rests on the assertion that the myth is true. The response of descriptive truth fails to address a threshold issue of normative truth: is it appropriate to use race as an independent variable or the suspect classification with which to make generalizations and draw conclusions? The proponent of the model minority myth implicitly must answer in the affirmative. But the data should be placed within a context for legal purposes. . . .

Specifically, the proponent of the model minority myth cannot avoid answering other questions. Which comparisons are apt: family income or individual income? Controlling for which other factors among many: citizen/immigrant status, gender, education, language skills, etc.? Overall, the proponent of the model minority myth also should be directed toward addressing the purpose of using the model minority myth—is it to attack affirmative action, or exclude Asian Americans from affirmative action?

Aside from the model minority myth, there are other "facts" about Asian Americans that may be considered as conundrums on this issue of social science in the law. One fact in particular conforms to stereotypes: it is true that today a majority of Asian Americans are foreign-born. . . .

Given the efforts to limit immigration, the foreign-born status of most Asian Americans will attract attention to them, even to those who are native-born citizens. If the majority of Asians in America are immigrants, and some unsubstantiated claims about undocumented immigration place it at a level equal to legal immigration, would that then make it "reasonable" under a statute similar to Proposition 187 . . . in California, to "suspect" that they were also undocumented immigrants?

These inquiries are meaningful if the law is to be purposive. In order to respond meaningfully to these queries—to give legal significance to the factual inquiries—the traditional test of invidious intent is important in constitutional law. . . . To the extent that the intent test may be divisive, requiring that a wrongdoer be identified, or that it may be inadequate, because of unconscious bias, it should be replaced by an approach that can weigh in the balance more than merely statistical data. None of this is to suggest that social science be disregarded.

The risks of relying on social science are well worth taking. The danger, however, is that courts will rely on empirical evidence without addressing the contested nature of the proof and the context in which it is generated. The courts must be willing to make normative judgments. . . . Otherwise, a Panglossian world will be the result, with what is becoming confused with what should be. . . .

The American dilemma is no longer an apt term. . . . There is the old American dilemma of black-white relations, but it has been joined by the new American dilemmas of multiple race relations, many disputes among even more contending groups, and still without a consensus on basic principles or guiding visions. It is too late to be optimistic, but too early to be pessimistic.

Discussion Notes

1. Is the Espinoza Court wrong in stating that Congress would not expect private employers to abide by requirements from which it exempted the federal government? Congress for many years exempted itself from Title VII coverage, leaving its staff with no federal remedy for sexual harassment.
2. Do you think the result in Espinoza would change if the statistical evidence had not been what it was, or did the Court's stress on legislative history render the statistical evidence merely persuasive rather than dispositive?
3. Recall the Court's discussion of preferences allocated on the basis of national origin. At least one court has applied this rationale to discrimination among Indian tribes. In *Dawavendewa v. Salt River Project Agricultural Improvement &*

Power District, 154 F.3d 1117 (9th Cir.), *cert. denied*, 528 U.S. 1098 (2000), presented below, the Ninth Circuit held that an American Indian who claimed that he was barred from working on a project because his tribe was Hopi and not Navajo stated a claim of national origin discrimination.

4. Should it be possible for a group of employees to claim that they are subjected to disparate treatment because their supervisor expects more of them due to his positive beliefs about their ethnic group? Strangely enough, this reverse-stereotyping has been held to violate Title VII. *See Kang v. U Lim America, Inc.*, 296 F.3d 810 (9th Cir. 2002) (Korean workers were berated by a supervisor who "viewed their national origin as superior"; although this sort of increased-expectation harassment is "unusual. . . . such stereotyping is an evil at which [Title VII] is aimed").

5. According to Judge Edward M. CHEN in the May 2003 *Asian Law Journal*, "of the 579 active district court judges nationwide, there are only five Asian Pacific Americans, including only one outside of California and Hawaii (Judge Denny CHIN of the Southern District of New York) [a]nd there are no Native American district court judges in the United States." What is the significance of these figures for the interpretation of Title VII when it comes to the unique factors involved in discrimination on the basis of Native American origin?

5. Perspectives on Discrimination Against Latina/os

Problem 44

Last spring, when he was 25 years old, Elvin Rodriquez moved to this country from his birthplace in Mexico. He knew some English, but he wasn't very comfortable speaking it. He obtained a position at the Lucern Widget Factory in Tucson, Arizona, as soon as he obtained the necessary working papers. Once he started on the factory line, he was informed by his supervisor that there was an "English only" policy at all times at work. He was fired when someone reported that he was speaking Spanish in the lunchroom during his break. Elvin wants to bring a claim of discrimination based on his national origin. Should this be considered a national origin claim?

The "LatCrit" movement engages scholars, activists, lawyers and members of the community in discussions that attempt to shift the discussion away from a focus on the Black/White paradigm of rights discourse. These critical theorists are raising important concerns about anti-essentialism and coalitions of minorities who work to achieve changes in structures of discrimination. Elizabeth Iglesias presents some of the key concepts of LatCrit theory in the following article.

Elizabeth M. Iglesias, Identity, Democracy, Communicative Power, Inter/National Labor Rights and the Evolution of LatCrit Theory and Community, 53 U. Miami L. Rev. 575 (1999).

(This is an edited version of this article and footnotes are deleted.)

Until relatively recently, the trials and tribulations. . . of the international peace movement, the labor movement, the environmental movement and the international movement for human rights, like the deconstruction of U.S. national security ideology or the critical analysis of the legal regimes organized by antitrust, tax and corporate laws have, for the most part, been cast as matters of universal concern, not particularly relevant to Latina/o and other minority communities, whose primary focus of attention has been thought to center on issues of discrimination and the meaning of equal protection. . . . LatCrit theory, by contrast, claims an interest in matters of universal concern, precisely because it rejects the metaphysical and epistemological assumptions that underpin the bifurcation of universal and particular. . . . By taking up and subjecting to critical anti-essentialist analysis such matters as the rhetoric and realities of the democratic project, the legal structures of communicative power and the future of the labor movement in and beyond the United States, these essays demonstrate how attention to the particularities of Latina/o experiences and perspectives can produce a richer and more contextual understanding of the broader contexts and multiple dimensions of the human struggle for justice and peace. . . .

guages are equally implicated in the such matters as the regulation of political speech. . . and the ownership and control of new technologies of communication. . . .

Indeed, in each of these contexts, the matter at stake is the power to communicate—to express oneself—meaningfully and effectively. Increasingly, the power to communicate is determined by access to, control of, or authority over the means of communication. . . . Indeed, the "means of communication" have become as central to the structure of power/lessness in our postmodern, hyperlinked, globalized, mass media society as the "means of production" were central to the class struggles of modernizing industrialism. Individuals and communities shut out of the information age and out-spent in a political system that casts the expenditure of money as protected political speech—such that effective speech comes to depend increasingly on the ability to spend money—are just as certainly robbed of the instruments of self-determination and the power of self-expression, as workers separated from and denied control over the means of production. By thematizing the linkages between language, meaning-making power and the struggle for self-determination, [this work] goes a long way toward delimiting a broad field ripe for anti-subordination theory and practice.

Language, Technology, and Communicative Power: From Language Rights to the Struggle for Control of the Means of Communication

Language rights have been a central issue in LatCrit theory since its inception. . . . [The LatCrit III Conference] was, however, the first time that LatCrit conference organizers sought intentionally and self-consciously to link the struggle against English-Only to a broader struggle for communicative power. This imagined project was forwarded to expand LatCrit theory's substantive agenda by encouraging a collaborative effort to develop a critical analysis of the way differential access to the means of communication is legally constructed across different sociolegal contexts and the way the resulting structures of communicative power/lessness should be addressed in LatCrit theory. In this expanded critical project, the struggle over language rights reflects only one instance in a more general struggle against relations of domination organized by and effectuated through the legal production of differential access to the means of communication. This is because the compelling personal and collective interests at stake in the struggle against the suppression of non-English lan-

Language Rights in Economic Analysis and Moral Theory

The [work of] Professors Bill Bratton and Drucilla Cornell is based on a collaborative project in which they join the anti-nativist struggle against initiatives to suppress the use of languages other than English.[171] Their objective is to make an economic and moral case for treating language based discrimination as an equal rights violation. Interestingly, they develop their arguments using two very different forms of discourse. Professor Bratton uses law and economic analysis to challenge key assumptions about the way English-Only laws and employment regulations affect the incentive structures through which individual language acquisition and group assimilation are mediated in this country. Professor Cornell articulates a moral theory of rights that casts respect for language rights as fundamental to "the basic moral right of personality," thereby moving

[171]See Drucilla Cornell & William W. Bratton, Deadweight Costs and Intrinsic Wrongs of Nativism: Economics, Freedom and Legal Suppression of Spanish, 84 Cornell L. Rev. 595 (1999).

the articulation of equality rights beyond the truncated formalism of an anti-discrimination framework to ground it, instead, on the concept of self-determination.

More specifically, Professor Bratton's objective is to use economic analysis to destabilize the nativist political project by challenging the assumption that English-only laws and workplace regulations will promote assimilation to the English-speaking norm that, for the nativist, defines "the essence" of American identity. He acknowledges that English-only laws and policies are, at least superficially, supported by a plausible economic argument that language regulation maximizes social utilities by increasing communicative efficiency and reducing barriers to social interaction otherwise associated with the Tower of Babel cacophony of multiple languages. . . . To be sure, Professor Bratton also challenges the initial assumption that "sameness" lowers costs. . . . However, his major contribution is in showing why English-only laws are unlikely to achieve their purported "efficiency" objectives. He does this through a detailed analysis of the incentive structures Spanish speakers confront in acquiring English language proficiency.

In a nutshell, Professor Bratton's economic analysis suggests that if nativists are really serious about promoting Latina/o assimilation into American society, they should focus on eliminating discrimination against Latinas/os, rather than suppressing Spanish. This is because the suppression of Spanish is neither necessary nor sufficient to achieve its purported objective of fostering Latina/o assimilation. Spanish suppression is unnecessary because Latinas/os have strong economic incentives to learn English. . . . Those incentives only increase when non-discriminatory practices enable English language acquisition to produce upward social mobility. Conversely, Spanish suppression is insufficient to promote assimilation precisely in those instances in which the reality Latinas/os confront in American society is discriminatory and exclusionary. From this perspective, enclave settlement, employment and commercial practices are simply a rational response to the discrimination experienced when Latinas/os venture outside the Spanish-speaking enclave. . . .

Professor Bratton's law and economics analysis of English-only is particularly interesting and valuable because it creates the point of departure for a more general and far-reaching attack on the oft-repeated assertions made by law and economics practitioners that civil rights and anti-discrimination laws constitute unwarranted "special interest" interventions in the otherwise efficient private ordering of American society. . . . It doesn't take a rocket scientist to see the ready uses of this discourse for the nativist project. Bilingual education programs and other public policies aimed at mitigating the exclusionary impact of language difference on non-English speakers are either manifestations of the concrete steps needed to give

meaning and effect to the vision of inclusion underlying the promise of equal protection and non-discrimination— or they are manifestations of the capture of public policy by special interests. Framed this way, it is clear that the initial debate is over the meaning of bilingual programs, on the one hand, and English-only, on the other.

In this debate, law and economics discourse gives the nativist substantial meaning-making power because the language of costs and efficiency is so readily wrapped in the mantle of purported objectivity and value-neutrality: English-only laws are not discriminatory because they are efficient, or so goes the argument. Against this backdrop, Professor Bratton's contribution maps the economic arguments that can effectively turn the tables to reveal English-only laws as special interest legislative interventions. Since—in the absence of discrimination—private ordering already ensures that non-English speakers will have strong incentives to acquire English language proficiency, there is no regulatory need to create such incentives through English-only laws. There being no regulatory need, English-only laws constitute the use of state power to reaffirm the exclusionary political project embedded in the presumption that Anglo culture defines what it means to be "an American," and, more specifically, to promote higher levels of English language acquisition and usage than the market would produce . . . in the absence of discrimination.

The implications of Professor Cornell's way of understanding the meaning of equality are profound and far-reaching. It entirely changes the public policy issue, for the issue is not whether public policy effectuates equal treatment among the similarly situated, but whether it treats those who are differentially situated as equally worthy of the respect and deference to which equals are entitled. Applying this framework to the analysis of English-only laws, it is immediately evident that the impact of English-only on the self-determination and self-expression of non-English speakers and bilingual or multilingual Americans cannot be reconciled with the imperative to treat all others as equals—each having the right of self-determination as defined and effectuated from their particular and altogether different perspectives. Thus, in this context, it is clear that the legitimacy of English-only laws depends on the projection of an equality norm that presupposes sameness as the predicate for equal treatment. Professor Cornell's great contribution is to show the profound inadequacy of this approach and to offer a more meaningful normative framework through which to resolve the indeterminacies otherwise generated by the instrumental analysis of public policy. . . .

. . . Otherness and difference are a gift, an avenue of insight beyond our own particularities, a window on the world we might behold if ever we could see beyond our own contingency and live beyond our finitude—a glimpse of God. An equality norm based on the imperative of treating others as equals operationalizes this understanding in ways that the norm of equal treatment neither does nor can, for it is only by treating others as equals that we activate an equality norm that enables us to focus, as Professor Wells suggests, on "the gift of otherness, the opportunities of multi-lingualism and the possibility that through difference we can find wholeness."[183]

Professor Wells makes another point worth further reflection. The power of self-expression is crucial to self-determination. Both presuppose access to language, not just any language, but a language in which the world, as one sees it, and one's own self-understandings can be meaningfully formulated and expressed. The language of law and economics has not been popular among critical legal scholars. Part of the reason is, as Professor Wells indicates, its failure to incorporate precisely those values, interests and cultural processes that resist translation into a cost-benefit analysis. The not-so implicit suggestion is that LatCrit theory should avoid speaking the language of law and economics. . . . Some might dismiss this suggestion out of hand: not only are the costs and benefits of any proposal substantively relevant to its proper assessment, but law and economics is the language of choice among policy-making elites and, increasingly, evident in the interpretative practices of many judges. . . .

Speaking the language of power is, from this perspective, imperative precisely because, and so long as, power is power. Indeed, there is no question that Professor Bratton's efforts to recast the debate over English-only laws in terms that destabilize the economic justifications routinely invoked to support the nativist agenda constitute a major contribution to the anti-nativist struggle precisely because law and economics analysis is the language of power. More importantly, however, the indeterminacy revealed by Professor Bratton's creative subversion of the law and economics analysis underlying English-only suggests that law and economics discourse may have become such a ready conduit for regressive and elitist political agendas precisely because critical legal scholars have rarely contested its articulation on its own terms. . . . Learning and using the language of power may thus be the best way to combat the legal production of subordination. Though not all LatCrit scholars need use law and economics analysis, certainly this suggests there is room for, and value in, counting it among the repertoire of critical methodologies through which we expand the scope of our anti-subordination agenda and enhance the depth of our analysis. . . .

Discussion Notes

1. Cases that are increasingly percolating through the courts involve language. Some employers have imposed English language requirements. Such require-

ments are legal if they meet the standards for a business necessity or bona fide occupational qualification defense in the eyes of the few courts that have examined the question. *See Garcia v. Rush-Presbyterian Med. Center*, 660 F.2d 1217 (7th Cir. 1981); *Vasquez v. McAllen Bag & Sup. Co.*, 660 F.2d 686 (5th Cir.), *cert. denied*, 458 U.S. 1122 (1982). The same is true where an employee's foreign accent makes it difficult for him to transact the employer's business because his communications are not understood by others. *Fragrante v. City of Honolulu*, 888 F.2d 591 (9th Cir.), *cert. denied*, 494 U.S. 1081 (1990) (Filipino man's accent interfered with public's ability to understand him); *Carino v. University of Okla.*, 750 F.2d 815 (10th Cir. 1984) (if foreign accent does not prevent employee from doing his job, it cannot be used as basis of adverse employment action).

English-only rules, however, are a source of disagreement between the EEOC and the courts. The EEOC position is as follows:

> Rules which require employees to speak English only at all times are presumptively unlawful because they unduly burden individuals whose language is one other than English, and tend to create a hostile or discriminatory environment based on national origin. An employer may have a more limited rule, requiring that employees speak only in English at certain times, where the employer can show that the rule is justified by business necessity.

EEOC Guidelines on Discrimination Because of National Origin, 29 C.F.R. § 1606.7; EEOC COMPLIANCE MANUAL § 23.

The Ninth Circuit has disagreed, allowing an English-only rule while employees are working. *See Garcia v. Spun Steak Co.*, 998 F.2d 1480, 1487 (9th Cir. 1993) ("It is axiomatic that an employee must often sacrifice individual self-expression during working hours. Just as a private employer is not required to allow other types of self-expression, there is nothing in Title VII which requires an employer to allow an employee to express [his] cultural identity."). *Accord Jurado v. Eleven-Fifty Corp.*, 813 F.2d 1406 (9th Cir. 1987) (radio station may prohibit announcer from using Spanish while broadcasting).

Questions

1. In what ways do Professors Wu and Iglesias deal with the problem of the "model minority" and the interaction between the interests of Latina/os and Asians? Does this work for the interaction between other minority interests? What about the commonalities that may exist between whites and other groups?
2. How is this scholarship relevant to the problems faced in a claim of discrimination on the basis of national origin? What are the issues that are identified by these theories?

---

[183]See Catharine Pierce Wells, Speaking in Tongues: Some Comments on Multilingualism, 53 U. Miami L. Rev. 787 (1999) at 988.

6. Issues of National Origin Discrimination After September 11, 2001

After September 11, 2001, the EEOC issued warnings to employers to be on guard against discrimination against Arabs, Sikhs, or Muslims by their employees. Given the intense response to the horrors of terrorism, the EEOC decided that it was important to inform employers of their obligations under Title VII. In April 2003, the EEOC reported that it had received more than 800 charge filings nationwide claiming post 9/11 discrimination as a backlash against employees perceived to be Muslim, Arab, Afghani, Middle Eastern, South Asian, or Sikh. According to the EEOC, "nearly 100 individuals aggrieved by 9/11 related employment discrimination have received over $1,425,000 in monetary benefits through the EEOC's enforcement, mediation, conciliation, and litigation efforts. The Commission has also been at the forefront of the federal government in conducting vigorous outreach and education to both the employer and labor communities at the national and grassroots levels to prevent such discrimination and promote voluntary compliance with the law." EEOC Chair Cari M. Dominguez stated that "[O]ur nation's tradition of religious tolerance and our laws prohibiting discrimination and ensuring equal employment opportunity must be honored. Employers must remain vigilant in guarding against backlash discrimination directed at innocent individuals due to their religion, ethnicity, or country of origin—especially after the tragic events of September 11 and during this time of war." Statement of EEOC Chair Cari M. Dominguez, EEOC Press Release, April 7, 2003.

B. Discrimination Against Native Americans

1. Introduction

The treatment of Native Americans in the employment context in the United States has been largely ignored in the past. Except for the focus on the exceptions specifically mentioned in Title VII of the Civil Rights Act of 1964 regarding Native American tribes, there have been very few legal opinions focused on the unique problems confronted by Native Americans. The attention, if any, has been focused on the role of Native Americans as employers of increasingly large numbers of employees in enterprises on Native American lands in their own sovereign jurisdiction. The exemptions in Title VII discussed below prevent non-Native-American employees from bringing successful claims against the tribal employers, and efforts to encroach upon the sovereign jurisdiction of Native American lands in order to impose U.S. liability for reverse discrimination have been unsuccessful.

Prohibitions against national origin discrimination apply to Native Americans according to the federal courts. The U.S. Supreme Court has not directly addressed indigenous peoples and their rights. As this movement grows, employers and legislators in the United States will need to take seriously the claims of Native American employees seeking a more complex acceptance of their position as members of sovereign tribes and as employees of U.S. companies.

Mary Ellen Turpel, INDIGENOUS PEOPLES' RIGHTS OF POLITICAL PARTICIPATION
AND SELF-DETERMINATION: RECENT INTERNATIONAL LEGAL DEVELOPMENTS and the CONTINUING
STRUGGLE FOR RECOGNITION (Symposium: The Nations Within: Ethnic Group Demands in a Changing World)
25 Cornell Int'l L.J. 579 (1992)

(This is an edited version of this article and footnotes are deleted.)

Introduction

It must be recognized that indigenous populations have their own identity rooted in historical factors which outweigh the phenomena of mere solidarity in the face of discrimination and exploitation, and that, by virtue of their very existence, they have a natural and original right to live freely on their own lands.[1]

The claims of indigenous[2] peoples have been vigorously advanced in the post-war era internationally and within nation states in key regions throughout the world, including the Americas, the Pacific, and Northern Europe. The unique character of these claims has challenged domestic and international legal and political regimes. Institutionally, the international trusteeship and decolonization process did not address indigenous claims. Indigenous peoples, especially in the Americas, have yet to witness political decolonization, and cultural decolonization is now nearly impossible. Moreover, politically, indigenous claims challenge a nation state's assertion of complete political and territorial sovereignty. . . .

Indigenous peoples are entrapped peoples-enclaves with distinct cultural, linguistic, political and spiritual attributes surrounded by the dominant society. Indigenous peoples find themselves caught in the confines of a subsuming, and frequently hostile, state political apparatus imposed by an immigrant or settler society following colonization. Moreover, indigenous peoples, particularly in the Americas, are surrounded by a dominant consumer culture that threatens their very way of life. Indigenous peoples are truly "nations within."[4]

Indigenous claims are multifaceted because they bring together requests for land, requests for autonomy from the political structures and cultural hegemony of dominant "settler" societies, and pleas for respect for their distinct indigenous cultural and spiritual world views. The claims also seek redress for systemic discrimination against indigenous peoples in the legal (criminal justice) and political systems, the social services sector, and the workforce. Indigenous claims unite legal, historical, political, moral, and humanitarian arguments in a body of doctrine that may be viewed as a third generation of international human rights law focusing on the uniquely collective nature of indigenous claims. This new generation of human rights has been termed the rights of peoples. . . .

The work of the United Nations during the past two decades has significantly legitimized indigenous peoples' claims.[6] Recent efforts of the United Nations Working Group on Indigenous Peoples in preparing a draft declaration of international principles on indigenous rights represents considerable advancement toward international acceptance of collective human rights and international recognition of the need for norms to respond to indigenous claims. In some states, there have also been rising efforts to respond to indigenous claims in the domestic context, often with terms of the debate set by international norms and developments. . . .

[Complaints of human rights violations made to the United Nations Human Rights Committee] must be submitted by named individuals in order to be admitted by the Committee and reviewed on the merits. . . .

. . . This requirement presents a conundrum for indigenous peoples because the human rights violations they suffer are not simply individual in nature; they are typically collective and include deprivations of lands, culture and political status. . . . Although indigenous people are individually affected by the denial of collective human rights, the source of their suffering is generally inseparable from the oppression experienced by the people as a group. The extent to which the complaint process can be adapted to address indigenous peoples communications will shape the capability (and illustrate the willingness) of United Nations human rights institutions to deal with these unique claims. . . .

. . . It is important in this context to consider the differences between collective and individual human rights complaints. While an abstract distinction between individual and collective human rights is often sustained in

[1]Martinez Cobo, Special Rapporteur, Study of the Problem of Discrimination Against Indigenous Populations, ¶578, U.N. Doc. E/CN.4/Sub.2/1983/Add.8.
[2]I use the term "indigenous" throughout this paper. I prefer this term to "Indian" or "native," which have paternalistic and offensive connotations. In Canada, [for example] the expression "aboriginal" is employed in the Constitution Act, 1982 to refer to indigenous peoples including the Metis and the Inuit. . . .
[4]It is important to remember that they are the first nations. Indeed the largest organization of indigenous peoples in Canada is called the Assembly of First Nations.

[6]For an overview, see Ashjborn Eide, Indigenous Populations and Human Rights: The United Nations Efforts at Midway, in NATIVE POWER: THE QUEST FOR AUTONOMY AND NATIONHOOD OF INDIGENOUS PEOPLES 196 (1985).

the literature, it is arguable that this distinction is unworkable. The collective enjoyment of human rights, such as self-determination, is a precondition for individual human rights protection; since individuals do not exist in isolation from a community, repression of the collective concretely affects individuals, particularly indigenous individuals whose identities are closely connected to their people. Moreover, the nature of diplomacy and international advocacy is such that it is individuals who bring forward collective complaints/situations to U.N. fora.

While the Human Rights Committee has established a jurisprudence that considers human rights violations of minorities, it is not entirely relevant to the indigenous context where peoples' or group rights are in issue.

2. Title VII Exemptions

Issues related to discrimination against Native Americans and issues of discrimination against persons born in other countries on the basis of their national origin applied to others have been ignored in the context of employment discrimination law. With respect to Native Americans, section 703(j) of Title VII of the Civil Rights Act of 1964 include recognition that preferences may be given to Native Americans by businesses or enterprises located on or near Indian reservations, and Section 701(b) exclude Native American tribes as employers subject to Title VII. Nothing else in the statute addresses the particular concerns that might apply to the employment concerns of Native American employees.

In the *Dawavendewa* case below, the U.S. Court of Appeals for the Ninth Circuit held that Title VII applies to the hiring practices of tribe-run corporations that do business outside tribal lands. The U.S. Supreme Court held in *Morton v. Mancari*, 417 U.S. 535 (1974), that Indian tribes, because of their sovereignty as separate nations from the United States, may conduct businesses, like casinos and other gambling enterprises, that may be illegal in contiguous lands of the United States. These casinos, on Native American lands, employ non-Native Americans. If they are within the sovereignty of the tribal lands, Title VII does not apply. However, if the tribe runs businesses outside of their sovereign land, Title VII will apply.

Discrimination based on tribal membership may be brought as either racial or national origin discrimination. In *Dawavendewa*, the plaintiff, a member of the Hopi tribe, did not receive a position with a private employer operating a facility on a Navajo reservation.

DAWAVENDEWA
v.
SALT RIVER PROJECT AGRICULTURAL IMPROVEMENT AND POWER DISTRICT
154 F.3d 1117 (9th Cir. 1998)

[The Employment Problem]

Salt River Project Agricultural Improvement and Power District (Salt River), an Arizona corporation, entered into a lease agreement with the Navajo Nation in 1969. The agreement allows Salt River to operate a generating station on Navajo land provided that it, among other things, grants employment preferences to members of the Navajo tribe living on the reservation, or, if none are available, to other members of the Navajo tribe. . . . This preference policy is consistent with Navajo tribal law. *See* 15 Navajo Nation Code § 604 (1995).

Dawavendewa, a member of the Hopi tribe, lives in Arizona less than three miles from the Navajo Reservation. . . . In 1991, he unsuccessfully applied for one of seven Operator Trainee positions at the Salt River generating station. He then filed a complaint alleging that Salt River was engaging in national origin discrimination in violation of Title VII. The complaint alleges that he took and passed a test for the position, ranking ninth out of the top twenty applicants, but was neither interviewed nor considered further for it because he was not a member of, or married to a member of, the Navajo Nation. . . .

Harold Dawavendewa. . . alleges that because he is a Hopi and not a Navajo, he was not considered for a position with a private employer operating a facility on the Navajo reservation. He contends that the employer's conduct constitutes unlawful employment discrimination under Title VII of the Civil Rights Act of 1964.

[The Legal Issue]

To determine whether Dawavendewa's Title VII complaint may proceed, we address, first, whether discrimination based on tribal affiliation constitutes "national origin" discrimination, and second, whether such discrimination is permitted under a Title VII provision that allows preferential treatment of Indians in certain specified circumstances.

[The Decision of the Trial Court]

Salt River moved to dismiss the complaint on the grounds that discrimination on the basis of tribal membership (as opposed to discrimination on the basis of status as a Native American) does not constitute "national origin" discrimination and that Title VII expressly exempts tribal preferences under § 703(i), 42 U.S.C. § 2000e-2 (i) (the "Indian Preferences exemption"). The district court granted the motion to dismiss. It held that Title VII exempts tribal preference policies, and therefore found it unnecessary to decide whether discrimination on the basis of tribal membership constitutes national origin discrimination under Title VII. Dawavendewa appeals.

[The Decision and Rationale of the U.S. Court of Appeals for the Ninth Circuit]

We first address the issue whether discrimination on the basis of tribal membership constitutes "national origin" discrimination for purposes of Title VII. . . . Although Title VII fails to define "national origin," we have observed that "the legislative history and the Supreme Court both recognize that 'national origin' includes the country of one's ancestors." *Pejic v. Hughes Helicopters, Inc.*, 840 F.2d 667, 673 (9th Cir. 1988); *see Espinoza v. Farah Mfg. Co.*, 414 U.S. 86, 88, (1973) (noting that "[t]he term 'national origin' on its

face refers to the country where a person was born, or, more broadly, the country from which his or her ancestors came"). Further, the regulations implementing Title VII provide that discrimination on the basis of one's ancestor's "place of origin"—not nation of origin—is sufficient to come within the scope of the statute. *See* 29 C.F.R. § 1606.1. . . . Accordingly, a claim arises when discriminatory practices are based on the place in which one's ancestors lived.

Consistent with the regulations, we have held that the current political status of the nation or "place" at issue makes no difference for Title VII purposes. In *Pejic v. Hughes Helicopters, Inc.*, we considered the issue whether discrimination against Serbians constituted "national origin" discrimination. 840 F.2d 667, 673 (9th Cir. 1988). The employer in *Pejic* contended that a Serbian employee could not bring a discrimination claim because Serbia as a nation had long been extinct. We rejected this argument and held that Serbians were a protected class:

> Unless historical reality is ignored, the term "national origin" must include countries no longer in existence. . . . Given world history, Title VII cannot be read to limit "countries" to those with modern boundaries, or to require their existence for a certain time length before it will prohibit discrimination. Animus based on national origin can persist long after new political structures and boundaries are established.

Id. (. . .)

Under the principles set forth in *Pejic* and the Code of Federal Regulations, we have no trouble concluding that discrimination against Hopis constitutes national origin discrimination under Title VII. The status of Indian tribes among the international community and in relation to the United States has, of course, a complicated history that cannot be summarized briefly, and we will not attempt to do so. It is elementary, however, that the different tribes were at one time considered to be nations by both the colonizing countries and later the United States. *See* William C. Canby, Jr., *American Indian Law* 68 (1998).. . .

We now consider whether Salt River's policy of favoring members of the Navajo tribe falls within the exception provided by 42 U.S.C. § 2000e-2(i) (the "Indian Preferences exemption").[7] The Indian Preferences exemption states that

---

[7]We note that the Indian tribes themselves are exempt from Title VII liability under § 701 (b).

[n]othing contained in this subchapter shall apply to any business or enterprise on or near an Indian reservation with respect to any publicly announced employment practice of such business or enterprise under which preferential treatment is given to any individual *because he is an Indian living on or near a reservation.*

42 U.S.C. § 2000(e)(2)(i) (emphasis added). Salt River maintains that its preferential treatment of Navajos is exempt from Title VII liability under this provision.

The issue whether the Indian Preferences exemption covers preferences on the basis of tribal affiliation has not been decided by the federal courts. The EEOC, however, addressed this precise issue in a 1988 Policy Statement. It concluded that the "extension of an employment preference on the basis of tribal affiliation is in conflict with and violates Section 703(i) of Title VII. *Policy Statement on Indian Preference Under Title VII*, Fair Empl. Prac. (BNA) 405:6647, 6653 (May 16, 1988). The Commission based its conclusion on three grounds. First, it interpreted the language of the exemption, which applies to preferential treatment towards "any individual because he is an Indian living on or near a reservation," as evidencing Congressional intent to disallow tribal distinctions and "to encourage the extension of employment opportunities to Indians generally." Fair Empl. Prac. 405:6654. It then considered two federal regulations, one issued by the Department of Labor, and the other by the Department of Interior, both of which specifically forbid federal contractors from discriminating on the basis of tribal affiliation as a part of general Indian preference policies. *See id.* (discussing 41 C.F.R. § 60–1.5(a)(6) (1987) and 48 C.F.R. § 1452.204–71 (1987). . . . Finally, the Commission reasoned that the allowance of tribal preferences could result in inequities in cases in which employers are situated near the reservations of two tribes or near a reservation shared by more than one tribe. *Id.* The EEOC, which has filed an amicus brief on this appeal, adheres to the position it adopted in the 1988 Policy Statement.

Generally, EEOC Guidelines are entitled to some deference. *See Albemarle Paper Co. v. Moody*, 422 U.S. 405 (1975). The level of deference, however, depends on the EEOC's thoroughness of consideration, validity of its reasoning, consistency with earlier and later pronouncements, and power of persuasion. *EEOC v. Arabian Am. Oil Co.*, 499 U.S. 244, 256 (1991). . . . "Ultimately, EEOC statements of policy 'should always be considered, but they should not be regarded as conclusive unless reason and statutory interpretation support their conclusion.'"

Yerdon v. Henry, 91 F.3d 370, 376 (2nd Cir. 1996). . . . We give the EEOC's Policy Statement due weight, and for reasons we make clear in the discussion which follows, we agree with its conclusion that the Indian Preferences exemption does not allow discrimination based on tribal affiliation.

We now examine the language and purpose of the statutory exemption. The exemption applies to "preferential treatment. . . given to any individual *because he is an Indian* living on or near a reservation." § 2000e-2 (i) (emphasis added). The term "Indian" is generally used to draw a distinction between Native Americans and all others. *See Perkins v. Lake County Dep't of Utilities*, 860 F. Supp. 1262, 1274 (N.D.Ohio 1994) (citing Felix S. Cohen's Handbook of Federal Indian Law 2 (1971)). An employment practice of giving preference to members of a particular tribe does not afford preference to an applicant "because he is an Indian," but rather because he is a member of "a particular tribe." Such a preference is not consistent with the objectives of the Indian Preferences exemption. While the statute exempts the hiring of Indians from the force of the anti-discrimination in employment provisions, it does so in order to compensate for the effects of past and present unjust treatment, not in order to authorize another form of discrimination against particular groups of Indians—tribal discrimination. It seems evident that, under the exemption, favored treatment could not be given to Indian males at the expense of Indian women, or to Indians of mixed blood in derogation of the rights of those who are entirely of Indian ancestry. The purpose of the Indian Preferences exemption is to authorize an employer to grant preferences to all Indians (who live on or near a reservation)—to permit the favoring of Indians over non-Indians. The exemption is not designed to permit employers to favor members of one Indian tribe over another, let alone to favor them over all other Indians. To so read the provision would be to immunize two forms of discrimination not just one—discrimination on account of Indian status and discrimination on account of tribal membership. The statute on its face reaches only the former. In short, we read the term "because he is an Indian" to mean precisely what it says. The reason for the hiring must be because the person is an Indian, not because he is a Navajo, a male Indian, or a member of any other formal subset of the favored class. . . .

. . . [W]e find that the recent amendment to the ISDA (Indian Self-Determination and Education Act 25 U.S.C. § 450 (a)(b)) supports the EEOC's position. The fact that Congress felt the need to pass the 1994 Amendment only bolsters the contention that general

Indian preference policies were not intended to allow distinctions among different tribes. When Congress decided that tribal affiliation preferences were appropriate in the context of self-determination contracts, it responded through the enactment of the 1994 Amendment. . . . It has passed no similar amendment with respect to Title VII. The fact that Congress now requires a narrowly-defined set of contracts to honor local tribal preference policies not only fails to support the argument that it intended to accomplish that same objective in 1964 when passing Title VII, but it suggests quite the opposite proposition. It shows us that when Congress wishes to allow tribal preferences, it adopts an appropriate amendment to the applicable statute. . . .

Salt River's final argument is that subjecting Salt River to Title VII liability would "frustrate" the purposes of the ISDA as amended in 1994. There is, however, no conflict between allowing tribal preferences under a self-determination contract, the entire purpose of which is to promote the *self-governance* of a tribe through the administration of federal programs, and not allowing those preferences in other private employment situations. . . . Further, other federal regulations that provide for general Indian preferences in employment contexts explicitly disallow discrimination based on tribal affiliation. *See, e.g.*, 23 C.F.R. § 635.117(d) (1997) (employment by state highway agencies); 25 C.F.R. § 256.3(b) (1997) (participation in Housing Improvement Program of BIA). . . . We conclude that Congress' decision to permit tribal preferences under the ISDA is in no way frustrated by our construction of Title VII as precluding such preferences in other types of employment. . . .

Finally, we note the possible inequities that would arise in allowing tribal affiliation discrimination, particularly in areas where there are many different tribal reservations. Under Salt River's interpretation of the provision, any private employer situated near a Hopi *and* Navajo reservation could arbitrarily institute a blanket-policy of preferential treatment towards members of one or the other of the tribes. Further, private employers would have license to pass over those Native Americans who live on a particular reservation but who do not share the same tribal affiliation as the governing body of the reservation. . . . Without a clear indication to the contrary, this appears to be the sort of individual discrimination wholly within the scope of Title VII.

Based on our reading of the Indian Preferences exemption, and informed by the 1994 Amendment to the ISDA, we conclude that the exemption does not include preferences based on tribal affiliation. If Congress wishes to amend Title VII to accommodate tribal preferences, as it did with respect to the ISDA, it may do so. Because Congress has not yet chosen that course, and because there is no dispute that the Salt River policy constitutes a tribal preference policy, the district court erred in dismissing the complaint.

Conclusion

We conclude that Salt River's conduct as described in the complaint constitutes "national origin" discrimination under Title VII and does not fall within the scope of the Indian Preferences exemption. Accordingly, the district court's Rule 12(b)(6) dismissal was improper, and we reverse.

chapter
11

Religious Discrimination

Problem 45

The police department runs a youth outreach unit. When the crisis counselor, Anna Moore, is hired, it is not known to the supervisor who hires her that she is not Christian. However, following an office conversation, the supervisor learns this and begins to harass the employee and to encourage co-workers to do so. When bonus time rolls around, the supervisor tells Anna that she is not getting one and mentions pointedly that she is not Christian. The supervisor then begins holding meetings to criticize the counselor's performance and does not allow Anna to attend. Does Anna have a Title VII claim?

Problem 46

A Pakistani Muslim woman, Ayesha Habib, works in a bank. At the time of hire, she explains that her religion requires her to pray five times daily, for 5 to 15 minutes at a time. The bank agrees. Later, however, her supervisor and co-workers make derogatory comments about her dress and diet, and her supervisor publicly criticizes the prayer breaks. Three times, the supervisor refuses to allow the prayers at the time Ayesha's religion requires. When she needs sick time, she is told to bring in a doctor's note explaining why she needs leave, and she fails to do so. She is fired by a different supervisor than the one who has troubled her in the past. If you are the lawyer representing the bank in her suit based on race, religion, and national origin discrimination, what might you argue?

A. Introduction and Meaning of "Religion"

The provisions of Title VII of the Civil Rights Act of 1964 set forth in Section 701(j) of the statute are broadly based: "The term 'religion' includes all aspects of religious observance and practice, as well as belief. . . . " Relatively little attention has been paid to whether a belief is actually a religion, as the courts tend to interpret this definition to include any sincerely held belief. The determination does not depend on whether the religion has an institutional structure. Title VII's religious protections encompass discrimination based both on the material terms and conditions of employment and on the atmosphere of a workplace environment; thus, a hostile environment claim can be brought based on religion.

A claim of discrimination based on religion may take many forms. In one such form, the employee claims that the employer has required the employee to work or perform some duty that interferes with the need for the employee to practice some part of his religious belief. For example, the employer may require the employee to work on Saturday, which may be the employee's day of religious observance, or the employer may forbid, at the workplace, the wearing of a yarmulke or other piece of clothing that has religious significance to the employee. In order to make out a prima facie claim of discrimination in these cases, the employee must demonstrate that (1) she has a sincere religious need that is being interfered with by an employment requirement and (2) she has notified the employer and the employer has refused to accommodate that need. The employer must then show that there is no reasonable accommodation that can occur without an undue hardship on the employer. The employer is not required to accept the employee's desired method of accommodation if there is another accommodation that the employer may choose.

B. Employer's Duty to Accommodate and Undue Hardship

Problem 47

Donald Ronfield, a postal carrier, is a member of the Worldwide Church of God, whose members observe the Sabbath by abstaining from work from sunset Friday to sunset Saturday. The postal service has a bona fide seniority system. Donald bid for and was given a rotating Saturday shift but then failed to show up for work on a Saturday. He was disciplined for being absent without excuse, but the postal service then offered him four different religious accommodations when he stated his religious needs. One of the accommodations the employer proposed was a transfer to at least three other post offices, all of which could have given him Saturdays off. Donald refused these accommodations because a transfer would have caused him to lose seniority for a period of 90 days. Some time later he applied for a promotion, which he did not get. The postal service cited his history of driving violations and his disciplinary record. The carrier sued for religious discrimination. The result?

Problem 48

The plaintiff, Monroe Fried, an Orthodox Jew, is hired as a correspondence analyst. Upon receiving a conditional offer of employment, he informs the recruiter of his faith and is told that he can have leave for the Jewish holidays. When the recruiter calls the department manager to tell him of the conditional offer, the department manager tells him to rescind the offer immediately because he thinks Monroe has been overly aggressive and obnoxious at a job fair. If Monroe sues, what if the decision maker who said to rescind the offer did not know of Monroe's religion?

Section 701(j) of the Civil Rights Act of 1964 imposes a duty on employers, employment agencies, labor unions, and joint labor-management committees to "reasonably accommodate" both candidates' and employees' modes of religious observance and practice except where doing so would impose an "undue hardship" on the employer's ability to run its business. As a general matter, secular employers are forbidden from considering religion in their hiring or firing decisions. Religious institutions and their associated educational institutions or organizations, however, are expressly allowed to give preference to persons who share the employer's religious affiliation, subject to some limitations.

The trend is toward narrow judicial construction of the scope of an employer's duty to reasonably accommodate an individual's religious observance or practice. The courts are also trending toward giving religious employers wide latitude in their hiring and firing decisions.

1. The Sabbath and Religious Holidays

There are numerous cases involving the claim that the employer refused to allow an employee to rearrange work schedules so that the employee could honor his or her religious day of worship. The employer experienced other demands that made it either difficult or annoying to adjust the previously understood schedule. Some of these cases are further complicated by the problems of contractual obligations that the employer may have to other employees based on collective bargaining agreements, seniority systems already in place, or other arrangements that give scheduling priorities to other employees. Does the employer have the obligation to change a schedule in a way that affects the contractual promises to other employees? The following Supreme Court case addressed these complications and further described the nature of the duty to accommodate religious beliefs and practices.

TRANS WORLD AIRLINES, INC.
v.
HARDISON
432 U.S. 63 (1977)

Mr. Justice WHITE delivered the opinion of the Court.

[The Employment Problem]

Petitioner Trans World Airlines (TWA) operates a large maintenance and overhaul base in Kansas City, Missouri. On June 5, 1967, respondent Larry G. Hardison was hired by TWA to work as a clerk in the Stores Department at its Kansas City base. Because of its essential role in the Kansas City operation, the Stores Department must operate 24 hours a day, 365 days per year, and whenever an employee's job in that department is not filled, an employee must be shifted from another department, or a supervisor must cover the job, even if the work in other areas may suffer.

Hardison, like other employees at the Kansas City base, was subject to a seniority system contained in a collective-bargaining agreement . . . that TWA maintains with petitioner International Association of Machinists and Aerospace Workers (IAM). . . . The most senior employees have first choice for job and shift assignments, and the most junior employees are required to work when the union steward is unable to find enough people willing to work at a particular time or in a particular job. . . .

In the spring of 1968 Hardison began to study the religion known as the Worldwide Church of God. One of the tenets of that religion is that one must observe the Sabbath by refraining from performing any work from sunset on Friday until sunset on Saturday. The religion also proscribes work on certain specified religious holidays.

When Hardison informed Everett Kussman, the manager of the Stores Department, of his religious conviction regarding observance of the Sabbath, Kussman agreed that the union steward should seek a job swap for Hardison or a change of days off; that Hardison would have his religious holidays off wherever possible if Hardison agreed to work the [more] traditional holidays when asked; and that Kussman would try to find Hardison another job that would be more compatible with his religious beliefs. The problem was temporarily solved when Hardison transferred to the 11 P.M.–7 A.M. shift. Working this shift permitted Hardison to observe his Sabbath.

The problem soon reappeared when Hardison bid for and received a transfer from Building 1, where he had been employed, to Building 2, where he would work the day shift. The two buildings had entirely separate seniority lists [and Hardison] was second from the bottom on the Building 2 seniority list.

In Building 2, Hardison was asked to work Saturdays when a fellow employee went on vacation. TWA agreed to permit the union to seek a change of work assignments for Hardison, but the union was not willing to violate the seniority provisions set out in the collective-bargaining contract, . . . and Hardison had insufficient seniority to bid for a shift having Saturdays off.

A proposal that Hardison work only four days a week was rejected by the company. Hardison's job was essential, and on weekends he was the only available person on his shift to perform it. To leave the position empty would have impaired supply shop functions, which were critical to airline operations; to fill Hardison's position with a supervisor or an employee from another area would simply have undermanned another operation; and to employ someone not regularly assigned to work Saturdays would have required TWA to pay premium wages.

When an accommodation was not reached, Hardison refused to report to work on Saturdays. A transfer to the twilight shift . . . still required Hardison to work past sundown on Fridays. After a hearing, Hardison was discharged on grounds of insubordination. . . .

Hardison . . . brought this action . . . claiming that his discharge by TWA constituted religious discrimination in violation of Title VII, 42 U.S.C. § 2000e-2(a)(1). He also charged that the union had discriminated against him by failing to represent him adequately in his dispute with TWA and by depriving him of his right to exercise his religious beliefs. . . .

[The Legal Issue]

The issue in this case is the extent of the employer's obligation under Title VII to accommodate an employee whose religious beliefs prohibit him from working on Saturdays.

[The Decision of the Trial Court and the U.S. Court of Appeals for the Eighth Circuit]

[The district court ruled that the union was not required to overlook its seniority system in order to accommodate Hardison's religious beliefs and that TWA could not accommodate them without working an undue hardship on it. The court of appeals left the ruling in favor of the union intact but reversed the district court's ruling covering the employer, finding that TWA had not satisfied its duty to accommodate.]

It might be inferred from the Court of Appeals' opinion . . . that TWA's efforts to accommodate were no more than negligible. The findings of the District Court, supported by the record, are to the contrary. In summarizing its more detailed findings, the District Court observed:

> TWA established as a matter of fact that it did take appropriate action to accommodate as required by Title VII. It held several meetings with plaintiff at which it attempted to find a solution to plaintiff's problems. It did accommodate plaintiff's observance of his special religious holidays. It authorized the union steward to search for someone who could swap shifts, which apparently was normal procedure.

It is also true that TWA itself attempted without success to find Hardison another job. The District Court's view was that TWA had done all that could reasonably be expected within the bounds of the seniority system.

The Court of Appeals observed, however, that the possibility of a variance from the seniority system was never really posed to the union. This is contrary to the District Court's findings and to the record. The District Court found that when TWA first learned of Hardison's religious observances in April, 1968, it agreed to permit the union's steward to seek a swap of shifts or days off but that "the steward reported that he was unable to work out scheduling changes and that he understood that no one was willing to swap days with plaintiff." 375 F. Supp. at 888. Later, in March 1969, at a meeting held just two days before Hardison first failed to report for his Saturday shift, TWA again "offered to accommodate plaintiff's religious observance by agreeing to any trade of shifts or change of sections that plaintiff and the union could work out. . . . Any shift or change was impossible within the seniority framework and the union was

not willing to violate the seniority provisions set out in the contract to make a shift or change." Id., at 889. As the record shows, Hardison himself testified that [the manager] Kussman was willing, but the union was not, to work out a shift or job trade with another employee. . . .

. . . [T]he [seniority] system itself represented a significant accommodation to the needs, both religious and secular, of all of TWA's employees. . . . [T]he seniority system represents a neutral way of minimizing the number of occasions when an employee must work on a day that he would prefer to have off. Additionally, recognizing that weekend work schedules are the least popular, the company made further accommodation by reducing its work force to a bare minimum on those days.

[The Decision and Rationale of the U.S. Supreme Court]

[T]he employer's statutory obligation to make reasonable accommodation for the religious observances of its employees, short of an undue hardship, is clear, but the reach of that obligation has never been spelled out by Congress or by [Equal Employment Opportunity Commission (EEOC)] guidelines. With this in mind, we turn to a consideration of whether TWA has met its obligation under Title VII to accommodate the religious observances of its employees.

. . . The emphasis of both the language and the legislative history of the statute is on eliminating discrimination in employment; similarly situated employees are not to be treated differently solely because they differ with respect to race, color, religion, sex, or national origin. . . . This is true regardless of whether the discrimination is directed against majorities or minorities. . . .

[In order to resolve some tension about the scope of the employer's "duty to accommodate" between EEOC Guidelines and a Sixth Circuit opinion that was affirmed by an equally divided Supreme Court], Congress included the following definition of religion in its 1972 amendments to Title VII:

> The term 'religion' includes all aspects of religious observance and practice, as well as belief, unless an employer demonstrates that he is unable to reasonably accommodate to an employee's or prospective employee's religious observance or belief or practice without undue hardship on the conduct of the employer's business. Title VII, Section 701(j), 42 U.S.C. § 2000e(j). . . .

We are also convinced, contrary to the Court of Appeals, that TWA cannot be faulted for having failed to work out a shift or job swap for Hardison. Both the union and TWA had agreed to the seniority system; the union was unwilling to entertain a variance over the objections of men senior to Hardison; and for TWA to have arranged unilaterally for a swap would have amounted to a breach of the collective-bargaining agreement.

Hardison . . . insist[s] that the statutory obligation to accommodate religious needs takes precedence over both the collective-bargaining contract and the seniority rights of TWA's other employees. We agree that neither a collective-bargaining contract nor a seniority system may be employed to violate the statute, . . . but we do not believe that the duty to accommodate requires TWA to take steps inconsistent with the otherwise valid agreement. Collective bargaining, aimed at effecting workable and enforceable agreements between management and labor, lies at the core of our national labor policy, and seniority provisions are universally included in these contracts. . . .

Any employer who, like TWA, conducts an around-the-clock operation is presented with the choice of allocating work schedules either in accordance with the preferences of its employees or by involuntary assignment. . . .

Whenever there are not enough employees who choose to work a particular shift, . . . some employees must be assigned to that shift even though it is not their first choice. Such was evidently the case with regard to Saturday work; even though TWA cut back its weekend work force to a skeleton crew, not enough employees chose those days off to staff the Stores Department through voluntary scheduling. In these circumstances, TWA and IAM [had] agreed to give first preference to employees who had worked in a particular department the longest.

Had TWA nonetheless circumvented the seniority system by relieving Hardison of Saturday work and ordering a senior employee to replace him, it would have denied the latter his shift preference so that Hardison could be given his. The senior employee would . . . have been deprived of his rights under the collective-bargaining agreement.

It was essential to TWA's business to require Saturday and Sunday work from at least a few employees even though these employees preferred those days off. Allocating the burdens of weekend work was a matter for collective bargaining. In considering criteria to govern this allocation, TWA and the union had two alternatives: adopt a neutral system, such as seniority, a lottery, or rotating shifts; or allocate days off in accordance with the religious needs of its employees. TWA would have had to adopt the latter in order to assure Hardison and others like him of getting the days off necessary for strict observance of their religion, but it could have done so only at the expense of others who had strong, but perhaps nonreligious reasons for not working on weekends. There were no volunteers to relieve Hardison on Saturdays, and to give Hardison Saturdays off, TWA would have had to deprive another employee of his shift preference at least in part because he did not adhere to a religion that observed the Saturday Sabbath.

Title VII does not contemplate such unequal treatment. The repeated, unequivocal emphasis of both the language and the legislative history of Title VII is on eliminating discrimination in employment, and such discrimination is proscribed when it is directed against majorities as well as minorities. . . . Indeed, the foundation of Hardison's claim is that TWA and IAM engaged in religious discrimination . . . when they failed to arrange for him to have Saturdays off. It would be anomalous to conclude that by "reasonable accommodation" Congress meant that the employer must deny the shift and job preference of some employees, as well as deprive them of their contractual rights, in order to accommodate or prefer the religious needs of others, and we conclude that Title VII does not require an employer to go that far.

Our conclusion is supported by the fact that seniority systems are afforded special treatment under Title VII itself. Section 703(h) provides in pertinent part:

> Notwithstanding any other provision of this subchapter, it shall not be an unlawful employment practice for an employer to apply different standards of compensation, or different terms, conditions, or privileges of employment pursuant to a bona fide seniority or merit system . . . provided that such differences are not the result of an intention to discriminate because of race, color, religion, sex, or national origin. . . .
>
> . . . Thus, absent a discriminatory purpose, the operation of a seniority system cannot be an un-

lawful employment practice even if the system has some discriminatory consequences. . . .

To require TWA to bear more than a *de minimis* cost in order to give Hardison Saturdays off is an undue hardship. . . . [T]o require TWA to bear additional costs when no such costs are incurred to give other employees the days off that they want would involve unequal treatment of employees on the basis of their religion. By suggesting that TWA should incur certain costs in order to give Hardison Saturdays off the Court of Appeals would in effect require TWA to fi-

nance an additional Saturday off and then to choose the employee who will enjoy it on the basis of his religious beliefs. . . .

Discussion Note

1. What about the circumstance in which an employee, rather than asking for religious holidays or the Sabbath off, asks to be relieved of particular job assignments that conflict with her religious beliefs? This poses a more interesting question, as explored below.

2. The Nature of Undue Hardship

Ten years after it heard *TWA*, the Supreme Court clarified whether the employer satisfies its burden of offering an accommodation where the accommodation it proposes is not the one that the employee would prefer. In *Ansonia Board of Education v. Philbrook*, 479 U.S. 60 (1986), a teacher observed holy days that caused him to miss six working days a year. The collective bargaining agreement between the school district and the teachers' union allowed for 3 religious holidays, 3 personal leave days, and 18 sick leave days a year. Philbrook asked to treat his three personal leave days as religious holidays. Because the personal leave was designated in the collective bargaining agreement as leave that was not for religious observance or sick time, the school board refused to make Philbrook's suggested accommodation. Philbrook sued, alleging that the school district had failed to accommodate him when it rejected his proposal and that it had also failed to prove that the accommodation he suggested would result in undue hardship to it.

The district court held that the collective bargaining provision providing for three religious holidays a year was a reasonable accommodation in itself. The Supreme Court likewise rejected Philbrook's argument about the showing the employer must make in a religious discrimination case. In addition to holding that the collective bargaining agreement accorded the neutral accommodation of three religious holidays for every employee, the Court instructed: "[W]here the employer has already reasonably accommodated the employee's religious needs, the statutory inquiry is at an end. The employer need not further show that each of the employee's alternative accommodations would result in undue hardship. . . . [T]he extent of undue hardship on the employer's business is at issue only where the employer claims that it is unable to offer any reasonable accommodation without such hardship."

Even in the absence of a collective bargaining agreement, it is not difficult for an employer to establish that accommodations involving shift substitutions constitute undue hardship. *See, e.g., Eversley v. MHank Dallas*, 843 F.2d 172 (5th Cir. 1988) (nonunionized employer is not required to accommodate employee's desire to observe his Sabbath if that involves conscripting co-workers to work his shift over their objections).

BRUFF

v.

NORTH MISSISSIPPI HEALTH SERVICES, INC.
244 F.3d 495 (5th Cir. 2001)

POLITZ, Circuit Judge

[The Employment Problem]

After graduating from the Reformed Theological Seminary in Jackson, Mississippi, with a master's degree in marriage and family counseling, Bruff was hired as a counselor by [the defendant and eventually was employed] as a counselor in its Employee Assistance Program (EAP). The Medical Center, a non-profit hospital in Tupelo, Mississippi, established the EAP to provide counseling to the employees of various businesses in the region.

Bruff was one of three EAP counselors, one of whom also acted as the program's supervisor. Counseling sessions were held during and after regular business hours in Tupelo and Oxford, Mississippi. Typically, only one counselor would travel to a given location on each occasion.

Early in 1996, Bruff counseled a woman identified only as Jane Doe. . . . Several months later, Doe returned for further counseling. At that time she informed Bruff that she was a [lesbian] and she asked for help in improving her relationship with her female partner. Bruff declined to counsel Doe on that subject, advising that homosexual behavior conflicted with her religious beliefs, but offered to continue counseling Doe on other matters. . . . [Doe] complained to her employer about Bruff's actions and her employer in turn complained to the Medical Center.

The supervisory counselor informed Bruff a complaint had been lodged and arranged a meeting to explore the matter. In that meeting, Bruff confirmed that she had declined to counsel Doe on improving her homosexual relationship because doing so would conflict with her religious beliefs. Bruff was then directed, per company policy, to put in writing exactly what aspects of her counseling responsibilities she wanted to be excused from. Bruff wrote a letter asking that she "be excused from . . . actively helping people involved in the homosexual lifestyle to have a better relationship with their homosexual partners. This would also include helping persons who have a sexual relationship outside of marriage have a better sexual relationship." She added that her problem was not with counseling the person *per se*, but only with providing assistance in improving the homosexual or extra-marital relationship.

In response to this letter, Medical Center management met several times to determine if Bruff's request could be accommodated by shifting responsibilities among the three EAP counselors. Eventually it was determined such an accommodation was not feasible. Management then gave her a letter denying her request, [which stated], "Individuals being seen in accordance with all of our EAP contracts obligates us to treat a wide variety of psychiatric disturbances and clinical issues. Our EAP contracts with our customers do not exclude certain categories or issues for individuals with certain types of issues. You also are not able to determine specific patient care issues in advance. Your request could create an uneven distribution of patient work load." . . . Bruff was relieved of her counseling responsibilities and placed on leave without pay.

Bruff appealed this decision to a vice president of the Medical Center who asked whether there would be any other situations when Bruff would not want to counsel a person. Bruff responded that she would not be willing to counsel anyone on any subject that went against her religion. When the possibility of transferring from the EAP to a section specifically performing pastoral or Christian counseling was discussed, she demurred, opining that the head of the section held religious views that were more liberal than hers, and that he likely would not tolerate her conservative perspective.

Based upon Bruff's letter and their discussion, the Medical Center's vice president wrote Bruff affirming the decision to deny her request to counsel only on topics that did not conflict with her religion. In his letter, the vice president referenced the small size of the EAP staff; the travel and extended hours the counselors must work; the inability to determine beforehand when a trait or topic might arise that would require referring the employee to another counselor, thus requiring either multiple counselors to travel, or scheduling additional counseling sessions at another time; and the additional sessions that introducing a new counselor might require to build the trust relationship necessary to be effective. He underscored that the logistics of accommodating her request would cause an undue hardship upon the Center, its clients, and the other EAP counselors.

Bruff then filed a complaint with the Equal Employment Opportunity Commission. The EEOC concluded its investigation without action, notifying Bruff that she had 90 days to file suit if she so desired. The instant action followed.

The matter was tried to a jury, which found that the Medical Center had discriminated against Bruff because of her religious beliefs, that it had not made a reasonable accommodation for those beliefs, and that it had acted with malice or reckless indifference. . . . The trial judge . . . reduced the total compensatory and punitive damages to the statutory maximum of $300,000.00. Back pay is not included in the statutory cap. Bruff's state law claims, which would not have been subject to a similar cap, previously had been dismissed on a motion for directed verdict. . . .

[The Legal Issues]

. . . The Medical Center . . . appeal[s] both the trial court's denial of its motion for judgment as a matter of law, and the jury's adverse verdict. Bruff cross-appeals the dismissal of her state law claims, and the denial of her motion for reinstatement, or alternatively, front pay in lieu thereof. [The issue of the sincerity of Bruff's religious beliefs was not challenged by the Medical Center. The court proceeded to discuss whether the Medical Center had discharged its duty to accommodate.]

[The Decision and Rationale of the U.S. Court of Appeals for the Fifth Circuit]

Accommodation can take place in two fundamental ways: (1) an employee can be accommodated in his or her current position by changing the working conditions, or (2) the employer can offer to let the employee transfer to another reasonably comparable position where conflicts are less likely to arise.

Retention as an EAP Counselor . . .

. . . [T]he Medical Center employed three counselors in its EAP program, one of whom handled supervisory duties in addition to her counseling responsibilities. Thus, any request by Bruff to refer all subjects desiring to be counseled on something that she felt conflicted with her religious beliefs meant, necessarily, that one of the two remaining counselors must assume that responsibility. . . .

. . . Bruff does not suggest that her request for accommodation was . . . flexible; instead, she contends that under Title VII the Medical Center must excuse her

from counseling on all subjects of concern at all times. Furthermore, unlike traditional requests for religious accommodation which merely seek to rearrange an employee's schedule, Bruff determined that she would not perform some aspects of the position itself, and her testimony makes it abundantly clear that she was aware of that before applying for the position. . . . [S]he apparently assumed she would only have to perform those aspects of the position she found acceptable. Title VII does not require an employer to accommodate such an inflexible position. . . .

. . . [G]iven the size of the EAP staff, the area covered by the program and the travel involved, and the nature of psychological counseling incorporating trust relationships over time, any accommodation of Bruff in the EAP counselor position would involve more than *de minimis* cost to the Medical Center. Requiring one or both counselors to assume a disproportionate workload, or to travel involuntarily with Bruff to sessions to be available in case a problematic subject area came up, is an undue hardship as a matter of law. . . . Requiring the Center to schedule multiple counselors for sessions, or additional counseling sessions to cover areas Bruff declined to address, would also clearly involve more than *de minimis* cost. . . .

. . . Title VII does not require an employer to actually incur accommodation costs before asserting that they are more than *de minimis*. . . .

Transfer to Another Counselor Position

Title VII does not restrict an employer to only those means of accommodation that are preferred by the employee. . . . Once the Medical Center establishes that it offered Bruff a reasonable accommodation, even if that alternative is not her preference, [it has], as a matter of law, satisfied [its] obligation under Title VII.

The Medical Center contends that its offer to give Bruff 30 days, and the assistance of its in-house employment counselor to find another position at the Center where the likelihood of encountering further conflicts with her religious beliefs would be reduced, fulfilled its obligations to offer her a reasonable accommodation. We agree. . . .

When the Medical Center gave Bruff 30 days to find another position, it also alerted its in-house employment counselor to the situation and directed that Bruff be given assistance in that effort. . . . Bruff was advised of, and applied for, another counselor position. Although she was not successful, the Medical Center was not obligated to give Bruff preference over others with superior credentials when filling the

Psychiatric Assessment Counselor position. . . . Bruff was also advised of other available positions, which she declined to apply for. . . . She declined to even consider a transfer to the pastoral counseling department because she speculated there might be a personal conflict with its director. . . . An employee has a duty to cooperate in achieving accommodation of his or her religious beliefs, and must be flexible in achieving that end. . . . Bruff displayed almost no such cooperation or flexibility.

[T]he facts and inferences point so strongly and overwhelmingly in favor of the Medical Center that . . . denial of the motion for judgment as a matter of law was error.

. . . Accordingly, we affirm the trial court's dismissal of Bruff's state law claims [and we reverse the judgment on the Title VII claim and render judgment for the appellant, dismissing all of Bruff's claims with prejudice].

Discussion Note

1. Sandra Bruff's claims, as the Fifth Circuit noted, are not traditional religious accommodation claims. Rather, they were directed at essential job functions that Bruff did not want to perform because of her religious beliefs. In this respect, Bruff's claims have something in common with claims premised on a conscientious objection to a workplace practice. Courts have been more sympathetic to employees who have conscientious objections to a practice that does not involve their actual job requirements. For example, courts have upheld the rights of employees whose religious beliefs proscribe the payment of union dues to give the dues to a charity instead and have found providing this option to be a reasonable accommodation on the employer's part. *International Ass'n of Mach. v. Boeing Co.*, 833 F.2d 165 (9th Cir.), *cert. denied*, 485 U.S. 1014 (1988); *Tooley v. Martin Marietta Corp.*, 648 F.2d 1239 (9th Cir.), *cert. denied*, 454 U.S. 1098 (1981); *EEOC v. Davey Tree Surgery Co.*, 671 F. Supp. 1260 (N.D. Cal. 1987).

   Bruff makes it clear that the employee who claims a conscientious objection to performing particular job functions acts at her peril if she refuses to cooperate with her employer in securing an accommodation. The attitude of the *Bruff* court toward reticent employees is not atypical. *See also Rodriguez v. City of Chicago*, 156 F.3d 771 (7th Cir. 1998) (police officer's request

to be excused from guarding abortion clinics because of his religious beliefs was reasonably accommodated when employer offered him a transfer to a district that did not have an abortion clinic, with no reduction in pay or benefits, which the officer refused). Also, courts are sensitive to the command of *Hardison* about *de minimis* expense; accommodating religious objections to performing essential job functions almost invariably involves more than *de minimis* expense to the employer. *See Weber v. Roadway Exp., Inc.*, 199 F.3d 270 (5th Cir. 2000) (over-the-road trucker, a Jehovah's Witness, requested that he never be assigned runs with a woman because his religious beliefs forbade traveling overnight with a woman other than his spouse; such an accommodation would involve more than *de minimis* expense).

Courts also have been hostile to the attempt to portray curtailment of coercive religious practices as "discrimination" or to extend "free-exercise" protection to them. Where government is the employer or has a contractual relationship with the employer, and where municipal antidiscrimination laws exist, free-exercise issues are sometimes raised. In *Spratt v. County of Kent*, 621 F. Supp. 594 (W.D. Mich. 1985), *aff'd*, 810 F.2d 203 (6th Cir.), *cert. denied*, 480 U.S. 934 (1987), Spratt had rather the opposite scruple from Bruff: He wanted not to abstain from counseling certain persons of whom he disapproved, but to counsel them precisely so that he could proselytize. When Spratt, a prison counselor, did not stop incorporating spiritual elements into his counseling of incarcerated persons when told to stop, he was fired. Spratt claimed to be a victim of religious discrimination, but the court rejected this argument, noting that the plaintiff's religious beliefs could be accommodated only to the extent that inmates could maintain their free exercise of religion. It also found that the state employer could conform with the establishment clause of the federal Constitution only by maintaining a strictly neutral policy toward religion (not affirmatively sponsoring it), especially in the captive-audience setting of a prison. *See also Knight v. Connecticut Dep't of Pub. Health*, 275 F.3d 156 (2d Cir. 2001) (nursing consultant under contract with Connecticut Department of Public Health paid a home visit to a gay couple, one of whom was in the end stages of AIDS, telling them that "although God created us and loves us, He doesn't like the homosexual lifestyle"; after being fired, nurse brought "hybrid" free-exercise and free-speech claims, rejected by the court because the state employer could not "accommodate" the nurse's need to evangelize her clients without running afoul of the establishment clause's command of official neutrality toward religion).

3. Religious Employers and Sectarian Preferences in Hiring

Title VII provides, in Section 702(a) that

[t]his title shall not apply . . . to a religious corporation, association or educational institution, or society with respect to the employment of individuals of a particular religion to perform work connected with the carrying on by such corporation, association, educational institution, or society of its activities.

In Section 703(e) of the Act, Congress further provided that

[n]otwithstanding any other provision of this title, (1) it shall not be an unlawful employment practice for an employer to hire and employ employees . . . on the basis of his religion, sex, or national origin in those certain instances where religion, sex, or national origin is a bona fide occupational qualification [BFOQ] reasonably necessary to the normal operation of that particular business or enterprise, and (2) it shall not be an unlawful employment practice for a school, college, university, or other educational institution or institution of learning to hire and employ employees of a particular religion if such school, college, university, or other educational institution . . . is, in whole or in substantial part, owned, supported, controlled, or managed by a particular religion . . . or if the curriculum of such school . . . is directed toward the propagation of a particular religion.

Neither Congress nor the judiciary has proscribed religious institutions from giving preference in hiring to members of their own sect; in 1979, Congress expressly amended Title VII to extend the exemption for religious activities of religious employers to the whole of a religious organization's activities. The Supreme Court upheld the exemption as applied to nonprofit secular activities against an establishment clause challenge and specifically allowed the Mormon Church to refuse to hire non-Mormons, even for jobs that were non-pastoral and secular in nature. *See Corporation of Presiding Bishop of the Church of Jesus Christ of Latter Day Saints v. Amos*, 483 U.S. 327 (1987). *See also Little v. Wuerl*, 929 F.2d 944 (3d Cir. 1991) (religious school may restrict employment to persons who share its doctrinal beliefs and may fire employees whose conduct, in its view, brings disrepute on the faith); *Pime v. Loyola Univ. of Chicago*, 803 F.2d 351 (7th Cir. 1986) (university founded and managed by Jesuits may restrict faculty to Jesuits; university may successfully claim that membership in Jesuit order is BFOQ for its philosophy faculty).

Where the employment is of a pastoral nature, the Title VII exemption as well as the free-exercise rights of the religious institution may be implicated. *See Rayburn v. Conference of Seventh-Day Adventists*, 772 F.2d 1164 (4th Cir.), *cert. denied*, 478 U.S. 1020 (1986). On the other hand, *Amos* notwithstanding, the Ninth Circuit has refused to allow schools that have a primarily secular—rather than religious—mission to show sectarian preference in hiring. *See*

EEOC v. Kamehameha Schls./Bishop Est., 990 F.2d 458 (9th Cir. 1993) (bequest by founder conditioned on schools' restriction of employment to Protestants cannot be enforced where schools are not primarily religious).

4. Sincerely Held Religious Beliefs of Private, For-Profit Actors

In construing both employment and public accommodations antidiscrimination provisions, the courts have drawn sharp distinctions between commercial and nonprofit activities of religious people and also between religious institutions and private individuals who are religious adherents. The Supreme Court has noted, in the public accommodations context, that when privately religious persons wander from the garden of religious devotion into the wilderness of commerce with the public, they generally cannot claim that complying with a mandate not to discriminate works a burden on their religious beliefs: "When followers of a particular sect enter into commercial activity as a matter of choice, the limits they accept on their own conduct as a matter of conscience and faith, are not to be superimposed on the statutory schemes which are binding on others in that activity." *United States v. Lee*, 455 U.S. 252, 261 (1982). *See also Braunfeld v. Brown*, 366 U.S. 599, 606 (1961) (for purposes of free-exercise jurisprudence, it is not a burden on for-profit landlord's religious rights if his choice to adhere to his private religious beliefs rather than to comply with an antidiscrimination law costs him money); *Smith v. Fair Empl. & Hous. Comm'n*, 913 P.2d 909, 925–26 (Cal. 1996) ("the landlord in this case does not claim that her religious beliefs require her to rent apartments; the religious injunction is simply that she not rent to unmarried couples. No religious exercise is burdened if she follows the alternative course of placing her capital in another investment"); *Swanner v. Anchorage Equal Rights Comm'n*, 874 P.2d 274, 283 ("[The religiously motivated discriminatory landlord] has made no showing of a religious belief which requires that he engage in the property-rental business. Additionally, the economic burden, or 'Hobson's choice,' of which he complains, is caused by his choice to enter into commercial activity that is regulated by anti-discrimination laws. . . . The [municipal] ordinance regulate[s] unlawful practices in the rental of real property and provides that those who engage in those activities shall not discriminate. . . . Voluntary commercial activity does not receive the same status accorded to directly religious activity.").

In the employment context, the courts have largely hewn to the same principles. While religious institutions have presumptive bona fides to discharge their spiritual mission, private persons operating businesses cannot claim sincerely held religious beliefs as *carte blanche* to discriminate or to coerce. For example, the federal courts have not been persuaded that the majority stockholders and operators of a manufacturing plant can claim either a free-exercise right to discriminate or an exemption to Title VII's religious discrimination provisions. *See Townley Eng. & Mfg. Co.*, 859 F.2d 610 (9th Cir.), *cert. denied*, 489 U.S. 1077 (1989) (religious beliefs of for-profit company's owners do not permit them to coerce employees into attending mandatory devotional services; private individuals' religious beliefs cannot be conflated with those of an entire enterprise); *Hyman v. City of Louisville*, 132 F. Supp. 2d 528, *judgment vacated*, 53 Fed Appx. 740 (6th Cir. 2002) [unpublished opinion] (court rejected gynecologist's assertion of free-exercise and freedom-of-association rights to refuse to comply with Louisville, Kentucky, municipal ordinance requiring equal treatment of homosexuals, writing that the mere fact that some persons did not want to comply with the ordinance did not work a burden on their religious rights and, moreover, sheerly commercial enterprises have no First Amendment associational right to discriminate; the court of appeals vacated its own opinion at a later date determing that the complaining physician lacked standing to file a claim.)

The courts have allowed established churches and religious entities far more latitude than they have individuals when construing both Title VII's religious exemption and state or municipal antidiscrimination laws. Contrast the result of the *Hyman* case described above—a case involving a private employer, a private medical practice, and the religious beliefs of the proprietor—with the results in the following cases: *Pedreira v. Kentucky Baptist Homes for Children*, 186 F. Supp. 2d 757 (W.D. Ky. 2001) (federal district court rejects lesbian counselor's claim that religiously affiliated youth home discriminated when it fired her upon learning of her sexual orientation; court upholds termination "because her admitted homosexual lifestyle is contrary to Kentucky Baptist Homes for Children's core values"); *Madsen v. Erwin*, 481 N.E.2d 1160, 1161, 1166 (Mass. 1985) (state law prohibiting sexual orientation discrimination unduly burdens church-published newspaper's free-exercise rights).

5. Religious Garb and Religious Speech in the Workplace

The courts have been less than sympathetic to claims of religious discrimination brought by employees who were not allowed to wear religious garb of their choosing in order to conform to their religious beliefs. They have also been generally unreceptive to claims of Title VII protection for proselytizing one's co-workers or members of the public while on the employer's time.

In *EEOC v. Heil-Quaker Corp.*, 55 Fair Empl. Prac. Cas. 1895 (BNA) (D. Tenn. 1990), the plaintiff worked an assembly line. The company had a rule requiring assembly-line workers to wear pants so that no loose clothing could get caught in the machinery and risk injury to the employee, equipment, and co-workers. When the employee refused to comply with the safety rule because her religious beliefs required women to wear dresses, she was fired. The court found that there was no duty to accommodate the employee's religious belief where doing so would create undue hardship by increasing safety hazards.

Questions involving more expressive speech elements have fared little better in the courts than have those involving religious garb. In *Wilson v. U.S. West Communications*, 58 F.3d 1337 (8th Cir. 1985), the employer fired an employee who, for religious reasons, wore an antiabortion button with a picture of a fetus on it. The court found that the button was offensive to co-workers and that permitting the employee to wear it constituted undue hardship. Conversely, a pregnant employee who was fired because she upset "very Christian" co-workers with talk of having an abortion stated a claim for religious discrimination when she alleged that she was fired because her religious views differed from those of her employer. *See Turic v. Holland Hospitality, Inc.*, 842 F. Supp. 971 (W.D. Mich. 1994). On what basis are the two employees' claims distinguishable from each other?

In *Slater v. King Soopers, Inc.*, 809 F. Supp. 809 (D. Colo. 1992), the employer fired a Ku Klux Klan member after he participated in a Hitler rally. The employee then brought a religious discrimination suit. The court held that the

Klan is "political and social in nature" and is not a religious organization within the meaning of Title VII.

In *Anderson v. U.S.F. Logistics (IMC), Inc.,* 274 F.3d 470 (7th Cir. 2000), a Christian Methodist Episcopal office coordinator for a large company regularly communicated with customers and vendors. Since being hired in 1995, Ms. Anderson had routinely signed off communications with the phrase "Have a Blessed Day." In 1999, a representative of Microsoft, the company's largest customer, complained about the "unacceptable" phrase. The company told Ms. Anderson to stop using the phrase when communicating with Microsoft. The next week, however, she sent an e-mail to Microsoft that contained the "Blessed Day" language. The employer again reminded her not to use the phrase with Microsoft. Ms. Anderson averred that the use of the phrase was part of her religious practice and told her supervisor that several Microsoft employees whom she had polled did not object to the phrase. Following this communication between Ms. Anderson and management, Ms. Anderson was issued a written reprimand, which informed her that continuing to use the phrase when communicating with Microsoft could result in termination.

For a few months, she abstained, but in February 2000, she sent an e-mail to Microsoft bearing the capitalized words "HAVE A BLESSED DAY." She received another reprimand. She filed suit under Title VII's religious accommodation provision, asking for a preliminary injunction allowing her to use the phrase. The Seventh Circuit held that no injunction could issue; no irreparable harm had been suffered by Ms. Anderson because she was allowed to use the phrase with her co-workers, just not with customers. Although her case could proceed to trial in the district court, the appellate court found that allowing the employee to use the phrase "Have a Blessed Day" with co-workers but not with customers until a decision on the merits was reached did not constitute the irreparable harm necessary to sustain injunctive relief.

Discussion Note

1. Employee Speech Rights: This curious ruling may be interpreted as ominous for the employee on the dispositive question of whether the employer's action in allowing her to wish co-workers but not customers a "Blessed Day" is a reasonable accommodation. When the case returns to the Seventh Circuit on appeal from a decision on the merits, hasn't the Seventh Circuit's ruling here really already determined the outcome?

   Consider the relationships among the actors in the *Anderson* case. Should a customer who is not in daily contact with the religious employee and who merely receives e-mail containing a religiously motivated phrase get the same degree of protection under Title VII that Ms. Anderson's co-workers would receive had they been the ones to complain? Should Ms. Anderson's rather rote, ritualistic incantation of a blessing be treated by the courts exactly as an employer's coercion of employees to pray would be? Should Ms. Anderson's phrase be treated the same way as an employee's button with a fetus on it of which co-workers complained?

   Recalling Title VII's "reasonable person" standard, as well as Title VII's benchmark of severe, recurrent, and pervasive conduct in order to state a hostile environment claim, does the Microsoft employee who complained seem to be so thin-skinned that, were he a regular employee complaining of the same conduct by a co-worker, his suit might be dismissed out of hand? Does it seem to you that such cases are appropriate uses of judicial resources? Does it appear that common sense has given way to bullying by one person at the employer's largest customer, and if so, doesn't *Hardison's* "undue hardship" holding allow for just such a result, assuming that the employer here would lose Microsoft's business if it ignored the Microsoft representative's complaint?

Conversely, how is this case distinguishable from the customer-preference cases in which the courts have refused to allow customers to dictate that employers discriminate in making work assignments? Does Microsoft have any more right to insist that an employee of a company with which it does business not express her religious beliefs than a white customer at a cafeteria has to insist that an African American not serve his selections to him? If not, did the *Hardison* Court reach the right result for any case that involves facts other than shift changes or days off?

6. Employees' Freedom to Disbelieve in a Deity

EEOC has taken the position that the employee's right not to subscribe to any religious belief is protected under Title VII, as have several courts. Thus, in *EEOC v. Townley Engineering and Manufacturing Company,* 859 F.2d 610 (9th Cir.), *cert. denied,* 489 U.S. 1077 (1989), the court held that an employee cannot be compelled to attend the employer's mandatory religious services. Nor can an employee who is an atheist be required to attend the employer's monthly staff meetings that feature devotional exercises to which she objects. *See Young v. Southwestern Sav. & Loan Ass'n,* 509 F.2d 140 (5th Cir. 1975). Public employees have a free-exercise right even if they make a mistake as to doctrine. Thus, if the employee believes that his religious doctrine requires a particular duty, but in fact it does not, or if the employee interprets his personal religious duty to demand more than the sectarian doctrine requires in practice, the employee is still entitled to seek an accommodation that will free him from a substantial burden on the free exercise of his religion. *Frazee v. Illinois Dep't of Emp. Sec.,* 489 U.S. 829 (1989).

7. Religious Organizations That Pay Women Less than Men

The EEOC has issued comprehensive Policy Guidance on the matter of religious organizations' paying women employees less than men. It has concluded:

> A religious organization or institution may not pay women less than men even if such a policy is pursuant to its religious beliefs. Religious institutions are covered by the Equal Pay Act (EPA) and Title VII of the Civil Rights Act of 1964, as amended (Title VII), in regard to sex discrimination in wages. They may not justify their refusal to comply with the Equal Pay Act or Title VII on constitutional grounds since the statutes neither infringe upon the organizations' free exercise of their religious beliefs nor violate the establishment clause of the first amendment.

Policy Guidance N-915.049 (2/1/90).

The courts have generally reached the same conclusion where the discrimination was directed at a lay, rather than a pastoral, position. In *EEOC v. Fremont Christian School*, 781 F.2d 1362 (9th Cir. 1986), the court held that neither the free-exercise clause nor any exemption in Title VII allowed the school to offer health benefits only to married males and not to married females because of the school's religious belief that only males could be heads of household. The Ninth Circuit had earlier ruled that a religiously affiliated publishing house could not provide male employees with remuneration it did not give to similarly situated female employees. *See EEOC v. Pacific Press Publishing Ass'n*, 676 F.2d 1272 (9th Cir. 1982). *Accord EEOC v. Mississippi Coll.*, 626 F.2d 477, 489 (5th Cir.), *cert. denied*, 453 U.S. 912 (1981). *See also Marshall v. Pacific Union Conf. of Seventh Day Adventists*, 14 Empl. Prac. Dec. (CCH) 7806, 1977 WL 885 (C.D. Cal. 1977) (EPA applies to laypersons employed by religious institution; free-exercise defense rejected); *Russell v. Belmont Coll.*, 554 F. Supp. 667 (M.D. Tenn. 1982) (same). Although the Sixth Circuit reached a contrary result, ruling that a state antidiscrimination statute could not be applied to bar gender discrimination at a parochial school when the school discriminated in accordance with its religious beliefs, the opinion was vacated by the Supreme Court without reaching the merits. *See Dayton Christian Schls. v. Ohio Civil Rights Comm'n*, 766 F.2d 932 (6th Cir.), *rev'd on other grounds and remanded*, 477 U.S. 619 (1986).

Pastoral positions, however, are treated quite differently. As the Fifth Circuit has explained:

> The minister is the chief instrument by which the church seeks to fulfill its purpose. Matters touching this relationship must necessarily be recognized as of prime ecclesiastical concern. Just as the initial function of selecting a minister is a matter of church administration and govern[ance], so are the functions which accompany such a selection. It is unavoidably true that these include the determination of a minister's salary, his place of assignment, and the duty he is to perform in the furtherance of the religious mission of the church. *McClure v. Salvation Army*, 460 F.2d 553, 559 (5th Cir.), *cert. denied*, 409 U.S. 896 (1972).

The Fifth Circuit thus rejected the claim of a minister who alleged that she was undercompensated because she was female. *See also Rayburn v. General Conf. of Seventh-Day Adventists*, 772 F.2d 1164 (4th Cir.), *cert. denied*, 478 U.S. 1020 (1986) (where duties are of a type associated with pastoral care, ministerial exemption to Title VII applies).

The Eleventh Circuit has dramatically extended church protection from suit under Title VII. In a sweeping ruling, one of its three-judge panels held that both the free-exercise and the establishment clauses prevent clergy from suing their churches under Title VII; the panel treated the ministerial exemption as conferring blanket immunity. *Gellington v. Christian Methodist Episcopal Church, Inc.*, 203 F.3d 1299 (11th Cir. 2000). Less-sweeping decisions, however, inquire into whether the ecclesiastical purpose was furthered by the alleged discrimination. Thus, in *Bollard v. California Province of the Society of Jesus*, 196 F.3d 940 (9th Cir. 1999), the court could find no ministerial purpose served by sexual harassment and thus declined to apply Title VII's ministerial exemption to shield such conduct from suit.

chapter 12

The Age Discrimination in Employment Act of 1967

Problem 49

Edgerton Academy is a private school with more than 20 employees. It operates a color guard and dance team. The color guard and dance team have for years been managed by 40- to 50-year-olds who are Beatles fans. The color guard and dance team have won many state and regional prizes for their *Let it Be* tribute that they perform at various community events and competitions. The school is nonetheless dissatisfied and wishes to give the program a new look that it believes will invigorate the program and make it more popular with teenagers; specifically, school administrators have surmised that the young people would rather participate in a program that does hiphop performances. They summarily dismiss the 40- to 50-year-olds with no explanation as to why and no conversation with them and replace them with 26-year-olds. As it turns out, however, the Beatles fans are also huge hiphop fans and have been planning a *Notorious B.I.G. Slammin' Show* for the next year.

Problem 50

Edgar Edmons, a 53-year-old regional sales manager, has worked for the Wallace Company for 20 years, and he has been successful at many different jobs at the company over that time. When he is fired at year 20 and replaced by a 36-year-old subordinate, the other sales managers ask about his retirement plans, and the company president meets with him and makes remarks about the plaintiff's bringing an age discrimination suit before he was fired. At summary judgment, the employer claims it fired the employee because he did personal business on the job and lied about this when caught and because he generally neglected his work.

Problem 51

The four oldest employees in a university printing department are laid off; they are aged 46–54. Each is replaced by a younger worker, some of them 10 years younger. A "campus layoff expert" approved the termination plan and encouraged university officials to write justifications for the terminations. These justifications are not written until after the termination decision were made. The terminated employees were never counseled about any of the performance deficiencies that showed up in the justifications. At trial, plaintiffs argue that certain "code words" employed in the justifications are proxies for age bias. These code words include such phrases as "pre-electronic" and the need for employees who are "up to speed" on "new trends." One of the decision makers testifies at trial that what is needed is "new vision" and that the "new vision" requires younger workers. He further testifies that the workers who will implement the "new vision" will be hired if the university can jump the "legal hurdle" of the ADEA. The terminations, he testifies, will "improve the agility" of the department. His testimony links youth and "agility."

A. Adding an Age Discrimination Statute to Federal Law

The Age Discrimination in Employment Act (ADEA) is not part of Title VII. It was enacted in 1967 as a separate statute. *See* 29 U.S.C. § 621 *et seq.* The ADEA outlaws discrimination against persons 40 years old and older. It differs from Title VII in its more stringent requirement for the number of employees an employer must have to be subject to the Act. Whereas Title VII exempts employers who do not have 15 employees on their payroll for 20 weeks within the current or preceding calendar year, the ADEA exempts employers who have fewer than 20 employees on the payroll during the same time period.

A labor organization is covered by the ADEA only if it operates a hiring hall or has 25 members and functions as the bargaining unit of the employees. Labor organizations, like other employers, are permitted to observe the terms of a bona fide employee benefit plan even if that results in unequal treatment, provided that they did not devise the plan in order to circumvent the ADEA. The same is true of a bona fide seniority system. *See* 29 U.S.C. § 623(f)(2)(A). Such seniority systems may not, however, require the involuntary retirement of any employee because of age. A seniority system is not bona fide unless it has been communicated to all affected employees and it applies equally to all affected employees regardless of age. Firefighters and law enforcement officers may legally be subjected to a specified age requirement for hire and to compulsory retirement at a specified age pursuant to congressional reenactment of Section 4(j) provisions that otherwise would have expired in 1993. A private company may enforce a mandatory retirement at age 65 for executives and policy makers if they would be entitled to a pension of $44,000 or more per year. Older Americans Act Amendments of 1984, Pub. L. 98-459, 98 Stat. 1767. Apart from the specific mandatory retirement programs allowed by the statute, only voluntary early retirement programs that are consistent with the purposes of the ADEA are allowed.

Elected state or local government officials, their staff, and their appointees who occupy policy-making positions are exempted from ADEA coverage; in its 1999 term, the Supreme Court ruled that a state employer enjoys sovereign immunity from ADEA suits. *Kimel v. Florida Board of Regents*, 528 U.S. 62 (2000).

Although Title VII clearly allows for recovery based on a disparate impact theory, some courts have refused to allow an age discrimination plaintiff to proceed with any claim other than disparate treatment. This is a creature of judicial construction, however. *See* Section E below. Most circuits apply *Faragher/Ellerth* [see Ch. 5] hostile environment claims, although the ADEA does not explicitly provide for this type of claim any more than Title VII explicitly provides for a gender-based hostile environment claim. EEOC Guidelines state that *Faragher/Ellerth* should be applied to all hostile environment claims. *See* EEOC Enforcement Guidance 915.002 (6/18/99), *reprinted in* EEOC COMPLIANCE MANUAL (BNA) N:4076.

Congress quite deliberately imposed the same procedural requirements on ADEA complainants as on other members of protected classes through amendments enacted in 1991. Prior to 1991, the statutes of limitations governing ADEA claims had corresponded to those of the Fair Labor Standards Act. After 1991, ADEA plaintiffs have 90 days after receipt of the notice of right to sue from the EEOC to file their suits. State courts have concurrent jurisdiction over ADEA claims, although a state action may be removable to federal court. *Baldwin v. Sears, Roebuck & Co.*, 667 F.2d 458 (5th Cir. 1982).

Punitive damages are not available under the ADEA. *See Pfeiffer v. Essex Wire Corp.*, 682 F.2d 684 (7th Cir. 1984). Some circuits likewise do not allow compensatory damages for pain and suffering. *Id.* Apart from this, injunctive and declaratory relief are available under the ADEA. Reinstatement is an available remedy. Back pay and front pay are available, as are attorney fees. Class action procedures are very different for ADEA cases than for Title VII cases. In Title VII class actions involving private employers, each class member is bound by the judgment unless she specifically "opts out" of the class; ADEA class members, by contrast, must "opt in" to the class. *See Thiessen v. General Elec. Cap. Corp.*, 255 F.3d 1221 (10th Cir.), *rev'd and remanded*, 267 F.3d 1095 (2001).

B. Prima Facie Case

The Supreme Court has stressed the flexibility of the *McDonnell Douglas* framework in addressing ADEA cases. In *O'Connor v. Consolidated Coin Caterers Corp.*, 517 U.S. 308 (1996), a 56-year-old was replaced by a 40-year-old. The Court held that an ADEA plaintiff need not show that he was replaced by a worker under 40 (40 being the age at which the ADEA draws the protected class) in order to state a prima facie case. The Court reasoned that because the statute is directed at discrimination "because of age," it is irrelevant that the plaintiff was replaced by another member of the protected class if the discrimination occurred because of the plaintiff's age. The Court noted that an inference of discrimination arises when there is a significant age difference between the plaintiff and his replacement and that being replaced by a person under 40 is not relevant to this inference: "Because the ADEA prohibits discrimination on the basis of age and not class membership, the fact that a replacement is substantially younger than the plaintiff is a far more reliable indicator of age discrimination than is the fact that the plaintiff was replaced by someone outside the protected class." *Id.* at 313.

Following *O'Connor*, the lower courts have focused on whether the ADEA plaintiff's replacement is "substantially younger" than the plaintiff. In *Showalter v. University of Pittsburgh Medical Center*, 190 F.3d 231 (3d Cir. 1999), the court applied *O'Connor* to layoffs and found that an age difference of eight years was sufficient to lead to an inference about whether the alleged discrimination was based on age. The Seventh Circuit relied on *O'Connor* to establish a presumption that a 10-year age difference between the ADEA plaintiff and her replacement is "substantial": "[W]e consider a ten-year difference in ages . . . to be presumptively 'substantial' under *O'Connor*. In cases where the disparity is less, the plaintiff may still present a triable claim if she directs the court to evidence that her employer considered her age to be significant. In that instance, the issue of age disparity would be less relevant." *Hartley v. Wisconsin Bell, Inc.*, 124 F.3d 887, 893 (7th Cir. 1997).

Question

1. Do you think that the fact that federal judges have life tenure influences their decisions in age discrimination cases, particularly those where forced retirement at a specified age is at issue?

C. "Because of" Age, or Something Else?

The courts have declined to equate an employer's economic incentive to avoid paying pensions with a motivation to discriminate based on age despite the obvious relationship pension-vesting might have to age. In *Hazen Paper Co. v. Biggins*, 507 U.S. 604 (1993), the plaintiff was fired only weeks before fully vesting in the employer's pension plan. Although the Court found that this termination violated the Employee Retirement Income Security Act (ERISA), it rejected the plaintiff's argument that the employer's termination before vesting constituted age discrimination:

> [T]here is no disparate treatment under the ADEA when the factor motivating the employer is some feature other than the employee's age. . . . Whatever the employer's decisionmaking process, a disparate treatment claim cannot succeed unless the employee's protected trait actually played a role in that process and had a determinative influence on the outcome. . . . It is the very essence of age discrimination for an older worker to be fired because the employer believed that productivity and competence declined with old age. . . . When the employer's decision is wholly motivated by factors other than age, the prob-

lem of inaccurate and stigmatizing stereotypes disappears. This is true even if the motivating factor is correlated with age, as pension status typically is. *Biggins*, 507 U.S. at 609–610.

The *Biggins* Court did leave open the possibility that some terminations that occurred close to full vesting might be a proxy for age discrimination, however; the Court noted that this might clearly occur where employees vested at a certain age rather than by a certain number of years of service. This caveat in *Biggins* is consistent with the Court's earlier decisions in *Trans World Airlines v. Thurston*, 469 U.S. 111 (1985), and *Western Air Lines, Inc. v. Criswell*, 472 U.S. 400 (1985). In each of those cases, the airlines had imposed age-based reassignment or mandatory retirement schemes on flight captains or flight engineers when age was not a BFOQ. To that extent, the airlines had not used age as a legitimate proxy for safety-related concerns.

Employee benefit plans present unique factual challenges. Age-based reductions in employee benefit plans are not illegal when they are based on actuarily significant cost considerations. *See* 29 C.F.R. § 1625.10(a)(1). Such reductions, however, are permissible only if the actual amount of the payment made or the cost incurred on behalf of an older employee is not less per benefit than those made or incurred for a younger employee. *See* 29 C.F.R. § 1625.10. Thus, as long as the employer spends equally on the older and the younger employee, a benefits plan does not violate the ADEA even if the older worker nets fewer benefits or less insurance coverage for each dollar expended.

Biggins notwithstanding, some lower courts have treated evidence of economic motivation to get rid of older workers as part of a mixed motive inquiry. *See Rose v. New York City Bd. of Educ.*, 257 F.3d 156 (2d Cir. 2001) (supervisor's observation that plaintiff could be replaced by someone "younger and cheaper" justified jury instruction on mixed motive).

D. Weighing the Evidence

Recall the case of *Reeves v. Sanderson Plumbing Products, Inc.*, 530 U.S. 133 (2000), discussed in Chapter 2. The case was introduced in the chapter on disparate treatment because, for the most part, decisions made about age discrimination parallel decisions made by the Supreme Court in *McDonnell Douglas Corp v. Green*. *Reeves* is an age discrimination case, holding that because "the plaintiff established a prima facie case of discrimination, and produced additional evidence of age-biased animus, there was sufficient evidence for the jury to find that respondent had intentionally discriminated." Reread the excerpt from the *Reeves* case at page 44–48, and focus on the Court's treatment of age-related comments and other evidence to support the jury's finding in that case.

Questions

1. Look at the summarized facts of *Reeves v. Sanderson Plumbing*. Imagine that the supervisor had been talking to an African-American employee

and that he is later directly involved with a decision to fire or not promote the employee. For the "Mayflower" remark, substitute a racially disparaging comment, and for "too damn old," substitute "too damn black." Is this now direct evidence? Using the same substitutions, now remove the supervisor from the realm of decision making on the plaintiff's future with the employer.

2. Suppose that the plaintiff is well over 40 and has the largest sales territory in the company, which is taken away from him and reassigned to two younger salespeople. Is this sufficient to state a prima facie age discrimination claim?

GENERAL DYNAMICS LAND SYSTEMS, INC.
v.
CLINE
540 U.S. 581 (2004)

Justice SOUTER delivered the opinion of the Court.

[The Employment Problem]

In 1997, a collective-bargaining agreement between petitioner General Dynamics and the United Auto Workers eliminated the company's obligation to provide health benefits to subsequently retired employees, except as to then-current workers at least 50 years old. Respondents (collectively, Cline) were then at least 40 and thus protected by the [Age Discrimination in Employment Act (ADEA)], see 29 U.S.C. § 631(a), but under 50 and so without promise of the benefits. All of them objected to the new terms, although some had retired before the change in order to get the prior advantage, some retired afterwards with no benefit, and some worked on, knowing the new contract would give them no health coverage when they were through. . . .

[The Legal Issue]

The question in this case is whether [the ADEA] also prohibits favoring the old over the young. We hold it does not.

[Decision of the Trial Court and the U.S. Court of Appeals for the Sixth Circuit]

. . . Cline brought this action against General Dynamics, combining claims under the ADEA and state law. The District Court called the federal claim one of "reverse age discrimination," upon which, it observed, no court had ever granted relief under the ADEA. . . . It dismissed in reliance on the Seventh Circuit's opinion in *Hamilton v. Caterpillar Inc.*, 966 F.2d 1226 (1992),

that "the ADEA 'does not protect . . . the younger *against* the older'". . . .

A divided panel of the Sixth Circuit reversed, 296 F.3d 466 (2002), with the majority reasoning that the prohibition of § 623(a)(1), covering discrimination against "any individual . . . because of such individual's age," is so clear on its face that if Congress had meant to limit its coverage to protect only the older worker against the younger, it would have said so. *Id.*, at 472. The court acknowledged the conflict of its ruling with earlier cases . . . but it criticized the cases going the other way for paying too much attention to the "hortatory, generalized language" of the congressional findings incorporated in the ADEA. . . . The Sixth Circuit drew support for its view from the position taken by the EEOC in an interpretive regulation.[2] *Id.*, at 471.

[The Decision and Rationale of the U.S. Supreme Court]

We granted certiorari to resolve the conflict among the Circuits . . . and now reverse. . . .

The common ground in this case is the generalization that the ADEA's prohibition covers "discriminat[ion] . . . because of [an] individual's age," . . . that helps the younger by hurting the older. In the abstract, the phrase is open to an argument for a broader

---

[2] 29 CFR § 1625.2(a) (2003) ("[I]f two people apply for the same position, and one is 42 and the other 52, the employer may not lawfully turn down either one on the basis of age, but must make such decision on the basis of some other factor"). . . .

construction, since reference to "age" carries no express modifier and the word could be read to look two ways. This more expansive possible understanding does not, however, square with the natural reading of the whole provision prohibiting discrimination, and in fact, Congress's interpretive clues speak almost unanimously to an understanding of discrimination as directed against workers who are older than the ones getting treated better.

Congress chose not to include age within discrimination forbidden by Title VII . . . being aware that there were legitimate reasons as well as invidious ones for making employment decisions on age. Instead, it called for a study of the issue by the Secretary of Labor, *ibid.*, who concluded that age discrimination was a serious problem, but one different in kind from discrimination on account of race.[2] The Secretary spoke of disadvantage to older individuals from arbitrary and stereotypical employment distinctions (including then-common policies of age ceilings on hiring), but he examined the problem in light of rational considerations of increased pension cost and, in some cases, legitimate concerns about an older person's ability to do the job. Wirtz Report 2. When the Secretary ultimately took the position that arbitrary discrimination against older workers was widespread and persistent enough to call for a federal legislative remedy, *id.*, at 21–22, he placed his recommendation against the background of common experience that the potential cost of employing someone rises with age, so that the older an employee is, the greater the inducement to prefer a younger substitute. The report contains no suggestion that reactions to age level off at some point, and it was devoid of any indication that the Secretary had noticed unfair advantages accruing to older employees at the expense of their juniors. . . .

. . . The hearings specifically addressed higher pension and benefit costs as heavier drags on hiring workers the older they got. See, *e.g.*, House Hearings 45 (statement of Norman Sprague) (Apart from stereotypes, "labor market conditions, seniority and promo-

tion-from-within policies, job training costs, pension and insurance costs, and mandatory retirement policies often make employers reluctant to hire older workers"). The record thus reflects the common facts that an individual's chances to find and keep a job get worse over time; as between any two people, the younger is in the stronger position, the older more apt to be tagged with a demeaning stereotype. Not surprisingly, from the voluminous records of the hearings, we have found (and Cline has cited) nothing suggesting that any workers were registering complaints about discrimination in favor of their seniors. . . .

In sum, except on one point, all the findings and statements of objectives are either cast in terms of the effects of age as intensifying over time, or are couched in terms that refer to "older" workers, explicitly or implicitly relative to "younger" ones. The single subject on which the statute speaks less specifically is that of "arbitrary limits" or "arbitrary age discrimination." But these are unmistakable references to the Wirtz Report's finding that "[a]lmost three out of every five employers covered by [a] 1965 survey have in effect age limitations (most frequently between 45 and 55) on new hires which they apply without consideration of an applicant's other qualifications." Wirtz Report 6. The ADEA's ban on "arbitrary limits" thus applies to age caps that exclude older applicants, necessarily to the advantage of younger ones. . . .

. . . As Justice THOMAS (*post*, at 1250) agrees, the word "age" standing alone can be readily understood either as pointing to any number of years lived, or as common shorthand for the longer span and concurrent aches that make youth look good. Which alternative was probably intended is a matter of context; we understand the different choices of meaning that lie behind a sentence like "Age can be shown by a driver's license," and the statement, "Age has left him a shut-in." So it is easy to understand that Congress chose different meanings at different places in the ADEA, as the different settings readily show. Hence the second flaw in Cline's argument for uniform usage: it ignores the cardinal rule that "[s]tatutory language must be read in context [since] a phrase 'gathers meaning from the words around it.' " . . . The point here is that we are not asking an abstract question about the meaning of "age"; we are seeking the meaning of the whole phrase "discriminate . . . because of such individual's age,"

[2]That report found that "[e]mployment discrimination because of race is identified . . . with . . . feelings about people entirely unrelated to their ability to do the job. There is *no* significant discrimination of this kind so far as older workers are concerned. The most closely related kind of discrimination in the non-employment of older workers involves their rejection because of assumptions about the effect of age on their ability to do a job *when there is in fact no basis for these assumptions*." Report of the Secretary of Labor, The Older American Worker: Age Discrimination in Employment 2 (1965) (hereinafter Wirtz Report) (emphasis in original).

where it occurs in the ADEA. . . . As we have said, social history emphatically reveals an understanding of age discrimination as aimed against the old, and the statutory reference to age discrimination in this idiomatic sense is confirmed by legislative history. For the very reason that reference to context shows that "age" means "old age" when teamed with "discrimination," the provision of an affirmative defense when age is a bona fide occupational qualification readily shows that "age" as a qualification means comparative youth. As context tells us that "age" means one thing in § 623(a)(1) and another in § 623(f)[9], so it also tells us that the presumption of uniformity cannot sensibly operate here. . . .

The second objection has more substance than the first, but still not enough. . . .

. . . Even from a sponsor, a single outlying statement cannot stand against a tide of context and history, not to mention 30 years of judicial interpretation producing no apparent legislative qualms. . . .

The third objection relies on [the deference to be given CFR § 1625.2(a)] with General Dynamics urging us that *Skidmore v. Swift & Co.*, 323 U.S. 134 (1944), sets the limit, while Cline and the EEOC say that § 1625.2(a) deserves greater deference under *Chevron*

[9]An even wider contextual enquiry supports our conclusion, for the uniformity Cline and the EEOC claim for the uses of "age" within the ADEA itself would introduce unwelcome discord among the federal statutes on employee benefit plans. For example, the Tax Code requires an employer to allow certain employees who reach age 55 to diversify their stock ownership plans in part, 26 U.S.C. § 401(a)(28)(B); removes a penalty on early distributions from retirement plans at age 59 1/2, § 72(t)(2)(A)(i); requires an employer to allow many employees to receive benefits immediately upon retiring at age 65, § 401(a)(14); and requires an employer to adjust upward an employee's pension benefits if that employee continues to work past age 70 1/2, § 401(a)(9)(C)(iii). The Employee Retirement Income Security Act of 1974 makes similar provisions. See, *e.g., 29 U.S.C. § 1002(24)* ("normal retirement age" may come at age 65, although the plan specifies later); § 1053(a) (a plan must pay full benefits to employees who retire at normal retirement age). Taken one at a time, any of these statutory directives might be viewed as an exception Congress carved out of a generally recognized principle that employers may not give benefits to older employees that they withhold from younger ones. Viewed as a whole, however, they are incoherent with the alleged congressional belief that such a background principle existed.

U.S.A. v. Natural Resources Defense Council, Inc., 467 U.S. 837 (1984). Although we have devoted a fair amount of attention lately to the varying degrees of deference deserved by agency pronouncements of different sorts . . . the recent cases are not on point here. In *Edelman v. Lynchburg College*, 535 U.S. 106 (2002), we found no need to choose between *Skidmore* and *Chevron* or even to defer, because the EEOC was clearly right; today, we neither defer nor settle on any degree of deference because the Commission is clearly wrong.

Even for an agency able to claim all the authority possible under *Chevron*, deference to its statutory interpretation is called for only when the devices of judicial construction have been tried and found to yield no clear sense of congressional intent. . . . Here, regular interpretive method leaves no serious question, not even about purely textual ambiguity in the ADEA. The word "age" takes on a definite meaning from being in the phrase "discriminat[ion] . . . because of such individual's age," occurring as that phrase does in a statute structured and manifestly intended to protect the older from arbitrary favor for the younger.

We see the text, structure, purpose, and history of the ADEA, along with its relationship to other federal statutes, as showing that the statute does not mean to stop an employer from favoring an older employee over a younger one. The judgment of the Court of Appeals is *Reversed*.

Justice THOMAS, with whom Justice KENNEDY joins, dissenting.

[Justice SCALIA's dissent is omitted.]

This should have been an easy case. The plain language of 29 U.S.C. § 623(a)(1) mandates a particular outcome: that the respondents are able to sue for discrimination against them in favor of older workers. The agency charged with enforcing the statute has adopted a regulation and issued an opinion as an adjudicator, both of which adopt this natural interpretation of the provision. And the only portion of legislative history relevant to the question before us is consistent with this outcome. Despite the fact that these traditional tools of statutory interpretation lead inexorably to the conclusion that respondents can state a claim for discrimination against the relatively young, the Court, apparently disappointed by this result, today adopts a different interpretation. In doing so, the Court, of necessity, creates a new tool of statutory interpretation, and then proceeds to give this newly created "social history" analysis dispositive weight. Because I cannot agree with the Court's new approach to interpreting anti-discrimination statutes, I respectfully dissent. . . .

The plain language of the ADEA clearly allows for suits brought by the relatively young when discriminated against in favor of the relatively old. The phrase "discriminate . . . because of such individual's age," is not restricted to discrimination because of relatively *older* age. If an employer fired a worker for the sole reason that the worker was under 45, it would be entirely natural to say that the worker had been discriminated against because of his age. I struggle to think of what other phrase I would use to describe such behavior. I wonder how the Court would describe such incidents, because the Court apparently considers such usage to be unusual, atypical, or aberrant. See *ante*, at 1243 (concluding that the "common usage of language" would exclude discrimination against the relatively young from the phrase "discriminat[ion] . . . because of [an] individual's age"). . . .

This plain reading of the ADEA is bolstered by the interpretation of the agency charged with administering the statute. A regulation issued by the Equal Employment Opportunity Commission (EEOC) adopts the view contrary to the Court's, 29 CFR § 1625.2(a) (2003), and the only binding EEOC decision that addresses the question before us also adopted the view contrary to the Court's, see *Garrett v. Runyon*, Appeal No. 01960422, 1997 WL 574739, (EEOC, Sept. 5, 1997). . . . Even if the Court disagrees with my interpretation of the language of the statute, it strains credulity to argue that such a reading is so unreasonable that an agency could not adopt it. To suggest that, in the instant case, the "regular interpretive method leaves no serious question, not even about purely textual ambiguity in the ADEA," *ante*, at 1248, is to ignore the entirely reasonable (and, incidentally, correct) contrary interpretation of the ADEA that the EEOC and I advocate. . . .

Strangely, the Court does not explain why it departs from accepted methods of interpreting statutes. It does, however, clearly set forth its principal reason for adopting its particular reading of the phrase "discriminate . . . based on [an] individual's age" in Part III-A of its opinion. . . . The Court does not define "social history," although it is apparently something different from legislative history, because the Court refers to legislative history as a separate interpretive tool in the very same sentence. Indeed, the Court has never defined "social history" in any previous opinion, probably because it has never sanctioned looking to "social

history" as a method of statutory interpretation. Today, the Court takes this unprecedented step, and then places dispositive weight on the new concept.

It appears that the Court considers the "social history" of the phrase "discriminate . . . because of [an] individual's age" to be the principal evil that Congress targeted when it passed the ADEA. . . . Hence, the Court apparently concludes that if Congress has in mind a particular, principal, or primary form of discrimination when it passes an antidiscrimination provision prohibiting persons from "discriminating because of [some personal quality]," then the phrase "discriminate because of [some personal quality]" only covers the principal or most common form of discrimination relating to this personal quality. . . .

The Court, however, has not typically interpreted nondiscrimination statutes in this odd manner. "[S]tatutory prohibitions often go beyond the principal evil to cover reasonably comparable evils, and it is ultimately the provisions of our laws rather than the principal concerns of our legislators by which we are governed." *Oncale v. Sundowner Offshore Services, Inc.*, 523 U.S. 75, 79 (1998). The oddity of the Court's new technique of statutory interpretation is highlighted by this Court's contrary approach to the racial-discrimination prohibition of Title VII of the Civil Rights Act of 1964. . . .

The congressional debates and hearings, although filled with statements decrying discrimination against racial minorities and setting forth the disadvantages those minorities suffered, contain no references that I could find to any problem of discrimination against whites. . . . I find no evidence that even a single legislator appeared concerned about whether there were incidents of discrimination against whites, and I find no citation to any such incidents.

In sum, there is no record evidence "that [white] workers were suffering at the expense of [racial minorities]," and in 1964, discrimination against whites in favor of racial minorities was hardly "a social problem requir[ing] a federal statute to place a [white] worker in parity with [racial minorities]. . . ." Thus, "talk about discrimination because of [race] [would] naturally [be] understood to refer to discrimination against [racial minorities]." *Ibid.* In light of the Court's opinion today, it appears that this Court has been treading down the wrong path with respect to Title VII since at least 1976. See *McDonald v. Santa Fe Trail Transp. Co.*, 427 U.S. 273 (1976) (holding that Title VII protected whites discriminated against in favor of racial minorities).

In *McDonald*, the Court relied on the fact that the terms of Title VII, prohibiting the discharge of "any individual" because of "such individual's race,"

42 U.S.C. § 2000e2(a)(1), "'are not limited to discrimi-nation against members of any particular race.'"... Admittedly, the Court there also relied on the EEOC's interpretation of Title VII as given in its decisions ... and also on statements from the legislative history of the enactment of Title VII.... But, in the instant case, as I have already noted ... the EEOC has issued a regulation and a binding EEOC decision adopting the view contrary to the Court's and in line with the in-terpretation of Title VII. And ... the only relevant piece of legislative history with respect to the ques-tion before the Court is in the same posture as the leg-islative history behind Title VII: namely, a statement that age discrimination cuts both ways and a rela-tively younger individual could sue when discrimi-nated against.... It is abundantly clear, then, that the Court's new approach to antidiscrimination statutes would lead us far astray from well-settled principles of statutory interpretation. The Court's examination of "social history" is in serious tension (if not outright conflict) with our prior cases in such matters. Under the Court's current approach, for instance, *McDonald*

and Oncale ... are wrongly decided. One can only hope that this new technique of statutory interpreta-tion does not catch on, and that its errors are limited to only this case....

... The Court does not seriously attempt to ana-lyze whether the term "age" is more naturally read narrowly in the context of § 623(a)(1).... [T]he Court concludes that the "common usage" of "age discrim-ination" refers exclusively to discrimination against the relatively old *only* because the "social history" of the phrase as a whole mandates such a reading. As I have explained here, the "social history" of the "whole phrase 'discriminate ... because of such indi-vidual's age,'" ... is no different than the "social his-tory" of the whole phrase "discriminate ... because of such individual's race." ...

As the ADEA clearly prohibits discrimination be-cause of an individual's age, whether the individual is too old or too young, I would affirm the Court of Appeals. Because the Court resorts to interpretive sleight of hand to avoid addressing the plain lan-guage of the ADEA, I respectfully dissent.

1. Stray Remarks

The question of whether age-related comments by supervisors constitute "di-rect evidence" of age discrimination or are merely "stray remarks" is often pre-sented. The courts have characterized as "stray remarks" any remarks by decision makers that are not uttered in the direct context of making the decision to take adverse employment action against the plaintiff and any statements of co-workers or others who had no part in making the decision to take the adverse employment action. *See generally Yates v. Douglas*, 255 F.3d 546, 549 (8th Cir. 2001) (distinguishing direct evidence of discriminatory animus from mere stray re-marks in the workplace). That this question is presented so often in age cases as compared to race cases is some testament to the fact that supervisors may use "code words" for age that they may be too shrewd to use for race; courts have been very reluctant to crack the code. Some supervisors are more blunt, how-ever, and the blunt supervisor can be rescued from liability for age-related com-ments by the fact that she made them prior to, and not in connection with, the actual adverse action. The following cases illustrate these principles.

In *Robin v. ESPO Engineering Corp.*, 200 F.3d 1081 (7th Cir. 2000), the em-ployer's CEO commented that the plaintiff, a salesperson, was an "old SOB" and that he was "getting too old." The Seventh Circuit found that these re-marks were "office banter" and not direct evidence of age discrimination be-cause the comments were made two years before plaintiff was fired and thus obviously were not made in the context of the decision to fire him. In another case involving older employees of a bank, the Seventh Circuit likewise found that the decision makers' choice of plaintiffs for an exit incentive program based on their comments that plaintiffs were not "flexible" or "energetic" did not constitute direct evidence of age discrimination. The court observed: "If 'flexible' and 'energetic' are to go the way of 'fresh blood' and 'you can't teach an old dog new tricks' as words or sayings purged from the lexicon of personnel management . . . supervisors will be rendered speechless in evaluating their subordinates." *Blackwell v. Cole Taylor Bank*, 152 F.3d 666, 671–72 (7th Cir. 1998). *But see Rose v. New York City Bd. of Educ.*, 257 F.3d 156 (2d Cir. 2001) (treating management's statement that plaintiff could be replaced by someone "younger and cheaper" as direct evidence of age discrimination).

The Supreme Court's decision in *Reeves v. Sanderson Plumbing Products, Inc.* is most frequently cited for the proposition that the plaintiff does not have to prove more than pretext to get to a jury. However, *Reeves* also treated, but did not resolve, the stray remark/direct evidence issue. The facts in *Reeves* included supervisor's statements to the plaintiff that he "must have come over on the Mayflower" and that he was "too damn old" to do his job, made shortly before the plaintiff was fired. The appellate court had found these statements to be "stray remarks" because they were not made while the supervisor was firing Mr. Reeves. The Supreme Court, however, found that the remarks were relevant evidence of discrimination because they were made by the decision maker close in time to the termination. *See Reeves*, 530 U.S. 133 (2000). At a minimum, even if *Reeves* does not establish that such remarks are in fact direct evidence, it does establish that remarks like these, made close in time to an adverse employment action by the decision maker, are not to be discarded as "stray remarks."

2. "Same Actor" or "Same Protected Class Member" Defense

In both Title VII and ADEA cases, the employer may argue for an inference or presumption of nondiscrimination when the manager who fired the employee is the same one who hired him or when the manager who fired the employee is a member of the same protected class as the employee. The circuits are split on whether an inference of nondiscrimination under these circumstances is permissible or mandatory. *See, e.g., Williams v. Vitro Servs. Corp.*, 144 F.3d 1438 (11th Cir. 1998) (breaking with Fourth, Fifth, Seventh, and Ninth Circuits, Eleventh Circuit comes closer to Third Circuit's rule that the evidence is relevant but should not be accorded presumptive value; Eleventh Circuit holds that inference of nondiscrimination is permissible only). The Second Circuit has issued at least some guidance about the weight to be assigned temporal factors. In *Carlton v. Mystic Transportation, Inc.*, 202 F.3d 129 (2d Cir.), *cert. denied*, 530 U.S. 1261 (2000), the court reversed summary judgment for the employer, which had prevailed on the "same actor" defense. In *Carlton*, seven years had elapsed between the hiring and firing dates; plaintiff had been 49 at the time of hire and was 56 when he was fired. The court ruled that the "same actor" defense weakens as time elapses. It found that a strong inference of nondiscrimination exists if the same person hired and fired the employee within two years' time, but not after seven years have gone by.

Since the circuits are split on whether the inference of nondiscrimination in "same actor" or "same protected class member" cases should be mandatory or permissible, and since particular panels might rule contrary to predecessor panels on the same question without acknowledging any disregard for circuit precedent, the law in this area is unsettled.

3. Reductions in Force (RIFs)

A reduction in force, or RIF, is simply the downsizing of personnel. RIFs often take a greater toll on older employees than others. The elements of a plaintiff's prima facie RIF case are (a) the plaintiff is over 40, (b) the plaintiff was performing the job in a qualified manner, (c) the plaintiff was terminated or demoted, and (d) the plaintiff was treated less favorably than employees who were not members of the protected class. *See Sauzek v. Exxon Coal USA, Inc.*, 202 F.3d 913 (7th Cir. 2000). RIF cases, as a species of disparate impact case, often but not always involve statistical proof. In the absence of very strong proof, either statistical or smoking-gun, it is difficult for plaintiffs to survive summary judgment in a RIF case. A few case summaries will give the flavor of how very difficult the plaintiff's task is.

In *Coleman v. Quaker Oats Co.*, 232 F.3d 1271 (9th Cir. 2000), *cert. denied*, 533 U.S. 950 (2001), the court upheld summary judgment for the employer. Even though the statistical evidence was that twice as many workers over 40 were laid off as workers under 40, the evidence was mitigated by factors such as education and job placement among the younger cohort. Although plaintiffs alleged that Quaker Oats used a rating system for these factors that was subjective and that was really intended to cloak age discrimination, the Ninth Circuit found that the nexus between subjective evaluations and proof of discriminatory intent was "weak." *Id.* at 1285. *Accord James v. New York Racing Ass'n*, 233 F.3d 149 (2d Cir. 2000) (affirming summary judgment in RIF case even though plaintiff was qualified and terminated while younger employees were kept on; evidence mitigated by fact that employer had recently hired employees in their sixties).

In *Cruz-Ramos v. Puerto Rico Sun Oil Co.*, 202 F.3d 381 (1st Cir. 2000), the employer reduced a seven-employee department to five employees. The plaintiff's duties were absorbed by the youngest person, who was kept on. The court rejected plaintiff's theory that consolidation of functions within another position was equivalent to being replaced by the younger person who took over the functions.

In *Stokes v. Westinghouse Savannah River Co.*, 206 F.3d 420 (4th Cir. 2000), the employer's RIF gave older employees the choice between severance pay and early retirement with augmentation of their pensions. The plaintiff alleged that he was discriminated against because he was forced to choose. The court, however, found that older workers were in fact treated more kindly by the company than others because they were permitted to "pick their poison" while others were not. Since the RIF itself was not motivated by a desire to get rid of older workers, the ADEA was not violated by the challenged aspect of the RIF.

The Seventh Circuit has allowed an employer to justify its RIF on grounds that some employees are more likely to contribute more to the employer over the long haul. This justification, in the Seventh Circuit's view, does not necessarily favor younger employees because it is balanced by the fact that older workers are less mobile than their younger counterparts. *See Thorn v. Sundstrund Aerospace Corp.*, 207 F.3d 383 (7th Cir. 2000).

E. Disparate Impact Generally

The circuits disagree on whether the ADEA allows disparate impact claims. The First, Third, Sixth, Seventh, Tenth, and Eleventh Circuits do not allow plaintiffs to bring disparate impact cases under the ADEA. The Second, Eighth, and Ninth Circuits have allowed ADEA disparate impact claims to proceed. The circuits that have disallowed the claims base their decisions on the differences between Title VII and the ADEA. Unlike Title VII, the ADEA explicitly shields an employer from liability if the employer's action is based on factors other than age; the courts that have disallowed impact claims have reasoned that the exemption would be meaningless if it did not vitiate disparate impact liability. *See, e.g., Adams v. Florida Power Corp.*, 255 F.3d 1322 (11th Cir. 2001), *cert. granted*, 534 U.S., 1054 (2001), *cert. dismissed*, 535 U.S. 228 (2002) *Mullin v. Raytheon Co.*, 164 F.3d 696 (1st Cir.), *cert. denied*, 528 U.S. 811 (1999). The Supreme Court granted and then dismissed certiorari on this issue, leaving it for another day perhaps, or leaving it to indefinite circuit conflict.

F. Relationship to State-Law Claims When the State Is the Employer

In its 1999 term, the Supreme Court decided that the ADEA does not abrogate the states' sovereign immunity; thus, when a state (as opposed to a private employer or a local governmental entity) is the employer, it cannot be sued for age discrimination without its express consent. *Kimel v. Florida Bd. of Regents*, 528 U.S. 62, 92 (2000).

In 2002, the Court assessed the interplay between state-law claims brought under the federal courts' supplemental jurisdiction and sovereign immunity for federal ADEA claims. It declined to toll the statute of limitations for remaining state-law claims when the federal court dismisses the federal claim. In *Raygor v. Regents of the University of Minnesota*, 534 U.S. 533 (2002), the Court held that even though the statute authorizing the federal court to assume jurisdiction of state-law claims intimately related to the plaintiff's federal claim specifically provided for the tolling of claims based on state law for 30 days after the plaintiff's federal claim is dismissed, the tolling period could not be applied where sovereign immunity barred the federal claim.

In *Raygor*, two employees of the University of Minnesota challenged the university's attempts to force them to take early retirement at age 52. When plaintiffs did not retire, the university reduced their salaries by reclassifying the plaintiffs' job descriptions. The employees filed claims with both the EEOC and the Minnesota Department of Human Rights (MDHR). They got their EEOC notice of right to sue on June 6, 1996 and filed a federal court action within 90 days of receipt of the right to sue. They brought age discrimination claims under both the ADEA and the Minnesota Human Rights Act (MHRA) in the federal court. The claim under the MHRA was brought under 28 U.S.C. § 1367, which allows federal courts to take jurisdiction of substantially related state-law claims. Section 1367 provides that, where the underlying federal action is dismissed, the federal court may in its discretion dismiss the state claims for refiling in the state court within 30 days of a dismissal without prejudice unless the state's law provides for a longer tolling period for refiling in state court. *See* 28 U.S.C. § 1367 c, d.

The plaintiffs received their MDHR right to sue on July 17, 1996. Minnesota law accords 45 days from receipt of the right to sue to file a state court action under the MHRA. The plaintiffs' federal action, which encompassed the claim under the state statute barring age discrimination, had been filed within the 45-day period after receipt of the notice of the right to sue on August 29.

In the federal court, the state of Minnesota raised sovereign immunity as a defense to both federal and state claims. On July 11, 1997, the district court ruled in favor of the university on the sovereign immunity issue and dismissed all claims, noting that it had no subject matter jurisdiction under Section 1367 for the state claim if it had no original jurisdiction for the federal claim because sovereign immunity barred the federal claim to begin with. Within 21 days of the dismissal of the state-law claims without prejudice, plaintiffs refiled the MHRA claim in the state court. Ultimately, the Minnesota Supreme Court held that, even though Section 1367(d)'s tolling provision facially applied to the plaintiffs' MHRA claims, according them 30 days to refile in state court, "[the] application of section 1367(d) to toll the statute of limitations applicable to state law claims against an unconsenting state defendant first filed in federal court but then dismissed and brought in state court is an impermissible denigration of [the state's] Eleventh Amendment Immunity." *Regents of the Univ. of Minn. v. Raygor*, 620 N.W.2d 680, 687 (Minn. 2001).

The Supreme Court, in affirming the Minnesota Supreme Court, noted that Section 1367 allows the federal courts to assume jurisdiction over state claims that are so related to federal claims as to form the same case or controversy—but that the federal courts must have to have original jurisdiction in order to extend their supplemental jurisdiction to the state-law claims initially. Because the ADEA has been previously held not to apply to state employers because of the bar of sovereign immunity, the Court reasoned, no jurisdiction over the federal claim existed as a predicate for the exercise of supplemental jurisdiction over state claims. Moreover, as to the statute of limitations issue, the Court held that federal tolling rules could not be applied if doing so would circumvent the Supreme Court's 2000 determination, in *Kimel*, that states enjoy sovereign immunity from ADEA claims. Congress, the Court held, could not prescribe a limitations period that effectively allowed actions to be tolled during their pendency in federal court if the tolling period would exceed the filing time allowed by state law, because that, too, infringes sovereign immunity.

G. Mixed Motive ADEA Retaliation Cases

Some confusion has surrounded the question of *Price Waterhouse*'s application to mixed motive ADEA retaliation claims. It has been suggested from time to time that the 1991 amendments to Title VII, rolling back *Price Waterhouse* on mixed motive by providing that damages and remedies may be lessened in such cases but that the presence of a mixed motive does not wholly defeat a claim, does not apply to the ADEA. The Eleventh Circuit has ruled that the amendments do not apply to ADEA retaliation cases, so that *Price Waterhouse* continues to govern them. *See Lewis v. YMCA* 208 F.3d 1303 (11th Cir. 2000).

H. Older Workers Benefits Protection Act

The Older Workers Benefits Protection Act (OWBPA) governs employers' voluntary early retirement incentive programs. The OWBPA allows employers to develop early retirement plans that do not violate the ADEA. An early retirement plan that is not truly at the election of the employee would violate the OWBPA. An employer may not coerce any employee into taking early retirement. Under the OWBPA, an employee may waive her rights under the ADEA if the waiver is made voluntarily and knowingly in writing and applies only to ADEA claims that existed prior to the date of the waiver (not to future or unknown claims) and if separate consideration supports the waiver. If the incentive program is offered to an individual employee, he must be given 21 days to consider it before execution; if it is offered to a whole class of employees, each member of that class must be given 45 days to consider it prior to execution. An employee who executed a waiver has seven days after execution to revoke it; if he does revoke it within that period, it is unenforceable.

chapter

13

The Americans with Disabilities Act of 1990—Part I: What Disabilities Are Covered?

Problem 52

Linda Read works as a laboratory assistant in a physics lab. She has a digestive disorder that causes her a great deal of pain when she eats hard-to-digest food such as meats and certain types of vegetables. Even accidentally eating a small amount of certain foods causes her great discomfort, and on a few occasions, the pain has been so great that her doctor has had to medicate her to alleviate the pain. There is no medication that is currently available to treat the condition itself. She has been harassed by her co-workers because of this disorder and recently filed a claim under the ADA. Of course, she must show that she is disabled as defined under the Act. Her employer has argued that her condition is not a disability because it is not an impairment.

A. Overview of the Americans with Disabilities Act (ADA)

This chapter and Chapter 14 will explore important issues relevant to claims of disability discrimination. The bulk of these chapters will focus on Title I (and to a lesser extent on Title II) of the Americans with Disabilities Act (ADA), 104 Stat. 327, 42 U.S.C. § 1201 *et seq.* which became law in 1990 and 1991, but we will also explore aspects of the Rehabilitation Act of 1973, 87 Stat. 361, as amended, 29 U.S.C. § 706(8)(B), an act that both set the stage for and has informed the interpretation of the ADA. Disability discrimination cases raise complex issues ranging from what a "disability" is and who a "qualified individual with a disability" is to issues of "reasonable accommodation" and "undue hardship." Each of these issues is interconnected and spawns a number of important subissues. Moreover, once the threshold requirements of the Act are met, many of the causes of action that should now be familiar to you may arise. For example, disparate treatment, disparate impact, and hostile work environment are all potential claims under the ADA. The extent to which the unique nature of disability discrimination alters these claims and the concomitant defenses is an important question to explore. Of course, there are also claims and defenses unique to disability discrimination.

This chapter will begin with an overview of the ADA, which will introduce the structure and terminology of the Act, as well as the basic elements of claims brought under it. This chapter will also introduce the administrative regulations and guidelines relevant to claims brought under Title I of the ADA. The overview will be followed by various issues related to the identification of disabilities covered by the ADA. Chapter 14 will address the requirements of employee qualifications to perform the position and the limits of the employer's obligations to make reasonable accommodations for the employee.

The ADA is a relatively complex statute. The protected class it covers is quite diverse, because there are numerous disabilities, both physical and mental, and these disabilities can affect people in many different ways. Thus, the provisions of the ADA must be applied to vastly different situations: for example, to those with epilepsy, to those with HIV, to paraplegics, and to those with mental illnesses. Even among people with a given disability, there may be varying levels of impairment. For example, epilepsy often can be treated with medications, but both the disease and the medications can affect people differently. Some may have little impairment of major life activities, while others are seriously affected. As we will see, the Supreme Court has muddied these waters by holding that whether one is disabled must be determined while considering the use of mitigating measures such as medication and prosthetics. This will be discussed further below.

There are several levels of analysis that one must engage in when considering an ADA claim. First, the claimant must be an individual with a disability. This might seem like an easy issue to address, but it is actually quite complex. This entire chapter covers the range of questions raised by the requirement. If the claimant is an individual with a disability, the claimant also must be a "qualified" individual with a disability. This means that the individual must be able to "perform the essential functions of the job with or without reasonable accommodation." As will be seen in Chapter 14, this is also a complex question. Further, if the claimant is a qualified individual with a disability, he or she must still prove that he or she was discriminated against. That means that the claimant must prove that he or she either was denied a reasonable accommodation or was the victim of disparate treatment, disparate impact or hostile work environment. Of course, there are a variety of defenses that arise as well. Some are specific to the ADA context, while others arise with the cause of action involved—for example, the use of legitimate, nondiscriminatory reasons in the disparate treatment context. Chapter 14 will address many of the issues after this chapter begins with the important preliminary question of who may be considered a person with a disability for purposes of the ADA.

As you read the cases that follow, you will notice that some of them were brought under the Rehabilitation Act of 1973 (Rehabilitation Act). This Act predated the ADA but applied only to the federal government and related entities, those receiving federal funding, and those contracting with the federal government. The ADA specifically notes that cases decided under the Rehabilitation Act should be treated as having precedential value under the ADA to the extent the Rehabilitation Act provisions being interpreted are consistent with the ADA. Thus, the ADA was enacted with a preexisting web of precedent that arose under the Rehabilitation Act.

Additionally, the EEOC has promulgated detailed regulations and guidelines interpreting Title I of the ADA. As will be seen, the Supreme Court has created some confusion as to the level of deference these guidelines are due, but it is safe to say that the EEOC regulations and interpretive guidelines are important to understanding Title I of the ADA. Thus, they will be referenced where relevant. Unless otherwise noted, all citations to EEOC materials will be to the Code of Federal Regulations (C.F.R.). Moreover, there are a number of state antidiscrimination laws that cover disability discrimination. While these laws are beyond the scope of this section, it is important to keep in mind that they exist. Some may provide better procedural or remedial benefits than federal law (for example, no caps on damages and no duty to file with an administrative agency), and a few may provide better substantive protection.

B. Bringing a Claim Under the ADA

1. The Disability Determination

To be covered under the ADA, a claimant must have a disability as defined in the Act. The ADA defines disability as "(A) a physical or mental impairment that substantially limits one or more major life activities of [an] individual; (B) a record of such an impairment; or (C) being regarded as having such an impairment." 42 U.S.C. § 12102(2) (1994). Many questions arise under this definition. Several of the most obvious are these: What qualifies as an impairment? What qualifies as a major life activity? When are major life activities substantially limited by an impairment? Less obvious questions also arise, such as whether mitigating measures (for example, medications and prosthetics) should be considered in making a disability determination and what qualifies as a "record of" disability or as "being regarded as" disabled. All of these questions are important. A substantial body of case law and EEOC regulations sheds some light on these issues.

a. Physical or Mental Impairments

The first element of a disability determination is the existence of "a physical or mental impairment." 42 U.S.C. § 12102(2)(A). This is, of course, connected to the other elements—i.e., the impairment must substantially limit a major life activity. Yet determining whether someone has an impairment is not always a simple question. Obviously, someone who is quadriplegic has an impairment, but what about someone who has HIV but has not yet developed AIDS (*see infra Bragdon v. Abbott*)? Is there any way to answer this question without looking at the other elements of the definition? This section will specifically explore the impairment element, but it should be noted that this will naturally touch on the other elements. Section (a) and sections (b) and (c) will give you a basic understanding of each element before moving to section (d), which will explore the definition in a more holistic manner.

The EEOC defines impairment as follows:

(h) Physical or mental impairment means:

1. Any physiological disorder, or condition, cosmetic disfigurement, or anatomical loss affecting one or more of the following body systems: neurological, musculoskeletal, special sense organs, respiratory (including speech organs), cardiovascular, reproductive, digestive, genito-urinary, hemic and lymphatic, skin, and endocrine; or
2. Any mental or psychological disorder, such as mental retardation, organic brain syndrome, emotional or mental illness, and specific learning disabilities.

Regulations to Implement the Equal Employment Provisions of the Americans with Disabilities Act, 29 C.F.R. § 1630.2.

This definition obviously covers a broad range of impairments. While courts are not bound by EEOC guidelines, generally they are given a great deal of deference. In the ADA context, however, the Supreme Court has muddied the deference issue. Compare *Bragdon v. Abbott* and *Sutton v. United Airlines*, both discussed below. Still, courts have relied on the definition of impairment in the EEOC and other agency guidelines interpreting the ADA and the earlier Rehabilitation Act of 1973.

The following is an excerpt from the U.S. Supreme Court's decision in *Bragdon v. Abbott. Bragdon* was brought under Title III of the ADA, which deals with public accommodations. The law was meant to ensure that people with disabilites could access facilities open to the public. Significantly, the definition of "disability" is the same for both Title I and Title III. The same is true in regard to administrative regulations. While the Department of Justice is responsible for drafting the administrative guidelines applicable to Title III, the basic definition of disability contained in those guidelines is virtually identical to the definition contained in the EEOC guidelines. We will return to *Bragdon* elsewhere in this chapter. The excerpt below deals only with the definition of impairment, but as you will see later in this chapter, one cannot end the inquiry there.

BRAGDON
v.
ABBOTT
524 U.S. 624 (1998)

Justice KENNEDY delivered the opinion of the Court.

[The Employment Problem]

Respondent Sidney Abbott . . . has been infected with HIV since 1986. When the incidents we recite occurred, her infection had not manifested its most serious symptoms. On September 16, 1994, she went to the office of petitioner Randon Bragdon in Bangor, Maine, for a dental appointment. She disclosed her HIV infection on the patient registration form. Petitioner completed a dental examination, discovered a cavity, and informed respondent of his policy against filling cavities of HIV-infected patients. He offered to perform the work at a hospital with no added fee for his services, though respondent would be responsible for the cost of using the hospital's facilities. Respondent declined.

Respondent sued petitioner under state law and § 302 of the ADA, 104 Stat. 355, 42 U.S.C. § 12182, alleging discrimination on the basis of her disability. The state-law claims are not before us. . . .

[The Legal Issue]

We address in this case the application of the Americans with Disabilities Act of 1990 (ADA), 104 Stat. 327, 42 U.S.C. § 12101 *et seq.*, to persons infected with the human immunodeficiency virus (HIV). We granted certiorari to review, first, whether HIV infection is a disability under the ADA when the infection has not yet progressed to the so-called symptomatic phase; and, second, whether the Court of Appeals, in affirming a grant of summary judgment, cited sufficient material in the record to determine, as a matter of law, that respondent's infection with HIV posed no direct threat to the health and safety of her treating dentist. . . .

[The Decision and Rationale of the U.S. Supreme Court]

We first review the ruling that respondent's HIV infection constituted a disability under the ADA. The statute defines disability as:

a. a physical or mental impairment that substantially limits one or more of the major life activities of such individual;
b. a record of such an impairment; or
c. being regarded as having such an impairment.

§ 12102(2).

We hold respondent's HIV infection was a disability under subsection (A) of the definitional section of the statute. In light of this conclusion, we need not consider the applicability of subsections (B) or (C).

Our consideration of subsection (A) of the definition proceeds in three steps. First, we consider whether respondent's HIV infection was a physical impairment. Second, we identify the life activity upon which respondent relies (reproduction and childbearing) and determine whether it constitutes a major life activity under the ADA. Third, tying the two statutory phrases together, we ask whether the impairment substantially limited the major life activity. In construing the statute, we are informed by interpretations of parallel definitions in previous statutes and

the views of various administrative agencies which have faced this interpretive question.

The ADA's definition of disability is drawn almost verbatim from the definition of "handicapped individual" included in the Rehabilitation Act of 1973, 87 Stat. 361, as amended, 29 U.S.C. § 706(8)(B) (1988 ed.), and the definition of "handicap" contained in the Fair Housing Amendments Act of 1988, 102 Stat. 1619, 42 U.S.C. § 3602(h)(1) (1988 ed.). Congress' repetition of a well-established term carries the implication that Congress intended the term to be construed in accordance with pre-existing regulatory interpretations. . . . In this case, Congress did more than suggest this construction; it adopted a specific statutory provision in the ADA directing as follows:

> Except as otherwise provided in this chapter, nothing in this chapter shall be construed to apply a lesser standard than the standards applied under title V of the Rehabilitation Act of 1973 (29 U.S.C. § 790 *et seq.*) or the regulations issued by Federal agencies pursuant to such title.

42 U.S.C. § 12201(a).

The directive requires us to construe the ADA to grant at least as much protection as provided by the regulations implementing the Rehabilitation Act. . . .

The first step in the inquiry under subsection (A) requires us to determine whether respondent's condition constituted a physical impairment. The Department of Health, Education and Welfare (HEW) issued the first regulations interpreting the Rehabilitation Act in 1977. The regulations are of particular significance because, at the time, HEW was the agency responsible for coordinating the implementation and enforcement of § 504 . . . [Section 504 prohibits discrimination against individuals with disabilities by recipients of federal financial assistance. 29 U.S.C. § 794.] The HEW regulations, which appear without change in the current regulations issued by the Department of Health and Human Services, define "physical or mental impairment" to mean:

a. any physiological disorder or condition, cosmetic disfigurement, or anatomical loss affecting one or more of the following body systems: neurological; musculoskeletal; special sense organs; respiratory, including speech organs; cardiovascular; reproductive, digestive, genito-urinary; hemic and lymphatic; skin; and endocrine; or

b. any mental or psychological disorder, such as mental retardation, organic brain syndrome, emotional or mental illness, and specific learning disabilities.

45 CFR § 84.3(j)(2)(i) (1997).

In issuing these regulations, HEW decided against including a list of disorders constituting physical or mental impairments, out of concern that any specific enumeration might not be comprehensive. 42 Fed. Reg. 22685 (1977), reprinted in 45 CFR pt. 84, App. A, p. 334 (1997). The commentary accompanying the regulations, however, contains a representative list of disorders and conditions constituting physical impairments, including "such diseases and conditions as orthopedic, visual, speech, and hearing impairments, cerebral palsy, epilepsy, muscular dystrophy, multiple sclerosis, cancer, heart disease, diabetes, mental retardation, emotional illness, and . . . drug addiction and alcoholism." *Ibid.*

In 1980, the President transferred responsibility for the implementation and enforcement of § 504 to the Attorney General. *See, e.g.,* Exec. Order No. 12250, 3 CFR § 298 (1981). The regulations issued by the Justice Department, which remain in force to this day, adopted verbatim the HEW definition of physical impairment quoted above. 28 CFR § 41.31(b)(1) (1997). In addition, the representative list of diseases and conditions originally relegated to the commentary accompanying the HEW regulations [was] incorporated into the text of the regulations. *Ibid.*

HIV infection is not included in the list of specific disorders constituting physical impairments, in part because HIV was not identified as the cause of AIDS until 1983. *See* Barre-Sinoussi et al., *Isolation of a T-Lymphotropic Retrovirus from a Patient at Risk for Acquired Immune Deficiency Syndrome (AIDS),* 220 Science 868 (1983). . . . HIV infection does fall well within the general definition set forth by the regulations, however.

The disease follows a predictable and, as of today, an unalterable course. Once a person is infected with HIV, the virus invades different cells in the blood and in body tissues. Certain white blood cells, known as helper T-lymphocytes or CD4+ cells, are particularly vulnerable to HIV. The virus attaches to the CD4 receptor site of the target cell and fuses its membrane to the cell's membrane. HIV is a retrovirus, which means it uses an enzyme to convert its own genetic material into a form indistinguishable from the genetic material of the target cell. The virus' genetic material migrates to the cell's nucleus and becomes integrated with the cell's chromosomes. Once integrated, the

virus can use the cell's own genetic machinery to replicate itself. Additional copies of the virus are released into the body and infect other cells in turn. Young, *The Replication Cycle of HIV-1*, in The AIDS Knowledge Base, pp. 3.1–2 to 3.1–7 (P. Cohen, M. Sande, & P. Volberding eds., 2d ed.1994) (hereinafter AIDS Knowledge Base); . . . . Although the body does produce antibodies to combat HIV infection, the antibodies are not effective in eliminating the virus. Pantaleo et al., *Immunopathogenesis of Human Immunodeficiency Virus Infection*, in AIDS: Etiology 79. . . .

The virus eventually kills the infected host cell. CD4+ cells play a critical role in coordinating the body's immune response system, and the decline in their number causes corresponding deterioration of the body's ability to fight infections from many sources. Tracking the infected individual's CD4+ cell count is one of the most accurate measures of the course of the disease. Greene, Medical Management of AIDS 19, 24. . . .

The initial stage of HIV infection is known as acute or primary HIV infection. In a typical case, this stage lasts three months. The virus concentrates in the blood. The assault on the immune system is immediate. The victim suffers from a sudden and serious decline in the number of white blood cells. There is no latency period. Mononucleosis-like symptoms often emerge between six days and six weeks after infection, at times accompanied by fever, headache, enlargement of the lymph nodes (lymphadenopathy), muscle pain (myalgia), rash, lethargy, gastrointestinal disorders, and neurological disorders. Usually these symptoms abate within 14 to 21 days. HIV antibodies appear in the bloodstream within 3 weeks; circulating HIV can be detected within 10 weeks. Carr & Cooper, *Primary HIV Infection*, in Medical Management of AIDS 89–91. . . .

After the symptoms associated with the initial stage subside, the disease enters what is referred to sometimes as its asymptomatic phase. The term is a misnomer, in some respects, for clinical features persist throughout, including lymphadenopathy, dermatological disorders, oral lesions, and bacterial infections. Although it varies with each individual, in most instances this stage lasts from 7 to 11 years. The virus now tends to concentrate in the lymph nodes, though low levels of the virus continue to appear in the blood. Cohen & Volberding, AIDS Knowledge Base 4.1-4, 4.1-8. . . . It was once thought the virus became inactive during this period, but it is now known that the relative lack of symptoms is attributable to the virus' migration from the circulatory system into the lymph nodes. Cohen & Volberding, AIDS Knowledge Base 4.1-4. The migration reduces the viral presence in other parts of the body, with a corresponding diminution in physical manifestations of the disease. The virus, however, thrives in the lymph nodes, which, as a vital point of the body's immune response system, represent[s] an ideal environment for the infection of other CD4+ cells. Staprans & Feinberg, Medical Management of AIDS 33-34. Studies have shown that viral production continues at a high rate. Cohen & Volberding, AIDS Knowledge Base 4.1-4; Staprans & Feinberg, Medical Management of AIDS 38. CD4+ cells continue to decline an average of 5% to 10% (40 to 80 cells/mm3) per year throughout this phase. Saag, AIDS: Etiology 207.

A person is regarded as having AIDS when his or her CD4+ count drops below 200 cells/mm^3 of blood or when CD4+ cells comprise less than 14% of his or her total lymphocytes. U.S. Dept. of Health and Human Services, Public Health Service, CDC, 1993 Revised Classification System for HIV Infection and Expanded Surveillance Case Definition for AIDS Among Adolescents and Adults, 41 Morbidity and Mortality Weekly Rep., No. RR-17 (Dec. 18, 1992). . . . During this stage, the clinical conditions most often associated with HIV, such as *pneumocystis carninii*

pneumonia, Kaposi's sarcoma, and non-Hodgkins lymphoma, tend to appear. In addition, the general systemic disorders present during all stages of the disease, such as fever, weight loss, fatigue, lesions, nausea, and diarrhea, tend to worsen. In most cases, once the patient's CD4+ count drops below 10 cells/mm^3, death soon follows. Cohen & Volberding, AIDS Knowledge Base 4.1–9. . . .

In light of the immediacy with which the virus begins to damage the infected person's white blood cells and the severity of the disease, we hold it is an impairment from the moment of infection. As noted earlier, infection with HIV causes immediate abnormalities in a person's blood, and the infected person's white cell count continues to drop throughout the course of the disease, even when the attack is concentrated in the lymph nodes. In light of these facts, HIV infection must be regarded as a physiological disorder with a constant and detrimental effect on the infected person's hemic and lymphatic systems from the moment of infection. HIV infection satisfies the statutory and regulatory definition of a physical impairment during every stage of the disease. . . . [The *Bragdon* court's discussion of "major life activity and the substantial limitation requirement appear in parts (b) and (c) respectively of this chapter.]

Reliance on Medical Science

As the discussion of impairment in *Bragdon* demonstrates, courts often look to medical data in determining what constitutes an impairment. In some cases, this determination is obvious because the claimant has a significant and apparent disability such as paraplegia. In other cases, such as *Bragdon*, the claimant may not exhibit obvious symptoms but may nonetheless have an impairment as defined in the Act and clarified in the regulations implementing the Act. Of course, as the Court reminds us in *Bragdon*, proving impairment is simply one step in establishing that one is disabled under the ADA.

Questions

1. How would a court address Linda's disability claim in Problem 52? What about her employer's assertion?
2. Think about the changes that have occurred in the treatment of AIDS. Should this make any difference to the Court?

b. Major Life Activities

Problem 53

Assume that Linda succeeds in showing that her digestive condition is an impairment. She must still demonstrate that her impairment substantially limits a major life activity. Assume that she asserts it affects her ability to work. In support of this assertion, she offers evidence that flare-ups of the condition make her so uncomfortable she cannot function at work without being in extreme pain, and sometimes she cannot work at all, although she has always been able to get her work done by coming in at odd hours to make up for work missed when she has flare-ups. What should happen?

Interpreting the Major Life Activity Requirement

As the *Bragdon* Court explained, the second element a court looks at in determining whether a claimant is disabled is actually the third element in the definition—what major life activities are affected by the disability. Of course, the impairment and major life activity inquiries are connected by the requirement that the impairment "substantially limit" a major life activity or activities. We will look at substantial limitation in the next section. This section will focus on the question of what counts as a major life activity.

The EEOC regulations define major life activity as follows:

§ 1630.2 Definitions. . . .
(i) Major Life Activities means functions such as caring for oneself, performing manual tasks, walking, seeing, hearing, speaking, breathing, learning, and working.

The EEOC Interpretive Guidance contained in the appendix to the regulations further clarifies this definition:

Section 1630.2(i) Major Life Activities
This term adopts the definition of the term "major life activities" found in the regulations implementing section 504 of the Rehabilitation Act at 34 C.F.R. part 104. "Major life activities" are those basic activities that the average person in the general population can perform with little or no difficulty. Major life activities include caring for oneself, performing manual tasks, walking, seeing, hearing, speaking, breathing, learning, and working. This list is not exhaustive. For example, other major life activities include, but are not limited to, sitting, standing, lifting, reaching. *See* Senate Report at 22; House Labor Report at 52; House Judiciary Report at 28.

The courts also have directly addressed the question of major life activities. *Bragdon* is an ideal case for exploring this element by itself because of the way the Court structured its discussion. Yet it is hard to address this element without also exploring the substantial limitation issue. Thus, this section will be immediately followed by the section addressing substantial limitations. The discussion in that section will further elucidate the issues surrounding the major life activities element. First, however, another piece of *Bragdon*. Before reading the following excerpt, go back and reread the facts of the case at pages 328–331.

BRAGDON
v.
ABBOTT
524 U.S. 624 (1998)

Justice KENNEDY delivered the opinion of the Court.

[Decision and Rationale of the U.S. Supreme Court]

. . . The statute is not operative, and the definition not satisfied, unless the impairment affects a major life activity. Respondent's claim throughout this case has been that the HIV infection placed a substantial limitation on her ability to reproduce and to bear children. . . . Given the pervasive, and invariably fatal, course of the disease, its effect on major life activities of many sorts might have been relevant to our inquiry. Respondent and a number of *amici* make arguments about HIV's profound impact on almost every phase of the infected person's life. . . . In light of these submissions, it may seem legalistic to circumscribe our discussion to the activity of reproduction. We have little doubt that had different parties brought the suit they would have maintained that an HIV infection imposes substantial limitations on other major life activities.

From the outset, however, the case has been treated as one in which reproduction was the major life activity limited by the impairment. It is our practice to decide cases on the grounds raised and considered in the Court of Appeals and included in the question on which we granted certiorari. . . . We ask, then, whether reproduction is a major life activity.

We have little difficulty concluding that it is. As the Court of Appeals held, "[t]he plain meaning of the word 'major' denotes comparative importance" and "suggest[s] that the touchstone for determining an activity's inclusion under the statutory rubric is its significance." 107 F.3d, at 939, 940. Reproduction falls well within the phrase "major life activity." Reproduction and the sexual dynamics surrounding it are central to the life process itself.

While petitioner concedes the importance of reproduction, he claims that Congress intended the ADA only to cover those aspects of a person's life which have a public, economic, or daily character. . . . The argument founders on the statutory language. Nothing in the definition suggests that activities without a public, economic, or daily dimension may somehow be regarded as so unimportant or insignificant as to fall outside the meaning of the word "major." The breadth of the term confounds the attempt to limit its construction in this manner.

As we have noted, the ADA must be construed to be consistent with regulations issued to implement the Rehabilitation Act. See 42 U.S.C. § 12201(a). Rather than enunciating a general principle for determining what is and is not a major life activity, the Rehabilitation Act regulations instead provide a representative list, defining the term to include "functions such as caring for one's self, performing manual tasks, walking, seeing, hearing, speaking, breathing, learning, and working." 45 CFR § 84.3(j)(2)(ii) (1997); 28 CFR § 41.31(b)(2) (1997). As the use of the term "such as" confirms, the list is illustrative, not exhaustive.

These regulations are contrary to petitioner's attempt to limit the meaning of the term "major" to public activities. The inclusion of activities such as caring for oneself and performing manual tasks belies the suggestion that a task must have a public or economic character in order to be a major life activity for purposes of the ADA. On the contrary, the Rehabilitation Act regulations support the inclusion of reproduction as a major life activity, since reproduction could not be regarded as any less important than working and learning. Petitioner advances no credible basis for confining major life activities to those with a public, economic, or daily aspect. In the absence of any reason to reach a contrary conclusion, we agree with the Court of Appeals' determination that reproduction is a major life activity for the purposes of the ADA.

Questions

1. Is Linda in Problem 53 likely to succeed on the working issue? Is there another life function(s) that would better support her claim? If so, which one(s)?
2. What other major life activities do you think might have been considered in the *Bragdon* case?

c. Substantial Limitation

The third element essentially serves as a bridge between the first two. The impairment must "substantially limit" a major life activity in order for a claimant to be disabled under the ADA. Substantial limitation was also addressed in *Bragdon*, but more recent cases before the U.S. Supreme Court, such as *Toyota v. Williams* and *Sutton v. United Airlines* may limit *Bragdon*'s analysis of this element. *Toyota v. Williams* is included in this section. *Sutton v. United Airlines* is included in the next section because it applies to the definition as a whole. Before looking at the cases, however, we will again turn to the definition of "substantial limitation" contained in the EEOC regulations. The regulations define "substantially limits" as follows:

§ 1630.2 Definitions. . . .
(j) Substantially limits—
  (1) The term substantially limits means:
    (i) Unable to perform a major life activity that the average person in the general population can perform; or
    (ii) Significantly restricted as to the condition, manner or duration under which an individual can perform a particular major life activity as compared to the condition, manner, or duration under which the average person in the general population can perform that same major life activity.
  (2) The following factors should be considered in determining whether an individual is substantially limited in a major life activity:
    (i) The nature and severity of the impairment;
    (ii) The duration or expected duration of the impairment; and
    (iii) The permanent or long term impact, or the expected permanent or long term impact of or resulting from the impairment.
  (3) With respect to the major life activity of working—
    (i) The term substantially limits means significantly restricted in the ability to perform either a class of jobs or a broad range of jobs in various classes as compared to the average person having comparable training, skills and abilities. The inability to perform a single, particular job does not constitute a substantial limitation in the major life activity of working.
    (ii) In addition to the factors listed in paragraph (j)(2) of this section, the following factors may be considered in determining whether an individual is substantially limited in the major life activity of "working":
    (A) The geographical area to which the individual has reasonable access;
    (B) The job from which the individual has been disqualified because of an impairment, and the number and types of jobs utilizing similar training, knowledge, skills or abilities, within that geographical area, from which the individual is also disqualified because of the impairment (class of jobs); and/or
    (C) The job from which the individual has been disqualified because of an impairment, and the number and types of other jobs not utilizing similar training, knowledge, skills or abilities, within that geographical area, from which the individual is also disqualified because of the impairment (broad range of jobs in various classes).

Working generally should be considered a life activity of last resort by counsel because it can be much harder to prove under the EEOC Guidelines (and most courts have agreed with this aspect of the EEOC Guidelines). Unfortunately, sometimes claims are brought under the life activity of working when other life activities might have been substantially limited. This is especially egregious when several life activities might have been substantially limited, but the only one asserted is working. Unless there is a good reason for doing so, this may be legal malpractice. While the following two cases are not focused on working, there is some discussion of that life activity in *Toyota v. Williams*.

Problem 54

Assume that Linda succeeds in demonstrating that her impairment limits two major life functions, working and eating. Could she demonstrate that her condition substantially limits either or both of these major life functions? What if instead of a digestive disorder, Linda has asthma? She rarely has asthma attacks, but when she does, she is at serious risk unless she uses an inhaler and takes adequate time (usually several minutes) to recover. She must sit down and cannot work until she is through the asthma attack and is back to breathing normally. She asserts that her impairment substantially limits her in the major life functions of working and breathing.

BRAGDON
v.
ABBOTT
524 U.S. 624 (1998)

Justice KENNEDY delivered the opinion of the Court.

[The Decision and Rationale of the U.S. Supreme Court]

... The final element of the disability definition in subsection (A) is whether respondent's physical impairment was a substantial limit on the major life activity she asserts. The Rehabilitation Act regulations provide no additional guidance. . . .

Our evaluation of the medical evidence leads us to conclude that respondent's infection substantially limited her ability to reproduce in two independent ways. First, a woman infected with HIV who tries to conceive a child imposes on the man a significant risk of becoming infected. The cumulative results of 13 studies collected in a 1994 textbook on AIDS indicate[s] that 20% of male partners of women with HIV

became HIV-positive themselves, with a majority of the studies finding a statistically significant risk of infection. . . .

Second, an infected woman risks infecting her child during gestation and childbirth, *i.e.*, perinatal transmission. Petitioner concedes that women infected with HIV face about a 25% risk of transmitting the virus to their children. 107 F.3d, at 942, 912 F. Supp., at 587, n.6. Published reports available in 1994 confirm the accuracy of this statistic. . . .

Petitioner points to evidence in the record suggesting that antiretroviral therapy can lower the risk of perinatal transmission to about 8%. . . . The United States questions the relevance of the 8% figure, pointing to regulatory language requiring the substantiality of a limitation to be assessed without regard to available mitigating measures. . . . We need not resolve this dispute in order to decide this case, however. It cannot be said as a matter of law that an 8% risk of transmitting a dread and fatal disease to one's child does not represent a substantial limitation on reproduction.

The Act addresses substantial limitations on major life activities, not utter inabilities. Conception and childbirth are not impossible for an HIV victim but, without doubt, are dangerous to the public health. This meets the definition of a substantial limitation. The decision to reproduce carries economic and legal consequences as well. There are added costs for antiretroviral therapy, supplemental insurance, and long-term health care for the child who must be examined and, tragic to think, treated for the infection. The laws of some States, moreover, forbid persons infected with HIV to have sex with others, regardless of consent. Iowa Code §§ 139.1, 139.31 (1997); Md. Health Code Ann. § 18-601.1(a) (1994); Mont. Code Ann. §§ 50-18-101, 50-18-112 (1997); Utah Code Ann. § 26-6- 3.5(3) (Supp. 1997); *id.*,

§ 26-6-5 (1995); Wash. Rev. Code § 9A.36.011(1)(b) (Supp.1998); see also N.D. Cent. Code § 12.1-20-17 (1997).

In the end, the disability definition does not turn on personal choice. When significant limitations result from the impairment, the definition is met even if the difficulties are not insurmountable. For the statistical and other reasons we have cited, of course, the limitations on reproduction may be insurmountable here. Testimony from the respondent that her HIV infection controlled her decision not to have a child is unchallenged. App. 14; 912 F. Supp., at 587, 107 F.3d, at 942. In the context of reviewing summary judgment, we must take it to be true. Fed. Rule Civ. Proc. 56(e). We agree with the District Court and the Court of Appeals that no triable issue of fact impedes a ruling on the question of statutory coverage. Respondent's HIV infection is a physical impairment which substantially limits a major life activity, as the ADA defines it. In view of our holding, we need not address the second question presented, *i.e.*, whether HIV infection is a *per se* disability under the ADA.

TOYOTA MOTOR MANUFACTURING, KENTUCKY, INC.
v.
WILLIAMS
534 U.S. 184 (2002)

Justice O'CONNOR delivered the opinion of the Court.

[The Employment Problem]

Respondent began working at petitioner's automobile manufacturing plant in Georgetown, Kentucky, in August 1990. She was soon placed on an engine fabrication assembly line, where her duties included work with pneumatic tools. Use of these tools eventually caused pain in respondent's hands, wrists, and arms. She sought treatment at petitioner's in-house medical service, where she was diagnosed with bilateral carpal tunnel syndrome and bilateral tendonitis. Respondent consulted a personal physician who placed her on permanent work restrictions that precluded her from lifting more than 20 pounds or from "frequently lifting or carrying . . . objects weighing up to 10 pounds," engaging in "constant repetitive . . . flexion or extension of [her] wrists or elbows," performing "overhead work," or using "vibratory or pneumatic tools." Brief for Respondent 2; App. 45–46.

In light of these restrictions, for the next two years, petitioner assigned respondent to various modified duty jobs. Nonetheless, respondent missed some work for medical leave and eventually filed a claim under the Kentucky Workers' Compensation Act [and an ADA claim]. . . . [As] part of the settlement, respondent returned to work in December 1993.

Upon her return, petitioner placed respondent on a team in Quality Control Inspection Operations (QCIO). QCIO is responsible for four tasks: (1) "assembly paint"; (2) "paint second inspection"; (3) "shell body audit"; and (4) "ED surface repair." App. 19. Respondent initially was placed on a team that performed only the first two of these tasks, and for a couple of years, she rotated on a weekly basis between them. In assembly paint, respondent visually inspected painted cars moving slowly down a conveyor. She scanned for scratches, dents, chips, or any other flaws that may have occurred during the assembly or painting process, at a rate of one car every 54 seconds. When respondent began working in assembly paint, inspection team members were required to open and shut the doors, trunk, and/or hood of each passing car. Sometime during respondent's tenure, however, the position was modified to include only visual inspection with few or no manual tasks. Paint second inspection required team members to use their hands to wipe each painted car with a glove as it moved along a conveyor. *Id.*, at 21–22. The parties agree that respondent was physically capable of performing both of these jobs and that her performance was satisfactory.

During the fall of 1996, petitioner announced that it wanted QCIO employees to be able to rotate through all four of the QCIO processes. Respondent therefore received training for the shell body audit job, in which team members apply a highlight oil to the hood, fender, doors, rear quarter panel, and trunk of passing cars at a rate of approximately one car per minute. The highlight oil has the viscosity of salad oil, and employees spread it on cars with a sponge attached to a block of wood. After they wipe each car with the oil, the employees visually inspect it for flaws. Wiping the cars required respondent to hold her hands and arms up around shoulder height for several hours at a time.

A short while after the shell body audit job was added to respondent's rotations, she began to experience pain in her neck and shoulders. Respondent again sought care at petitioner's in-house medical service, where she was diagnosed with myotendonitis bilateral periscapular, an inflammation of the muscles and tendons around both of her shoulder blades; myotendonitis and myositis bilateral forearms with nerve compression causing median nerve irritation; and thoracic outlet compression, a condition that causes pain in the nerves that lead to the upper extremities. Respondent requested that petitioner accommodate her medical conditions by allowing her to return to doing only her original two jobs in QCIO, which respondent claimed she could still perform without difficulty. [The employer refused to make any accommodation.] . . .

Respondent's ADA claim [alleged] that she was "disabled" under the ADA on the ground that her physical impairments substantially limited her in (1) manual tasks; (2) housework; (3) gardening; (4) playing with her children; (5) lifting; and (6) working, all of which, she argued, constituted major life activities under the Act. Respondent also argued, in the alternative, that she was disabled under the ADA because she had a record of a substantially limiting impairment and because she was regarded as having such an impairment. *See* 42 U.S.C. §§ 12102(2)(B–C) (1994 ed.)

[The Legal Issue]

We granted certiorari . . . to consider the proper standard for assessing whether an individual is substantially limited in performing manual tasks. We now reverse the Court of Appeals' decision to grant partial summary judgment to respondent on the issue of whether she was substantially limited in performing manual tasks at the time she sought an accommodation. We express no opinion on the working, lifting, or other arguments for disability status that were preserved below but which were not ruled upon by the Court of Appeals. . . .

The question presented by this case is whether the Sixth Circuit properly determined that respondent was disabled under subsection (A) of the ADA's disability definition at the time that she sought an accommodation from petitioner. 42 U.S.C. § 12102(2)(A). The parties do not dispute that respondent's medical conditions, which include carpal tunnel syndrome, myotendonitis, and thoracic outlet compression, amount to physical impairments. The relevant question, therefore, is whether the Sixth Circuit correctly analyzed whether these impairments substantially limited respondent in the major life activity of performing manual tasks. Answering this requires us to address an issue about which the EEOC regulations are silent: what a plaintiff must demonstrate to establish a substantial limitation in the specific major life activity of performing manual tasks.

[The Decision and Rationale of the Trial Court and the U.S. Court of Appeals for the Sixth Circuit]

. . . The District Court granted summary judgment to petitioner, finding that respondent's impairments did not substantially limit any of her major life activities. The Court of Appeals for the Sixth Circuit reversed, finding that the impairments substantially limited respondent in the major life activity of performing manual tasks, and therefore granting partial summary judgment to respondent on the issue of whether she was disabled under the ADA. . . .

. . . The Court of Appeals held that in order for respondent to demonstrate that she was disabled due to a substantial limitation in the ability to perform manual tasks at the time of her accommodation request, she had to "show that her manual disability involve[d] a 'class' of manual activities affecting the ability to perform tasks at work." *Id.*, at 843. Respondent satisfied this test, according to the Court of Appeals, because her ailments "prevent[ed] her from doing the tasks associated with certain types of manual assembly line jobs, manual product handling jobs and manual building trade jobs (painting, plumbing, roofing, etc.) that require the gripping of tools and repetitive work with hands and arms extended at or above shoulder levels for extended periods of time." *Ibid.* In reaching this conclusion, the court disregarded evidence that respondent could "ten[d] to her personal hygiene [and] carr[y] out personal or household chores," finding that such evidence "does not affect a determination that her impairment substantially limit[ed] her ability to perform the range of manual tasks associated with an assembly line job," *ibid.* . . .

[The Decision and Rationale of the U.S. Supreme Court]

. . . We conclude that the Court of Appeals did not apply the proper standard in making this determination because it analyzed only a limited class of manual tasks and failed to ask whether respondent's impairments prevented or restricted her from performing tasks that are of central importance to most people's daily lives. . . .

. . . Under the Americans with Disabilities Act of 1990 (ADA or Act) a physical impairment that "substantially limits one or more . . . major life activities" is a "disability." 42 U.S.C. § 12102(2)(A) (1994 ed.). . . .

Our consideration of this issue is guided first and foremost by the words of the disability definition itself. "[S]ubstantially" in the phrase "substantially limits" suggests "considerable" or "to a large degree." See Webster's Third New International Dictionary 2280 (1976) (defining "substantially" as "in a substantial manner" and "substantial" as "considerable in amount, value, or worth" and "being that specified to a large degree or in the main"); see also 17 Oxford English Dictionary 66–67 (2d ed. 1989) ("substantial": "[r]elating to or proceeding from the essence of a thing; essential"; "[o]f ample or considerable amount, quantity, or dimensions"). The word "substantial" thus clearly precludes impairments that interfere in only a minor way with the performance of manual tasks from qualifying as disabilities. Cf. *Albertson's Inc. v. Kirkingburg*, 527 U.S. at 565. . . (explaining that a "mere difference" does not amount to a "significant restric[tion]" and therefore does not satisfy the EEOC's interpretation of "substantially limits").

"Major" in the phrase "major life activities" means important. *See* Webster's, *supra*, at 1363 (defining "major" as "greater in dignity, rank, importance, or interest"). "Major life activities" thus refers to those activities that are of central importance to daily life. In order for performing manual tasks to fit into this category—a category that includes such basic abilities as walking, seeing, and hearing—the manual tasks in question must be central to daily life. If each of the tasks included in the major life activity of performing manual tasks does not independently qualify as a major life activity, then together they must do so. . . .

We therefore hold that to be substantially limited in performing manual tasks, an individual must have an impairment that prevents or severely restricts the individual from doing activities that are of central importance to most people's daily lives. The impairment's impact must also be permanent or long term. See 29 CFR 1630.2(j)(2)(ii)–(iii) (2001).

It is insufficient for individuals attempting to prove disability status under this test to merely submit evidence of a medical diagnosis of an impairment. Instead, the ADA requires those "claiming the Act's protection. . . to prove a disability by offering evidence that the extent of the limitation [caused by their impairment] in terms of their own experience . . . is substantial." *Albertson's Inc. v. Kirkingburg, supra.,* at 567. . . .

An individualized assessment of the effect of an impairment is particularly necessary when the impairment is one whose symptoms vary widely from person to person. Carpal tunnel syndrome, one of respondent's impairments, is just such a condition. While cases of severe carpal tunnel syndrome are characterized by muscle atrophy and extreme sensory deficits, mild cases generally do not have either of these effects and create only intermittent symptoms of numbness and tingling. . . . Studies have further shown that, even without surgical treatment, one quarter of carpal tunnel cases resolve in one month, but that in 22 percent of cases, symptoms last for eight years or longer. . . . Given these large potential differences in the severity and duration of the effects of carpal tunnel syndrome, an individual's carpal tunnel syndrome diagnosis, on its own, does not indicate whether the individual has a disability within the meaning of the ADA. . . .

. . . The Court of Appeals' analysis of respondent's claimed disability suggested that in order to prove a substantial limitation in the major life activity of performing manual tasks, a "plaintiff must show that her manual disability involves a 'class' of manual activities," and that those activities "affec[t] the ability to perform tasks at work." *See* 224 F.3d, at 843. Both of these ideas lack support. . . .

While the Court of Appeals in this case addressed the different major life activity of performing manual tasks, its analysis circumvented *Sutton* by focusing on respondent's inability to perform manual tasks associated only with her job. This was error. When addressing the major life activity of performing manual tasks, the central inquiry must be whether the claimant is unable to perform the variety of tasks central to most people's daily lives, not whether the claimant is unable to perform the tasks associated with her specific job. Otherwise, [the Supreme Court decision in *Sutton v. United Air Lines*, 527 U.S. 471 (1999) infra at pp. 965 and its] restriction on claims of disability based on a substantial limitation in working will be rendered meaningless because an inability to perform a specific job always can be recast as an inability to perform a "class" of tasks associated with that specific job.

There is also no support in the Act, our previous opinions, or the regulations for the Court of Appeals' idea that the question of whether an impairment constitutes a disability is to be answered only by analyzing the effect of the impairment in the workplace. Indeed, the fact that the Act's definition of "disability" applies not only to Title I of the Act, which deals with employment, but also to the other portions of the Act, which deal with subjects such as public transportation . . . and privately provided public accommodations . . . demonstrates that the definition is intended to cover individuals with disabling impairments regardless of whether the individuals have any connection to a workplace.

Even more critically, the manual tasks unique to any particular job are not necessarily important parts of most people's lives. As a result, occupation-specific tasks may have only limited relevance to the manual task inquiry. In this case, "repetitive work with hands and arms extended at or above shoulder levels for extended periods of time," 224 F.3d, at 843, the manual task on which the Court of Appeals relied, is not an important part of most people's daily lives. The court, therefore, should not have considered respondent's inability to do such manual work in her specialized assembly line job as sufficient proof that she was substantially limited in performing manual tasks.

At the same time, the Court of Appeals appears to have disregarded the very type of evidence that it should have focused upon. It treated as irrelevant "[t]he fact that [respondent] can . . . ten[d] to her personal hygiene [and] carr[y] out personal or household chores." *Ibid.* Yet household chores, bathing, and brushing one's teeth are among the types of manual tasks of central importance to people's daily lives, and should have been part of the assessment of whether respondent was substantially limited in performing manual tasks.

The District Court noted that at the time respondent sought an accommodation from petitioner, she admitted that she was able to do the manual tasks required by her original two jobs in QCIO. App. to Pet. for Cert. A-36. In addition, according to respondent's deposition testimony, even after her condition worsened, she could still brush her teeth, wash her face, bathe, tend her flower garden, fix breakfast, do laundry, and pick up around the house. App. 32–34. The record also indicates that her medical conditions caused her to avoid sweeping, to quit dancing, to occasionally seek help dressing, and to reduce how often she plays with her children, gardens, and drives long distances. *Id.*, at 32, 38–39. But these changes in her life did not amount to such severe restrictions in the activities that are of central importance to most people's daily lives that they establish a manual task disability as a matter of law. On this record, it was therefore inappropriate for the Court of Appeals to grant partial summary judgment to respondent on the issue of whether she was substantially limited in performing manual tasks, and its decision to do so must be reversed. . . .

Accordingly, we reverse the Court of Appeals' judgment granting partial summary judgment to respondent and remand the case for further proceedings consistent with this opinion.

Question

1. After reading the Supreme Court's decisions, how should Linda's claim in Problems 53 and 54 be analyzed? What major life functions are involved in her case and how should she try to prove her disability interferes with that major life function?

d. Mitigating Measures

Problem 55

Jane recently took a job as an accountant for a large financial planning company. She has epilepsy. Her condition is well controlled with medication, and she has been seizure-free for several years. Her doctor has advised her, however, that certain types of fluorescent light bulbs could trigger a seizure because of their flicker rate, especially in an enclosed area such as an office. As it turns out, her employer has installed the problematic light bulbs throughout the office. Jane has requested that her employer change the bulbs to a different kind of bulb that would fit in the same fixtures. The added cost of installing this type of bulb throughout the building would be $700 per year, but the new bulbs would last longer than those currently used, which would save the employer an estimated $300 per year. Her employer is a multibillion-dollar company. The employer agrees that replacing the bulb would be a reasonable accommodation but has refused to do so because it argues that Jane is not disabled and that it does not want to set a precedent of accommodating every minor request that employees make. Moreover, Jane's boss, who did not know that Jane is epileptic until she requested the accommodation, began to treat her differently after she made the request. He has denied her the opportunity to work on several major accounts that require a good deal of travel, and this will affect her bonus at the end of the year.

Problem 56

Donald works at a car dealership as a sales associate. He has mild Tourette's Syndrome. The disease is well controlled by medication, and he is fortunate that the medication prevents him from having outbursts. The only outward sign that Donald has Tourette's is a slight facial tic that occasionally manifests itself. It has not interfered with his job, and in fact, he is consistently among the top three salesmen at the dealership. When his co-workers learned of his condition, however, they began to make fun of him by mimicking the symptoms of uncontrolled Tourette's Syndrome, such as more severe facial tics and outbursts. They often yelled curses when he walked by (not all people with Tourette's syndrome curse when they have outbursts, but, needless to say, Donald's colleagues do not exactly have a detailed understanding of the condition). Donald complained to his supervisor about the harassing conduct, but his supervisor responded, "They are just joking around. They make fun of everyone." The conduct has gotten worse, and Donald has finally decided to file a claim for hostile work environment based on disability.

(continued)

> His attorney is confident that if they can reach the hostile work environment issue, Donald will win, but first Donald must prove that he has a disability.

As the materials above demonstrate, determining who has a disability is a complex process involving analysis of all three elements of the definition and their interaction with each other. There are other issues that can have a profound impact on disability determinations under the ADA. Perhaps the most significant of these is whether mitigating measures such as medications and prosthetics should be considered when determining if an individual has an impairment that substantially limits one or more major life activities. The Supreme Court addressed this issue in three cases decided in 1999. *Sutton v. United Air Lines*, 527 U.S. 471 (1999), is probably the most significant of the cases. *Sutton* is one of a number of cases decided by the U.S. Supreme Court in the last few years that have dramatically limited the ability of claimants to successfully bring and prove ADA claims (in fact, several of these cases, such as *Sutton* and *Toyota v. Williams* exclude claimants from coverage under the ADA because they are no longer considered "disabled" for ADA purposes). *Bragdon* is the exception to this trend.

Sutton is especially interesting because the Court went against the view of all three agencies charged with interpreting the ADA, views expressed on the record in both houses of Congress, and the precedent in every federal court of appeals but one that had addressed the issue. Amazingly, despite the virtually unanimous interpretation going against the Court's approach, the Court appears to have relied on plain meaning in reaching its decision. Consider why the Court concludes as it does and whether the dissent is correct in its characterization of the majority's approach.

SUTTON
v.
UNITED AIR LINES, INC.
527 U.S. 471 (1999)

Justice O'CONNOR delivered the opinion of the Court.

[The Employment Problem]

Petitioners are twin sisters, both of whom have severe myopia. Each petitioner's uncorrected visual acuity is 20/200 or worse in her right eye and 20/400 or worse in her left eye, but "[w]ith the use of corrective lenses, each . . . has vision that is 20/20 or better." App. 23. Consequently, without corrective lenses, each "effectively cannot see to conduct numerous activities such as driving a vehicle, watching television or shopping in public stores," *id.*, at 24, but with corrective measures, such as glasses or contact lenses, both "function identically to individuals without a similar impairment," *ibid.*

In 1992, petitioners applied to respondent for employment as commercial airline pilots. They met respondent's basic age, education, experience, and Federal Aviation Administration certification qualifications. After submitting their applications for employment, both petitioners were invited by respondent to an interview and to flight simulator tests. Both were told during their interviews, however, that a mistake had been made in inviting them to interview because petitioners did not meet respondent's minimum vision requirement, which was uncorrected visual acuity of 20/100 or better. Due to their failure to meet this requirement, petitioners' interviews were terminated, and neither was offered a pilot position.

In light of respondent's proffered reason for rejecting them, petitioners filed a charge of disability discrimination under the ADA with the Equal Employment Opportunity Commission (EEOC). After receiving a right to sue letter, petitioners filed suit in the United States District Court for the District of Colorado, alleging that respondent had discriminated against them "on the basis of their disability, or because [respondent] regarded [petitioners] as having a disability" in violation of the ADA. App. 26. Specifically, petitioners alleged that due to their severe myopia they actually have a substantially limiting impairment or are regarded as having such an impairment, see *id.*, at 23–26, and are thus disabled under the Act.

[The Decisions of the Trial Court and the U.S. Court of Appeals for the Tenth Circuit]

The District Court dismissed petitioners' complaint for failure to state a claim upon which relief could be granted. . . . [T]he Tenth Circuit affirmed the District Court's judgment. 130 F.3d 893 (1997).

[The Legal Issue]

The Tenth Circuit's decision is in tension with the decisions of other Courts of Appeals. *See, e.g., Bartlett v. New York State Bd. of Law Examiners*, 156 F.3d 321, 329 (C.A.2 1998) (holding self-accommodations cannot be considered when determining a disability), *cert. pending*, No. 98-1285; *Baert v. Euclid Beverage, Ltd.*, 149 F.3d 626, 629–630 (C.A.7 1998) (holding disabilities should be determined without reference to mitigating measures); *Matczak v. Frankford Candy & Chocolate Co.*, 136 F.3d 933, 937-938 (C.A.3 1997) (same); *Arnold v. United Parcel Service, Inc.*, 136 F.3d 854, 859–866 (C.A.1 1998) (same); *see also Washington v. HCA Health Servs. of Texas, Inc.*, 152 F.3d 464, 470-471 (C.A.5 1998) (holding that only some impairments should be evaluated in their uncorrected state), *cert. pending*, No. 98-1365.

[W]hether petitioners have stated a claim under subsection (A) of the disability definition, that is, whether they have alleged that they possess a physi-cal impairment that substantially limits them in one or more major life activities is the first question. [The Court also addressed a second question: Were the plaintiffs "regarded as" having a disability under subsection (2)c) of the Act?]

[The Decision and Rationale of the U.S. Supreme Court]

We granted certiorari, 525 U.S. 1063 (1999), and now affirm.

. . . We conclude that the complaint was properly dismissed. In reaching that result, we hold that the determination of whether an individual is disabled should be made with reference to measures that mitigate the individual's impairment, including, in this instance, eyeglasses and contact lenses. In addition, we hold that petitioners failed to allege properly that respondent "regarded" them as having a disability within the meaning of the ADA. . . .

. . . Because petitioners allege that with corrective measures their vision "is 20/20 or better," App. 23, they are not actually disabled within the meaning of the Act if the "disability" determination is made with reference to these measures. Consequently, with respect to subsection (A) of the disability definition, our decision turns on whether disability is to be determined with or without reference to corrective measures.

Petitioners maintain that whether an impairment is substantially limiting should be determined without regard to corrective measures. They argue that, because the ADA does not directly address the question at hand, the Court should defer to the agency interpretations of the statute, which are embodied in the agency guidelines issued by the EEOC and the Department of Justice. These guidelines specifically direct that the determination of whether an individual is substantially limited in a major life activity be made without regard to mitigating measures. See 29 CFR pt. 1630, App. Section 1630.2(j); 28 CFR pt. 35, App. A § 35.104 (1998); 28 CFR pt. 36, App. B § 36.104.

Respondent, in turn, maintains that an impairment does not substantially limit a major life activity if it is corrected. It argues that the Court should not defer to the agency guidelines cited by petitioners because the guidelines conflict with the plain meaning of the ADA. The phrase "substantially limits one or more major life activities," it explains, requires that the substantial limitations actually and presently exist. Moreover, respondent argues, disregarding mitigating measures taken by an individual defies the statutory command to examine the effect of the impairment on the major life activities "of such individual." And even if the statute is ambiguous, respondent claims, the guidelines' directive to ignore mitigating measures is not reasonable, and thus this Court should not defer to it.

We conclude that respondent is correct that the approach adopted by the agency guidelines—that persons are to be evaluated in their hypothetical uncorrected state—is an impermissible interpretation of the ADA. Looking at the Act as a whole, it is apparent that if a person is taking measures to correct for, or mitigate, a physical or mental impairment, the effects of those measures—both positive and negative—must be taken into account when judging whether that person is "substantially limited" in a major life activity and thus "disabled" under the Act. Justice STEVENS relies on the legislative history of the ADA for the contrary proposition that individuals should be examined in their uncorrected state. See *post*, at 2154–2155 (dissenting opinion). Because we decide that, by its terms, the ADA cannot be read in this manner, we have no reason to consider the ADA's legislative history.

Three separate provisions of the ADA, read in concert, lead us to this conclusion. The Act defines a "disability" as "a physical or mental impairment that *substantially limits* one or more of the major life activities" of an individual. Section 12102(2)(A) (emphasis added). Because the phrase "substantially limits" appears in the Act in the present indicative verb form, we think the language is properly read as requiring that a person be presently—not potentially or hypothetically—substantially limited in order to demonstrate a disability. A "disability" exists only where an impairment "substantially limits" a major life activity, not where it "might," "could," or "would" be substantially limiting if mitigating measures were not taken. A person whose physical or mental impairment is corrected by medication or other measures does not have an impairment that presently "substantially limits" a major life activity. To be sure, a person whose physical or mental impairment is corrected by mitigating measures still has an impairment, but if the impairment is corrected it does not "substantially limi[t]" a major life activity.

The definition of disability also requires that disabilities be evaluated "with respect to an individual" and be determined based on whether an impairment substantially limits the "major life activities of such individual." . . . Thus, whether a person has a disability under the ADA is an individualized inquiry. See *Bragdon v. Abbott*, 524 U.S. 624, 641–642 (1998) (declining to consider whether HIV infection is a *per se* disability under the ADA); 29 CFR pt. 1630, App. Section 1630.2(j) ("The determination of whether an individual has a disability is not necessarily based on the name or diagnosis of the impairment the person has, but rather on the effect of that impairment on the life of the individual").

The agency guidelines' directive that persons be judged in their uncorrected or unmitigated state runs directly counter to the individualized inquiry mandated by the ADA. The agency approach would often require courts and employers to speculate about a person's condition and would, in many cases, force them to make a disability determination based on general information about how an uncorrected impairment usually affects individuals, rather than on the individual's actual condition. For instance, under this view, courts would almost certainly find all diabetics to be disabled, because if they failed to monitor their blood sugar levels and administer insulin, they would almost certainly be substantially limited in one or more major life activities. A diabetic whose illness does not impair his or her daily activities would therefore be considered disabled simply because he or she has diabetes. Thus, the guidelines approach would create a system in which persons often must be treated as members of a group of people with similar impairments, rather than as individuals. This is contrary to both the letter and the spirit of the ADA.

The guidelines approach could also lead to the anomalous result that in determining whether an individual is disabled, courts and employers could not consider any negative side effects suffered by an individual resulting from the use of mitigating measures, even when those side effects are very severe. . . . This result is also inconsistent with the individualized approach of the ADA.

Finally, and critically, findings enacted as part of the ADA require the conclusion that Congress did not intend to bring under the statute's protection all those whose uncorrected conditions amount to disabilities. Congress found that "some 43,000,000 Americans have one or more physical or mental disabilities, and this number is increasing as the population as a whole is growing older." § 12101(a)(1). This figure is inconsistent with the definition of disability pressed by petitioners. . . .

Regardless of its exact source, however, the 43 million figure reflects an understanding that those whose impairments are largely corrected by medication or other devices are not "disabled" within the meaning of the ADA. The estimate is consistent with the numbers produced by studies performed during this same time period that took a similar functional approach to determining disability. For instance, Mathematica Policy Research, Inc., drawing on data from the National Center for Health Statistics, issued an estimate of approximately 31.4 million civilian noninstitutionalized persons with "chronic activity limitation status" in 1979. Digest of Data on Persons with Disabilities 25 (1984). The 1989 Statistical Abstract offered the same estimate based on the same data, as well as an estimate of 32.7 million noninstitutionalized persons with "activity limitation" in 1985. Statistical Abstract, *supra*, at 115 (Table 184). In both cases, individuals with "activity limitations" were those who, relative to their age-sex group could not conduct "usual" activities. . . .

Because it is included in the ADA's text, the finding that 43 million individuals are disabled gives content to the ADA's terms, specifically the term "disability." Had Congress intended to include all persons with corrected physical limitations among those covered by the Act, it undoubtedly would have cited a much higher number of disabled persons in the findings. That it did not is evidence that the ADA's coverage is restricted to only those whose impairments are not mitigated by corrective measures.

The dissents suggest that viewing individuals in their corrected state will exclude from the definition of "disab[led]" those who use prosthetic limbs, see *post*, at 2153–2154 (opinion of STEVENS, J.), *post*, at 2161 (opinion of BREYER, J.), or take medicine for epilepsy or high blood pressure, see *post*, at 2158, 2159 (opinion of STEVENS, J.). This suggestion is incorrect. The use of a corrective device does not, by itself, relieve one's disability. Rather, one has a disability under subsection (A) if, notwithstanding the use of a corrective device, that individual is substantially limited in a major life activity. For example, individuals who use prosthetic limbs or wheelchairs may be mobile and capable of functioning in society but still be disabled because of a substantial limitation on their ability to walk or run. The same may be true of individuals who take medicine to lessen the symptoms of an impairment so that they can function but nevertheless remain substantially limited. Alternatively, one whose high blood pressure is "cured" by medication may be regarded as disabled by a covered entity, and thus disabled under subsection (C) of the definition. The use or nonuse of a corrective device does not determine whether an individual is disabled; that determination depends on whether the limitations an individual with an impairment *actually* faces are in fact substantially limiting.

Applying this reading of the Act to the case at hand, we conclude that the Court of Appeals correctly resolved the issue of disability in respondent's favor. As noted above, petitioners allege that with corrective measures, their visual acuity is 20/20, App. 23, Amended Complaint ¶36, and that they "function identically to individuals without a similar impairment," *id.*, at 24, Amended Complaint ¶ 37e. In addition, petitioners concede that they "do not argue that the use of corrective lenses in itself demonstrates a substantially limiting impairment." Brief for Petitioners 9, n.11. Accordingly, because we decide that disability under the Act is to be determined with reference to corrective measures, we agree with the courts below that petitioners have not stated a claim that they are substantially limited in any major life activity. . . .

Our conclusion that petitioners have failed to state a claim that they are actually disabled under subsection (A) of the disability definition does not end our inquiry. Under subsection (C), individuals who are "regarded as" having a disability are disabled within the meaning of the ADA. Subsection (C) provides that having a disability includes "being regarded as having," "a physical or mental impairment that substantially limits one or more of the major life activities of such individual.". . . There are two apparent ways in which individuals may fall within this statutory definition: (1) a covered entity mistakenly believes that a person has a physical impairment that substantially limits one or more major life activities, or (2) a covered entity mistakenly believes that an actual, non-limiting impairment substantially limits one or more major life activities. In both cases, it is necessary that a covered entity entertain misperceptions about the individual—it must believe either that one has a substantially limiting impairment that one does not have or that one has a substantially limiting impairment when, in fact, the impairment is not so limiting. These misperceptions often "resul[t] from stereotypic assumptions not truly indicative of . . . individual ability.". . .

There is no dispute that petitioners are physically impaired. Petitioners do not make the obvious argument that they are regarded due to their impairments as substantially limited in the major life activity of seeing. They contend only that respondent mistakenly believes their physical impairments substantially limit them in the major life activity of working. To support this claim, petitioners allege that respondent has a vision requirement that is allegedly based on myth and stereotype. Further, this requirement substantially limits their ability to engage in the major life activity of working by precluding them from obtaining the job of global airline pilot, which they argue is a "class of employment." See App. 24–26, Amended Complaint ¶ 38. In reply, respondent argues that the position of global airline pilot is not a class of jobs and therefore petitioners have not stated a claim that they are regarded as substantially limited in the major life activity of working.

Standing alone, the allegation that respondent has a vision requirement in place does not establish a claim that respondent regards petitioners as substantially limited in the major life activity of working.... By its terms, the ADA allows employers to prefer some physical attributes over others and to establish physical criteria. An employer runs afoul of the ADA when it makes an employment decision based on a physical or mental impairment, real or imagined, that is regarded as substantially limiting a major life activity. Accordingly, an employer is free to decide that physical characteristics or medical conditions that do not rise to the level of an impairment—such as one's height, build, or singing voice—are preferable to others, just as it is free to decide that some limiting, but not *substantially* limiting, impairments make individuals less than ideally suited for a job....

When the major life activity under consideration is that of working, the statutory phrase "substantially limits" requires, at a minimum, that plaintiffs allege they are unable to work in a broad class of jobs. Reflecting this requirement, the EEOC uses a specialized definition of the term "substantially limits" when referring to the major life activity of working:

> significantly restricted in the ability to perform either a class of jobs or a broad range of jobs in various classes as compared to the average person having comparable training, skills and abilities. The inability to perform a single, particular job does not constitute a substantial limitation in the major life activity of working. § 1630.2(j)(3)(i).

The EEOC further identifies several factors that courts should consider when determining whether an individual is substantially limited in the major life activity of working, including the geographical area to which the individual has reasonable access, and "the number and types of jobs utilizing similar training, knowledge, skills or abilities, within the geographical area, from which the individual is also disqualified." Sections 1630.2(j)(3)(ii)(A), (B). To be substantially limited in the major life activity of working, then, one must be precluded from more than one type of job, a specialized job, or a particular job of choice. If jobs utilizing an individual's skills (but perhaps not his or her unique talents) are

available, one is not precluded from a substantial class of jobs. Similarly, if a host of different types of jobs are available, one is not precluded from a broad range of jobs.

Because the parties accept that the term "major life activities" includes working, we do not determine the validity of the cited regulations. We note, however, that there may be some conceptual difficulty in defining "major life activities" to include work, for it seems "to argue in a circle to say that if one is excluded, for instance, by reason of [an impairment, from working with others] . . . then that exclusion constitutes an impairment, when the question you're asking is, whether the exclusion itself is by reason of handicap." Tr. of Oral Arg. in *School Bd. of Nassau Co. v. Arline*, O.T.1986, No. 85-1277, p. 15 (argument of Solicitor General). Indeed, even the EEOC has expressed reluctance to define "major life activities" to include working and has suggested that working be viewed as a residual life activity, considered, as a last resort, *only* "[i]f an individual is not substantially limited with respect to *any other* major life activity.". . .

Assuming without deciding that working is a major life activity and that the EEOC regulations interpreting the term "substantially limits" are reasonable, petitioners have failed to allege adequately that their poor eyesight is regarded as an impairment that substantially limits them in the major life activity of working. They allege only that respondent regards their poor vision as precluding them from holding positions as a "global airline pilot." See App. 25–26, Amended Complaint ¶ 38f. Because the position of global airline pilot is a single job, this allegation does not support the claim that respondent regards petitioners as having a *substantially limiting* impairment.... ("The inability to perform a single, particular job does not constitute a substantial limitation in the major life activity of working"). Indeed, there are a number of other positions utilizing petitioners' skills, such as regional pilot and pilot instructor to name a few, that are available to them. Even under the EEOC's Interpretative Guidance, to which petitioners ask us to defer, "an individual who cannot be a commercial airline pilot because of a minor vision impairment, but who can be a commercial airline co-pilot or a pilot for a courier service, would not be substantially limited in the major life activity of working." 29 CFR pt. 1630, App. § 1630.2 (1998).

Petitioners also argue that if one were to assume that a substantial number of airline carriers have similar vision requirements, they would be substantially limited in the major life activity of working. See Brief for Petitioners 44–45. Even assuming for the sake of argument that the adoption of similar vision requirements by other carriers would represent a substantial limitation on the major life activity of working, the argument is nevertheless flawed. It is not enough to say that if the physical criteria of a single employer were *imputed* to all similar employers one would be regarded as substantially limited in the major life activity of working *only as a result of this imputation.* An otherwise valid job requirement, such as a height requirement, does not become invalid simply because it *would* limit a person's employment opportunities in a substantial way *if it* were adopted by a substantial number of employers. Because petitioners have not alleged, and cannot demonstrate, that respondent's vision requirement reflects a belief that petitioners' vision substantially limits them, we agree with the decision of the Court of Appeals affirming the dismissal of petitioners' claim that they are regarded as disabled.

For these reasons, the judgment of the Court of Appeals for the Tenth Circuit is affirmed. [Justice Ginsburg's concurring opinion is omitted.]

Justice STEVENS, with whom Justice BREYER joins, dissenting.

When it enacted the Americans with Disabilities Act of 1990 (ADA or Act), Congress certainly did not intend to require United Air Lines to hire unsafe or unqualified pilots. Nor, in all likelihood, did it view every person who wears glasses as a member of a "discrete and insular minority." Indeed, by reason of legislative myopia it may not have foreseen that its definition of "disability" might theoretically encompass, not just "some 43,000,000 Americans, . . ." but perhaps two or three times that number. Nevertheless, if we apply customary tools of statutory construction, it is quite clear that the threshold question whether an individual is "disabled" within the meaning of the Act—and, therefore, is entitled to the basic assurances that the Act affords—focuses on her past or present physical condition without regard to mitigation that has resulted from rehabilitation, self-improvement, prosthetic devices, or medication. One might reasonably argue that the general rule should not apply to an impairment that merely requires a nearsighted person to wear glasses. But I believe that, in order to be faithful to the remedial purpose of the Act, we should give it a generous, rather than a miserly, construction.

There are really two parts to the question of statutory construction presented by this case. The first question is whether the determination of disability for people that Congress unquestionably intended to cover should focus on their unmitigated or their mit-

igated condition. If the correct answer to that question is the one provided by eight of the nine Federal Courts of Appeals to address the issue,[1] and by all three of the Executive agencies that have issued regulations or interpretive bulletins construing the statute—namely, that the statute defines "disability" without regard to ameliorative measures—it would still be necessary to decide whether that general rule should be applied to what might be characterized as a "minor, trivial impairment." *Arnold v. United Parcel Service, Inc.*, 136 F.3d 854, 866, n.10 (C.A.1 1998) (holding that unmitigated state is determinative but suggesting that it "might reach a different result" in a case in which "a simple, inexpensive remedy," such as eyeglasses, is available "that can provide total and relatively permanent control of all symptoms").. . .

. . . I shall therefore first consider impairments that Congress surely had in mind before turning to the special facts of this case.

"As in all cases of statutory construction, our task is to interpret the words of [the statute] in light of the purposes Congress sought to serve". . . . Congress expressly provided that the "purpose of [the ADA is] to provide a clear and comprehensive national mandate for the elimination of discrimination against individuals with disabilities.". . .

The Act's definition of disability is drawn "almost verbatim" from the Rehabilitation Act of 1973, 29 U.S.C. § 706(8)(B). The ADA's definition provides:

> The term "disability" means, with respect to an individual—
> (A) a physical or mental impairment that substantially limits one or more of the major life activities of such individual; (B) a record of such an impairment; or (C) being regarded as having such an impairment . . .

---

[1]See *Bartlett v. New York State Bd. of Law Examiners*, 156 F.3d 321 (C.A.2 1998), cert. pending, No. 98-1285; *Washington v. HCA Health Servs. of Texas*, 152 F.3d 464, 470–471 (C.A.5 1998), cert. pending, No. 98-1365; *Baert v. Euclid Beverage, Ltd.*, 149 F.3d 626, 629–630 (C.A.7 1998); *Arnold v. United Parcel Service, Inc.*, 136 F.3d 854, 859–866 (C.A.1 1998); *Matczak v. Frankford Candy & Chocolate Co.*, 136 F.3d 933, 937–938 (C.A.3 1997); *Doane v. Omaha*, 115 F.3d 624, 627 (C.A.8 1997); *Harris v. H&W Contracting Co.*, 102 F.3d 516, 520–521 (C.A.11 1996); *Holihan v. Lucky Stores, Inc.*, 87 F.3d 362, 366 (C.A.9 1996). While a Sixth Circuit decision could be read as expressing doubt about the majority rule, *see Gilday v. Mecosta County*, 124 F.3d 760, 766–768 (1997) (KENNEDY, J., concurring in part and dissenting in part); *id.*, at 768 (GUY, J., concurring in part and dissenting in part), the sole holding contrary to this line of authority is the Tenth Circuit's opinion that the Court affirms today.

The three parts of this definition do not identify mutually exclusive, discrete categories. On the contrary, they furnish three overlapping formulas aimed at ensuring that individuals who now have, or ever had, a substantially limiting impairment are covered by the Act.

An example of a rather common condition illustrates this point: There are many individuals who have lost one or more limbs in industrial accidents, or perhaps in the service of their country in places like Iwo Jima. With the aid of prostheses, coupled with courageous determination and physical therapy, many of these hardy individuals can perform all of their major life activities just as efficiently as an average couch potato. If the Act were just concerned with their present ability to participate in society, many of these individuals' physical impairments would not be viewed as disabilities. Similarly, if the statute were solely concerned with whether these individuals viewed themselves as disabled—or with whether a majority of employers regarded them as unable to perform most jobs—many of these individuals would lack statutory protection from discrimination based on their prostheses.

The sweep of the statute's three-pronged definition, however, makes it pellucidly clear that Congress intended the Act to cover such persons. The fact that a prosthetic device, such as an artificial leg, has restored one's ability to perform major life activities surely cannot mean that subsection (A) of the definition is inapplicable. Nor should the fact that the individual considers himself (or actually is) "cured," or that a prospective employer considers him generally employable, mean that subsections (B) or (C) are inapplicable. But under the Court's emphasis on "the present indicative verb form" used in subsection (A), *ante*, at 2146, that subsection presumably would not apply. And under the Court's focus on the individual's "presen[t]—not potentia[l] or hypothetica[l]"—condition, *ibid.*, and on whether a person is "precluded from a broad range of jobs," *ante*, at 2151, subsections (B) and (C) presumably would not apply.

In my view, when an employer refuses to hire the individual "because of" his prosthesis, and the prosthesis in no way affects his ability to do the job, that employer has unquestionably discriminated against the individual in violation of the Act. Subsection (B) of the definition, in fact, sheds a revelatory light on the question whether Congress was concerned only about the corrected or mitigated status of a person's impairment. If the Court is correct that "[a] 'disability' exists only where" a person's "present" or "actual" condition is substantially impaired, *ante*, at 2146, there would be no reason to include in the protected class those who were once disabled but who are now fully recovered. Subsection (B) of the Act's definition, however, plainly covers a person who previously had a serious hearing impairment that has since been completely cured. . . . Still, if I correctly understand the Court's opinion, it holds that one who *continues to wear* a hearing aid that she has worn all her life might not be covered—fully cured impairments are covered, but merely treatable ones are not. The text of the Act surely does not require such a bizarre result.

The three prongs of the statute, rather, are most plausibly read together not to inquire into whether a person is currently "functionally" limited in a major life activity, but only into the existence of an impairment—present or past—that substantially limits, or did so limit, the individual before amelioration. This reading avoids the counterintuitive conclusion that the ADA's safeguards vanish when individuals make themselves more employable by ascertaining ways to overcome their physical or mental limitations.

To the extent that there may be doubt concerning the meaning of the statutory text, ambiguity is easily removed by looking at the legislative history. As then-Justice REHNQUIST stated for the Court in *Garcia v. United States*, 469 U.S. 70 (1984): "In surveying legislative history we have repeatedly stated that the authoritative source for finding the Legislature's intent lies in the Committee Reports on the bill, which 'represen[t] the considered and collective understanding of those Congressmen involved in drafting and studying the proposed legislation.' " *Id.* at 76, (quoting *Zuber v. Allen*, 396 U.S. 168, 186 (1969)). The Committee Reports on the bill that became the ADA make it abundantly clear that Congress intended the ADA to cover individuals who could perform all of their major life activities only with the help of ameliorative measures.

The ADA originated in the Senate. The Senate Report states that "whether a person has a disability should be assessed without regard to the availability of mitigating measures, such as reasonable accommodations or auxiliary aids." S. Rep. No. 101–116, p. 23 (1989). The Report further explained, in discussing the "regarded as" prong:

[An] important goal of the third prong of the [disability] definition is to ensure that persons with medical conditions that are under control, and that therefore do not currently limit major life activities, are not discriminated against on the basis of their medical conditions. For example, individuals with controlled diabetes or epilepsy are often denied jobs for which they are qualified. Such denials are the result of negative attitudes and misinformation." *Id.*, at 24.

When the legislation was considered in the House of Representatives, its Committees reiterated the Senate's basic understanding of the Act's coverage, with one minor modification: They clarified that "correctable" or "controllable" disabilities were covered in the first definitional prong as well. The Report of the House Committee on the Judiciary states, in discussing the first prong, that, when determining whether an individual's impairment substantially limits a major life activity, "[t]he impairment should be assessed without considering whether mitigating measures, such as auxiliary aids or reasonable accommodations, would result in a less-than-substantial limitation." H.R. Rep. No. 101-485, pt. III, p. 28 (1990). The Report continues that "a person with epilepsy, an impairment which substantially limits a major life activity, is covered under this test," *ibid.*, as is a person with poor hearing, "even if the hearing loss is corrected by the use of a hearing aid." *Id.*, at 29.

The Report of the House Committee on Education and Labor likewise states that "[w]hether a person has a disability should be assessed without regard to the availability of mitigating measures, such as reasonable accommodations or auxiliary aids." *Id.*, pt. II, at 52. To make matters perfectly plain, the Report adds:

> For example, a person who is hard of hearing is substantially limited in the major life activity of hearing, *even though the loss may be corrected through the use of a hearing aid.* Likewise, persons with impairments, such as epilepsy or diabetes, which substantially limit a major life activity are covered under the first prong of the definition of disability, *even if the effects of the impairment are controlled by medication. Ibid.* (emphasis added).

All of the Reports, indeed, are replete with references to the understanding that the Act's protected class includes individuals with various medical conditions that ordinarily are perfectly "correctable" with medication or treatment. . . .[2]

In addition, each of the three Executive agencies charged with implementing the Act has consistently interpreted the Act as mandating that the presence of disability turns on an individual's uncorrected state. We have traditionally accorded respect to such views when, as here, the agencies "played a pivotal role in setting [the statutory] machinery in motion." *Ford Motor Credit Co. v. Milhollin*, 444 U.S. 555, 566 (1980). . . . At the very least, these interpretations "constitute a body of experience and informed judgment to which [we] may properly resort" for additional guidance. *Skidmore v. Swift & Co.*, 323 U.S. 134, 139–140 (1944). See also *Bragdon*, 524 U.S., at 642 (invoking this maxim with regard to the Equal Employment Opportunity Commission's (EEOC) interpretation of the ADA).

The EEOC's Interpretive Guidance provides that "[t]he determination of whether an individual is substantially limited in a major life activity must be made on a case by case basis, without regard to mitigating measures such as medicines, or assistive or prosthetic devices.". . . The EEOC further explains:

> [A]n individual who uses artificial legs would . . . be substantially limited in the major life activity of walking because the individual is unable to walk without the aid of prosthetic devices. Similarly, a diabetic who without insulin would lapse into a coma would be substantially limited because the individual cannot perform major life activities without the aid of medication. *Ibid.*

The Department of Justice has reached the same conclusion. Its regulations provide that "[t]he question of whether a person has a disability should be assessed without regard to the availability of mitigating measures, such as reasonable modification or auxiliary aids and services." 28 CFR pt. 35, App. A, § 35.104 (1998). The Department of Transportation has issued a regulation adopting this same definition of "disability." See 49 CFR pt. 37.3 (1998).

In my judgment, the Committee Reports and the uniform agency regulations merely confirm the message conveyed by the text of the Act—at least insofar as it applies to impairments such as the loss of a limb, the inability to hear, or any condition such as diabetes that is substantially limiting without medication. The Act generally protects individuals who have "correctable" substantially limiting impairments from unjustified employment discrimination on the basis of those impairments. The question, then, is whether the fact that Congress was specifically concerned about protecting a class that included persons characterized as a "discrete and insular minority" and that it estimated that class to include "some 43,000,000 Americans" means that we should construe the term "disability" to exclude

[2]The House's decision to cover correctable impairments under subsection (A) of the statute seems, in retrospect, both deliberate and wise. Much of the structure of the House Reports is borrowed from the Senate Report; thus it appears that the House Committees consciously decided to move the discussion of mitigating measures. This adjustment was prudent because in a case in which an employer refuses, out of animus or fear, to hire an individual who has a condition such as epilepsy that the employer knows is controlled, it may be difficult to determine whether the employer is viewing the individual in her uncorrected state or "regards" her as substantially limited.

individuals with impairments that Congress probably did not have in mind.

The EEOC maintains that, in order to remain allegiant to the Act's structure and purpose, courts should always answer "the question whether an individual has a disability. . . without regard to mitigating measures that the individual takes to ameliorate the effects of the impairment." Brief for United States et al. as *Amici Curiae* 6. "[T]here is nothing about poor vision," as the EEOC interprets the Act, "that would justify adopting a different rule in this case." *Ibid.* . . .

This case . . . is not about whether petitioners are genuinely qualified or whether they can perform the job of an airline pilot without posing an undue safety risk. The case just raises the threshold question whether petitioners are members of the ADA's protected class. It simply asks whether the ADA lets petitioners in the door in the same way as the Age Discrimination in Employment Act of 1967 does for every person who is at least 40 years old, see 29 U.S.C. § 631(a), and as Title VII of the Civil Rights Act of 1964 does for every single individual in the work force. Inside that door lies nothing more than basic protection from irrational and unjustified discrimination because of a characteristic that is beyond a person's control. Hence, this particular case, at its core, is about whether, assuming that petitioners can prove that they are "qualified," the airline has any duty to come forward with some legitimate explanation for refusing to hire them because of their uncorrected eyesight, or whether the ADA leaves the airline free to decline to hire petitioners on this basis even if it is acting purely on the basis of irrational fear and stereotype. . . .

. . . [I]t seems to me eminently within the purpose and policy of the ADA to require employers who make hiring and firing decisions based on individuals' uncorrected vision to clarify why having, for example, 20/100 uncorrected vision or better is a valid job requirement. So long as an employer explicitly makes its decision based on an impairment that in some condition is substantially limiting, it matters not under the structure of the Act whether that impairment is widely shared or so rare that it is seriously misunderstood. Either way, the individual has an impairment that is covered by the purpose of the ADA, and she should be protected against irrational stereotypes and unjustified disparate treatment on that basis. . . .

. . . While not all eyesight that can be enhanced by glasses is substantially limiting, having 20/200 vision in one's better eye is, without treatment, a significant hindrance. Only two percent of the population suffers from such myopia. . . . Such acuity precludes a person from driving, shopping in a public store, or viewing a

computer screen from a reasonable distance. Uncorrected vision, therefore, can be "substantially limiting" in the same way that unmedicated epilepsy or diabetes can be. Because Congress obviously intended to include individuals with the latter impairments in the Act's protected class, we should give petitioners the same protection. . . .

. . . I agree that the letter and spirit of the ADA is designed to deter decision making based on group stereotypes, but the agencies' interpretation of the Act does not lead to this result. Nor does it require courts to "speculate" about people's "hypothetical" conditions. Viewing a person in her "unmitigated" state simply requires examining that individual's abilities in a different state, not the abilities of every person who shares a similar condition. It is just as easy individually to test petitioners' eyesight with their glasses on as with their glasses off.[5] . . .

In this case the quality of petitioners' uncorrected vision is relevant only because the airline regards the ability to see without glasses as an employment qualification for its pilots. Presumably it would not insist on such a qualification unless it has a sound business justification for doing so (an issue we do not address today). But if United regards petitioners as unqualified because they cannot see well without glasses, it seems eminently fair for a court also to use uncorrected vision as the basis for evaluating petitioners' life activity of seeing.

Under the agencies' approach, individuals with poor eyesight and other correctable impairments will, of course, be able to file lawsuits claiming discrimination on that basis. Yet all of those same individuals can already file employment discrimination claims based on their race, sex, or religion, and—provided they are at least 40 years old—their age. Congress has never seen this as reason to restrict classes of antidiscrimination coverage. . . .

Occupational hazards characterize many trades. The farsighted pilot may have as much trouble seeing the instrument panel as the nearsighted pilot has in identifying a safe place to land. The vision of appellate judges is sometimes subconsciously obscured by a concern that their decision will legalize issues best left to

---

[5]For much the same reason, the Court's concern that the agencies' approach would "lead to the anomalous result" that courts would ignore "negative side effects suffered by an individual resulting from the use of mitigating measures," *ante*, at 2147, is misplaced. It seems safe to assume that most individuals who take medication that itself substantially limits a major life activity would be substantially limited in some other way if they did not take the medication. . . .

the private sphere or will magnify the work of an already-overburdened judiciary. See *Jackson v. Virginia*, 443 U.S. 307, 326, 337–339 (1979) (STEVENS, J., dissenting). Although these concerns may help to explain the Court's decision to chart its own course—rather than to follow the one that has been well marked by Congress, by the overwhelming consensus of circuit judges, and by the Executive officials charged with the responsibility of administering the ADA—they surely do not justify the Court's crabbed vision of the territory covered by this important statute.

Accordingly, although I express no opinion on the ultimate merits of petitioners' claim, I am persuaded that they have a disability covered by the ADA. I therefore respectfully dissent. [Justice BREYER's dissent is omitted.]

Questions

1. How might a court analyze Jane's claim in Problem 55 after *Sutton*? For an analysis of a situation similar to this, see Frank S. Ravitch and Marsha B. Freeman, *The Americans with "Certain" Disabilities Act: Title I of the ADA and the Supreme Court's Result Oriented Jurisprudence*, 77 Denv. U. L. Rev. 119 (1999).
2. Which argument seems more persuasive in *Sutton*? Why?

ALBERTSON'S, INC. v. KIRKINGBURG
527 U.S. 555 (1999)

Justice SOUTER delivered the opinion of the Court: [Justice STEVENS and Justice BREYER joined only in Parts I and III of the opinion.]

[The Employment Problem]

In August 1990, petitioner, Albertson's, Inc., a grocery-store chain with supermarkets in several States, hired respondent, Hallie Kirkingburg, as a truck driver based at its Portland, Oregon, warehouse. Kirkingburg had more than a decade's driving experience and performed well when petitioner's transportation manager took him on a road test.

Before starting work, Kirkingburg was examined to see if he met federal vision standards for commercial truck drivers. . . . For many decades the Department of Transportation and its predecessors have been responsible for devising these standards for individuals who drive commercial vehicles in interstate commerce. . . . Since 1971, the basic vision regulation has required corrected distant visual acuity of at least 20/40 in each eye and distant binocular acuity of at least 20/40. See 35 Fed. Reg. 6458, 6463 (1970); 57 Fed. Reg. 6793, 6794 (1992); 49 CFR § 391.41(b)(10) (1998). . . . Kirkingburg, however, suffers from amblyopia, an uncorrectable condition that leaves him with 20/200 vision in his left eye and monocular vision in effect. . . . Despite Kirkingburg's weak left eye, the doctor erroneously certified that he met the DOT's basic vision standards, and Albertson's hired him. . . .

In December 1991, Kirkingburg injured himself on the job and took a leave of absence. Before returning to work in November 1992, Kirkingburg went for a further physical as required by the company. This time, the examining physician correctly assessed Kirkingburg's vision and explained that his eyesight did not meet the basic DOT standards. The physician, or his nurse, told Kirkingburg that in order to be legally qualified to drive, he would have to obtain a waiver of its basic vision standards from the DOT. . . . The doctor was alluding to a scheme begun in July 1992 for giving DOT certification to applicants with deficient vision who had three years of recent experience driving a commercial vehicle without a license suspension or revocation, involvement in a reportable accident in which the applicant was cited for a moving violation, conviction for certain driving-related offenses, citation for certain serious traffic violations, or more than two convictions for any other moving violations. A waiver applicant had to agree to have his vision checked annually for deterioration, and to report certain information about his driving experience to the Federal Highway Administration (FHWA or Administration), the agency within the DOT responsible for overseeing the motor carrier safety regulations. . . . Kirkingburg applied for a waiver, but because he could not meet the basic DOT vision standard Albertson's fired him from his job as a truck driver. . . . In early 1993, after he had left Albertson's, Kirkingburg received a DOT waiver, but Albertson's refused to rehire him. . . .

[The Legal Issue]

The question posed is whether, under the Americans with Disabilities Act of 1990 (ADA or Act), 104 Stat. 327, as amended, 42 U.S.C. § 12101 *et seq.* (1994 ed. and Supp. III), an employer who requires as a job qualification that an employee meet an otherwise applicable federal safety regulation must justify enforcing the regulation solely because its standard may be waived in an individual case. We answer no. [The case also addressed the mitigation issue and the portion of the opinion excerpted here addresses that question as well. The qualification issue is addressed later in this chapter.]

[The Decision and Rationale of the U.S. Supreme Court]

Though we need not speak to the issue whether Kirkingburg was an individual with a disability in order to resolve this case, that issue falls within the first question on which we granted certiorari,[8] and we think it worthwhile to address it briefly in order to correct three missteps the Ninth Circuit made in its discussion of the matter. . . .

. . . There is no dispute either that Kirkingburg's amblyopia is a physical impairment within the meaning of the Act. . . (defining "physical impairment" as "[a]ny physiological disorder, or condition. . . affecting one or more of the following body systems: . . . special sense organs"), or that seeing is one of his major life activities, see Section 1630.2(i) (giving seeing as an example of a major life activity). . . . The question is whether his monocular vision alone "substantially limits" Kirkingburg's seeing.

In giving its affirmative answer, the Ninth Circuit relied on a regulation issued by the Equal Employment Opportunity Commission (EEOC), defining "substantially limits" as "[s]ignificantly restrict[s] as to the condition, manner or duration under which an individual can perform a particular major life activity as compared to the condition, manner, or duration under which the average person in the general popula-

tion can perform that same major life activity." Section 1630.2(j)(ii). The Ninth Circuit concluded that "the manner in which [Kirkingburg] sees differs significantly from the manner in which most people see" because, "[t]o put it in its simplest terms [he] sees using only one eye; most people see using two." 143 F.3d, at 1232. The Ninth Circuit majority also relied on a recent Eighth Circuit decision, whose holding it characterized in similar terms: "It was enough to warrant a finding of disability . . . that the plaintiff could see out of only one eye: the *manner* in which he performed the major life activity of seeing was different. . . ."

But in several respects, the Ninth Circuit was too quick to find a disability. First, although the EEOC definition of "substantially limits" cited by the Ninth Circuit requires a "significant restrict[ion]" in an individual's manner of performing a major life activity, the court appeared willing to settle for a mere difference. By transforming "significant restriction" into "difference," the court undercut the fundamental statutory requirement that only impairments causing "substantial limitat[ions]" in individuals' ability to perform major life activities constitute disabilities. While the Act "addresses substantial limitations on major life activities, not utter inabilities," *Bragdon v. Abbott*, 524 U.S. 624, 641 (1998), it concerns itself only with limitations that are in fact substantial.

Second, the Ninth Circuit appeared to suggest that in gauging whether a monocular individual has a disability, a court need not take account of the individual's ability to compensate for the impairment. The court acknowledged that Kirkingburg's "brain has developed subconscious mechanisms for coping with [his] visual impairment and thus his body compensates for his disability. . . ." But in treating monocularity as itself sufficient to establish disability . . . , the Ninth Circuit apparently adopted the view that whether "the individual had learned to compensate for the disability by making subconscious adjustments to the *manner* in which he sensed depth and perceived peripheral objects . . . was irrelevant to the determination of disability. . . . We have just held, however, in *Sutton v. United Airlines, Inc.*, 527 U.S., at 482 that mitigating measures must be taken into account in judging whether an individual possesses a disability. We see no principled basis for distinguishing between measures undertaken with artificial aids, like medications and devices, and measures undertaken, whether consciously or not, with the body's own systems.

Finally, and perhaps most significantly, the Court of Appeals did not pay much heed to the statutory obligation to determine the existence of disabilities on a case-by-case basis. The Act expresses that mandate

---

[8]"Whether a monocular individual is 'disabled' per se, under the Americans with Disabilities Act.". . .

clearly by defining "disability" "with respect to an individual . . . " and in terms of the impact of an impairment on "such individual," § 12102(2)(A). . . . While some impairments may invariably cause a substantial limitation of a major life activity, cf. *Bragdon, supra*, at 642, (declining to address whether HIV infection is a *per se* disability), we cannot say that monocularity does. That category, as we understand it, may embrace a group whose members vary by the degree of visual acuity in the weaker eye, the age at which they suffered their vision loss, the extent of their compensating adjustments in visual techniques, and the ultimate scope of the restrictions on their visual abilities. These variables are not the stuff of a *per se* rule. While monocularity inevitably leads to some loss of horizontal field of vision and depth perception,[12] consequences the Ninth Circuit mentioned . . . , the court did not identify the degree of loss suffered by Kirkingburg, nor are we aware of any evidence in the record specifying the extent of his visual restrictions.

This is not to suggest that monocular individuals have an onerous burden in trying to show that they are disabled. On the contrary, our brief examination of some of the medical literature leaves us sharing the Government's judgment that people with monocular vision "ordinarily" will meet the Act's definition of disability, Brief for United States et al. as *Amici Curiae* 11, and we suppose that defendant companies will often not contest the issue. We simply hold that the Act requires monocular individuals, like others claiming the Act's protection, to prove a disability by offering evidence that the extent of the limitation in terms of their own experience, as in loss of depth perception and visual field, is substantial. . . .

[12]Individuals who can see out of only one eye are unable to perform stereopsis, the process of combining two retinal images into one through which two-eyed individuals gain much of their depth perception, particularly at short distances. At greater distances, stereopsis is relatively less important for depth perception. In their distance vision, monocular individuals are able to compensate for their lack of stereopsis to varying degrees by relying on monocular cues, such as motion parallax, linear perspective, overlay of contours, and distribution of highlights and shadows. See von Noorden, *Binocular Vision and Ocular Motility* at 23–30 (4th ed. 1990). . . .

Discussion Notes

As the preceding cases demonstrate, the threshold question of whether one is disabled is quite complex. Under Title VII or the ADEA, the question of whether someone is actually protected by the statute rarely is a substantial issue, yet that question was complex under the ADA even before the Supreme Court's highly controversial decision in *Sutton*. Losing the battle at this threshold level means that one is not covered under the ADA, and thus one cannot get to the merits of one's claim.

Sutton is controversial because it could result in situations where someone who is discriminated against because of a stereotype regarding his or her condition (one of the central concerns underlying the ADA) is denied protection because he or she functions normally in a mitigated state. This might be less problematic in situations involving impairments that are not generally recognized as disabilities, but when one considers that *Sutton* may remove well-controlled epileptics diabetics, and asthmatics or those who have lost a limb but can effectively function with a prosthesis—even if they are the targets of stereotyping and discrimination—one can see why the issues surrounding the disability determination are so important.

In the next two sections, we will explore the "record of" and "regarded as" elements of the definition. These might provide an alternative to those denied coverage under the *Sutton* doctrine. As you will see, however, these elements have been limited in their reach as well.

Question

1. How would a court analyze Donald's assertion in Problem 56 above that he is disabled? Would the fact that Donald has been harassed based on his condition affect this analysis?

e. Record of Impairment

Problem 57

Bob had a serious glandular disorder when he worked at Mertco, the largest manufacturer of widgets. Two years ago, Bob was cured with a new gene therapy. Prior to being cured, he missed a number of days at work because of his condition, which would make him immobile for periods of time. Since he was cured, he has missed no work, and he has received excellent performance evaluations. Recently Mertco was bought out by Bigco, and Bob was one of the few Mertco employees that Bigco laid off. Bob believes he was laid off because of his prior disability. He brings a claim asserting that he was fired because of a record of his impairment.

The "record of impairment" element in the definition of disability under the ADA applies when an employer relies on a record indicating a history of disability or misclassifies an employee as disabled based on his or her past of having a disability record. The record element generally applies to past disabilities. A currently disabled individual would proceed under the general definition of disability. *See* 42 U.S.C. § 12102(2)(A). Significantly, however, it is not enough that an employer rely on a record of impairment. The language of the definition is "a record of *such* an impairment." 42 U.S.C. § 12102(2)(B) (emphasis added). This harkens back to the general definition of disability—i.e., the record must be of an impairment that substantially limits one or more major life activities. Moreover, as the cases below demonstrate, the employer must actually rely on the record, and the information relied on must qualify as a "record" for purposes of the definition. Thus, it is not always easy to establish a "record of" disability. The following cases, one of which arose after the Exxon Valdez oil spill, show why.

EQUAL EMPLOYMENT OPPORTUNITY COMMISSION
v.
EXXON CORPORATION
124 F. Supp. 2d 987 (N.D. Tex. 2000)

BOYLE, United States Magistrate Judge.

[The Employment Problem]

In the wee hours of March 24, 1989, a drunken Captain Joseph Hazelwood caused the *Exxon Valdez* supertanker to run aground on Bligh Reef, spilling eleven million gallons of oil into the waters of Prince William Sound, Alaska. . . . The accident, which captured national attention, cost Exxon more than eight billion dollars in clean-up costs, settlements, and outstanding judgments. . . . The *Valdez* disaster also resulted in the government's criminal indictment of Exxon for offenses related to the accident. . . . Within weeks after the mishap, Exxon began the process of instituting a stiff new substance abuse policy aimed at eliminating another *Valdez* calamity. . . . In July 1989, Exxon formally adopted its "Statement of Policy Regarding Employee Alcohol and Drug Use,". . . which barred all employees with "substance abuse problem[s]" from holding designated "safety-sensitive" positions.[8] In conjunction with its policy, Exxon designated approximately ten percent of its jobs as "safety-sensitive," affecting approximately 1,500 positions. . . . Exxon instituted its policy in all of its regions and affiliates in the United States and it remains in full effect today. . . .

Under Exxon's substance abuse policy, employees who have participated in rehabilitation programs are considered to have a "substance abuse problem" and are, consequently, precluded from all of the designated jobs. . . . Exxon's policy does not require individualized assessments of each rehabilitated employee to determine their fitness for these positions. Rather, these employees are, without exception, precluded from the "safety-sensitive" jobs. . . . Exxon justifies its across-the-board policy by claiming that the inability to predict when a former substance abuser will relapse prevents it from employing any rehabilitated employee in a designated spot due to the attendant safety risk. . . . The safety risk, according to Exxon, was determined by examining the nature of the jobs. . . . Exxon's official criteria for the safety-sensitive designations is in jobs where: (1) there is high exposure to catastrophic public, environmental, or employee incident; (2) the person in such position performs a key and direct role in the operating process where failure could cause a catastrophic incident; and (3) there is either no direct supervision or very limited supervision to provide an operational check. . . .

All of the plaintiffs in this case have been through substance abuse rehabilitation. As a consequence of their participation in rehabilitation programs, each has also been removed from or prevented from attaining one or more of Exxon's designated jobs. It is on this basis that they have filed suit against Exxon challenging its policy under the ADA. . . .

[The Legal Issue]

The Equal Employment Opportunity Commission (EEOC) brought this action pursuant to the Americans With Disabilities Act (ADA), challenging the manner in which Exxon Corporation . . . treats reha-

bilitated substance abusers. The plaintiffs, represented by the EEOC, are all present or former employees of Exxon who, in the past, have been treated for drug or alcohol abuse. They contend that Exxon's drug and alcohol policy, which bars rehabilitated substance abusers from certain safety-sensitive jobs, violates the ADA. Exxon filed the instant summary judgment motion addressing the sole issue of whether the plaintiffs are "disabled" as defined under the ADA. . . .

[The Decision and Rationale of the U.S. District Court for the Northern District of Texas]

Exxon moves for summary judgment, contending that the plaintiffs are not "disabled" within the meaning of the ADA [only the discussion of the record of impairment element is included here]. . . .

"Record of" or "Regarded as" Substantially Limited In Work

Both sides to this dispute agree that none of the plaintiffs *currently* have an impairment that substantially limits a major life activity. What plaintiffs do assert is that Exxon's substance abuse policy *treats* employees who participated in a rehabilitation program as if they are disabled with respect to their ability to perform certain designated jobs. Specifically, plaintiffs argue that, based on their prior substance abuse and rehabilitation histories, they are protected by the ADA under the "record of". . . pron[g] of the definition of disability. The Court, therefore, must determine: (1) whether Exxon, by relying on the plaintiffs' rehabilitation history, discriminated against them on the basis of a *record* of a disability. . . .

Record of Disability

While the ADA does not define "record of" a disability, the regulations provide, "[h]as a record of such impairment means has a history of, or has been misclassified as having, a mental or physical impairment that substantially limits one or more major life activities." 29 C.F.R. § 1630.2(k). Under this prong for the ADA's definition of disability, an individual is protected if an employer relies on a record which indicates that the individual has or has had a substantially limiting impairment. 29 C.F.R. App. § 1630.2(k). Such a record may include educational, medical, or employment records. *Id.* The purpose of this provision is to protect individuals from discrimination based on a history of disability or because they have been misclassified as disabled. *Id.*

---

[8]The policy provides: No employee with alcohol or drug dependency will be terminated due to the request for help with overcoming that dependency or because of involvement in a rehabilitation effort. However, an employee who has had or is found to have a substance abuse problem will not be permitted to work in designated positions identified by management as being critical to the safety and well-being of employees, the public, or the Corporation. . . . Def.'s App. at 541, Ex. 29.

Therefore, it applies only to those individuals who have been classified or misclassified as having a substantially limiting impairment.... *Sherrod*, 132 F.3d at 1120–21 (**plaintiff's record of impairment failed to show a substantially limiting impairment to satisfy definition of disability**); *Ray*, 85 F.3d at 229 (same).

In addition to showing a substantially limiting impairment, the record of the disability must be relied on by the employer as a basis for discriminating against the individual. *See* 29 C.F.R. App. § 1630.2(k). Thus, the employer must have some knowledge of the record establishing the disability....

In this summary judgment context, the EEOC has failed to raise a genuine fact issue regarding the plaintiffs' disabled condition under this definition. Specifically, the EEOC has failed to establish that the information regarding their substance abuse histories constitutes a record of disability within the meaning of the Act, and that Exxon relied on that record in discriminating against them.

The EEOC claims that the plaintiffs have a record of an impairment that substantially limits the major life activities of remembering, thinking, concentrating, sleeping, caring for one's self, interacting with others, eating, and the "awareness associated with consciousness."... Their primary evidence on this issue consists of declarations from seven of the plaintiffs wherein each plaintiff recalls how their prior substance abuse interfered with their personal lives, detailing incidences from drinking binges, blackouts, loss of memory and consciousness, difficulty in thinking and concentrating, difficulty in interacting with others, difficulty in eating and sleeping, to the physical pains of withdrawal from substance abuse.... Even assuming these effects of the plaintiffs' prior substance abuse constitute substantial limitations on major life activities, ... their declarations, the Court finds, do not constitute a record of a disability as contemplated by the ADA, the regulations, and the case authority. The plaintiffs' declarations merely recount their past problems with substance abuse, and in no way suggest the existence of a "record" relied upon by Exxon that classifies or misclassifies these plaintiffs as having a substantially limiting impairment. *See Taylor*, 214 F.3d at 961 ("In order to have a record of a disability, an employee's documentation must show that she has a history of or has been subject to misclassification as disabled.") ... *See also Hilburn*, 181 F.3d at 1229 (plaintiff furnished no evidence that employer

had any record of a substantially limiting impairment); *Sorensen v. Univ. of Utah Hosp.*, 194 F.3d 1084, 1087–88 (10th Cir. 1999). The EEOC has failed to provide any medical, educational, or employment records as mentioned in the regulations. *See* 29 C.F.R. App. § 1630.2(k). Nor are there any treatment, counseling or hospitalization records currently before the Court. In short, the undisputed evidence establishes that these plaintiffs were affected by Exxon's policy based solely on their past participation in some sort of rehabilitation program for substance abuse. As noted earlier, alcoholism and substance abuse are not *per se* disabilities. *See Burch*, 119 F.3d at 316; *Zenor*, 176 F.3d at 859. And hospitalization, inpatient counseling, or record of a mere medical diagnosis alone does not establish a substantially limiting impairment. *See Gallagher*, 181 F.3d at 655; *Demming v. Housing and Redevelopment Auth.*, 66 F.3d 950, 955 (8th Cir. 1995); *Byrne v. Bd. of Educ.*, 979 F.2d 560, 566 (7th Cir. 1992).

The Court should not be misunderstood to say that declarations are always insufficient to establish a record of a disability. Rather, the plaintiffs' reliance on these declarations is misplaced. The declarations were created only recently after the filing of Exxon's summary judgment motion.... They cannot, therefore, constitute a record of a disability that was relied on by Exxon in implementing its substance abuse policy. The affidavits contain nothing to indicate that Exxon was aware of the effects of the plaintiffs' prior substance abuse problems, or that Exxon was aware of anything beyond the mere fact that each plaintiff had participated in some substance abuse rehabilitation.... And the plaintiffs' proof fails to show that such rehabilitation constitutes an impairment that substantially limits any major life activity. Consequently, the EEOC has failed to meet its burden of establishing that the plaintiffs are disabled under the "record of" prong of the ADA's definition of disability and therefore are unable to invoke its protection on this ground.[35]

---

[35]Although the plaintiffs have failed to establish that their substance abuse history constitutes a record of a disabling impairment, the existence of a record of rehabilitation remains relevant in the Court's analysis of whether Exxon regarded the plaintiffs as disabled.

TAYLOR
v.
PHOENIXVILLE SCHOOL DISTRICT
113 F. Supp. 2d 770 (E.D. Pa. 2000)

JOYNER, District Judge.

[The Employment Problem]

. . . The essential facts of the case are as follows. Plaintiff was employed by Defendant as the principal's secretary for the East Pikeland Elementary School (East Pikeland) from September 1974 until her termination on October 28, 1994. During her tenure as secretary, Plaintiff worked for several different principals, each of whom gave Plaintiff consistently positive work reviews. In August 1993, a new principal, Christine Menzel (Menzel), was assigned to East Pikeland. Unfortunately, after working with Menzel for only one week, Plaintiff became ill and was forced to take a leave of absence from work.

Plaintiff's leave of absence began on August 30, 1993. The next day she was admitted to the Coastal Plains Hospital and Counseling Center in North Carolina (Coastal Plains) where she was diagnosed with bipolar disorder. While under care at Coastal Plains, Plaintiff was treated with the prescription drugs Navane and Lithium Carbonate. She remained hospitalized until September 20, 1993, at which time she was discharged to the care of Louise Sonnenberg, M.D. (Dr. Sonnenberg), a psychiatrist practicing in Phoenixville, Pennsylvania. Plaintiff currently remains under the care of Dr. Sonnenberg and continues to take Lithium.

With her doctor's permission, Plaintiff returned to work in mid-October 1993. Almost immediately upon her return, Plaintiff encountered difficulties performing her job. These problems were exacerbated by a number of changes in office procedure that had been implemented by Menzel during Plaintiff's absence. As a result of the problems, Menzel became dissatisfied with Plaintiff's performance, and the working relationship between the two women became strained. Over the next year, Menzel documented Plaintiff's errors in a series of disciplinary memoranda that culminated with Plaintiff being placed on probation for unsatisfactory performance on September 8, 1994. Finally, on October 28, 1994, Plaintiff was informed that she had failed to improve her performance during the probationary period and that she was being terminated from her position. . . .

[The Legal Issue]

This is an employment discrimination case presently before the Court on remand from the United States Court of Appeals for the Third Circuit. . . . In her Complaint, Taylor claimed that the School District discriminated against her in violation of the Americans with Disabilities Act, 42 U.S.C. § 12101, *et seq.* (the ADA) and the Pennsylvania Human Relations Act, 43 P.S. § 951, *et seq.* (the PHRA). The essence of Taylor's claims was that the School District failed to provide reasonable accommodations for her mental illness. . . .

. . . [W]e consider whether Taylor is disabled under the ADA by virtue of having a "record of impairment." *See* 42 U.S.C. § 12102(2)(B). . . . To meet this [record of unpairment definition], an individual must have a history of, or been misclassified as having, an impairment that substantially limited a major life activity. . . .[2]

[The Decision and Rationale of the U.S. District Court for the Eastern District of Pennsylvania]

Taylor blends her "record of impairment" claim and her "regarded as" claim together into a single argument. In doing so, she fails to offer any specific evidence that she has a record of an impairment that substantially limits a major life activity. To the contrary, her argument, and the evidence in support of that argument, appear to apply solely to whether Defendant regarded her as disabled. As described *infra,* "regarded as" disability is a distinct way to establish a disability under the ADA, and we will consider Taylor's evidence in support of that claim in turn. However, for purposes of meeting the definition of a

[2]The EEOC guidelines further state: "This part of the definition is satisfied if a record relied on by an employer indicates that the individual has or has had a substantially limiting impairment. The impairment indicated in the record must be an impairment that would substantially limit one or more of the individual's major life activities." 29 C.F.R. App. § 1630.2(k).

disability by virtue of a "record of impairment," Taylor has failed to provide sufficient evidence to support her claim. To the extent a record of an impairment exists at all, nothing in that record suggests that the impairment substantially limited a major life activity. Such a showing is insufficient to establish disability based upon a record of impairment. . . . As a result, we will grant Defendant's Motion with respect to claims premised on "record of impairment" disability. . . .

Question

1. In Problem 57, what must Bob do to prevail on the disability determination issue? What might Bigco argue in response to Bob's claim? How would the situation be analyzed if Bob never had a disability but rather a temporary condition? What if there is evidence that based on Mertco company records, Bigco believed Bob was disabled?

f. The "Regarded As" Element

As with the "record of" element, the "regarded as" element requires that the employee be regarded as having an *impairment that substantially limits one or more major life functions*. *Sutton* takes away the best means for those with mitigated impairments to avoid the strange result that they are not covered under the ADA even when an employer discriminates against them based on stereotypes. For example, a well-controlled epileptic may not be covered under the initial definition of disability under *Sutton*, even where an employer discriminates based on stereotype, because the employee can never reach the discrimination issue if she is not considered disabled and thus not protected under the Act. An obvious way around this would be to argue that she is still covered because the employer regarded her as disabled even if she did not meet the definition of disability, but what if the employer regarded her only as impaired but not as substantially limited in a major life function? Or what if the employer felt that she could not perform a particular job because he or she had a stereotyped view of the employee's condition but did not regard the employee as substantially limited in regard to working or any other life function?

Although the regarded as element is not a universally effective means to avoid some of the seemingly odd results of *Sutton*, it is still an important element of the disability definition. The Supreme Court has held that the regarded as element applies when a person without an impairment is mistakenly believed to have an impairment that substantially limits one or more major life functions or where a nonlimiting (or more accurately nonsubstantially limiting) impairment is regarded as though it were limiting. *Sutton*, 527 U.S. at 489. As noted above, the nonlimiting impairment must be regarded as though it substantially limits a major life function or functions. This was discussed in *Sutton*, but it was also addressed in the following case that was decided by the Supreme Court on the same day as *Sutton*. Following the Supreme Court decision is a lower court decision that also addresses the regarded as element.

MURPHY
v.
UNITED PARCEL SERVICE, INC.
527 U.S. 516 (1999)

Justice O'CONNOR delivered the opinion of the Court.

[The Employment Problem]

Respondent United Parcel Service, Inc. (UPS), dismissed petitioner Vaughn L. Murphy from his job as a UPS mechanic because of his high blood pressure. . . .

Petitioner was first diagnosed with hypertension (high blood pressure) when he was 10 years old. Unmedicated, his blood pressure is approximately 250/160. With medication, however, petitioner's "hypertension does not significantly restrict his activities and . . . in general he can function normally and can engage in activities that other persons normally do.". . . (discussing testimony of petitioner's physician).

In August 1994, respondent hired petitioner as a mechanic, a position that required petitioner to drive commercial motor vehicles. Petitioner does not challenge the District Court's conclusion that driving a commercial motor vehicle is an essential function of the mechanic's job at UPS. . . . To drive such vehicles, however, petitioner had to satisfy certain health requirements imposed by the Department of Transportation (DOT). . . . One such requirement is that the driver of a commercial motor vehicle in interstate commerce have "no current clinical diagnosis of high blood pressure likely to interfere with his/her ability to operate a commercial vehicle safely." Section 391.41(b)(6).

At the time respondent hired him, petitioner's blood pressure was so high, measuring at 186/124, that he was not qualified for DOT health certification. . . . Nonetheless, petitioner was erroneously granted certification, and he commenced work. In September 1994, a UPS medical supervisor who was reviewing petitioner's medical files discovered the error and requested that petitioner have his blood pressure retested. Upon retesting, petitioner's blood pressure was measured at 160/102 and 164/104. See App. 48a (testimony of Vaughn Murphy). On October 5, 1994, respondent fired petitioner on the belief that his blood pressure exceeded the DOT's requirements for drivers of commercial motor vehicles.

[The Legal Issues]

Petitioner filed suit under Title I of the Americans with Disabilities Act of 1990 (ADA or Act), 104 Stat. 328, 42 U.S.C. § 12101 *et seq.*, in Federal District Court. The District Court granted summary judgment to respondent, and the Court of Appeals for the Tenth Circuit affirmed. We must decide whether the Court of Appeals correctly considered petitioner in his medicated state when it held that petitioner's impairment does not "substantially limi[t]" one or more of his major life activities and whether it correctly determined that petitioner is not "regarded as disabled." *See* § 12102(2).

[The Decision and Rationale of the U.S. Supreme Court]

In light of our decision in *Sutton v. United Air Lines, Inc.*, 527 U.S. 471, we conclude that the Court of Appeals' resolution of both issues was correct. . . .

The first question presented in this case is whether the determination of petitioner's disability is made with reference to the mitigating measures he employs. We have answered that question in *Sutton* in the affirmative. Given that holding, the result in this case is clear. The Court of Appeals concluded that, when medicated, petitioner's high blood pressure does not substantially limit him in any major life activity. Petitioner did not seek, and we did not grant, certiorari on whether this conclusion was correct. Because the question whether petitioner is disabled when taking medication is not before us, we have no occasion here to consider whether petitioner is "disabled" due to limitations that persist despite his medication or the negative side effects of his medication. Instead, the question granted was limited to whether, under the ADA, the determination of whether an individual's impairment "substantially limits" one or more major life activities should be made without consideration of mitigating measures. . . .

The second issue presented is also largely resolved by our opinion in *Sutton*. Petitioner argues that the Court of Appeals erred in holding that he is not "regarded as" disabled because of his high blood pressure. As we held in *Sutton*, . . . a person is "regarded as" disabled within the meaning of the ADA if a covered entity mistakenly believes that the person's actual, nonlimiting impairment substantially limits one or more major life activities. Here, petitioner alleges that his hypertension is regarded as substantially limiting him in the major life activity of working, when in fact it does not. To support this claim, he points to testimony from respondent's resource manager that respondent fired petitioner due to his hypertension, which he claims evidences respondent's belief that petitioner's hypertension—and consequent inability to obtain DOT certification—substantially limits his ability to work. In response, respondent argues that it does not regard petitioner as substantially limited in the major life activity of working but, rather, regards him as unqualified to work as a UPS mechanic because he is unable to obtain DOT health certification.

As a preliminary matter, we note that there remains some dispute as to whether petitioner meets the requirements for DOT certification. As discussed above, petitioner was incorrectly granted DOT certification at his first examination when he should have instead been found unqualified. See *supra*, at 2136. Upon retesting, although petitioner's blood pressure was not low enough to qualify him for the 1-year certification that he had incorrectly been issued, it was sufficient to qualify him for optional temporary DOT health certification. App. 98a–102a (Medical Regulatory Criteria). Had a physician examined petitioner and, in light of his medical history, declined to issue a temporary DOT certification, we would not second-guess that decision. Here, however, it appears that UPS determined that petitioner could not meet the DOT standards and did not allow him to attempt to obtain the optional temporary certification. *Id.*, at 84a–86a (testimony of Monica Sloan, UPS' company nurse); *id.*, at 54a–55a (testimony and affidavit of Vaughn Murphy). We need not resolve the question whether petitioner could meet the standards for DOT health certification, however, as it goes only to whether petitioner is qualified and whether respondent has a defense based on the DOT regulations, *see Albertson's Inc. v. Kirkingburg*, 527 U.S. 555, issues not addressed by the court below or raised in the petition for certiorari.

The only issue remaining is whether the evidence that petitioner is regarded as unable to obtain DOT certification (regardless of whether he can, in fact, obtain optional temporary certification) is sufficient to create a genuine issue of material fact as to whether petitioner is regarded as substantially limited in one or more major life activities. As in *Sutton*, we assume, *arguendo*, that the Equal Employment Opportunity Commission (EEOC) regulations regarding the disability determination are valid. When referring to the major life activity of working, the EEOC defines "substantially limits" as: "significantly restricted in the ability to perform either a class of jobs or a broad range of jobs in various classes as compared to the average person having comparable training, skills and abilities." 29 CFR § 1630.2(j)(3)(i) (1998). The EEOC further identifies several factors that courts should consider when determining whether an individual is substantially limited in the major life activity of working, including "the number and types of jobs utilizing similar training, knowledge, skills or abilities, within [the] geographical area [reasonably accessible to the individual], from which the individual is also disqualified." Section 1630.2(j)(3)(ii)(B). Thus, to be regarded as substantially limited in the major life activity of working, one must be regarded as precluded from more than a particular job. . . .

Again, assuming without deciding that these regulations are valid, petitioner has failed to demonstrate that there is a genuine issue of material fact as to whether he is regarded as disabled. Petitioner was fired from the position of UPS mechanic because he has a physical impairment—hypertension that is regarded as preventing him from obtaining DOT health certification. . . .

The evidence that petitioner is regarded as unable to meet the DOT regulations is not sufficient to create a genuine issue of material fact as to whether petitioner is regarded as unable to perform a class of jobs utilizing his skills. At most, petitioner has shown that he is regarded as unable to perform the job of mechanic only when that job requires driving a commercial motor vehicle—a specific type of vehicle used on a highway in interstate commerce. 49 CFR § 390.5 (1998) (defining "commercial motor vehicle" as a vehicle weighing over 10,000 pounds, designed to carry 16 or more passengers, or used in the transportation of hazardous materials). Petitioner has put forward no evidence that he is regarded as unable to perform any mechanic job that does not call for driving a commercial motor vehicle and thus does not require DOT certification. Indeed, it is undisputed that petitioner is generally employable as a mechanic. Petitioner has "performed mechanic jobs that did not require DOT certification" for "over 22 years," and he secured another job as a mechanic shortly after leaving UPS. . . . Moreover, respondent presented uncontroverted evidence that petitioner could perform jobs such as diesel mechanic, automotive mechanic, gas-engine repairer, and gas-welding equipment mechanic, all of which utilize petitioner's mechanical skills. See App. 115a (report of Lewis Vierling).

Consequently, in light of petitioner's skills and the array of jobs available to petitioner utilizing those skills, petitioner has failed to show that he is regarded as unable to perform a class of jobs. Rather, the undisputed record evidence demonstrates that petitioner is, at most, regarded as unable to perform only a particular job. This is insufficient, as a matter of law, to prove that petitioner is regarded as substantially limited in the major life activity of working. See *Sutton*, 527 U.S., at 492–493. . . . For the reasons stated, we affirm the judgment of the Court of Appeals for the Tenth Circuit.

Justice STEVENS, with whom Justice BREYER joins, dissenting.

For the reasons stated in my dissenting opinion in *Sutton v. United Airlines, Inc.*, 527 U.S., at 495, I respectfully dissent. I believe that petitioner has a "disability" within the meaning of the ADA because, assuming petitioner's uncontested evidence to be true, his very severe hypertension—in its unmedicated state—"substantially limits" his ability to perform several major life activities. Without medication, petitioner would likely be hospitalized. See App. 81. Indeed, unlike *Sutton*, this case scarcely requires us to speculate whether Congress intended the Act to cover individuals with this impairment. Severe hypertension, in my view, easily falls within the ADA's nucleus of covered impairments. See *Sutton*, 527 U.S., at 496–503 (STEVENS, J., dissenting).

Because the Court of Appeals did not address whether petitioner was qualified or whether he could perform the essential job functions . . . I would reverse and remand for further proceedings.

TAYLOR
v.
PHOENIXVILLE SCHOOL DISTRICT
113 F. Supp. 2d 770 (E.D. Pa. 2000)

JOYNER, District Judge.

[The Decision and Rationale of the U.S. District Court for the Eastern District of Pennsylvania]

[See the section above on "record of" disability for the facts of this case. This excerpt includes only the discussion of the regarded as element.]

Regarded as Disabled

Finally, we examine whether Plaintiff has established a disability by virtue of having been "regarded as" disabled. *See* 42 U.S.C. § 12102(2)c. Under the ADA, a person is regarded as having a disability if the person:

1. has a physical or mental impairment that does not substantially limit major life activities but is treated by the covered entity as constituting such limitation;
2. has a physical or mental impairment that substantially limits major life activities only as a result of the attitudes of others toward such impairment; or
3. has [no such impairment] but is treated by a covered entity as having a substantially limiting impairment. 29 C.F.R. § 1630.2(1).

In the instant case, we find that there is adequate evidence for Plaintiff to withstand summary judgment on her "regarded as" claim. Genuine issues of material fact exist concerning the School District's initial notice of Taylor's ailment, its understanding of Taylor's medical condition when she returned to work, and its later conduct toward Taylor based on that understanding. Viewing these facts in the light most favorable to Taylor, we find that a reasonable jury may be able to conclude that the School District regarded Taylor as disabled when she was discharged. *See, e.g., Deane*, 142 F.3d at 145 (holding that summary judgment inappropriate where factual disputes exist over degree of impairment compared with perception thereof); *see also*

Taylor v. Pathmark Stores, Inc., 177 F.3d 180, 191 (3d Cir. 1999) (noting that "regarded as" plaintiff can make out a claim even if employer is innocently wrong about extent of impairment). Accordingly, we will deny Defendant's motion with respect to claims based upon regarded as disability.

The cases above demonstrate that the "regarded as" element of the ADA definition of disability is not an easy one to meet in many cases. One other possible piece of the definition comes from the EEOC Guidelines. The Guidelines include persons who have an impairment "that substantially limits major life activities only as a result of the attitudes of others toward such impairment." 29 C.F.R. § 1630.2(l)(2). The district court cited to the guidelines in *Taylor*, but significantly, the Supreme Court does not address the guidelines in either *Murphy* or *Sutton*.

Questions

1. Look again at the problems addressed earlier in this chapter. How would Jane, the accountant with well-controlled epilepsy, and Donald, the car salesman with well-controlled Tourette's Syndrome, fare under the regarded as element? Even if their medication adequately mitigates their conditions so that they are not disabled under the first element of the disability analysis, might they prevail under this element? Remember that they must be regarded as having an impairment that substantially limits one or more major life functions. What might their employers assert in response to their regarded as claims?
2. What do you think of the Supreme Court rationale in making these determinations? Do you think the purposes of the ADA are promoted by these decisions? Explain your answer and try to refer to the various critical perspectives in Chapter 1 for support of your argument.

chapter 14

The Americans with Disabilities Act of 1990—Part II: Employee Qualifications and Employer Obligations to Provide Reasonable Accommodations

Problem 58

Leonard Abner works as a regional bank manager for a major national bank. He oversees the work at three branch locations in his region. Leonard sustained a severe injury to his leg that has caused him to have great difficulty walking and has also prevented him from driving a car. A big part of Leonard's job is visiting each branch at least once a week to meet with the branch managers, and he must work daily at the main branch in his region, where he is the defacto branch manager. Otherwise, he must visit the other branches only once a month for two days each to make sure their daily operations are running smoothly. Leonard is able to get transportation to work and to the branch offices for the monthly visits, but he is unable to go to the branch offices to meet with the managers weekly. As a result, his employer terminates his employment. Prior to being terminated, Leonard had asked the bank to allow him to conduct the weekly meetings by conference call or to have the branch managers come to his office for the meetings. He pointed out that the meetings occur before the branch offices open, and thus nothing would be lost if he was not physically there for the meetings. In response to Leonard's claim under the ADA, the bank argues that Leonard is no longer qualified for his former position because he cannot perform the essential functions of the job. The bank argues that going to the branch offices for the weekly meetings is an essential function.

A. Qualified Individual with a Disability

Demonstrating that one is an individual with a disability simply establishes that one is covered under the Americans with Disabilities Act (ADA). In order to win one's case under the ADA, it is also necessary to demonstrate that one is a "qualified individual with a disability"—i.e., that one can perform the essential functions of the job with or without reasonable accommodation. 42 U.S.C. § 12111(8). After this, one must still establish his or her actual claim—i.e., disparate treatment, failure to accommodate, hostile work environment, and so on. Yet proving that one is qualified for purposes of the ADA is not always an easy matter. A number of issues arise in this context, such as these: What are the essential functions of the job? Who gets to decide what functions are essential? What counts as a reasonable accommodation for purposes of this analysis? What happens if a claimant can perform the essential functions of the job but there is a possibility his or her condition might pose a threat to the claimant or others if he or she performs the job?

B. The Essential Functions of the Job

The ADA states that a qualified individual with a disability is one who can perform the essential functions of the job with or without reasonable accommodation. But what are the essential functions of the job? The Equal Employment Opportunity Commission (EEOC) has further defined the term 29 CFR 1630.2:

(m) Qualified individual with a disability means an individual with a disability who satisfies the requisite skill, experience, education and other job-related requirements of the employment position such individual holds or desires, and who, with or without reasonable accommodation, can perform the essential functions of such position. . . .

(n) Essential functions—

(1) In general. The term essential functions means the fundamental job duties of the employment position the individual with a disability holds or desires. The term "essential functions" does not include the marginal functions of the position.

(2) A job function may be considered essential for any of several reasons, including but not limited to the following:

(i) The function may be essential because the reason the position exists is to perform that function;

(ii) The function may be essential because of the limited number of employees available among whom the performance of that job function can be distributed; and/or

(iii) The function may be highly specialized so that the incumbent in the position is hired for his or her expertise or ability to perform the particular function.

(3) Evidence of whether a particular function is essential includes, but is not limited to:

(i) The employer's judgment as to which functions are essential;

(ii) Written job descriptions prepared before advertising or interviewing applicants for the job;

(iii) The amount of time spent on the job performing the function;

(iv) The consequences of not requiring the incumbent to perform the function;

(v) The terms of a collective bargaining agreement;

(vi) The work experience of past incumbents in the job; and/or

(vii) The current work experience of incumbents in similar jobs.

29 C.F.R. § 1630.2.

The EEOC regulations fill in a number of significant gaps in the statutory definition of essential functions. Yet in *Sutton*, the Supreme Court did not show great deference to the EEOC regulations and has been rather cryptic on the subject since. The *Sutton* Court relied heavily on the fact that the EEOC was not specifically charged to interpret the definition section of the ADA, and thus *Sutton's* treatment of the regulations may be irrelevant for purposes of the essential function inquiry, as it derives directly from Title I of the ADA, which the EEOC is charged to interpret.

The question of qualification and essential functions is a complex and fact-sensitive one, as the EEOC regulations demonstrate. The following two cases address the question of essential functions in two very different contexts. *Davis* is a classic case decided under the Rehabilitation Act of 1973. Cases decided under the Rehabilitation Act have precedential value under the ADA so long as they are consistent with the language of the ADA. *Davis* is generally instructive on the question of qualification, but it is not consistent (especially with Title I of the ADA) in aspects of its discussion of reasonable accommodation (or what the *Davis* Court sometimes refers to as "affirmative action"). *Davis* involved a claim for access to a program and not a claim of employment discrimination, but it should be noted that the notion that one is not qualified if a program must be fundamentally altered in order for one to participate does apply to employment claims in that an employer ordinarily need not fundamentally restructure a position in order to accommodate an individual. 29 C.F.R. § 1630.2(p)(2)(v); EEOC Interpretive Guidance, 29 C.F.R. app. to § 1630.2(p). In the *Kirkingburg* case, already discussed in Chapter 13, the Court addressed the interaction between the essential function analysis and government regulations, but it is also a good case through which to analyze the essential functions inquiry more generally.

SOUTHEASTERN COMMUNITY COLLEGE
v.
DAVIS
442 U.S. 397 (1979)

Mr. Justice POWELL delivered the opinion of the Court.

[The Employment Problem]

Respondent, who suffers from a serious hearing disability, seeks to be trained as a registered nurse. During the 1973–1974 academic year, she was enrolled in the College Parallel program of Southeastern Community College, a state institution that receives federal funds. Respondent hoped to progress to Southeastern's Associate Degree Nursing program, the completion of which would make her eligible for state certification as a registered nurse. In the course of her application to the nursing program, she was interviewed by a member of the nursing faculty. It became apparent that respondent had difficulty understanding questions asked, and on inquiry she acknowledged a history of hearing problems and dependence on a hearing aid. She was advised to consult an audiologist.

On the basis of an examination at Duke University Medical Center, respondent was diagnosed as having a "bilateral, sensori-neural hearing loss." App. 127a. A change in her hearing aid was recommended, as a result of which it was expected that she would be able to detect sounds "almost as well as a person would who has normal hearing." *Id.*, at 127a–128a. But this improvement would not mean that she could discriminate among sounds sufficiently to understand normal spoken speech. Her lipreading skills would remain necessary for effective communication: "While wearing the hearing aid, she is well aware of gross sounds occurring in the listening environment. However, she can only be responsible for speech spoken to her, when the talker gets her attention and allows her to look directly at the talker." *Id.*, at 128a.

Southeastern next consulted Mary McRee, Executive Director of the North Carolina Board of Nursing. On the basis of the audiologist's report, McRee recommended that respondent not be admitted to the nursing program. In McRee's view, respondent's hearing disability made it unsafe for her to practice as a nurse. . . . In addition, it would be impossible for respondent to participate safely in the normal clinical training program, and those modifications that would be necessary to enable safe participation would prevent her from realizing the benefits of the program: "To adjust patient learning experiences in keeping with [respondent's] hearing limitations could, in fact, be the same as denying her full learning to meet the objectives of your nursing programs." *Id.*, at 132a–133a.

After respondent was notified that she was not qualified for nursing study because of her hearing disability, she requested reconsideration of the decision. The entire nursing staff of Southeastern was assembled, and McRee again was consulted. McRee repeated her conclusion that on the basis of the available evidence, respondent "has hearing limitations which could interfere with her safely caring for patients." *Id.*, at 139a. Upon further deliberation, the staff voted to deny respondent admission.

[The Legal Issue]

This case presents a matter of first impression for this Court: Whether § 504 of the Rehabilitation Act of 1973, which prohibits discrimination against an "otherwise qualified handicapped individual" in federally funded programs "solely by reason of his handicap," forbids professional schools from imposing physical qualifications for admission to their clinical training programs. . . .

[The Decision and Rationale of the Trial Court and the U.S. Court of Appeals for the Fourth Circuit]

Respondent . . . filed suit in the United States District Court for the Eastern District of North Carolina, alleging both a violation of § 504 of the Rehabilitation Act of 1973 . . . [2] and a denial of equal protection and due process. After a bench trial, the District Court entered judgment in favor of Southeastern. . . .

[T]he District Court concluded that respondent was not an "otherwise qualified handicapped individual" protected against discrimination by § 504. . . . [3]

On appeal, the Court of Appeals for the Fourth Circuit reversed. . . . It did not dispute the District Court's findings of fact, but held that the court had misconstrued § 504. In light of administrative regulations that had been promulgated while the appeal was pending . . . the appellate court believed that § 504 required Southeastern to "reconsider plaintiff's application for admission to the nursing program without regard to her hearing ability." . . . It concluded that the District Court had erred in taking respondent's handicap into account in determining whether she was "otherwise qualified" for the program, rather than confining its inquiry to her "academic and technical qualifications." *Id.*, at 1161. The Court of Appeals also suggested that § 504 required "affirmative conduct" on the part of Southeastern to modify its program to accommodate the disabilities of applicants, "even when such modifications become expensive." . . .

[The Decision and Rationale of the U.S. Supreme Court]

Because of the importance of this issue to the many institutions covered by § 504, we granted certiorari. . . . We now reverse. . . .

As previously noted, this is the first case in which this Court has been called upon to interpret § 504. It is elementary that "[t]he starting point in every case involving construction of a statute is the language itself." . . . Section 504 by its terms does not compel

---

[2]The statute, as set forth in 29 U.S.C. § 794 (1976 ed., Supp. II) provides in full: "No otherwise qualified handicapped individual in the United States, as defined in section 706(7) of this title, shall, solely by reason of his handicap, be excluded from the participation in, be denied the benefits of, or be subjected to discrimination under any program or activity receiving Federal financial assistance. . . . "

[3]The District Court also dismissed respondent's constitutional claims. The Court of Appeals affirmed that portion of the order, and respondent has not sought review of this ruling.

educational institutions to disregard the disabilities of handicapped individuals or to make substantial modifications in their programs to allow disabled persons to participate. Instead, it requires only that an "otherwise qualified handicapped individual" not be excluded from participation in a federally funded program "solely by reason of his handicap," indicating only that mere possession of a handicap is not a permissible ground for assuming an inability to function in a particular context. . . .

The court below, however, believed that the "otherwise qualified" persons protected by § 504 include those who would be able to meet the requirements of a particular program in every respect except as to limitations imposed by their handicap. . . . Taken literally, this holding would prevent an institution from taking into account any limitation resulting from the handicap, however disabling. It assumes, in effect, that a person need not meet legitimate physical requirements in order to be "otherwise qualified." We think the understanding of the District Court is closer to the plain meaning of the statutory language. An otherwise qualified person is one who is able to meet all of a program's requirements in spite of his handicap.

The regulations promulgated by the Department of HEW to interpret § 504 reinforce, rather than contradict, this conclusion. According to these regulations, a "[q]ualified handicapped person" is, "[w]ith respect to postsecondary and vocational education services, a handicapped person who meets the academic and technical standards requisite to admission or participation in the [school's] education program or activity. . . ." 45 CFR § 84.3(k)(3) (1978). An explanatory note states:

> The term "technical standards" refers to *all* nonacademic admissions criteria that are essential to participation in the program in question. 45 CFR pt. 84, App. A, p. 405 (1978) (emphasis supplied).

A further note emphasizes that legitimate physical qualifications may be essential to participation in particular programs. . . . We think it clear, therefore, that HEW interprets the "other" qualifications which a handicapped person may be required to meet as including necessary physical qualifications. . . .

The remaining question is whether the physical qualifications Southeastern demanded of respondent might not be necessary for participation in its nursing program. It is not open to dispute that, as Southeastern's Associate Degree Nursing program currently is constituted, the ability to understand speech without reliance on lipreading is necessary for patient safety during the clinical phase of the pro-

gram. As the District Court found, this ability also is indispensable for many of the functions that a registered nurse performs.

Respondent contends nevertheless that § 504, properly interpreted, compels Southeastern to undertake affirmative action that would dispense with the need for effective oral communication. . . .

We note first that on the present record it appears unlikely respondent could benefit from any affirmative action that the regulation reasonably could be interpreted as requiring. Section 84.44(d)(2), for example, explicitly excludes "devices or services of a personal nature" from the kinds of auxiliary aids a school must provide a handicapped individual. Yet the only evidence in the record indicates that nothing less than close, individual attention by a nursing instructor would be sufficient to ensure patient safety if respondent took part in the clinical phase of the nursing program. . . . Furthermore, it also is reasonably clear that [the regulation] does not encompass the kind of curricular changes that would be necessary to accommodate respondent in the nursing program. In light of respondent's inability to function in clinical courses without close supervision, Southeastern, with prudence, could allow her to take only academic classes. Whatever benefits respondent might realize from such a course of study, she would not receive even a rough equivalent of the training a nursing program normally gives. Such a fundamental alteration in the nature of a program is far more than the "modification" the regulation requires. . . .

We do not suggest that the line between a lawful refusal to extend affirmative action and illegal discrimination against handicapped persons always will be clear. It is possible to envision situations where an insistence on continuing past requirements and practices might arbitrarily deprive genuinely qualified handicapped persons of the opportunity to participate in a covered program. Technological advances can be expected to enhance opportunities to rehabilitate the handicapped or otherwise to qualify them for some useful employment. Such advances also may enable attainment of these goals without imposing undue financial and administrative burdens upon a State. Thus, situations may arise where a refusal to modify an existing program might become unreasonable and discriminatory. Identification of those instances where a refusal to accommodate the needs of a disabled person amounts to discrimination against the handicapped continues to be an important responsibility of HEW.

In this case, however, it is clear that Southeastern's unwillingness to make major adjustments in its nursing program does not constitute such discrimination. The uncontroverted testimony of several members of Southeastern's staff and faculty established that the purpose of its program was to train persons who could serve the nursing profession in all customary ways. . . . This type of purpose, far from reflecting any animus against handicapped individuals, is shared by many if not most of the institutions that train persons to render professional service. It is undisputed that respondent could not participate in Southeastern's nursing program unless the standards were substantially lowered. Section 504 imposes no requirement upon an educational institution to lower or to effect substantial modifications of standards to accommodate a handicapped person. . . .

One may admire respondent's desire and determination to overcome her handicap, and there well may be various other types of service for which she can qualify. In this case, however, we hold that there was no violation of § 504 when Southeastern concluded that respondent did not qualify for admission to its program. Nothing in the language or history of § 504 reflects an intention to limit the freedom of an educational institution to require reasonable physical qualifications for admission to a clinical training program. Nor has there been any showing in this case that any action short of a substantial change in Southeastern's program would render unreasonable the qualifications it imposed. . . .

Accordingly, we reverse the judgment of the court below, and remand for proceedings consistent with this opinion.

ALBERTSON'S
v.
KIRKINGBURG
527 U.S. 555 (1999)

Justice SOUTER delivered the opinion of the Court.

[The Employment Problem]

[The facts of this case and the analysis of whether Mr. Kirkingburg was disabled can be found in Chapter 13 in section C.4, addressing mitigating measures under the definition of disability. The following excerpt from the opinion is focused on the requirement that plaintiff prove he or she is a qualified individual with a disability issue.]

[The Decision and Rationale of the U.S. Supreme Court]

[Albertson's] primary contention is that even if Kirkingburg was disabled, he was not a "qualified" individual with a disability . . . because Albertson's merely insisted on the minimum level of visual acuity set forth in the DOT's Motor Carrier Safety Regulations, 49 CFR § 391.41(b)(10) (1998). If Albertson's was entitled to enforce that standard as defining an "essential job functio[n]" of the employment position,"

see 42 U.S.C. § 12111(8), that is the end of the case, for Kirkingburg concededly could not satisfy it.[13]

Under Title I of the ADA, employers may justify their use of "qualification standards . . . that screen out or tend to screen out or otherwise deny a job or benefit to an individual with a disability," so long as such standards are "job-related and consistent with

---

[13]Kirkingburg asserts that in showing that Albertson's initially allowed him to drive with a DOT certification, despite the fact that he did not meet the DOT's minimum visual acuity requirement, he produced evidence from which a reasonable juror could find that he satisfied the legitimate prerequisites of the job. See Brief for Respondent 36, 37; see also *id.,* at 6. But petitioner's argument is a legal, not a factual, one. In any event, the ample evidence in the record on petitioner's policy of requiring adherence to minimum DOT vision standards for its truck drivers, see, e.g., App. 53, 55–56, 333, would bar any inference that petitioner's failure to detect the discrepancy between the level of visual acuity Kirkingburg was determined to have had during his first two certifications and the DOT's minimum visual acuity requirement raised a genuine factual dispute on this issue.

business necessity, and . . . performance cannot be accomplished by reasonable accommodation. . . . " § 12113(a). See also § 12112(b)(6) (defining discrimination to include "using qualification standards . . . that screen out or tend to screen out an individual with a disability . . . unless the standard . . . is shown to be job-related for the position in question and is consistent with business necessity").[14] . . .

. . . When Congress enacted the ADA, it recognized that federal safety rules would limit application of the ADA as a matter of law. The Senate Labor and Human Resources Committee Report on the ADA stated that "a person with a disability applying for or currently holding a job subject to [DOT standards for drivers] must be able to satisfy these physical qualification standards in order to be considered a qualified individual with a disability under title I of this legislation." S. Rep. No. 101-116, pp. 27–28 (1990). The two primary House Committees shared this understanding, see H.R. Rep. No. 101-485, pt. 2, p. 57 (1990) (House Education and Labor Committee Report); id., pt. 3, at 34 (House Judiciary Committee Report). Accordingly, two of these Committees asked "the Secretary of Transportation [to] undertake a thorough review" of current knowledge about the capabilities of individuals with disabilities and available technological aids and devices, and make "any necessary changes" within two years of the enactment of the ADA. S. Rep. No. 101-116, at 27–28; see H. R. Rep. No. 101-485, pt. 2, at 57; see also id., pt. 3, at 34 (expressing the expectation that the Secretary of Transportation would "review these requirements to determine whether they are valid under this Act"). Finally, when the FHWA instituted the waiver program it addressed the statutory mandate by stating in its notice of final disposition that the scheme would be "consistent with the safe operation of commercial motor vehicles," just as 49 U.S.C.App. § 2505(f) (1988 ed.) required, 57 Fed.Reg. 31460 (1992). . . .

. . . Is it reasonable, that is, to read the ADA as requiring an employer like Albertson's to shoulder the general statutory burden to justify a job qualification that would tend to exclude the disabled, whenever the employer chooses to abide by the otherwise clearly applicable, unamended substantive regulatory standard despite the Government's willingness to waive it experimentally and without any finding of

its being inappropriate? If the answer were yes, an employer would in fact have an obligation of which we can think of no comparable example in our law. The employer would be required in effect to justify *de novo* an existing and otherwise applicable safety regulation issued by the Government itself. The employer would be required on a case-by-case basis to reinvent the Government's own wheel when the Government had merely begun an experiment to provide data to consider changing the underlying specifications. And what is even more, the employer would be required to do so when the Government had made an affirmative record indicating that contemporary empirical evidence was hard to come by. It is simply not credible that Congress enacted the ADA (before there was any waiver program) with the understanding that employers choosing to respect the Government's sole substantive visual acuity regulation in the face of an experimental waiver might be burdened with an obligation to defend the regulation's application according to its own terms.

The judgment of the Ninth Circuit is accordingly reversed.

Justice THOMAS, concurring.

As the Government reads the Americans with Disabilities Act of 1990 (ADA or Act) . . . it requires that petitioner justify the Department of Transportation's (DOT) visual acuity standards as job related, consistent with business necessity, and required to prevent employees from imposing a direct threat to the health and safety of others in the workplace. The Court assumes, for purposes of this case, that the Government's reading is, for the most part, correct. *Ante*, at 2170, and n.15. I agree with the Court's decision that, even when the case is analyzed through the Government's proposed lens, petitioner was entitled to summary judgment in this case. As the Court explains, *ante*, at 2174, it would be unprecedented and nonsensical to interpret Section 12113 to require petitioner to defend the application of the Government's regulation to respondent when petitioner has an unconditional obligation to enforce the federal law.

As the Court points out, though, *ante*, at 2169, DOT's visual acuity standards might also be relevant to the question whether respondent was a "qualified individual with a disability" under 42 U.S.C. § 12112(a). That section provides that no covered entity "shall discriminate against a qualified individual with a disability because of the disability of such individual." Presumably, then, a plaintiff claiming a cause of action under the ADA bears the burden of proving, *inter alia*,

[14]The EEOC's regulations implementing Title I define "[q]ualification standards" to mean "the personal and professional attributes including the skill, experience, education, physical, medical, safety and other requirements established by a covered entity as requirements which an individual must meet in order to be eligible for the position held or desired." 29 CFR § 1630.2(q) (1998).

that he is a qualified individual. The phrase "qualified individual with a disability" is defined to mean:

> an individual with a disability who, *with or without reasonable accommodation*, can perform the *essential functions* of the employment position that such individual holds or desires. For the purposes of this subchapter, consideration shall be given to the employer's judgment as to what functions of a job are essential, and if an employer has prepared a written description before advertising or interviewing applicants for the job, this description shall be considered evidence of the essential functions of the job. Section 12111(8) (emphasis added).

In this case, respondent sought a job driving trucks in interstate commerce. The quintessential function of that job, it seems to me, is to be able to drive a commercial truck in interstate commerce, and it was respondent's burden to prove that he could do so.

As the Court explains, *ante*, at 2171, DOT's Motor Carrier Safety Regulations have the force of law and bind petitioner—it may not, by law, "permit a person to drive a commercial motor vehicle unless that person is qualified to drive." 49 CFR § 391.11 (1999). But by the same token, DOT's regulations bind respondent, who "shall not drive a commercial motor vehicle unless he/she is qualified to drive a commercial motor vehicle." *Ibid.*; see also § 391.41 ("A person shall not drive a commercial motor vehicle unless he/she is physically qualified to do so"). Given that DOT's

regulation equally binds petitioner and respondent, and that it is conceded in this case that respondent could not meet the federal requirements, respondent surely was not "qualified" to perform the essential functions of petitioner's truck driver job without a reasonable accommodation. The waiver program might be thought of as a way to reasonably accommodate respondent, but for the fact, as the Court explains, *ante*, at 2171–2174, that the program did nothing to modify the regulation's unconditional requirements. For that reason, requiring petitioner to make such an accommodation most certainly would have been *unreasonable*.

The result of this case is the same under either view of the statute. If forced to choose between these alternatives, however, I would prefer to hold that respondent, as a matter of law, was not qualified to perform the job he sought within the meaning of the ADA. I nevertheless join the Court's opinion. . . . I join the Court's opinion, however, only on the understanding that it leaves open the argument that federal laws such as DOT's visual acuity standards might be critical in determining whether a plaintiff is a "qualified individual with a disability."

Question

1. In Problem 58, given the discussion by the Supreme Court in these cases, how might a court analyze the bank's "essential functions" argument? How might Leonard respond?

C. The Direct Threat Defense

Whether someone is a qualified individual with a disability may depend on whether that person poses a direct threat to herself or others. If so, the individual may be physically and mentally able to perform the essential functions of the job but cannot do so safely. As a practical matter, the direct threat argument is generally used as a defense. For example, if a school teacher had active tuberculosis, she might be able to teach her classes, but the contagiousness of the disease would be a defense that her employer could use to show she is not qualified. If the tuberculosis is in remission, however, the situation is different, as you will see in one of the cases below.

Section 12113(b) of the ADA states, "The term 'qualification standards' may include a requirement that an individual shall not pose a direct threat to the health or safety of other individuals in the workplace." This language raises several major questions, perhaps the most important of which is what constitutes a "direct threat." The definitions section of the Act, Section 12111(3), defines "direct threat" as follows: "The term 'direct threat' means a significant risk to the health or safety of others that cannot be eliminated by reasonable accommodation." The definition doesn't add much clarity does it? Fortunately, the EEOC regulations do add some clarity. Section 1630.2(r) of 29 C.F.R. defines the term Direct Threat as follows:

> Direct Threat means a significant risk of substantial harm to the health or safety of the individual or others that cannot be eliminated or reduced by reasonable accommodation. The determination that an individual poses a "direct threat" shall be based on an individualized assessment of the individual's present ability to safely perform the essential functions of the job. This assessment shall be based on a reasonable medical judgment that relies on the most current medical knowledge and/or on the best available objective evidence. In determining whether an individual would pose a direct threat, the factors to be considered include:
>
> 1. The duration of the risk;
> 2. The nature and severity of the potential harm;
> 3. The likelihood that the potential harm will occur; and
> 4. The imminence of the potential harm.

The EEOC definition closely tracks the Supreme Court's decision in a famous case that dealt with the direct threat issue under the Rehabilitation Act of 1973. That case follows. As you will see, the direct threat analysis is highly fact sensitive and highly dependent on medical judgments based on the state of current medical knowledge, which, of course, changes over time. Relying on medical judgment makes a great deal of sense in this context, because Congress and the Court have clearly stated that stereotypes and fear should not be a valid basis for decisions that exclude disabled individuals from programs, jobs, and the like.

Reliance on medical judgments can lead to a battle of the experts, where each side hires experts who they hope will support their side's contentions (and often their hopes are met). Of course, such use of experts is common in other areas of the law, and there must be some medical basis for an expert's opinion. For example, it is unlikely that an employer could find an expert who would testify that chronic asthma is contagious like the common cold, and even if an employer could, it would be easy to discredit an expert who espoused such a ridiculous opinion, given the current state of medical knowledge.

Moreover, the fact-sensitive nature of the direct threat analysis makes sense as well because one must determine what threat a disabled individual poses based on that individual's condition.

SCHOOL BOARD OF NASSAU COUNTY
v.
ARLINE
480 U.S. 273 (1987)

Justice BRENNAN delivered the opinion of the Court.

[The Employment Problem]

From 1966 until 1979, respondent Gene Arline taught elementary school in Nassau County, Florida. She was discharged in 1979 after suffering a third relapse of tuberculosis within two years. After she was denied relief in state administrative proceedings, she brought suit in federal court, alleging that the school board's decision to dismiss her because of her tuberculosis violated § 504 of the Act. . . .

A trial was held in the District Court. . . . According to the medical records. . . Arline was hospitalized for tuberculosis in 1957. . . . For the next 20 years, Arline's disease was in remission. . . . Then, in 1977, a culture revealed that tuberculosis was again active in her system; cultures taken in March 1978 and in November 1978 were also positive. . . .

The superintendent of schools for Nassau County . . . testified as to the school board's response to Arline's medical reports. After both her second relapse, in the spring of 1978, and her third relapse in November 1978, the school board suspended Arline with pay for the remainder of the school year. . . . At the end of the 1978–1979 school year, the school board held a hearing, after which it discharged Arline, "not because she had done anything wrong," but because of the "continued reoccurence [*sic*] of tuberculosis." . . .

[The Legal Issue]

Section 504 of the Rehabilitation Act of 1973 . . . prohibits a federally funded state program from discriminating against a handicapped individual solely by reason of his or her handicap. This case presents the questions whether a person afflicted with tuberculosis, a contagious disease, may be considered a "handicapped individual" within the meaning of § 504 of the Act, and, if so, whether such an individual is "otherwise qualified" to teach elementary school. . . .

[The Decision by the Trial Court and the U.S. Court of Appeals for the Eleventh Circuit]

The District Court held . . . that although there was "[n]o question that she suffers a handicap," Arline was nevertheless not "a handicapped person under the terms of that statute." . . . The court found it "difficult . . . to conceive that Congress intended contagious diseases to be included within the definition of a handicapped person." The court then went on to state that, "even assuming" that a person with a contagious disease could be deemed a handicapped person, Arline was not "qualified" to teach elementary school. . . . The Court of Appeals reversed, holding that "persons with contagious diseases are within the coverage of section 504," and that Arline's condition "falls . . . neatly within the statutory and regulatory framework" of the Act. . . . The court remanded the case "for further findings as to whether the risks of infection precluded Mrs. Arline from being 'otherwise qualified' for her job and, if so, whether it was possible to make some reasonable accommodation for her in that teaching position" or in some other position. . . .

[The Decision and Rationale of the U.S. Supreme Court]

We granted certiorari, and now affirm. . . .

. . . Section 504 of the Rehabilitation Act reads in pertinent part:

> No otherwise qualified handicapped individual in the United States, as defined in section 706(7) of this title, shall, solely by reason of his handicap, be excluded from participation in, be denied the benefits of, or be subjected to discrimination under any program or activity receiving Federal financial assistance. . . . 29 U.S.C. § 794.

In 1974, Congress expanded the definition of "handicapped individual" for use in § 504 to read as follows: . . .

> [A]ny person who (i) has a physical or mental impairment which substantially limits one or more of such person's major life activities, (ii) has a record of such an impairment, or (iii) is regarded as having such an impairment. 29 U.S.C. § 706(7)(B).

The amended definition reflected Congress' concern with protecting the handicapped against discrimination stemming not only from simple prejudice, but also from "archaic attitudes and laws" and from "the fact that the American people are simply unfamiliar with and insensitive to the difficulties confront[ing] individuals with handicaps. . . . "

Allowing discrimination based on the contagious effects of a physical impairment would be inconsistent with the basic purpose of § 504, which is to ensure that handicapped individuals are not denied jobs or other benefits because of the prejudiced attitudes or the ignorance of others. By amending the definition of "handicapped individual" to include not only those who are actually physically impaired, but also those who are regarded as impaired and who, as a result, are substantially limited in a major life activity, Congress acknowledged that society's accumulated myths and fears about disability and disease are as handicapping as are the physical limitations that flow from actual impairment. . . . Few aspects of a handicap give rise to the same level of public fear and misapprehension as contagiousness. . . . Even those who suffer or have recovered from such noninfectious diseases as epilepsy or cancer have faced discrimination

based on the irrational fear that they might be contagious. . . . The Act is carefully structured to replace
such reflexive reactions to actual or perceived handicaps with actions based on reasoned and medically
sound judgments: the definition of "handicapped individual" is broad, but only those individuals who are
both handicapped *and* otherwise qualified are eligible
for relief. The fact that *some* persons who have contagious diseases may pose a serious health threat to others under certain circumstances does not justify
excluding from the coverage of the Act *all* persons with
actual or perceived contagious diseases. Such exclusion would mean that those accused of being contagious would never have the opportunity to have their
condition evaluated in light of medical evidence and a
determination made as to whether they were "otherwise qualified." Rather, they would be vulnerable to
discrimination on the basis of mythology—precisely
the type of injury Congress sought to prevent. . . . We
conclude that the fact that a person with a record of a
physical impairment is also contagious does not suffice
to remove that person from coverage under § 504. . . .

The remaining question is whether Arline is otherwise qualified for the job of elementary school-
teacher. To answer this question in most cases, the
district court will need to conduct an individualized
inquiry and make appropriate findings of fact. Such
an inquiry is essential if § 504 is to achieve its goal of
protecting handicapped individuals from deprivations based on prejudice, stereotypes, or unfounded
fear, while giving appropriate weight to such legitimate concerns of grantees as avoiding exposing others to significant health and safety risks.[16] The basic
factors to be considered in conducting this inquiry are
well established.[17] In the context of the employment

of a person handicapped with a contagious disease,
we agree with *amicus* American Medical Association
that this inquiry should include:

> [findings of] facts, based on reasonable medical
> judgments given the state of medical knowledge,
> about (a) the nature of the risk (how the disease is
> transmitted), (b) the duration of the risk (how long
> is the carrier infectious), (c) the severity of the risk
> (what is the potential harm to third parties) and
> (d) the probabilities the disease will be transmitted
> and will cause varying degrees of harm. Brief for
> American Medical Association as *Amicus Curiae* 19.

In making these findings, courts normally should
defer to the reasonable medical judgments of public
health officials. . . . The next step in the "otherwise-
qualified" inquiry is for the court to evaluate, in light
of these medical findings, whether the employer
could reasonably accommodate the employee under
the established standards for that inquiry. . . .

Because of the paucity of factual findings by the
District Court, we, like the Court of Appeals, are unable at this stage of the proceedings to resolve whether
Arline is "otherwise qualified" for her job. The District
Court made no findings as to the duration and severity of Arline's condition, nor as to the probability that
she would transmit the disease. Nor did the court determine whether Arline was contagious at the time she
was discharged, or whether the School Board could
have reasonably accommodated her. . . . Accordingly,
the resolution of whether Arline was otherwise qualified requires further findings of fact. . . .

We hold that a person suffering from the contagious disease of tuberculosis can be a handicapped
person within the meaning of § 504 of the Rehabilitation Act of 1973, and that respondent Arline is such a
person. We remand the case to the District Court to
determine whether Arline is otherwise qualified for
her position. The judgment of the Court of Appeals is
Affirmed.

Chief Justice REHNQUIST, with whom Justice SCALIA joins, dissenting.

In *Pennhurst State School and Hospital v. Halderman*, 451
U.S. 1 (1981), this Court made clear that, where Congress intends to impose a condition on the grant of
federal funds, "it must do so unambiguously." . . .
This principle applies with full force to § 504 of the Rehabilitation Act, which Congress limited in scope to
"those who actually 'receive' federal financial assistance." . . . Yet, the Court today ignores this principle,

[16]A person who poses a significant risk of communicating an in-
fectious disease to others in the workplace will not be otherwise
qualified for his or her job if reasonable accommodation will not
eliminate that risk. The Act would not require a school board to
place a teacher with active, contagious tuberculosis in a classroom
with elementary school children. Respondent conceded as much
at oral argument. . . .

[17]"An otherwise qualified person is one who is able to meet all of
a program's requirements in spite of his handicap." *Southeastern
Community College v. Davis*, 442 U.S. 397, 406 (1979). In the employment context, an otherwise qualified person is one who can
perform "the essential functions" of the job in question. 45 CFR
§ 84.3(k) (1985). When a handicapped person is not able to perform the essential functions of the job, the court must also consider whether any "reasonable accommodation" by the employer
would enable the handicapped person to perform these functions.
Ibid. Accommodation is not reasonable if it either imposes "undue
financial and administrative burdens" on a grantee . . . or requires
"a fundamental alteration in the nature of [the] program," . . . .

resting its holding on its own sense of fairness and implied support from the Act. . . . Such an approach, I believe, is foreclosed not only by *Pennhurst*, but also by our prior decisions interpreting the Rehabilitation Act.

Our decision in *Pennhurst* was premised on the view that federal legislation imposing obligations only on recipients of federal funds is "much in the nature of a contract." . . . As we have stated in the context of the Rehabilitation Act, " 'Congress apparently determined it would require . . . grantees to bear the costs of providing employment for the handicapped as a *quid pro quo* for the receipt of federal funds.' . . . The legitimacy of this *quid pro quo* rests on whether recipients of federal funds voluntarily and knowingly accept the terms of the exchange. . . . There can be no knowing acceptance unless Congress speaks "with a clear voice" in identifying the conditions attached to the receipt of funds. . . .

The requirement that Congress unambiguously express conditions imposed on federal monies is particularly compelling in cases such as this where there exists longstanding state and federal regulation of the subject matter. From as early as 1796, Congress has legislated directly in the area of contagious diseases. . . . Congress has also, however, left significant leeway to the States, which have enacted a myriad of public health statutes designed to protect against the introduction and spread of contagious diseases. . . . When faced with such extensive regulation, this Court has declined to read the Rehabilitation Act expansively. . . .

Applying these principles, I conclude that the Rehabilitation Act cannot be read to support the result reached by the Court. The record in this case leaves no doubt that Arline was discharged because of the contagious nature of tuberculosis, and not because of any diminished physical or mental capabilities resulting from her condition. . . . Thus, in the language of § 504, the central question here is whether discrimination on the basis of contagiousness constitutes discrimination "by reason of . . . handicap." Because the language of the Act, regulations, and legislative history are silent on this issue, . . . the principles outlined above compel the conclusion that contagiousness is not a handicap within the meaning of § 504. It is therefore clear that the protections of the Act do not extend to individuals such as Arline.

In reaching a contrary conclusion, the Court never questions that Arline was discharged because of the threat her condition posed to others. Instead, it posits that the contagious effects of a disease cannot be "meaningfully" distinguished from the disease's effect on a claimant under the Act. . . . To support this position, the Court observes that Congress intended to extend the Act's protections to individuals who have a condition that does not impair their mental and physical capabilities, but limits their major life activities because of the adverse reactions of others. This congressional recognition of a handicap resulting from the reactions of others, we are told, reveals that Congress intended the Rehabilitation Act to regulate discrimination on the basis of contagiousness. . . .

This analysis misses the mark in several respects. To begin with, Congress' recognition that an individual may be handicapped under the Act solely by reason of the reactions of others in no way demonstrates that, for the purposes of interpreting the Act, the reactions of others to the condition cannot be considered separately from the effect of the condition on the claimant. In addition, the Court provides no basis for extending the Act's generalized coverage of individuals suffering discrimination as a result of the reactions of others to coverage of individuals with contagious diseases. Although citing examples of handicapped individuals described in the regulations and legislative history, the Court points to nothing in these materials suggesting that Congress contemplated that a person with a condition posing a threat to the health of others may be considered handicapped under the Act. . . . Even in an ordinary case of statutory construction, such meager proof of congressional intent would not be determinative. The Court's evidence, therefore, could not possibly provide the basis for "knowing acceptance" by such entities as the Nassau County School Board that their receipt of federal funds is conditioned on Rehabilitation Act regulation of public health issues. . . .

In *Alexander v. Choate, supra*, 469 U.S., at 299, this Court stated that "[a]ny interpretation of § 504 must . . . be responsive to two powerful but countervailing considerations—the need to give effect to the statutory objectives and the desire to keep § 504 within manageable bounds." The Court has wholly disregarded this admonition here.

The *Arline* case addresses the threat posed by an employee to others in the workplace. What if the employee is primarily a threat only to himself? The language of the Act would seem to suggest that under such circumstances the direct threat "defense" is unavailable, but the EEOC has issued regulations that recognize direct threat to the health and safety of the employee himself as adequate to support a direct threat argument by the employer. The Supreme Court addressed this issue in the following case.

CHEVRON U.S.A. INC.
v.
ECHAZABAL
536 U.S. 73 (2002)

Justice SOUTER delivered the opinion of the Court.

[The Employment Problem]

Beginning in 1972, respondent Mario Echazabal worked for independent contractors at an oil refinery owned by petitioner Chevron U.S.A. Inc. Twice he applied for a job directly with Chevron, which offered to hire him if he could pass the company's physical examination. . . . Each time, the exam showed liver abnormality or damage, the cause eventually being identified as Hepatitis C, which Chevron's doctors said would be aggravated by continued exposure to toxins at Chevron's refinery. In each instance, the company withdrew the offer, and the second time it asked the contractor employing Echazabal either to reassign him to a job without exposure to harmful chemicals or to remove him from the refinery altogether. The contractor laid him off in early 1996.

[The Legal Issue]

A regulation of the Equal Employment Opportunity Commission authorizes refusal to hire an individual because his performance on the job would endanger his own health, owing to a disability. The question in this case is whether the Americans with Disabilities Act of 1990 . . . permits the regulation. . . . We hold that it does.

[The Decision of the Trial Court and the U.S. Court of Appeals for the Ninth Circuit]

Echazabal filed suit, ultimately removed to federal court, claiming, among other things, that Chevron violated the Americans with Disabilities Act (ADA or Act) in refusing to hire him, or even to let him continue working in the plant, because of a disability, his liver condition. . . . Chevron defended under a regulation of the Equal Employment Opportunity Commission . . . permitting the defense that a worker's disability on the job would pose a "direct threat" to his health. . . . Although two medical witnesses disputed Chevron's judgment that Echazabal's liver function was impaired and subject to further damage under the job conditions in the refinery, the District Court granted summary judgment for Chevron. It held that Echazabal raised no genuine issue of material fact as to whether the company acted reasonably in relying on its own doctors' medical advice, regardless of its accuracy.

On appeal, the Ninth Circuit asked for briefs on a threshold question not raised before, whether the EEOC's regulation recognizing a threat-to-self defense, *ibid.*, exceeded the scope of permissible rulemaking under the ADA. . . . The Circuit held that it did and reversed the summary judgment. [The Supreme Court reversed on this issue. The rationale of the Court on this issue is omitted here.] . . . The court went on to reject Chevron's further argument that Echazabal was not "'otherwise qualified'" to perform the job, holding that the ability to perform a job without risk to one's health or safety is not an "'essential function'" of the job. . . .

[The Decision and Rationale of the U.S. Supreme Court]

The decision conflicted with one from the Eleventh Circuit . . . and raised tension with the Seventh Circuit case of *Koshinski v. Decatur Foundry, Inc.*, 177 F.3d 599, 603 (1999). We granted certiorari . . . and now reverse. . . .

Section 102 of the ADA prohibits "discriminat[ion] against a qualified individual with a disability because of the disability . . . in regard to" a number of actions by an employer, including "hiring." . . . The statutory definition of "discriminat[ion]" covers a number of things an employer might do to block a disabled person from advancing in the workplace, such as "using qualification standards . . . that screen out or tend to screen out an individual with a disability. " § 12112(b)(6). By that same definition, *ibid.*, as well as by separate provision,

§ 12113(a), the Act creates an affirmative defense for action under a qualification standard "shown to be job-related for the position in question and . . . consistent with business necessity." Such a standard may include "a requirement that an individual shall not pose a direct threat to the health or safety of other individuals in the workplace," § 12113(b), if the individual cannot perform the job safely with reasonable accommodation, § 12113(a). By regulation, the EEOC carries the defense one step further, in allowing an employer to screen out a potential worker with a disability not only for risks that he would pose to others in the workplace but for risks on the job to his own health or safety as well: "The term 'qualification standard' may include a requirement that an individual shall not pose a direct threat to the health or safety of the individual or others in the workplace." 29 CFR § 1630.15(b)(2) (2001).

Chevron relies on the regulation here, since it says a job in the refinery would pose a "direct threat" to Echazabal's health. In seeking deference to the agency, it argues that nothing in the statute unambiguously precludes such a defense, while the regulation was adopted under authority explicitly delegated by Congress, 42 U.S.C. § 12116, and after notice-and-comment rulemaking. . . . Echazabal, on the contrary, argues that as a matter of law the statute precludes the regulation, which he claims would be an unreasonable interpretation even if the agency had leeway to go beyond the literal text. . . .

Since Congress has not spoken exhaustively on threats to a worker's own health, the agency regulation can claim adherence under the rule in *Chevron*, 467 U.S., at 843, so long as it makes sense of the statutory defense for qualification standards that are "job-related and consistent with business necessity." 42 U.S.C. § 12113(a). Chevron's reasons for calling the regulation reasonable are unsurprising: moral concerns aside, it wishes to avoid time lost to sickness, excessive turnover from medical retirement or death, litigation under state tort law, and the risk of violating the national Occupational Safety and Health Act of 1970. . . .

Nor can the EEOC's resolution be fairly called unreasonable as allowing the kind of workplace paternalism the ADA was meant to outlaw. It is true that Congress had paternalism in its sights when it passed the ADA, see § 12101(a)(5) (recognizing "overprotective rules and policies" as a form of discrimination). But the EEOC has taken this to mean that Congress was not aiming at an employer's refusal to place disabled workers at a specifically demonstrated risk, but was trying to get at refusals to give an even break to classes of disabled people, while claiming to act for their own good in reliance on untested and pretextual stereotypes. . . . Its regulation disallows just this sort of sham protection, through demands for a particularized enquiry into the harms the employee would probably face. The direct threat defense must be "based on a reasonable medical judgment that relies on the most current medical knowledge and/or the best available objective evidence," and upon an expressly "individualized assessment of the individual's present ability to safely perform the essential functions of the job," reached after considering, among other things, the imminence of the risk and the severity of the harm portended. 29 CFR § 1630.2(r) (2001). The EEOC was certainly acting within the reasonable zone when it saw a difference between rejecting workplace paternalism and ignoring specific and documented risks to the employee himself, even if the employee would take his chances for the sake of getting a job. . . .

Finally, our conclusions that some regulation is permissible and this one is reasonable are not open to Echazabal's objection that they reduce the direct threat provision to "surplusage," see *Babbitt v. Sweet Home Chapter, Communites for Great Ore.*, 515 U.S 687, 698 (1995). The mere fact that a threat-to-self defense reasonably falls within the general "job related" and "business necessity" standard does not mean that Congress accomplished nothing with its explicit provision for a defense based on threats to others. The provision made a conclusion clear that might otherwise have been fought over in litigation or administrative rulemaking. . . .

Accordingly, we reverse the judgment of the Court of Appeals and remand the case for proceedings consistent with this opinion.

Questions

1. You are a lawyer representing the school board in Arline's district, but unlike in the case above, Arline's TB is currently contagious. What may your client do legally, and how would you argue your case under the direct threat defense? Now change the facts a bit. You are in the same role, but rather than TB, the teacher has a relatively new respiratory disease about which little is known. Most scientists think the disease can be transmitted only by direct contaminant contact, as when an infected person sneezes on another person or shares a cup with another person, but some scientists argue that it is an airborne disease and can be easily transmitted. There is no clear proof either way. How would you advise your client if your client wants to place the teacher on leave?

2. You are the manager of a new restaurant in town. You recently hired an excellent chef with top credentials. Several days after hiring him you learn that he has HIV. You are concerned about customer reaction and decide you want to fire him. Your lawyer advises you that you have no basis for doing so unless his condition combined with his duties as a chef poses a direct threat. The current state of scientific evidence suggests that even if he bleeds into the food, he is not likely to infect anyone, and you know as a restaurant manager that the chances of him actually bleeding into the food are slim. Can you terminate him because of his condition without being potentially liable under the ADA? How would a court be likely to address your direct threat defense? What if the facts are the same, but rather than happening now, the situation occurred in 1985, when medical experts knew much less about the transmission of HIV?

D. With or Without Reasonable Accommodation

Laura L. Rovner, *Disability, Equality and Identity*; Symposium: Disability Law, Equality, and Difference: American Disability Law and the Civil Rights Model, 55 Ala. L. Rev. 1043 (2004)

(This is an edited version of the article and footnotes are deleted.)

. . . For over forty years . . . the disability rights movement has sought to reframe the way people with disabilities are understood by American law, social policy, and society. One of the central tenets of modern disability theory is a shift away from the "medical" model of disability, which "characterizes people with disabilities as having pathological individual attributes, typically linked to incapacity and dependence, which in turn may lead to social and economic isolation," . . . and toward the view of disability as a socially constructed condition, through which the 'problem' is defined as "a dominating attitude by professionals and others, inadequate support services when compared with society generally, as well as attitudinal, architectural, sensory, cognitive and economic barriers." . . .

The enactment of the Americans with Disabilities Act . . . (ADA), was viewed as a watershed in the disability community, not only because of the substantive rights it guaranteed to disabled people, but also because it reflected a departure from the medical model and an adoption of the movement's socio-political model of disability. This is particularly true of what has been referred to as the statute's "reasonable accommodation" mandate, which requires both public and private entities to make those modifications to physical structures as well as rules, policies, and practices that are necessary to ensure that people with disabilities have the opportunity to participate in or benefit from society's employment opportunities . . . public entities . . . and places of public accommodation. . . . As such, the reasonable accommodation mandate is grounded in two assumptions: first, that many of the structures and institutions of society—the "built environment" . . . —

were (and are) not constructed with disabled people in mind; and second, that in many situations, accommodations to that environment are necessary to ensure that disabled people have meaningful access to society. By including the reasonable accommodation mandate in the ADA, Congress did more than seek "to address the major areas of discrimination faced day-to-day by people with disabilities." . . . It also embraced and endorsed the socio-political model of disability.

Over the past decade, however, the success of the disability community in infusing the socio-political model of disability into federal law has begun to be eroded by judicial decisions interpreting the ADA that appear to be grounded in—and espousing—the medical model of disability. . . . While such challenges are fundamentally jurisdictional questions . . . the analytical framework by which these questions are decided requires courts to make determinations about . . . what equality means for people with disabilities. In the process of answering those questions, some courts also have made implicit judgments about people with disabilities—and disability itself—that appear to signify a retrenchment to the medical model of disability that is profoundly at odds with the movement's vision of disability as a societally-constructed condition. . . .

According to the medical model, the disabled individual is the unfortunate victim of some twist of fate, and that misfortune is seen as essentially a personal or family matter—not a misfortune that society is obligated to remedy. For if disability is essentially biological, then the social disadvantages and exclusion that accompany the disability can be explained as natural and not ascribable to any social cause. Because disability is not socially caused, the disabled individual has no claim of right to social remediation, and any benefits or assistance that society chooses to bestow on persons with disabilities can be viewed as a charitable response of 'doing special things.' . . .

. . . The move away from viewing disability purely as the 'problem' of the 'unfortunate victim,' toward an approach that views disability as a societally constructed condition made its first significant headway in the late 1960s and early 1970s with the enactment of the Architectural Barriers Act[39] and section 504 of the Rehabilitation Act of 1973. . . . People with disabilities, however, particularly those at the forefront of the independent living movement,[47] quickly realized the importance of section 504, and the fight to get implementing regulations promulgated under the statute was the first significant social protest of the modern disability rights movement. . . . A central feature of this movement was the reframing of disability from a medical defect residing in the individual, to a recognition that the major problems associated with disability could be attributed to the external environment. . . .

In addition to viewing disability as primarily caused by the built environment, the socio-political model of disability also emphasizes the idea that disability is culturally constructed. . . . The lack of realistic cultural representations of the lives of disabled people in the media and films contributes to nondisabled society's sense that disabled people are "other," which further contributes to their exclusion. . . . While a handful of films, television programs, and news stories portray people with disabilities as part of the mainstream,[59] the majority of media and artistic portrayals continue to feature disabled people as either helpless cripples . . . or courageous overcomers . . . (sometimes referred to by the disability community as "supercrips").[62] These media and artistic messages frequently operate on a subtextual level for many viewers, and therefore remain an unexamined and powerful shaper of cultural attitudes toward disabled people. . . .

A large part of the justification for the civil rights model derives from the idea that people with disabilities "collectively occupy a stigmatized social position . . . a social status analogous to that of racial and ethnic minorities." . . . Particularly damaging to people with disabilities are the stereotypes of "dependence on others and a general incapacity to perform social and economic activities," because these assumptions "can result in exclusion and social isolation, including lack of access to employment, public facilities, voting, and other forms of civic involvement." . . . The opportunity to participate in these types of institutions and activities has, in our society, traditionally been defined as a civil right, and the exclusion from them as discrimination.

Yet in other ways, the nature of discrimination against people with disabilities is not identical to that based on race or sex, and consequently, the American civil rights construct, at least as it has been historically developed and understood (which has been primarily in the context of race), is not a perfect fit for either describing the nature of the discrimination encountered by disabled people, or for crafting the remedial measures necessary to address it. . . .

A logical outgrowth of the socio-political and civil rights models of disability is the idea that since disability is understood as an interaction between the individual and an inhospitable environment, what is therefore necessary to enable disabled people to participate equally is

[39]42 U.S.C. §4151-57 (2003). The Architectural Barriers Act of 1968 provides for the removal of architectural barriers from new federally-funded buildings. *Id.* An interagency Architectural and Transportation Barriers Compliance Board was created in 1973 to ensure compliance with the Act. 29 U.S.C. § 792 (2000).

[47]The independent living movement is built on the philosophy that people with disabilities should have the same civil rights, options, and control over choices in their own lives as do people without disabilities. Shapiro, supra note 23, at 53–54. The movement arose in the early 1970s, largely as a result of the advocacy of Ed Roberts (who is widely regarded as the father of the movement) and other disability activists in Berkeley. *Id.* These activists at the University of California-Berkeley established the nation's first Center for Independent Living (CIL) in 1972 following their successful development of the Physically Disabled Students Program at Berkeley. *Id.* The core philosophical principles of the CIL were: (1) that it was run by people with disabilities; (2) it viewed disability as socially caused; (3) was open to people with a wide range of disabilities; and (4) had community integration as one of its central goals. *Id.* at 54. For a fascinating account of the rise of the independent living movement, see Shapiro, supra note 23, at 41–58; see also Doris Zames Fleischer & Frieda Zames, The Disability Rights Movement: From Charity to Confrontation 37–48 (2001).

[59]Artistic and media portrayals of people with disabilities that some in the disability community believe to present realistic portrayals of disabled people include films such as Waterdance (Samuel Goldwyn Company 1992), Notting Hill (PolyGram Filmed Entertainment 1999), The Replacements (Warner Brothers 2000) and Twin Falls Idaho (Sony Pictures Classics 1999); and television programs such as E.R. (NBC), The West Wing (NBC), and the children's program Pelswick (Nickelodeon).

[62]. . . Author Jack Nelson has identified a total of six ways in which people with disabilities are negatively portrayed in the media in the book, Images that Injure: Pictorial Stereotypes in the Media, which are (1) The Victim; (2) The Hero/Supercrip; (3) The Threat—Evil and Warped; (4) Unable to Adjust—"Just buck up!", (5) To Be Cared For—The Burden; and (6) One Who Shouldn't Have Survived. Jack A. Nelson, The Invisible Cultural Group: Images of Disability, in Images that Injure: Pictorial Stereotypes in the Media 119 (Paul Martin Lester ed., 1996).

not simply a mandate to treat them the same as anyone else, but a recognition and a requirement that in many situations, people with disabilities must be provided with something different to allow them the equal opportunity to participate. As many disability rights lawyers, scholars, and policy analysts have noted . . . the problem with applying the traditional civil rights approach (i.e., a formal equality construct) in situations involving discrimination on the basis of disability is that in most cases, treating people with disabilities in the same way as nondisabled people will result in their exclusion from societal institutions and structures, rather than inclusion. . . .

. . . While the statutory language of the ADA demonstrated a legislative understanding and acceptance of the socio-political model of disability . . . that same understanding and acceptance had not permeated much of American society at the time the statute was enacted into law. . . .

What remains largely unknown to the general public is that the ADA is a self-described antidiscrimination statute that implicitly and explicitly frames the claims of disabled people "as congruent with traditional and broadly accepted values such as equality, fair play and meritocracy." . . . Of particular significance to the characterization of the ADA as a civil rights statute is the way the statute describes people with disabilities and the systemic barriers to participation they have encountered in American society. The "Findings and Purposes" section of the statute identifies people with disabilities as a discrete and insular minority who have been faced with restrictions and limitations, subjected to a history of purposeful unequal treatment, and relegated to a position of political powerlessness in our society, based on characteristics that are beyond the control of such individuals and resulting from stereotypic assumptions not truly indicative of the individual ability of such individuals to participate in, and contribute to, society. . . . [T]he ADA did more than simply reflect/embody traditional civil rights principles—it expanded on those principles to create a broader version of equality. . . .

. . . [T]o address these types of exclusions, disability advocates recognized that "framing their political demands as purely a claim to equal treatment on a level playing field" would not achieve equality . . . because in most cases, treating people with disabilities in the same manner as people without disabilities serves to exclude people with disabilities from mainstream society, rather than include them. . . . Standing at the top of the courthouse steps and telling a litigant who uses a wheelchair, "You may come in," is a disingenuous statement of equal opportunity. . . . Explaining to deaf person that his right to participate in a trial has been met by virtue of his physical presence in the courtroom when the proceedings have been conducted in spoken English and without a sign language interpreter does

not constitute meaningful access to a fundamental right. . . . Consequently, a different paradigm for equality needed to be used in the ADA—one that would give recognition to the incontrovertible fact that "to provide individuals with disabilities with equal opportunities(,) the civil rights model must be amended or expanded to incorporate the concept of accommodations." . . .

For this reason, Robert Burgdorf, the principal drafter of the original version of the statute, calls the ADA "a second-generation civil rights statute that goes beyond the 'naked framework' of earlier statutes and adds much flesh and refinement to traditional nondiscrimination law."[110] Arguably, the most significant aspect of this 'flesh' and 'refinement' is the reasonable accommodation mandate, which appears in varying forms in Titles I . . . II . . . and III . . . of the ADA, but which may be generally understood as requiring both public and private entities to make those changes to the "built environment" that are necessary to ensure that people with disabilities are able to participate in society's institutions (so long, of course, as those changes are not too expensive or burdensome to make). . . . The reasonable accommodation mandate has two premises embedded in it, both of which are rooted in the socio-political model of disability. First, that the 'problem' of disability is not solely located in the person who, for example, uses a wheelchair for mobility, but rather that the problem resides in many of our societal structures and institutions that have been constructed without a range of needs and abilities in mind, such as streets without curb cuts, narrow doorways and entrances without ramps. . . . The second premise is that given these hard-wired, systematic social exclusions, society therefore has an obligation to make reasonable modifications to those structures and institutions as part of any meaningful commitment to equality for people with disabilities. . . .

The reasonable accommodation mandate has been called a "transformative" aspect of the law because it "challenge(s) preexisting consensus definitions of particular categories or concepts, and . . . attempt(s) to redefine, or 'reinstitutionalize' them with a different set of constituent social meanings, values, and normative principles." . . . Indeed, by acknowledging that there must be modifications made to the built environment in order to allow for participation by disabled people, the reasonable accommodation mandate necessarily embraces the socio-political approach to disability. . . . With this transformation comes a different understanding not only of disability, which is no longer "a container holding tragedy, or occasion for pity, charity, or exemption

---

[110]Robert L. Burgdorf, The Americans with Disabilities Act: Analysis and Implications of a Second-Generation Civil Rights Statute, 26 Harv. C.R.-C.L.L.Rev 413, 415 (1991) at 415.

from the ordinary obligations attending membership in society," but now "also, or to a certain extent instead, contains rights to and societal responsibility for making enabling environmental adaptations." . . .

Many scholars and theorists have written about the reasonable accommodation mandate and how to con-

strue it. . . . Some consider the failure to provide such accommodations as disparate treatment discrimination . . . while others view such refusals as disparate impact discrimination. . . . Still others . . . consider the reasonable accommodation mandate to constitute a "mild regime of affirmative action." . . .

Problem 59

Edger works on an assembly line for a major automobile manufacturer. His job is to inspect the sides and bottoms of cars as they pass by him on the line. Edger does one side of the car, and a colleague on the other side of the assembly line inspects the other side. Edger has suffered for years from scoliosis, a disease that effects the vertebrae. He has always been able to do his job, but doing so has caused him chronic and serious back pain. His doctor finally advises him that he needs a spinal fusion, a procedure that fuses rods to the spine in order to provide more support and correct the alignment of the vertebrae. Edger's doctor hopes that after Edger recovers, he will have significantly less back pain and more mobility, but he warns Edger that he will need to minimize bending. As part of Edger's job, he bends over to look underneath the cars as they pass by. The bottom of the cars pass at about four feet from the ground to enable the inspectors to view both the side and bottom of the vehicles. Edger has requested accommodation from his employer. The employer and Edger have discussed the situation, and Edger has proposed the following accommodations: (1) transferring Edger to another job on the line that does not require bending as much, (2) providing Edger with a chair that he could raise and lower with a switch (the chair would cost $1,300), (3) allowing Edger to inspect only the sides of the cars but not the bottoms, or (4) raising the cars by a foot and a half as they pass Edger and his colleague (this is feasible with the current equipment but might limit what Edger and his colleague could spot on the upper sides of the cars). Which, if any, of these proposed accommodations are reasonable and why? Would it make a difference if the employees at Edger's plant are unionized and there is a collective bargaining agreement that specifically requires that transfers be based on seniority and that employees transfer only to vacant positions?

Problem 60

Tammy works as an insurance agent at a branch office of a major national insurance company. The branch is owned by the national company but generates enough revenue to both cover its operating costs and make a profit and thus is self-sufficient in this regard. Tammy's job entails sales and service of insurance policies. She networks to develop business and also takes "through the door business," which refers to clients who contact the agency in person, via telephone, or over the Internet. All agents in the branch are trained to service any existing account, so Tammy shares this duty with the other agents whenever she is in the office.

The branch has been quite successful at recruiting clients, and as a result, the company recently began requiring agents to be on site (at the office) at least 35 hours per week during business hours to service clients and work with the increasing number of "through the door" clients who are referred by existing clients. Most agents spend at least 10 hours a week out of the office meeting with clients or developing new business.

Tammy has a serious disorder for which she takes medication. The medication does not mitigate the effects of the disorder, but none of those effects prevent her from doing her job. The medication, however, has a side effect. It makes her extremely drowsy in the morning (she must take it before she goes to bed, or she would be drowsy all day). This has never been a problem because Tammy has generally been able to begin work at 1:00 P.M. and stay at the office until 5:00 P.M. (when the office closes). After that, she generally goes out to develop new business, usually until at least 9:00 P.M. She usually works six days a week for a total of about 48 hours. She is unable to work 35 hours per week in the office due to her extreme drowsiness in the morning, but she asks for an accommodation.

Her boss acknowledges that she is an excellent employee and that she is wonderful at developing new business, but he says she needs to be there for the 35 hours because it is essential that the office be able to service its now large client base. Tammy offers to work in the office past closing to service clients, but her boss explains that one person cannot run the office (especially if word gets out the office is open), and thus she would need the receptionist and another agent to be there. She then asks for an exception to the 35-hour rule, but her boss says that other agents would have to pick up the time she is not at the office because the branch is having problems servicing clients even with the 35-hour rule. Her boss offers to let her work part-time and hire another part-time agent, but he says that he cannot afford to hire another full-time agent, which would cost at least $70,000. Can Tammy be reasonably accommodated? Do the proposed accommodations constitute an undue hardship on her employer?

Whether or not someone is a qualified individual is determined based on whether that person can "perform the essential functions of the job with or without reasonable accommodation." The concept of "reasonable accommodation" is thus relevant to the qualification question. For that reason alone, it is important to better understand the concept. Significantly, the failure to provide a reasonable accommodation when such an accommodation is available and does not pose an undue hardship can itself be the basis for a claim under the ADA. Thus, the term is also relevant because it can be the center of an important class of claims brought under the ADA.

The meaning of the term "reasonable accommodation" is quite different under the ADA than it is in the religious discrimination context under Title VII, *see* Chapter 11. To better understand the concept, we must answer three questions: (1) What is an accommodation? (2) When is an accommodation "reasonable" for ADA purposes? (3) When does an accommodation pose an undue hardship on an employer? The language of the ADA and the EEOC regulations help to answer these questions, but the "reasonable accommodation" inquiry is fact sensitive, and thus whether an accommodation is required under the ADA must be determined on a case-by-case basis.

The ADA defines reasonable accommodation and undue hardship at 42 U.S.C. § 12111 as follows:

(9)   Reasonable accommodation

The term "reasonable accommodation" may include—

(A) making existing facilities used by employees readily accessible to and usable by individuals with disabilities; and

(B) job restructuring, part-time or modified work schedules, reassignment to a vacant position, acquisition or modification of equipment or devices, appropriate adjustment or modifications of examinations, training materials or policies, the provision of qualified readers or interpreters, and other similar accommodations for individuals with disabilities.

(10) Undue hardship

(A) In general

The term "undue hardship" means an action requiring significant difficulty or expense, when considered in light of the factors set forth in subparagraph (B).

(B)   Factors to be considered

In determining whether an accommodation would impose an undue hardship on a covered entity, factors to be considered include—

(i)   the nature and cost of the accommodation needed under this chapter;

(ii)   the overall financial resources of the facility or facilities involved in the provision of the reasonable accommodation; the number of persons employed at such facility; the effect on expenses and resources, or the impact otherwise of such accommodation upon the operation of the facility;

(iii) the overall financial resources of the covered entity; the overall size of the business of a covered entity with respect to the number of its employees; the number, type, and location of its facilities; and

(iv) the type of operation or operations of the covered entity, including the composition, structure, and functions of the workforce of such entity; the geographic separateness, administrative, or fiscal relationship of the facility or facilities in question to the covered entity.

Most accommodations are relatively inexpensive and pose little or no hardship to employers. Yet some accommodations can be quite expensive or disruptive to an employer's operations. Examples of the former include allowing employees to take a five-minute break to take medication, using light bulbs that don't have a high flicker rate to keep someone who is epileptic from having seizures, and providing a chair with a straighter back. An example of the latter is provided by the case below, where the question presented is whether an accommodation under the ADA trumps an employer's usual seniority system. Another example is the provision of expensive equipment to enable an employee to use a computer. This may have little impact on a large employer but could have a big impact on a smaller employer. Thus, the ADA focus on the size of the employer as an aspect of the undue hardship analysis. It is important to remember that the accommodation inquiry is fact specific and can be further affected by the variety of ways a given employee may be accommodated. If the individual does not get his or her ideal accommodation because it poses an undue hardship, an employer may still have a duty to provide a different accommodation.

In addition to the definitions of reasonable accommodation and undue hardship and the provision mentioning reasonable accommodation in the qualification context, the ADA has a provision, 42 U.S.C. § 12112(b), that directly makes the failure to accommodate actionable:

> As used in subsection (a) of this section, the term "discriminate" includes—. . .
>
> (5)(A) not making reasonable accommodations to the known physical or mental limitations of an otherwise qualified individual with a disability who is an applicant or employee, unless such covered entity can demonstrate that the accommodation would impose an undue hardship on the operation of the business of such covered entity; or
>
> (B) denying employment opportunities to a job applicant or employee who is an otherwise qualified individual with a disability, if such denial is based on the need of such covered entity to make reasonable accommodation to the physical or mental impairments of the employee or applicant. . . .

The U.S. Supreme Court has recently addressed the definition of reasonable accommodation under the ADA. That case arose in the context of seniority systems, but it contains some significant discussion of the accommodation issue generally. When reading the case, it is useful to remember that the accommodation issue is fact specific and consider whether the accommodation sought by Barnett would have been reasonable when he initially received it and in the absence of a seniority system (the Court suggests that the answer is yes).

U.S. AIRWAYS, INC.
v.
BARNETT
535 U.S. 391 (2002)

Justice BREYER delivered the opinion of the Court.

[The Employment Problem]

In 1990, Robert Barnett, the plaintiff and respondent here, injured his back while working in a cargo-handling position at petitioner U.S. Airways, Inc. He invoked seniority rights and transferred to a less physically demanding mailroom position. Under U.S. Airways' seniority system, that position, like others, periodically became open to seniority-based employee bidding. In 1992, Barnett learned that at least two employees senior to him intended to bid for the mailroom job. He asked U.S. Air-

ways to accommodate his disability-imposed limitations by making an exception that would allow him to remain in the mailroom. After permitting Barnett to continue his mailroom work for five months while it considered the matter, U.S. Airways eventually decided not to make an exception. And Barnett lost his job.

[The Legal Issue]

The Americans with Disabilities Act of 1990 . . . prohibits an employer from discriminating against an "individual with a disability" who, with "reasonable accommodation," can perform the essential functions of the job. . . . This case, arising in the context of summary judgment, asks us how the Act resolves a potential conflict between: (1) the interests of a disabled worker who seeks assignment to a particular position as a "reasonable accommodation," and (2) the interests of other workers with superior rights to bid for the job under an employer's seniority system. In such a case, does the accommodation demand trump the seniority system?

[Decision by the Trial Court and the U.S. Court of Appeals for the Ninth Circuit]

Barnett then brought this ADA suit claiming, among other things, that he was an "individual with a disability" capable of performing the essential functions of the mailroom job, that the mailroom job amounted to a "reasonable accommodation" of his disability, and that U.S. Airways, in refusing to assign him the job, unlawfully discriminated against him. U.S. Airways moved for summary judgment. . . .

The District Court found that the undisputed facts about seniority warranted summary judgment in U.S. Airways' favor. The Act says that an employer who fails to make "reasonable accommodations to the known physical or mental limitations of an [employee] with a disability" discriminates "*unless*" the employer "can demonstrate that the accommodation would impose an *undue hardship* on the operation of [its] business." 42 U.S.C. § 12112(b)(5)(A) (emphasis added). The court said:

> [T]he uncontroverted evidence shows that the US-Air seniority system has been in place for "decades" and governs over 14,000 USAir Agents. Moreover, seniority policies such as the one at issue in this case are common to the airline industry. Given this context, it seems clear that the USAir employees were justified in relying upon the policy. As such, any significant alteration of that policy would result in undue hardship to both the company and its non-disabled employees. App. to Pet. for Cert. 96a.

An en banc panel of the United States Court of Appeals for the Ninth Circuit reversed. It said that the presence of a seniority system is merely "a factor in the undue hardship analysis." . . . And it held that "[a] case-by-case fact intensive analysis is required to determine whether any particular reassignment would constitute an undue hardship to the employer." *Ibid.*

[The Decision by the U.S. Supreme Court]

In our view, the seniority system will prevail in the run of cases. As we interpret the statute, to show that a requested accommodation conflicts with the rules of a seniority system is ordinarily to show that the accommodation is not "reasonable." Hence such a showing will entitle an employer/defendant to summary judgment on the question—unless there is more. The plaintiff remains free to present evidence of special circumstances that make "reasonable" a seniority rule exception in the particular case. And such a showing will defeat the employer's demand for summary judgment. . . .

In answering the question presented, we must consider the following statutory provisions. First, the ADA says that an employer may not "discriminate against a qualified individual with a disability." 42 U.S.C. § 12112(a). Second, the ADA says that a "qualified" individual includes "an individual with a disability who, *with* or without *reasonable accommodation,* can perform the essential functions of" the relevant "employment position." § 12111(8) (emphasis added). Third, the ADA says that "discrimination" includes an employer's "*not making reasonable accommodations* to the known physical or mental limitations of an otherwise qualified . . . employee, *unless* [the employer] can demonstrate that the accommodation would impose an *undue hardship* on the operation of [its] business." § 12112(b)(5)(A) (emphasis added). Fourth, the ADA says that the term "'reasonable accommodation' may include . . . reassignment to a vacant position." § 1211(9)(B). . . .

US Airways' claim that a seniority system virtually always trumps a conflicting accommodation demand rests primarily upon its view of how the Act treats workplace "preferences." Insofar as a requested accommodation violates a disability-neutral workplace rule, such as a seniority rule, it grants the employee with a disability treatment that other workers could not receive. Yet the Act, U.S. Airways says, seeks only "equal" treatment for those with disabilities. . . . It does not, it contends, require an employer to grant preferential treatment. . . . Hence it does not require the employer to grant a request that, in violating a disability-neutral rule, would provide a preference.

While linguistically logical, this argument fails to recognize what the Act specifies, namely, that sometimes preferences will sometimes prove necessary to achieve the Act's basic equal opportunity goal. The Act requires preferences in the form of "reasonable accommodations" that are needed for those with disabilities to obtain the *same* workplace opportunities that those without disabilities automatically enjoy. By definition, any special "accommodation" requires the employer to treat an employee with a disability differently, *i.e.*, preferentially. And the fact that the difference in treatment violates an employer's disability-neutral rule cannot by itself place the accommodation beyond the Act's potential reach.

Were that not so, the "reasonable accommodation" provision could not accomplish its intended objective. Neutral office assignment rules would automatically prevent the accommodation of an employee whose disability-imposed limitations require him to work on the ground floor. Neutral "break-from-work" rules would automatically prevent the accommodation of an individual who needs additional breaks from work, perhaps to permit medical visits. Neutral furniture budget rules would automatically prevent the accommodation of an individual who needs a different kind of chair or desk. Many employers will have neutral rules governing the kinds of actions most needed to reasonably accommodate a worker with a disability. See 42 U.S.C. § 12111(9)(b) (setting forth examples such as "job restructuring," "part-time or modified work schedules," "acquisition or modification of equipment or devices," "and other similar accommodations"). Yet Congress, while providing such examples, said nothing suggesting that the presence of such neutral rules would create an automatic exemption. . . .

In sum, the nature of the "reasonable accommodation" requirement, the statutory examples, and the Act's silence about the exempting effect of neutral rules together convince us that the Act does not create any such automatic exemption. The simple fact that an accommodation would provide a "preference"—in the sense that it would permit the worker with a disability to violate a rule that others must obey—cannot, *in and of itself*, automatically show that the accommodation is not "reasonable." As a result, we reject the position taken by U.S. Airways and Justice SCALIA to the contrary.

U.S. Airways also points to the ADA provisions stating that a "'reasonable accommodation' may include . . . reassignment to a *vacant* position." Section 12111(9)(B) (emphasis added). And it claims that the fact that an established seniority system would assign that position to another worker automatically and always means that the position is not a "vacant" one. Nothing in the Act, however, suggests that Congress intended the word "vacant" to have a specialized meaning. And in ordinary English, a seniority system can give employees seniority rights allowing them to bid for a "vacant" position. The position in this case was held, at the time of suit, by Barnett, not by some other worker; and that po-

sition, under the U.S. Airways seniority system, became an "open" one. Moreover, U.S. Airways has said that it "reserves the right to change any and all" portions of the seniority system at will. . . . Consequently, we cannot agree with U.S. Airways about the position's vacancy; nor do we agree that the Act would automatically deny Barnett's accommodation request for that reason.

Barnett argues that the statutory words "reasonable accommodation" mean only "effective accommodation," authorizing a court to consider the requested accommodation's ability to meet an individual's disability-related needs, and nothing more. On this view, a seniority rule violation, having nothing to do with the accommodation's effectiveness, has nothing to do with its "reasonableness." It might, at most, help to prove an "undue hardship on the operation of the business." But, he adds, that is a matter that the statute requires the employer to demonstrate, case by case.

In support of this interpretation Barnett points to Equal Employment Opportunity Commission (EEOC) regulations stating that "reasonable accommodation means . . . [m]odifications or adjustments . . . that *enable* a qualified individual with a disability to perform the essential functions of [a] position." 29 CFR § 1630(*o*)(ii) (2001) (emphasis added). . . . Barnett adds that any other view would make the words "reasonable accommodation" and "undue hardship" virtual mirror images—creating redundancy in the statute. And he says that any such other view would create a practical burden of proof dilemma.

The practical burden of proof dilemma arises, Barnett argues, because the statute imposes the burden of demonstrating an "undue hardship" upon the employer, while the burden of proving "reasonable accommodation" remains with the plaintiff, here the employee. This allocation seems sensible in that an employer can more frequently and easily prove the presence of business hardship than an employee can prove its absence. But suppose that an employee must counter a claim of "seniority rule violation" in order to prove that an "accommodation" request is "reasonable." Would that not force the employee to prove what is in effect an absence, *i.e.*, an absence of hardship, despite the statute's insistence that the employer "demonstrate" hardship's presence?

These arguments do not persuade us that Barnett's legal interpretation of "reasonable" is correct. For one thing, in ordinary English, the word "reasonable" does not mean "effective." It is the word "accommodation," not the word "reasonable," that conveys the need for effectiveness. An *ineffective* "modification" or "adjustment" will not *accommodate* a disabled individual's limitations.

Nor does an ordinary English meaning of the term "reasonable accommodation" make of it a simple, redundant mirror image of the term "undue hardship." The statute refers to an "undue hardship on the operation of the business." 42 U.S.C. § 12112(b)(5)(A). Yet a demand for an effective accommodation could prove unreasonable because of its impact, not on business operations, but on fellow employees—say because it will lead to dismissals, relocations, or modification of employee benefits to which an employer, looking at the matter from the perspective of the business itself, may be relatively indifferent.

Neither does the statute's primary purpose require Barnett's special reading. The statute seeks to diminish or to eliminate the stereotypical thought processes, the thoughtless actions, and the hostile reactions that far too often bar those with disabilities from participating fully in the Nation's life, including the workplace. . . . These objectives demand unprejudiced thought and reasonable responsive reaction on the part of employers and fellow workers alike. They will sometimes require affirmative conduct to promote entry of disabled people into the workforce. . . . They do not, however, demand action beyond the realm of the reasonable.

Neither has Congress indicated in the statute, or elsewhere, that the word "reasonable" means no more than "effective." The EEOC regulations do say that reasonable accommodations "enable" a person with a disability to perform the essential functions of a task. But that phrasing simply emphasizes the statutory provision's basic objective. The regulations do not say that "enable" and "reasonable" mean the same thing. . . .

Finally, an ordinary language interpretation of the word "reasonable" does not create the "burden of proof" dilemma to which Barnett points. Many of the lower courts, while rejecting both U.S. Airways' and Barnett's more absolute views, have reconciled the phrases "reasonable accommodation" and "undue hardship" in a practical way.

They have held that a plaintiff/employee (to defeat a defendant/employer's motion for summary judgment) need only show that an "accommodation" seems reasonable on its face, *i.e.*, ordinarily or in the run of cases . . .

Once the plaintiff has made this showing, the defendant/employer then must show special (typically case-specific) circumstances that demonstrate undue hardship in the particular circumstances . . .

Not every court has used the same language, but their results are functionally similar. In our opinion, that practical view of the statute, applied consistently with ordinary summary judgment principles, see Fed. Rule Civ. Proc. 56, avoids Barnett's burden of proof dilemma, while reconciling the two statutory phrases ("reasonable accommodation" and "undue hardship").

The question in the present case focuses on the relationship between seniority systems and the plaintiff's need to show that an "accommodation" seems reasonable on its face, *i.e.*, ordinarily or in the run of cases. We must assume that the plaintiff, an employee, is an "individual with a disability." He has requested assignment to a mailroom position as a "reasonable accommodation." We also assume that normally such a request would be reasonable within the meaning of the statute, were it not for one circumstance, namely, that the assignment would violate the rules of a seniority system. . . . Does that circumstance mean that the proposed accommodation is not a "reasonable" one?

In our view, the answer to this question ordinarily is "yes." The statute does not require proof on a case-by-case basis that a seniority system should prevail. That is because it would not be reasonable in the run of cases that the assignment in question trump the rules of a seniority system. To the contrary, it will ordinarily be unreasonable for the assignment to prevail.

Several factors support our conclusion that a proposed accommodation will not be reasonable in the run of cases. Analogous case law supports this conclusion, for it has recognized the importance of seniority to employee-management relations. This Court has held that, in the context of a Title VII religious discrimination case, an employer need not adapt to an employee's special worship schedule as a "reasonable accommodation" where doing so would conflict with the seniority rights of other employees. *Trans World Airlines v. Hardison*, 432 U.S. 63, 79–80 (1977). The lower courts unanimously have found that collectively bargained seniority trumps the need for reasonable accommodation in the context of the linguistically similar Rehabilitation Act. . . . And several Circuits, though differing in their reasoning, have reached a similar conclusion in the context of seniority and the ADA. . . . All these cases discuss *collectively bargained* seniority systems, not systems (like the present system) which are unilaterally imposed by management. But the relevant seniority system advantages, and related difficulties that result from violations of seniority rules, are not limited to collectively bargained systems.

For one thing, the typical seniority system provides important employee benefits by creating, and fulfilling, employee expectations of fair, uniform treatment. These benefits include "job security and an opportunity for steady and predictable advancement based on objective standards." . . . They include "an element of due process," limiting "unfairness in personnel decisions." . . . And they consequently encourage employees to invest in the employing company, accepting "less than their value to the firm early in their careers" in return for greater benefits in later years. . . .

Most important for present purposes, to require the typical employer to show more than the existence of a seniority system might well undermine the employees' expectations of consistent, uniform treatment—expectations upon which the seniority system's benefits depend. That is because such a rule would substitute a complex case-specific "accommodation" decision made by management for the more uniform, impersonal operation of seniority rules. Such management decision-making, with its inevitable discretionary elements, would involve a matter of the greatest importance to employees, namely, layoffs; it would take place outside, as well as inside, the confines of a court case; and it might well take place fairly often. . . . We can find nothing in the statute that suggests Congress intended to undermine seniority systems in this way. And we consequently conclude that the employer's showing of violation of the rules of a seniority system is by itself ordinarily sufficient.

The plaintiff (here the employee) nonetheless remains free to show that special circumstances warrant a finding that, despite the presence of a seniority system (which the ADA may not trump in the run of cases), the requested "accommodation" is "reasonable" on the particular facts. That is because special circumstances might alter the important expectations described above. *Cf. Borkowski*, 63 F.3d, at 137 ("[A]n accommodation that imposed burdens that would be unreasonable for most members of an industry might nevertheless be required of an individual defendant in light of that employer's particular circumstances"). . . . The plaintiff might show, for example, that the employer, having retained the right to change the seniority system unilaterally, exercises that right fairly frequently, reducing employee expectations that the system will be followed—to the point where one more departure, needed to accommodate an individual with a disability, will not likely make a difference. The plaintiff might show that the system already contains exceptions such that, in the circumstances, one further exception is unlikely to matter. We do not mean these examples to exhaust the kinds of showings that a plaintiff might make. But we do mean to say that the plaintiff must bear the burden of showing special circumstances that make an exception from the seniority system reasonable in the particular case. And to do so, the plaintiff must explain why, in the particular case, an exception to the employer's seniority policy can constitute a "reasonable accommodation" even though in the ordinary case it cannot.

In its question presented, U.S. Airways asked us whether the ADA requires an employer to assign a disabled employee to a particular position even though another employee is entitled to that position under the employer's "established seniority system." We answer that *ordinarily* the ADA does not require that assignment. Hence, a showing that the assignment would violate the rules of a seniority system warrants summary judgment for the employer—unless there is more. The plaintiff must present evidence of that "more," namely, special circumstances surrounding the particular case that demonstrate the assignment is nonetheless reasonable.

Because the lower courts took a different view of the matter, and because neither party has had an opportunity to seek summary judgment in accordance with the principles we set forth here, we vacate the Court of Appeals' judgment and remand the case for further proceedings consistent with this opinion.

It is so ordered.

In *Barnett*, the Court held that exceptions to a bona fide seniority system are rarely reasonable accommodations, but the Court did not base its decision on the undue hardship exceptions might create for employers. While the Court did not discuss the factors relevant to a determination of undue hardship in any depth, it did answer an important question, namely, the allocation of the burden of proof. The Court held that the employee has the initial burden to show that a given accommodation is reasonable by showing that it is "reasonable on its face—i.e., ordinarily or in the run of cases." If this burden is met by the employee, the employer then has the burden of showing why the accommodation would pose an undue hardship under the facts of the given case. Prior to *Barnett,* there was some disagreement about the burden of proof.

As noted above, *Barnett* is primarily about the reasonable accommodation part of the equation. The following case analyzes both the reasonable accommodation and the undue hardship concepts. It is important to remember that like the question of when an accommodation is reasonable, the question of when an accommodation poses an undue hardship is highly fact sensitive. The *Vande Zande* case, below, was decided before the Supreme Court's decision in *Barnett*. After reading the excerpt from the case, consider whether the decision in *Barnett* alters Judge POSNER'S discussion of the reasonableness of an accommodation. Judge POSNER points out that cost can be a factor in both the reasonableness and the undue hardship analyses. The EEOC's definition and guidance on undue hardship will be provided after the *Vande Zande* case excerpt.

VANDE ZANDE
v.
STATE OF WISCONSIN DEPARTMENT OF ADMINISTRATION
44 F.3d 538 (7th Cir. 1995)

POSNER, Chief Judge.

[Decision and Rationale of the U.S. Supreme Court]

In 1990, Congress passed the Americans with Disabilities Act. . . . The stated purpose is "to provide a clear and comprehensive national mandate for the elimination of discrimination against individuals with disabilities," said by Congress to be 43 million in number and growing. . . . "Disability" is broadly defined. . . . Many . . . impairments are not in fact disabling but are believed to be so, and the people having them may be denied employment or otherwise shunned as a consequence. Such people, objectively capable of performing as well as the unimpaired, are analogous to capable workers discriminated against because of their skin color or some other vocationally irrelevant characteristic. . . .

The more problematic case is that of an individual who has a vocationally relevant disability—an impairment such as blindness or paralysis that limits a major human capability, such as seeing or walking. In the common case in which such an impairment interferes with the individual's ability to perform up to the standards of the workplace, or increases the cost of employing him, hiring and firing decisions based on the impairment are not "discriminatory" in a sense closely analogous to employment discrimination on racial grounds. The draftsmen of the Act knew this. But they were unwilling to confine the concept of disability discrimination to cases in which the disability is irrelevant to the performance of the disabled person's job. Instead, they defined "discrimination" to include an employer's "not making reasonable accommodations to the known physical or mental limitations of an otherwise qualified individual with a disability who is an applicant or employee, unless . . .

[the employer] can demonstrate that the accommodation would impose an undue hardship on the operation of the . . . [employer's] business." . . .

The term "reasonable accommodations" is not a legal novelty. . . . It is one of a number of provisions in the employment subchapter that were borrowed from regulations issued by the Equal Employment Opportunity Commission in implementation of the Rehabilitation Act of 1973, 29 U.S.C. § 702 *et seq.* . . . Indeed, to a great extent, the employment provisions of the new Act merely generalize to the economy as a whole the duties, including that of reasonable accommodation, that the regulations under the Rehabilitation Act imposed on federal agencies and federal contractors. We can therefore look to the decisions interpreting those regulations for clues to the meaning of the same terms in the new law.

It is plain enough what "accommodation" means. The employer must be willing to consider making changes in its ordinary work rules, facilities, terms, and conditions in order to enable a disabled individual to work. The difficult term is "reasonable." The plaintiff in our case, a paraplegic, argues in effect that the term just means apt or efficacious. An accommodation is reasonable, she believes, when it is tailored to the particular individual's disability. . . . Considerations of cost do not enter into the term as the plaintiff would have us construe it. Cost is, she argues, the domain of "undue hardship" (another term borrowed from the regulations under the Rehabilitation Act, *see* S. Rep. No. 116, *supra*, at 36)—a safe harbor for an employer that can show that it would go broke or suffer other excruciating financial distress were it compelled to make a reasonable accommodation in the sense of one effective in enabling the disabled person to overcome the vocational effects of the disability.

These are questionable interpretations both of "reasonable" and of "undue hardship." To "accommodate" a disability is to make some change that will enable the disabled person to work. An unrelated, inefficacious change would not be an accommodation of the disability at all. So "reasonable" may be intended to qualify (in the sense of weaken) "accommodation," in just the same way that if one requires a "reasonable effort" of someone this means less than the maximum possible effort, or in law that the duty of "reasonable care," the cornerstone of the law of negligence, requires something less than the maximum possible care. . . . It would not follow that the costs and benefits of altering a workplace to enable a disabled person to work would always have to be quantified, or even that an accommodation would have to be deemed unreasonable if the cost exceeded the benefit however slightly. But, at the very least, the cost could not be disproportionate to the benefit. Even if an employer is so large or wealthy—or, like the principal defendant in this case, is a state, which can raise taxes in order to finance any accommodations that it must make to disabled employees—that it may not be able to plead "undue *hardship*," it would not be required to expend enormous sums in order to bring about a trivial improvement in the life of a disabled employee. . . .

The concept of reasonable accommodation is at the heart of this case. The plaintiff sought a number of accommodations to her paraplegia that were turned down. The principal defendant as we have said is a state, which does not argue that the plaintiff's proposals were rejected because accepting them would have imposed undue hardship on the state or because they would not have done her any good. The district judge nevertheless granted summary judgment for the defendants on the ground that the evi-

dence obtained in discovery, construed as favorably to the plaintiff as the record permitted, showed that they had gone as far to accommodate the plaintiff's demands as reasonableness, in a sense distinct from either aptness or hardship—a sense based, rather, on considerations of cost and proportionality—required. . . . On this analysis, the function of the "undue hardship" safe harbor, like the "failing company" defense to antitrust liability . . . is to excuse compliance by a firm that is financially distressed, even though the cost of the accommodation to the firm might be less than the benefit to disabled employees.

This interpretation of "undue hardship" is not inevitable—in fact it probably is incorrect. It is a defined term in the Americans with Disabilities Act, and the definition is "an action requiring significant difficulty or expense." 42 U.S.C. § 12111(10(A). The financial condition of the employer is only one consideration in determining whether an accommodation otherwise reasonable would impose an undue hardship. See 42 U.S.C. § 12111(10)(B)(ii), (iii). The legislative history equates "undue hardship" to "unduly costly." . . . These are terms of relation. We must ask, "undue" in relation to what? Presumably (given the statutory definition and the legislative history) in relation to the benefits of the accommodation to the disabled worker as well as to the employer's resources.

So it seems that costs enter at two points in the analysis of claims to an accommodation to a disability. The employee must show that the accommodation is reasonable in the sense both of efficacious and of proportional to costs. Even if this *prima facie* showing is made, the employer has an opportunity to prove that upon more careful consideration the costs are excessive in relation either to the benefits of the accommodation or to the employer's financial survival or health. . . .

The EEOC regulations addressing undue hardship, 29 C.F.R. § 1630.2(p), read as follows:

(p) Undue hardship—

(1) In general. Undue hardship means, with respect to the provision of an accommodation, significant difficulty or expense incurred by a covered entity, when considered in light of the factors set forth in paragraph (p)(2) of this section.

(2) Factors to be considered. In determining whether an accommodation would impose an undue hardship on a covered entity, factors to be considered include:

(i) The nature and net cost of the accommodation needed under this part, taking into consideration the availability of tax credits and deductions, and/or outside funding;

(ii) The overall financial resources of the facility or facilities involved in the provision of the reasonable accommodation, the number of persons employed at such facility, and the effect on expenses and resources;

(iii) The overall financial resources of the covered entity, the overall size of the business of the covered entity with respect to the number of its employees, and the number, type and location of its facilities;

(iv) The type of operation or operations of the covered entity, including the composition, structure and functions of the workforce of such entity, and the geographic separateness and administrative or fiscal relationship of the facility or facilities in question to the covered entity; and

(v) The impact of the accommodation upon the operation of the facility, including the impact on the ability of other employees to perform their duties and the impact on the facility's ability to conduct business.

Additionally, the ADA Interpretive Guidance on undue hardship, 29 C.F.R. app. to § 1630.2(p), reads as follows:

Section 1630.2(p) Undue Hardship

An employer or other covered entity is not required to provide an accommodation that will impose an undue hardship on the operation of the employer's or other covered entity's business. The term "undue hardship" means significant difficulty or expense in, or resulting from, the provision of the accommodation. The "undue hardship" provision takes into account the financial realities of the particular employer or other covered entity. However, the concept of undue hardship is not limited to financial difficulty. "Undue hardship" refers to any accommodation that would be unduly costly, extensive, substantial, or disruptive, or that would fundamentally alter the nature or operation of the business. See Senate Report at 35; House Labor Report at 67.

For example, suppose an individual with a disabling visual impairment that makes it extremely difficult to see in dim lighting applies for a position as a waiter in a nightclub and requests that the club be brightly lit as a reasonable accommodation. Although the individual may be able to perform the job in bright lighting, the nightclub will probably be able to demonstrate that that particular accommodation, though inexpensive, would impose an undue hardship if the bright lighting would destroy the ambience of the nightclub and/or make it difficult for the customers to see the stage show. The fact that that particular accommodation poses an undue hardship, however, only means that the employer is not required to provide that accommodation. If there is another accommodation that will not create an undue hardship, the employer would be required to provide the alternative accommodation.

An employer's claim that the cost of a particular accommodation will impose an undue hardship will be analyzed in light of the factors outlined in part 1630. In part, this analysis requires a determination of whose financial resources should be considered in deciding whether the accommodation is unduly costly. In some cases the financial resources of the employer or other covered entity in its entirety should be considered in determining whether the cost of an accommodation poses an undue hardship. In other cases, consideration of the financial resources of the employer or other covered entity as a whole may be inappropriate because it may not give an accurate picture of the financial resources available to the particular facility that will actually be required to provide the accommodation. . . .

If the employer or other covered entity asserts that only the financial resources of the facility where the individual will be employed should be considered, part 1630 requires a factual determination of the relationship between the employer or other covered entity and the facility that will provide the accommodation. As an example, suppose that an independently owned fast food franchise that receives no money from the franchisor refuses to hire an individual with a hearing impairment because it asserts that it would be an undue hardship to provide an interpreter to enable the individual to participate in monthly staff meetings. Since the financial relationship between the franchisor and the franchise is limited to payment of an annual franchise fee, only the financial resources of the franchise would be considered in determining whether or not providing the accommodation would be an undue hardship. . . .

If the employer or other covered entity can show that the cost of the accommodation would impose an undue hardship, it would still be required to provide the accommodation if the funding is available from another source, e.g., a State vocational rehabilitation agency, or if Federal, State or local tax deductions or tax credits are available to offset the cost of the accommodation. If the employer or other covered entity receives, or is eligible to receive, monies from an external source that would pay the entire cost of the accommodation, it cannot claim cost as an undue hardship. In the absence of such funding, the individual with a disability requesting the accommodation should be given the option of providing the accommodation or of paying that portion of the cost which constitutes the undue hardship on the operation of the business. To the extent that such monies pay or would pay for only part of the cost of the accommodation, only that portion of the cost of the accommodation that could not be recovered—the final net cost to the entity—may be considered in determining undue hardship. . . .

Question

1. Is the Seventh Circuit's decision in *Vande Zande* consistent with the EEOC's definition of undue hardship in 29 C.F.R. § 1630.2(p) and the examples provided in the interpretive guidance excerpt above?

E. Causes of Action

Once an individual with a disability is found to be a qualified individual with a disability, the individual must still make out a claim of discrimination. Such claims can be based on the theories you are familiar with from earlier sections of this book. Thus, claims of disparate treatment, disparate impact, and hostile work environment all have been recognized under the ADA. Moreover, as mentioned in the preceding section, failure to make a reasonable accommodation is a form of discrimination under the ADA. A failure to accommodate claim might interact with other claims such as a claim of disparate treatment.

There are, of course, differences between such claims under Title VII and the ADA. The most significant is that a claimant under the ADA must demonstrate that he or she is a qualified individual with a disability in addition to whatever claim he or she is asserting. Moreover, disability may be relevant to a number of employment decisions that are challenged, while other protected classifications such as race generally are not (gender also may be relevant in rare circumstances, as you saw with the bona fide occupational qualifications material earlier in this book). Significantly, disability is a somewhat unique classification in employment discrimination law because there are a large number of disabilities that affect numerous bodily functions, and thus "disability" is a classification that covers an immensely diverse and varied group of conditions, conditions that may affect individuals differently depending on their severity and other characteristics.

This diversity within the classification has ramifications when analyzing claims of disability discrimination under the traditional causes of action. For example, what objective reasonableness standard should be used in the hostile work environment context? Should it be a reasonable individual with a disability? If so, what if the conduct is aimed at a specific disability—i.e., would someone with asthma feel harassed by conduct aimed at someone with a hearing impairment? Does this mean a "reasonable person with the same or similar disability" standard should be used? How would this work? Would a simple reasonable person standard work better? What about the fact that the ADA was drafted in part because of the stereotypes most people have of individuals with disabilities? How would this compare to the standard applied to hostile work environment claims under Title VII? This question has not been answered definitively, and there is still a great deal of debate on the subject. Compare Frank S. Ravitch, *Beyond Reasonable Accommodation: The Availability and Structure of a Cause of Action for Workplace Harassment Under the Americans with Disabilities Act*, 15 Cardozo L. Rev. 1475 (1994); and Christine Neagle, Comment, *An Analysis of the Applicability of Hostile Work Environment Liability to the ADA*, 3 U. Pa. J. Lab. & Emp. L. 715 (2001), with Holland M. Tahvonen, Note, *Disability-Based Harassment: Standing and Standards for a "New" Cause of Action*, 44 Wm. & Mary L. Rev. 1489 (2003). This issue is a good example of the potential complexity involved in applying "traditional" employment discrimination causes of action to the disability discrimination context.

Two important issues that arise under the ADA relate to claims of disparate treatment and disparate impact, respectively. The first is how the concept of reasonable accommodation affects disparate treatment claims. The second is how some specific language in the ADA affects disparate impact claims.

Consider a traditional disparate treatment case. As you learned in Chapter 2, the plaintiff must make out a *prima facie* case of discrimination. At that point, the burden of production (but not the burden of proof) shifts to the defendant to demonstrate that it had legitimate, nondiscriminatory reasons for its action(s). If the defendant asserts such reasons, the plaintiff has the opportunity to demonstrate that the proffered reasons are a pretext for discrimination. In the ADA context, the concept of reasonable accommodation could have an effect on this analysis. For example, what if the employer asserted, as a legitimate, nondiscriminatory reason for termination of a disabled employee, the disabled employee's inability to do the job as quickly or efficiently as other employees? Assume the disabled employee is qualified but simply not as efficient. Is the employer's reason legitimate? Assume further that there is no accommodation that would enable the employee to be as efficient as other employees. Does this make a difference? Is tolerating a lower level of efficiency from an employee who can perform the essential function of the job a reasonable accommodation? Does it make a difference if the employer does or does not tolerate other employees who are less efficient than most employees?

Obviously, an employer would have a duty to accommodate a disabled employee where a reasonable accommodation is possible without imposing an undue hardship. The failure to do so could be challenged in a claim for failure to accommodate regardless of whether the employer engaged in disparate treatment such as failure to promote or the like, and undue hardship could be asserted as a defense where supportable. Relatedly, an employer could not deny a reasonable accommodation and use the resulting impact of the disability as a legitimate, nondiscriminatory reason for an adverse job action.

Yet this does not answer the question of whether an employer can use the effects of a disability on job performance as a legitimate, nondiscriminatory reason when the employee is qualified but simply not as efficient, quick, and so forth. The employer might try to argue that efficiency or speed is an essential function of the job, and thus the employee is not qualified, but in many cases, efficiency and speed may be preferred by the employer but are not essential. If so, we must address the disparate treatment and accommodation questions. Here, the accommodation question is relevant only where the employer could accommodate the employee to enable her to perform as efficiently or quickly as the other employees. If not, the employer is taking action against a qualified employee because of the effects of that employee's disability on job performance, but the effects are real. Some courts have suggested that such real effects can be used as legitimate, nondiscriminatory reasons for disparate treatment aimed at qualified individuals with disabilities when accommodation is not possible, but the answer is not clear. Of course, the employee would still have the opportunity to prove that the employer's proffered reasons are pretextual.

Claims of disparate impact are also possible under the ADA, but included within the ADA are some provisions that may add some force to such claims. For example, the definition of the term "discriminate" in Title I of the ADA, 42 U.S.C. § 12112(b), includes the following provisions:

(3) utilizing standards, criteria, or methods of administration—
(A) that have the effect of discrimination on the basis of disability; or
(B) that perpetuate the discrimination of others who are subject to common administrative control; . . .
(6) using qualification standards, employment tests or other selection criteria that screen out or tend to screen out an individual with a disability or a class of individuals with disabilities unless the standard, test or other selection criteria, as used by the covered entity, is shown to be job-related for the position in question and is consistent with business necessity;

In addition, 42 U.S.C. § 12113, which sets forth the defenses to claims of discrimination, includes the following provision:

(a) In general
It may be a defense to a charge of discrimination under this chapter that an alleged application of qualification standards, tests, or selection criteria that screen out or tend to screen out or otherwise deny a job or benefit to an individual with a disability has been shown to be job-related and consistent with business necessity, and such performance cannot be accomplished by reasonable accommodation, as required under this subchapter.

Thus, both disparate impact and the traditional defense to disparate impact are recognized under the ADA, but with added textual force via 42 U.S.C. § 12112(b)(3), which adds specific types of behavior or requirements that could give rise to disparate impact claims. Section 12112(b)(6) of 42 U.S.C. reflects the traditional disparate impact cause of action, and thus subsection (3) can be viewed as augmenting the types of policies and practices that are covered under (6).

Significantly, disparate impact claims under the ADA can raise two additional concerns: What impact do qualification standards have on disparate impact claims for determining who is a qualified individual with a disability? What is the relationship between reasonable accommodation and disparate impact under the ADA? As to the first, 42 U.S.C. § 12113(a) specifically sets forth a defense where an employer uses valid qualification standards. Of course, if a qualification standard is not job related and consistent with business necessity, it is not valid and thus cannot be used to demonstrate that the employee is unqualified and will fail as a defense to a disparate impact claim.

Employers also have a duty to accommodate employees so that they can meet any criteria necessary for the job so long as the accommodation is reasonable and does not pose an undue hardship. Thus, an employer must provide reasonable accommodation where possible to an employee or job applicant to enable her to compete fairly under any selection criteria, standards, or tests used to determine who is hired, fired, promoted, and so on. Moreover, the inability to provide reasonable accommodation or the existence of undue hardship would enable an employer to defend against a disparate impact claim where the challenged criteria are job related and consistent with business necessity. Of course, when an employer fails to accommodate under such circumstances, the employee may also bring a claim for failure to accommodate.

In *Raytheon v Hernandez*, 540 U.S. 44 (2003), the Supreme Court vacated and remanded the decision by the Ninth Circuit and held that the Court of Appeals had impermissibly relied on a disparate impact analysis in an ADA claim. The Court refused to consider whether the ADA could have been an appropriate claim because the disparate impact claim was not properly raised below.

F. A Note on the ADA and "Gender Identity Disorder" or Dysphoria

The ADA specifically excludes "transsexualism," more recently termed "transgenderism." However, it excludes "gender identity disorders" only if they do not result from "physical impairments." 42 U.S.C.A. § 12211(b)(1). Theoretically, then, it is possible for a transgender individual to obtain ADA protection if there is a qualifying long-term condition resulting from physical causes. For example, it is possible that long-term physical effects may accompany the arduous progress toward sex-reassignment. The hormone treatment that is part of the extended transition from male to female, for example, may arguably produce symptoms that are themselves disabling under the regime of *Sutton* and its progeny, discussed in Chapter 13. Pleading an ADA claim may seem to some practitioners a way to state a claim for a transgender client or a client who is making the transition from the biological gender to the gender with which the client identifies, since a Title VII claim is barred. The practitioner should carefully evaluate the ramifications of doing so, however.

On one hand, the American Psychiatric Association (APA) recognizes gender identity disorder or dysphoria as a psychiatric disorder, which may be helpful in establishing an ADA case if the proponent of an ADA claim can parse physical impairments from an APA-listed psychiatric disorder. On the other hand, there are those who would question the designation of such a psychiatric disorder as inherently stigmatizing and those who would assail the language and criteria that the APA has selected to identify and describe gender identity disorder in the Fourth Edition of its DIAGNOSTIC AND STATISTICAL MANUAL (DSM-IV) (1994) as pejorative.

Section 302.85 of DSM-IV provides the following diagnostic criteria for identifying gender identity disorder among adolescents and adults:

a. A strong and persistent cross-gender identification (not merely a desire for any perceived cultural advantages of being the other sex). In adolescents and adults, the disturbance is manifested by symptoms such as a stated desire to be the other sex, frequent passing as the other sex, desire to live or be treated as the other sex, or the conviction that he or she has the typical feelings and reactions of the other sex.

b. Persistent discomfort with his or her sex or sense of inappropriateness in the gender role of that sex. In adolescents and adults, the disturbance is manifested by symptoms such as preoccupation with getting rid of primary and secondary sex characteristics (e.g., request for hormones, surgery, or other procedures to physically alter sexual characteristics to simulate the other sex) or belief that he or she was born the wrong sex.

c. The disturbance is not concurrent with a physical intersex condition.

d. The disturbance causes clinically significant distress or impairment in social, occupational, or other important areas of functioning.

Students should note that until 1973, the APA's MANUAL (DSM-II) listed homosexuality as a psychiatric disorder.

Critics of DSM-IV's classification and language believe that it invites clinicians to supply their own content to the definitions, courting subjective perceptions of "appropriate" gender roles. They fear that the DSM-IV classification and language will harm the very people they were intended to help. *See, e.g.,* K. Wilson, *Gender as Illness: Issues of Psychiatric Classification* (reprinted in E. Paul, ed., TAKING SIDES—CLASHING VIEWS ON CONTROVERSIAL ISSUES IN SEX AND GENDER (2000) at 31–38. The ADA does not bar a claim premised on "gender identity disorder" or "gender dysphoria" if the condition is the result of a physical impairment. DSM-IV, however, would rule out such a diagnosis where the "disturbance" appears in an intersex person; that is, a person born with ambiguous sexual characteristics.

Medical experts have pointed to several factors as contributors to a person's sex: chromosomal sex (e.g., XX or XY); gonadal sex (testes or ovaries as reproductive organs); internal morphologic sex (seminal vesicles, vagina, fallopian tubes—which are not apparent until three months' gestation); external morphologic sex (e.g., penis, labia); hormonal sex (androgens, estrogens); and phenotypic sex (secondary sex characteristics such as facial hair or breasts). *See* Greenberg, *Defining Male and Female: Intersexuality and the Collision Between Law and Biology,* 41 Ariz. L. Rev. 265 (1992). More controversially, some medical experts would add to two factors: (1) the sex assigned by the culture and the gender in which one was raised and (2) one's own sexual identity/identification. *Id.* Whether the latter two factors can "trump" the factors that are more easily identified as biologically based has been grist for the judicial pen and is the issue that lies at the heart of the debate over extending a variety of legal protections to transgender citizens.

Professor Julie Greenberg is a leading scholar and proponent of using all of the factors listed above in determining sex. As Professor Greenberg has observed, all of these factors, including the ones addressing assigned gender and sexual identity, usually coalesce. Coalescence is not invariable, however. In some individuals, a particular factor may dominate. As Professor Greenberg explains:

> For most people, these factors are all congruent, and one's status as a man or woman is uncontroversial. For intersexuals, some of these factors may be incongruent, or an ambiguity within a factor may exist.
>
> The assumption is that there are two separate roads, one leading from XY chromosomes at conception to manhood, the other from XX chromosomes at conception to womanhood. The fact is there are not two roads, but one road with a number of forks that turn in the male or female direction. Most of us turn in the same direction at each fork.
>
> The bodies of millions of intersexed people [, however,] have taken a combination of male and female forks and have followed the road less traveled. These individuals have noncongruent sexual attributes. For these individuals, the law must determine which of the eight sexual factors will determine their sex and whether any one factor should be dispositive for all legal purposes.

Id. at 269. Professor Greenberg points out that, for the initial seven weeks after conception, all human embryos have gonads that are not differentiated. At eight weeks, a fetus with one X chromosome and one Y chromosome will typically form testes from the gonads, which will begin to produce male hormones. The fetus with two X chromosomes, however, will develop ovaries from the undifferentiated gonads at about 13 weeks' gestation, which will begin to produce female hormones. For either the XX or the XY fetus, the presence of one sex's hormone will generally destroy the possibility that sex organs generally associated with a different sex will develop. *Id.* It is actually the hormones that direct an individual's sexual development and not the chromosomes.

Rarely, an individual may differ from the XX or XY norm. For example, 1 in 5,000 female newborns has an XO chromosome (Turner Syndrome). There are no clearly defined ovaries or testes because neither male nor female hormones were produced in sufficient quantity to cause the development of ovaries or testes. People with Turner Syndrome have female external genitalia but, due to the lack of estrogen, no mammary development. The closest male equivalent of Turner Syndrome is Swyer Syndrome. Whereas Turner Syndrome is characterized by the lack of a chromosome, Swyer Syndrome is characterized by the typical XY pattern, but there has been no development to cause the male hormones to kick on, resulting in a fetus with a uterus but no ovaries. One in 500–1,000 males is affected by Klinefelter Syndrome, in which the individual will have two or more than two X chromosomes even though phenotypically male. With a condition known as Persistent Mullerian Duct Syndrome, the embryo has a male XY chromosomal pattern and develops testes to secrete androgens but does not secrete hormones to destroy the development of a uterus. These individuals have male secondary sexual characteristics. *Id.* Even more rarely, hormonal disorders can create "hermaphroditism," in which an individual's external genitalia are ambiguous. *Id.*

The courts, however, prefer tidy rules of law for determining sex, since it has obvious implications for matters such as the right to marry and spousal inheritance rights. The *Ulane* court decision, included in Chapter 4, for example, noted that the plaintiff's sex-reassignment surgery would not enable her to procreate because the surgery could not create a uterus or ovaries. *Ulane v. Eastern Airlines, Inc.*, 742 F.2d 1081, 1083 (7th Cir. 1984). It also noted that "Ulane is a transsexual—a biological male who takes female hormones, cross-dresses, and has surgically altered parts of her body to make it appear to be female." *Id.* at 1083. The judicial opinions on whether chromosomal makeup at birth determines one's sex and on the relative weight to be assigned to one's physical ability to procreate as the sex with which one identifies have been highly controversial for a number of reasons. These cases tend to arise in the context of family law, generally in marriage or inheritance rights.

Scientific research, largely undertaken over the past 30 years, seems to support the view that determining sex based on chromosomal characteristics is simplistic. An influential study conducted in 2000 drew its findings from autopsies of the brains of homosexuals, heterosexual males and females, and male-to-female transgender subjects. The study concluded:

> Regardless of sexual orientation, men had almost twice as many somatostatin neurons as women. The number of neurons in . . . male-to-female transsexuals was similar to that of the females. . . . In contrast, the neuron number of female-to-male transsexuals was found to be in the male range. . . . The present findings of somatostatin neuronal sex differences . . . in the brain . . . and its sex reversal in the transsexual brain, clearly support the paradigm that in transsexuals sexual differentiation of the brain and genitals may go in opposite directions and point to a biological basis of gender identity disorder.

Kruijver, Zhou, Pool, Hoffman, Gooren, & Swaab, *Male-to-Female Transsexuals Have Female Neuron Numbers in a Limbic Nucleus*, 85 J. Clin. Endocrinology & Metabolism 2034 (2000).

The courts have not always caught up to the science, however, sometimes preferring instead to announce bright-line rules that are easily administered. Consider the following cases.

In *Matter of Anonymous v. Weiner*, 50 Misc. 2d 380, 270 N.Y.S.2d 319 (1966), a postoperative male-to-female petitioned the State of New York for a new birth certificate issued in her new female name. The court declined to order the Bureau of Vital Statistics to reissue the birth certificate in the new name because it accepted the Bureau's conclusion that male-to-female transgender persons are "still chromosomally males while ostensibly females." 50 Misc. 2d at 382. It also affirmed the Bureau's conclusion that "it is questionable whether laws and records such as the birth certificate should be changed and thereby used as a means to help psychologically ill persons in their social adaption." *Id. Accord K. v. Health Div.*, 277 Or. 371, 560 P.2d 1070 (1977); *Matter of Hartin v. Director of Bur. of Recs.*, 75 Misc. 2d 229, 232, 347 N.Y.S.2d 515 (1973); *In re Ladrach*, 32 Ohio Misc. 2d 6, 513 N.E.2d 828 (1987). *But see Matter of Anonymous*, 57 Misc. 2d 813, 816, 293 N.Y.S.2d 834 (1968) (criticizing, without overturning, New York Bureau of Vital Statistics' practice of denying reissued birth certificates changing name and gender to postoperative petitioners; "where, with or without medical intervention, the psychological sex and the anatomical sex are 'harmonized,' then the social sex or gender of the individual should conform to the harmonized status of the individual, and if such conformity requires a change in statistical information, the changes should be made").

In *M.T. v. J.T.*, 140 N.J. Super. 77, 355 A.2d 204, *cert. denied*, 71 N.J. 345 (1976), a husband who had paid for the wife's sex-reassignment surgery prior to their marriage argued that upon divorce, he owed no alimony because his wife was a man. The court found that alimony was owed because the marriage was valid. The court rebuffed a sheerly chromosomal or reproductive-capacity inquiry, ruling that, for marriage purposes, "if the anatomical or genital features of a genuine transsexual are made to conform to the person's gender, psyche or psychological sex, then identity by sex must be governed by a congruence of these standards." 140 N.J. Super. at 87. The court further observed:

> In this case the transsexual's gender and genitalia are no longer discordant; they have been harmonized through medical treatment. Plaintiff has become physically and psychologically unified and fully capable of sexual activity consistent with her reconciled sexual attributes of gender and anatomy. Consequently, plaintiff should be considered a member of the female sex for marital purposes. It follows that such an individual would have the capacity to enter into a valid marriage relationship with a person of the opposite sex and did so here. In so ruling we do no more than give legal effect to a fait accompli, based upon medical judgment and action which are irreversible. Such recognition will promote the individual's quest for inner peace and personal happiness, while in no way disserving any societal interest, principle of public order or precept of morality.

Id. at 89–90.

In sharp contrast to the attitude represented in the decision of the New Jersey Superior Court is the decision of the Texas Court of Appeals in *Littleton v. Prange,* 9 S.W.2d 223 (Tex. Civ. App. 1999), *cert. denied,* 531 U.S. 872 (2000). Christie Littleton had been born a man. About a decade after undergoing sex-reassignment surgery, she married a man to whom she was married for some seven years before his death. Upon her husband's death, Christie Littleton sued her husband's doctor for medical malpractice under Texas's wrongful death statute. The doctor defended based on Texas law regarding surviving spouses, arguing that since Christie had been born a man and Texas law defined marriage as the legal union between one man and one woman, the marriage was never valid. The Texas court relied on Christie's chromosomal makeup at birth, as well as Christie's lack of ovaries and female reproductive capacity, to conclude that she remained male: "Her female anatomy . . . is all man-made. The body that Christie inhabits is a male body in all aspects other than what the physicians have supplied." *Id.* at 231. Accordingly, her marriage was a same-sex one void under Texas law.

At least one lower state appellate court incorporated all of Professor Greenberg's scholarship about the criteria to be used in identifying sexual identify and repudiated the rationale of the Texas appellate court. *In re Estate of Gardiner,* 273 Kan. 191, the Supreme Court of Kansas was called on to determine whether J'Noel Gardiner, who had had her birth certificate changed under Wisconsin law to reflect her female postoperative sex, had a valid marriage to a man so that she could collect the statutorily set share of his estate provided under Kansas law to a surviving spouse whose spouse died without a will.

J'Noel underwent sex-reassignment surgery at the age of 37. Shortly thereafter, she married Marshall Gardiner, who was an influential benefactor and trustee of the rural college where she taught finance. He was in his eighties at the time of the marriage. Approximately one year after the marriage, Marshall Gardiner died without a will and left an estate worth approximately $2.3 million. His sole surviving son, in his forties, from whom he had been estranged for years, hired a private detective who discovered that J'Noel had been Jay Ball, a man. Because Kansas law restricts marriage to one man and one woman, he sued to have the marriage declared invalid, which would leave him in sole possession of his deceased father's entire estate. The trial court ruled for him, finding that gender was chromosomally set at birth and did not change with sex-reassignment surgery. The intermediate appellate court disagreed and reviewed some of the scientific literature. The appellate court opinion relied extensively on Greenberg, *Defining Male and Female: Intersexuality and the Collision Between Law and Biology*, 41 Ariz. L. Rev. 265, 278-92 (1992). The Court of Appeals, stated in relevant part:

> This court rejects the reasoning of the majority in the *Littleton* case as a rigid and simplistic approach to issues that are far more complex than addressed in that opinion.

> We conclude that a trial court must consider and decide whether an individual was male or female at the time the individual's marriage license was issued and the individual was married, not simply what the individual's chromosomes were or were not at the moment of birth.
> The [trial court, on remand] may use chromosome makeup as one factor, but not the exclusive factor, in arriving at a decision.
> Aside from chromosomes, we adopt the criteria set forth by Professor Greenberg. On remand, the trial court is directed to consider factors in addition to chromosome makeup, including: gonadal sex, internal morphologic sex, external morphologic sex, hormonal sex, phenotypic sex, assigned sex and gender of rearing, and sexual identity. The listed criteria we adopt as significant in resolving the case before us should not preclude the consideration of other criteria as science advances.
> . . . Last, we note the conclusion of William Reiner, M.D., a researcher at the Johns Hopkins Hospital, [one of three world-renowned sex-reassignment surgical centers in the world]:

> > In the end it is only the children themselves who can and must identify who and what they are. It is for us as clinicians and researchers to listen and learn. Clinical decisions must ultimately be based not on anatomical predictions, nor on the "correctness" of sexual function, for this is neither a question of morality nor of social consequence, but on that path most appropriate to the likeliest psychosexual developmental pattern of the child. In other words, the organ that appears to be critical to psychosexual development and adaptation is not the external genitalia, but the brain.

Id. (quoting Reiner, *To Be Male or Female—That Is the Question*, 151 Arch. Pediatr. Adolesc. Med. 225 (1997)). The opinion is revolutionary in its acceptance of scientific knowledge as the basis for determining gender. It was short-lived; however. The Kansas Supreme Court, on further appeal, entirely repudiated the intermediate appellate court's reasoning and wrote an opinion almost identical to *the Littleton* opinion.

Conclusion

This section is meant to provide a basic overview of several of the complex issues that sometimes arise when traditional causes of action are used in the ADA context. These two chapters as a whole are meant to give a strong basic foundation in Title I of the ADA. It is important to remember, however, that the issues addressed in these two chapters are not the only ones that arise under Title I of the ADA. For example, the question of pre- and post-employment medical examinations raises important issues but is beyond the scope of this book. When confronted with an issue under the ADA, it is important to remember how fact sensitive most ADA inquiries are and to remember the various stages of ADA analysis set forth in Chapter 13 and in this chapter.

FOUR

Conclusion

chapter

15 The Future of Antidiscrimination Efforts

A. Introduction

It is difficult to predict whether the present antidiscrimination laws will survive future congressional revisions or whether these statutes are adequate to deal with the dilemma facing employers and employees alike when discrimination exists in the workplace of the future. Some have argued for the elimination of federal antidiscrimination laws, placing confidence instead in the market to regulate, where the demand for good workers should allow for equal opportunity. Others claim that this will never happen and, in fact, the opposite occurs. There are also proponents of new ways of analyzing the problem of discrimination and the role of government in addressing the harm done to all of society. The excerpts from articles throughout this book have been offered to provide students with a window into the vast literature available to help think about new approaches and institutional reforms that might be more effective than the present system. This book concludes with a few excerpts from forward-thinking scholars in economics and critical theory that provide a different vision of the future.

B. Challenge to Contemporary Understandings of "Merit" Based Selection

Affirmative action remains a highly diverse issue in modern society. One of the most important challenges for a reexamination of the acceptance of "Merit" selection practices has emerged from the work of professors Susan Sturm and Lani Guinier.

Susan Sturm and Lani Guinier, *The Future of Affirmative Action, Promoting diversity in education and employment requires us to rethink testing and "meritocracy"*, Boston Review, December 2000/2001

(This is an edited version of the article and footnotes are deleted.)

For more than two decades, affirmative action has been under sustained assault. In courts, legislatures, and the media, opponents have condemned it as an unprincipled program of racial and gender preferences that threatens fundamental American values of fairness, equality, and democratic opportunity. Such preferences, they say, are extraordinary departures from prevailing "meritocratic" modes of selection, which they present as both fair and functional: fair, because they treat all candidates as equals; functional, because they are well suited to picking the best candidates.

... Defenders argue that affirmative action is still needed to rectify continued exclusion and marginalization. And they marshal considerable evidence showing that conventional standards of selection exclude women and people of color, and that people who were excluded in the past do not yet operate on a level playing field. But this response has been largely reactive. Proponents typically treat affirmative action as a crucial but peripheral supplement to an essentially sound framework of selection for jobs and schools.

We think it is time to shift the terrain of the debate. We need to situate the conversation about race, gender and affirmative action in a wider account of democratic opportunity by refocusing attention from the contested periphery of the system of selection to its settled core. The present system measures merit through scores on paper-and-pencil tests. But this measure is fundamentally unfair. In the educational setting, it restricts opportunities for many poor and working-class Americans of all colors and genders who could otherwise obtain a better education. In the employment setting, it restricts access based on inadequate predictors of job performance. In short, it is neither fair nor functional in its distribution of opportunities for admission to higher education, entry-level hiring, and job promotion.

To be sure, the exclusion experienced by women and people of color is especially revealing of larger patterns. The race- and gender-based exclusions that are the target of current affirmative action policies remain the most visible examples of bias in ostensibly neutral selection processes. Objectionable in themselves, these exclusions also signal the inadequacy of traditional methods of selection for everyone, and the need to rethink how we allocate educational and employment opportunities. And that rethinking is crucial to our capacity to develop productive, fair, and efficient institutions that can meet the challenges of a rapidly changing and increasingly complex marketplace. By using the experience of those on the margin to rethink the whole, we may forge a new, progressive vision of cross-racial collaboration, functional diversity, and genuinely democratic opportunity. . . .

... [F]undamentally, arguments about merit are functional: a person merits a job if he or she has, to an especially high degree, the qualities needed to perform well in that job. Many critics of affirmative action equate merit, functionally understood, with a numerical ranking on standard paper-and-pencil tests. Those with higher scores are presumed to be most qualified and therefore most deserving.

Fairness, like merit, is a concept with varying definitions. The stock story defines fairness formally. Fairness, it assumes, requires treating everyone the same: allowing everyone to enter the competition for a position, and evaluating each person's results the same way. If everyone takes the same test, and every applicant's test is evaluated in the same manner, then the assessment is fair. So affirmative action is unfair because it takes race and gender into account, and thus evaluates some test results differently. A crucial premise of this fairness challenge to affirmative action is the assumption that tests afford equal opportunity to demonstrate individual merit, and therefore are not biased.

Underlying the standard claims about merit and fairness, then, is the idea that we have an objective yardstick for measuring qualification. Institutions are assumed to know what they are looking for (to continue the yardstick analogy, length), how to measure it (yards, meters), how to replicate the measurement process (using the ruler), and how to rank people accordingly (by height). Both critics and proponents of affirmative action typically assume that objective tests for particular attributes of merit—perhaps supplemented by subjective methods such as unstructured interviews and reference checks—can be justified as predictive of performance, and as the most efficient method of selection.

Merit, Fairness and Testocracy

The basic premise of the stock narrative is that the selection criteria and processes used to rank applicants for jobs and admission to schools are fair and valid tests of merit. This premise is flawed. The conventional system of selection does not give everyone an equal opportunity to compete. Not everyone who could do the job, or could bring new insights about how to do the job even better, is given an opportunity to perform or succeed. The yardstick metaphor simply does not withstand scrutiny.

Fictive Merit

For present purposes, we accept the idea that the capacity to perform—functional merit—is a legitimate consideration in distributing jobs and educational opportunities. But we dispute the notion that merit is identical to performance on standardized tests. Such tests do not fulfill their stated function. They do not reliably identify those applicants who will succeed in college or later in life, nor do they consistently predict those who are most likely to perform well in the jobs they will occupy. Particularly when used alone or to rank-order candidates, timed paper-and-pencil tests screen out applicants who could nevertheless do the job.

Those who use standardized tests need to be able to identify and measure successful performance in the job or at school. In both contexts, however, those who use tests lack meaningful measures of successful performance. In the employment area, many employers have not attempted to correlate test performance with worker productivity or pay. In the educational context, researchers have attempted to correlate standardized tests with first-year performance in college and post-graduate education.[3] But this measure does not reflect successful overall academic achievement or performance in other areas valued by the educational institution.

Moreover, "successful performance" needs to be interpreted broadly. A study of three classes of Harvard alumni over three decades, for example, found a high correlation between "success"—defined by income, community involvement, and professional satisfaction—and two criteria that might not ordinarily be associated with Harvard freshmen: low SAT scores and a blue-collar background.[4] When asked what predicts *life success*, college admissions officers at elite universities report that, above a minimum level of competence, "initiative" or "drive" are the best predictors.[5]

By contrast, the conventional measures attempt to predict successful performance, narrowly defined, in the short run. They focus on immediate success in school and a short time frame between taking the test and demonstrating success. Those who excel based on those short-term measures, however, may not in fact excel over the long run in areas that are equally or more important. For example, a study of graduates of the University of Michigan Law School found a negative relationship between high LSAT scores and subsequent community leadership or community service.[6] Those with higher LSAT scores are less likely, as a general matter, to serve their community or do pro bono service as a lawyer.

. . . Standardized tests may thus compromise an institution's capacity to search for what it really values in selection. Privileging the aspects of performance measures by standardized tests may well screen out the contributions of people who would bring important and different skills to the workplace or educational institution. It may reward passive learning styles that mimic established strategies rather than creative, critical, or innovative thinking.

Finally, individuals often perform better in both workplace and school when challenged by competing perspectives or when given the opportunity to develop in conjunction with the different approaches or skills of others.

The problem of standardized tests to predict performance is particularly acute in the context of employment. Standardized tests may reward qualities such as willingness to guess, conformity, and docility. If they do, then test performance may not relate significantly to the capacity to function well in jobs that require creativity, judgment, and leadership. In a service economy, creativity and interpersonal skills are important, though hard to measure. In the stock scenario of civil service exams for police and fire departments, traits such as honesty, perseverance, courage, and ability to manage anger are left out. In other words, people who rely heavily on numbers to make employment decisions may be looking in the wrong place. While John Doe scored higher on the civil service exam, he may not perform better as a police officer.

---

[3]No tester claims that the LSAT or SAT, which is designed to predict academic performance, has ever been validated to predict job performance or pay. One study by Christopher Jencks finds that people who had higher paying jobs also had higher test scores. One problem with this conclusion is that higher test scores were used to screen out applicants from earlier, formative opportunities. Another study, by David Chambers, et al., of graduates of the University of Michigan Law School finds no correlation between LSAT and either job satisfaction or pay.

[4]See David K. Shipler, "My Equal Opportunity, Your Free Lunch," New York Times, 5 March 1995.

[5]As Walter Willingham, an industrial psychologist who consults with the Educational Testing Service (the organization that prepares and administers the SAT), points out, leadership in an extracurricular activity for two or more years is also a good proxy for academic performance, future leadership, and professional satisfaction.

[6]"In all decades, those with higher index scores tend to make fewer social contributions than those with lower index scores." See Richard O. Lempert, David L. Chambers, and Terry K. Adams, "The River Runs Through Law School," Journal of Law and Social Inquiry 25 (2000); See also, William G. Bowen and Derek Bok, The Shape of the River: Long-Term Consequences of Considering Race in College and University Admissions (Princeton, N.J.: Princeton University Press, 1998).

Fictive Fairness

Scores on standardized tests are, then, inadequate measures of merit. But are the conventional methods of selecting candidates for high-stakes positions fair? The stock affirmative action narrative implicitly embraces the idea that fairness consists in sameness of treatment. But this conception of fairness assumes a level playing field—that if everyone plays by the same rules, the game does not favor or disadvantage anyone.

An alternative conception of fairness—we call it "fairness as equal access and opportunity"—rejects the automatic equation of sameness with fairness. It focuses on providing members of various races and genders with opportunities to demonstrate their capacities and recognizes that formal sameness can camouflage actual difference and apparently neutral screening devices can be exclusionary. The central idea is that the standards governing the process must not *arbitrarily advantage* members of one group over another. It is not "fair," in this sense, to use entry-level credentials that appear to treat everyone the same, but in effect deny women and people of color a genuine opportunity to demonstrate their capacities.

On this conception, the "testocracy" fails to provide a fair playing field for candidates. Many standardized tests assume that there is a single way to complete a job, and the tests assess applicants solely on the basis of this uniform style. In this way, the testing process arbitrarily excludes individuals who may perform equally effectively, but with different approaches. . . .

In addition to arbitrarily favoring certain standards of performance, conventional selection methods advantage candidates from higher socioeconomic backgrounds and disproportionately screen out women and people of color, as well as those in lower income brackets. When combined with other unstructured screening practices, such as personal connections and alumni preferences, standardized testing creates an arbitrary barrier for many otherwise-qualified candidates.

The evidence that the testocracy is skewed in favor of wealthy contestants is consistent and striking. Consider the linkage between test performance and parental income. Average family income rises with each 100-point increase in SAT scores, except for the highest SAT category, where the number of cases is small. Within each racial and ethnic group, SAT scores increase with income.

Reliance on high school rank alone excludes fewer people from lower socioeconomic backgrounds. When the SAT is used in conjunction with high school rank to select college applicants, the number of applicants admitted from lower-income families decreases. This is because the SAT is more strongly correlated with every measure of socioeconomic background than is high school rank.[10]

Existing methods of selection, both objective and subjective, also exclude people based on their race and gender. For example, although women as a group perform worse than males on the SAT, they equal or outperform men in grade point average during the first year of college, the most common measure of successful performance. Similar patterns have been detected in the results of the ACT and other standardized college selection tests.[11]

Supplementing class rank with the SAT also decreases black acceptances and black enrollments.[12] Studies show that the group of black applicants rejected based on their SAT scores includes both those who would likely have failed and those who would likely have succeeded, and that these groups offset each other. Consequently, the rejection of more blacks as a result of using SAT scores "does not translate into improved admissions outcomes. The SAT does not improve colleges' ability to admit successful blacks and reject potentially unsuccessful ones." . . .

Thus, it is incontestable that the existing meritocracy disproportionately includes wealthy white men. Is this highly unequal outcome fair? Even if the "meritocracy" screens out women, people of color, and those of lower socioeconomic status, it could be argued that those screens are fair if they serve an important function. But the testocracy fails even on this measure; it does not reliably distinguish successful future performers from unsuccessful ones, even when supplemented by additional subjective criteria. Therefore, racial, gender, and socioeconomic exclusion cannot legitimately be justified in the name of a flawed system of selection.

By allowing partial and underinclusive selection standards to proceed without criticism, affirmative action perpetuates an asymmetrical approach to evaluation. In addition to arbitrarily favoring certain standards of performance, conventional selection methods advantage candidates from higher socioeconomic backgrounds and disproportionately screen out women and people of color, as well as those in lower income brackets. When combined with other unstructured screening

[10]See James Crouse and Dale Trusheim, The Case Against the SAT (Chicago: University of Chicago Press, 1988), p. 128.

[11]"Research . . . shows the GRE under-predicts the success of minority students. And an ETS Study concluded the GRE particularly under-predicts for women over 25, who represent more than half of female test-takers." See Phyllis Rosser, The SAT Gender Gap: Identifying the Causes (Washington D.C.: Center for Women's Policy Studies, 1989), p.4 Also, "ETS Developing 'New' GRE," Fair Test Examiner, Fall/Winter 1995–96.

[12]Crouse and Trusheim, fn. 10, supra at p. 103.

practices, such as personal connections and alumni preferences, standardized testing creates an arbitrary barrier for many otherwise-qualified candidates. . . .

An Emerging Model

Because of the importance in a democracy of ensuring opportunities to perform, we can start by shifting the model of selection from prediction to performance. This model builds on the insight that the opportunity to participate helps to create the capacity to perform, and that actual performance offers the best evidence of capacity to perform. So instead of making opportunity depend on a strong prior showing of qualification, we should expand opportunities as a way of building the relevant qualifications.

To follow this model, organizations need to build assessment into their activities, integrate considerations of inclusion and diversity into the process of selection, and develop mechanisms of evaluation that are accountable to those considerations. The result would be a dynamic process of selection, with feedback integrated into productivity. At the level of individual performance assessment, it would mean less reliance on one-shot predictive tests and more on performance-based evaluation.

One fundamental change resulting from our framework would be a shift away from reliance on tests as a means of distinguishing among candidates. Tests would be limited to screening out individuals who could not learn to perform competently with adequate training and mentoring, or be simply discontinued as a part of the selection process. Of course, decreasing reliance on tests to rank candidates would create the need to develop other ways of distinguishing among applicants. There is no single, uniform solution to this problem. One approach would be a lottery system that would distribute opportunity to participate among relatively indistinguishable candidates by chance. Concerns about a lottery's insensitivity to particular institutional needs or values could be addressed by increasing the selection prospects of applicants with skills, abilities, or backgrounds that are particularly valued by the institution. A weighted lottery may be the fairest and most functional approach for some institutions. . . .

A more institutionally grounded approach might work in non-educational contexts. In some jobs, for example, decision-makers would assume responsibility for constructing a dynamic and interactive process of selection that is integrated into the day-to-day functioning of the organization. Recent developments in the assessment area, such as portfolio-based and authentic assessment, move in this direction. These might build on the tradition and virtues of apprenticeship, and indeed might "more closely resemble traditional apprenticeship

measures than formal testing." . . . They would build from and acknowledge the effects of context on performance and the importance of measuring performance in relation to context . . .

. . . The central challenge is to develop systems of accountable decision-making that minimize the expression of bias, and structure judgment around identified, although not static, norms. For each assessment, decision-makers would articulate criteria of successful performance, document activities and tasks relevant to the judgment, assess candidates in relation to those criteria, and offer sufficient information about the candidate's performance to enable others to exercise independent judgment.

For this model to work, institutions would also need to change the relationship between race, gender, and other categories of exclusion to the overall decision-making process. Institutions would continue to assess the impact of various selection processes on traditionally excluded groups. But institutions would use that information in different ways. Rather than operating as an add-on, after-the-fact response to failures of the overall process, race and gender would serve as both a signal of organizational failure and a catalyst of organizational innovation. . . .

Consider the case of Bernice, now the general counsel of a major financial institution. Initially, she was hired as local general counsel to a bank, after having previously been partner in a prestigious law firm. (She left the firm after reaching the glass ceiling, unable to bring in enough new clients to progress further.) Bernice ultimately became general counsel to a major national corporation that previously had no women in high-level management positions. Her promotion resulted from the opportunities presented in an interactive and extended selection process. Her local bank merged with a larger company. In part to create the appearance of including women, she was permitted to compete for the job of general counsel for the new entity. Three lawyers shared the position for nine months. She initially did not view herself as in the running for the final cut.

During this time period, Bernice had a series of contacts with high-level corporate officials, contacts she never would have had without this probationary team approach. As it turned out, Bernice was able to deal unusually well with a series of crises. If standard criteria, such as recommendations and interpersonal contacts, had been used to select a candidate, it is doubtful Bernice would have been picked. But teamwork, decentralized management, and collaborative and flexible working relationships allowed her to develop the contacts and experiences that trained her. The opportunity to interact over a period of time allowed her to demonstrate her strengths to those who made promotion decisions. Bernice did not know she had those strengths until she took the job. . . .

Now, as general counsel, she is positioned to expand opportunities for women and corporate culture in general. She can structure the same kind of collaborative decision-making in selection that provided her the opportunity to work her way into the job. She determines who is promoted within the legal department, and who is hired as outside counsel. She is also in a position to influence how women are assessed as managers within the company.

This story illustrates the potential for integrating concerns about diversity into the process of recruitment and selection. It also shows the value of using performance to assess performance. At the core of this integrative move is a functional theory of diversity animated both by principles of justice and fairness (the inclusion of marginalized groups and the minimization of bias) and by strategic concerns (improving productivity). It is crucial to this integration that decision-makers and advocates understand and embrace a conception of diversity that comprises normative and instrumental elements. . . . Too often, the different strands of diversity remain separate, with those concerned about justice emphasizing racial and gender diversity as a project of remediation, and those concerned about productivity emphasizing differences in background and skills. Without an articulated theory that links diversity to the goals of particular enterprises and to the project of racial justice, public discussion and public policy-making around race and gender issues is more complicated. . . .

One argument for more closely integrating selection and performance is that doing so has the potential to improve institutions' capacity to select productive workers, pursue innovative performance, and adapt quickly to the demands of a changing economic environment. . . .

Instead of relying on standardized tests, the system of performance-based selection would focus decision-makers' attention on creating suitable scenarios for making informed judgments about performance. This would improve the capacity of institutions to find people who are creative, adaptive, reliable, and committed, rather than just good test-takers. In some instances, these structured opportunities could directly contribute to the productivity of the organization.

A more interactive process of selection also provides an ongoing opportunity to assess and monitor organizational performance and to perceive and react to the changing character and needs of clients and employees. . . .

A performance-based framework of selection is the equivalent, in employment and education, to the elimination of poll taxes and restrictive registration laws in the arena of voting. We seek to open up a conversation about issues that many people treat as resolved. Our institutions do not currently function as fair and functional meritocracies. Only by rethinking our assumptions about the current system and future possibilities can we move toward the ideals that so many Americans share. . . .

C. Collaboration and Shared Goals for the Future

This casebook has introduced a number of excerpts from the work of critical race scholars who have identified ways in which the dominant perspective in the law and in the workplace have left out the viewpoint or needs of particular minority groups in our society. In Chapter 1, excerpts from the work of Professors Kimberle Crenshaw, and Jerome McCristal Culp, Jr., provide important insight on the need to reexamine standard views of identity and privilege in society and the workplace. Professor Valdes joins others in suggesting that all of these voices share much in common and have been engaged in a joint process of finding the commonalities as much as identifying their unique characteristics that will be critical in the future analysis and formation of new laws concerning the workplace.

Francisco Valdes, *Outsider Scholars, Legal Theory and OutCrit Perspectivity: Postsubordination Vision as a Jurisprudential Method*, 49 DePaul L. Rev. 831 (2001)

(This is an edited version of the article and footnotes are deleted.)

Introduction

. . . Postsubordination vision grounded in substantive security. . . conjures a time and place wherein people of color, women, sexual minorities, and other traditionally subordinated groups no longer are the targets of social disdain, hate crime, and backlash democracy. . . . It imagines a society wherein these traditionally marginalized populations are well represented in popular culture, Congress, and the corridors of the corporate world. It describes a nation of peaceably and multiply diverse playgrounds, schools, workplaces, neighborhoods, and governments. It demands the restructuring of social, legal, and economic conditions to eradicate the systematic imposition of poverty, violence, and exploitation based on racism, sexism, xenophobia, homophobia, and similar ideologies of prejudice and repression.

By offering postsubordination vision as jurisprudential method, this essay also strives to recast extant sameness/difference questions as relevant, but not threshold or conclusive, determinants of the possibility for critical coalitions as vehicles of social justice and substantive security. By "critical coalitions" I mean "alliances based on a thoughtful and reciprocal interest in the goal(s) or purpose(s)" of a collaborative and collective project. . . . Critical coalitions signify intergroup collaborations grounded explicitly and substantively in joint convictions and mutual commitments rather than in the happenstance of coinciding self-interest. Critical coalitions therefore stand in sharp contrast to the convergence of White-Black group interests that produced yesteryears' Civil Rights triumphs. . . .

By "OutCrit" I mean "those scholars that identify and align themselves with outgroups in this country, as well as globally.". . . Therefore, among them are the legal scholars who in recent times have launched CRT (Critical Legal Theory), Feminist, Queer, and LatCrit legal discourses, including critical race feminists, Asian American and Native American scholars. But this OutCrit denomination also is a conscious effort to conceptualize and operationalize a mutual and proactive interconnection of the social justice analyses and struggles of varied and overlapping—yet "different"—subordinated groups in the United States and globally. . . .

The cumulative experience and record of outsider jurisprudence illustrates how CRT, Feminist, Queer, and LatCrit experiments in critical legal theory converge and diverge in numerous significant ways, both substantively and structurally. . . . In different ways and to different degrees, these outsider discourses strive similarly

to: represent certain marginalized viewpoints; espouse critical, egalitarian, progressive, and diverse antisubordination projects; accept discursive subjectivity, political consciousness, and social responsibility; recognize postmodernism; favor praxis; and seek community. . . . In addition, these outsider discourses have imagined and alluded to, but have not explicitly described, their vision of a postsubordination order to orient our collective antisubordination work. . . .

The rhetorics and ambitions of outsider scholars indicate that we are striving collectively toward a sociolegal alternative to the Euroheteropatriarchal status quo. . . which, by definition, must entail some vision of a postsubordination alternative. Yet no such vision has been expressly denoted in CRT or similar outsider venues. Accordingly, among the pending and interrelated queries for all OutCrit scholars and activists are: How does the post-homophobic society appear from today's QueerCrit perspective? . . . How does the post-white supremacy society appear from today's RaceCrit and LatCrit positions? . . . How does the post-patriarchal society appear from today's FemCrit viewpoint? How do these visions overlap? . . . How can legal theory and praxis help to engineer such transformation? Clearly, these questions of vision implicate at the threshold issues of "sameness" and "difference" in outsider jurisprudence. . . .

Some of the foundational insights produced during CRT's first decade are associated with this exploration of sameness and difference. Concepts like intersectionality, multiplicity, antiessentialism, and multiple consciousness arise from issues of sameness and difference in critical legal analysis, antisubordination discourse, and contemporary identity politics. . . . These concepts have provided strong foundations, helping CRT and other OutCrit scholars to elucidate multidimensional analyses that foster interconnection of antisubordination insights and projects. . . . Thus, this turn to outgroup experience and struggle no doubt has helped to illuminate important issues and mediate some sameness/difference tensions. Indeed, this potential utility explains why OutCrit scholars must continue to learn lessons from self-critical assessments of our collective jurisprudential experience. . . .

If outsider scholars are serious about using critical legal theory to catalyze social transformation, this potentially powerful dialogue about identity and dis/continuity cannot become an impediment to, nor a substitution for, acts of solidarity through theory in the service of antisubordination community and action. Depending on its use, this dialogue can be, but is neither automatically nor always, a form of progressive or effective jurisprudential method. Thus, sameness/difference dialogue is empowering only if deployed to ensure substantive security for the socially and/or legally subordinated. . . .

Postsubordination vision expands the prevailing focus of OutCrit inquiry beyond experience and struggle to include aspiration and hope. . . as another way of approaching and assessing the efficacy and design of critical coalitions. But this method also can help OutCrit scholars begin to delineate as concretely as possible the substance of critical coalitions grounded in the pursuit of substantive security for all. Postsubordination vision can help to provide the principles and purposes of intergroup cooperation and coalescence. . . .

This focus thus asks not whether OutCrit scholars and outgroup communities can travel together based first and foremost on present or past positions, but whether overlapping yet distinct outgroups can work together to arrive at a common destination based on shared goals.

Rather than prompting outsiders to determine whether our past and present are sufficiently alike to create a common path toward social justice and substantive security, postsubordination vision prompts us to determine first and foremost whether our destination coordinates are compatible—whether our critical conceptions of substantive social justice match, or can be made to. By shifting the focus to goals, agendas, and projects, postsubordination vision may help coalition-building where backward-looking assessments of sameness and difference may not. By emphasizing a forward-looking basis for intergroup coalescence toward substantive security, the shift from victimhood to vision can advance mutual recognition and accommodation of dis/continuities within and across multiple diverse outgroups. Postsubordination vision, therefore, is best viewed as a complement to, not a substitute for, constructive and progressive sameness/difference dialogue.

Postsubordination vision also may be useful as OutCrit method because it sometimes is helpful to begin a project by first envisioning as concretely as possible where one wants to be at its end, and then to work back from that vision to plan the journey. And sometimes it is useful to imagine and spell out for one's self (and others) not only what the project is "against" but also what it is "for." This utility is magnified when the project or journey is long, controversial, complex, or arduous. Because coalitional antisubordination projects and journeys are each of these, and more, critical legal scholars from varied subject positions constructively can begin coalitional OutCrit theorizing by imagining and articulating the substantive end-goal of our respective yet collective antisubordination activities and communities. . . .

Postsubordination discourse entails a positive articulation of substantive visions about reconstructed social

relations and legal fields. By focusing attention on the specific sociolegal character of a postsubordination era, this move encourages identity critiques to go beyond oppositional criticism and to set forth the alternative(s) to the status quo that motivate our work.

Postsubordination vision as jurisprudential method, therefore, calls for some hard-thinking and honest-talking about the type of postsubordination society that "we" are struggling toward. This concreteness might reveal differences of vision and produce conflict, as our collective record of comparative jurisprudential experience already illustrates. . . .

Postsubordination vision as jurisprudential method thus calls for OutCrit scholars to focus on an omnipresent sociolegal formation that appropriately might be called "Euroheteropatriarchy.". . . This term signifies the commingling and conflation of various supremacies: white supremacy, Anglo supremacy, male supremacy, and straight supremacy. This term, therefore, seeks to capture the interlocking operation of dominant forms of racism, ethnocentrism, androsexism, and heterocentrism—all of which operate in tandem in the United States and beyond it to produce identity hierarchies that subordinate people of color, women, and sexual minorities in different yet similar and familiar ways.

In this way, Euroheteropatriarchy also encompasses issues of language, religion, and other features of "culture" and community that help to produce and sustain hierarchical social and legal relations. . . . Euroheteropatriarchy therefore denotes a specific form of subordination in a specific context, which encompasses and enforces white racism and Anglo ethnocentrism, as well as androsexism and heterosexism, normatively, politically, and legally. Precisely because Euroheteropatriarchy is a system of interlocking rules, traditions, and structures that jointly legitimate and perpetuate today's sociolegal status quo, its dismantlement is a prerequisite common to the postsubordination hopes and visions of all OutCrits and outgroups. . . .

The vision I pursue here and elsewhere is a society where "difference" is not only tolerated and accepted but cultivated and celebrated, a society where legal principles and cultural practices accommodate and affirm, rather than burden or disdain, the public performance of difference across multiple axes of social and legal personhood. Rather than utopian, this vision seeks to reclaim and apply the demand for human agency and dignity proclaimed stirringly at the founding of this nation, but betrayed since then by the many acts of de jure or de facto domination and exploitation that have wracked the nation's soul, and that still do. . . . Thus, for legal scholars of whatever affiliation willing to share and toil for this progressive postsubordination vision, the pressing question is: How do we help to theorize and materialize this vision of a multiply diverse and socially just inter/national community?. . .

Progressive postsubordination vision can help Out-Crits imagine and animate critical coalitions by underscoring how "different" forms of hegemony or supremacy may combine to produce mutually reinforcing vectors of oppression that mutate in myriad ways time and again to oppose or co-opt any effort toward material transformation on any single front. In this way, postsubordination vi-

sion may help to interconnect the historic quests for substantive security that many OutCrits and outgroups continue today still to pursue. If OutCrit scholars practice critical legal theory in this way, and if we do so responsibly, insistently, collectively, and mutually, our respective and shared visions of a progressive postsubordination order just may help bring us together during CRT's second decade to build a common table of justice, dignity, and prosperity for all. . . .

D. Changes in the Structure of the Labor Market

In the first chapter of this book, you were introduced to the debate between Judge Richard Epstein and Professor Erwin Chemerinsky concerning the role of law and economics in solving the problems of discrimination in the workplace. In Chapter 8, the work of John Donohue analyzed the economic effects of the disparate impact analysis in employment discrimination laws. In Chapter 9, the work of Judge Richard POSNER, Professor Margaret Chon, and Professor Kingsley Browne raised further interdisciplinary concerns about the effects of the economic perspective on equality and discrimination in the workplace. The economic perspective is an important tool in the analysis of the workplace. The following review of a relatively new book by four economists from the Massachusetts Institute of Technology offers another perspective of the need for restructuring the workplace and labor market in the coming years.

Orly Lobel, *Orchestrated Experimentalism in the Regulation of Work*, 101 Mich. L. Rev. 2146 (2003) (reviewing Paul Osterman, Thomas A. Kochan, Richard M. Locke, & Michael J. Piore, WORKING IN AMERICA: A BLUEPRINT FOR THE NEW LABOR MARKET (2001)).

(This is an edited version of this article and footnotes are deleted.)

Since the advent of the New Deal vision, work and the workplace have undergone dramatic changes. Policies and institutions that were designed to provide good working conditions and voice for workers are no longer fulfilling their promise. In *Working in America: A Blueprint for the New Labor Market* (*Blueprint*), four MIT economists take on the challenge of envisioning a new regulatory regime that will fit the realities of the new market. The result of several years of deliberation with various groups in business and labor, academia, and government, *Blueprint* provides a thoughtful yet unsettling vision of the future of work. . . .

The authors strongly advocate the need to recognize new types of worker organization and eliminate the limits on employee participation and consultation in the workplace. They suggest that instead of seeing employee participation as a way for employers to compete over workers' loyalties and avoid unionization, union leaders should embrace participation and become visi-

ble champions and skilled facilitators of employee voice at work (p. 123). . . .

It is this very question about the relationship between employee involvement and profitability, however—which *Blueprint* leaves open—that is precisely the key challenge to any legal reform in the new market realities. Initiatives to improve working conditions depend on larger economic and political processes and on a strong public commitment to a new social contract. The reader is left with a big question mark as to the ability of firms to remain competitive while ensuring real voice and benefits to their workers. But more than that, *Blueprint* leaves the reader wishing for more explicit acknowledgment that such novel arrangements in the employment relationship, whether initiated by the market or by government, will not result simply in "efficient" outcomes in the narrow economic sense. The tension between social provision and economic competition continues to underlie other suggestions that are part of *Blueprint's*

3

comprehensive vision. This is precisely the tension that the authors, themselves prominent economists, do not sufficiently engage.

Written by prominent labor economists, *Blueprint* starts with the recognition that the market alone is insufficient in governing the economy, and will produce neither efficient nor equitable results. *Blueprint* rejects the competitive-market model that equates economic welfare with social welfare, and instead embraces an institutional perspective, which recognizes that labor regulation should be informed by additional values that include the notion of work as a source of dignity and self-fulfillment, the right to worker voice, association, participation, and equity and equality of opportunity. Whether government and the public will accept, promote, and legally require significant market redistribution will determine the future of labor, employment, and welfare regulation in the United States. *Blueprint*'s strength is in its recognition of the economy as an embedded social structure and its understanding that policymakers should operate within a framework that reconciles economic considerations with a set of moral values distinct from economic considerations. Yet, in the book's substantive reform proposals, as well as its organizational model of decentered experimentalism, the tensions between corporate profitability and worker protection are often lost: *Blueprint* risks reaffirming rather than resisting an ongoing process of declining governmental commitment to the regulation of the new workplace. . . .

Blueprint provides a linear description of a shift from the "old economy" to the "new economy." The old economy was based on the assumption that the U.S. economy is relatively self-contained and immune from foreign competition. It was also based on a sharp distinction between the marketplace and the household, and on the model of a male breadwinner. Employment relations were informed by the "old social contract," which viewed work as stable, secure, long-term, full-time, and typically in a large industrial firm. The new economy challenges all of these assumptions. Dramatic increases in global trade and capital mobility, as well as rapid technological innovations, augment pressure for flexibility, productivity, and competition. . . . As firms face increased risk of hostile takeovers and tough competition, employers are shifting to leaner and more flexible organizational and hiring structures, focusing on their core competencies while outsourcing other functions. The diversification of the workforce presents another dramatic change. Increased participation of women elevates the importance of work/family issues. The increased participation of immigrants, women, and minorities in the workforce contributes to the growth of contingent, part-time, temporary, leased, and other atypical workforces. . . . The number of people working for temporary employment agencies on an average day is growing rapidly, and staffing and leasing firms are among the fastest growing industries in the country. . . .

All of these developments have dramatically altered the nature of the employment relationship. In part a result of these shifting realities and in part a result of factors such as the weaknesses of existing American labor laws and negative public attitudes toward unionism, collective bargaining has declined sharply. The New Deal assumptions that collective bargaining and employment protections sustain adequate social protections and voice for workers have proved inconsistent with current realities of economic and social life. As traditional mechanisms of employee voice eroded and new workplace conditions have emerged, many workers are experiencing material insecurity, instability, social dislocation, and a loss of balance between work and family. *Blueprint* is thus concerned that the old social contract has been broken. The authors of the book set as their goal the articulation of an updated vision of institutional and policy reform that will match the new market realities while enabling the construction of a new social contract. . . .

In the context of unemployment, *Blueprint* rightly recognizes the importance of the ability of a welfare recipient to move from welfare to work. Globalization and technology advancements have exposed a new fault line in the workforce. . . . Highly skilled professionals have shifted the notion of job security from the ability to maintain a stable job to the ability to get jobs, while firms now offer increased premiums for skill and experience. . . . *Blueprint* argues for modernizing unemployment insurance, which currently covers less than half of the unemployed (p. 160). But more than just expanding coverage, unemployment insurance could be broadened to be viewed as part of an effort for structural adjustment, which would include investment in training and other measures designed to foster job mobility for the unemployed. In one of the book's more ambitious and exciting proposals it suggests the possibility of setting up funds that would allow workers to take time off work to refresh their skills (p. 155). . . .

Although *Blueprint* is sensitive to the existence of the many types of workers that constitute today's workforce, it does not sufficiently explore the vast inequalities between different social classes and between workers employed in various industries. Moreover, many of the book's structural-reform proposals do not adequately take into account the pervasive racial, gendered, and cross-generational gaps, and the inadequacy of antidiscrimination laws to address these ongoing structural inequalities.

Historically, part of the weakness of the labor movement has been its failure to encompass the diversity of the workforce. The American Labor Movement has a complex history of discrimination against women, people of color, and migrants. Today, the new fault lines dividing the labor market remain patterned along gender, race, and national origin lines. A comprehensive reform agenda of workplace regulation, as well as a revival of work-reform activism, must include a systematic rethinking of antidiscrimination regulation and its enforcement.

The problems of the new labor market are not only those of inadequate laws. Any reform agenda for the new market must be attentive to the problems of increasing labor-market informalization and the underenforcement of existing regulations. Within a globalized contingent workforce, an underground economy thrives. . . . The main problem in such informal sectors is not the lack of protective labor legislation, but the lack of enforcement of such legislation. Most labor standards are not linked to citizenship or residency. Therefore, in theory, even undocumented workers are protected by fair-labor-standards laws, such as those involving minimum wage, overtime pay, and leave. . . . Similarly, all workers, including undocumented workers, are protected by employment-discrimination laws. . . . Yet, in practice, many workers are paid less than the minimum wage, receive no overtime or health-care benefits, and do not find adequate venues to resist discrimination and abusive practices. . . . When employed informally, these workers are unable to receive social-security benefits upon retirement, unemployment benefits, or workers' compensation and disability benefits in case of illness or accident. . . .

. . . Employees do not seem to feel free to make use of worker-friendly regulations, often because they fear negative consequences to their career.

An ongoing obstacle to comprehensive labor-market reform is the lack of constructive public debate on workplace issues. Despite periodical coverage of distinct issues such as work/family balance, there has been little public discussion about the underlying fundamental questions of workplace justice. According to *Blueprint*, the lack of public debate has stemmed both from the prosperity during most of the 1990s as well as a lack of an adequate framework of thinking about the new economy. Indeed, some of the most challenging questions left unanswered by the book concern the ability of different types and classes of workers to view themselves as part of one workforce and to collaborate in challenging the prevailing conceptions of work relations and the declining commitment to market redistribution. In the context of enforcement, some of *Blueprint*'s most important suggestions focus on the ability of workers to challenge actual practices, focusing less on substantive provisions of employment standards, but rather on process rights, including the right to organize and the encouragement of participation, self-regulation, and engagement of multiple nongovernmental actors (pp. 181–90). A central part of *Blueprint*'s vision concerns a model in which government draws on the potentials of private institutions, in-

cluding individual firms, union-based dispute-resolution institutions, and community-based organizations to assist the traditional enforcement mechanisms (pp. 165–68). . . .

. . . In its broad vision, *Blueprint* confirms the need to think about economic and social needs as complementary concerns rather than as a zero-sum game. Yet to do so requires political commitment to intervene publicly in market processes and direct distributive outcomes. *Blueprint* begins its exploration of the new market with a mixed description (pp. 1–3). On the one hand, it describes the prosperity that the United States has experienced in the last decade. On the other hand, many American workers are facing great difficulties and dissatisfaction in their work lives due to the persistence of a large low-wage market, the growing gaps in earnings, and a general lack of voice and participation in the workplace. This paradox with which the book opens is key to understanding the problems underlying the regulation of work. The vast power imbalances between workers and the perseverance of dominant market ideologies systematically prevail over local attempts to produce significant change in the workplace. Blueprint provides interesting case studies of different firms, from Kodak to United Airlines, which demonstrate the vast variations in business organization in today's American corporations. Yet, it is perhaps the weakness of *Blueprint* that it insists on focusing on the great variety and differences among workplaces. Emphasizing diversity often conceals the ongoing links within the labor market and the nature of work relations that affect all workers and inhibits broader coalition building and a comprehensive vision for labor-market reform. In order to provide a blueprint for the new labor market, policymakers must recognize that the needs of the workforce have changed but are still often in direct conflict with those of business. Enabling market flexibility and global competitiveness are not seamlessly aligned with ensuring fair employment practices. By returning to the book's initial notions of work as a social institution, it is possible to articulate the need for equitable distribution among the competing stakeholders of the new economy and to advocate an orchestrated scaling-up of local democratic experimentalism.

Questions

1. Each of the authors presented in this chapter discusses ideas for change. Which ones make sense to you? Which ideas seem impractical? Why? Are there common themes in these approaches?
2. How would you change Title VII and other federal antidiscrimination laws? What are the social, economic, moral, or other concerns that affect your thinking about this problem?

Cases

The main cases presented in each chapter are highlighted in bold letters. The case excerpt begins on the bold page number. Cases contained within excerpted cases are not included in this table.

ductivity but rather depended on the discriminatory tastes of customers and the employer. This is the distinction between what the labor market achieves in terms of equating price and contingent value and what would be achieved if the labor market functioned in the same fashion as the capital market.

. . . Those who find intrinsic equality to be insufficient believe that a higher level of what I call "constructed equality" should be the aim of the law. Interestingly, while the first success in the law of employment discrimination was the acknowledgement, if not the attainment, of the right to intrinsic equality, over time this demand for equality has come to be overshadowed in much the same way that the early demands of blacks for the equal protection of the laws subsequently came to be seen as wholly inadequate. . . .

. . . [T]he civil rights movement sought to achieve what the market had yet to offer to black Americans—wages equal to the true value of their labor in a nondiscriminatory environment. This aspect of the civil rights movement was virtually a complete success, at least at the doctrinal and aspirational levels. At one point, the idea that the government could coerce private employers to hire individuals that they did not wish to have as employees had little widespread support; today there is a staunch consensus that such coercion is appropriate to guarantee to protected workers what they would secure in a nondiscriminatory free market. . . . As the goal of eradicating the appalling mistreatment of black Americans provided the battering ram against the doctrine of freedom of contract in employment, other disadvantaged groups—initially women and then the elderly and the disabled—attached themselves to this quest for legal equality in the workplace. Once this initial version of equality became widely accepted, the demands for a more aggressive employment discrimination policy began to grow.

In the same way that the doctrine of "separate but equal" came to be seen as the embodiment of inequality—even though for decades it was the basis of a legal strategy to advance the status of blacks—the initial phase of employment discrimination law that tried to confer what a perfectly competitive market would provide has come to be seen by many as a stunted form of equality that represents an impediment to needed change. These claims to go beyond the protections of an idealized market are seen in the argument that the special burdens of childbirth and childrearing require preferential treatment of female employees. . . . Women are not to be given only what a pure profit-maximizing, nonmisogynistic employer would offer them; instead they should receive what the modern conception of gender equality demands.

The Age Discrimination in Employment Act . . . emerged in 1967 from the combined support of those who sought to guarantee the intrinsic notion of equality—that is, what a non-ageist, idealized free market would yield to

workers who were over the age of forty—and those who thought older workers needed to be protected from the market. . . . The latter group was uncomfortable with the relentless logic of disregarding the surface attributes of race, color, religion, sex, or age and focusing exclusively on those traits purely related to productivity. In their opinion, the single-minded focus on worker productivity, which is the very essence of the intrinsic notion of equality, could itself be the enemy of female and older workers.

The requirement that employers shift their focus away from what an idealized market would offer to what fairness requires was taken a step further with the passage of the Americans with Disabilities Act (ADA). . . . Like the Age Discrimination in Employment Act before it, the ADA incorporates a component of the market protection conception of antidiscrimination in that it prohibits employers from irrationally discriminating on the basis of a disability. A disabled worker who can perform the essential functions of a job may not be rejected because of an employer's irrational aversion to the worker's disability. This conforms precisely to the intrinsic notion of equality—workers should receive what they would get in a nondiscriminatory free market. But, at the same time, the ADA is not content with this notion of equality. The Act goes much further by requiring employers to make reasonable accommodations that would enable disabled workers to perform adequately on the job. . . . Clearly, given a choice between two equally productive workers, one requiring the expenditure of significant sums in order to accommodate him and one requiring no such expenditures, the profit-maximizing firm would prefer the worker who is less costly to hire. Thus, the transformation that has occurred in the realm of civil rights is that the ideal nondiscriminatory market solution, which previously was both the benchmark of intrinsic equality and what the law demanded, is now regarded as the obstacle to social justice. . . .

The framework of contingent, intrinsic, and constructed equality offers insights into some of the major issues of employment discrimination law. For example, some have argued that the Supreme Court's creation of the disparate impact doctrine represented a departure from the congressional intent to prohibit only intentional discrimination. . . . The claim is that the disparate impact standard represents an unwarranted shift in Title VII's purpose from guaranteeing equality of opportunity to ensuring equality of result. But the move to a disparate impact standard, which was ultimately endorsed by Congress in the Civil Rights Act of 1991, is consistent with the goal of trying to guarantee intrinsic equality. Neutral rules that adversely affect protected workers without being tightly tied to their productivity are obstacles to the attainment of intrinsic equality, because the use of such neutral rules reflects the existence of statistical discrimination. As we saw above, intrinsic equality, which is defined by what would exist in a market that was as perfectly competitive as the capital market, cannot coincide with statistical discrimination. . . .

In addition, the tripartite equality framework can also be used to focus discussion concerning the likely success of various legal interventions. Intrinsic equality will necessarily be easier to generate than constructed equality because the pressures of the market at least push in the direction of intrinsic equality, but they steadfastly resist the attainment of constructed equality. This is not to say that the attainment of intrinsic equality is relentlessly encouraged by the market. For example, pure market forces do not encourage the hiring of groups that are disfavored by the employer, fellow employees, or customers, nor do they dictate the disregard of low-cost statistical proxies that generate a reasonably productive work force. Still, if workers could be properly sorted throughout the economy, a market equilibrium could exist in which every worker was being paid precisely his or her intrinsic value. . . . This could not happen with respect to constructed equality, because any employer who was paying a worker more than the worker's intrinsic value would find it advantageous to replace the worker. . . . This implies that intrinsic equality is at least in theory a goal that is attainable for all workers. Conversely, ambitious efforts to extend the enlarged demands of constructed equality to a growing array of protected workers moves society away from a conceptually attainable goal to an amorphous objective, which can only be defined through wrangling among conflicting interests in the political process. This fact in no way undermines the desirability of certain objectives, but it does suggest that political power may play a greater role than principled discourse in determining the future contours of constructed equality.

Conclusion

. . . Primarily through litigative efforts on behalf of female and elderly employees, the courts began to broaden the notion of equality beyond what a perfect market could give to what a perfect market would negate. Advocates of affirmative action began not only to seek the idealized market solution but to push for broader social justice. In this vision of constructed equality, the dictates of law are defined no longer through some abstract market paradigm but rather through considering what steps would be necessary to define a fair society. Releasing the law and its goals from the theoretical confines of a market paradigm has the advantage of freeing it to promote a more refined notion of justice, especially in light of the nonmarket roles of women as childbearers and caretakers, than would otherwise have been possible. On the other hand, freed from the theoretical mooring that the market paradigm provided, the malleable claims for constructed equality began to proliferate in ways that have weakened the moral force of antidiscrimination law. Employment discrimination law began to provide avenues for windfall gains rather than opportunities for promoting corrective justice, and the moral imperative that impelled the civil rights movement has been blunted to the extent that employment discrimination protections have been extended by special interest legislation to groups, such as smokers, with little to commend their legislative demands other than the political power of tobacco companies.

The ADA has imposed perhaps the greatest demands of constructed equality by explicitly requiring that employers take reasonable measures to make the disabled equal. Rather than the early Title VII insistence that employers disregard the traits of protected workers, the ADA requires employers to identify the traits of the disabled that undermine their productivity and to seek whenever possible to overcome these traits. The ADA has paved the way for the possibility that economically disadvantaged minorities such as blacks, whose position as the central focus of employment discrimination law has gradually diminished, will employ the ADA's rationale to argue that the effects of the factors that have undermined their productivity—including very poor schooling and broken families—are now to be corrected by employers. Although the conceptual groundwork for this step has been laid, the fracturing of the consensus forged by the civil rights movement may render this next step unattainable in the current political environment.

D. The Relationship Between Neutral Policies and Unconscious Discrimination

The Civil Rights Act of 1991 ensured that disparate impact would remain a viable approach under Title VII. In addition to the debate about the viability of disparate impact analysis, there has been much consideration about the meaning of disparate treatment discrimination and whether unconscious gender stereotyping can be considered disparate treatment under Title VII.

All of these questions force one to consider the issue of responsibility for discrimination. Is one relieved of discrimination claims if one acted in a way that created discriminatory results as long as the person didn't understand the nature of the discrimination? What then of the way that affects the victim of that discrimination? If we recognize that the harm has occurred, does it make a difference in the degree of discrimination, or is it discrimination at all? In criminal law, a similar problem is resolved by distinguishing between the more serious crimes and lesser crimes when the level of "mens rea," or conscious intent to do the act, varies. The punishment is less for the lack of a motive or intent to cause the harm, but society recognizes that reckless or negligent behavior can also cause serious harm. Society imposes some measure of responsibility on the one who caused the harm.

Consider the questions raised by Professor Charles Lawrence regarding the role of unconscious discrimination. In what ways does his analysis question underlying assumptions about your understanding of the nature of discrimination?

Charles R. Lawrence III, *The Id, the Ego, and Equal Protection*: *Reckoning with Unconscious Racism*, 39 Stan. L. Rev. 317 (1987)

(This is an edited version of this article and footnotes have been deleted.)

Prologue

It is 1948. I am sitting in a kindergarten classroom at the Dalton School, a fashionable and progressive New York City private school. My parents, both products of a segregated Mississippi school system, have come to New York to attend graduate and professional school. They have enrolled me and my sisters here at Dalton to avoid sending us to the public school in our neighborhood where the vast majority of the students are black and poor. They want us to escape the ravages of segregation, New York style.

It is circle time in the five-year old group, and the teacher is reading us a book. As she reads, she passes the book around the circle so that each of us can see the illustrations. The book's title is *Little Black Sambo*. Looking back, I remember only one part of the story, one illustration: Little Black Sambo is running around a stack of pancakes with a tiger chasing him. He is very black and has a minstrel's white mouth. His hair is tied up in many pigtails, each pigtail tied with a different color ribbon. I have seen the picture before the book reaches my place in the circle. I have heard the teacher read the 'comical' text describing Sambo's plight and have heard the laughter of my classmates. There is a knot in the pit of my stomach. I feel panic and shame. I do not have the words to articulate my feelings—words like 'stereotype' and 'stigma' that might help cathart the shame and place it outside of me where it began. But I am slowly realizing that, as the only black child in the circle, I have some kinship with the tragic and ugly hero of this story—that my classmates are laughing at me as well as at him. I wish I could laugh along with my friends. I wish I could disappear.

I am in a vacant lot next to my house with black friends from the neighborhood. We are listening to *Amos and Andy* on a small radio and laughing uproariously. My father comes out and turns off the radio. He reminds me that he disapproves of this show that pokes fun at Negroes. I feel bad—less from my father's reprimand than from a sense that I have betrayed him and myself, that I have joined my classmates in laughing at us.

I am certain that my kindergarten teacher was not intentionally racist in choosing *Little Black Sambo*. I knew even then, from a child's intuitive sense, that she was a good, well-meaning person. A less benign combination of racial mockery and profit motivated the white men who produced the radio show and played the roles of Amos and Andy. But we who had joined their conspiracy by our laughter had not intended to demean our race.

A dozen years later I am a student at Haverford College. Again, I am a token black presence in a white world. A companion whose face and name I can't remember seeks to compliment me by saying, "I don't think of you as a Negro." I understand his benign intention and accept the compliment. But the knot is in my stomach again. Once again, I have betrayed myself.

This happened to me more than a few times. Each time my interlocutor was a good, liberal, white person who intended to express feelings of shared humanity. I did not yet understand the racist implications of the way in which the feelings were conceptualized. I am certain that my white friends did not either. We had not yet grasped the compliment's underlying premise: To be thought of as a Negro is to be thought of as less than human. We were all victims of our culture's racism. We had all grown up on *Little Black Sambo* and *Amos and Andy*.

Another ten years pass. I am thirty-three. My daughter, Maia, is three. I greet a pink-faced, four-year old boy on the steps of her nursery school. He proudly presents me with a book he has brought for his teacher to read to the class. 'It's my favorite,' he says. The book is a new edition of *Little Black Sambo*.

Introduction

Much of one's inability to know racial discrimination when one sees it results from a failure to recognize that racism is both a crime and a disease.... This failure is compounded by a reluctance to admit that the illness of racism infects almost everyone.... Acknowledging and understanding the malignancy are prerequisites to the discovery of an appropriate cure. But the diagnosis is difficult, because our own contamination with the very illness for which a cure is sought impairs our comprehension of the disorder.

1. "Thy Speech Maketh Thee Manifest": A Primer on the Unconscious and Race

We have found—that is we have been obliged to assume—that very powerful mental processes or ideas exist which can produce all the effects in mental life that ordinary ideas do (including effects that can in their turn become conscious as ideas), though they themselves do not become conscious....

A. Racism: A Public Health Problem

Not every student of the human mind has agreed with Sigmund Freud's description of the unconscious, but few today would quarrel with the assertion that there is an unconscious—that there are mental processes of which we have no awareness that affect our actions and the ideas of which we are aware. There is a considerable, and by now well respected, body of knowledge and empirical research concerning the workings of the human psyche and the unconscious.... Common sense tells us that we all act unwittingly on occasion. We have experienced slips of the tongue and said things we fully intended not to say, ... and we have had dreams in which we experienced such feelings as fear, desire, and anger that we did not know we had.

The law has, for the most part, refused to acknowledge what we have learned about the unconscious. Psychiatrists and psychologists are called to court to discuss the mental state of the criminal defendant or the sus-

pected incompetent or to report on the mental pathology produced by an alleged tort, a neglectful parent, or the deprivation of a civil right.... But in most other legal matters, students of the unconscious are excluded, and we pretend that what they have learned is unknown.

It is hardly surprising that lawyers resist recognizing theories that describe the effects of unknown forces on our lives. For the most part, this reluctance is appropriate. The law is our effort to rationalize our relationships with the other. It is a system through which we attempt to define obligations and responsibilities. Denial of the irrational is part of that system, as is our notion that one should not be held responsible for any thoughts or motives of which one is unaware....

... Racism is irrational in the sense that we are not fully aware of the meanings we attach to race or why we have made race significant. It is also arguably dysfunctional to the extent that its irrationality prevents the optimal use of human resources. In this light it seems an appropriate candidate for study and/or treatment by the psychoanalyst as well as for exclusion from law, the discipline that attempts to govern or influence the actions of rational people. But unlike other forms of irrational and dysfunctional behavior, which we think of as deviant or abnormal, racism is "normal." It is a malady that we all share, because we have all been scarred by a common history. Racism's universality renders it normal....

Racism's ubiquity underscores the importance of incorporating our knowledge of the unconscious into the legal theory of equal protection. The law has traditionally used psychological theory to define abnormality in order to exclude the irrational from the law's protection or sanction. But where the law's purpose is to eradicate racial discrimination, it must recognize that racism is both irrational and normal. We must understand that our entire culture is afflicted, and we must take cognizance of psychological theory in order to frame a legal theory that can address that affliction ...

Whatever our preferred theoretical analysis, there is considerable commonsense evidence from our everyday experience to confirm that we all harbor prejudiced attitudes that are kept from our consciousness.

... Another manifestation of unconscious racism is akin to the slip of the tongue. One might call it a slip of the mind: While one says what one intends, one fails to grasp the racist implications of one's benignly motivated words or behavior. For example, in the late 1950s and early 1960s, when integration and assimilation were unquestioned ideals among those who consciously rejected the ideology of racism, white liberals often expressed their acceptance of and friendship with blacks by telling them that they "did not think of them as Negroes." Their conscious intent was complimentary. The speaker was saying, "I think

Index